PENGUIN BOOKS

BEYOND THE MYTHS

Dr Shelley Phillips is a psychological consultant, counsellor and popular community lecturer. She has degrees in History, English Literature and Psychology, and for fifteen years she was a senior academic at the University of New South Wales. She has also held visiting posts at universities in both Britain and the USA.

Over the past decade, as Director of the Foundation for Child and Youth Studies, she discovered that she was being asked to counsel mothers and daughters in increasing numbers, and as a result she became particularly interested in this relationship. *Beyond the Myths* is a comprehensive research investigation, which reveals shrewd insights into psychology, history, literature and everyday life.

SHELLEY PHILLIPS

BEYOND THE MYTHS

MOTHER–DAUGHTER RELATIONSHIPS IN PSYCHOLOGY, HISTORY, LITERATURE AND EVERYDAY LIFE

PENGUIN BOOKS

For Cathy, Odette, Inika, Jane, Lauren and Beth

PENGUIN BOOKS

Published by the Penguin Group
Penguin Books Ltd, 27 Wrights Lane, London W8 5TZ, England
Penguin Books USA Inc., 375 Hudson Street, New York, New York 10014, USA
Penguin Books Australia Ltd, Ringwood, Victoria, Australia
Penguin Books Canada Ltd, 10 Alcorn Avenue, Toronto, Ontario, Canada M4V 3B2
Penguin Books (NZ) Ltd, 182–190 Wairau Road, Auckland 10, New Zealand

Penguin Books Ltd, Registered Offices: Harmondsworth, Middlesex, England

First published in Australia by the Hampden Press 1991
Published in Penguin Books 1996
1 3 5 7 9 10 8 6 4 2

Printed in England by Clays Ltd, St Ives plc

Acknowledgements

My gratitude goes to the many mothers and daughters who urged me to devise a research programme that might address the issues behind their feelings and behaviours toward each other. I also want to thank those who participated in my research with such enthusiasm and my research assistants who helped with the tedious analyses of mountains of data.

I must acknowledge all my supportive friends, colleagues, acquaintances and students who took interest in the writing of *Beyond The Myths*. I thank them for drawing my attention to articles, books, films and persons of value. Unfortunately, they are too numerous to mention by name.

I also thank my daughters for their belief in the project. The memories left me by my grandmothers and great grandmothers and the life and childhood of my mother also added to my insights into the situation of mothers and the courage and potential of women.

Finally my thanks are offered to my editor, Loretta Barnard. Her enthusiasm was just what was needed to keep my spirits up during the final stages of the editing.

∾

Disclaimer

All names and identifying details of individual case studies have been changed. Some are composite characters based on the author's professional experience.

CONTENTS

❧

Book I

The Psychology of Mother-Daughter Relationships

❧

BOOK II — Retrieving Our Heritage

ॐॐ

ॐॐ

Preface

Why Mother-Daughter Relationships?

Here under one cover are two books about mother-daughter relationships. The first explores the psychology of the relationship. The second finds a wealth of information about the relationship in the legends, essays, short stories and novels written by mothers and daughters from antiquity to the present day. Obviously, these two books could have been about the relationships between fathers and sons, or husbands and wives, or family relationships, but I have concentrated on relationships between mothers and daughters for the following reasons.

There is extensive research on the relationships between fathers and sons and mothers and sons but, until recently, very little on the relationships between mothers and daughters. This is not surprising, since the pillars of research into the human condition, psychology and psychiatry, have been concerned with seeing that human beings adjust to the status quo. These disciplines have preserved traditional doctrines, with roots in a patriarchal society, which has tended to regard the male perspective as the universal reality and male norms as "normal adjustment", by which women can be assessed.[1] Thus, psychology, with few exceptions, has based its findings on half of reality. As a consequence, it is half a science.

These two books focus on a major aspect of the other half of reality, namely mother-daughter relationships. The aim is to recount something of the psychology and experiences of women by focusing on mother-daughter relationships — be they good, bad or indifferent. Suggestions for healing rifts in the mother-daughter relationship are made throughout the book.

Using Research, Case Studies and Fiction

Unfortunately, many papers and books on mother-daughter relationships go no further than describing what is wrong with the relationship.[2] They also often rely totally on reports of individual cases or on individual speculation. Individual opinion is not always reliable. It is very hard to generalise from one case to many. This is why, in this book, case studies are combined with systematic research that is specifically designed to unearth the needs and demands of mother-daughter relationships.[3] I had to undertake my own research to get a comprehensive and realistic picture of the questions mothers and daughters were bringing to me. This research is not isolated from the participants. Unlike the procedures in much academic research, the participants were involved in its construction and were given the feedback to use in their own lives.

I have supplemented research and case studies with cameo descriptions of mother-daughter relationships found in the novels of several well-known contemporary women authors. Because they are more realistic than the theories of psychology and psychiatry, I have borrowed mother and daughter stories from Tillie Olsen, Alice Walker, Alice Munro, Marilyn French, Doris Lessing and many others.

The purpose of this borrowing is twofold. One of my objectives is to draw together strands of thought and debate, which are often kept separate because of disciplinary boundaries. Book I synthesises psychology and literature in order to enlarge the picture of mother-daughter relationships.

The Use of Bibliotherapy

The second purpose is to offer a selection of novels that can be used as a Bibliotherapy. By this I mean that they can help with the development of self insights and strategies for coming to terms with mother-daughter relationships. As we identify with the trials and solutions of a novel's characters, we may learn strategies for coping with motherhood and daughterhood. While some of this Bibliotherapy has been selected to illustrate particular points in several chapters, there is also a more comprehensive Bibliotherapy, which covers a broader range of experiences, in the concluding chapter of Book I. In addition, at the end of each chapter of Book I, the novels and stories that are relevant to the issues discussed are indicated.

I have tried and tested this approach in my work with women and found that their everyday reading can offer sources which help them understand themselves and their mothers or daughters. It can provide a means for each to become their own therapist. The reading suggested here can also be used for group discussion among neighbours and friends or as a guide for a course on mother-daughter relationships. In fact, the entire book is based on such a course, which was generated by my work with mothers and daughters. The chapters are ordered in the logical sequence that grew out of the progressive needs and questions of the participants. However, this does not mean that the book must be read in the order presented. Some may prefer to begin with the Bibliotherapy in Chapter 9.

A Warning

Before I give more details of the content, I should warn the reader that I am not presenting a repetitive treatise on the nature and predicament of women in contemporary society. Bookshelves are bulging with books on this topic. The political situation of women is undoubtedly relevant to the relationship between mothers and daughters but, rather than duplicate the countless discussions on women's roles or attitudes to women, I have selected and synthesised the issues that are most specifically relevant to mother-daughter relationships. The criteria for relevance is based on the experience of the mothers and daughters quoted throughout Book I.

Similarly, while in-depth analyses of how social forces influence and shape the female psyche are the foundation of some of the material presented here, to regurgitate it all is unnecessary. There are many such feminist analyses around and for those who want to delve into the philosophy and theory construction in this area, I give many references throughout the book.

My aim is to go beyond the polemic of political, social or philosophical theories to the practical day to day issues and strategies for mothers and daughters wanting to build good relationships.

Embracing the Complexity of Mother-Daughter Relationships

Like any other relationship, there is no one factor that explains why a mother-daughter relationship is working or not working. We cannot pinpoint one issue, one psychological factor or one social factor and say that is the answer. This has been the trouble with most analyses. Some posit the influential biases of a male-dominated society as the only important factor.

Others posit so-called intra-psychic factors — the concepts of Freudian psychological theories such as the id, ego and superego. Yet these are merely constructs — models — which practitioners find useful. They do not exist as entities. Any practitioner, worth his or her salt, knows that the use of such constructs in explanations involves ignoring some aspects of human psychology and selecting special features for attention. They present a simplistic picture. In reality, human psychology is more complex. It is not possible to say how much our behaviour is a product of either outer or inner forces. Endless tomes have theorised about this question. The point is that the intra-psychic and the social are inextricably interwoven.

Obviously, we are, in part, products of a particular culture, a particular society, a particular family. Each has conditioned us to have certain expectations of mothers and daughters and how they are supposed to relate to each other. These expectations can become hidden agendas and influential self-fulfilling prophecies. But interwoven with social influences are psychological factors and a web of individual responses and behaviours, all of which have outcomes for mother-daughter relationships. For example, were we taught to value ourselves and others when we were children? If so, how did we respond? Was autonomy encouraged? If not, are we taking responsibility for developing it now? Self-esteem and autonomy are crucial to satisfying mother-daughter interaction.

Gender is also important. Social and family attitudes toward females are incorporated into our view of ourselves as women, mothers and daughters. The politics of gender in a family are expressed through a variety of behaviours, for example, different treatment of sons and daughters that may have long term effects on our feelings about ourselves and our female sexuality. How we value or devalue ourselves as sexual beings is very much related to the value we put on mother-daughter relationships.

Often forgotten is how much a father's attitudes, both to himself as a sexual being and to his wife, influences mother-daughter relationships. The research outlined in Chapter 5 of Book I suggests that fathers have significant impact on our behaviours toward our mothers and our daughters. There are many such factors interwoven into the fabric of mother-daughter relationships.

Thus, mother-daughter relationships have to be approached on many fronts and these two books attempt to explore the many interlocking facets of these relationships as clearly as possible.

PLAN — BOOK I

The Psychology of Mother-Daughter Relationships

Now to the plan of the books. Book I is for those wanting an overview of the significant work in the psychology of mother-daughter relationships. It provides a survey of much of the relevant research that is currently available. I have combined this with my own research and the most effective preventive and healing procedures generated by it. Any new interpretations are based on my own extensive work with mothers and daughters.

A major objective is to help mothers and daughters recognise and resist the hidden agendas and self-fulfilling prophecies that set up a psychological pattern of conflict from the moment of birth. Chapter I introduces the most powerful of these agendas and prophecies. The psychological impact of these at various stages of development is explored throughout. Awareness is a preventive strategy. In Chapters 2 — 4, the developmental psychology of daughters in infancy, childhood and adolescence is discussed. Chapters 6 and 7 look at many of the stresses of adult daughter-mother relationships. There are practical illustrations taken from case studies, many of which demonstrate positive measures.

Because it creates stress in mother-daughter relationships, Chapter I takes a critical look at the traditionally accepted and extensive literature on the responsibility of mothers — especially the literature of the past century and a half. Western society does not accept that mothers are simply fallible human beings like anyone else. We are encouraged to be angry with our mothers for failing and letting us down. Impossible expectations combined with the fact that women are treated as the second sex make relationships between mothers and daughters particularly difficult because daughters feel trapped in the same syndrome. Chapter 6 supplements the historical observations of Chapter 1 with the soap opera, super-mum expectations of contemporary daughters and the tragedy that these expectations create in their relationships with their mothers. It explains why so many mothers don't enjoy being mothers and why many daughters dread becoming mothers.

Because they appear to be crucial to good relationships between mothers and daughters, the early chapters of Book I describe how self-awareness and self-esteem develop in daughters from infancy and early childhood, through primary school, adolescence and young adulthood. In later chapters, daughters from everyday families talk about the experiences they saw as significant in relation to their mothers in their childhood and young adulthood. Many mention their growing ambivalence about their sexuality as having a major influence on their relationships with their mothers. The chapters on psychological growth reverse the old tradition of using "he" to embrace both sexes. "She" and "her" often denote experiences that apply to boys also and the reader will recognise the common features.

These chapters on psychological growth in Book I also consider the points at which conflict between mothers and daughters may in fact be conflict that both parents experience in relation to all their children. This has been done because there is a danger of exchanging the male bias in psychology for a female one and missing the commonality of experience.[4] Moreover, if women are always studied separately by feminists, their work may be seen as having little general application, or women's issues may become separated from debates of crucial importance.

These chapters also refer to the development of bisexuality and lesbianism. Unfortunately, the research is so deficient in these areas, it is slight and speculative. Nevertheless, there is a discussion of why these issues are important for mother-daughter relationships and some misconceptions are tackled.

Chapters 6 and 7 consider why traditional psychology has taught us that healthy daughters must "separate" from their mothers. What does this really mean? How is autonomy achieved without putting continents and seas between mothers and their daughters? And what of that longing for mothering that extends into adulthood and is never satisfied? Were our mothers deficient or is the longing due to something in ourselves? How do we negotiate the guilt that bedevils so many mother-daughter relationships?

Chapter 8 discusses some relevant aspects of psychoanalysis and is for those who want an overview of some of the psychoanalytic ideas that relate to mothers and daughters, but don't have time to struggle with the often formidable primary sources. Psychoanalysis has had a tremendous impact on the theories of mother-daughter relationships and familiarity with it is important for an in-depth understanding.

It seems that old theories and practices have not provided the means of healing mother-daughter relationships. Facing up to this fact, Book I asks whether feminist reinterpretations and adaptations of the great patriarchal theories in psychology, psychiatry or philosophy are helpful. It questions whether the boundaries, set by patriarchal thinkers, allow new sources of consciousness to develop, or whether they keep mothers and daughters marginal and secondary and therefore in conflict?

We need new approaches and Book I suggests some.

PLAN — BOOK II

Retrieving Our Heritage:

Forgotten Mothers and Daughters in History and Literature

Book II extends the major theme of Book I — the theme that the process of healing mother-daughter relationships lies in as full an understanding of our relationships as possible. Understanding does not simply embrace self-insight and knowledge of the forces that influence us. It also involves knowledge of where we fit in immediate and extended relationships and our history as mothers and daughters. We need to know more about other mother-daughter relationships, both present and past.

Book II is concerned with the fact that these necessities were often sadly neglected in our early teaching. It attempts to renegotiate them.

At school, some of us were obliged to read *Jane Eyre* by Charlotte Brontë or *Wuthering Heights* by her sister, Emily. Some of us were fascinated by these novels and most at least found the films based on them absorbing. The big question is the source of this fascination. The conclusion, that it is due to the magnetic descriptions of passionate sexual relationships, gives only a partial answer, yet it was the answer many of us were given at school. What was rarely discussed was the enormous influence that the loss of their mother had on the Brontë daughters and the consequent insatiable hunger of their heroines for motherly love. This hunger finds substitutes in surrogate mothers and sexual love — an experience common to most of us. Sometimes, stereotypes about women confuse or destroy that love. The distortions of pornography, for example, inculcate attitudes that lead some women to betray other women and mothers their daughters. All this is in the Brontë novels. They are novels about the psychology of mothers and daughters under patriarchy.

Exploration of these themes, when we first read these books, could have equipped us better to cope with our present doubts about mother-daughter relationships. Similarly, it might have been helpful to look at what Jane Austen contributed to the liberation of daughters. Instead, we learnt about her patriarchal sympathies and her attack on the feminine use of sentiment. Did we learn how Colette or Virginia Woolf negotiated their problems with their mothers? Had we traced their lives and read their books with that question in mind, we might have gained not only useful information but a sense of community with mothers and daughters through generations. Book II renegotiates some of these neglected opportunities.

In the process of amending a number of the omissions and biases of the literature of our school or university years, Book II overviews the work of several feminist writers who have tried to put mother-daughter relationships in a woman-centred historical perspective. The objective is to give us some insight into where we came from and why we are as we are. There is no attempt to be comprehensive about this in a pedantic fashion. Old and well-known historical facts are not regurgitated here. Rather, together with original material, there is a deliberate selection of the work of others, in order to offer a serendipity of some uncommon changes in thinking. Hopefully, this saves the reader time-consuming excursions into primary sources. Like Book I, Book II synthesises research and ideas from a number of fields.

In the course of endeavouring to expose many of the myopisms, which inhibit thorough understanding of mother-daughter relationships, Book II introduces us to those who dare to challenge the patriarchal myth-making of Christianity.[5] Some feminists extend the challenge further and assert that, if men have been able to identify with an all-powerful male God and his Christ through mythology, then women have the right to create strong myths that allow them to identify with an all powerful Goddess. They believe it would "work miracles" with the self confidence of women. Identifying with the submissive Virgin Mary is not enough. Chapters 1 — 3 of Book II also try to interpret the psychology of men and women in societies where a strong Goddess was, or is, worshipped. It examines whether such a situation increases the self-confidence of mothers and daughters and consequently their acceptance of each other.

From there, Book II takes us through the experiences of mothers and daughters in biblical times, among the knights of medieval romances and as Shakespeare saw them. We find the significance for mothers and daughters in the tragedy of Marie Antoinette. We can read what Mary Wollstonecraft and other feminists of the seventeenth and eighteenth centuries observed about mother-daughter relationships. Feminism and women friendships are not simply a phenomenon of the late twentieth century. It is important for mothers and daughters to include this fact in their self understanding, if they are to develop respect for each other.

As with Book I, it is not necessary to read the chapters in Book II consecutively. Selecting chapters as a source for reading about issues of particular interest is an alternative, although this approach may miss the comprehensive sense of our history.

What is Patriarchy?

Because of its relevance to contemporary mother-daughter relationships, much of the material in both books concerns mothers and daughters in the shadow of patriarchy. Patriarchal society is the prism through which mothers and daughters are seen and through which their relationships are constructed, so it is important to know how patriarchy is defined here. I must emphasise, however, that the books are not a detailed study of women under patriarchy. There are innumerable analyses of this phenomenon. The books are confined to a study of some of the psychological outcomes for the mother-daughter relationship and how to recognise and be armed against patriarchy's divisiveness.

Also, to avoid misunderstanding, it should be noted that patriarchy is also the prism through which father-son relationships are shaped. Men suffer under patriarchy too and are also strait-jacketed by its stereotypes and expectations.[6] This is illustrated in many parts of Books I and II.

Patriarchy is used here in a much broader sense than it was defined by Engels or Freud. In its narrower definition, patriarchy is a system in which the male head of the household has absolute legal and economic power over his dependent female and male members. In the broader perspective, there can be no general definition of patriarchy.[7] It manifests itself differently in different economic and social structures, at different historical periods and in different classes. It not only includes the dynamics of relationships within the family, but in labour relations, power hierarchies and the spheres of gender and procreativity.

In its wider definition, patriarchy as an institution does not imply that women are either totally powerless or totally deprived of rights, influence and resources, but it does mean that men tend to hold power in social relationships and in all the major organisations in society. Its survival depends upon domination by a particular group, be it billionaires, bureaucrats, the aristocracy or the military, over the rest of the population and most importantly one sex over the other, or men over women. Patriarchy is a system of political and economic control, based upon hierarchy and power conflicts. It is not egalitarian, humanistic or genuinely attentive to the needs of the majority. It accepts enormous wealth for the few, alongside poverty and starvation for millions. It has mismanaged the environment and is out of harmony with it. It has brought the world to the brink of nuclear war and annihilation.

Many of patriarchy's inherent problems are due to its need for compartmentalisation. For instance, marking distinct boundaries between fields of endeavour, study, research, business applications or marketing, flourishes under patriarchy, because it is a social and economic organisation that is constructed out of competition and power. Each dominant person in its innumerable hierarchies must have his sphere of influence, control and profit. Since an education system reflects the dominant values of any culture, it follows that learning under patriarchy is rarely directed toward synthesis and co-operation.

For example, science has been studied and applied independently of the environment and as a result, the world is heading for ecological disaster. Technologies have been developed that take no account of human beings. Medicine and its treatments have been studied independently of the psychology of people. The list is endless.

This narrowness is compounded by élitism. Unfortunately, an all too common aspect of patriarchal institutions of higher learning and research is contempt for, and segregation from, the ordinary citizen. There is a reluctance to forsake purism because it offers power by exclusion, so there is an unwillingness to present ideas in a generalised and palatable form for ordinary human beings.

Each of these tendencies have special implications for mothers and daughters. It is only through synthesising and bringing together many fields of endeavour that their full position can be recognised. Only then is an integrated plan for effective action possible, instead of the piecemeal approach we have at present. Furthermore, they must have access to the debates and research that throw light on their position. These books attempt to negotiate both these problems.

Why do Mothers and Daughters Aquiesce?

Having given a brief definition of how patriarchy is defined in this book, there follows an important question. Why have mothers and daughters acquiesced in and reinforced a patriarchal system that sets them in a some-times antagonistic and frustrated relationship?

In broad terms, the answer seems to lie in the fact that, for centuries, women have participated in the process of their own subordination. They have been psychologically shaped to internalise the idea of their inferior-ity. As Gerda Lerner, in her book *The Creation of Patriarchy*, puts it:

> The system of patriarchy can function only with the co-operation of women. This co-operation is secured by a variety of means: gen-der indoctrination; educational deprivation; the denial to women of the knowledge of their history; the dividing of women, one from the other, by defining "respectability" and "deviance" according to women's sexual activities; by restraints and outright coercion; by discrimination in access to economic resources and political power; and by awarding privileges to conforming women.[8]

We all have some experience of what Lerner is talking about. Perhaps the most valuable contribution her impressive research makes is that it emphasises that we cannot attribute our secondary status to any definite or single cause. That would be typical of patriarchal interpretations, which many rightly see as bedevilling not only traditional theory, but feminist theory.[9] Lerner allows for chance and accident in the processes that have placed women on the margins of economic and political power.

Her work shows that, whereas in the beginning of their history, women, mothers and daughters agreed to an equitable and rational division of labour, throughout later patriarchal history a woman only shared the priv-ileges of the ruling class when she was under the protection of, or married to, a man. In a society divided by class, it is difficult for people who them-selves have some power, however limited and circumscribed, to see

themselves as deprived and subordinated. Class and racial privileges serve
to undermine the ability of women to see themselves as part of a coherent
group, which they are not. Uniquely of all oppressed groups, women
occur in all strata of society. The connection of women to family structures
has also made any large scale development of group cohesiveness difficult.
Women have been secured to male kin and to their paternally-legitimised
children through their associated emotional family obligations and ties in
all patriarchal societies.

Other oppressed classes and groups are united by awareness of their
past history and the conditions of their subordination and can clearly distinguish between themselves, their families and their oppressors. Indeed,
the family may protect and support them in resistance to oppression. On
the other hand, women in early patriarchal societies learned that their families would cast them out should they ever rebel against their
subordination and the mother-daughter alliance could not always be relied
upon for salvation. In many tribes, families and communities, there are
instances where women have participated in the punishment, torture or
death of a girl who has transgressed patriarchal, sexual rules for women.

Another factor that contributes to the marginal economic and political
position of women is that since antiquity, the official systems of communication, ie language, religion and more recently, newspapers and
television, have been part of the patriarchal system. The interests of powerful men, since such men control communication systems, have largely
been given central place. An example is the way in which patriarchy has
utilised the pronoun "he" to signify all of humanity. Thus from an early
age the female child learns that the pronoun that is significant for her is secondary. By this device her marginality is incorporated into her concept of
self. Perhaps initially, there is some questioning, but so persistent is the
indoctrination that later she loses awareness of it and its effect upon her.[10]
She learns that female experience is repeatedly defined in a derogatory gender-specific fashion. "Women's knowledge becomes mere "intuition";
women's talk becomes "gossip".[11]

As an adult, she finds that the symbolic constructs, or models, in psychology and psychiatry have implied that the male is the norm and the
female unfinished and that patriarchal castration of female personality
principally offers women but two alternatives: an impossibly idealised
motherhood or an emphasis on the kind of sexual attraction that turns
women into objects. The sex symbol aspect of womanhood, which
excludes personality and character, has become more and more salient as
the need to emphasise motherhood for population growth declines. This is
discussed in Chapter I of Book I.

The sex symbol device also reflects the increasing shallowness and
emptiness of the patriarchal socialisation process in contemporary society.
The plastic women of the advertising world, the "dumb blond", the Miss
World contests and the current exploitation of the young, female adolescent in the fashion industry offer degraded models that restrict and

undermine personality development. Respect for one's sex is an essential basis for a good relationship between mother and daughter.

These books do not take a passive view of women or children. Mothers and daughters have participated in their own hostility to each other and are not totally the victims of brain-washing. They argue that we have reached a stage when mothers and daughters can personally stop thinking of themselves as victims and reject all the other labels that have set them in conflict.

Why Interdisciplinary?

The mothers and daughters with whom I work find the interdisciplinary approach — the combination of psychological explanation with illustration from fiction and history — attractive, interesting and effective. In contrast, academic purists, who are enmeshed in one discipline, may find it difficult to cope with the synthesis that is presented in these books. The books are not intended for them. They are for ordinary women and men who seek more comprehensive understanding and hypotheses.

A non-sexist interdisciplinary approach is essential if we are to gain new insights into mother-daughter relationships. We need to recognise the restrictiveness inherent in knowledge that has rigid boundaries.[12] Learning in our schools and universities is compartmentalised into tight disciplines. Rigid divisions between disciplines are typical of patriarchal thinking and are becoming increasingly unproductive, especially in the study of mother-daughter relationships, as is illustrated throughout the following chapters.

Achieving this interdisciplinary approach is a mammoth task, not only because of the patriarchal antagonism it arouses, but because there are very few writers, lecturers and critics who have sufficient interdisciplinary background to attempt the integration. This is the unfortunate heritage of our predominantly patriarchal education system. Patriarchal thinking inevitably pervades everything. Formal education, which is supposed to assist us to think more clearly, is often full of unrecognised indoctrination about patriarchal views that are hostile to mothers and daughters.

Unfortunately, it cannot be expected that all women teachers and academics are open to interdisciplinary thinking. Even some members of Women Studies' Departments, many of which are trying to undo the compartmentalisation of traditional thinking and its stifling of multi-disciplinary approaches, are occasionally prone to the age-old rigidities.

There is a related and more commonly aired problem. Dale Spender gives her experience of it in her book, *The Writing Or The Sex.*[13] Her thesis is that the powers that be in universities, publishing houses and newspapers (and also classrooms and everyday conversation) prejudge everything on the basis of the sex of the contributor. She argues that many female reviewers are schooled in patriarchal values and prejudiced against women.

Academics and the literati are not alone in their patriarchal and single track approach. Many vocations share it. Hopefully, some who are products of these may come to accept and enjoy the interdisciplinary synthesis that is basic to an understanding of the new approaches and consciousness-raising outlined in this book. It is not for those who cannot or will not step outside patriarchal patterns of thought.

Conclusion

This collection of ideas, research and case studies — real and fictional — is for ordinary women and men. It does not toe a party line. It neither advocates nor constructs a particular theory. Using one line, one theory, is a patriarchal way of thinking. Moreover, a theory is only a theory. By its very nature it excludes some aspects of reality.

Instead, the objective is very practical. For example, Book I tells of everyday realities for individual mothers and daughters. It utilises theories only where they have some meaning for these everyday realities. It synthesise theories. It rejects some aspects of some theories and retains others. The test is whether there are genuine insights about mother-daughter relationships or whether the theories are patriarchally biased and obscure a clear view of mother-daughter relationships.

The material brought together here is not for those who must have one model, one framework. It is not for those who prefer to keep literature in one department and psychology in another. It is for those who enjoy eclecticism and see it as a useful way to explore most issues, including mother-daughter relationships.

The need for a one way approach to information gathering — can easily degenerate into authoritarian and totalitarian ways of thinking.[14] Intolerance of another's perspective leads to anxiety and vilification, which does not advance understanding and knowledge. Those who become apoplectic should their favourite theory become subject to a little constructive criticism — be it psychoanalysis, feminism, behaviourism, psychology, sociology or whatever — are not creators of new ideas.

Those who are looking for easy solutions to mother-daughter relations will find these books are not for them. The lack of motherly affection, the loss of a mother, or poor relations with her in childhood, are not presented as leading to emotional disabilities that inevitably mar all future relationships. Instead, it is argued that the mishaps of childhood can be reconstructed. Indeed, the processes of working through the unfinished business of childhood, and resolving the stresses of old relationships in new ones, is an essential and positive force for personal growth.

Since the aim is to concentrate on everyday relationships and general trends in mother-daughter relationships, it has not been possible to dwell on special problems of pathology, child abuse or incest, because the psychology and politics of these warrant examination in works devoted to them exclusively. Here, the concern is for those who are interested to know more about the relationships of mothers and daughters, in "ordinary" and reasonably nurturing families.

The overall theme is that we live in a society which has many negative attitudes about mothers and mother-daughter relationships. In families where mothers and daughters create a just community for themselves as well as everyone else, the negative hidden agendas of patriarchy are freely discussed and laughed out of countenance. This process is the basis of any good mother-daughter relationship. Once hidden agendas are demolished, we can turn to enhancing self esteem in ourselves and our daughters. We can seek out and nourish all the psychological processes that ensure we have good relationships. We can sustain a good relationship through consciousness-raising by rediscovering our heritage in the literature that abounds in our libraries and bookshops.

It is important to re-emphasise that before we can confront the means of achieving these conditions, we need to know more about how we got into the mess we are in. To this end, the first chapter of Book I looks at the patriarchal propaganda against mothers and mothering over the last 150 years. Longer term influences, going back to antiquity, are explored in Book II. The point is that if we recognise the origins of the attitudes which devalue mothers and daughters and their relationship, we may be more wary of them in future. This is the message of Chapter 1.

To emphasise the importance of the message, the chapter begins with a description of a mother-daughter relationship by Doris Lessing. It was chosen because, first of all, it is a good illustration of the destructive and unhappy relationship which many mothers and daughters have and secondly it shows how urgent it is to be aware of the kind of traditional teachings and attitudes that have set them at loggerheads.

ℰℐ

BOOK I

The Psychology of Mother-Daughter Relationships

CHAPTER 1

The Roots of Mother-Daughter Conflict

A Century and a Half of Unreal Expectations and Myths About Mothers

Mothers have long had an ambivalent status and a bad reputation for messing up the personalities of their daughters. Indeed, many adults hold that their mothers crippled them emotionally for life and assume that mothers and daughters are inevitably at loggerheads. Conflict between them is expected as part of the natural order of things. This expectation and the bad reputation of mothers are among the major influences on mother-daughter relationships.

An excellent illustration of how pervasive these attitudes are is given by Doris Lessing, in her best-selling five-part *Children of Violence* series.[1] In the beginning of the series, we find the adolescent daughter, Martha, and her mother, Mrs Quest, living with their family on a poor farm in Southern Rhodesia. The mother's lot is circumscribed by her immigrant background, her conservatism and colonialism. Martha strives to become something other than her mother. She sees her mother as having little existence apart from her children.

Martha has the usual adolescent dreams of independence, but claims that they are frustrated by the expectation that she will follow in her mother's footsteps — marriage and motherhood. In particular, she believes her mother resists her independence, as if it is the end of her purpose in life — a kind of death. Failing to recognise that wider social and economic pressures are at the root of her frustration[2], she focuses her problems entirely on her mother and her rigid devotion to what she sees as her limited model of motherhood. She despises her mother for exemplifying the traditionally passive female role and expecting her to play the role of the marriageable daughter. On the one hand, Martha is dissatisfied with such limitations but on the other, she has difficulty in defining herself as anything other than as a non-mother.

We are given a not uncommon picture of an adolescent girl who feels engulfed by her mother — totally chained to her. She contrasts her lot with her brother's independence. Unlike him, she believes she can be nothing but a link in the chain of motherhood. Lessing doesn't describe Martha and her mother as enjoying affectionate family bonds but as locked in the fatal pattern of an ancient curse.[3] To Martha, Mrs Quest is the dark and terrible mother — symbolising the devouring womb[4] — who leaves her no room to be her own person and no choice but to follow in her degraded footsteps.

Having no other role models than her mother, Martha is uncertain of her own identity. Instead of finding in her mother a model to emulate, she finds one she fears because her mother is not free. However, her own plans for independence go no further than her plan to remain single. In her resolution to both defy her mother and be unlike her, she fluctuates wildly between wanting to be independent and wanting to be mothered.

Because she is blinded by her obsession with blaming her mother, Martha is unable to accept the responsibility for her own character and future. She cannot rally sufficiently out of her lethargy to take her matriculation examination, which would allow her a job and an escape from home. Instead, she accuses her mother of putting a spell on her.

Martha's adolescent behaviour is not unusual. The problem is that she never entirely works through its confusions. In the second novel, *A Proper Marriage*, we see her grappling with yet another aspect of her conflict with her mother. Like many women, she is influenced by the stereotypes about female beauty and is consequently ambivalent about her body.[5] Martha is rather boyish looking, with a long, lean narrow body, and is obsessed with thinness. This is as close as a female can be to the supposed ideal figure of freedom, namely the young male.[6] She fears her mother's body, because any physical resemblance between them is a reminder that she could become like her. She feels physical revulsion at her touch and that of any other woman. Martha is terrified of losing the beauty and wholeness of her body to the varicose veins of her mother's friend, Mrs Van Rensberg, for they are, to her, evidence of her bondage to child-bearing.

When her body betrays her and she becomes pregnant, she loses her idealised self-image of what an independent woman should be like and rejects her body as an instrument of oppression. Here we have a situation that classical psychoanalytic theory described as an eternal human dilemma, namely that biology is destiny. Martha has no choice but to become a mother and feels the victim of a conspiracy.[7] She unsuccessfully attempts an abortion. Her mother is no consolation, stating that having a baby is the greatest experience in a woman's life.

Martha, who set out to be different from her mother, finds she is repeating what she sees as her mother's inadequacy as a mother. Moreover, in her quest for independence and non-complacent motherhood, she finds she cannot enjoy her baby daughter and gives her husband Douglas custody of her upon their divorce. She claims this was a political decision because, at the time, her communist affiliations led her to believe it best if the family withered away. Later, she regrets having let her daughter go.

Experience tells her that she lives in a socio-economic system which is maintained by subordination of one human being to another, but she never truly grasps that the root cause goes beyond her mother. She never becomes sufficiently autonomous to function independently of her mother and judge the workings of the world rationally. She is obsessed with what she thinks her mother represents.

It could be said that ultimately Martha benefited psychologically from the struggle with her mother, because it marked boundaries between her mother's values and her own. This allowed her to define who she was and develop her individual philosophy of life. The conflict with her mother was the impetus for her later idealised dream of a utopian, four-gated city, beyond domestic squabbles, political differences, the sex war and the oppressive characteristics of mothering. However, the social structures and doctrines that spawn people like her mother are never understood fully. Instead, she says that bigoted, neurotic or old fashioned people, like her mother, would have to be excluded, if her four-gated city were to function. Thus her own growth was only to be achieved by rejecting her mother.

The denigration of mothers and the pernicious and ghastly patriarchal images of them created an enormous gulf between this mother and daughter. It is typical of the tragedy of many mother-daughter relationships in the 1950s and 1960s, the time in which Lessing's novels are set. These were possibly some of the most difficult decades for mothers and daughters and their problems are still with us. How did this come about?

As always, the psychological context owes much to the socio-economic one. By the 1950s, advanced industrial society, in its search for more consumers, was willing to support theories that encouraged daughters to work outside the home before marriage.[8] Where these changing forces were not understood, many daughters saw their mothers' past as representing a bondage of their own construction. Thus in both the psychological and economic spheres, daughters were coerced into believing that their lack of abundance and freedom was due to their mothers.[9] Of course, their mothers had grown up in a time where women who worked outside the domestic sphere were held in contempt. Understandably, many were unable to swiftly change from disapproval to acceptance of daughters who entered the working world they'd been taught was the province of men.

This situation invited conflict between mothers and daughters. It also gave rise to a spate of women writers who looked back with nostalgia to the time of their great grandmothers, when mothers and daughters formed a strong and supportive alliance. This was a time when little changed and experience followed the same pattern from generation to generation. Daughters participated in a system of apprenticeship, through the accumulated female wisdom of their mothers. Because daughters had few options, they accepted their mothers' reality which, although restrictive, nevertheless offered mutual support and understanding.[10] The contrast with the mother-daughter experience in the 1950s could not be greater and is vividly depicted in Doris Lessing's *Children of Violence* series.

Obviously, the socio-economic changes of the 1950s were not the only

factors used to sanction a daughter's conflict with her mother and the kind
of denigration and rejection that Martha directed at Mrs Quest. There is a
long history of contributing factors — social, economic and cultural — the
discussion of which is better left to the historical and literary explorations
of Book II. Here at the beginning of Book I, I will address the attitudes that
are handed on, generation after generation, within families — attitudes that
shaped the relationship between our great grandmothers and our grandmothers and down the line to our mothers and ourselves. I am talking
about attitudes that are based on the traditions and the myths that can be
found in our immediate family history over the past 150 years.

If we want to improve relationships, we need to know more about these
hidden agendas and how much they were part of our education, our
mother's education as well as her mother's and our great grandmother's
education. The expectations that they endorse are handed on in families
and fashion the mother-daughter relationship. If we are to avoid Martha
Quest's obsession and unhappiness with her mother, we need to know the
myths and traditions that created her tragedy.

A good course for beginning any such information gathering is Barbara
Ehrenreich's and Deidre English's book *For Her Own Good — 150 Years
of the Experts' Advice to Women* and I am much indebted to it. There are
also many other sources and references that are acknowledged throughout
the chapter.

ᘒ

From Great Grandmother to Mother to Daughter

Myths And Tenets That Have Spoilt Relationships

We begin in the mid-nineteenth century when our great grandmothers and
their daughters were rather like hostages. They couldn't go out and get an
education, work in the male work place, own property or vote. They were
told their minds and bodies were inferior to male minds and bodies.
Women were forced into a parasitic situation, in which they performed sexual and reproductive duties for financial support. They were not however
totally submissive. Although many accepted their imprisonment, they also
used it to fight back. At the same time, defiance was tempered by the need
to survive. Like hostages everywhere, they learnt to adulate their gaolers[11]
— the patriarchal heads of families — because they were powerful. As a
result, mothers and daughters learnt to denigrate each other because of their
plight and "weaknesses". What were these so called weaknesses?

One of them is exemplified in the first myth I will highlight, the myth
of the pathology of the female body and its functions. It is always coupled
with the myth of the inferiority of the female psyche and mentality. If
mothers and daughters want respectful relationships, these are major

patriarchal myths that they need to be vigilant about. These myths are so essential to reinforcing the patriarchal system, they have become tenets that survive to this day.[12]

Myth No. 1:
The Female Body Is Imperfect Because It Isn't Male

We are not always fully conscious of being influenced by this myth, but sometimes the discomfort surfaces when we hear a dirty joke about our sexual organs or we feel unhappy about menstruating. I explore its effect on mother-daughter relationships further in Chapters 4 and 6. For the present, suffice it to say that there are many subtle "put downs" about women's moods and physical functions that have had an impact on our mothers, grandmothers and great grandmothers and how their daughters related to them. How and why did they accept them?

Step back 150 years and the reasons are more obvious and less camouflaged than they are today. The leaders and entrepreneurs of Victorian society were engrossed in an unabashed and ruthless pursuit of capitalism, expanding industry, profits and empire without the democratic and humanitarian constraints that some governments now have in place. Their mainstay was a strongly patriarchal value system: power, competition and exploitation. It was a very male-dominated society structured in many ways to enlarge the male ego. Delicate women made men feel masculine and powerful. The possession of such women became a status symbol and set the sexual, romanticist ideal of femininity for all classes. A successful man could have no better indication of his class and masculinity than a wife who was an idle, social ornament, delicate and cultured, with a childlike ignorance of the male world. Even the less affluent favoured such a wife, as in the case of David Copperfield's first doll-like wife, Dora. A virtuous wife and mother spent a secluded life sewing, sketching, planning menus and supervising the servants and the children — or being ill. Masculinity was further endorsed by a belief that the female condition was a pathological deviation from the male. The Victorians expected invalidism of mothers and daughters.

In this context, the curious epidemic that swept through the middle and upper-middle class female population in the United States and England, during the mid-nineteenth century, becomes more comprehensible. It did not afflict the working women of the lower classes. Diaries and journals of the time give hundreds of examples of middle class mothers and daughters becoming hopeless invalids. We find diagnostic labels such as "neurasthenia", "nervous prostration", "hyperesthesia", "cardiac inadequacy", "dyspepsia", "rheumatism" and "hysteria". Symptoms included headache, muscular aches, weakness, depression, menstrual difficulties, indigestion and general debility.

By the mid-nineteenth century, mothers and daughters had made invalidism a way of life and a way of filling in time, as well as a form of passive resistance.

Alice James, sister of Henry James, the novelist and William James, the psychologist, is an example of one who began her career as an invalid at nineteen. Although it is not known whether her invalidism had an organic basis, it is known that she had a gift for writing, but was never encouraged to go to college. In her time, women could be charming, highly strung or imaginative, but not brilliant or culturally productive. Literature and art dwelt on the sensuous, languid passivity of the beautiful invalid. Novels for mothers and daughters followed suit, with the loveliest of heroines, too good and too pure for this life, dying young. A good example is Alcott's *Little Women*, which was a very popular novel with generations of young girls.

Female fashion was an imprisonment which ensured the frailty that made the conventional male feel confidently masculine and powerful. Tight-laced corsets had a crippling effect on body and health, applying anywhere between 20 and 80 pounds (9-36 Kg) of pressure to internal organs. Hence the shortness of breath, indigestion, weakness and bent and fractured ribs recorded in the literature of the time. In some cases, the uterus could even be forced out through the vagina by the pressure of the corset!

In the following passage, Ehrenreich and English summarise the hypocrisy behind the demand for the kind of female beauty that enhances masculinity in men:

> The morbidity of nineteenth-century tastes in female beauty reveals the hostility which never lies too far below the surface of sexual romanticism. To be sure, the romantic spirit puts women on a pedestal and ascribes to her every tender virtue absent from the Market. But carried to an extreme the demand that woman be a negation of man's world left almost nothing for women to actually be: if men are busy, she is idle; if men are rough, she is gentle; if men are strong, she is frail; if men are rational, she is irrational; and so on. The logic which insists that femininity is negative masculinity necessarily romanticises the moribund woman and encourages a kind of paternalistic necrophilia.[13]

In this vein, theories, which guided medical practice from the late nineteenth century to the early twentieth century, held that women's normal state was to be sick. Medicine believed female functions were inherently pathological and used as evidence childbirth, menopause and menstruation — female functions that have always been described as alarming and threatening to men in patriarchal myths. This is why a normal female function such as menstruation was seen as a period of ill health, when ordinary activities, riding, shopping, dancing should be avoided. Pregnancy was an indisposition and after delivery, a protracted period of convalescence was required. Menopause was a terminal illness — the death of the woman in the woman. All this meant, among other things, that women could not be doctors, being physically and mentally unstrung. In this way the medical profession kept an exclusive men's club and made a fortune out of sickly, middle class women. As the feminist writing of the time underlined, attention was now paid to women's health as never before, because it was lucrative, and medical literature perpetuated the epidemic of female invalidism for that reason.

Working class women received no such attention from the medical profession. Their employers gave them no time off for pregnancy or childbirth. They were regarded as robust and coarse. These dichotomies in attitudes, these double standards, are typical of the patriarchal thinking of the time. Either way, women were deprived of pride in their bodies — a pride that is essential to any accepting relationship between mothers and daughters. As we have seen, lack of pride in her own and her mother's body contributed to Martha Quest's wish to reject her mother.

This brings us to another divisive myth. Patriarchy not only regarded women as physically abnormal, since they weren't men, but denigrated their ability to create life.

Myth No 2:
Women's Life-giving Processes Indicate Their Inferiority and Their Danger

This belittling view of female functions makes mothers and daughters embarrassed with each other and leads to a loss of pride in their ability to create life. It has a long history which is discussed in Book II.

Here, if we take a look at more recent history beginning in the 1860s, we find the medical profession openly denigrating women because they give birth. Natural scientists equated women's place on the evolutionary scale with Negroes, who were seen as subhuman at that time.[14] Even today, there are male gynaecologists who regard a woman as retreating down the evolutionary scale during childbirth, because inevitably she needs to abandon conventional standards of female modesty as she labours to deliver her baby.[15]

By the 1880's, the medical profession had developed the psychology of the ovary, whereby a woman's entire personality was seen as directed by her ovaries. It was claimed that any abnormalities, from nervousness to insanity, could be traced to some ovarian disease. Female personality disorders, masturbation and nymphomania were controlled by various surgical assaults, such as removal of the clitoris or, most often, by the removal of the ovaries. Such cases ran into hundreds of thousands. Some doctors claimed the removal of the ovaries improved a woman's moral sense, since she became less like a woman. It was argued that ovarian function made women inherently artful and deceitful. It is a myth that has not been completely surrendered to this day.

However, defining women exclusively in terms of their reproductive capacities did not make them sexual beings. Female sexuality was regarded as unfeminine and detrimental to reproduction. An over-sexed woman was seen as a sperm-draining vampire, who would leave men weak, effeminate and spent. For this reason, sportsmen, for example, were advised to avoid sexual intercourse before a major sporting competition and only recently has the advice been challenged. This attitude to women's sexuality causes mothers and daughters to lose respect for each other and the damage this does to mother-daughter relationships to this day is discussed in Chapter 4.

Whenever women fought to regain pride, nineteenth century patriarchy put them in a no-win situation. For example, during the later part of the century, feminists and founders of the suffragette movement persuaded many women to forsake the passive, sick model of femininity and demand the right to the same education and work opportunities as men. In response, the threatened medical profession raised the battle cry of the uterus versus the brain. It was said one could only be developed at the expense of the other. Doctors took the lead in the ongoing debate over female education and argued vociferously about its dangers.

Myth No 3:
Education Reduces Women's Reproductive Capacity

Mothers and daughters lived in terror and were subdued after reading medical and psychological books, such as Hall's *Adolescence*, which doomed them to a pathological existence if they rebelliously partook of education. Nevertheless, feminists attacked the idea that women did not have the stamina for education and increasingly ignored the doctors' advice. This heightened the medical profession's view that women were "neurasthenic" and they advocated the rest cure, involving total isolation and sensory deprivation — a form of brain-washing.

During the economic depression of the 1890s, women turned to abortion as a means of fertility control and that combined with other factors, such as puerperal fever in childbirth, meant that the birth rate fell. The drop was said to be due entirely to feminine invalidism and the patriarchally-dominated medical profession began to describe the previously, honoured invalidism as malingering. Thus, there emerged the theory of hysteria and the petty, female tyrant, whose invalidism gave her power over her husband, children, servants and her doctor.

So on the one hand, women's physique was regarded as less perfect than males' and prone to illness and disease and, on the other, women who were sick were seen as malingering. This epitomises the double bind — the no-win situation of disrespect for women — in which mothers and daughters find themselves. As Ehrenreich and English explain, sickness was both a way of coping and a form of defiance:

> In the epidemic of hysteria women were both accepting their inherent "sickness" and finding a way to rebel against an intolerable social role. Sickness having become a way of life, became a way of rebellion, and medical treatment, which had always had strong overtones of coercion revealed itself as frankly and brutally oppressive.[16]

Women continued to be regarded as the "weaker" sex, yet were expected to fulfil themselves in motherhood and bear as many children as possible. They were intended to suffer in childbirth.[17] This brings us to the third patriarchal myth that set Martha Quest against her mother and still fills many daughters with fear and anger that they will end up in the martyred role of their mothers.

Myth No. 4:
Becoming the Ideal Mother is Women's Vocation

Victorian patriarchy insisted that women devote themselves to becoming perfect mothers. We all know that perfection is impossible. To this day, the unrealistic expectations of mothers make daughters behave irrationally towards their mothers.[18]

Yet despite the impossible demands upon motherhood and looking back over the past 150 years, we see how mothers have struggled to make the best of their mothering role and tried to strengthen and dignify mother-daughter relationships through it. For example, some believed in the possibility of motherhood as a political weapon. Nineteenth century feminist writers and women of the intelligentsia, such as George Eliot, whose work as it bears upon her relationship with her mother is discussed in Book II, attempted to salvage some dignity for the tearful and gentle mothers of the Victorian era by espousing the catch phrase: "The hand that rocks the cradle rules the world".

The idea had grown from the fact that the importance of mother love was stressed in many patriarchal treatises of the period. Women, it was argued, are responsible for the home and for raising their children. The middle class mother willingly accepted such responsibility, since it gave her status that her female forebears had not had.[19]

At the same time, we find the experts doing an about-turn and agreeing that higher education would not destroy the mothering instinct, but help it. So motherhood began to be regarded as a profession. Excited by Darwin's theory of evolution and his methods of observation, the experts instructed mothers how to be professional by observing their babies and children systematically. Baby biographies became the fashion. These fashions were supported by many feminists of the time, for were they not a way to the kind of education that had previously been denied them?

This acceptance of the importance of mothers by a strongly patriarchal society was not entirely driven by concern for women and children, but was tied to economic and social changes. It highlights how often what is said to be "good" for mothers and daughters is in fact manipulative propaganda to ensure the stability of traditional society. By the closing decades of the nineteenth century, the Industrial Revolution had driven most men from domestic industries into the factories and offices and they now worked in locations apart from their wives and children. It was important that women took control of the domestic world, which provided sustenance for the factory worker and, through babies, more hands for the factories.

Rapid industrial development meant that the men who worked in the factories required some education. At the same time, the need for appropriately literate managers was growing. Thus more schools and a longer preparation for adulthood became important, in order to develop the abilities needed to survive in industrial society. In parallel, those in charge of the domestic world must have the skills necessary to cope with the basics of shopping and marketing. Basic education was valued for economic and social reasons and to a limited degree became open to women. This was a step forward, since education opened the way for mothers and daughters to acquire greater understanding of the system that limited them.

But the limited education permitted women, based on the philosophy of maternal responsibility, was not straightforward. A woman's purpose in life was still said to lie entirely in her children and her capacity for repro-duction. Consequently, she was seen as needing the kind of education about children that would ensure she brought them up "correctly" or, in other words, to support and perpetuate the status quo. Thus the patriar-chal child experts found a raison d'être and became a strong force in maintaining the status quo. Subsequently, the twentieth century became known as the century of the child.

Those who followed Freud and the psychoanalytic movement were among many child experts who gained recognition around the beginning of the twentieth century. They too acknowledged women's intelligence, but the acceptance was double edged, for they became engrossed in what women *ought* to be doing, or not doing, with their children. The tyranny of *ought* became increasingly strident over the next four or five decades, culminating in an obsession with the guilt of mothers. This kind of guilt is very destructive of mother-daughter relationships and is examined in sub-sequent chapters.

In many ways, focusing on the child was an argument against the social-ist, marxist and feminist revolutionaries of the late nineteenth and early twentieth centuries, for it implied that the social structure could not be changed within a single generation, even after a revolution. Instead, it was argued that concentrating on the methods of raising children would achieve the just society painlessly, over a number of generations. This argument reinforced the power of the child-raising expert.

Thus the child expert and psychological theories about mothering came to be seen as superior to the mother and her experience, which brings us to a special characteristic of patriarchy — the tendency to create mutually exclusive myths about mothers and mothering. Contradictory myths are impossible to implement and undermine the mother's status and therefore the mother-daughter relationship.

Myth No 5:
Mothers Knowing Everything About Child-rearing versus Mothers Should Follow the Child Expert

One of the major problems with following child experts is that they dis-agree and their theories change frequently. The ever-changing attitudes to what mothers should and should not be doing encourages daughters to hold their mothers in contempt. Changing fashions in child-rearing deprive mothers of authority and autonomy. Any help and advice they might give their daughters can easily be described as old fashioned and therefore worthless.[20]

As Ehrenreich and English point out, motherhood as a profession requiring intelligence was dogged from the start by the expert, who made it his business to tell mothers what to do. He was given the authority to do this through the status that his alignment with science gave him. In all quarters, industrial society extolled science as the hope of the future and the fountain of progress and child study was no exception. The public was impressed by pragmatic psychologists such as William James and John Dewey, who attempted to prove that psychology was a science by philosophical reasoning.[21] Many admired Stanley Hall who, at the turn of the century, pioneered crude surveys of children's attitudes, fears and games, which passed for "science" and which won the admiration of the motherhood movements.

Mothers were nevertheless confused, because advice from one quarter was in direct conflict with that from another. For example, what Freud had to say was criticised by many who regarded his theories as mere generalisations, based on subjective interpretations of a limited number of clinical cases. His concepts were said to be unscientific and, inevitably, contrary advice to mothers came from those who regarded themselves as more "scientific" than Freud.[22]

Many of these theories "reflected the means of production".[23] In other words, they were based purely on industrial changes and did not spring from the "nature" of the child. This is why we find that the newly emerging, mechanical age spawned mechanical theories of child-raising and development. For example, the psychologist James Watson advocated behaviourism — the core of which was conditioning. This was described as a mechanistic approach to bringing up children.[24]

Many of Watson's contemporaries criticised his ideas as the ultimate in patriarchal inhumanity and mindlessness, for they removed mind and consciousness from psychology and reduced emotion and thought to the mechanics of physiology. The feminine perspective, which was said to belong to the province of feeling was totally banished from psychology. Raising children became a mere matter of conditioning. The child could be trained, by the mother, to become like a machine, and thus acquire the necessary regularity and discipline to survive in industrial society.[25]

Mothers were exhorted to feed their babies every three hours, precisely on the hour and pot them in similar fashion. An example is seen in the advice of the famed and regimented Truby-King, who ruled in large numbers of middle class households, in the 1930s and 1940s.

Most of all, the way in which behaviourism removed the feminine perspective from psychology meant that women were subsumed under male psychology. This blocked explorations that would further understanding about female relationships and mother-daughter relationships.

By the 1940s, the experts had taken another about-turn and had proclaimed that mothers were doing violence to their children's innate nature by over-regulation. A child's spontaneous impulses were good and sensible. The child, instead of being mindless putty, actually knew what was best for its development. He (never she) was viewed as harmless and purposefully inquisitive. Thumb sucking or exploring genitals, once highly suspect, were now perfectly normal. Mothers were to follow the line of the new breed of scientific experts and be permissive, in order to respond appropriately to their children's needs.

These were the days of Arnold Gesell and Dr Spock, from whom mothers learnt that almost everything their offspring did was normal and that all their behaviour was understandable and excusable, because "children go through stages". In the texts of Spock and Gesell, bewildered mothers found reassurance and inexhaustible patience for their children's tantrums, stubborness and moods.

As behaviourism lost ground, several descendants of the Freudian school rallied mothers to their flag with warnings about stress and trauma. Mothers were instructed in techniques for protecting their children from stress. Traumatisation of children's natural sexual and aggressive instincts was to be avoided. Instinctual theories that reduced all human needs to biological urges became popular.[26]

If by now you are feeling bemused and your mind is wandering, imagine the effect all these changes had on mothers and still do and how much they confuse daughters who have to choose between their mothers' advice and the experts' latest decree. What does this do to their relationship?

While the disagreements between experts and the changes in their advice made mothers less confident in relationship to their children, inherent in each change was always some factor that undermined the mother-daughter relationship further. Instinctual theory is a good example. A mother's role, as a scientific observer checking off charts or writing diaries, gave way to one which regarded her as an instinctual being who exuded love. This brings us to the sixth patriarchal tenet or myth — a myth that sets any mother up as the failing mother.

Myth No. 6:
Mothers Provide Unlimited and Bountiful Love

This expectation is fraught with disappointments that do great damage to mother-daughter relationships and is discussed in Chapters 3 and 6. By the 1940s, the expectation was entrenched. Love was a mother's job. Mother love had become a kind of inexplicable nourishment which oozed from mothers. It was seen as rooted in biological instincts, which meant mothers should find total fulfilment in meeting the needs of their children.

Education once more became suspect, because it might put women out of line with their motherly instincts. The conflicts and coercions which were put upon mothers by the conventional child experts in this era, are well expressed in Mary McCarthy's novel of the period, The Group. They are summed up in the words of one of the characters, Norinne, who comments: "Our Vassar education made it tough for me to accept my womanly role".

By the 1950s, professional acceptance and community reinterpretation of old psychoanalytic theories and the tyranny of "ought" had combined to create an intolerable burden of responsibility for mothers in western society. Popular interpretations of psychoanalysis generated our seventh myth — one that encourages adult daughters to renege on self-responsibility and use their mothers as scapegoats.

Myth No. 7:
Mothers Are Responsible For All Our Problems

If after 20 or 30 years of employment, our employer expected us to take total responsibility for all the problems created by all the employees of the firm for which we worked, most of us would change jobs. We would see it as an impossible and unjust responsibility. Yet this is what is expected of mothers. Inevitably, impossible expectations lead to the belief that mothers are inadequate and depriving. Consequently, daughters — children, adolescents and adults — feel justified in regarding mothers as the mainspring of their personal maladjustments and mothers become the butt of social resentment and hostility. As a result, mothers often feel guilty of having failed their children: "Am I doing what is right? Am I doing enough? Am I doing too much?"

By the 1950s these attitudes and feelings were widespread. Whenever a child had anything, from a behaviour problem to a personality disorder, psychiatry and psychology emphasised the role of the mother. For example, until recently, asthma, autism and schizophrenia were all said to be the outcome of cold and dominating mothering. In cases of school phobia or school avoidance (not to be confused with truancy) it was fashionable to dwell entirely upon the mother's role. The mother of a child with school phobia was described as a dependent person, who'd had unsatisfactory relationships with her own parents and reversed roles with her child in order to make him or her a substitute parent. The child stayed home, albeit unconsciously, to allay the mother's anxiety about being left without support.

More recently, it has been recognised that fathers may also reverse roles and augment the problems of their children by neglect, ineffectualness, lack of support or constant absence. For example, a father may be passive and dependent, making no attempt to give emotional support to his wife and child. Alternatively, he may be excessively masculine — again incapable of emotional support. He may be frequently absent from home, because he's a workaholic or pursuing his career or sporting interests.[27] In cases of childhood deprivation or malfunction, both parents generally interact in some dyadic fashion.

The 1950s brought other confusions for mothers.

Myth No. 8:
Working Mothers Are Not Good For Their Children

Whereas during World War 11, women had been persuaded to work in munitions and essential services, after the war, attitudes about their function and purpose took a somersault. As ever, changing attitudes had much to do with social and economic changes. As men returned from the war, patriarchy was concerned that women might compete with them for jobs. Moreover, the unprecedented prosperity and full employment of the 1950s made the idealisation of the "mother at home" viable.

As a result, conventional child experts and other pillars of society admonished mothers who worked and said they were doing damage to their inner, feminine instincts and depriving their children.

In the 1950s and 1960s, a common assumption was that a working mother was neglecting her children. Maternal employment and maternal deprivation were equated. However, we now know that the non-working mother is not necessarily interacting with her child as successfully as these assumptions suggested. If she has inadequate support or is unhappy about her role, she is likely to transmit it to her children. Positive self-esteem seems to be the significant factor in successful child-raising, rather than whether a mother is in outside employment.

Before and during the 1950s and 1960s, there was so much disapproval of mothers working that there was often conflict between a daughter and her mother, if the daughter worked after marriage and especially if she had children. Social disapproval created tension between many mothers who had never worked and daughters who had always worked before and after the birth of their babies. This was not universal, as we shall see in the story of Anastasia and her mother in the Bibliotherapy (Chapter 9).

Contrary to earlier research and negative attitudes toward working mothers, the research of the 1970s, 1980s and 1990s, indicated that maternal employment can positively affect the child's concept of the female role. This is because the child learns sex roles from observations of parents. Contemporary daughters of working mothers tend to view work as something they will want to do when they are mothers. They see women as competent and effective, while sons of working mothers see men as warm and expressive, if their fathers have shared responsibility for child care with their wives.[28]

In the late 1970s and 1980s, research showed that daughters of employed women are significantly different from daughters of full-time housewives, in that they do not devalue female achievements to the same extent. Among tertiary students, both male and female, maternal employment is related to positive attitudes about social equality between the sexes. Adolescent daughters of working mothers are more likely to name their mothers as the person they most admire. Tertiary women students, with working mothers, are more likely to name their mothers as the person they most resemble and the one they most want to be like. In short, this myth is shown up for the destructive piece of false propaganda it is. In favourable circumstances, working mothers have very respectful and close relationships with their daughters.

In this period, it was observed that daughters of working mothers have higher academic and career aspirations and show a higher level of actual achievement. They also have higher self esteem, when any of the following conditions exist: the mother works for self-oriented reasons, is very satisfied with her work, is a professional, has adequate home and child care arrangements so that her dual role does not involve undue strain and where she does not feel so guilty that she over-compensates. When the mother's employment involves conflict and difficulties, the daughter's self-esteem is not enhanced.[29] However, these observations were not widely accepted, until the late 1970s and early 1980s.

The tendency to blame working mothers heralded the twentieth century's most vociferous period of mother-blaming. Ehrenreich and English argue that the romantic and simple ideal of motherly love disappeared, when psychoanalysis took over completely and reduced motherhood to a regression to, and a psychological re-enactment of, the problems of the mother's own infancy and her relationship with her mother.[30] This view, which is explored further in Chapter 8, condoned a blaming attitude towards mothers — an attitude which is a variation on Myth 7, but is more vicious in its content.

Myth No. 9:
Blaming Mothers Is Justified

By the 1950s, psychoanalysis was directed at probing the maternal unconscious and searching for the neuroses that had begun in the mother's childhood and was now leading to behavioural and mental problems in her offspring. Mothers were haunted by images of their fundamental neuroticism, which were said to cause them to be rejecting mothers or over-protective mothers or mothers who were both rejecting and over-protective and, as a result, destructive of their children. Daughters were encouraged to resent their mothers for causing their personality and relationship problems.

The over-protective mother became a particular obscenity, said to be especially apparent among Jewish mothers, as exemplified in *Portnoy's Complaint*. Such mother-monsters, created by patriarchally aligned writers, are much maligned literary figures of this period. They are depicted as the all-engulfing nurturers, who devour the very soul of their children with every mouthful of gefilte fish. At least Jewish women writers, on the whole, portrayed mothers as both the devourer and the devoured. They understood that they sacrifice themselves, yet are helpless to prevent the sacrifice of their daughters.[31]

The hidden agenda in this obsession with the pathological influence of mothers soon became apparent. It was aimed at undermining what was seen as the threatening power of mothers. In the beginning, the doctrine of maternal responsibility had been a convenient "cop-out". It was a way in which men could forego responsibility, by projecting their personal inadequacies onto mothers. Popular books, that were written on the subject at the time, relieved their readers of any responsibility for themselves as individuals.

However the doctrine had its down-side. It implied that women had a more salient role in the family than had previously been acknowledged.

What was now believed to be the extreme power of women, as mothers, created alarm and anxiety.

In later chapters, there are discussions of the many and varied forms of men's fear of the power of women and their origins. Unfortunately, fear of feminine power is incorporated by women themselves. Women become anxious that expression of their strength is threatening to men. As a consequence, they repress it and re-direct it against themselves and their mothers.[32] Fear of stepping outside the submissive stereotype of femininity has far-reaching effects on how mothers and daughters value and relate to each other. It is at the root of many conflicts.

Myth No.10:
Mother-Power Is Dangerous

During the 1950's, anxiety about the power of mothers found many forms of expression — one of them being the spectre of "Momism". One of a number of books on the topic was *The Lonely Crowd* by David Reisman, who stated that the decline of ambition and individualism in men was due to "Momism", or the devouring and controlling nature of mothers. Cartoons poking fun at domesticated or cowed and foolish husbands and fathers, such as Dagwood, became popular. It became fashionable to say that women were castrating men.

Even the frustrations of the marketplace were projected into hostile images of women. They became the scapegoats for patriarchal misman-agement and disintegration. Society was seen as declining, not through the inhumanity of competitiveness and materialism, but because women were failing as mothers. It was said that the only way to invigorate society was for fathers to resume power. Fathers, however, did not recognise that they were being hoist by their own petard, since they'd been encouraged to hand their children over to women during the Industrial Revolution. The "mother is responsible" philosophy had led inevitably to a situation whereby the courts were giving custody of children pre-dominantly to mothers.[33] Fathers found the impetus to retake a hand in child-raising.

Research was now unearthed, or designed, which demonstrated that fathers are crucial to their children's self-esteem. It was discovered that they are needed to guide sons to masculinity and daughters to femininity. In Chapter 5, I explore this further and point to research which negates the old patriarchal view that child-raising should be entirely a mother's job and underlines that fathers are the forgotten influence in the mother-daughter relationship. But first we must consider another tenet or myth.

Myth No. 11:
Fathers Have More Important Things To Do Than Rearing Children

In the research of the 1950s, this myth was partly reversed and fathers were described as particularly necessary in order to keep their wives sexually satisfied. It was said that much of poor mothering lay in sexual frustration. This partly derogatory view had some value, in that it recognised that mothers could be sexual beings. Unfortunately, the recognition that fathers are as important as mothers and that parenting is a mutual responsibility did not always go beyond the theory and often came about for the wrong reasons. It was frequently tainted by the tendency to see children as personal property — a tendency that is aggravated by conflict during family breakdown. Thus children's needs became secondary in many divorce court battles.[34]

In 1986, Phyllis Chesler's *Mothers On Trial: The Battle for Children and Custody*, reported the results of a seven year study of custodial challenges to mothers. She is not sure that custodial-seeking fathers always have genuine feelings for their children, are discriminated against, or that mothers are always deliberately withholding their children from them. She concludes that children are only on loan to their mothers and that the new-age man is really a mother-father, who typically suffers womb envy, hates women and wants to replace them as the better parent.

This is a very angry view, no doubt born of observing the undermining of the mother's role in the 1970s and 1980s. Despite Chesler's pessimism, it is certainly evident that many fathers and mothers work out custodial arrangements that are in the child's interests without legal battles. Custodial battles often signify a conflicted marriage situation, that was not in the child's interests in the first place.[35]

The attention to fathers, which generated the new line about sexier mothers, certainly had its negative connotations. It revived old patriarchal divisive teachings that women — mothers and daughters — are in competition for men. The psychological impact on mother-daughter relationships of this divisive propaganda is discussed in Chapters 4-6. It is an outcome of the following phallocentric myth.

Myth No.12:
The Value of Women Lies In Their Sexual Attractiveness To Men

The promotion of this attitude meant that the mothers and daughters who believed it, tried to emulate the plastic females of advertisements. A new commercially-viable literature, directed at telling mothers and daughters how to be sexy in the most vacuous and demeaning way, was born. Often the stereotypes of sexiness set up disrespect and anxiety between mothers and daughters. Ageing mothers could be scorned. Like Martha Quest, a daughter's anxiety about the loss of her youth could justifiably become focused on the wrinkles and varicose veins of her mother. For a mother, a daughter who was not as slim and well-groomed as the models in the television advertisements, was evidence of her failure as a mother. The conflicts and criticisms generated through trying to measure up to the stereotypes is well known to most mothers and daughters.

The 1960s and 1970s were a particularly difficult time for mother-daughter relationships in other ways. Many daughters adopted markedly different behaviours from their mothers and not infrequently these differences became a source of conflict. Some daughters became flower children and abandoned the decorum and sexual monogamy their mothers had been taught to value. They went on anti-Vietnam marches and became political activists outside the domestic world in which patriarchy had tried to confine their mothers.

In this period, increasing numbers of women began to question many of the old attitudes and particularly whether women must make themselves little more than sex objects for men. They were also questioning whether motherhood was the only possible role for women. Their questions challenged some of the myths already discussed, including myths 4 and 5, which are offshoots of the most central of all patriarchal myths, namely that biology is everything as far as women are concerned.

Myth No. 13:
A Woman's Purpose Is To Become a Biological Mother

More open access to contraception, which had begun in earlier decades, did not necessarily mean that women's choices about motherhood had come totally under their control. Many had still felt pressured by the widespread social support for the myth that a woman's purpose is to become a biological mother and settled for having at least two children. But smaller families often meant there was even greater pressure to become a perfect mother — a super-mum. Some were consoled by the fact that the establishment allowed them to shift blame for their less than perfect offspring onto the very child experts, whom they'd previously been admonished to follow.

The Vietnam war and the rebellious behaviour of the young protesters of the 1960s and 1970s had much to do with this official change in the attitude to the child experts. "Permissive" child-raising advocates, such as Spock, were accused and blamed for encouraging parents to raise a generation of undisciplined and disrespectful youth. Mothers were advised to replace permissive parenting with a stricter approach. Child-raising jargon was augmented by the term "authoritative" parenting. Authoritative parents were those who praised, set limits and had high expectations for their children.[36]

Another alternative was not to have children at all. Many a mother was at odds with a daughter who would not give her grandchildren, as she had her mother. Not to have children flew in the face of something that had been instilled into generation upon generation of women.

By the 1970s it had begun to be fashionable to be childless. Articles appeared in the popular press, describing children as an obstacle to women's freedom. As this view became more popular and there were fewer voters with children, governments could freely make spending cuts in child welfare and stall on day care. Ehrenreich and English conclude that the "Century of the Child" was over by the beginning of the 1980s. Since patriarchy had always measured women's value by the number of off-spring they produced, this became a very confusing time for women who questioned whether they should become mothers or not.

The 'fulfilled' mother of five or more children of earlier decades, was now reviled as a menace to zero population movements. But, as ever, there was a hidden socio-economic agenda in this exhortation. For one thing, such is the paradoxical nature of post-industrial society, it cannot sustain a large population that demands a higher and higher standard of living, because this depends on the limited resources and poverty of the third world. Moreover, since large families have less money to spend on material goods, they are of little value to a society that is sustained by consumerism.

Even in smaller families, full-time motherhood became financially untenable in the post-industrial societies of the 1980s and 1990s. Housewifery lost whatever status it once had. Women felt pressured to get into the work-force and help their families partake of the material possessions, promoted as essential to a better lifestyle.

In the movement to make mothers redundant, daughters were seduced by the images of the television soapies where the single, working girl, sexy and clever, with money in her pocket, outshone the sickly, sweet mum on a restricted family budget. They were encouraged to believe that it was the former, whom men valued, not the virtuous and the long-suffering mother — a complete reversal of the previous stereotype. Women, who all their lives had faithfully followed patriarchal demands to be passive and devoted wives and mothers, found themselves abandoned. While they were the losers, the marketplace found value in their plight. Assertiveness training for women flourished.

The spectacle of the abandoned mother can create an enormous gulf between a mother and her daughter. The daughter fears becoming a victim like her mother. But a divorce can be used constructively to rework relationships between a mother and her daughter. An example is given in the story of Ally in the Bibliotherapy in Chapter 9.

Eventually, many women learnt how to cope after divorce and live outside the family unit, by which patriarchy had previously defined them. Many single mothers formed very close ties with their daughters. Those who remarried, often found a new and complicated motherhood in blended or step-families. The myth of the wicked stepmother reappeared and women tried to be angels to their stepchildren.[37]

Overall, by the mid 1980's, motherhood had become less important as a role model for women. The conditions of post-industrial society had largely brought this about, in a destructive way for the mother-daughter relationship, by giving mothers less and less status. There were women and some feminists who jumped on this bandwagon.[38] They denigrated mothers and children, because to them they represented the sources of past bondage. In doing so, they could appeal to another of patriarchy's contradictory myths.

Myth No. 14:
Motherhood is an Inferior Role

This myth has always created confusion and conflicting feelings between mothers and daughters. Fortunately, in this period, many women and feminists positively redirected current thinking about women and mother-daughter relations. They promoted a searching analysis of patriarchy's ambivalent and hypocritical definitions of maternal love and responsibility. They exposed the repressiveness of contradictory sets of myths. Ehrenreich and English, who have been quoted frequently in this chapter, are good examples of leaders in this critical examination of mothers under patriarchy. There are many others, including Park and Heaton, Eichenbaum and Orbach, Firman and Firman, Strom and Strom, Fischer, Rabuzzi and Walters. Several books by these authors can be found in the Bibliography. As a result of these explorations, mothers were re-valued and daughters encouraged to rethink their relationship with them. This book presents much of this literature as Bibliotherapy for mothers and daughters.

By the 1980's, many women were prepared to join feminists who questioned the experts and their ideas about children, mothers, daughters and femininity. More and more gave support to the feminist argument, that they could not assimilate into patriarchal society and its excesses without doing violence to their own nature and their relationships. Female writers and some male writers, such as Marcuse, argued that feminine values are the human principles that can save civilisation. They are certainly the values that construct good mother-daughter relationships.

These explorations were augmented by re-examination of the female psyche in the context of humanistic psychology. Whereas patriarchally-oriented psychology had long concentrated upon aggression, humanistic themes were revived and explored. The human characteristics of altruism or empathy, which had previously been devalued as primarily female propensities, found their place in texts, courses and research. Similarly, the study of child development became concerned with the child's perspective and what it is like to be a child, rather than theories that were machismo projections about children being driven by the power motives and aggression of adult men. Such projections had occasioned books with titles like *The Terrible Two's* or *Taming Tinies* and their assumptions were now examined in public discussion.[39] The study of the female child, and the role of language and social expectations in her developing psyche, began to equal studies in the relationships and development of boys.[40] These are re-examinations that added insight and value to female psychology and development. They did much to help the understanding of mother-daughter relationships and are discussed throughout this book.

The revaluing process also meant that the views of women could more easily find space in the media. They could air and discuss the pressures on mothers and were able to clear away some of the dross that had undermined mother-daughter relationships. Their discussions made it more difficult for the patriarchally indoctrinated to lapse into old and common denigrations, such as hostile jokes about wives or mothers-in-law, which had made mothers and daughters devalue each other.

But as patriarchy became less likely to deflect its hostility onto mothers, there was a down-side. It now found an outlet in open violence against women.

Myth No. 15:
Women Enjoy Sexual Violence

This is an age-old myth, examples of which can be found in the pornography of the Victorian era and the earlier writings of the Marquis de Sade. In the late twentieth century, examples are readily available in the marketplace through pornographic videos which exhibit the mutilation and the savage rape of women. Mothers and daughters find it hard to escape these images. Some even believe the myth that women enjoy sexual violence and fail to recognise how much it degrades women by presenting them as victims. The image of the victim means anxiety about one's sex and less respect for femaleness. This is tragic for mother-daughter relationships and later chapters explain why. In fact, this theme is explored throughout both books. In Book I, see Chapter 4 on sexuality and Chapter 8 on masochism.

Overview

The best protection against the myths, tenets and traditions that destroy mother-daughter relationships is to recognise the true nature of the society that encourages them. By the 1980s alongside women, many men — some of them with power — began to realise that the inequities and deprivations of patriarchy — sexual discrimination, rampant consumerism, environmental degradation and general deterioration of living standards — were doing them injustice. Recognition of these obvious paradoxes created a climate that made it is easier for mothers and daughters to acknowledge the harm patriarchy and its myths have done their relationship.

This chapter has outlined in historical setting some of the traditions, myths and tenets that spoil mother-daughter relationships. Many of these are aimed at destroying mothers' and daughters' pride in their femininity, their sexuality, their bodies and their bodily functions and powers. Many set up a distance, an embarrassment and even a loathing between mothers and daughters, as was seen in the case of Martha Quest at the beginning of the chapter.

The saga of changing "shoulds" and "oughts" has had profound implications for mother-daughter relationships. Quite apart from the guilt, anxieties and pressures to conform involved, it means child-rearing fashions change so rapidly in the hands of the experts, that mothers can no longer hand on their experience to their daughters. They have lost credibility by the time their daughters become adults or mothers. Above all, the prevailing misogyny, inherent in every change in the fashion of child-rearing methods, inculcates disrespect between mothers and daughters.

It has been suggested that we overcome this insidious erosion of self respect by examining old traditions and myths and the true nature of the patriarchal society that constructs them.

But most important of all is building our own self-esteem. Patriarchy will not do it for us. This book tries to show how mothers and daughters can do it for themselves.

We begin the process by acquiring some understanding of how we develop as persons from birth, through childhood, adolescence and young adulthood. We can rework the events that undermined our self-esteem, but we have to recognise their true nature first. If we have daughters, we can use the understanding generated by our renegotiations of self to ensure that the processes that undermined our self confidence are resisted. If we don't have daughters, we can help others. We are all daughters and we all have mothers. There are also mother and daughter relationships that are non-biological, found in friendships and the workplace.

The next chapter looks at the development of self-concept and self-esteem in young children and their importance for good mother-daughter relationships. Subsequent chapters explore mother-daughter relationships in adolescence and adulthood.

෴

BIBLIOTHERAPY

For further reading about myths that encourage us to blame mothers and poison relationships between mothers and daughters read Paula Caplan's *Don't Blame Mothers*.

To pursue further the history of the influence of patriarchy on mothers and daughters and their relationships, read Chapters 1-4 of Book II.

Mothers and daughters have been battling the experts for centuries. Read about Mary Wollstonecraft's battle with Rousseau in Chapter 6 of Book II.

References to patriarchal attitudes to women's sexuality and how they influence mother-daughter relationships are indicated throughout the book. For specific historical context, see Pauline Weideger: *History's Mistress*.

෴

CHAPTER 2

Self-esteem and Gender in Infancy and Childhood

The Foundations of Mother-Daughter Relationships

We cannot respect others unless we respect ourselves. This is why self-esteem is essential for a good relationship between a mother and her daughter. But how is self-esteem built in infancy and childhood, so that mothers and daughters come to respect each other? In the following description you will note that many of the early milestones in the development of self-esteem are similar for both sexes. But here the emphasis is on the young daughter and we look beyond the generalities to issues that are especially significant for her. How important are gender differences in the development of self-esteem? Is shared parenting a way of ensuring that mothers are not the prime target for their daughters' ambivalent feelings? Before exploring these issues, it is important to make it clear how self-esteem is being used here.[1]

Self-esteem. What Is It? Can It Be Changed?

Self-esteem is part of the self-concept or how we see ourselves. Initially, it might be useful to distinguish between self-concept and personality. Personality is as others see us. Self-concept is the way we see ourselves. If you were to complete a sentence beginning with "I am" several times on paper, or in your head, you would have said something about your self-concept. For example, you may have said: "I'm a female" or "I'm a male", "I'm easy going" or "I get uptight", "I'm a swinging voter" or "I'm a greenie". Self-concept includes descriptions of our character, ideas, attitudes, values and commitments. It involves a sense of personal continuity through childhood, adulthood and old age. You may have changed your behaviours in the last ten years, but you are still you. People lacking a sense of continuity, as in the case of people with so-called multiple personalities, have disintegrated self-concepts.[2]

Self-concept is learnt. It grows in childhood as we learn new skills, relate to more and more people and get more feedback about ourselves. Each stage of development adds specific features. Some of these features can be distorted by social pressures and have some long term consequences for mother-daughter relationships and are discussed in this and subsequent chapters.

Developing a reasonably stable self-concept also involves learning to distinguish two types of experiences — those that don't have self reference and those that do. In other words, mature self-concept development ensures the ability to distinguish our own thoughts and actions from those of others. Adults who cannot do this vary from those with seriously disturbed self-concepts to those in the normal range who defend, project or thrust responsibility for their actions onto others. Obviously, such behaviours can influence mother-daughter relationships and are considered here.

If self-concept is how we see ourselves, than self-esteem is the evaluative aspect of our self-concept — the degree to which we can accept ourselves. It involves feeling competent in the things that matter to us. For example, if you are not very good at telling jokes and it is not important to you, it's not a self-esteem issue. Self-esteem involves a sense of security: "I can manage this thing or event and achieve support if I need it". It involves a feeling of emotional confidence and stability: "I'm not going to go to pieces". It also includes self-confidence in our capacity to relate to and communicate with others. It embraces self-assertion and the ability to express and gain self-respect. This book explores why these latter attributes can have conflicting connotations for mothers and daughters and how they affect their relationship.[3]

In children, the content of self-esteem varies at different ages and relates to achieving those skills which children understand to be appropriate to their age, through observing others. At two years of age, riding a two wheeled bicycle is seen as something that is accomplished by older children. At six, conquering it can be a self-esteem issue. A six year old accepts that her mother can control the children at her birthday party better than she can, but at 12 she wants to do it herself.

Because it is central to achieving good mother-daughter relationships, the important question is can self-esteem be changed? The answer is yes, because self-esteem is based on our own evaluations of how we are behaving in particular situations. Years of observing children and people in many settings have demonstrated to me how much people are in control of building their own self-esteem. For example, mature age students, enrolling for a university course in developmental psychology — some middle-aged mothers, some grandmothers and some grandfathers — present themselves apologetically on the first day: "I'm very rusty". "I'm not going to be as good as the young ones". Six months later, when they have obtained credits for case study work, because they have worked harder and have had more experience with children than young unmarried students, their attitudes to themselves have changed completely.

Children also alter their behaviour and improve their self-esteem:

> Ten year old Sandra came home from school in tears every day. She could not explain to her mother why she was so upset. A little observation of Sandra in class, in the playground and in the family soon explained why. She lacked the communication and social skills to interact with other children. Sandra's parents were 57 and 64 respectively. Her mother invested her care for her family in domestic chores. Dad invested his caring in workaholism. There was little social and personal communication. All Sandra's siblings were in their twenties and thirties and her parents believed children were "naturally" happy. Sandra had been instructed in what not to do, but not in what to do. Three months of practising some simple communication skills — how to smile at other children, how to invite, how to share and initiate social exchange — and Sandra had friends and someone to sit next to in class and eat her lunch with. She had acquired self-esteem through her changed behaviours.[4]

The question of whether self-esteem can be changed is a complicated one for mother-daughter relationships because these are formed in a patriarchal society, amidst patriarchal stereotypes, that can put mothers and daughters in contempt of each other. Here, I hope to show how we can be wary of the pitfalls of such stereotypes and how many mothers and daughters have constructed their self-esteem in the face of some terrible odds.

As we saw in the last chapter, once the idea that our unconscious controlled us completely was accepted dogma. Nowadays, more rational theories are popular and research indicates that by the time we are adults, we can get to know the reasons for our behaviour and can re-educate ourselves.[5] This means taking responsibility for ourselves, rather than eternally blaming our mothers. Understanding can be achieved by reading, observing others, acquiring knowledge from others, counselling, participating in self-help groups and exercising introspection.

Said Dawn:

> "I used to be very shy. We lived in the bush when I was a kid and never saw anyone outside the family until I was sent away to school in the town. I was 12 and that was pretty harrowing, but I found a book in the school library about a girl like me and how she practised speaking up. Then, when I married and we moved to the city, I took lots of opportunities to go to meetings and meet people and build up my confidence. I went to debating classes. I still don't shine at parties. I can't hold the floor in a group, but I'm good on a one-to-one basis. I'm a good listener. I enjoy people as individuals".

She went on to speak about her 16 year old daughter:

"Jessica is much more outgoing than I am, partly because I helped her overcome the problems I'd had to confront on my own. She can be the life of the party, but those very characteristics mean she hasn't the patience I have with people. I wouldn't have her any other way. I'm very proud of her".

Said Jessica:

" Mum is quieter than I am, and I feel so proud when I see her having a heart to heart with someone".

Dawn knew her own good points and could accept her shortcomings and the individuality between herself and her daughter. Her good self-esteem was transmitted to her daughter and they had a very good relationship. Their self-descriptions also indicate that having good self-esteem does not involve being perfect. Above all, it does not involve being arrogant — quite the opposite.

As in Jessica's case, a child's self-esteem is most of all influenced by how his or her parents see themselves. Parents with good self-esteem transmit it to their children, because children model themselves on parental behaviour. This is why a father's self-esteem is as important as the mother's as a model for his children. This influence does not limit itself to his sons. If the child is female, the father's self-esteem and his attitude to his wife has profound outcomes for the mother-daughter relationship. Discussion of this can be found in the chapter on fathers.

A Mother's Self-esteem and the Birth of Her Baby Daughter

The self-concept of a mother differs from that of a non-mother. Changed responsibilities and relationships mean that when a woman becomes a mother, new definitions are included in her self-concept. She must also negotiate social attitudes to herself as a mother. Undeniably, not all women can or should become mothers. As we shall see later, many are miserable in the role.[6] If women accept that motherhood is inferior to what men do in the public sphere, their self-esteem will be affected. If they accept any of the other myths and tenets about mothers which were discussed in the first chapter, their self-esteem is also threatened. They devalue themselves and have conflicting feelings about giving birth to daughters. Fathers do not experience the same kind of profound change in their self-concept when they become parents.

One of the most obvious differences is that it is the mother who gives birth to her child. If pride in the power to give birth is converted to indignity and a sense of powerlessness, as it often was by some of the old fashioned procedures in obstetrics, the mother-child relationship can be put under strain even at the moment of birth. Because the mother knows that her daughter will grow into a woman and perhaps also give birth in this way, she can experience some confusing feelings about welcoming her daughter into the world. These can include a mixture of euphoria, anger, guilt and depression.[7]

Anastasia, in Marilyn French's novel, *Her Mother's Daughter*, describes how a mother's self-esteem can be severely shaken, if the birthing process is coerced into the age-old pattern, as it was for her in the 1950s. She describes the birth of her daughter Arden:

> ...I was shocked, incredibly shocked at myself, at the utter abject humiliation I felt with this thing coming out of my vagina, with my legs in those stirrups, with the nurses and aides and doctors milling around..........And then she came, Arden, and I felt eradicated, I felt like an animal doing what nature decrees all female animals must do.[8]

Sometimes, women feel even less competent as though they have failed to do what women "ought" to do naturally. For example, if the birth is induced, in a way that subordinates a woman to the convenience or attitudes of the obstetrician, then she may well feel as though she has failed. Judith Traill, a psychiatrist, has described the consequent loss of self-esteem that many women experience after unnecessary inducements.[9] Her research suggests that this may adversely influence their interaction with their infants in the first months. Obviously, if the mother is allowed to feel that she can control how she gives birth and can look back with pride on her birthing experience and share it with someone close and equally proud, she is likely to feel more positive about her new baby. She is less likely to have conflicting feelings about bringing a daughter into the world and less likely to have feelings of anger or irritation towards her own mother. She is less likely to experience post-natal depression.

A woman obstetrician described the procedures in a hospital unit with a reputation for a high rate of successful natural births:

> "In our pre-natal classes, we've introduced self-esteem building and particularly pride in being a woman and having the power to give birth. There are also sessions with the mothers of the mother-to-be and small daughters, if any, to build up that sense of pride in female continuity. Husbands and fathers are involved too. The mothers are given a sense of responsibility and power over their own bodies and the birthing process. They are listened to because they know best when the birth is about to take place. I'm just the assistant. I've worked under the old system and this is incomparable — less complications, less post-natal depression and marvellous relationships between mothers and babies. I would advise women to change their obstetrician, mid-wife or whomever, if during pregnancy they are not treated as a responsible person. Only by women taking action can we change things."

Later I met some mothers who had given birth in this Unit. Said Julie whose response was typical:

> "With Alice (her five year old daughter), it was the best pregnancy and birth I ever had. It was hard work, and when the baby came I

was so proud of myself. Of all my children I feel a kind of sunny radiance when I'm with Alice. I tell her about the joy I felt when I was carrying her and my pride when she was born. She feels that she is special and her kindergarten teacher says she is one of the happiest most self-confident little girls she's come across."

After the birth, if all has gone well, the process of falling in love with the baby begins.[10] In one mother it may happen quickly. In another it may take months and if she is expecting an immediate sense of bonding and feels she is inadequate because she doesn't fit the theories, it may influence her self-esteem as a mother and her relationship with her baby.[11] Nicole, a young mother who had recently given birth to Sally said:

"I wouldn't like anything to happen to her, but I don't have a magic feeling that we are bonded together. I'm sure there is something wrong with me. The doctor looked at me queerly when I described how I felt and the nurses avoided saying anything when I told them."

A little discussion of the facts restored Nicole's self-esteem and she became more relaxed with her baby daughter.

Another complication can happen when the expectation of a certain kind of baby is not met. This happened to Aggie, whom we will meet in Chapter 7. Aggie expected a fun-loving child. Instead, her serious fretful baby seemed not to be the one with whom she had established a relationship during pregnancy. Aggie's expectations were fuelled by her unsatisfactory marriage. She eventually tried to mend the relationship by settling for being a "good enough" mother.

These are the hidden agendas in early relationships, especially as a baby absorbs into her self-awareness the behaviour of her mother and other caretakers towards her. She develops a feeling of comfort through repeated cuddling during feeding and other times. If the caretaker is angry or full of self doubts, the baby may not receive wholehearted physical endorsement.

Mothers are not Solely Responsible for Self-esteem

However a word of caution is needed. Hopefully, the era when mothers were held completely responsible for the way their offspring behaved from the cradle to the grave is on its way out. As we saw in the last chapter, mother blaming influences mothers' self-esteem and therefore the mother-daughter relationship. Nowadays, if babies have unloving caretakers or ones who treat them with hostility or unwitting ineptitude, it is no longer believed that their ability to trust and love others is irreparably damaged for the rest of their lives.[12] More recently, psychology has been influenced by humanistic research, which is less deterministic and suggests that good caretaking can make up for earlier difficulties.[13]

Above all, a total rethink of who shares in the child-raising is needed. There are societies in which fathers take an equal share in child care. In some, the community sees it as a group responsibility[14] and children are not left entirely to the private and sometimes erratic responsibility of their parents, nor regarded as private property.

Because fathers play such a small part in infant care in contemporary western society, we cannot tell whether interaction with a male nurturer might be an important omission in developing self-awareness in infants. Certainly, it appears that babies delight in the vigorous type of physical play their fathers often adopt, for example, tossing the baby in the air.

The idea that mothers and fathers should equally share in the responsibility of parenting is becoming popular, but tends to be more often theoretical than practical. Unfortunately, the idea is thwarted because men are not trained in the nurturing role and often have enormous difficulty with it. Many escape through work or recreation and empathise little with their children. They are often afraid of children and attribute manipulative and controlling intentions to them which are beyond a child's cognitive ability.[15] What is needed are educational and child development experiences for males, as much as for females.

While the present situation persists, mothers carry an unfair burden of responsibility, not only in the domestic work-load but in the aftermath of having been the primary caretaker. In their early years, children do not see their mothers as independent persons, but as their providers and comforters — extensions of themselves. Thus, it is usual for toddlers, preschoolers and young primary school children to describe mothers only in terms of what they do for them.[16] Young children rarely describe their fathers as solely existing to take care of them.

Mothers are the major nurturers. They are also the major teachers and in the process they must frustrate and deny. Fathers are not around to frustrate on a regular basis. What little time is given may be limited to playful interchanges. An outcome of this differential experience of parenting is that an infant may experience her mother as overwhelming and denying and incorporate this alongside recognition of her nurturance. This reaction may become a lasting emotionally charged disposition, its origins lost to consciousness and therefore unavailable for rational assessment.

Men, as non-nurturers of infants, are not necessarily seen as overwhelming and denying in the same way as mothers are. Therefore, fathers are not targeted with the same ambivalence. Many mothers endure emotional hostility from their offspring from pre-adolescence until old age, especially if the offspring have not constructed a sense of their own autonomy. They often blame their mothers for their lack of independence.

In summary, the part-time father coupled with the image of the denying mother is often the setting for long term mother-daughter conflict. Equal parenting by mothers and fathers or consistent multiple mothering (as in a good and stable day care situation) or greater utilisation of the extended family are commonly suggested ways of easing the emotional load carried by mothers and dispersing the ambivalence directed at them. Obviously, pragmatics may not make these solutions open to all. In that event, understanding the pressures on mothers helps enormously and from eight years of age the issues can be discussed with daughters in a developmentally appropriate way. Why eight? I will explain this in the following section.

Some Developmental Milestones

Encouraging Autonomy in Infancy and Early Childhood

A sense of autonomy in both mother and daughter is essential for respectful mother-daughter relationships. Autonomy exists in embryo in infants and needs encouraging if it is to flourish.

At first, newborn babies probably do not experience themselves as separate from their environment and their caretakers. There is little sense of demarcation between their bodies and those of others. Exploration of toes and fingers, learning to co-ordinate hand and eye and the physical sensations aroused by contact with others establishes a sense of the physical me and mine.[17] It is facilitated by the primary caretaker which, in western culture, is usually the mother. Awareness of physical separateness develops through experience of the mother's departure and return and originates in the early months, when an infant begins to sense that the mother's activities do not always coincide with those of her own.

It is through the continuity of the relationship with the mother or caretaker that the baby learns that her own body is a constant. If the relationship is warm, then the baby develops a sense of a comfortable physical self; if it is not, there is the beginning of a negative, self-feeling.[18] Thus, the groundwork for the development of the self-concept and self-esteem occurs at the sensory and physical level because babies think through their bodies and their senses and not in abstractions. They lack the capacity for intention in the adult or psychological sense, despite prevailing folklore to the contrary.[19] Kerry's response to her daughter is typical of this fundamental misunderstanding.

Kerry was a new mother who had arranged that she breast feed her baby while listening to a radio talk back programme:

> "She always cries. She knows I want to listen to the programme and she does it to spite me".

Needless to say this mother-daughter relationship was fraught with misunderstanding about motivation and intent.

A baby's awareness of self develops, not only through the incorporation of the physical actions and expressions of others towards them, it also grows out of the sensations aroused by reciprocal exchanges with others. For example, a baby's smiles are returned by the parents or the parents respond positively to their baby's attempts at peek-a-boo and other games. In infancy, games of social interaction with caretakers, such as dropping objects for others to pick up or imitating speech sounds enhance the baby's awareness as a social being.

The capacity to respond to a baby as though she is an individual and not just an extension of her mother or father is important if the process of achieving a sense of physical autonomy is to be successful. Unfortunately, some caretakers become anxiously absorbed in their babies in the hope of discovering the love that they missed out on with their own mothers and fathers or are not receiving from their spouses. Sometimes absorption in their baby is a bolster for poor self-esteem. They see their babies, not as "him" or "her", but "mine" or "me" — a projection of themselves. As in Kerry's case, if a baby cries unduly, she may be seen as deliberately distressing the mother or father, not as acting independently and motivated by her own discomfort.[20] The caretaker's response of anger or anxiety is incomprehensible and overwhelming for the baby and so she begins to learn to inhibit the expression of independent needs.

Another important step in the early development of self-esteem is the baby's emerging attempts at self-initiation. By 12 to 15 months, infants are beginning to demonstrate self-choice and preference and may resist being dressed or taking a bath. Driven by the concerns of a power-oriented society, some parents are threatened by the loss of the physically passive baby. They do not appreciate that these emerging, individual behaviours are the foundations for a developing sense of will and purpose. Head on power struggles ensue and the infant learns that her attempts at independence invite punishment. She comes to fear her embryonic attempts at independence and may be set on a path to withdrawn, repressed or aggressive behaviour. Fortunately, most parents have skills which allow the infant to practise some self initiation, yet ensure that necessary and safe routines are followed. For example, they may turn the infant's resistance into a game, or use diversion of one sort or another.[21]

This milestone — the emergence of will — sometimes attracts differential treatment on the basis of gender. Most of it is unwitting and a product of social beliefs about male and female behaviour. But it can have a negative impact on mother-daughter relations.[22] If parents convey a message that assertion and resistance is to be expected more from boys than girls, this often lays the basis for the lack of drive said to be characteristic of females. Unfortunately, it is not unusual for daughters to later blame their mothers for their lack of assertiveness.[23]

Peter said of his 15 month old daughter, Inez:

"I feel out of control and very anxious when she runs away, says 'No'! or starts screaming when I want her to do something, especially as she's a girl. I've always found bossy women very threatening. I'd hate her to become one, so I'm stopping her now. I smack her hard when she wants to do something other than what I tell her to".

Fortunately, Inez's mother, Andrea, nipped this stereotyping in the bud.

She took Peter along to some child development seminars. The information about self-concept and self-esteem development in infancy won him over and he learnt to interact successfully with Inez. Andrea recognised that her intervention would benefit her later relationship with her daughter.

Mother-Daughter Fusion During Infancy and Early Childhood

While seeing a baby's behaviour as motivated by her own needs, as distinct from adult projections, is a problem in any baby-caretaker relationship, it can be especially so for a mother and her daughter, because it is easier to project our motives, wishes and hopes onto children of the same sex as ourselves. The daughter is expected by society to be like her mother, both as a person and in her female attributes and roles. So there is less recognition of the need for her to develop her own individuality, character and talents. A classical example of this can be found in the Bibliotherapy, Chapter 9, in the portrayal of a mother-daughter relationship in Tennessee Williams' play *The Glass Menagerie*. The mother, Amanda, wants her daughter, Laura, to live out her unfulfilled expectations and thus resolve the disappointment of her own girlhood and marriage. Laura is not allowed an identity of her own.

Jane Flax, an American psychotherapist, records how she observed that mothers tend to identify more strongly with their girl babies. In her experience, very disturbed mothers were enmeshed with their daughters and did not seem to have a clear awareness of the physical boundaries between themselves and their girl children, as do mothers of boys. She writes:

> "Women in therapy have frequently said that they have no sense where they end and their mothers begin, even in a literal physical way. The very fact of gender differences with boy babies enforces, on the mother's part, a sense that the child is 'not me', is other than me".[24]

Flax found that daughters, who came to her clinic, frequently remembered being confused from as early as three years of age as to exactly who was the mother and who the child in the relationship. Their mothers had not been able to enjoy the sensual and emotional closeness of the relationship without losing their own sense of separateness. Further, in early and later childhood, these daughters had served as confidants and friends in a way that was not only inappropriate to the daughter's developmental process but retarded the ability for the two of them to recognise the autonomy of each other. This leads to conflict later and is discussed in more detail in Chapters 3 and 6.

Said Anne-Marie:

> "Brigitte (her three year old daughter) has no understanding at all. I think she's a mean little bitch. I'm going through a divorce and she just runs off and plays when I tell her how upset I am".

Actually, Brigitte did try to comfort Anne-Marie in her childish way by offering her mother things that comforted her, such as her favourite toys.

She was also very distressed by the departure of her father and her tantrums expressed her deep sadness. A child of three does not have the cognitive ability to grasp the complexity of the psychological interaction of adults and cannot yet empathise in an adult way. After reading some descriptions of a three year old's cognitive capacities, Anne-Marie looked much happier. Weeks later she said:

> "Brigitte is nicer than I used to think. We are getting along much better".

While Flax's argument about mothers who enmesh their identities with their children's is valid, it must be put into perspective. Not all cultures aim for the distinct ego boundaries revered in contemporary western society. In some other cultures, even subcultures within our own, where multiple mothers or extended families are the norm, the concept of self and mother-daughter relationships can develop differently from the way that is described here. Moreover, the psychoanalytic insistence that a mother and daughter must separate can be confusing and wrongly interpreted. As we shall see in Chapter 3, daughters want to stay close to their mothers. There is nothing unhealthy about closeness between mothers and daughters. What is unhealthy is where a daughter's developmental characteristics and individuality are not acknowledged. Kerry and Anne-Marie blocked their daughters' individuality by using them as vehicles for their adult needs. They did not see their daughters as separate persons.

To sum up, the ability of a mother (or a father) to recognise her baby as a responding, spontaneous and separate individual is the basis of the earliest development of autonomy. Autonomy is encouraged in boys, but not always in girls. Mothers and daughters who have a fully developed sense of their own autonomy are close, because they are sufficiently confident to allow each other their own space and individuality.

Encouraging Self-Respect and Competency in Daughters During the Preschool and Middle Childhood Years

Letting a small daughter know she is valued and encouraging her to feel competent will make it easier for her to value her mother. Obviously, this lays the basis for good mother-daughter relationships and means the continuation of the encouragement and support begun in infancy.

The process of building a sense of differentiation from others and a unique self-concept takes a qualitatively different form at each developmental stage. Having learnt that they are physically autonomous from others, toddlers and preschoolers can tell you quite a lot about their self-concepts. They will proudly tell you their names and ages. They will tell you something about their physical appearance and things they can do. They are also learning that their thoughts are separate from others. At four, planning to wag kindergarten with a friend, Lizzy reconsidered, "My mother knows everything I think". By six, after having been naughty many times and not found out, Lizzy was beginning to realise her thoughts were hers alone. The experiences of primary school including clashing with the points of view of other children convinced her.

In toddlerhood and the early preschool years, children are also using interaction around toys to define boundaries between themselves and other children. This is not only because at this age children's understanding of themselves is largely limited to what they know of their physical capacities and possessions. It is also because care with possessions is a major feature of western households and a learning process for the preschooler. Thus, claiming toys is not simply negative and aggressive behaviour, but an important part of children's definition of themselves. It is a positive sign of self-awareness and an attempt to make sense of the other child as a separate social being.[25] Not only is this not the age to insist on sharing and attack the child who does not, it is not productive, for either sex, to expect girls to be more prepared to share things than boys.[26]

This can generalise into the expectation that girls should be more attentive to the needs of others, so creating an enormous gender difference. As they get older, daughters can become more and more resentful about the one-sided burden of caring and direct their anger at their mothers for allowing it to happen.

Blanche, a mother of three daughters, made an important point about the way in which parents and society construct gender differences at this age:

> "I don't just teach my girls to value their so-called feminine abilities for caring, I teach them how to stand up for them." While she was making this point, through the living room window, I watched a four year old boy, son of a neighbour, climb a fence into Blanche's garden. He kicked over a tower of blocks, which was being built by Blanche's two year old daughter. Blanche's four year old daughter, Libby, knocked the boy to the ground, stood over him and said, "You are never, never kind. You've got to learn to be kind like girls are. I'm telling your Mummy to put you into the kennel with Boozie". (Boozie was the family dog.)

Said Blanche:

> "Libby's very confident about being a girl. We talked about gender differences from the moment we started reading to all our girls. Libby recognises stereotyping on television and her kindy teacher tells me she hears her instructing other children about it in a very sophisticated way. She's popular with both boys and girls at kindy. It helps that Andy (Blanche's husband) teaches us all karate. He also runs karate classes for girls and boys at the local community centre. He sprinkles the activities with cracks about stereotyping. You can pick out the girls in his classes at the local school by their confidence in the playground. The teachers tell us that these girls are never teased and bullied by the boys. My sisters-in-law are always inviting the girls over to their houses. They've got lots of boys and reckon our girls civilise them. Our girls don't sit on the

side lines. They are in there organising things the way they want them. I praise the girls for it".

The girls in this family were notable for their pride in themselves and their mother.

Of course, in these years, young children do not fully understand that other things may change, but their sex and the language labels that go with it do not. For example, sometimes three and four year olds will tell you that a girl can become a boy if she cuts her hair and puts on boys' clothes. A toddler told me that she was now a little girl and would grow into a Mummy and then a Daddy.[27]

Toddlers and preschoolers of both sexes spend most of their time exploring the active dimensions of self: "What can I do"? "Where can I go"? They test the boundaries of their physical skills. They often reject attempts to help and insist on doing things for themselves. When frustrated in this self-learning process, they may throw temper tantrums. Temper tantrums are particularly prevalent at two and four years of age, which seem to be peak years for trying to develop new skills.

Most temper tantrums express a struggle to develop a competent sense of self. Brief positive instructions, accompanied by diversion, unobtrusive assistance or rapid unemotional removal, achieve more than power struggles at this early age when children lack the abstract ability to see their behaviour objectively.

Unfortunately, even something as obvious as temper tantrums can be submitted to the hidden agenda of sexual politics at this age. Temper tantrums are more likely to be seen as 'will' in boys and 'temperament' in girls.[28] So the same behaviour is evaluated and treated differently and incorporated differently in boys and girls, setting up long term patterns. This in turn influences mother-daughter relationships, because things female are devalued. Said Olly, observing his two year old daughter throwing a tantrum:

"What a shrew she's going to be by the time she's 20 — all those female bitchinesses are beginning to come out. I say 'No'! and 'Stop it'!, but it makes no difference. It's clearly innate".

Because he applied a male chauvinistic yardstick, Olly could not encourage his daughter's self-esteem. He not only projected his biased interpretations onto her behaviour, but understood little about her developmental capacities.

Children under four years of age tend to be unable to inhibit behaviour in response to negative verbal instructions, because this is an age when language is tied to doing things. Observations of hundreds of mothers (and a few fathers) show that those who use any form of confirmative instruction, which imparts an expectation of competence, have children with good self-esteem. These parents act out their instructions and speak positively, for example: "Let me see you lift it like this", rather than "Don't drop it".[29]

Perhaps the greatest contribution to the way in which we devalue, or value, ourselves comes from how we were instructed or disciplined as children. Western society is still influenced by the old Christian idea that children are stained by original sin. This has created an environment that justifies a hostile approach to them, as found in 'little monster' theories.[30] It has also led to the survival of a negative approach to disciplining and instructing children, with devastating effects on self-esteem. When asked to describe themselves, children who have never been encouraged to feel competent give a string of negative descriptions: "I am not nice". "I'm a bad girl". "I don't help Mum". "I don't share my sweets".[31]

Some societies and particularly those where group co-operation, rather than competition, is the means of survival, are more aware of developmental processes in children than are others. For example, Fabian and Loh describe child-raising among the Australian Aboriginals before the coming of the whites. The raising of young children was based on positive encouragement and practising skills with them that would make them competent tribe members. Negative instructions, which are typical of western societies, were not in evidence.[32] The old Aboriginal way is more in tune with the pre-schooler's and toddler's learning processes. Above all, allowing daughters to feel competent and valued will help them, not only to acquire self-respect, but the capacity to value their mothers.

The Mirrored Self:

Its Role In Mother-Daughter Relationships

Much of the process of becoming a person involves taking on board verbal and unspoken messages about ourselves and interpreting and acting upon them. Parents act as mediators of social expectations about how children, boys and girls, should behave.[33] The responses of parents and significant others to their behaviours play an important role in building a child's self-concept. If told often enough that they have certain characteristics or tendencies, children tend to develop them and incorporate them into their self-view: "You are a good girl". "You are pretty". "You are clever and helpful". "You are especially good at swimming and art". "Girls are sillier than boys". "Girls would not make good engineers".

In some families much needed positive appraisals and realistic feedback may be missing and the child does not accurately incorporate her abilities into her self-view. Almost unwittingly, parents, teachers and playmates, may induce a child to see herself as clumsy, stupid or inferior. For example, Charlotte Brontë in *Jane Eyre*, which is discussed later, depicts Jane's childhood as one in which there was excessive negative criticism and discipline leading to severe damage to Jane's self-esteem.

It is through their appraisal by adults that children learn about their special qualities: "I am a good runner". These appraisals act as a mirror in which children see and assess themselves. Parents and teachers who positively and realistically mirror their daughter's activities are laying the basis for her self-acceptance and self-esteem. Margaret Mead, whose childhood is described in the Bibliotherapy, Chapter 9, is an example of a daughter who had these experiences in childhood. She grew into a highly achieving woman who could express herself more freely than most and had a good relationship with her mother.

Sometimes, the mirroring process is not in accordance with the child's needs. In Christina Stead's novel, *The Man Who Loved Children*, we find a distressing example of a father who could not mirror his children's needs. One of almost endless demonstrations of his inadequacy occurred when his daughter, Louie, composed a play in an invented language in honour of his birthday and he was unable to accept her gift in a developmentally appropriate way. Instead, he said, "Damn my eyes if I've ever seen anything so stupid and silly". The result of a stream of such occasions is Louie's poor self-esteem. She weeps, "I am so miserable and poor and rotten and so vile and melodramatic, I don't know what to do. I don't know what to do. I can't bear the daily misery. I can't bear the horror of every day life".[34] Her distress was not mitigated by a good relationship with her mother, for she too lacked self-esteem.

The experiences of this child are in contrast to Elizabeth's. Her mother, Georgia, spoke of the influence on her child-rearing practices of the French author, Colette, and her relationship with her mother, which is described in Chapter 10 of Book II:

> "I'm a great admirer of Colette. Her descriptions of how her mother gave her such pride in her capabilities, her talent with words and her female body have influenced how I interact with Elizabeth. I let her know when I'm overcome with joy at the sight of her. When I'm helping her get dressed or we are snuggling up, I tell her that her little limbs are cuddly and beautiful. My mother was never outspoken about these things. One wasn't in those days. I felt unsure of myself with her and therefore with myself. Elizabeth is totally sure that I love her and is very proud of being a girl. She says to me,'Mummy I'm glad you are a girl like me. I love you'."

Childhood Autonomy and Mother-Daughter Relationships

In middle childhood, a daughter continues to respond emotionally in a different way to her mother and her father. This happens with boys too, but their mothers are not of the same sex and they are urged to identify with fathers and escape into the non-domestic world. Daughters identify with their mothers and do not necessarily want to escape their mothers in the way that boys do under patriarchy. This difference has enormous advantages for intimacy in the mother-daughter relationship, but it is also behind its fractious intensity and Chapters 3 and 6 explore this further.

In the primary school years, children learn more about who they are through their achievements in school tasks and how their teachers react to them. They obtain realistic estimates of their skills through play with school mates. By eight years of age, they are concerned with how they measure up to others and they need a lot of support from home. They become more insightful and capable of self-criticism.[35] They are keen to develop more autonomy in their activities with other children and spend less time with the family. This push for autonomy involves some minor clashes with authority. Parents may complain that they find their nine and ten year olds less angelic, more secretive and occasionally defiant.

That autonomy is not yet equally resolved for both sexes in middle childhood can be seen by observing mothers and daughters in any outdoor setting. You will notice that girls both play and are kept closer to their mothers than are boys.

Questions of autonomy and individuality for girls in middle childhood need as much attention as they do for boys. A daughter who lacks a sense of her uniqueness and competence becomes dependent or rebels in adolescence and adulthood. Either way, there is dissatisfaction with her lot. She may lose respect for her mother, whom she sees as giving her neither opportunity for, or providing a model of, autonomy. The way the daughter sees it is not necessarily the case, but society sanctions her mother-blaming.

Psychology and psychiatry reinforce these attitudes. They generally describe mothers as the chief inhibitors of female autonomy, but it seems such generalisations are theoretical rather than factual. Research suggests that it is generally the father who insists most on sex-stereotyped behaviour for his male and female children.[36] Thus, mothers who limit the autonomy of their daughters may do it in response to paternalistic and cultural pressures, rather than their own psychological needs. Not all mothers do this. This is a story about nine year old Gina, told by Martine, her mother:

> "Gina wants to be a billiard player. Her father is dead against it and says it is not for girls. I can't see any logic in that. Gina often stays with her Nanna who is a jolly good billiard player and she's learnt a love of the game from her. Nanna has friends who have daughters and granddaughters who play and we've persuaded one of the men's clubs to let Gina and the other girls compete. I'm going to do everything I can to see she gets expert coaching and goes as far as she wants".

Positive Continuity in the Development of a Daughter's Self-concept

Girls have several developmental advantages during middle childhood which enhance mother-daughter relationships. These advantages have largely been ignored or distorted in patriarchally-oriented developmental psychology.

Paradoxically, the heart of a major advantage is found in the social expectation that girls and boys should be different in their personal behaviours and in relation to the mother. Since mothers are the primary caretakers in early childhood, both sons and daughters incorporate the mother's behaviour. But, when boys enter school, the major thing demanded of them by their peers, their teachers and their fathers, is that they overcome many of the feminine gentlenesses they have learnt from their mothers. Above all, they learn that it is important not to be "a sissy". The impact of this injunction was underlined in a study on children's sexist attitudes. It showed that primary school boys exhibited a great deal of anxiety about any trace of feminity in themselves and projected this anxiety into fierce denigration and rejection of females in general. Their self-esteem was poor.[37]

Because of the primacy of the mother in early life and because of the absence of a male nurturer, learning what it is to be masculine, for a boy, comes to mean learning not to be feminine, or womanly.[38] This repression and self-denial is an essential aspect of male personality development in patriarchy. Male identity depends upon rejection of the mother's characteristics: "Don't be a mummy's boy". The necessity for an often quite drastic change in behaviour and feeling means the early primary school years can be a period in which boys are at greater risk of depression and suicide.[39] It appears that the repression of emotion and tenderness and the encouragement of aggression and competition, which is characteristic of wider peer contact, is a disturbing process for some boys. Sadly, the very processes that cause unhappiness in boys lay the bases for their later patriarchal attitudes to women.

Girls in primary school do not have these assaults on their sense of personal continuity and self-esteem. They are not required to reject and split off the earlier self, incorporated from the mother. This is a positive force for good self-concept development and needs to be emphasised more in studying female psychology. It means that girls have a stronger sense of their identity and continuity. This enhances self-esteem and mother-daughter relationships.

It is not until the later primary school years and in secondary co-ed schools, that this self-esteem often diminishes.[40] It seems that girls develop less respect for their femaleness, when they are increasingly interacting with boys who are learning to reject the female aspect of themselves and trying to become toughies. In this situation, girls tend to denigrate females and female characteristics in general.[41] Thus, for good mother-daughter relationships, self-esteem in daughters must be well established in middle childhood, so that daughters can resist these early onslaughts on their female identity and their self-esteem. They benefit from parental support and the opportunity to talk about these issues.

Educating Daughters for Gender Inferiority:

A Major Factor in Mother-Daughter Conflict

So far the discussion of childhood development has mentioned only a few instances where stereotyped expectations about gender can influence a daughter's self-esteem. They need exploring further.

The task of building good self-esteem in daughters involves not only giving praise for competence and achievement, but developing a resistance to defining themselves as marginal, deficient or inferior, simply because they are female. They need to learn to recognise the hidden agendas which inculcate these false beliefs. An example of how it might be done is given in the case of Susi.[42]

> Susi was an attractive five year old, with a confident mother as a model. When she started school, she was subject to denigratory teasing from the boys which included the lifting of her skirt, accompanied by rude words. This raised her first questions as to what was wrong with being a girl and marked the beginning of some reticence about herself.
>
> Fortunately, her mother explained that it was the boys who had the problem, not she. They didn't know how to express their liking for her, except in a stupid way. They were afraid of becoming kind and gentle like her. They thought it was important to be tough and rude, when in fact it was an unkind way to behave. Susi's mother also talked to other mothers whose daughters were being treated in this way. Together, at a school parents meeting, they raised the issue of the right of the girls in the school to be as self-respecting as the boys. The headmaster and staff accepted the premise and took appropriate action. Boys and girls were encouraged to empathise with one another through co-operative games and tasks. Prejudice and anxiety were included in the curriculum in a developmentally appropriate way.

Susi's case is not unusual. As daughters grow older, they hear their female genitalia and other sexual features used as abusive and vile adjectives and expletives. They also encounter metaphors for the feminine gender which imply innate female inferiority, such as "sissies", "bitches" or "nags". They may see their fathers actively rejecting invitations to join groups of women on the grounds that a lone male in women's company is something that a self-respecting male will not suffer. Daughters may hear their mothers agreeing that women's conversation is second rate in contrast to that of men's and other similar comments which endorse the lower status of women.[43] In this way, daughters learn to see themselves as second class citizens and come to disrespect their mothers for also being members of the "second sex".

From the moment she learns to read, the female child learns that she is not as important as a boy, but marginal or on the fringes of all that is 'significant' in society. For example, five year old Molly was learning a religious song about children, which used the pronoun "he" to cover all children. "Why does it only say 'he'?", said Molly. "I aren't a 'he'. Where are the girls"? In Western literature, female readers are required to be a "generic man" and an invisible woman.[44] Lakoff, in defence of the use of "he" to cover both sexes in everyday language, argues that the point is trivial.[45] Is it? When you consider Molly's dilemma, it is not. In fact, the use of "he" to embrace all of humanity, when it effectively excludes half the population, has all the characteristics of a propaganda technique. It is a subtle and powerful force for shaping the attitude that anything female is secondary. The young female child inevitably internalises it.[46]

In the same category is the use of stereotyped language, such as describing all girls as "weak", "dumb", "bitches", "hags"[47] We can expose these negative stereotypes in the family. Schools also need to treat them as a form of prejudice which is as destructive as calling children from other races "wogs", "greasies" or any other derogatory name.

The language of many children's books and school texts also reinforces the incorporation of marginal self-perceptions in females. Despite attempts to remedy the situation, in many texts and stories men are over-represented and depicted as participating in a much broader range of activities than women. Given the fact that the sex ratio of the population is approximately 50-50, such portrayals suggest that the activities in which women participate are not important enough to be written about in school readers.[48]

Fairy tales can be a mixed bag. Many witches and fairy queens are strong and powerful and good role models for girls. Others, as Bettelheim points out, socialise girls into the passivity and subordination expected of them under patriarchy.[49] I deal with the story of Snow White as an example in Chapter 4.

On the whole, if books for children portray women in leadership roles, they are not always depicted as being as capable as men and are sometimes described as disagreeable.[50] Much of the fame of the women in school texts is attributed to the fact that they are the wives or mistresses of famous men. As this book and others attest, there have been plenty of remarkable women who need to be included equally in texts if children of both sexes are to get a clear picture of reality and of the important contributions of women to society.

Fortunately, many women writers have written children's fiction in which girls and women are central or equally significant. These can be used in self-esteem building. Recognising the worthiness of women and their contribution to society is the basis of a respectful mother-daughter relationship.

The sexist literature for children is a product of a society that is anxious to preserve the status quo and perpetuate age-old inequalities between the sexes. It establishes conformity in the early years. It extends into adulthood and divides men and women in almost every aspect of life. It offers destructive solutions to relationships. Men are encouraged to maintain their self-esteem by regarding female attributes, and therefore mothers and daughters, as having less value than male attributes and fathers and sons. It encourages gender differences which mean that men and women have difficulty communicating. Women are taught to be more empathetic and intuitive and less aggressive than men. The outcome is that women are better at thinking wholistically, but these attributes are valued less than the aggressive, competitive and analytic attributes and endeavours which are encouraged in boys and men.[51]

This sexual division of attributes is achieved by repressing different aspects of self. Men repress their caring tendencies and women their assertiveness. This repression tends to erupt into personality disorders. Sociopathy (exhibiting no feelings or caring or concern for others) tends to occur more frequently in males than females, while significantly more females than males suffer from anxiety disorders, such as depression and obsessive-compulsive reactions.[52]

Even when one casts culturally recognised pathology aside, the research suggests that children are deprived when gender stereotypes are all that are offered to them. Their personalities become half personalities. Instead of aiming to educate sons and daughters toward a rounded capacity for both global and analytic thinking and to have both empathetic and assertive characteristics, we have created the myth that they are incompatible opposites and so deprive our sons and daughters of optimum intellectual and personality development.

These divisions have their impact on mother-daughter relations, for where the accepted personality attributes of one sex are valued less than those of the other, mothers and daughters devalue each other.

I come across many networks among women aimed at countering these influences. Some are within women's pressure groups, others are informal groups arising out of school associations or baby-sitting networks. They alert one another to sexism in programmes or advertisements their children might see on television. They arrange outings to special concerts by feminist singers or collect their records. Morale building activities are numerous. Women in these groups are generally very aware that their actions give their daughters a sense of power and competence and that this ensures respectful mother-daughter relationships.

Communication

The marked feature of many of the happy mother-daughter relationships that I have described in this chapter is the open communication between mother and daughter. A mother cannot expect her daughter to suddenly start communicating with her in adolescence or adulthood, if her daughter hasn't been encouraged to talk with her from early childhood. Mothers who encourage a sense of competence and self-esteem in their children open the channels of communication from infancy. Unlike Olly (page 37), they can respect a child's ways of thinking and communicating. They adjust to their daughters' developmental capacities. They don't inhibit their daughters' attempts at communication with adult projections, negative stereotypes and destruction of self-esteem. They offer open affection, rather than expressing it all through domestic chores as did Sandra's mother (page 27). They don't try to be perfect mothers. They behave like human beings. They communicate.

Overview

Both sexes have ambivalent feelings toward their mothers, since she is the primary educator and controller in infancy and early childhood. She is seen as dominating, depriving and loving. Until fathers share in child-raising, they will miss the kind of intimacy a mother has with her children and fail to ease the emotional intensity directed at mothers.

The fact that the daughter is the same sex as her prime nurturer permits a sense of security, continuity and intimacy as the daughter's self-concept develops. This makes for good self-esteem and a special closeness between mothers and daughters in early and primary school childhood.

It has been argued in this chapter that self-esteem is essential for a good relationship between a mother and her daughter. How to make a good beginning in infancy and childhood has been suggested.

Where mothers ensure their own good self-esteem and teach their daughters to scorn prejudice against women, mother-daughter relationships are accepting and largely respectful. Patriarchy may not teach mothers and daughters self-esteem. This does not mean that they cannot and do not create their own counter-culture and support networks to build and maintain self-esteem. This is essential.

Under patriarchy, either sex faces special hazards. Here I have paid attention to those that may hinder self-esteem development in mothers and daughters — hindrances that are constructed out of stereotypes of gender. Gender differences in the building of self-esteem are crucial factors in the mother-daughter relationship.

Providing the role of gender differences is taken into account, self-esteem has been presented as essential to good relationships between parents and children in general. Daughters have not been treated as the only offspring requiring self-esteem, otherwise we become enmeshed in the sexist attitudes we wish to oppose. Good self-esteem in boys will also contribute to respect for themselves and make it less necessary for them to indulge in "put-downs" of the opposite sex. Ultimately, respect for females in families generates a good setting for respectful and fond mother-daughter relationships.

Our view of ourselves (our self-concept) is constructed out of social pressures, attitudes of others towards us and our conquering of social and physical skills stage by stage in childhood. A sense of competence grows as the specific tasks of each stage are mastered by the child. Some idiosyn-cratic aspects of each stage of a child's self-concept development have been described to draw attention to misunderstandings that may hinder the development of self-esteem.

By adulthood we are ultimately responsible for our self-construction. If we are unhappy about some aspect of our behaviour and personality, it is our responsibility to do some reconstruction. Adolescence is the time we begin to learn to take that responsibility and renegotiate our self-concept and our relationship with our mothers. By then, the special closeness of mothers and daughters may be both reinforced and undergoing some stress. Why? This is addressed in the next chapter.

ↄ

BIBLIOTHERAPY

In the Bibliotherapy (Chapter 9, Book I), the stories of Margaret Mead and Kim Chernin are about childhoods which encouraged good self-esteem. Colette's story in Book II is another example. Also in Book II, are accounts of Charlotte Brontë's *Jane Eyre*, which begins as a saga about inducing poor self-esteem in a child, who as an adult learns to create her own self-esteem and become an independent daughter. Virginia Woolf is another whose childhood contributed to poor self-esteem, which she worked through and in doing so learnt to value her mother. See Chapter 11, Book 2 and also DeSalvo's account (1989) of Virginia Woolf's child-hood which is listed in the bibliography.

Conversations with Mothers & Daughters by Celia Dodd, describes how important for the mother-daughter relationship birthing experiences can be. It also addresses the significance of gender in the first years. As the title indicates, the book is devoted to mothers and daughters experiences as told by themselves and touch on topics raised in the first and later chap-ters. Their conversations are full of the traditionalisms which set mothers and daughters apart, including impossible expectations, adult-centred pro-jections about the meaning of a child's behaviour, mother-blaming, fear of being like the mother, over-emphasis on the mother as a model, using the menopause as a "biologically" based reason for stressed behaviours that have social origins, ignorance about sex and menstruation, the biased over-valuing of sons, mothers who avoid emotional closeness and invest all in domestic routines, anorexic daughters, runaway daughters, etc. The author offers little discussion of the historical, social and economic traditions that influence negative attitudes about women and affect mother-daughter relationships, but the conversations make good discussion points for these issues.

ↄ

CHAPTER 3

Adolescent Daughters and Their Mothers

"We Fight Because We Want a Relationship"

Most daughters report that they spent their adolescence and young adulthood arguing with their mothers more than with anyone else. Their conflicts centered around simple things such as keeping rooms tidy, outings, peers and boyfriends, yet seemed to have an emotional content out of all proportion to the matters at issue. These daughters say they were both more intimate and more fractious with their mothers. Why is this?

In part, tensions arise because patriarchal propaganda creates ambivalence in daughters about the value of their relationship with their mothers. Daughters long for closeness with their mothers but they are confused by images of mothers as the enemy, mothers as having low status, mothers as neurotic.[1]

Unreasonable Expectations Disrupt the Reworking of Old Ties

As we saw in the last chapter, a daughter's relationship with her mother has a special quality. From the time they enter school, patriarchy drives boys into a world apart from their mothers and their world of feeling and caring. The psychological problems this creates do not disrupt the personality development of daughters. Their self-definition — their self-concept — remains more intact. In childhood, daughters are allowed to accept their attachment to their mothers and their characteristics of feeling and caring. Their task in adolescence is to rework that attachment and give it adult form. The reworking of old and deep ties to their mothers is a central theme of female development and a life-long task.

In the previous chapter, I also spoke of the mirroring process and the way in which young children learn who they are. A mother's mirroring role continues to be important to her daughter, in fact more so, in adolescence.[2] At a time when enormous physical and psychological changes are taking place in her daughter, a mother's recognition, selective approval and validation plays an important role in her maturing.

This is not some new-fangled idea. Jane Austen wrote of it in the character of Anne Elliot in *Persuasion*, 180 years ago. Anne's mother dies when Anne is in early adolescence. We find her in late adolescent years losing her pretty youthful bloom, misguided by her surrogate mother in affairs of the heart and in a state of mourning and depression. In company, she is requested to play the piano but is described by Jane Austen as lacking:

> ....fond parents to sit by and fancy themselves delighted by her performance...excepting one short period in her life, she had never, since the age of fourteen, never since the loss of her dear mother, known the happiness of being listened to, or encouraged by any just appreciation of real taste.[3]

Jane Austen attributes much of Anne's depression and loss of her youthful bloom to her lack of a mother to validate her as a person. She presents Anne's father as an inadequate substitute.

This does not mean that mothers have to be perfect. That demand is destructive. Yet patriarchy encourages adolescent daughters to have unreasonably high expectations of how their mothers should behave toward them.[4] They feel cheated when their mothers don't live up to their expectations. This causes stress. This disappointment is well expressed in Anne Frank's diary.[5] Anne is disappointed with her mother for having ceased to be the idealised figure of her childhood imagination. She becomes unremittingly critical of her and at times is full of rage and hate. Not until late adolescence is she able to be shocked at her own unreasonableness and recognise that her mother has redeeming qualities and that Anne herself has contributed to their poor relationship.

Every mother of an adolescent daughter can supply similar examples. When her mother began a university course, Mireille sneered at the time and interest her mother devoted to her reading and assignments. She wanted to be the sole and only interest her mother had. Another adolescent daughter, Francesca, enjoyed the benefits of the extra income her mother brought to the family and was not prepared to give up the pocket money it provided, but complained when her mother's job took her out of town a couple of days every two or three months, "Mothers are not supposed to go away, even for a couple of days". Yet another, Kate, expected her mother to tolerate her friends visiting and raiding the refrigerator when it suited them. Like most adolescents, these daughters complained endlessly about their mothers' fallibilities and inability to be the angel in the house. Their unjust expectations created special tensions for their mothers.

Mothers cannot cast off motherhood as easily as fathers can fatherhood. Being a mother remains central to the mother's identity, even if she is working in a fulfilling job. Working mothers often tell me how they carry their adolescent's sulky face and tantrums to work, feel hated, lie awake at night, feel sub-human and lose their self-esteem.

Fathers bear only intermittent conflict. Mothers, because of domestic responsibilities and their special intimacies with daughters, carry the burden of most of it. They are often at sea. When faced with their daughters' moodiness or unhappiness, they feel helpless, perhaps emotionally exhausted if it goes on too long. They may resort to denial, "It's not so bad" or "Others are worse off".

The mutually exclusive and contradictory myths about mothers put them in a no-win situation. If mothers are sympathetic, this is described as intrusiveness in the media and much of the professional literature. This belittling propaganda sanctions and perpetuates the barbarous behaviour of many adolescents.

Much of any adolescent's negative behaviour lies in the permission — the encouragement — society gives to use mothers as scapegoats for almost every personal and social problem.

Mothers Take the Brunt of Adolescent Frustrations

Adolescents have a lot of difficulty in coping with self-responsibility and independence. They tend to externalise their inner conflicts and motives. This is why they see school, society, parents or authority figures in general as the obstacle to their full independence rather than recognising their own immaturity, lack of confidence or tendency to cling to childish supports. Most of all, they see mothers as the chief inhibitors of their drive toward autonomy because patriarchy is organised in such a way that mothers take the brunt of their personal frustrations. Why and how does this happen?

As I discussed in Chapter 2, mothers are seen as nurturers more so than their fathers and this creates ambivalence towards the mother in infancy and childhood.[6] In the early years, nurturance is closely linked with dependence. In adolescence, dependence becomes an obstacle to autonomy and independence. Overcoming dependence requires a great deal of energy.

The origins of these confusing and emotionally charged urges are not always clear to the adolescent daughter and her mother. More often than not, an adolescents does not understand that she is fighting an inner battle with her own dependency or that she deflects her inner anger onto her mother. This is why mothers who encourage independence may still be targets for rudeness and abuse.

It is not necessary to take this like an angel. Some discussion of developmental urges and the effect their brash expression is having on others is important if adolescents are to obtain any self-insight.

The Cruel Testing Behaviour

All adolescents are critical, watchful, touchy and read unwarranted meanings into things, but daughters have a special touchiness about being controlled by mothers. The childhood ambivalence about the mother as the nurturer and the controller and the depriver is so deeply embedded, it cannot be brought out in the open and examined rationally. When the daughter is heading toward the independence and responsibilities of adulthood, this ambivalence seethes below the surface. Why?

The mother is the same sex. She is her daughter's female model. She is the person with whom her daughter is most closely identified. For all these reasons and because the adolescent daughter cannot yet clearly define who she is, it is the mother who seems to be taking up her space. "Stop trying to run me", screamed Helen, when her mother helpfully offered her a lift to a party. She wanted to hurt her mother for her solicitude, because it was what she had done for her when Helen was a child. She wanted her mother to register that she was no longer a child but another person. She did not want a rift from her mother. She was trying to re-negotiate the relationship.

Some mothers understand the symptoms of the autonomy seeking better than others; some feel rejected. Perhaps in childhood the daughter has been used to confiding in her mother. In adolescence, she is likely to decide to select what she will tell her mother. Some mothers can cope with the closed door, withdrawals and silences or the accusations about prying — others are devastated.

Adolescents can be surprisingly mature one minute and behave like two year olds the next. All adolescents can be irritable, petulant, disconsolate creatures, unsatisfied with their physical appearance, their social skills and their behaviour among friends. All adolescents have enormous difficulty seeing themselves as other see them. They fixate on their view of things.[7] This makes them argumentative with both parents.

But adolescent daughters tell you they argue most with their mothers. They know how to hurt their mothers — more than their fathers — by rejection. They know how to set up situations so they are misunderstood and their mothers can be criticised for responding poorly. Mothers of adolescent daughters will tell you how painful and one-sided it often is. The special egocentricity of adolescents in relation to their mothers is summed up by Marla, aged 16:

"I told my mother I hated her and she said, 'You make me hate you'. I couldn't believe it. Mothers are supposed to love you, no matter what. I thought I was asking for help".

Anna's behaviour is also typical. When she started going to university, she moved into a rented house with some other students. She never rang her mother or remembered her birthday and when her mother visited her she went to bed or refused to eat any of the goodies she brought. Her deeply offended mother decided to let her be and didn't contact her or hear from her for months. However, she rang Anna a day before her birthday and suggested she might like to call at her office. The next day Anna walked into her mother's office and said, "Where's my present?" Her mother handed her a parcel and Anna said, "I knew there would be one". The mother was completely confused by the one-sided expectation.

Anna was trying to be as hurtful as possible so she could see her mother's pain and validate her mother's love for her. It indicated to her that her mother took her seriously. The aim of her testing and argumentative behaviour was to get acknowledgement of herself as she believed she had become now. She explained that she didn't just want love because she was once a baby and then a child in the family, but because of whom she had changed into mentally and physically. She didn't want to be agreed with and bought goodies as though she was still a small child but appreciated on her own terms, as a person who could survive away from home, who could keep house and shop and study.

Said Felicity:

> "Mum always praised me when I was a child. I know it was good for my self-esteem, but I'm older now. I want to throw up when she does it now. I want to be treated as a person who has different values, who has made a lot of decisions. I'm going to be religious. Mum isn't. I want her to say, 'O.K you are religious. That's you now. I'm glad you can make decisions for yourself'. I'd like her to argue with me about it, but allow me to be me".

On other occasions, Marla, Anna and Felicity behaved like six year olds and were annoyed if their mothers treated them like adults. This vacillation is nerve-wracking and more so if it's not seen as the adolescent's struggle to overcome her own childishness. It is not necessarily an indication that there is something wrong with ourselves as mothers.

The Aim is to Recreate the Relationship

Unfortunately, these struggles with their inner childishness have been treated in the past as daughters wanting to make a complete break with their mothers — separating from them in every way. In my experience, most daughters do not want a 'just calling in for Sunday dinner once a month and exchanging pleasantries about the weather' sort of relationship with their mothers. Daughters want to separate by becoming individuals, perhaps with some different values and choices, but they don't want to cut ties and feelings. They know they are joined to their mothers by gender and feeling. Most care deeply about their mothers.

Most accounts of adolescence have been based on all-male research, or on the desired patriarchal model of the male who departs from his mother and her domestic world to the world of the male work-place. These accounts do not address the relationship needs and attachments which are important to adolescent girls.[8] To an adolescent daughter, becoming a separate person does not mean breaking the relationship. Daughters want to transform their relationships with their mothers, not abandon them. They quarrel because they don't want to give up on their mothers — "I just want to get her to see how I am now and how I feel."

Being confused as to who she is, the adolescent daughter may behave outrageously in order to shock her mother into taking a new and appreciative look at her. She wants her mother to be bowled over by her new personality. She teases and coaxes her mother in all manner of ingenious ways in order to make her sit up and take notice of her. The ploys are numerous. Adolescent daughters may try to discomfort their mothers by distorting stories of childhood — "That time you were so proud because you thought I didn't join in with the kids who stole the apples — well I told you a lie". An adolescent daughter may try to shake her mother out of her complacent attitude toward her by causing her anxiety — "We used to swim in the flooded river when you weren't home". She may revise long accepted beliefs and say she thought her mother was a dill or looked awful in a situation that had previously been seen as a highly successful event. Said Edwina, describing a school outing — an outing on which it had previously been agreed that her mother was among the most appropriately dressed — "I was ashamed when you wore slacks to the bush picnic and all the other mothers had on dresses and high heels".

A daughter may remind her mother of ideas they don't share — "I think your favourite music is pathetic". These are shock tactics to make her mother stop in her tracks and reassess her. Said one adolescent girl:

> "I'm me, me, me. Mum thinks I'm her, twenty years ago. She keeps on saying, 'I know what you feel like. I used to feel like that'. Well she's got to see I'm not like she was at all. I'm much more remarkable".

Quarrelling is Constructive

Often the mother is extremely proud of her adolescent daughter, but she doesn't express it in the extravagant way her daughter wants. This is not to say the mother is in the wrong. On the contrary, the mother is the catalyst for her daughter's growth. Her responses disappoint her daughter but they push her toward maturity. Her adolescent daughter needs to learn to cope with reality, because in adulthood extravagant, supportive responses will be few and far between.

Nor should it be said that the quarrelling is wrong. Tension between mothers and daughters allows daughters to define their own boundaries more clearly. Through fighting with her mother about what she wants and believes, an adolescent daughter learns about herself and how to cast off childhood. She learns how to define her differences with her childish self. She learns how to define her difference from her mother. It is the mother who pushes her to become an individual. The more the daughter argues with her mother, the more she understands how she herself thinks and feels. A mother who questions and can argue with a father about arrangements and ideas with which she does not agree, thus indicating she is an independent person, also sets a good example. Diplomacy is not the answer. A daughter needs a good fighting partner in her mother.

All adolescents are notoriously touchy. A mother's list of instructions may seem right enough to an outsider. To an adolescent, they are an onslaught on her self-esteem. She wants to let her mother know she is no longer a malleable child and knows she gets more response from her if she is unreasonable. She's expert at glances that could kill and stares and looks full of projected meaning. One adolescent girl, Jenny, sobbed and screamed when her mother told her not to wash woollen socks in the washing machine. "Leave me alone. You are always telling me what to do", was her response, meanwhile thrusting the socks into the machine. The outraged mother shouted, "Don't do that". Her mother's unusual outburst bewildered and terrified Jenny. To her the issue was gaining recognition for her new independent self and that seemed to be making her mother angry. But her mother's response also made her face her egocentricity. Her mother made it clear that the issues were selfishness and economics and handed Jenny her independence, "I'm the one who has to pay for new socks when they come out hard as a board and you won't wear them. I suggest you buy your own socks out of your allowance from now on. Then you can do with them whatever you want."

Adolescent daughters can intersperse violent and vindictive statements about their mothers with statements that their mothers understand and support them. Adolescent daughters confide in mothers rather than fathers. They enjoy time with their fathers, but they don't just sit and talk with them as they do with their mothers. They engage in specific activities with Dad. He teaches them to ride a bike and takes them camping.

Adolescent daughters know how to hurt their mothers, but they also know that a time to heal will come — "She gets mad, but she calms down". They are much better at seeing things from their mothers' perspective than their fathers and can explain why their mothers behave as they do.[9] They know their mothers try to understand and try to reciprocate, but fathers "don't want to know" or "they try to control you". Although they know that their fathers care about them, they have learnt that their fathers' lesser emotional involvement in their lives means less insight. Most adolescent daughters have a greater sense of intimacy with their mothers and this makes them feel more secure about conflicts with them. An adolescent daughter is less likely to avoid conflict with her mother than her father. It may be painful but she wants to analyse and explain things to her mother. Fathers rarely allow room for that.

This is why daughters tend to avoid discussion and conflict with fathers. Said Wendy, who wanted to go interstate to a school for Nannies.

> "My Mum starts off by saying, 'Oh No you don't'. Then, after a couple of days, she's thought it through and is more enthusiastic than I am. With Dad I just think, 'forget it'. We laugh about what he doesn't notice".

Said Alison, "Mum's sensible on some issues and hopeless on others. Dad's always hopeless."

Daughters Want to Think Well of Their Mothers

Daughters like to admire their mothers — "I gave Mum a bad time when she kept me studying, but all the time I admired her for making me stick to it". "She makes these marvellous chocolate cakes". "She made all our clothes" "Mum's the one who has done up the house. She's like Rosie the Riveter with the electric drill".

Even if daughters do not feel close to their mothers, they still care about what their mothers think of them. They give up on drug-addicted or alcoholic mothers less easily than they do wayward fathers. They tend to refrain from the criticisms they level at healthy mothers and forego the need to be understood by their mothers.

Adolescent daughters like intimate conversations with their mothers but they don't want to be conversed with as equals. They resist friendship and equal sharing of emotional problems with their mothers — "I feel embarrassed when she asks my advice about breaking up with Dad". They like to think of their mothers as supporters, not the ones to be supported. "I don't mind her telling me she's upset or she's having a bad time. I just don't want her to ask me how to solve her problems. She's supposed to be the one who is grown up."[10]

Adolescent daughters' plans for the future either involve doing what their mothers have or haven't done — "I don't want my husband to treat me like Dad treats Mum". "I'm not going to work and raise kids". If we return to Jane Austen's *Persuasion*, written almost 200 years ago, we find the same theme. Under pressure, Anne Elliot is tempted to marry her cousin — a man like her father — and fill her dead mother's place in her role as Lady Elliot. But she remembers how her mother humoured her father's feelings and promoted his respectability and was never particularly happy. She decides to marry a man totally unlike her father in temperament and position.

To sum up what has been said so far, it is the conflict between mothers and daughters that causes stress for most mothers, not the fear of their daughters separateness — their wish to develop a separate identity — as traditional psychology and psychiatry have argued. Most mothers and daughters fight because they don't want to give up on each other. A good fight may be warranted. A mother's presentation of her point of view can be the catalyst for the daughter's maturing. However, the use of humiliation, destruction of self-esteem or distortion of facts can destroy the adolescent's psychological growth. Just listening without comment is often all that is needed.

Adolescent girls tend to be obsessed that their mothers are trying to control them, because they see themselves as having a new self, a new individuality and they want to shock their mothers into recognition. The adolescent of course wants to hear that she is totally unique. She quarrels with her mother because she feels secure enough to do so and because she wants to have a relationship with her.

❧

Conflict and Adolescents in General

Conflict is Not Peculiar to Mothers and Daughters

Many conflicts of concern to mothers during their daughters' adolescence are not specific to the mother-daughter relationship, as the myths would have. Most clashes arise from the challenges of the changes that take place during the adolescence of both sexes. Many are due to quite normal features of any adolescent's development. They concern and can discomfort both parents, not mothers alone. In the rest of the chapter, I shall confine myself to normal changes during adolescence which, while elaborating on the issues I've already discussed, can be important for boys also. I do this in order to clear away the false projections about the inevitability of mother-daughter conflict. I shall continue to use her/she and female case studies to cover both sexes. I shall not cover all features of adolescence, but those I've found to be most often misconstrued. There are innumerable books on the psychology of adolescents and why adolescence takes the form it does in western society.[11]

Separation Rituals

It is the critical nature of adolescents, that most parents find hardest to cope with. For example, Anastasia, the leading character in Marilyn French's novel, *Her Mother's Daughter*, whom we met in Chapter 2, tried to fathom why it was that, in adolescence, her daughter, Arden, felt compelled to challenge everything she said, why she screamed at her and called her mean and accused her of not caring for her. Why was it that after Anastasia's work had taken her away for a few days, even at the age of 16, Arden was invariably in a bad mood and refused to keep her room tidy or help with the domestic chores?

Until Arden went to College, Anastasia was utterly intimidated by her and was always edgy with her, living in fear as to what would set her off. Marilyn French describes how they both looked forward to her vacations which quickly deteriorated:

> ... as if she went around a corner and found herself suddenly in a dark place, or fell over an edge — she'd lash out and move into a morose rage, in which she took every remark addressed to her, or any omission of her, any plan that didn't involve her, as a slight, an attack, darts aimed at her, lethal. Then she would retire to the corners of chairs using her eyes to shoot poison darts of her own at all of us, especially me. And these states would last for days, would not end until it was time for her to leave again.[12]

So common are these behaviours in adolescence, they can be described as separation rituals. They are rehearsals for psychological autonomy, which begin in pre-adolescence, around nine or ten years of age. If she has been permitted reasonable autonomy, a small girl gradually learns to be self-reliant in many ways while she is at school, playing at a friend's house or staying with grandparents. Even so, children of this age do not see themselves as psychologically independent human beings. For instance, they still believe their parents know better than they do what they are like deep down inside.[13]

Working towards physical autonomy began in infancy. In toddlerhood and during the pre-school years, it expressed itself in temper tantrums, refusing to follow instructions and practising physical skills. The first marked attempts at psychological separation commence in mid-primary school years, when the daughter (or son) recognises the imperfection of parents. There may follow a period of acute embarrassment if, in the offspring's eyes, parents don't measure up to other parents, or fall short of expectations. Ten year old Debra told her mother:

"I felt really ashamed of you when you told the Cubs' mistress that you didn't go to Church. The best mothers go to Church".

At 13, Anne Frank wrote in her diary about how far her mother was from the ideal. She described how she looked elsewhere to find larger than life heroes and heroines to replace the lost idealised role of her parents — royal families of Europe, gods, goddesses and film stars.

As the parent tumbles from the pedestal, the daughter (or son) may begin to be more secretive, less co-operative and even less affectionate. These are early testings for psychological autonomy. The child is experimenting with emotional independence. Later, with the same objective, adolescents may use excessive criticism and moodiness as a battering ram, as Arden did. At this stage, parents may feel rejected, not being able to recognise their offsprings' clumsy attempts at independent behaviour for what it is.

The push for psychological autonomy is aided by cognitive and neurological development and the accumulated learning and experiences of childhood.[14] Adolescents have acquired a growing capacity to differentiate, to abstract and to integrate ideas. The capacity to differentiate ideas appears to precede the ability to integrate them and thus see multiple points of view. The ability to see multiple points of view usually doesn't happen until later adolescence and early adulthood. So in the earlier stages of this development, younger adolescents (12-13 years) usually begin by being critical of the values of salient others, such as their parents.

Until they are about 15 or 16, adolescents seem to be driven by a need to critically differentiate themselves from those who have been closest and dearest. Mothers are most often the closest and adolescents know their mothers are the ones on whom they have been most dependent in the past. So their first attempts at developing their own independent system of values and ideas may take the form of criticism of their mothers. Unfortunately, in sexist families, the general denigration of female values makes those of the mother the more obvious starting point.

Because the capacity to integrate different perspectives is a skill that usually does not develop until late adolescence or early adulthood, many adolescents are unable to think objectively about themselves or others. Unfortunately, many are confined to their own perspectives and remain concrete thinkers, with a consequent restricted view of others, for the rest their lives.

However, theoretically, by 18 or 19 years of age, teenagers should be able to grasp that others are also selves with fears, doubts and hopes and strengths that may be similar to or different from their own. So at this stage, they should be able to accept the independent selfhood of their mothers.

Unfortunately, in patriarchal society, the recognition of the individuality of mothers is particularly difficult for children and teenagers, because the infant, the child and the teenager are seen as primary and the mother as secondary. The mother is seen foremost in the caretaking role and hence as an object of gratification and frustration, not as an independent self. Harriett, 15 years, illustrates the point:

> "Mum's just got a part-time job. About once a week she gets home about half an hour after I do. I have to let myself in. I hate it. I want her to be there when I get home, with afternoon tea ready, so we can sit down and have a chat. I need her to be there. Aren't I supposed to be all she's got to think about"?

This naive, egotistical view of mothers is retained by many throughout adulthood, even when mothers display interests and pursuits of their own outside the family. But at 19, Harriett had matured sufficiently to be able to say: "Mum's got to have a life of her own — not just me, Dad and Johnno".

Although adolescents see mothers as extensions of themselves much more than they do fathers, relationships between mothers and daughters do not have a monopoly on emotional strain and convolution. For example, where autonomy seeking takes the form of quite brash and even callous behaviours which are testing the parents' affection and control, both parents may feel threatened.

The behaviour of their offspring may exacerbate their growing awareness of middle-age. It may arouse in them a sense of loss — the loss of their youth, the loss of the hoped-for ideal family, the loss of the dream of a compliant son or daughter who lives out the projections of their own hopes. Coping with their adolescents' challenges may confront them with the realisation that they will not reach the heights they'd wished for in their jobs or their lives. At this stage, fathers often become very depressed and worry about the ebb of their sexuality. Their compensatory manoeuvres are well documented — chasing younger women or belittling their offspring, because they themselves feel belittled. These are parental separation anxieties and ways of responding to those of their offspring.

One separation ritual that frequently confuses or upsets both parents is where an adolescent or young adult leaves home, only to return again, perhaps repeating the exit and re-appearance several times. It is a ritual common to both sons and daughters and their way of testing whether they can cope in the outside world. Obviously, there are limits to the parents' indulgence. Said Valentine, aged 50:

> "Maria went off to live with friends about 6 years ago when she was 18 and got a job. Two months ago she re-appeared with all her luggage. Didn't ring to ask if it was convenient for us. She's taken over her old room which is O.K. but she wants to control the T.V every night she's in. She's critical and rude when our friends come over and she expects me to cook her meals and do her washing as I did when she was 6, 10 or 13. Maurice (Valentine's husband) and I have adjusted to the children leaving home and have independent arrangements now. I love her but she seems to want to take over my personal space completely."

Although now an adult, Maria was still struggling with immature adolescent ideas about mothers and anxieties about her own psychological independence and autonomy. Not until she had children of her own, three years later, did she appreciate that her mother was a separate being with needs and interests of her own. For two of those three years, Valentine and Maurice had to establish limits and explain their point of view, while making it clear that they loved her.

While this was not the case with Valentine, some parents compound their own and their adolescents' separation difficulties by inventing special ways of binding them to the family. Perhaps mother waits on the adolescent hand and foot or Dad supplies every gratification, so that the adolescent has no impetus to try living away from home. Adolescents can also be bound to the family home by mixed messages: "You are no good at coping on your own". Mothers are particularly accused of not letting go of their daughters, but in my experience this applies as much to fathers.

Sometimes, an adolescent's failure in school, or in relationships, is the result of mixed messages, for there are parents who do not want their children to succeed where they themselves have failed. Others want their children to make up for everything they did not do when they were young. Some parents involve themselves in their adolescents' successes and failures in order to vicariously relive part of their own lives, as Amanda Wingfield tried to do with her daughter, Laura, in *The Glass Menagerie*. This means the parents are using their offspring as extensions of themselves and have not established their own autonomy. In my experience, fathers do this as often as mothers and sometimes more so.

Helm Stierlen, a psychiatrist,[15] believes parents delegate their adolescents to be this or that and that some of this unrecognised and indirect pressure is healthy and some of it is unhealthy. For example, how many students study medicine to satisfy parents? Less obvious are cases where a daughter (or a son) is delegated to adventurous roles, for example a backpacking trip to the Himalayas, promiscuity or taking illegal drugs. The adolescent hears the parents condemnation, but picks up the hidden agenda through the parents excitement or interest. Sometimes even 'unwanted' pregnancies are delegated.[16]

Candida said with humour:

"My Mum enjoys me going out in these outrageous clothes and she gets a hype from the way Dad looks shocked. But she knows it and she laughs about how her Dad would have killed her if she'd worn some of the things I do. That's my Mum and I get some fun out of her wackiness. It makes me see the differences between us — her life and mine — me and her".

Not all adolescents and their mothers are as honest with themselves as Candida and her mother were. Where the agendas are hidden, inexplicable emotion and anger can surface over a mother criticising or commenting on how her daughter dresses or acts.

Mutual Feelings of Inferiority

Many mothers (and fathers) complain that they feel totally inadequate as parents and human beings in the face of their adolescents' constant barrage of criticism, moodiness, sulking and withdrawal. They don't always realise that adolescents don't really think their parents are stupid — quite the reverse. They are usually behaving like this because they themselves feel inadequate. They know how to hurt parents. Hurting parents is their immature way of getting parents to value them.

The youth cult of post-industrial society, which has brought untold profits to the clothing and record industries, means that parents are behind in the tastes, fads, crazes, philosophies and values of the younger generation. As a consequence, not only mothers, but both parents, have to share their advisory role with the media, the fashion houses and the record industry.

These trends have inevitably given adolescents more status than they had generations ago. The youth cult has particularly given them a strong advantage over their parents. Nowadays, it is not only mothers but also fathers who try to emulate their sons and daughters in dress and behaviour.[17] Some even affect an exaggerated egalitarianism with them. In doing so, researchers suggest that they have failed to recognise that adolescents basically perceive themselves as inferior.[18] They are likely to look down on those who show similar behaviour patterns. Many studies report that adolescents are seeking direction from adults, despite the fact that they protest about it.

Exploited and pushed by business into a leading role as consumers and setters of fashion in dress, music or lifestyle, contemporary adolescents are in an advantageous position to manipulate their parents. Angry at feeling inferior to adults, teenagers do their best to make their parents feel inferior and in the last decades, research suggests that they have been rather successful.[19]

Living with an adolescent often threatens a parent's self-esteem enor mously. Parents find it hard to cope with the constant criticism about their values, habits or "old fashioned" ideas. Yet the seemingly negative behaviour of adolescents is often no more than their clumsy attempts to test their wings. Adolescents are not always as rejecting as parents think.

Nevertheless, constantly coping with the criticism of a teenager can have a negative effect on the mother's self-esteem in particular, especially if it has already been undermined by the social expectations of her as a female and a mother. Guilt can be a major inhibiting factor for mothers (and fathers) in trying to maintain self-esteem — "Where did I go wrong?" "I must have done something wrong to cause her to be this way. It's my fault".

The sadness of this situation is that it leads parents to believe that they have failed. Diana Baumrind,[20] who has worked with middle class families over many decades, found that parents who had an egalitarian or extremely democratic approach in bringing up their children tended to be most dissatisfied with their adolescents. However, the suggestion is that these relationships improve considerably and satisfactorily, once the autonomy-seeking, rebellious phase of adolescence and young adulthood is over.

The psychological reasons for this are many, but the most obvious one is that democratic parents have encouraged their children to evaluate adults, as well as themselves. To test and to be rebellious toward the demo-cratically-minded adult is not as threatening as it is in the authoritarian family. Hence, many democratically-oriented parents wistfully envy the sometimes seemingly good order and control of the authoritarian family and wonder if they did the right thing.

In such situations, mothers, or parents in general, may like to review their objectives in their children's development and the messages they imparted and realise that they did not fail. The following extract from some unpublished case notes is pertinent:

> Joanne, aged 40, was confronted by continual critical assessment of her values and her appearance by her 15 year old daughter, Bettina. Bettina had also recently dropped out of school, complaining that it was a waste of time. Joanne considered the situation: "I daresay I've got to live with that and learn to assert myself. I also criticised the education system a lot and she's acting out just what I think about it. Now what I've got to get across to her firmly is that despite this, she's got to maximise her abilities, using a poor educa-tion system where she can."

The Brash Behaviour of Adolescents

Due to a state of uncertainty, confusion and frustration, adolescent behaviour is often compensatorily brash and arrogant, even bullying.[21] Hard as they may be to deal with, it is a relief to know that upheavals dur-ing adolescence have to do with the normal processes of adolescent development and the kind of world we live in.[22]

For adolescents, the major challenge is discovering who they are in today's world and forming their individual identity. This is often the theme of their favourite songs or topics of conversation. If adolescents prematurely fall in with their parents views without question, conflict with their parents may be minimal. Conflict is more likely to arise if an adolescent is actively working at discovering his or her individual identity. Conflict will probably be greatest, if an adolescent steps outside the prevailing morés and tries to create an unconventional identity.[23]

Examples of the latter can be seen in those who live alternative lifestyles, or in the punks of the 1970s and 1980s, with their violent dress and spiky hair. Their differences, since they drew attention, reduced the threat of being a nonentity in today's world. Punks were also making a statement about the violence and false values of the society that adults support. Discussion of the point of view of an adolescent with an alternative lifestyle, rather than rejection of it because it's different from the parental lifestyle, is important for good relationships.[24]

Many parents give illustrations of their confusions about the origins of seemingly antagonistic behaviours in their adolescents. Much of it is incorrectly blamed on the inevitability of mother-daughter conflict. For example:

> One father brought his wife and daughter to me complaining that his daughter was behaving oddly because she and his wife were "not getting on". He added apologetically, "One has to expect fights between mothers and daughters. They are just built that way".[25]

> Through his 'failure' to recognise that his daughter was a typical adolescent, the father was hoping to absolve himself from any need to respond and listen to her. She had been telling both her parents that she wanted "to do my own thing" and that the family lifestyle did not suit her. She wanted to give up the family religion and try something else. She showed me the poetry she had written about her love for her parents. Her poetry expressed deep emotional pain. As she saw it, her parents could not love her enough to let her try her wings and they misconstrued her attempts to construct her own identity as hatred of them.

> In fact, this adolescent was doing what all healthy adolescents do. She was not involved in some peculiar brand of mother-daughter conflict. She simply wanted to test her family's values and herself in different settings. There was no need for either of her parents to feel rejected and threatened, as they did. She loved them dearly and had been trying to let her parents know this, albeit in a rather belligerent and incomprehensible fashion.

> Another father complained about much the same kind of behaviour, except in his case the daughter's choice of vocation was

his problem. She wanted to be a car mechanic. He attributed her choice to the mother's lack of proper guidance and an outcome of the usual "aggravation that one must expect between mothers and daughters". He told me that he had an upper middle class background — that he was in an occupation with a high professional status, that his father was in the same profession and so was his grandfather. He added that he lived in an upper middle class suburb in a substantial house and he expected his children to end up in professional careers with high status.

Parental concern about the downward mobility of their offspring of either sex is not unusual today.[26] The following story is another example:

> Louisa was the daughter of a barrister. She was herself headed for a legal career, until she dropped out of university and moved to a country area to work on a small farm with friends. She is now back in the metropolis happily working as a gardener with a large institution. Her female friends admire her for doing what she likes best and for doing it well. Her mother and father are most apologetic for the way she earns her livelihood. They wonder where they failed as parents, instead of accepting their daughter on her terms.[27]

If you are coping with an adolescent right now, you may want to go further than the reassurance offered here. Reading a variety of books on the psychology of adolescent development,[28] along with forming a support group to exchange experiences about living with adolescents helps parents and especially mothers. Many may find some kind of Bibliotherapy useful. Stories of other mothers and daughters struggling with their relationships with each other may indicate just how normal our own experiences are. Examples are given in this book. Above all a sense of humour helps. When none of this works you may decide to seek the help of a professional.[29]

Professional Help and False Propaganda

What happens when we consult professionals about our adolescents and they use outdated theories which blame mothers? Unfortunately, there are some such theories which continue to be widely used in professional practice and which do mother-daughter relationships a disservice.

An outstanding example is a theory by Eric Erikson,[30] which is still taught in many professional training courses and embodies the outdated view that a female depends on male support for the formation of her psychological identity. While Erikson maintains that a male achieves his identity through the typical, male stereotypes of autonomy, initiative and industry, he describes the female as holding her identity in "abeyance" until she finds a man who rescues her from her inner "emptiness" and loneliness, by filling "the inner space". This view, that a woman is totally dependent on a man for her identity, is patriarchally oriented and socially induced — a point which Erikson failed to discuss.

Fortunately, Erikson's theory has been subjected to some rigorous testing. I shall address just one aspect of that testing here. It is associated with the assertion that a woman feels physically incomplete as a person unless she is having a sexual relationship with a man. This implies that, until this happens, females lack a sense of physical self-esteem and are focused upon the incompleteness of their inner bodies. Males, whose genitalia are externalised, derive self-esteem from their outward appearance and behaviour. This is a very patriarchal way of interpreting sexual desire.

Lerner and Spanier[31] found the research data to give only partial support for this theory. In several studies, although the females had more knowledge about their inner bodies (womb, vagina, etc.) than did males about theirs, their inner physiology was not more crucial to their feelings of self-esteem and effectiveness, than it was to males. In fact, their outer body parts were more crucial to such factors, than they were to males. This runs counter to what Erikson saw as the male's presumably greater external orientation. It appears that females are just generally more attuned to their bodies, both internal and external, than are males.[32]

The point is that 'experts' should not make unverified generalisations about the psychological outcomes of physical differences between males and females. It is unjust to use them to try and justify "biology is destiny" type theories which claim that females are dependent on penetration by a penis, or being pregnant, for a sense of self-worth.

Where attitudes encourage a female adolescent to believe her identity depends entirely on sexual partnership with a male, they create special problems for mother-daughter relationships. Autonomy for women, it is implied, involves escape from the mother to the protective custody of a male. The division is encouraged by the all too common tendency to paint mothers in a hostile fashion. Mother-in-law jokes are part of this propaganda.

Mothers and daughters need to be wary of jokes and theories that make them feel ashamed of their friendship with one another. They need to know about the many negative influences that try to keep them in opposition to each other. Autonomy and friendship are possible and a good friendship should not allow itself to be, jealously and destructively, described as lack of autonomy.

Adrienne Rich argues that the negative attitudes of theorists and clinicians, such as Erikson, arise because, like most close relationships between women, the relationship between mother and daughter has been profoundly threatening to men.[33]

Nothing could illustrate the petty, daily propaganda and pressures that are used to set mothers and daughters asunder better than a story by Tess Slessinger: *Mother To Dinner*.[34] Slessinger describes how the newly married Katherine reflects on the pressures from Gerald, her husband, to give up her friendship with her mother:

But suppose he had come upon her telephoning her mother; she could hear him say, as he said last Sunday, catching her at the telephone (and of course one thought of one's mother on a long Sunday), Oh for God's sake Katherine, like a two year old baby you are always running home to mother ... Cut off from her mother. Yet Gerald was right, she musn't, she musn't.[35]

Katherine reflects on the difference at home with her parents during her adolescence and young adulthood, where the mother-daughter relationship was accepted. Her father, Mr Benjamin, beside his work downtown:

...mailed their letters, called for their purchases, or did any of the little errands which they had spent the day pleasantly avoiding. If he entered the room where Katherine and her mother were talking, it had seemed quite natural for Mrs Benjamin to say, "Dear, we are talking"; it seemed quite natural because of the peaceful expression with which Mr Benjamin picked up his Saturday Evening Post on the way out of the room. All Katherine's uncles were disposed in the same way by her aunts.[36]

In contrast to this acceptance of the mother-daughter relationship are the experiences of many women — mothers and daughters — when they consult a therapist. Paula Caplan, a therapist herself, argues that mother-blaming among therapists is as bad today as it was in 1969, when she began her graduate training. In her experience, if anyone in the family is depressed, aggressive or otherwise emotionally disturbed, the mother is likely to be blamed.[37] This is quite the reverse of what is needed in mother-daughter counselling.

The emotional health of female clients is contingent on their being treated by counsellors who respect women and are sensitive to their emotional needs. Yet many feel that the kind of help they have received from professional sources aggravated their problems, because the counsellor used a male yardstick to assess them.[38] Research indicates that male counsellors often have expectations of stereotyped female behaviour.[39] The facts are that many therapists, both male and female, have different standards of mental health for men and women. They require women to to be more submissive, emotional, sensitive, dependent and less competitive. Their assumptions about mother-daughter conflict often exacerbate, rather than help, the situation.

Research also indicates that both female and male counsellors recall fewer facts relating to female clients, while physicians attach greater importance to the complaints of male patients, than to the complaints of female patients.[40] Studies suggest that similar kinds of devaluations of female clients' concerns occur in most counselling processes.[41]

One must be careful not to be lulled out of vigilance where the therapist is a woman.[42] Although women are generally more able to empathise with their female clients than males, the therapist may unwittingly be using a male yardstick for a female problem. Because there is a strongly patriarchal bias in psychological and psychoanalytic theories and professional training, a women therapist may be unaware that her assessment is prejudiced.[43]

Many mothers and daughters find more effective therapy through self-initiation and self-learning, together with discussion with friends.

Overview

During adolescence, mother-daughter relationships do not have a monopoly on fractiousness. Both parents describe adolescents of both sexes who are behaving cruelly or like frightful four year olds. They conclude they have somehow caused this behaviour by not being good parents. Mothers are most prone to this self-condemnation. They are relieved to hear that their adolescents' behaviour is not unusual and not abnormal. They are surprised, as well as relieved, when they come to observe that the tantrums and negativisms have a lot to do with their adolescents' feelings of inferiority about how they are coping with major problems of developing autonomy and identity.

They also take heart when they know that researchers argue that if parents are not coming in for some criticism from their adolescents, they should be concerned that their adolescents do not feel free to engage in the testing of their ideas and ways. Not to test parental values, or to accept them without question, may be a suppression of the development of autonomy. At the same time, the parent should not 'surrender', but put her point of view. This clash of perspectives helps an adolescent to see her opinions from other standpoints and hence reduces her egocentricity. It increases her ability to see herself objectively and therefore assists her autonomous, identity development. It encourages her to allow her mother a separate identity.

Mother-daughter relationships in adolescence can be both intimate and fractious. The reasons for this have been discussed. It has been recognised that the quarrelling often stems from the fact that mothers and daughters do not want to give up on developing a good relationship. A mother is the catalysts for her daughter's maturity. A mother can feel demoralised in the face of an adolescent daughter's boorish manoevures and game playing as she struggles to build her 'grown-up' self.

The kind of family that best lays the foundation for good mother-daughter relationships is one where the mother's contribution is valued along with all others and where co-operation and responsibility is expected and given by all family members equally. This is a 'just community' — a concept that is gaining increasing popularity among counsellors and recipients of family counselling. A mother who deprives and subordinates herself in order to dance attendance on her husband and her offspring has lost sight of her equal right to justice. She does not provide a model that makes her daughter proud of her female identity and her relationship with her mother.

The emotionally charged content of mother-daughter relationships in adolescence and young adulthood is explored further in the next two chapters. Sexuality, which is the seat of much conflict and resentment, is looked at first.

∞

BIBLIOTHERAPY

Stories about adolescent daughters can be found in *Between Mothers and Daughters: Stories across a Generation*, edited by Susan Koppelman. Some of the stories are outlined in the Bibliotherapy in Chapter 9. The stories by Alice Munro such as *Ottowa Valley, Winter Wind and Princess Ida* are also relevant to issues discussed in this chapter. The extracts about Anastasia and her adolescent daughter, Arden, come from Marilyn French's, *Her Mother's Daughter*.

Some of the following give marvellous insights into adolescent daughters: Shakespeare's *Romeo and Juliet*, Jane Austen's *Persuasion*, Muriel Spark's *The Prime of Miss Jean Brodie* and *The Diary of Anne Frank*. Katherine Dalsimer, in *Female Adolescence*, draws attention to the insights given into adolescence by each of these.

∞

CHAPTER 4

The Snow White Syndrome

Sexuality and Mother-Daughter Conflict

During adolescence, sexuality comes to occupy an important place in the definition of self. How an adolescent daughter experiences her sexuality is crucial to the mother-daughter relationship at this time. The question is whether patriarchy allows mothers and daughters to value their sexuality? If not, what can be done about it? This chapter addresses these issues.

Physical changes take place during adolescence that make both girls and boys capable of procreation and intensely interested in sex. The sexual interest of girls should not be underestimated. A humorous reminder that this interest is not simply a product of the women's liberation movements of the 1970s and 1980s is found in *The Prime of Miss Jean Brodie* — a comic novel by Muriel Spark. It describes just how much adolescent girls are pre-occupied with and mystified by sex.[1]

Miss Brodie's young pupils speculate among themselves about how sexual intercourse might feel and how the impulse to do it occurs. They ask each other whether the sexual urge might not be dampened by the time it takes to remove clothes. In attempting to fathom what it means to be swept away by the sexual impulse, they eavesdrop on adults and are fascinated by media accounts of sexual encounters — even sexual crime.

Boys are equally pre-occupied but do not have the same sense of mystery. They've had concrete experience of erections and ejaculations. They have a current folklore, slang and jokes to confirm their sexuality. Because, until recently, our patriarchally biased society has been anxious to deny sexuality in girls, there is little positive folklore about female sexuality — unlike the situation in the ancient woman-centered societies discussed in Book II.[2]

Even contemporary text books on the subject generally have a strongly patriarchal bias. For example, as Katherine Dalsimer, a clinical psychologist influenced by psychoanalysis, points out, the language of psychoanalysis is rooted in the sexual experience of males : "upsurge", "flood", "spurt of sexual drive". It has also defined away the pleasure, delight or pride on the part of the female in her own genitalia.[3] Menarche, the signal of female puberty, has been described as a fresh wound. This lack of positive validation of the female sexual experience is a hurdle which the mother-daughter relationship has to overcome. How can this be done?

Obviously, the first step is to understand the defenses adolescent girls resort to when they begin to experience the feelings and crushes of early sexuality. Many of these defenses are an outcome of patriarchal problems with sex in general and female sexuality in particular.[4]

Sometimes, novels by women give more genuine insight into the early reactions of girls to their sexuality than traditional theories. *The Prime of Miss Jean Brodie* is an example. With humour, Muriel Spark shows how the deep concern of adolescent girls for their own sexuality is dealt with by proxy. Their curiosity finds safe outlet in speculating about the sex life of their teacher, Miss Jean Brodie, who tells them she is in her prime. The girls are fascinated by her relationship with two male teachers, Mr Lloyd and Mr Lowther. Is she having a sexual relationship with one of them?

Claudine at School by Colette, the legendary French author, is another novel by a woman writer which describes how intensely adolescent girls are interested in the subject of sex. Their urge to know more makes them pry indefatigably into the sex lives of their teachers. Claudine lusts after her pretty young teacher, Aimée. She conjectures endlessly about Aimée's relationship with the headmistress who is having an affair with the District Superintendent of Schools. The novel is packed with heterosexual and homosexual triangles.

Parental Anxiety and Daughter's Resentment

Parents can be frightened by their adolescents' emerging sexuality. As a result, adolescents often feel that their sexual knowledge has been attained in an embarrassed and furtive way. Daughters may be angry because their mothers have told them very little about sex, menstruation and the female biological processes. "All she ever said to me", said one, "was, 'Don't let men touch you *there*'. One had to deduce what she meant by *there*."[5]

These quotes and findings come from a research study which I began in 1982 and which is still in progress. It has involved hundreds of daughters who are adolescents, young adults, middle aged or very old. Generally, these daughters claim that not only was information from their mothers inadequate, but sexuality was seen as secretive — even furtive — by the entire family. Little information was given about sexuality or its pleasures. These daughters harboured considerable resentment about their mothers' failure to endorse a fundamental aspect of themselves and said it inhibited good relationships with them.

Younger women remembered being warned of menstruation, but sometimes in an embarrassed or discomforting fashion. When it commenced, they said it was rarely treated as a celebration of womanhood. It was often kept a secret from fathers and brothers, as though it was shameful or something they were bound to be teased about. This did not make them feel proud to be female. It did not make them proud of their mothers.

In contrast, in Merlin Stone's book, *Ancient Mirrors of Womanhood*, we find accounts of women's ceremonies at the time of a young girl's menstruation. Menstruation rituals honour and esteem daughters and establish a proud sense of continuity with their mothers and all women.[6] This is validating literature and folklore for mothers to read and hand on to their daughters.

Some find *The Diary of Anne Frank* helpful. On her thirteenth birthday Anne was given some money and bought *The Myths of Greece and Rome*. She wrote:

I go into ecstasies every time I see the naked figure of a woman, such as Venus ... It strikes me as so wonderful and exquisite that I have difficulty in stopping the tears rolling down my cheeks.[7]

She speaks of the "sweet secret" of her menarche:

Each time I have a period — and that has only been three times — I have the feeling that in spite of the pain, unpleasantness, and nastiness, I have a sweet secret, and that is why, although it is nothing but a nuisance to me in a way, I always long for the time I shall feel that secret within me again.[8]

The pity of it is that patriarchal attitudes link the arrival of menarche with trauma and early fantasies of castration.[9] Where these negative attitudes are scorned and positive folklore is substituted, the mother-daughter relationship benefits. Said Corinne, who obviously had a good relationship with her daughter, Stephie:

"Stephie went through this period of being mad on anything about goddesses and The Diary of Anne Frank. I used both to encourage pride in her female body and its power for creating life — something I'd always tried to do. We discussed how Anne felt. I remember she liked the bit where Anne says, 'I think what is happening to me is so wonderful, and not only what can be seen on my body, but all that is taking place inside'".[10]

Sexuality and Mother-Daughter Intimacy

Unfortunately, most contemporary daughters say that it was hard to reconcile awareness of their sexuality in adolescence with intimacy with their mothers. They claimed that sexual awareness made them feel more awkward — even distanced them from their mothers. There was little or no sense of a joint sexual heritage with their mothers, or of their sexuality as a continuity with the generations of women in their families. There was no discovery that sexuality was something to be proudly shared and used to strengthen the mother-daughter relationship.[11] Few had thought through the role that the politics of patriarchy played in their and their mothers' predicaments.[12] Consequently, few could forgive their mothers for their inadequacies as informants and models.

Some remembered being shamed, in sexual curiosity games and explorations in childhood, by both parents. A story frequently told was about a sense of shame because of a mother's unwarranted suspicion that her unmarried daughter might be pregnant — "I felt untrusted". Some said mothers gave a curiously ambivalent tolerance to sexual relationships, with boyfriends — "She wouldn't let me do 'it' in 'her' house. Said it was inconsiderate, disrespectful. She knew my boyfriend and I were having sex and put on an air of open mindedness, but she never wanted to know whether where we did it was safe".[13]

In turn, adolescents are uncomfortable with the notion of their mothers' (and fathers') sex lives and begin their denial of it in primary school. *The Prime of Miss Jean Brodie* captures the ambivalence. Despite their avid curiosity about the sex life of Miss Brodie, her pupils seem to lack any interest in the sex lives of their mothers. Similarly, Claudine's obsession with the sex lives of her teachers and Anne Frank's concern with her own awakening sexuality, are in contrast to a seeming indifference to the sexuality of their parents. When recalling childhood and adolescence, most daughters talk of their embarrassment at the thought of their mothers' sexuality.

For example, one daughter described how her mother complained that her father gave her no sexual satisfaction. This daughter said she disliked her mother confiding in her, not only because she found it embarrassing, but also because it made her angry about being female:

> "Sometimes she cried when my father put pressure on her to go to bed with him when she didn't want to, and I felt an overwhelming identification with the victim. Once I remember, on a Saturday afternoon, my mother came out of my father's room shouting: 'Now you've finished with me you are just going to sleep'. I was only about eight but intuitively understood. I was profoundly embarrassed and felt that my mother was inadequate because she allowed herself to be used for something from which she got no pleasure. But I felt the situation also applied to me. I remember feeling that. I think this was the beginning of my fear of being used by men in sex.
>
> Later, when I used to hear men speaking about their wives as though they should have sex with them and were monsters if they didn't, I grew angrier. There are male jokes about wives' headaches."[14]

The reaction of many adolescents to such situations is less insightful and simply one of uncomprehending anger, which is deflected to their mothers. They are angry with their mothers for their problematic, female heritage and because the sexual models they provided were inhibited, restrictive and poorly defined. Not until they are adults, if then, do most daughters understand, that in handing on a restrained model of female sexuality, their mothers may have seen themselves as preparing their daughters in the best possible way for their roles in a patriarchal society.

Fortunately, things are not as bad as they used to be. This fact was underlined when my interviews with mothers and daughter brought to light some past child-rearing practices restraining sexuality in girls. For example, Adrienne described how her mother, Mavis, always complained that Adrienne was not physically affectionate. Then one day in a flash of insight, Mavis, who was born in the early 1900s, recalled a common teaching about raising girl babies:

> "We were advised not to cuddle our female children too much as it might make them overly affectionate and hence promiscuous and turn them into fallen women."

Here we have in a nutshell the sadness of cultural prescriptions that disregard the basic needs of female children to satisfy a one-sided stereotype.[15]

Overcoming Embarassment and Forming a Positive Identity

Finding ways to overcome the destructive influence these furtive attitudes about sex and female sexuality have on mother-daughter relationships is not as difficult as it may seem at first glance. Eva described her experience with her daughter, Mandy:

> "I was as inhibited as anyone else about my sexuality. I noticed Mandy becoming quite furtive after her first period. So I got together with some other mothers from Mandy's school. We experimented. We compared notes about the effect of leaving certain books around the house for our girls to read, going to selected films and the way to raise sensitive topics. The school is an all girls' school and we found the Biology and Phys. Ed. teachers were very sympathetic to what we were trying to do. We all worked together on pride in female sexuality, its creative power, its enjoyment. Then I threw a party to celebrate the arrival of my second daughter's first period. It was a great success. Mind you, one of my friends tried to throw the same kind of party for her daughter and it was initially most embarrassing. You've got to genuinely believe in what you are doing. Mandy keeps telling me that we have a much better relationship than any of her friends have with their mothers. She cites our open pride in our sexuality and me overcoming my apologetic behaviour about it, as two of the reasons for this."

Unfortunately, despite improvements in attitudes, embarrassment still hinders parents and adolescents from communicating about sexuality, although adolescents claim they would rather hear the facts from their parents. Daughters (and sons) need support to integrate feelings, fantasies and realities about sexual encounters. Without parental guidance, many young people are engaging in risky behaviour.[16] Confused by the half truths and plastic portrayals on television as well as pressures from peers, they prefer to think of sex as emotional and spontaneous. They feel it is not something that should be prepared for. There is a double edge to such myths, as they relieve one of responsibility. They are also an outcome of insufficient education about responsibility in sexual relationships and the undervaluing of the creation of life. Where these issues are aired and values and limits made clear, the disruptive tensions and anxieties arising out of the adolescent's immature behaviour are lessened, because the parent feels she is trying to act competently. Despite their protests, adolescents recognise competence in parents.

Maintaining Self-respect

Old patriarchal myths continue to confuse our daughters, unless we discuss them. For example, "good girls don't", is still alive to the extent that "good girls" are not supposed to be sexually active, unless the passion of the moment carries them away. Forethought, such as carrying a diaphragm, or even worse, taking a contraceptive pill daily, means that a girl has sex on her mind even when she was not involved in love-making. She is therefore "bad".[17] Adolescent girls often incorporate the attitudes of male peers that they are "slack" and without self-respect, if they practise sexual freedom in the way society allows boys to do. Poor respect for her sexual self may generalise to all women and her mother in particular. Communication between mothers and daughters about such illogicalities and their consequences is obviously important for self-respecting relationships.

Understanding the psychology of adolescence in general, empowers mothers (and fathers) to feel less frustrated and self-blaming. Getting rid of the feelings of guilt and incompetence improves the mother-daughter relationship enormously. If mothers (and fathers) do not understand the fundamentals of adolescent development, they can be totally confused by their daughters' irresponsible behaviour and feel the relationship is failing. They are more easily bullied into surrendering the limits that their good sense tells them they must set.

For example, mothers (and fathers) often complain that a daughter has been carefully instructed about the consequences of sexual experimentation yet becomes pregnant. Why is it that girls often fail to apply the facts of contraception to which they have been exposed? Something seems to prevent them from taking the possibility of their becoming pregnant seriously. The answer has a lot to do with cognitive immaturity. Adolescents have difficulty with pursuing the logic of hypothetical arguments such as, "What if I became pregnant?" or "What if I got AIDS?". They feel omnipotent and that they cannot be touched by the ills that beset others.[18]

Thus adolescents need information about themselves, as developing persons, from parents. If parents feel inadequate they should look for suitable articles and books. Of course, the adolescent may well resist and test parental advice but most prefer authoritative (as distinct from authoritarian) guidance from their parents, despite their protests.[19]

Roberta, now aged 30, said:

"When I was an adolescent, I gave Mum a bad time when she tried to tell me about sexual relationships. I called her old-fashioned and sneered at the books she gave me. I was furious when she wouldn't let me go to parties where there would be alcohol. But all the time, deep down inside I knew she was right. I respected her. I knew she was being firm because she cared. The best part about Mum was that she was never phased by me. She understood adolescents better than any mother I know. It made me feel secure. I knew she'd know best how to put the reins on me when I felt myself getting out of hand. This is why we get on so well now. I respect her for helping me to keep my self-respect, until I could do it all for myself."

An example of the confusion and self-denigration which many daughters experience in relation to their sexuality and female physiology is provided by the following two excerpts from a diary provided by a teenage girl. Her pseudonym is Sophie:

"I am 14 and my life is all to do with what I do at school. I do not like it at all. The female teachers are all frustrated spinsters who hate me and the other girls are silly like all girls. I just watch them getting around with their fat legs and boobs and think what a messy lot they are. The only friend I have is Phil. He's my boyfriend. I'd feel terrible if I didn't have a boyfriend. The girls who don't have boyfriends are ugly and stupid — nobody wants them."

"When I got my period I was 12. I was scared and embarrassed. I was terrified my mother would tell my father and brothers who would tease me. I felt unclean."

These two extracts are not uncommon to teenage girls and tell us a lot about the female condition, even in contemporary society — ambivalence about her sex and her body, disgust at female biology, and dependence on the male for feelings of self-worth. The attitudes of distaste for her own femaleness were later revealed to be the basis for Sophie's rejection of her mother.

Females of all ages must contend with gentle but basically derogatory sneers and sniggers about boobs, tits or fat bottoms, which can subtly destroy confidence in their bodies or encourage distaste for certain physical aspects of themselves. There are sick jokes about cunts. Patriarchal ambivalence, in the form of attraction, fear and repulsion toward female bodies and sexuality, appears in art (Picasso for example), in pornography and in advertising. By way of illustration, the following story was told by Jocelyn, upon overhearing her husband, Simon, comment on, a Picasso type picture of a woman with bits and pieces juxtaposed in all directions.

> "He said, 'That's a jolly good picture. Women's bodies are a mess — bits stuck on the front, wide bottoms, blobs of fat in the wrong place, painted mouths and eyes — it's all a great jumble'. We were not long married and I realised with a mortal blow to my self-esteem that his view of me had not been entirely what I thought.
>
> I suddenly realised that there had been a long line of such blows to my physical self-esteem. I remembered times as a child, dressing with my girlfriends after swimming, and being spied on by boys who made rude jokes about our female bodies, and another occasion when a gang of boys grabbed my girlfriend, aged eight, and pulled her pants down to look at her. 'Isn't that awful?', they shouted and went away sniggering and sneering. We complained to our parents but it was dismissed with: 'Boys will be boys,' as though the boys had been doing a fun thing for them. But what about us? Their attitude caused us to feel ashamed to be female. We felt angry and confused, because surely it was the boys who should have been ashamed for behaving meanly."

In patriarchal society, ordinary mothers and daughters often have to battle to maintain respect and affection for their own bodies and not to view them as unclean or as depersonalised sex objects. A woman, who feels pride in her female body, will not visit self-deprecation upon her female child. She will wordlessly transmit to her daughter that a woman's body is a good and healthy place to live.[20] As Adrienne Rich aptly puts it:

> Until a strong line of love, confirmation and example stretches from mother to daughter, from woman to woman across the generations, woman will still be wandering in the wilderness.[21]

Fortunately, there are daughters with positive memories of mothers' attitudes to sexuality. Through her attitudes, they have learnt pride and pleasure in female sexuality. One wrote:

> My mother didn't regard sex as obscene. It was never discussed much but, because of the accepting attitude to sex at home, I find it really hard to relate to English lavatory humour. I find it hard to understand why girls like Martha Quest found her mother's body so repulsive. I can see how attractive and sexual my mother is. I think I am sexually attractive. I'm not a masochist like some women. It's due to the independent model Mum gave me. It's why we have such a good relationship.[22]

In her novels, Colette describes how she found physical beauty in her mother: in her expression, her face, her body, her work-worn hands. She saw her unconventional confirmation of female sexuality as the basis of their good relationship.[23] Margaret Mead's daughter also describes how her mother transmitted pride in her female body and sexuality. How fundamental this was to their good relationship is outlined in the Bibliotherapy, Chapter 9, in the discussion of Mead's life. Tess Slessinger is another who intimates that her life as a child with her mother had the same positiveness. A neighbour reported her astonishment at the sight of Tess's brothers singing and dancing around a table in celebration of her first menstrual period.[24]

The Fluidity of Female Sexuality and the Mother-Daughter Relationship

The discussion so far has suggested that a daughter's sexuality is unequivocally directed at heterosexual union. It is not as simple as patriarchal teaching would have us believe. Sexuality appears to be more fluid and complex in females than it is in males and this creates another difference between boys and girls in the psychological ramifications of puberty. The difference relates to the fact that a daughter's first love object is typically of the same sex — her mother. Her mother is her chief nurturer in early infancy.

The infant daughter's relationship with her mother leads to an association of her nurturing and caring responses — cuddling, stroking, patting etc. — with pleasurable physical experience. Dinnerstein is one who has described this process as establishing a "homoerotic" potential in women.[25] Nancy Chodorow has also suggested that the early physical pleasure and emotional nurturance given by mothers to their infant daughters lays the psychic foundation for "homoemotional" needs and capacities.[26]

The problem is that patriarchy uses sexual taboos to maintain power. Closeness between mothers and daughters and women in general threatens that power.[27] It has therefore diminished the special bond between mothers and daughters by denigration and the arbitrary decree that the flexibility inherent in the homoerotic and homoemotional capacities of women is immature.[28] It has made it taboo to include in descriptions of normal aspects of development any erotic content the early mother-daughter relationship may have. As a consequence, during adolescence there are considerable social and personal pressures to give up physical closeness with mothers.[29]

Under patriarchy, the process of giving up the physical closeness with mothers takes a typical course. As the daughter experiences menarche and becomes aware of her emerging sexuality and society's confusions about sex and sin and homosexual taboos, she becomes embarrassed with any thought of her mother's sexuality. She tries to distance herself, but she needs transitional support. To this end, she may develop crushes on older women or other girls.[30]

These are safe transitional supports, while she renegotiates her powerful bond with her mother. As we saw earlier, her recollection of her mother's nurturance is also accompanied by anger at the frustrations meted out by her mother in childhood. As she becomes an autonomous person, she needs to put this anger in context and reconsider it. Much of the anger may also be directed at the martyred role of her mother and her subordination of herself as a female under patriarchy.[31] As we shall see in subsequent chapters, the daughter needs to rework these feelings. Understanding the traditional coercions upon her mother helps enormously.

Many daughters renegotiate these angers and feelings successfully. They resist the pressures to reject the significance of their mothers in their lives and remain close and friendly with them. Others learn to cope with the demand that they repress their yearnings for physical closeness with their mothers. In achieving this, the use of transitional support from persons of the same sex is a very common strategy. Some go to greater lengths than others. Colette and Virginia Woolf are among many famous women writers, discussed in Book II, who emphasise how important loving other women was in successfully working through their relationships with their mothers.

Ultimately, patriarchal society endeavours to shape female pride in sexuality so that it centres entirely on attracting men. But what about daughters whose sexuality does not have the opposite sex as its object? What about lesbian daughters? There have been many changes in social attitudes which allow the more open expression of homosexuality than was permitted decades ago. As a consequence, many mothers are learning to accept lesbian daughters. An example of this is given in the novel *Peeling* in the Bibliotherapy, Chapter 9. Mothers of lesbian daughters often have to surrender many dreams — not the least of which is having grand-children. There is grief and a sense of loss about things that can no longer be taken for granted. The daughter also has to come to terms with her identity. How does this affect mother-daughter relationships? I shall address this question in the next section of the chapter.

Relationships Between Lesbian Daughters and Their Mothers

On the whole, developmental psychology assumes a heterosexual model. This heterosexual chauvinism excludes children and adults who are anywhere else on the sexual continuum. Yet, it seems probable that none of us is born with a fixed sexual orientation. We learn it.[32] Even Freud, who was much influenced by Victorian patriarchy, was convinced of the basic bisexuality of human beings, while to Jung no man is exclusively male, no woman exclusively female. Both these men were interested in the manner in which society has required that we repress opposite sex traits and the extent to which this builds up tension in the unconscious.

Gender identity, that is, accepting oneself as male or female, is established in late pre-school. Sexual orientation or determination of sexual choice, on the other hand, seems in many cases to be closely related to acceptance or rejection of the role that one is expected to play in society as a man or a woman. This is thought to be fixed by the time a child starts school, if not sooner.[33] In middle childhood, children become clearer about their sex role identities and it is at this stage that some children begin to feel different from other members of their sex. They feel that they are not meeting the "ought" prescription of gender, even though they cannot yet give their sexual preference a label.

Most of western social conditions push toward heterosexuality. In the midst of these pressures, there is little to explain how a person becomes homosexual, lesbian or bisexual.[34] Many explanations, such as dominant mothers, weak fathers, family constellation, seduction, imitation of homo-sexuals in the child's environment, or the lack of support from an opposite sexed person, have proved to be myths.

The model of the typical happy family is not helpful as at best, it only approximates lived experience. Role theory is equally simplistic and deter-ministic, while the socialisation model helps little, because it embodies value judgements about being adequately or inadequately gender stereo-typed.[35] One can generalise about social forces, but the question is how did the individual child see those forces and internalise them? Nor is there much help from many lesbian and bisexually oriented explanations. These tend egocentrically, in adult hindsight, to focus on remembered childhood or adolescent crushes or sexual attraction to members of the same sex, but overlook that heterosexual children also have these experiences, as I have indicated.

More useful is the argument that children are not passive recipients of family and social pressures. They are human beings who make choices and act upon them. Admittedly, their choices are restricted by the fact that they are under adult constraint and do not yet have the abstract ability to accu-rately assess the motives of those who judge them. Nevertheless, parents give different messages to their children — some of them based on sex-stereotyped expectations.[36] A young child is quite capable of both recognising that these descriptions do not make her feel comfortable and deciding to be otherwise. Similarly, a child observing how her parents treat each other may decide to step outside the prescription that she is supposed to follow as a girl.

While some lesbians feel their sexual preferences are a matter of nature, for others it has been a matter of political and personal choice.[37] How early this happens and why is as yet open to conjecture. Many argue that their rela-tionship with their mothers, or view of their mothers role, was central. Some of this literature is hostile to the mother, while much recent work takes a more positive view. Certainly, by adulthood and contrary to a popular myth, lesbianism often has more to do with relationships than sexuality. As women have been trained to foster and sustain relationships more than men, such women tell us that they find a lesbian partnership more rewarding than partnerships with men, who are poorly trained in this area. Moreover, women tend to pay more attention to women's needs in sexual arousal. Several studies, including the Kinsey report, show that women bring each other to orgasm more effectively than a man usually can.[38]

Sexuality is but one aspect of identity and, in some, it can be more fluid than it is in others. Thus, an adolescent may define her gender as feminine and be sexually attracted to other females. At one time of life, some women may be contentedly heterosexual — at other times lesbian or bisexual. I have already indicated that it is argued that this fluidity has much to do with the infant daughter's relationship with her nurturing mother. As she becomes an adolescent and an adult, there are many other internal and external circumstances that influence the shape of her tentative or consistent sexual experience.

The observations of Margaret Mead at single sex institutions and studies of prison inmates, are examples of fluidity in female sexuality. Heterosexual females may develop lesbian relationships during detention and return to heterosexual relationships on release.[39]

In a college study, Carla Golden found much evidence of diversity in self-definitions and a degree of incongruence between the women students' sexual activities and their sexual identification.[40] Even so, they did not suffer the internal distress that traditional psychoanalytic theory predicts. She concludes that identity is constructed both societally and psychologically and that it is both a social and a personal process. Certainly, changing contemporary attitudes permit more open personal decisions. A 1984 poll of the Boston Bisexual Women's Network revealed that 90 percent of bisexual women are under 40. This suggests that the recent relaxed attitude to homosexuality has allowed greater expression of bisexual inclinations in the younger groups. However, we cannot conclude that this is a uniquely modern phenomenon. The same experiences applied when Colette and Virginia Woolf were alive.[41]

In our society, women are generally less threatened than men by the knowledge that they are capable of homosexual love, perhaps because of their early relationships with their mothers. They do not suffer as much fear of sexual inadequacy, nor identify homosexual orientation with an effeminancy that society regards as discordant with their outward sexual characteristics. Golden suggests that, because of these differences, male homosexuals do not experience their sexuality in the fluid manner that some lesbian and heterosexual women do.[42]

Consideration of these matters is important to mother-daughter relationships for many reasons — one being that many contemporary mothers are learning to accept daughters who do not conform to the heterosexual model. In doing so, some tell us that they acquire another, loving daughter in their child's partner.

In a study of gay children and their parents, Fairchild and Hayward observed that some mothers (and fathers) do not wish to acknowledge, or are angered by, the fact that their daughters are not heterosexuals.[43]

Fairchild and Hayward point out that their daughters are still the same persons that they, the parents, knew as children and that they need a lot of support, given society's prejudices.

Some parents experience profound guilt and conflict when one of their children tells them he or she is homosexual, lesbian or bisexual — "I must have done something". Instead of being pleased that their child wanted to confide in them, many parents respond with, "I don't want to talk about it", or "You'll grow out of it", or "This is a tragedy. How could you do it to me?" This head in the sand approach, drives a wedge between themselves and their homosexual child. It ignores how their child feels.[44] Their daughter may have needed to do a lot of painful soul-searching simply to acknowledge that she is a lesbian. She is now needing support to validate herself as a good person. But it must be a two way process, with the daughter also endeavouring to understand the parents' difficulties.

I find that when mothers begin to appreciate the difficulties their daughters face as lesbians, a huge step is taken toward healing rifts in the relationship. For example, the mother benefits from understanding that if a child does not conform to the heterosexual model and is a lesbian or bisexual, she has few positive role models in fiction or in the media. Instead, such children largely see negative images of homosexuals, who lisp, are bitchy, or act out their negative stereotypes in outrageous behaviour and gear. Television or fiction may have offered them little more than portrayals of man-hating, butch lesbians, who are mentally ill, perverted and violent. Since they have incorporated these images by the time they learn their sexual identity, many young lesbians are submerged in self-hate and rejection. Due to social taboos, in their first homosexual encounters, they may decide they are sick, dirty, insane or perverted. In this state of self-condemnation a lesbian may reject the woman she is attracted to, as an addiction.[45] Mothers and other nurturing women can play an important countering role and help build a sense of self-worth.

Fortunately, social acceptance of homosexuals has been growing over recent years. The facts of non-heterosexual identity have been opened up for discussion in the media. Important professional groups, such as the American Psychiatric and Psychological Associations, have declared that gays are not sick. By letting go of social taboos, lesbian women and homosexual men are freer to accept their sexuality as a healthy part of their identities.

In spite of the relaxation of social attitudes, however, lesbians and bisexuals experience greater oppression and conflict than their heterosexual sisters. They must contend, not only with the marginality of their female sex, but also with social hostility toward lesbians and toward their own internalised homophobia. Shuster stresses that they continually face misunderstanding and mistreatment because they break cultural rules about intimacy, sex and gender.[46] The Boston Lesbian Psychologies Collective, in a book entitled *Lesbian Psychology*, describes just how difficult their lives can be in an intolerant heterosexual society.[47]

Difficulties are compounded because families, mothers, fathers, society and schools largely find sex and sexuality uncomfortable subjects. There is little open discussion of sexuality and little fulsome pride in it.[48] Because of this discomfort, an adolescent is unlikely to come home and discuss her crushes on female teachers, prefects or other girls. Yet these are common experiences of both lesbian and heterosexual adolescent girls. Obviously, a little more discussion of sexuality and sexual experience — with mothers and in families — would be constructive for relationships.

As we have seen, early same-sex crushes are not sufficient to make a person decide that she is a lesbian. Even where it does seem congruent with later self-definitions, it cannot be said that the first encounters are experienced as homosexual desire. Some lesbians enter marriage without any idea that they are sexually attracted primarily to women.

Éspin observes that many cultures are more tolerant of their lesbian daughters than is western patriarchal society.[49] The intolerance of lesbianism in our society means that lesbians are often misunderstood. For example, it is commonly believed that lesbians and bisexual women see men as the enemy. Some do and some don't.[50] A bisexual feminist, for one, is often both opposed to sexism and also accepts heterosexual relationships as a viable option.

Nor is the age-old heterosexual relationship involving one dominant and one submissive partner necessarily mirrored in every lesbian partnership. It rarely corresponds to the reality of most lesbian relationships.[51] Even so, the stereotype which offers a picture of one dominant butch type and one passive partner is commonly accepted. Sheila Jeffreys indicates that lesbians, who mirror the dominance and submission of age-old patriarchal marriages and go so far as to see their feminine partners and heterosexual women as lesser beings, are a minority.[52] She says these hierarchical attitudes are not endorsed by feminist lesbians. Knowledge of the facts are essential if mothers are to understand their lesbian daughters

It is unfortunate that some of the lesbian and bisexual literature defensively infers, or argues, that either lesbianism or bisexuality are superior states. This will get us nowhere. What is needed is acceptance that sexuality is a continuum and an acknowledgement of its diversity. Understanding and acceptance outside patriarchal value judgements will improve relationships between lesbian daughters and their mothers.

Many lesbian and bisexual women who are trying to understand or are searching for their identities, have focused on the roles of their mothers. They have led the movement against the mid-century antipathy to mothers which was discussed in Chapter 1. They realise that in denying or denigrating their mothers' sexuality and gender they are denying their own.

While it has not been possible in this section to explain why some daughters are lesbian and others are not, I hope the description of what it is like to be a lesbian daughter increases understanding between mothers and daughters and helps the relationship between them.

A Fairy Tale For Daughters

I will conclude this chapter by recounting a fairy tale — a fairy tale that underlines the pervasive influence of patriarchal myths about female adolescent sexuality and mother-daughter conflict. In particular, I shall refer to Bruno Bettelheim's psychoanalytic interpretation of the fairy story of Snow White, in his book *The Uses of Enchantment* [53] As Bettelheim sees it, fairy stories prepare children for their lot in society. Bettelheim is not talking about patriarchy as such, but we can see what he means. Among other things, stories such as Snow White teach small girls (and boys) to expect enmity and conflict between mothers and daughters. I am not saying that our children should stop reading Snow White — on the contrary. One can both enjoy such stories and discuss whether everything in the story applies to everyone. In my experience, children ask pertinent questions about them anyway. These questions then become useful ways of helping our daughters understand subtle patriarchal propaganda, in much the same way that questions about media images make them aware of the ploys of advertising.

It is recognised that Bettelheim's psychoanalytic interpretation of the story of Snow White offers some fascinating insights into the adolescent's struggle for identity. It is when his interpretations miss the patriarchal overtones, that we realise how insidious patriarchal indoctrination is. I will recount the main points Bettelheim makes and distinguish some of his insights from the usual stereotypes. Recognition of much of the obvious stereotyping is left to the reader.

He believes the story of Snow White prepares young girls for their menstruation and sexuality. The story begins with Snow White's mother pricking her finger so that three drops of blood fall upon the snow. Bettelheim writes: "Fairy tales prepare the child to accept what is otherwise a most *upsetting* event: sexual bleeding, as in menstruation and later in intercourse when the hymen is broken".[54] The italics are mine to underline an example of how menstruation is conveyed to our children as a curse rather than cause for celebration.[55]

Bettelheim goes on to make the point, already made in this book, that children project their anxieties onto their mothers. He puts this theme in a psychoanalytic framework. The child is jealous of her mother's power, so she believes the mother is jealous of her growing, emerging sexual power. She thinks the mother will find her sexual maturing a threat, so she reverses the threat. If the child cannot permit herself to feel jealous of the parent, she projects her feeling onto the parent. Bettelheim writes, "Then, 'I am jealous of all the advantages and prerogatives of Mother' turns into the wishful thought 'Mother is jealous of me'".[56] This is why in adolescence the mother becomes the wicked stepmother. The only problem is that there is no discussion of how the use of this stereotype can become a self-fulfilling prophecy. Nor is there a lot of evidence that sexual maturing is the issue above all else that is fundamental to adolescent rebelliousness. Nevertheless, Bettelheim offers some useful insights in the following quotation. The use of "he" and "his" to cover both sexes comes from an earlier era.[57]

> The pubertal child is ambivalent in his wish to be better than the parent of the same sex because the child fears that if this were actually so, the parent, still much more powerful, would take terrible revenge. It is the child who fears destruction because of his imagined or real superiority, not the parent who wishes to destroy. The parent may suffer pangs of jealousy if he, in his turn, has not succeeded in identifying with his child in a very positive way, because only then can he take vicarious pleasure in his child's accomplishments. It is essential that the parent identify strongly with his child of the same sex for the child's identification with him to prove successful.[58]

According to Bettelheim, Snow White's stepmother cannot let her daughter identify with her and move onto beautiful adulthood. This is because the stepmother is "fixated to a primitive narcissism and arrested on the oral incorporative stage".[59] In other words, she is a person who cannot positively relate to anyone, nor can anybody identify with her. One is left wondering whether all mothers are supposed to be like this? The stepmother also tries to compete with Snow White's beauty. Like all mothers? Patriarchal theory says yes to both these questions.[60] Whether these generalisations apply to all real-life mothers and daughter is discussed in the next chapter.

The hunter stands in for the father, as in many fairy stories. He does not kill Snow White at the behest of the jealous queen, but he doesn't protect her. He leaves her in the forest. Bettelheim suggests that the frequent appearance of such figures in fairy tales "suggests that wife-dominated husbands are not exactly new to this world".[61] This stereotype has long been used to shift blame for almost anything from the failing father to the mother. Note the fear of women controlling men — an anathema under patriarchy.

When the hunter brings the queen the lungs and liver of an animal to prove he has executed her command, the bad woman eats them in the belief that she is eating Snow White's lungs and liver. Bettelheim writes, "In primitive thought and custom, one acquires the powers or characteristics of what one eats. The queen, jealous of Snow White's beauty, wanted to incorporate Snow White's attractiveness, as symbolised by her internal organs".[62]

The dwarfs are unable to protect Snow White and her mother continues to have power over her — as symbolised by Snow White permitting the queen (in her various disguises) into the dwarf's house. Bettelheim makes an obvious and worthwhile observation about the symbolism of this aspect of the story: "One cannot free oneself from the impact of one's parents and one's feeling about them by running away from home".[63] On the other hand, Snow White's "behaviour in restraining herself in eating and drinking, her resisting sleeping in a bed that is not just right for her shows that she also learned to control to some degree her id impulses".[64]

As Snow White becomes an adolescent, she begins to experience the sexual desires which, according to Bettelheim were repressed and dormant during childhood.[65] This idea that sexuality is repressed or 'latent' in childhood has always been part of traditional psychoanalytic theory and is based on the observation that boys and girls avoid one another in the primary school years. In defining almost anything in terms of sexual repression, it overlooks the influence of social attitudes- a point which has already been discussed in Chapter 2. Bettelheim adheres to the traditional explanation and describes how the stepmother, who represents the consciously denied elements of Snow White's internal conflict, reappears on the scene and shatters Snow White's inner peace.[66] The apple with which the queen tempts her, represents mature sexual desire. It stands for love and sex in many myths and fairy tales. Eating the red (erotic) part of the apple is the end of Snow White's innocence. The redness of the apple evokes sexual associations, as did the three drops of blood which led to Snow White's birth. It also symbolises menstruation, the event which marks the beginning of sexual maturity.[67]

Ultimately, it is the prince who rescues Snow White from her fears and envy of her mother — the incorporated bad object which is represented in the poisonous apple. He "causes her to spit out the poisonous apple and come to life, ready for marriage".[68] The patriarchal tenet that men rescue women from their mothers and themselves is obvious. The queen, who wanted to remain fairest forever, is punished by having to dance to her death, in red hot shoes. Down with mothers!

I recommend everyone read Bettelheim's *The Uses of Enchantment*. It does not set out to highlight the patriarchal stereotypes which fairy tales introduce to young children. Nor does it analyse how these stereotypes help to colour mother-daughter conflict during a daughter's menstruation and adolescent sexual growth. Nevertheless, it's a marvellous source for recognising them instantly. It is also a very enjoyable book to read — the psychoanalytic imagery is quite evocative.

Overview

In this chapter, I have dealt with the patriarchal tenet that the daughter's first menstruation and emerging adult sexuality marks the end of mother-daughter intimacy. This self-fulfilling prophecy springs from the patriarchal fear of women's sexuality and their powerful role in child-bearing.[69] These twin fears fuse into dread of the mother-daughter alliance. Thus, adolescence is wishfully interpreted as the end of mother-daughter closeness. Positive measures have been suggested for mothers and daughters to resist the indoctrination and share a sense of pride in their menstruation and sexuality.

So far in speaking about sexuality, I have largely concentrated on adolescent daughters and their relationships with their mothers. What about fathers? Do their attitudes figure in mother-daughter relationships? This important question is taken up in the next chapter.

೬౩

BIBLIOTHERAPY

There are many specialist issues in mother-daughter relationships which individuals may wish to pursue; adoptive mothers and daughters, step-mothers, mothers-in-law as substitute mothers, bulimic or anorexic daughters, severely disturbed daughters. *Mothers and Daughters: Loving and Letting Go* by Evelyn Bassoff, with a neo-psychoanalytic emphasis, discusses many of these. Lucy Rose Fischer's book, *Linked Lives*, also deals with some of these issues.

Book II introduces a number of sources for building pride in sexuality and menstruation. The Bibliotherapy, Chapter 9, includes a good example in Margaret Mead's and her daughter's lives. Tess Slessinger and Katherine Dalsimer have already been mentioned. Good books on generational pride among mothers and daughters are also morale builders. An example based on Australian women is *Generations: Grandmothers, Mothers and Daughters*, edited by Diane Bell and published by McPhee Gribble.

There are a number of books about lesbian daughters. *Peeling* is an Australian example and given in the Bibliotherapy, Chapter 9. An English example is *Oranges are not the only fruit* by Jeannette Winterson, which became a major BBC TV drama in 1989. 'Meet My Mother' by Michele Wandor in *Close Company*, edited by Christine Park and Caroline Heaton, is an amusing account of a Jewish mother's reaction, when her daughter tells her she is a lesbian. Humour is very much needed in mother-daughter relationships.

೬౩

CHAPTER 5

Fathers

Their Influence on Mother-Daughter Relations

The forgotten factor in mother-daughter relationships is the father. How he relates to the mother influences how his daughter values her mother and herself. The sexual style of a father shapes how a daughter relates to both men in general and her mother in particular. Whether he finds femininity threatening, or likes sensual women, defines how a daughter experiences her own sexuality. He can make or break the pride in feminine sexuality that contributes to a good relationship between mother and daughter.

The loss of a daughter's virginity may be especially threatening to both father and daughter. It can be seen as a rite of separation between them or as a celebration of maturity. How a father feels about mature and experienced sexual women is crucial to how a daughter sees herself, other women and her mother.

Some daughters have fathers, who behave like interrogators from the CIA. They question; they spy; they check; they imply that their daughters are headed for a life of depravity, thus arousing guilt, inhibition and fear of dominance. Some daughters become so addicted to out-manoeuvring the supervisory tactics of their fathers, that they are left with a yen for police-style drama in their sexual relationships for the rest of their lives. These daughters cannot value themselves as responsible, independent sexual beings and this self-devaluation disrupts their relationship with women in general and their mothers in particular.

While not all fathers act like puritanical extremists during their daughters' adolescence, it is true that large numbers behave like over-suspicious wardens — albeit inconsistently. One daughter described how her bra was torn in the washing machine and her father questioned her closely, suspicious that she and a male friend had been "up to no good". "I felt really dirty when he'd read nasty connotations into things that had quite ordinary explanations".

Among the many fathers I meet in my work with families one, who behaved like this regularly with his daughter, explained that he did it because he'd taken advantage of girls sexually "when he was a lad". Another, who was extremely strict about tight blouses or short skirts, said he wanted to reduce the temptations of his daughter's sexuality for his own sake. Daughters tend to recognise that their fathers are projecting their guilty impulses onto them. However, the recognition leaves them with a feeling that feminine sexuality is tainted. They don't feel trusted and some act this out in self-destructive, promiscuous behavior, as well as extending their resulting self-contempt to contempt for their mothers' sexuality. Mothers are described as more tolerant in these matters and certainly as more at ease with their daughters' boyfriends — a fact that daughters appreciate.

Fathers who are not at ease with their own sexuality, transmit this unease to their daughters. Their daughters become uncomfortable with their fathers as masculine sexual beings. Some of these daughters feel an aversion to their fathers' masculine physical features — perhaps thick black hair on arms and legs, bulging muscles or body odour. It is not unusual for women to complain about fathers (and men in general) who adopt the arrogant patriarchal sitting style — spreading their legs wide apart, so taking up far more than their share of space. Many daughters recall that as adolescents they'd disliked their fathers appearing in the nude. "Because he was so big I felt threatened. I think it had to do with his sexual jokes that made sex appear dirty or put women down".[2] It is also not unusual for daughters to report feeling ashamed of any indication that their fathers found them sexually attractive in adolescence or later. Anita recalls:

"I remember how my coarse, middle-aged father looked at me on a bus once. It was a mixture of sexual attraction and poking fun to put me down, as men often do with women they find attractive. He made me ashamed of my sexuality — part of my identity."[3]

Said another:

"My stupid father flirts with me. He tells everyone I'm jealous, if he talks to another woman. I'm angered by his belief that his own wishes are mine also. I feel imprisoned and denied separate rights and existence as a person. He has that special technique of making you feel that he cannot afford to let the true you out, because it will be too damaging to his views and beliefs about his importance."[4]

Both these fathers were threatened by their adolescent daughters' sexuality. As a result, their daughters felt discouraged and insecure about their development as feminine sexual adults. They were deprived of the right to open acknowledgement of, and pleasure in, an important phase of growth.[5] They were left without a sense of joint pride with their mothers in their sexuality. Instead, they often blamed their mothers for their feelings of shame and anger.

Some of the more discerning adolescent girls stated that their fear of their fathers' sexuality had something to do with the power of males over females — the patriarchal distortion of sexuality. Some had been sexually abused. Incest is not examined here and there follow only a few observations that have significance for all women.[6] They are included because the sexually-abused girls who took part in my research project wanted the observations made. They particularly stressed the need to understand why social indoctrination caused them to reject themselves. Sadly, despite the fact that they were used against their will, most had incorporated negative feelings about their sexuality. They said they felt dirty and questioned whether there was something fundamentally sluttish about them. In other words, their sexual self-respect had been severely damaged. Some of the daughters had hidden what was happening from their mothers, because they feared losing their mothers. They'd also been threatened by their fathers with dire punishment if they did tell.

The daughters, whose mothers had known of their abuse, were in a state of acute distress at their mothers' failure to support them. Some felt that the lack of support was because they were unworthy. Here one sees an unfortunate example of how much a child's concept of self is imparted by the behaviours of significant others toward her.[7] All the sexually-abused girls in the study suffered major self-esteem problems and had poor relationships with their mothers.

The worst cases were where the blame was shifted from the perpetrator to the abused daughter. Adrienne Rich points out a significant and tragic factor in situations where the sexually-abused girl gets no support from her mother, because the mother has been demoralised by the patriarchal stereotype that "sluts invite what they get".[8] Due to her indoctrination, the mother accepts without question that she would feel guilty and dirty had she been sexually abused. Her attempt to protect her daughter can go no further than telling her to hide what is happening, as in the following case described by one of the participants in my research project:

> Mrs M's husband sexually abused their eight year old daughter. Ashamed for him, protective of him, and ashamed on account of her daughter for the violation of her sexuality, she said to the eight year old, 'Don't ever tell anyone this has happened'. Thus, the shocked and distressed child, sexually subjugated by the father, did not obtain support and protection from her mother. Not understanding the pressures on her mother, bewildered by what she was told was her own degradation, she understandably grew up angry about being female. The anger grew into self-loathing and self-rejection and ultimately created an enormous gulf between this mother and daughter.

A famous case, which contributed greatly to changing attitudes about child and maternal compliance in incest cases in Australia was reported in the Sydney press in 1981.[9] It highlighted how much power, and threats of power, are the means by which a parent is able to divide and dominate members of his family and destroy the sexual pride of his daughters. This particular father had sexually abused his five young daughters over a period of 15 years, and set them against each other and their mother, by manipulative and brutal threats. He allowed his daughters a brief and occasional sense of power, which made them even more vulnerable in his hands and confused them greatly. Moreover, an abusive — or deserting father — may give a daughter a legacy of trouble with men all her life.

Feminist writers have tackled the issue of how sexual abuse disrupts mother-daughter relations more extensively than can be done here and their books are recommended for further reading.[10]

How Fathers' Attitudes to Women and Mothers Affect Mother-Daughter Relationships

Undoubtedly in reasonably nurturing families, a daughter's relationship with her father affects many aspects of her adult life: her choice of friends and lovers, how she feels about herself as a person and how she values women and her mother in particular. The father who cannot surrender his daughter to adulthood may leave her acting out the little girl role, thus resulting in difficulty in relationships with lovers, her husband and her mother in later life. More fortunate is a daughter with a warm and supportive father, who accepts his daughter as an individual, nurtures her self-esteem appropriately and doesn't cramp her style in order to cope with his own problems.

Virginia Woolf is an example of a daughter with a father who could manage little of this. Her father wrote a famous and magnificent treatise on English Literature, but at the expense of his wife and daughters. Their mental health was threatened by his violent temper and domineering and self-pitying behaviour.[11] Virginia Woolf's diaries and letters graphically tell of the effect on her of a father who believed the women in his family must be at his service. The way he treated her mother, and her sacrificial behaviour toward him, left Virginia angry with her mother, until she understood the destructiveness of the patriarchal family. Her story is told in Book II.

While the father plays an important part in his daughter's self-esteem through his attitudes and behaviour to her directly, research also indicates that fathers may play an influential role in their daughters' self-esteem through their attitudes to their wives as mothers, as women and as sexual beings.[12]

While one must be very careful in any research about making associations that might have other causes, or multiple causes, it is nevertheless significant that, in the minds of many women, their fathers were influential in the kind of relationship that they had with their mothers. We cannot leave fathers out of research into mother-daughter relationships and indeed family relationships, as is often done.

The attitude of significant others to a daughter's most important childhood role model, who is usually her mother, is important in her identity development. If her most consequential role model is denigrated by important others, then it is likely that negative or ambivalent attitudes will develop toward those aspects of herself which are identified with the role model.

Fathers are usually one of the most significant figures in a child's life. They influence the value that children put upon their mothers. Said Emma, who had a fond relationship with her mother:

"Dad had enormous respect for Mum's opinion and ideas. If they went to a play or film together, he valued her analysis of what they'd seen. He respected her assessment of people. This made us respect and value her too. I can see that I value my Mum a lot more than my friends value their mothers. I've watched how their fathers put their mothers down or speak to them with impatience. I thank Dad because he taught me to value Mum."

In my research, approximately half the women interviewed claimed to have been influenced by positive messages about their mothers from their fathers. As children, they were aware that their fathers had admired their mothers' physical appearance, for instance. In turn these daughters felt good about themselves physically. Said Beatrice:

"You could often see Dad looking at Mum with such admiration. I remember how he'd watch her dancing when we went to family bush dances. I'd hear him saying things to her like, 'I felt so proud watching you dance with Bill' or 'You looked so attractive and sexy on the tennis court'. It made me feel good about Mum and good about being the same sex as her."

However, a small percentage remembered their fathers' attitudes to their mothers as almost totally negative. That negativism took the form of rarely looking at her, or not associating with her on social outings. They specified, in some cases, that he did not admire her sexuality; in others that he complained of her overweight condition or sloppiness. The daughters of these men felt strongly that they'd not had an important other who had positively assessed the same sexed parent with whom they'd identified as children and adolescents. Most had incorporated ambivalent notions about their own sexuality and were excessively concerned with being over-weight. Most felt that these things would not have been important if fathers as well as social expectations had not underlined them.

The fathers of these women had also tended to reinforce traditional feminine stereotypes. For example, they admired things in their wives that were almost exclusively related to the impossibly idealised picture of mother-hood, such as good management of the home, children and finance, care of others, active interest in and support of the father, sense of humour, good nature, care, kindness, gentleness, endurance, perseverance and resilience.

These women remembered their fathers criticising their mothers for characteristics that did not fit patriarchal female stereotypes. The fathers were very ambivalent about wives who were at all independent. At the same time, they were irritated by dependent wives. Many of the women spoke of the confusion this ambivalence created in them. They were never certain how assertive they should be. Said Marianne:

"I was really confused by my father as to how I should behave as a girl. I was either accused of being too confronting and unladylike or pathetically timid. I'm still confused and anxious about being assertive. Dad treated Mum the same way. There was no way she could win. The worst of it is that I find myself not only hating her when she's timid and indecisive but also when she speaks up and defends herself."

One third of the daughters who took part in the research saw their fathers as not liking their mothers' shyness, unassertiveness and anxiety. Almost one fifth of the women described fathers who did not admire mothers who were outspoken and aggressive. Fathers denigrated anger, nagging, negativism and lack of emotional response in their wives — even when it was justified or a last resort to curb thoughtlessness or authoritarianism. Usually, a father's reaction to any of these behaviours was to infer, either directly or subtly, that they were irrational female pettinesses. As a result, many women had accepted that these denigrated characteristics were an inherent part of the female personality and therefore their own. They described how these attitudes disrupted their relationship with their mothers.

Daughters Who Identify With Fathers

While children copy traits of both parents, they are more likely to identify with the same sexed parent and incorporate their particular characteristics into their self-concepts. The underlying negative messages about mothers lead some daughters to take on a devalued sense of their femaleness. Other daughters cope in a different way. They redirect their processes of identification.

During middle childhood, a daughter may begin to over-identify with her father, seeing him as the more valued member of society. In the family, she sees him behaving as though he has every right to deny his wife's attributes and to devalue her to his children, albeit in indirect ways. As a child, she does not understand that as a representative of patriarchy, he must maintain his masculinity and domination. He needs to deny his feminine characteristics, in order to be masculine.[13] This is done by denying the value of the mother as an independent identity. He strips her of any power she may gain in the family by winning her children's respect.

Where fathers feel driven to represent the patriarchal image, they can be jealous of their role as the larger provider of the family needs, possessions and status. They prefer to be the ones who earn more money. The power derived from these factors means that their employment is generally the determining factor in where the family lives, meal-times and holidays. Their work schedule may also determine who uses the family car and whether and when the mother works. The father represents autonomy and in these situations, some daughters go so far as to take on the father's devaluation of, and contemptuous attitude toward, their mothers and women in general. Sometimes, such daughters have difficulty in growing up and retain a "little girl" relationship with their fathers.

In summary, the dilemma for the daughter is whether to be loved by her mother and continue to practise the caring values her mother embodies or to forsake all that her mother imparted in favour of the values of the male-dominated work-place. In short, should she reject her mother and learn to endorse the inhumanity and alienation of the patriarchal world order? Jane Flax stresses that when a woman devalues and mistrusts her mother and other women, "she loses the possibility that they will nurture her".[14] She and Adrienne Rich argue that mistrust is encouraged by patriarchal ideology, which devalues women. How that can work in the family has been described here. Flax and Rich also believe that patriarchy has to devalue women because it is threatened and discomforted by strong female bonds.[15] This belief is supported by reports from daughters. They describe fathers who were often jealous of their closer bonds with their mothers and who had tried to implement divisive tactics.[16]

Daughters give a contrasting picture of fathers and their relationship with them. At one extreme, some fathers are described as authoritarian and dominating or just plain disinterested. These fathers are less likely to build up self- confidence in their daughters. They are far less supportive than mothers. At the other extreme are fathers who are described as more supportive than mothers. They are said to be trusting, interested, tolerant and sympathetic. They pay compliments to their daughters. They are likely to demonstrate that they enjoy being in the company of their daughters. However, the percentage of such fathers is small.

Some daughters revise their beliefs about "admired" fathers once young adulthood is passed. They decide that their fathers' "good" relationship with them had contained some deliberately divisive manoeuvres which affected the mother-daughter relationship. Maturity, experience, having to cope with a husband and children and greater understanding of the position of women are all factors that contribute to these changes. For example, Beth described how she gave her mother a bad time during adolescence but later changed her behaviour toward her:

> "During adolescence I had this crazy attitude that Mum was taking up my space and was the root of all my difficulties in becoming an independent person. I thought Dad was marvellous, but looking back I can see he encouraged and got a lot out of my conflict with Mum. I married a man who is just like Dad. Now that I have to cope with someone who is sometimes selfish and inconsiderate, I can see what Dad really did to Mum. I yell at my husband like Mum yelled at Dad and now understand why she did it. I've also got children now and that made me understand Mum's situation more. My hus-

band loves the children but he's never really prepared to do anything for them that puts him out at all and I now recognise that Dad
did the same with us and left the worst bits to Mum. That was really
why he never lost his temper with us. I thought it was because he
was nicer than Mum, but it was because he had it easier."

If fathers respect their wives and honour them to their daughters, the
mother-daughter relationship is usually good.[17]

Attitudes to Fathers Who Make Themselves Peripheral

Overall, if all other factors are straightforward, a good relationship
between the parents and toward the children augurs well for mother-
daughter relationships. Unfortunately, most fathers appear to be but
peripherally involved with their daughters. Most fail to live up to their
daughters' expectations of what fathers should be like. They may fail in
their daughters' estimations because they are remembered as having said
consistently damaging things to their daughters when they were children
and adolescents — "You are dumb". "You can't do anything right". "You
get on my nerves". Such messages affect daughters' self-esteem negatively.
Fathers were also said to have failed if they were punitive, authoritarian
and too strict.

In general, many more fathers were seen to have failed as parents than
mothers. Mothers were preferred far more often than fathers. Despite
this, there was less anger among daughters about the deficiencies of
fathers, than for the shortcomings of mothers. Fathers may be described
as having massive shortcomings as parents, but the deficiencies of mothers concern daughters more. That concern is full of highly-charged
emotion.

By default, fathers leave responsibilities to mothers which contribute to
ambivalent mother-daughter relationships. Fathers' lack of involvement in
child-raising largely explains why their daughters are not so ambivalent
about them. The problems that were apparent in early childhood remain.
The child and adolescent experiences her mother as both nurturer and
inhibitor. A mother frustrates because it is she who has the responsibility
of training the child to become a socially acceptable human being. This
control is combined with emotional closeness.

When the time comes for emotional separation in adolescence, these
two factors are fused to such an extent that the mother can be seen as overwhelming and denying. As I have indicated in Chapter 3, on the whole, this
projection is an expression of the adolescent's struggle with her own emotional dependency. However, this projection thrusts a burden of
highly-charged emotion upon the mother, which in turn puts major strain
upon the mother-daughter relationship.[18] If fathers took a greater share in
child-raising and nurturing, the ambivalence would be shared between the

parents. There would be less mother-blaming because the origins of the ambivalence would be better understood.

An ordinary and common illustration of the point was given by Petra, aged 30, whose father was an alcoholic.[19] She said her father took little interest in her as a child, yet she was able to describe him affectionately as a "no hoper". In contrast, her mother, who seemed to have filled in as both parents and helped her fulfill her ambitions through school and university, was described with hostility. After a series of telephone calls and visits that stretched over two years, Petra admitted that, as a child, she'd known her mother had tried to make up for the lack of love from her father, but she'd felt angry, because "mothers should be able to make fathers love their children".

Although she could now see how self-centered her father was, the mistaken belief in the omnipotence of mothers remained. With some insight, she described how she expected her mother to be in two or three places at once and to support her, yet fail her.

> "My whole attitude to mothers is one big soap opera. I've been brainwashed by every play, every book, every film I've read or seen that contained a mother. I've got a two year old girl. What shall I do about her and me?"

Literature and film give many examples of how our society tends to forgive the man who is not a good father. Karl Marx, A.A. Milne and Tolstoy are but a few forgiven, honoured, neglecting fathers. In contrast, attitudes to neglecting or inadequate mothers are much more highly-charged with negative emotion, ambivalence and hostility. Fathers who murder their children in custody battles, for example, do not warrant extensive condemnation in the press, beyond the initial sensationalism. This contrasts with the protracted hate campaign that surrounded Lindy Chamberlain after the disappearance of her baby daughter Azaria, in the now infamous case that was made into a movie entitled *Evil Angels*.

So far, I have looked at the important role fathers play in mother-daughter relationships by their attitudes to both the mother and the daughter. Fathers stand in as patriarchal representatives in other ways. I've already indicated that they can give currency to stereotypes about the nature and behaviour of females, which adolescent girls and young women find particularly threatening, during the time when they are incorporating awareness of themselves as women into their identities. These daughters deflect the anxiety generated by these stereotypes onto their mothers.

When a young daughter is trying to discover who she is, negative stereotypes about women and mothers can have profound effects on how she values herself and her mother. They often begin to have effect in the preadolescent stage (11-12 years) in western society, as evidenced in a daughter's first open recognition of her ambivalent attitude to her mother, both as a mother and a woman. This recognition is not necessarily exposed to the mother at this stage. Secret letters and notes may be written about the problem. *The Diary of Anne Frank* is a marvellous testimony of some of the attitudes of an adolescent daughter toward her mother in a traditional family.

Some of these ambivalent attitudes stem from the adolescent's concern about sexual development and sexual attractiveness. Often, this is because this development is accompanied by growing awareness of negative stereotypes about loss of "sexiness" in females.

In the rest of this chapter, I shall pay some attention to two stereotypes which most adolescent daughters suggest their fathers endorse and which figure strongly in their attitudes to their mothers. They are, that ageing makes women valueless and women are inevitably neurotic.

Hidden Agendas in Mother-Daughter Relationships

Ageing Women are Valueless

Many adolescent girls believe that youth is their only advantage and are vulnerable to the patriarchal myth that ageing is the worst thing that can happen to women. Fear of this seems to be a hidden agenda in their ambivalent feelings toward their mothers.

Said one adolescent, in a passing state of vindictiveness toward her 40-year-old mother, "She's an old bag. How can you respect an old bag?" She went on to reveal where the anxiety behind her vindictiveness really lay: "She's got grey hair and wrinkles. I'm going to kill myself when I get grey hair and wrinkles".

The media, the advertising industry and fathers, who bolster their egos and position in the family by means of negative patriarchal stereotypes, play important roles in perpetuating their daughters' anxieties about the nature and lot of becoming women. Phoebe said:

> "My father reinforced my mother's preoccupation with the loss of her youth by pulling out photos of her when she was young and saying, 'Your mother trapped me when she was young and beautiful, like that' or 'It's hard on men that women age faster than their husbands' or 'I think I'll look for a new edition'. He'd pretend he was joking, but you knew he really meant these things. Once, I heard him telling my uncle that when he went to bed with her, he could only get an erection if he closed his eyes and thought of her as she was when she was young. He no doubt said things like that to her. It all gave me a rather disrespectful view of my mother as a sexual being and in the end of myself."

Ingrid, who is a well-educated professional woman, recounted a story that showed how much fear of ageing can affect the mother-daughter relationship:

> "My mother was obsessed with staying young and beautiful and

lived in dread that Dad would leave her for a younger woman. On one occasion, when I'd 'upset her' and was numb with anxiety as to how or why, she began to cry and said, 'I haven't got much of my youth left'. I was about 9. She would have been 29. I felt responsible for ageing her and therein began my own anxiety about ageing. It also increased my contempt for her, for I had something she did not. Youth!"

Another daughter, who came from what she described as a traditionally patriarchal Middle Eastern family, said, "My father won't let my mother work. She sits at home all day and cries for her lost youth. She gives me the pip".

How do we combat these absurd anxieties that set mothers and daughters adrift? Family discussion of the issues helps. Of value are discussions of how age is over rated in female identity and how the emphasis put upon it lies in the past. In their rebellious phase, adolescents enjoy criticising outdated attitudes. So they are ready to see the absurdity of prejudices that have survived from ancient patriarchal societies, such as the belief that only young, nubile women were valuable because they produced male children. Adolescents recognise the role wars and aggrandisement played in these beliefs. They can comprehend why the patriarchs thought their power to be threatened by experienced women and why they devalued women in general. These issues are discussed in more detail in Book II.

Drawing attention to some of the absurdities and illogicalities of patriarchy not only appeals to adolescents, it challenges one-sided social expectations they may have incorporated — for example, society's willingness to accept an older-man-younger-woman liaison, while the opposite is often ridiculed. One mother described how her adolescent son took particular delight in theories that attributed this dichotomised thinking to anxiety in older men about losing sexual potency and social and economic power to younger men, with whom they are in competition. "I daresay he used it to rationalise his conflict with his father, but at least it aroused some discussion that also helped his sisters."

Zoe, an ardent feminist, described how discussion of these matters among her friends, with their children present from an early age, had good long term effects:

"I never instructed my daughter, Leonie, about any of these things. All the time I thought that they were beyond her, she was picking up bits here and there that interested her. Now she's 16, she astonishes me. She and her friends did a project on patriarchy for school and got A+ for it. They are now into collecting stories of older-women-younger-men liaisons and marriages — Napoleon and Josephine — and the like. She reckons they are going to write a book about it as a morale booster for some of the girls at her school whom she describes as pathetic. By this she means that they are already worrying about getting old."

Leonie has a point. The recounting of such liaisons can be morale boosters for mothers and daughters. It can also put the record straight about hidden realities. Although they are most often not openly acknowledged in patriarchy, older-women-younger-men liaisons are common and several are well-known — for example Sybil Burton and Princess Margaret received much publicity when they had affairs with younger men. The French writer, Colette, wrote of women's lives and had little difficulty in portraying and understanding older-women-younger-men liaisons. She herself had a love affair with her stepson, who was very much younger than she was.[20]

The effect of Margaret Mead on younger men is documented by Jane Howard in her biography of Mead.

> "You should have seen the way she operated at seminars", said a man who went to many meetings with Mead in the late 1960s. "Men who generally would chase after anybody's secretary, or any attractive woman who might wander in, would take one first look at Margaret and think, 'Oh my God, a lady intellectual', but then, as she talked, they'd all end up at her knees. The sex appeal of that mind of hers was absolutely captivating". A handsome and accomplished man 30 years Mead's junior, who met her at a dinner party in 1973, remembered her vividly several years later. "If she had pointed to me and said , 'You! You're the one I choose! Come off with me!' " he said, "I would have gone with her. Anywhere."[21]

Yet, whatever evidence is produced about the attractiveness of mature women and the illogicality of prejudice about them, the belief that ageing makes women unattractive seems to dog the mother-daughter relationship from an early age.

Many young mothers, perhaps with infant or pre-school daughters, will often speak of their fear about ageing and loss of sexual attractiveness. They believe that when that happens they will be in conflict with their daughters, perhaps in as little as a dozen years. These young women generally tell stories about men mocking older women or treating them as nobodies. Often, it is a story about their mothers or grandmothers. Sadly, they may go on to say that they themselves find these women to be without sexual attraction and that they dread becoming like them.[22] Generally, these daughters acknowledge that fear of becoming like their mothers is causing them to reject them. Thus, the acceptance of the patriarchal stereotype has created unnecessary anxiety, which in turn becomes a self-fulfilling prophecy.

Barbara, a successful, imaginative and attractive doctor in her sixties offers the antidote:

> "Women should be proud of their years. Margaret Mead said that post menopausal women, freed of menstruation and fear of pregnancy, can turn their creative talents to so much and she did just that."

Indeed Mead was a champion of what she described as post-menopausal zest.[23] Barbara continues:

"Yet so many are imprisoned by the stereotype of the aged, sterile crow. Mothers have got to combat this stereotype, discuss it as nonsense with their daughters and inspire them to look forward to and enjoy middle and old age. They need to know that women wear better than men. Did you know that a healthy woman at 60 is only slightly diminished in the physical agility that she had at 20? With men it is not so. The stereotype flies in the face of fact."[24]

Ultimately, Barbara's attempts at encouraging mothers and daughters to be self-confident and respectful of ageing runs into the counter propaganda that middle-aged mothers must, by nature, be excessively concerned with sexual competition with their daughters. Propaganda needs sorting from fact. In general, it is where the dynamics of the patriarchal family have undermined the mother-daughter relationship that mothers may feel the need to compete with their daughters. Demoralised mothers, who have been physically and sexually abused as children, mothers who are jeered at for their ageing and accept patriarchal stereotypes which debase them, are mothers who may have so little sense of worth that even their own daughters are a threat.

Evelyn Bassoff, an American psychologist, argues that mothers who fear their daughters, often have special problems — problems hidden by patriarchy. Some of these mothers are blamed for their husbands' impotence. They accept the blame because they see themselves as nothing more than sexual objects and are accustomed to sexual exploitation by men. Usually, in these cases, the husband's doubts about his own sexual desirability are projected onto his wife. He preserves his self-esteem by seeing the wife as the problem.[25] The daughter is likely to absorb the disrespect for her mother.

The Snow White and the jealous mother syndrome still influences many. Instead of turning mothers into wicked stepmothers, let us not forget the influence of the patriarchal family.

Certainly, some daughters report that their middle-aged mothers have tried to imitate younger fashions and make-up, sometimes successfully.[26] But do not let the negative stereotype about competition between women always spring to mind. By the time daughters reach adolescence, mothers are less tied to dependent children. They may be reaching 40 and the forties can be years in which many women blossom physically. Naturally, they enjoy looking their best. Most daughters are immensely proud of such mothers.

Very few women believe that their mothers tried to compete with them. In my research, most were proud of attractive mothers. However, many daughters report feeling jealous of their mothers and the stereotype that mothers compete with their daughters was generally in reverse.

One daughter said:

"My mother was attractive and intelligent. She was very feminine and it soon became apparent to me that men of all ages found her attractive. She never tried to attract men. I used to wonder if she preferred women. My boyfriends, who were half her age, always liked her and some fell in love with her. I remember feeling jealous."

Later, this daughter could recognise what a pity it was that she could not enjoy and take pride in her mother's sexual attractiveness. Instead, she had been indoctrinated into the belief that women vie with each other for men.

Women are Neurotic

In relating exchanges between their parents, some daughters describe hearing their fathers repeatedly dismissing their mothers as neurotic and this description being accepted without protest by their mothers. Usually, these accusations came after a mother's response of anger, tears or protest to some unreasonable action by the father. Many daughters said the endless repetition of these kinds of judgements by their fathers prevented them from taking pride in women's talent for emotional responsiveness. These daughters were indoctrinated by the patriarchal stereotypes that to engage in emotion is neurotic and that the capacity for emotion is the greatest female weakness.[27]

This belief still has a surprisingly strong currency. Many young and older women accept the stereotype of the neurotic mother and fear that they will follow suit. One mother, Laura, described with sadness a letter she had received from her teenage daughter. It began: "I see us all, you me and Isabelle (her sister) as neurotic. I'm neurotic like you". The letter then went on in great anger that the daughter should have to inherit her mother's neuroticism. The daughter saw the mother as both responsible for, and a passive recipient of, the nature of woman.

Interestingly, the father in this case was very concerned with his maleness. He had been humiliated at a private boys school and unable to defend himself. He had a very poor relationship with his mother. He was aggressive in a passive way. For example, he had many 'accidents' which destroyed people's favourite and private possessions. He was frequently obtuse and ignored signals that he was hurting people's feelings. He took little responsibility for the family.

The father also drank excessively and was rather touchy. Paradoxically and like many men in the same situation, he believed his marriage was a happy one. A closer look at the family interactions revealed that the father's basically poor self-esteem, as a male, was strengthened through his belief that his wife was neurotic. She acted out this stereotype, rather than confronting him with the frustrations of her situation.

The father had a not unusual underlying hostility to women. He had occasional affairs — always with "neurotic" women, who became even more "neurotic" during the affair and were aggressive to his wife Laura.

Ultimately, his wife divorced him and went on to a successful career. Without his wife as a smoke-screen for his problems, he faced up to his massive projections, as did his daughters.

The essence of this case is perhaps well summarised in Virginia Woolf's description of how patriarchy functions:

> Women have served all these centuries as looking-glasses, possessing the magic and the delicious power of reflecting the figure of man at twice its natural size. Without that power the earth would still be a swamp and jungle. ...That is why Napoleon and Mussolini both insist so emphatically upon the inferiority of women, for if they were not inferior, they would cease to enlarge.[28]

Laura's story reinforces Virginia Woolf's point and indicates how much attitudes and behaviours are handed on in families — generation after generation of mothers and daughters. Her story also demonstrates how the inheritance does not have to be accepted. Mothers and daughters can help each other to destroy the stereotypes. This encourages respect for one another.

Laura's relationship with her husband had possibly repeated a relationship her own mother, Charlotte, had had with Laura's father. Charlotte, in turn, had had an intelligent mother, Henrietta, frustrated by the domesticity and the child bearing that was a woman's almost exclusive lot in the early 1900s.

Outbursts of anger, crying and blaming, due to little opportunity or ability to assert themselves and fulfil their potential, had been repeated in generations of attractive and intelligent women. These are normal reactions to frustration which, in women, are described as neuroticism. The pattern was broken when Laura achieved a satisfactory and successful career. It is important to note that the change in social attitudes to women helped this process. Said one of Laura's daughters:

> "Thank God mum got herself together. The family female tradition really suffocated me as a child. I used to lie awake at night thinking about all those frustrated females and get angry and feel like a potential victim. Now Mum has done something, I feel as though I can get up and be a person. I admire her a lot for what she has done."

There is a process whereby children take on parental characteristics in their play and daily behaviour. Gradually, they are absorbed into the child's own personality. This is the process of identification and there is a strong tendency to identify with or take on the personality characteristics of the same sexed parent. Thus children need a competent, self-confident role model which, as we have seen, is not always the case, given the retention of the patriarchal family style. Parents need good self-esteem in order to have children with good self-esteem.[29]

Phillipa describes how she felt about her mother in adolescence:

"My mother was my father's doormat. She wasn't a person. She never stood up to him. I remember getting really depressed when I was about eight and thinking this was going to be my lot. It was worse when I was an adolescent. I began to feel that I was like my mother — a dull doormat. I was really afraid about my future and being like her. I became angrier and angrier with her and began to criticise her and loathe her and myself."

Adrienne Rich has claimed that the mother's bondage (doormat behaviour to both father and children) is not untypically the seat of the mother-daughter conflict. Often, it begins in adolescence, as in Phillipa's case. The criticisms or rejections of their mothers, by daughters like Phillipa, seemed to be an attempt to reject and overcome the victim — the martyr in themselves. It is also an expression of their fear that they will become like their mothers.

Moreover, emotional and behavioural responses to the frustrations created by the bondage, that some mothers experience, have led to the belief that mothers and daughters are inevitably unstable.

Overview

Fathers play a vital role in mother-daughter relationships. Where they take on the role of patriarchal representatives, they can inflict divisive attitudes and disturbing stereotypes on their daughters, in a way that affects their self-esteem and identity development. Children typically identify with the same sexed parent. Young daughters identify with their mothers. If the father transmits negative messages about the mother, as a woman and a sexual being, to the daughter, she may not learn to esteem her femininity and that of women in general. In this way, fathers can create mother-daughter conflict. Where fathers are caring and share in the responsibility of child-raising, they do a great deal for their own relationship with their daughters as well as mother-daughter relationships.

Most daughters report more involvement and a greater sense of continuity with their mothers than their fathers. They also tend to engage in more intense separation struggles with their mothers during adolescence and young adulthood — sometimes all their lives. These autonomy seeking behaviours are often more emotionally charged than separation rituals involving fathers. The difference in degree of emotionality has a lot to do with the fact that fathers are usually less involved in the upbringing of their daughters than are mothers. Fathers are not as close emotionally and as a consequence, during the separation rituals of adolescence, their relationships with their daughters can be calmer.

Daughters forgive their fathers their failures as parents much more than they do mothers. Because they are not as involved as mothers, fathers avoid the ambivalence directed at mothers. On the other hand and more importantly, fathers miss out on genuinely close communication and relationships with their daughters. Many daughters who do speak of their father's involvement, also imply that his role was secondary to their mother's.

Daughters grow up with a greater feeling of familiarity and intimacy with their mothers.[30] At the same time, their mothers also had most to do with their day to day discipline. Mothers, much more than fathers, are argued with, withdrawn from, and rebuffed — although daughters continue to rely on their mothers for nurturance.[31] Research suggests that, as a result, mothers with teenagers experience anxiety and lowered self-esteem.

There is of course enormous variety in mother-daughter relationships. Some mothers and daughters are not close — either one or both may be withdrawn.[32] Other mothers and daughters are highly involved, particularly where the mother is single, divorced or widowed. In some families, there is a tight mother-daughter alliance against the father. This often happens where the father is a problem — perhaps abusive, a philanderer or an alcoholic.[33] Such a problem case can be seen in the novel, *Love Child*, mentioned in the Bibliotherapy, Chapter 9. In this novel, the daughter protects the mother from an alcoholic father.

While many daughters are unhappy in the role, daughters who willingly become confidants understand the marital difficulties of their mothers and are more likely to protect their mothers. Where the mother is a problem, daughters turn to fathers for support or as allies. However, they rarely see themselves as protecting fathers in the same way they do mothers.[34]

The mother-daughter relationship has a particular quality. So far, we have looked at aspects of that special quality in childhood and adolescence. The next chapter concentrates on the relationship between mothers and daughters in adulthood. It looks at guilt, the super mum and why so many daughters continue to resent their mothers. It also faces up to the fact that many mothers do not enjoy being mothers and why this is so.

 св

BIBLIOTHERAPY

More reading in this area can be found in *Linked Lives*, by Lucy Rose Fischer. From the Bibliotherapy, Chapter 9, *The Colour Purple, Love Child* and *Her Mothers' Daughter* describe fathers who have an impact on mother-daughter relationships, including alcoholic and sexually-abusing fathers.

For insights into some of the damaging things fathers and mothers in conflict can do to a daughter's identity development read Christina Stead, *The Man Who Loved Children*. More disturbing are Virginia Woolf's diaries and letters and Louise DeSalvo's book: *Virginia Woolf: The Impact of Childhood Sexual Abuse on her Life and Work*. This book is about daughters in patriarchal families. Virginia Woolf's childhood was not spent in a cosy Victorian family as many biographers would have us believe. In fact, it seems the Victorian family was a very dangerous and violent place for daughters.

Tiger Country by Penelope Rowe, is about a tyrannical father and a submissive mother and how their situation destroys the mother-daughter relationship and leads to the daughter's breakdown. It also portrays the lack of pride in the female body and menstruation and how it is dealt with in a very patriarchal family.

Mood Indigo by Mandy Sayer describes a child's relationship with a much-loved unreliable father and a mother who finds it hard to cope. It is the failing father who has the most destructive impact on the child.

The influence of a positive father, who supported the mother is seen in Kim Chernin's book, *In My Mother's House*.

✧

CHAPTER 6

Adult Daughters and Their Mothers

Guilt and Super Mum

Mothers, instilled with nurturing and over-responsible attitudes, tend to feel guilty about the rebellious, often rude, cruel and barbarous behaviour of their sons and daughters in adolescence and young adulthood. "What did I do wrong? Where have I failed?" Their self-esteem is shattered by the criticisms of growing persons who were once compliant children. They are distressed to hear that their daughters would prefer to confide in friends. They try to be perfect, ever nurturing mothers, centred wholly on their offsprings' demands and needs. Their daughters are often most demanding of this perfection, because they fear their own inadequacies as young women. For some the demand continues until the grave.

For example, in some of my earlier research,[1] when asked whether they could define "good" mothering, scores of women, ranging in age from 18 to 70, said they could. They said that a "good" mother was loving, affectionate, accepting, non-judgmental, non-critical, understanding and easy to communicate with. A "good" mother was also seen to be a person with whom one can enjoy sharing thoughts, feelings and experiences and who builds a child's self-confidence by means of praise. She trusts her daughter and treats her as an individual. A "good" mother, they said, also needs to be encouraging, helping, supportive and give opportunities for the child to develop. She gives devotion, loyalty and commitment to the family.

Here we have the super mum, reified by the mid-twentieth century in the patriarchal theories of the child experts, the politicians, the press and now living on in television soap operas. By their own expectations, these women revealed how much the concept of the super mum creates anxieties and tragedies for every day mothers. They clearly demonstrated how it especially puts strains upon mother-daughter relationships, because the attainment of perfect motherhood, as conceived in patriarchal society, is an impossible task. Yet, generations of mothers have handed on the pursuit to their daughters without challenging its falsity.

These daughters, with impossible soap opera expectations of their own mothers, inevitably felt inadequate in their role as mothers and many held their mothers responsible for providing poor role models. Many of the poor models they described were the strict and harsh ones, prescribed by tradition and the child experts of earlier decades. Others were quite the reverse and similar to the child-rearing manuals of the 1960s. They are typified in the following account by Jane, a mother aged 30, with a two and half year old daughter, Deanne, and a three month old baby son:

> "I'm having a lot of trouble managing Deanne. She throws terrible tantrums. They scare me. I do everything I can to avoid conflicts with her. Problem is I got a very permissive message about children from my mother — you know, that you should not overcontrol them. My mother confused me. I have no firm example to follow."[2]

It would appear from this example, and many like it, that whatever model they pursue, mothers cannot win.

At the rational level, most daughters saw that their mothers had tried to be "good" mothers. They indicated that they understood the origins of their mothers' shortcomings and described their mothers' difficulties, such as lack of support, loneliness or social isolation. They recognised that their mothers often had too many pressing problems, such as economic worries, difficult marriages or demanding and a dogmatic husbands. Even so, the same daughters said they were overwhelmed by inexplicably hostile and intensely ambivalent attitudes toward their mothers — attitudes that distorted rational understanding and aroused guilt. Only a few recognised that their highly charged emotions arose from their definitions of the "good "mother and the "good" daughter — definitions that embody such unattainable perfectionism that feelings of frustration are inevitable.

Some even felt guilty about the things they had written about their mothers in the research questionnaires, which were confidential and recorded without names. The number is probably larger in the general population, because some felt so guilty about what they had written, that they said they could not return the questionnaires. The reasons given for feeling guilty included — their mothers had sacrificed a lot or they had a lot to cope with; it was not loyal to criticise one's mother who would be hurt and feel unloved; one should be good friends with one's mother.

In fact, in general, there was considerable guilt about being dutiful daughters, about being sufficiently affectionate to their mothers and about being hurtful to them. Many daughters were confused by remembered accusations of causing headaches or by a belief that they'd made their mothers ill. Many found themselves distressed and resentful about caring for their aged mothers.

In her research reported in *Our Mothers' Daughters*, Judith Arcana found daughters defined themselves as persons who are to give parents unconditional love and respect, display affection for them, maintain a certain acceptable level of physical appearance, marry, stay married, re-marry if necessary and bear and raise children. They believed mothers felt affronted if daughters did not care about the same things as they did. In reality the reverse was also true. As a result of these cultural role prescriptions, mothers and daughters have impossible expectations of each other.[3]

In responding to the questions asked in my own research, it is interesting to note that, although nearly a quarter of the women felt guilty about what they'd written about their mothers, only four percent felt guilty about what they had written about their fathers, yet many had been severe in their criticism of them. This matches their lesser anger with fathers for their perceived shortcomings, which was discussed in the last chapter. Both these results yet again underline how emotionally charged the relationship between mothers and daughters remains in contemporary society. It is little wonder some mothers don't enjoy motherhood.

The Women Who Don't Enjoy Being Mothers

There is an expectation in our society that all women enjoy being mothers. Admittedly, there is a growing recognition that some women don't want children, but the recognition is often accompanied by a belief that such women are somewhat unnatural. Despite the influence of feminism and the increase in the numbers of childless couples, the expectation that all women should not only be mothers but "good" mothers, remains coercive.

Society finds it easier to accept denial, guilt, overconscientiousness, hostility or child abuse, rather than permit the unhappy or inadequate mother to openly admit her dilemma and have it dealt with. The advantage to the children of this second course is also often denied in western culture. Demystifying motherhood and recognising its realities can do nothing but improve mother-daughter relationships.

Almost half of the women, who were interviewed in my research study, said they did not enjoy being mothers.[4] They stated that they'd spoken of their unhappiness, or indifference as mothers, for the first time, because they were protected by the anonymity of the questionnaire, the interview methods of the research and the non-judgmental, research procedures. Many said they had unthinkingly stepped into motherhood, not realising they had a choice in the matter. Motherhood was seen as something every woman inevitably did, if she had the opportunity.

Several women felt that their husbands made better primary carers than they. Some had tried going out to work, while their husbands had stayed at home. For some, this had worked out reasonably well, but social expectations had created problems. Neighbours had "ganged up" on many a "mothering" father and had refused to allow their children to visit his house, or play with his children under his supervision. Some fathers, initially happy and successful as caregivers, had ultimately found the social disapproval and snubs too much and the family had unhappily reverted to traditional sex role divisions.

The reasons given by the women for not enjoying mothering involved many things to do with mother-daughter relationships. There were memories of the inadequacies or difficulties of their own mothers and, as a consequence, like Martha Quest in Doris Lessing's novel of the same name, they feared that they may also be inadequate as mothers.[5] Although they were not always prepared to admit it, this fear was accompanied by a good deal of anxiety about child-rearing. The excessive responsibility which is thrust upon mothers in patriarchal society, together with a fear that they could be the cause of emotional and behavioural problems in their children, were also given as reasons for not enjoying mothering. Stress, fatigue, lack of independence, lack of privacy and unclear definitions of mothering were also factors contributing to the lack of enjoyment of motherhood.

A very small minority said they disliked children because, as a result of the way they were treated in childhood, they had learnt to see children as pests. In other words, they had come to reject or deny the child in themselves. Some also felt they'd never had any choice other than to become mothers. As a result, they were angry not only with society, but also with their mothers for limiting their horizons. Yet, it seemed that their fathers had figured more strongly in the stereotyped expectations of traditional female behaviour.

The Loss of a Motherhood Identity versus the Daughter's Autonomy

Even if a woman works outside the home or has other consuming interests, motherhood is most often the central factor in her self-definition. She cannot escape from the uncertainties of being a "good" mother. The more central her concern about being a "good" mother, the more likely it is that the final and permanent departure of her daughters (or sons) from the family home will be seen as a blow to her self-esteem. To the daughter, the departure can confirm the arrival of young adulthood. To the mother, it may be seen as a major catastrophe, if her sense of identity comes entirely from within the family. Women have been trained to need and be needed by a "strong" partner and dependent children, in order to have an identity. If they have come to believe that their identity depends entirely upon caring for their children, it is not surprising that some resist their children's departure, since it implies that they are no longer significant as persons. Without their major source of self-esteem, they may sink into depression and despair.

This time can be especially difficult for daughters. More often than a son, a daughter is seen as an extension of her mother's self. Even if the relationship doesn't seem close, it is nevertheless a fact that the daughter is of the same sex and a "piece of the mother's self" in a way that sons cannot be. Thus, the daughter's departure can be more threatening and she is likely to feel guilty for seeking independence.

In recent decades, changes in social and economic pressures have allowed mothers and daughters, more so than their grandmothers, greater opportunities to enter the work-force. Many overcome their loneliness and sense of purposelessness in this way, when their offspring depart or become more independent. If they are not so inclined, others, as did their grandmothers, develop new pursuits or help voluntary organisations. Indications are that once the distresses of the emotional and physical separation are over, a great many find satisfaction in their new won freedom and time for themselves. An example is seen in the character, Ally, in the novel *Peeling*, by Grace Bartram, which is discussed in the Bibliotherapy, Chapter 9.

It is clear that the mothers, who are best equipped to survive family changes, are those who have maintained independent interests.[6] Such women are not so subject to the kind of identity disintegration, which is overly ascribed to the biological changes of the menopause. More often, the root causes are psychological factors, associated with a sense of redundancy in the context of patriarchal society, once child-bearing and caring are finished.

Because females are more often trained to pay attention to inner feelings and emotional relationships, it is usually the daughter, rather than the son, who feels responsible for the mother, who may be suffering unduly after the departure of her offspring. Daughters in this situation sometimes confess that they wish or long privately for their mother's death, in order to free themselves from the guilt occasioned by their leaving their mothers to a life of purposelessness and anonymity.[7]

Others feel that they must rescue their mothers before they can work out their own problems. They may press her to independence, assertiveness training, a university course, or a divorce. These can be creative solutions. But many a daughter may behave as though she must destroy her mother's identity (her values and her past), if she is to develop her own. Hence, she may become excessively critical of, and antagonistic, toward her. Even so, as Adrienne Rich suggests, she may not achieve the identity she wishes through the destruction of her mother's values. Many of the independent roles that she longs for are not achieved in this way and are, in any event, denied her by patriarchy.

Even in the best of relationships, separation usually occasions some turmoil and defensive manoeuvres. Where the situation is not good, the experience can be exceedingly disturbing — even traumatic. For example, in her psychotherapy with disturbed mothers and daughters, Jane Flax observed how often a mother sees separation as abandonment of herself by her daughter. In turn, this belief is accompanied by the daughter's fear that the mother will abandon her. Flax's women patients tended to feel guilty that they were somehow betraying their mothers in their attempts to terminate the symbiotic or enmeshed ties with them.[8]

Flax feels that the root of these special problems, which daughters face in separating from their mothers and achieving autonomy in patriarchal society, lies in the fact that the patriarchal family separates nurturance and autonomy. Autonomy is the province of fathers who mirror at home the behaviour that is demanded in the outside economic and political structures in which they work. In this situation, the mother, who is herself without a nurturing figure, is often the only source of nurturance for both father and daughter.

Given the one-sided nature of these emotional demands, it is little wonder that Flax found that her women patients complained, that they often felt pressure from their own mothers to provide the care the mothers themselves had lacked in childhood or in marriage. Thus separation became a major source of conflict and distress for many daughters. Mothers are less likely to have as many expectations about their sons as carers. Because men are not seen as nurturers in our culture, they are not expected to provide the same degree of emotional support for their mothers.

The irony, as Flax sees it, is compounded because women mother sons, who must grow contemptuous of her in order to become manly. Thus the patriarchy perpetuates itself. The mother makes herself powerful by overvaluing the son, through whom she vicariously experiences the power men have in the outside world. She thereby fulfills her own repressed wishes for autonomy and achievement. Her only source of emotional security is her daughter, whom she cannot allow to individuate. Thus her daughter ends up in the same situation as herself.

Carla, now in a highly successful career, gave an example of this situation.

> "Mum worshipped my brother, Andy. She took extra jobs to see there was enough money for him to study medicine. I had to work part-time to put myself through University. Andy has ended up as a mediocre G.P. but Mum talks about 'my son the doctor' whenever she can. She delights in his power over his patients and basks in the reflected glory of his having a high status profession. One of my girl friends took her to task for never boasting about me. Mum replied, 'Carla is a woman. She won't stay at the top long. Once she has babies she'll disappear into oblivion, like I did. I'm looking forward to her giving me grandchildren. Then we will be close again, like we used to be."

Some mothers encourage daughters to escape their dilemma by encouraging autonomous behaviour, but often in the process they convey a double message of "do not be like me" but also "be like me".[9] This can be exemplified in mothers who encourage their daughters to make careers for themselves but are disappointed if their daughters don't get married. They may encourage them not to be slaves to convention as they were, yet are concerned should their daughters live with a male partner outside marriage. They may feel that their daughters' unconventional behaviour is not acceptable and due to their failure as mothers. They worry that they granted too much autonomy. Mothers may be especially ambivalent about their daughters' autonomy, because patriarchy abhors overly independent women and therefore teaches that they are unfeminine.

In some situations, ambivalence about autonomy is based on outside realities, which the daughter also accepts. In as much as society infantilises, dominates and terrorises women, for example, by rape and other forms of violence, the fear of taking the steps toward one's autonomy is more easily exacerbated. In many other ways, women learn that autonomy and self-assertion on their part results in rejection in social and work situations. Women need to overcome the fear of punishment for the expression of autonomy. Here their best helpmates and supporters are likely to be other women, for they understand the double bind best.

Resentful Daughters:

Who is Responsible?

Flax also points out another dilemma for mothers and daughters. In patriarchal society, it would be difficult for a woman not to feel conflict about being female, albeit unconsciously. It is not only that a mother might value a son more, reflecting the higher social esteem enjoyed by men. Knowing the difficulties of being a female in a man's world, she might also wish for her daughter's own sake that she could have been born male. Yet, because the mother identifies so strongly with a girl child, she also wants the child to be just like her.[10] As a result of these conflicts, it is more difficult for her to be as emotionally generous and unreserved as her daughter needs her to be.

Flax underlines that what women want is the experience of nurturance and autonomy within an intimate relationship. What makes this wish so strong and, for many women, so unattainable, is that psychological development occurs within the patriarchal family. The process of learning about one's gender means recognising that men and women are not valued equally and that men are socially more esteemed than women. This influences how a woman values herself, as an individual and as a mother, and the type of mothering she provides. It also means she relates differently to her daughters and her sons. This is the origin of daughters' claims that they did not get enough nurturance, encouragement and strength for autonomy from their mothers.

Such beliefs among ordinary daughters prompted Judith Arcana to ask: "If I am to love myself — love women, what about my mother"?[11] This is a difficult question. On the one hand, the prevailing ethos, which expects perfect nurturance from mothers, inevitably makes daughters feel disappointed with the fallibility of their mothers. On the other hand, if mothers do not have self-esteem, it is difficult for them to transmit it to their daughters and be emotionally generous in Flax's sense. We must like ourselves in order to begin to like others, which is the essence of Arcana's question. If I am to love myself — what about my mother?

In my own research,[12] daughters highlighted how complex the issues that have been raised by Flax and Arcana are. Many had no doubt suffered as children. But, even though they were now adults, there remained a crippling concern with everlasting maternal responsibility, rather than self-responsibility. That they could remake their self-esteem in adulthood was not apparent to them. They had surrendered to the "blame your mother" school of thought. They allowed themselves to be embittered by childhood memories. Lost in past resentments, they were not creating their own possibilities.

Instead, these daughters dwelt on the shortcomings of their mothers in encouraging a sense of their possibilities as children or adolescents. In particular, they were concerned at their mothers' failure to instill in them, as children, a sense of themselves as competent female persons, so building a feeling of self-confidence.

Undoubtedly, the things they wanted were desirable for the best nurturance of children. As we have seen, it is through the appraisals of adults[13], that the young child begins to learn about her special qualities — "I have rosy cheeks", "I am a good runner". These appraisals act as a mirror in which children see and assess themselves. Parents and teachers who positively and realistically mirror their child's activities are laying the basis for that child's self-acceptance and self-esteem. Sometimes this mirroring process is not in accordance with the child's needs.

Three quarters of the women interviewed in my research, felt that this had been their lot and that their mothers had consistently imparted damaging and negative criticisms about their personalities, physical characteristics, behaviour and friends. While fathers were seen as doing this also, and more so, there was special concern about the mothers' actions. Loretta's story was typical of many:

> "I was a very good child, shy and not at all spontaneous — the sort of child grandparents, aunts and mothers approve of. In fact, I was the favourite grandchild of my maternal grandmother. I'm told now that I always looked tidy and attractive and could sit still for a long time when adults were present. My cousins, who were a rowdy scruffy lot, hated me and were jealous. This made me unhappy but I could not overcome the restraint that had been emotionally hammered into me from birth. My mother watched and criticised every move that I made. I was accused of being clumsy if I had any kind of childish accident. I was told I was stupid unless I said exactly what my mother told me to say — even then I was told I didn't say it right. If I couldn't keep up with her, I was accused of loitering deliberately to annoy her.
>
> Everyday and every hour that I was with her there was a string of negative criticisms. I think I should have been defeated utterly had it not been that occasionally my father, teachers and family friends took me aside and said my mother was too hard on me and too critical. Nevertheless, it took years to overcome the self-uncertainty and lack of spontaneity she instilled into me."[14]

Others, while not subject to such unrelenting criticism, reported that they were subject to regular bouts of criticism, which negated their child-ish right to self-respect or existence. Some reported, for example, that comments, such as the following were applied to them quite often:

"If you hadn't been born I could have continued with my stud-ies/dancing/writing/have more time to garden/ read/ improve myself."

"It would have been better if you hadn't been born."

"You were an accident."

"I'll kill myself if you keep bothering me."

"You are a financial burden. We could have travelled more without you."

"You give me no peace. I shall go mad."

"When you are naughty you make Mummy sick."

"You give Mummy headaches."

"I'm sick because you worried me so much."

"You should not stay out late. You do it deliberately to upset me. You are selfish and self-centred."

It was clear that these women were not talking about an occasional off day or negative remark by their mothers. They were talking about nega-tive messages so often repeated that, as children, they'd come to see themselves entirely as the negative reflection of their mothers' remarks. As a result, they devalued themselves as females and as persons. The problem was that as adults, they were not re-assessing themselves on their own terms.

The level of parental interest in their children is another important fac-tor in building children's self-esteem. As we have seen, the father's interest is of considerable influence.[15] Most daughters described fathers who took very little interest in them, but they largely overlooked the effects of that on their self-esteem. Instead, they concentrated upon maternal responsi-bility and were angry about their mothers' level of interest. To them, it was an important area in which mother-daughter relationships had foundered. Approximately one quarter of the women felt that their mothers had taken an interest in them only sometimes or rarely. Nearly one third felt that their mothers did not like them. Said Sadie, aged 42 and of working class background:

"My mother was always yelling, ordering, criticising and hitting me. She sneered at and belittled everything in which I was interested. I wanted to be a writer, largely because she set me that model and I began keeping a diary in pre-adolescence. She found it and tore it to shreds. I felt violated. I think this had been the way of handling children in the family for generations back to England. She protests now that she loves me and I'm ungrateful, but her methods of bringing me up just didn't convey it."[16]

Here we have generation after generation of mothers, with poor self-esteem and little capacity to express emotional generosity, providing models of poor self-esteem for their daughters. Albert Ellis in his books on "Rational Emotive Therapy" argues that in these situations children can develop "crazy hypotheses" about themselves, for example that they are absolutely no good. The problem is that as adults they may not take responsibility for shaking off "the original, crazy hypotheses about themselves". They rigidly stick to stupid inferences and the "shoulds" and dependencies of childhood.

Moreover, many go on believing that because they lacked sufficient nurturing as children, they are still owed its replacement in adulthood. They still see themselves as unnurtured four year olds. The problem is that their infantile greediness for nurturing can never be satisfied in any relationship in adult life. Instead, it disrupts it, because of the childish content of must and should: "People should care for me", instead of "I must take care of myself".

In a few cases, part of letting go of the demand for bountiful and sacrificial love from parents throughout adult life may require facing up to the fact that they were, and still are, neither caring or nice people. From here, one can move forward and take responsibility for oneself. For most, letting go involves acknowledging that their mothers are fallible characters in their own right. Their mothers might have made a hash of bringing up their children, but they equipped them as best they could, given the limitations of their environment and their upbringing.

Margaret Attwood is an example of one daughter who let go in this way. Her story, "Significant Moments in the Life of My Mother",[17] is told with tolerance and humour. Jeanette Winterson's "Psalms" and *Oranges are not the only fruit*[18] are other examples. Both these women report that throughout childhood they challenged their mothers' quirks in their own devious, and sometimes funny, ways. Their childhood and their mothers' childhood became cherished family archives — giving a sense of continuity.

In the same way, one third of the daughters who were interviewed, had positive hypotheses about their mothers' attempts at child-raising. They exhibited good self-esteem and believed that their mothers had also had good self-esteem. They felt that their mothers had been as emotionally generous to them as they could. They were honestly able to accept their mothers as courageous individuals and on their own terms. That is, they saw their mothers as struggling with personal and domestic difficulties, overcoming folklore, social stereotyping and resisting prevailing child-rearing fashions, in order to consistently build up their daughters' self-confidence and sense of competence as females.

These daughters maintained that their mothers had been able to come to terms with Adrienne Rich's call for "courageous" mothering which recognises that culture impresses on women a false image of their limits.[19] So the most important thing a mother can do for her daughter is to expand her sense of her possibilities, for example as Margaret Mead's mother and grandmother did for her, as we shall see in the Bibliotherapy, Chapter 9. Most believed that they were now doing this to their own daughters.

Unlike the resentful daughters, a small percentage felt that their mothers had meted out discipline in a positive way, which did not destroy their self-esteem, but made them realise they were capable of better — "My mother was very firm, but you always knew you were appreciated for a job well done and that if you had done something badly, you could do better and she knew it. My grandmother was the same to mum". This description came from a self-confident daughter, who described a self-confident mother, aged 70, who was running a small farm, almost single handed.

Enough Mothering

Like the daughters I've described here, Flax found that resentful daughters commonly depict their mothers as emotionally depriving and as having poor self-esteem. I have observed in my research, and Flax also believes, that such mothers had ambivalent ties to their own mothers and experienced conflicts about being female. As a consequence, she says they have a narcissistic relation to their daughters. By this she means they are unable to nurture their daughters and provide them with a satisfactory, loving relationship from the moment of birth. This is the background of daughters who are terrified by their feelings of a deep, greedy need for unconditional love and, as a result, deny those feelings.

Flax's insights, in a psychoanalytic framework, are drawn from *disturbed* mother-daughter relationships. They are nevertheless pertinent to the general experiences of daughters, as my research confirmed. Malika, one of many daughters says:

"I feel like going home to Mum and being tucked up in bed and cuddled and listened to, but she does all these things and I still feel dissatisfied and then I get angry with her. She needs to do more and be a better mother to me. (Pause ... she laughs) I know that I'm unreasonable. She is a good mother and has to make up to me for my problems with Dad and Beeta and Marc. I wish I weren't so unreasonable. Why am I?"[20]

Adult women, like Malika, who constituted more than one fifth of the women interviewed in my research study, claimed that they felt unmothered.[21] They described enough mothering as showing affection, warmth, care, acceptance, understanding and the ability to communicate easily and with sympathy.

Most were not conscious of how much their insatiable need for affectionate mothering had been induced by the soap opera expectations of patriarchal society, although at least one mother, Edith, in her early fifties, described the following episode by way of demonstration:

"Jill, my daughter, is at university. She comes home once a week and immediately starts talking about everything that is going on in the house where she lives with half a dozen other students — their fights — the things that irritate her — the things she likes. If I say anything, I'm accused of not understanding what she is saying. If I take my eyes off her face, I'm not listening. I've learnt it's best to shut up and just listen, but sometimes she has me glued to the chair for three to four hours and if I try to get up and make a cup of coffee, I'm accused of not being sympathetic. How does one be a good mother? Enough mothering is a bottomless pit."

Despite her own experience, this mother did not recognise that the double bind she'd described with her daughter, also applied to her relationship with her own mother. Her mother complained that Edith was making little allowance for the fact that she was getting on in years and had a life of her own — expecting her to listen to her lengthy telephone calls at any time and be ever available to help with her domestic problems and children. Edith complained that her mother was sometimes reluctant to put her own plans aside and respond to calls for help "as you'd expect a mother would". She was not unusual.

In my research, nearly half the daughters described factors that made them feel as though they were not mothered enough. They revolved around their perceptions of whether or not their mothers had valued them as persons and had been sensitive to their need for self-esteem. Included were recollections that their mothers only sometimes, or rarely, gave support when needed, when they were children. It was said that now, as then, their mothers did not understand them. Some described their mothers as self-centred, preoccupied with their own problems, unresponsive and as providing little physical and emotional contact and expression of feelings.

In hindsight, there is no way of being absolutely certain that these responses describe inadequate mothers. They may be a product of the impossible pursuit of enough mothering.

As long as the patriarchal socialisation processes predominate, women will feel unmothered. First, because suppressed emotion and restraint of physical expression of affection are seen as models of manliness and ideal behaviours for both sexes. In addition, due to social pressures, most adult women learn to repress or negate their yearnings for the physical closeness they had with their mothers as children. As a result, women find it very difficult to discuss early, erotic feelings aroused by their mothers or daughters.

In secret moments, most mothers remember the erotic and sensual pleasures of caressing their babies. They remember the ecstatic delight with which their babies responded to their caresses. I find that when women verbalise these feelings they define "eroticism" and "sensuality" contextually. In short, for them these words have different meanings in different settings. Generally, men have less flexible responses . More often than not, men have been socialised into directing sensuality and affection into sexual channels. Affection is not seen as manly unless it has sex and sexual intercourse as its object and equates that intercourse with power and domination.

For women, the sensual and erotic exchanges with their babies do not have this kind of sexual objective. Their caresses are not directed at achieving self-gratification and power, but are genuinely loving and affectionate exchanges with the intent of providing physical pleasure, comfort and security for their babies. At the same time, they are stimulating their babies' senses and by these means their babies come to realise and enjoy their own separate physical identity. But because patriarchal society has a major problem about sensuality and equates it almost exclusively with sexual desire and fulfilment, the sensual caresses between mothers and babies are not approved of when the infant becomes a child and obviously a separate person. Expressions of sensuality in affection between mothers and school age children are taboo. From adolescence through adulthood, eroticism is channelled into heterosexual relationships.

In adulthood, society encourages men to fondle and caress female bodies and obtain whatever satisfaction they can from them. Thus a male can replace his mother and satisfy his erotic yearnings with another female. But for most women, once childhood is over, the mother's body is lost forever as a source for close and comforting physical contact, as are her caresses which soothe, banish pain and provide security — in short the original mothering sensations. This is one of the many reasons why so many women feel unmothered.

Penny, who was happily married with two lively children, illustrated this point:

> "My Mum may look ordinary and a bit dumpy to you, but I've always thought her physically beautiful. I love cuddling her and being cuddled and kissed by her. She strokes my back when I am tired and I massage her feet when they are swollen with too much standing. It gives us both a warm luxurious feeling. It smooths away anxieties and tension. It makes me feel secure. I don't understand what it is like to feel unmothered. My friends envy me and say their upbringing inhibited expression of physical affection. There is one friend who thinks I'm kinky. She never cuddles her Mum and finds her physically repulsive. . . . . . She's always talking about not being mothered enough."

Women are expected to give up their need for mothering once adulthood is reached. They do not find substitute mothers in their husbands and partners. Few women growing up in patriarchal society feel mothered enough because, whereas men may find a substitute mother in their female partners, men are not trained or expected to offer motherly nurturance to their wives and girlfriends. Thus, females are trained to need and give more nurturance than men and yet receive less. This, many lesbians tell us, is why they prefer relationships with other women.

Even if the existing heterosexual situation is relatively nurturing, other factors may hinder the kind of closeness daughters, as wives, are seeking. As men are educated to be aggressive and competitive and women are trained to develop their emotional, caring and affectionate traits, there is often a partial communication gap, even in the best of marriages. As a result, when the daughter becomes a mother, she may turn to her daughter to fill the gap. The child becomes the major source of gratification, affection, close friendship and even advice and support.

On the face of it, a relationship between a mother and daughter, which can be described as a friendship, may seem ideal. Unfortunately, in the situation just described, the emotional demands are not always appropriately reciprocal or supportive of the young daughter's needs. Even if they are, there is something in the nature of the expectations which adult daughters have of mothers, which makes simply a friendship with them unpalatable. For example, Judith Arcana, author of *Our Mothers' Daughters* ,[22] gives many case studies of women who resented that their mothers wanted to be friends, rather than their mothers — a mother being someone who gives but never demands equality as friends do. These women felt angry as adults, because mothers are needed, they said, to provide mothering which is more than and different from friendship.

Many other tensions are created when the unsatisfied female need for nurturance causes mothers to look to their daughters for the affection they feel they are not getting from their husbands. The mother's need may be exacerbated by recollection of her own imperfect parents. In this situation, subtle pressures emerge which may mean the daughter is also expected to make up for dissatisfactions with her mother's own mother. This is a distressingly ambivalent role for the child because, at the same time, the mother expects the daughter to fail her as a nurturer, just as her own mother did and her husband has. She may continually accuse a quite compliant child of not loving her and we see such a case in Marilyn French's novel, *Her Mother's Daughter*, which is discussed in the Bibliotherapy in Chapter 9.

Reversal of mother-child roles, with children of both sexes, is well recognised in the psychiatric literature; what is not always acknowledged is the frequent socialisation of the male into an inadequate partner. He is unable to give emotional support and yet is demanding of it for himself, for men too, have recollections of non-perfect mothers. They also reverse roles with their children.

Given the frequency of feelings of insufficient mothering, daughters may engage in one of several inadequate manoeuvres to try to satisfy their needs. They may mother others.[23] They may reverse roles with their mothers. They may be unwilling to share their mothers or allow them an independent life. These daughters are usually enraged by the conflicts their manoeuvres bring upon themselves, as in the following case:

> Janice had not been her father's favourite daughter. She was recognisably jealous of her brother and her two sisters. Psychotherapy revealed her to be also intensely jealous of her mother, for the attention her father paid her, and hostile toward her mother for not making the father love her. In fact, the mother had remonstrated with the father continually and, according to reliable observers, who were either within the family or were close neighbours, she had considerably improved the child's lot. She had devoted extra love and time to Janice to compensate for the irritation, the father sometimes expressed toward her. The father was aware of the problem but described Janice as "too bossy" and "assertive" for his liking. He preferred his more "feminine" daughters.

> As an adult, Janice adopted a very controlling attitude toward her mother, interfering continually in her affairs and constantly criticising her. The mother had made a good adjustment to middle age and the departure of her family and had developed a thriving business. Janice resented her independence to such an extent, that she began stealing from her mother's firm. Those events led to family therapy. During therapy, Janice began to understand her mother's difficulties and efforts and why her rage against her father had been projected onto her mother.

Janice's rage was covered by an expressed concern to protect her mother. Daughters like Janice, typically become greedy for unconditional love. Their concern with nurturance has been distorted and misdirected, by the unrealistic expectations of mothers in a patriarchal society.

The stresses of the enough mothering issue often reach unmanageable proportions during the mother's old age. My study confirmed other research in this area. Many daughters have difficulty permitting their mothers to age and cannot cope with the power and nurturance reversal this period involves. The reversal clearly puts a great strain on the mother-daughter relationship. Remembered resentments about their treatment as children, feelings that they were not mothered enough and the mother's growing dependence and demands, create overwhelming ambivalence in many daughters. If the aged mother has been placed in a nursing home, guilt about the amount of visiting is considerable. Nursing home staff can unthinkingly expose and exacerbate many a daughter's guilt, with excessive demands and criticism.

This uncalled for guilt is clearly a mammoth social problem, born of the over expectations of the mother-daughter relationship and the loss of the extended family. Certainly old people have a right to a happy, comfortable ending. However, their care needs to be shared by all family members and the community at large. The total responsibility for their care, typically accorded to daughters, can clearly do much damage to the final years of the mother-daughter relationship.

Overview

In this chapter, I have discussed why mother-daughter relationships often have an angry emotional content and why so many daughters feel unmothered. These feelings of deprivation are sometimes compounded by the inability of mothers to be emotionally generous to their daughters, due to the politics of the patriarchal family. I have described why women are left with a feeling of being unmothered, while men can replace their mothers with wives. In this situation, mothers may turn to daughters to supply the mothering they themselves lack. This creates conflict and guilt in daughters.

Over-expectations of mothers have created a tragedy — the super mum. It is a tragedy because no mother can attain the perfection dictated by this model. Because mothers can't live up to the impossible dreams and the soap opera expectations about motherhood, daughters are resentful. As long as the false ideals remain, there is absolutely no way mothers can win.

A humourous picture of this truism is found in Michele Wandor's story: "Meet My Mother".[24] She describes the "once upon a time" with her orthodox Jewish mother, to whom she'd stopped bothering to talk: her mother's crusade to see her married and settled, her criticisms; her emotional blackmail; the fights;

One day she tells her mother, "There is no revolutionary hope for the heterosexual, and I have therefore decided to love myself and become a lesbian".[25] Her mother does not react as emotionally to this news as her daughter expected. Instead, when she learns the daughter's lover is not Jewish and is called Rowena, she sniffs, "What kind of a goyische (non-Jewish) name is that"? She orders her daughter to bring Rowena home to meet her.

On the crucial day, Rowena cannot be dissuaded from wearing her usual punk gear and appears with cerise and purple hair, tight black satin trousers and sequins. The shock for the daughter is that her mother and Rowena become friends and the result is her mother's metamorphosis. Her mother joins an older women's group, becomes involved in pensioner rights, goes to protest at Greenham Common, joins a Jewish feminist group and harangues her daughter about how patriarchal the Judaeo-Christian heritage is. She is now altogether too busy to remember her daughter's birthday or to sew for her or to criticise her.

The daughter has always wanted "the perfect social-feminist mother-daughter relationship". Now it looks possible, she is still not happy with her mother: The daughter says to Rowena:

> "You must think I'm around the twist ... once upon a time I had a
> mother who was just what she should be. Manipulative, bigoted, a

pain in the neck, didn't understand me, didn't want to understand me, wanted me to be all the things she thought I should be. Once upon a time I could dread going round to visit her on Sunday... Once upon a time I had a mother. Now she's gone. And I don't know what I'm going to do".[26]

It is little wonder that many mothers do not enjoy being mothers.

Despite the feelings of being unmothered — feelings that I have described in this chapter — more than half the women who were interviewed thought their mothers were more influential, than their fathers, in making them what they'd become and more were friendlier and closer to their mothers now, than they were to their fathers. Forty percent remembered a good relationship with their mothers as children and half claimed they had a good relationship with their mothers now.

Courageous mothering — handing on self-esteem, seeing through patriarchal propaganda — is good enough mothering. It is neither possible nor necessary to be an infallible super woman. In fact, it is through the process of recognising a mother's fallibility, that a daughter grows emotionally and can separate from her. A mature, adult daughter with good self-esteem can accept the foibles and quirks of her mother with humour. She can recognise that her mother was limited by a set of social values as she will be in her turn. She can take self-responsibility now.

The problem is that the idealised mothering role is made central to the definition of women in patriarchal society. Even when women work, the mothering role is often the core of a woman's self-definition and she ceases to feel like a person of significance when her children leave home. The departure of the daughter can be traumatic and the manoeuvres of mothers and daughters in this situation have been discussed in this chapter.

The impositions of the idealised mothering role is accompanied by overexpectations of daughters. Daughters are guilty people. They are guilty about abandoning their mothers. They feel they must rescue their mothers and solve their problems, before they can separate from them. Separation is a major issue in mother-daughter relationships and is discussed in the next chapter.

ख

BIBLIOTHERAPY

Almost all the issues concerning guilt and super-mothering that have been discussed in this chapter are portrayed in Marilyn French's book, *Her Mother's Daughter*. Also in Chapter 9, see the discussion under the heading, "Unfinished Business Between Mothers and Daughters" and the story, *Love Child* by Jean Bedford. How far a daughter can go in rescuing her mother from a violent home, without surrendering herself, is discussed in Kim Chernin's *In My Mother's House*. *Close Company* edited by Park and Heaton, deals with mother-daughter relationships in many cultures. Amy Tan's *The Joy Luck Club*, is well worth reading. It is a courageous story about Chinese-American daughters and their mothers struggling to come to terms with each other and their cultural identity.

Poppy by Drusilla Modjeska, deals with many of the conflicts that emerge between young adult daughters and their mothers. It is also a story of the quest for the dead mother in order that the daughter may understand herself. It portrays how the attempt to be the perfect mother sent many mid-century mothers to psychiatric institutions and is in part an indictment of psychiatric excesses against women.

Resolving conflicts with mothers crops up often in the writings of many authors, such as George Eliot, Colette and Virginia Woolf. Their special ways of coping are discussed in Book II.

॰ॐ

CHAPTER 7

Therapeutic Rethinking About Separation

Some of the most refreshing women writers in the last decades of the twentieth century are the Canadian women writers, who trace their heritage in their pioneering mothers. Margaret Attwood, Margaret Laurence and Alice Munro are examples. Lorna Irvine believes they have the advantage of citizenship of a relatively young country, without a long literary tradition.[1] Thus, instead of reacting to an established patriarchal literary perspective, they are in a position to co-operate in creating new horizons. These writers depict their leading female characters as persons who aim for autonomy as part of the natural course of events. They are not preoccupied with female protagonists who met tragedy because they strove for independence. Victimisation is precluded because these women take responsibility and are, as a result, reconciled with their mothers.

Irvine suggests that what makes Canadian fiction particularly significant, for anyone interested in studies of female development, is the seriousness with which it treats women's quests and its emphasis on a past that, for women, is bound up with their mothers.[2] Perhaps the anger with mothers and the dreams of radical independence, during the 1950s, were a necessary stage in a process culminating in the willingness of contemporary daughters to accept responsibility for themselves. In turn, this acceptance enables reconciliation with their mothers. To a certain extent, this theme can be found in Margaret Laurence's *Rachel, Rachel*, Sylvia Fraser's *Pandora* and Margaret Attwood's *Lady Oracle*, which is discussed later.

Some of the daughters depicted by the Canadian women writers complete their search for identity, by fulfilling many of their mothers' ambitions. In the 1950s, such a mother and daughter would have been accused of being enmeshed or narcissistic extensions of each other. These writers dismiss these labels with contempt and look at the mother-daughter relationship through female eyes. The images of mothers, cast as threatening by patriarchal psychology and psychiatry, can be reversed and seen positively in their true light. Women possess an enormous potential for creativity and for the co-operative and empathetic skills that are found in humanitarian endeavours. Mothers are not alien beings. They are not dissimilar from the rest of their sex. They share the same circumstances, anxieties and capacities that are special to all women. These recognitions can be therapeutic, since they release daughters from destructive views of themselves and their mothers — views which so many have sadly incorporated.

In this chapter, I will look at novels by two Canadian writers, which reject negative, patriarchal images of mothers and offer a range of candidly expressed feelings between mothers and daughters. In particular, I've chosen novels which give insight into the stresses and strains which were seen as major ones by the mothers and daughters who took part in my research.[3] After looking at the ideas of the Canadian women, we will move on to a novel by Doris Lessing which offers some suggestions about reworking an uneasy mother-daughter relationship. The novels all deal with some aspect of separation, which is at the core of the difficulties raised in the previous chapter. Finally there is an account of the very supportive relationships between working class mothers and daughters in Bethnal Green.

The Therapy of Emotional Separation from Mothers

More than half the women in my study were in accord with the psychoanalytic literature, which asserts that mothers do not "let go" of their daughters sufficiently. They said it was an accurate description of their experiences with their mothers. Few of these women understood the processes of separation and rebellion that take place in adolescence and young adulthood, which were discussed in Chapters 3 — 6. Few indicated any understanding of the degree to which mothers are unwitting agents of patriarchal agendas. In summary, it was clear that, as yet, the new "feminist consciousness" has had little affect on large numbers of women.

Although well beyond their youth, many were still angry with their mothers. This fact raised questions as to whether they had successfully taken responsibility for their own independence. Had they separated emotionally from their mothers?

Some daughters had tried to achieve independence by physical separation. This is generally an ineffective manoeuvre as will be illustrated later when Margaret Attwood's *Lady Oracle* is discussed. If daughters have not emotionally separated from their mothers, they are not sufficiently responsible to achieve independence. Emotional separation emerges when one knows one's own identity and who one is. Once achieved, it is possible to live in the same house as one's mother, yet be a separate individual.

Where daughters felt emotionally trapped, their ambivalence was exhibited in both their fury and their closeness with their mothers. They visited several times a week, but they felt they were living out a dream of the dutiful daughter, which had diminished their certainty of independent selfhood. In fact, they had not let go of their mothers. Had the daughter left her mother more time and space to develop her own interests and resources, she'd have had more reason to give up the mothering role as a major part of her life. Many of these daughters, who had been critical of their mothers' failure to grant separation, were often repeating these behaviours with their own daughters.

What is equally significant is that these daughters were furious when their mothers exhibited some independent behaviour that did not maintain the centrality of the daughters' needs. By contrast, in *My Mother's House*, Colette describes how she could accept and admire her mother, Sido, when she preferred to stay home to see a rare flower bloom, rather than visit her daughter. The daughter, Colette, nevertheless knew she was loved.[4]

In my study, daughters described their mothers as having many of the controlling behaviours that Sido had exhibited when Colette was a child. However as adults, there was an immense difference between their's and Colette's perspectives of the behaviour of mothers. Their recollections were resentful, rather than fond. Their chief complaints were overprotection, the imposition of ideas, feelings and opinions and dominating behaviour. Many believed that their mothers had restricted their character development when they were children. They claimed that all of these behaviours had continued beyond developmentally appropriate stages and had limited their ability to regard themselves as independent and competent persons. Some of the stories, if taken out of cultural context, could be described as obsessive.

For example:

> "I(Sheila, now aged 52) was not even permitted a sense that I controlled my own bodily processes. My mother (Clare) clearly had the idea that I had lots of nasty thoughts inside me about her and I think she confused it with my faeces when I was a child. This was the bad inside me that she wanted to get out and control. She was obsessed with constipation. I was watched everyday to see if I'd had a bowel motion. Inevitably, probably as a means of asserting my independence and anger, I would become constipated, despite a good diet. Then she'd give me an enema. I was terrified as a littly, at this water being pumped inside me and then rushing out. I'd beg and plead for her not to do it, but grimly she insisted. I felt it was a violation and a losing of myself. I still remember my terror and immense fear. I felt she hated me. How could anyone be so insensitive and cruel to a little kid? I felt she was obsessed with controlling every aspect of me. She did it regularly until I was about eight."[5]

This story with several versions, some not so unrelenting, was told by many daughters. Certainly, such procedures are today seen as a serious violation of children in the early and middle childhood years, since in this period their concept of self revolves largely around their bodies and physical activities.[6] At this age, children fear damage to their bodies or the loss of a limb or an eye. For the same reason, disabled persons can be very worrying to young children. They fear the same thing may happen to them.

Yet one cannot judge Clare, the mother, in isolation. She came from an era when it was considered in the best interests of children to control their bowels. It was also an era obsessed with controlling girls, in case they lost their virginity or became pregnant. However, the issue is not a simple matter of social pressures. Clare was insecure and used her daughter as a device for purging any threat to herself. She could not treat her daughter as a separate person, but only as an extension of her own needs. The cultural morés enabled her to rationalise her actions toward her daughter. Whether her daughter chooses to allow resentment of her mother's inappropriate actions to rule her life is a matter open to her as an autonomous adult.

Certainly, we are more fortunate if we have mothers who are more thoughtful about cultural morés and ask, What is this doing to my daughter? What is her perspective? What is my perspective? Why do I feel compelled to act this way? Is it meeting my daughter's needs and my needs as a self-respecting individual?

However, one can well understand the confusion of the mothers in the study. Who is to blame? Is it the mother? Is it the daughter? Is anyone to blame? Since a clear-cut response to such questions is not possible, according blame between mothers and daughters is not productive. Instead, the social and psychological pressures on mother-daughter relationships need examination. Well chosen novels can often bring these pressures to light, without personal recrimination.

For example, Margaret Attwood's novel *Lady Oracle*, underlines how much a daughter's "mother as monster" obsessions are an indication of her own failure to separate from her mother emotionally.[7] Her book can be used for therapeutic exploration of this issue.

Initially, it is a story about a daughter's smouldering resentment of a mother, whom she describes as a three headed-monster. The mother is forever critical and forever disappointed. Her daughter, Joan, feels constantly watched. Ultimately, in order to try and achieve emotional separation from her mother and establish a new identity for herself, she fakes her own drowning. Despite this drastic measure, she does not achieve the sense of independence she craves. She makes many other ineffectual manoeuvres, yet her feeling of enmeshment with her mother always remains. In her teenage years, Joan defies her mother by becoming enormously fat, a weapon to protect herself from becoming thin and beautiful, like her mother.

She leaves home and severs all physical connection with her mother, but stays in touch with her father, a doctor. She believes her mother has destroyed their relationship. Joan recognises that her father has not rescued her from the destructive conflict in which she is engaged with her mother, but excuses him on the grounds that her mother was too overpowering.

Joan, now independent and fending for herself, is to others slim and beautiful, but she cannot rid herself of the inner fat image. She becomes a hack writer of gothic costume novels. In melodramatic form, her characters take on facets of herself and her mother. These insights are helped by the fact that she has telepathic abilities — something she learnt long ago with the help of an aunt who became her surrogate mother.

In times of crisis, Joan experiences increasing visions of her mother. To the reader, it becomes increasingly obvious that Joan is not emotionally separate from her mother, although she herself is not fully aware of it. Interwoven in her visions and her gothic novels is a man of many disguises, good and evil, who may represent her father. She learns later that her father had a sinister job as an agent and hitman during the war.

Her mother appears to Joan at her moment of death. Joan hurries home and finds that without her mother's presence she has nothing to say to her father. Indeed, she realises that her mother held them together. Did he kill her mother? That question cannot be answered, but the discovery of the mutilation of the family photo album establishes her mother's fury, anger and frustration. Why had the mother always behaved as though her father owed her something and had destroyed her life? Why was her mother so horrid to her? Joan becomes convinced that she was an unwanted baby and an embodiment of her mother's failure, through a forced pregnancy and marriage.

Her mother continues to have enormous influence upon her, even after her death. In fact, Joan begins to experience some of the mother's despair. Eventually, under a kind of psychic influence, she writes a best seller, an angry novel about a woman's relationship with a husband, presumably her mother's story. Despite this bloodletting, the malevolent, maternal image does not fade but continues to haunt her. She wants freedom. Eventually, she realises that it is she who has never let her mother go. Joan has been her mother's reflection, although she has overtly rejected her. She also recognises the affection that was buried beneath the hostility. The journey is not complete. It may never be, but at least it has begun.

The Imagined Child and the Therapy of Unlocking Roles

A mother's use of her daughter as an extension of herself is another symptom and setting for separation difficulties. For example, during pregnancy the mother may hope to fulfil her own thwarted dreams, hopes and needs through the unborn child. Indeed, it was not unusual for mothers in my study to remember hoping that their babies would match an ideal image they'd had before the birth. If the baby is other than expected, for example is a girl instead of a boy, or cries unduly instead of being cuddly, or looks like Uncle Bill, whom nobody likes, or fusses, when one dreamed of a smiling, easy going baby, the situation is very hard for some mothers to accept. In their disappointment, the charms and individuality of the baby are not recognised. The baby is not endorsed as a person and this can lead to a poor relationship between the mother and her child.

These processes are not to be confused with the perfectly normal sense of the fusing of the baby and self, which may happen to some mothers in the early weeks after the birth, especially if they are more satisfied with the appearance and behaviour of their newborn. For example, one young mother of 27 reported:

"I was on a high after Avril was born and kept thinking that she was me. It was not until she was about one month old that I began to feel detached and see her as separate from my own self. Now that she's three, I can see that she's lovable but not perfect."

This daughter will become an individual, free to develop her own style and a separate identity. She will be loved for her uniqueness and her relationship with her mother will be better for it.

Others felt that they did not have this choice: Said Esna:

"My mother boasted about me as though I was especially clever, because I was her daughter. I did always come top of the class but felt deprived as though the achievement was not mine but inevitable, because I was her daughter. I grew up feeling I was a reflection of what others, and chiefly my mother, wanted. I was frustrated and angry. I broke free when I went to university and increasingly avoided her because she never gave me space to be an individual in my own right."

Where mothers and daughters see each other as extensions of themselves, there is often poor self-esteem and conflict between them. For example, each is constantly on the alert for minute shortcomings in the other. One very attractive and smartly dressed mother, Julia, hid her poor self-esteem beneath an air of arrogance. She was not aware of these feelings, but expressed them by constantly pulling at her daughter's clothes, telling her to brush her hair or apologising that her daughter did not look her best today.

Joan Barfoot's novels, *Duet for Three* and *Gaining Ground* deal with some of these issues, without blaming mothers.[8] In fact, Barfoot would probably argue that mothers are not responsible for the self-esteem and neuroticism of their offspring. In *Gaining Ground*, she describes the mother's attitude toward children, as similar to the attitudes she has to the squirrels she saves from starvation in her bush retreat. They can survive on their own and she has no right other than to let them be, especially if it interferes with her own self-sufficiency. To her daughter she says, "Just be yourself, Katie. If we like each other, we'll like each other. If we don't, we won't."[9] Barfoot's ideas provide a good basis for discussion about the limits on mothers, as servants to the needs of others, whether or not one thinks her isolationist images are constructive.

The therapy of *Duet for Three* lies in its exploration of the way the individuality and personality of mothers and daughters can be obscured to each other by failing husbands, rigid self-projections and locked roles. Not allowing oneself to be controlled by expectations means one can be a separate and independent individual, who gets the most out of life.

The mother and daughter in *Duet for Three* are not heroines, but are very ordinary persons who compound their own difficulties through their stereotyped expectations of each other. The mother is looking at her child solely as a daughter and the daughter is seeing only a mother, rather than the woman as a whole. These two not untypical processes lock Aggie, the mother, and her daughter, June, in an arid relationship until the end of the book, when a discussion of their past and what has made each as they are, offers a glimmer of understanding between them. It may do the same for the reader.

The story begins in the early part of this century. The main character, Aggie, is a country girl from a happy farming family and has the advantage of a sterling mother. Aggie, at the instigation of her mother who wants the best for her daughter, marries a seemingly good prospect, the antiseptic Neil — the local schoolteacher from England. There is no great expression of love, but he is kind until married, when he sees Aggie as his property. In accordance with the then current expectations of women, she is to behave with decorum, duty and obedience to him. The demand is compounded by his own conformity. In fact, Neil is depicted as a most pathetic victim of patriarchy and his adherence to its rules destroys a potentially good relationship between himself and Aggie and leads to his isolation and disappointment. To Neil, the house he has purchased in the town is his house not theirs. Aggie has no share in it and must decorate it and do with it only as he pleases.

Aggie does her duty in cooking and keeping house and submitting to his sporadic, unaffectionate, penis-thrusting. She does all this, having been trained to be a wife and mother, but she refuses to surrender her will, to become submissive, and their life together becomes a battlefield. Neil is seen by her as cold, meticulous, unspontaneous. She eats a great deal and feels more power as she grows fatter, for he is very thin. She becomes self-educated and reads widely. She invests her all in the house, decorating some rooms as she wants. It is the scene of her victories and her bruises.

Throughout her pregnancy, she communicates with the child within her body, tells it about her own childhood, promises story telling and singing, looks forward to sharing riddles and jokes, only to find after the birth that the baby, a daughter, appears not to be the one with whom she has developed a relationship. The baby is not in any way as she expected. For one thing, she looks like her husband. Later, as a small child, she develops his good and orderly and puritanical characteristics, which run counter to Aggie's happy-go-lucky style. As well, Neil chose to call their newborn daughter "June" and registered the name without consulting Aggie. It is a name Aggie does not like. She feels her own child, the hoped for child, has been stolen, and, by comparison with Neil's love for the child, she falls short.

June grows into a pale and hostile little girl, with a poor appetite, who glides away from her mother's embrace. So Aggie gives up the hope for a robust husband and an adventurous child. She comes to feel detached from her own immediate flesh, because it is stamped with the features and character of the man who does not respect her integrity. Lacking independent means, she is a prisoner until Neil dies suddenly. Now the independent training of her own mother suddenly blooms. Thereafter, Aggie thrives as she utilises her cooking skills and develops a successful bakery business. She is no longer the girl she has been. There are parts of her that will not be touched again, places that have been hurt that now will feel no pain.

Aggie's potential for relationships was impaired by the dominating stance of her husband. Then her own imprisoning expectations thwarted any possibility of close ties between herself and her daughter. They are all losers in this process. Neil did not have an affectionate wife and Aggie does not have the love of her daughter. But Aggie is a survivor. She succeeds in having a good life, on her own terms, and develops a rewarding, platonic friendship with the dairy man who supplies her bakery.

June blames her mother for her father's death and cannot remember any motherliness in Aggie. She accuses her of never being interested in her. She forgets her cuddling, her reading, her singing, her concern and attention. June, conditioned by and longing for the unreal expectation of the "ideal" mother, remembers only the denying mother, especially as Aggie, like most, is no more than a good enough mother — a slapdash mother. In other circumstances, unconstrained by patriarchal ideals, such mothering would be considered sufficient.

June, missing out on the whole-hearted endorsement of her mother, becomes a schoolteacher and trudges pale faced through her days with a keen sense of duty. Barfoot's presentation does not lead one to accord blame to Aggie for bad mothering. She is accepted as she is — a survivor and a good enough mother. June, as a child, made a choice when her father died, so one may feel sorry for her. But there is no urge to find fault with one more than the other. This is not to say Aggie is not protective and concerned. She is, as long as it does not interfere with her precept that June should learn to stand on her own two feet.

Aggie remembers her own sterile sexual relationship and hopes June's will be better with her husband. She painstakingly sews a flimsy, seductive gown for her wedding night saying, "I hope it works for you. I hope you'll be happy". However, like her father, June is sexually restrained — frustrated by her husband's belief in her pureness. Aggie's gown is misplaced. June repeats her mother's history — a bad marriage, crucified on a mattress by her husband and then a daughter unlike her — not the expected baby.

June badly wanted to show her mother what a real mother should be like and did not want to bring up her daughter, Frances, in the slapdash, irregular way she had been raised. But reality makes her expectations impossible. She cannot live up to the ideal motherhood that patriarchy has taught her to expect of both her mother and herself. Nor does she understand the destructive effect such expectations have on mother-daughter relations.

Frances is more like Aggie and they have a good relationship. Poor June, who only dared small and timorous movements — how could she be expected to take pleasure in her daughter's capacity for risk — a child with appetite and curiosity. Aggie, having experienced detachment from her daughter, is astounded when she discovers her love for her granddaughter. Looking into Frances's eyes, she sees her own. The loss of this recognition in her daughter and its consequences, underline the tragedy of having hoped her daughter would be an extension of herself.

Aggie plays an important role in bringing Frances up, at considerable sacrifice. Each stage has its remembered joys: A five year old coming home at noon from kindergarten, running into the shop calling, "See the picture I made, Grandma? I made a picture of you". The crayoned portrait of a tiny head mounted on a massive body, bigger than the trees beside it, was taped to the door of the refrigerator.

Then there is the recollection of Frances as a seven year old, home with the measles, and Aggie running up and down stairs and sticking signs on the shop door — "Back in 10 minutes" — or the little girl examining her spotted face in Aggie's hand mirror, and saying, "Oh Grandma, make them go away. They're ugly".[10] Finally, Frances grows up, becomes a separate person and leaves home to make her own independent life. Aggie is satisfied. She wishes June had done the same.

By the time she reaches her eighties, Aggie is grossly fat. She can see her body is unattractive.

> But looking at it from the inside, as its inhabitant, she finds it pleasing and comforting, cosy, like a warm house. There is a sharp Aggie like a needle safely embedded inside this rippling pincushion, and there is an imposing Aggie whose bulk is perfectly expressive.[11]

But sometimes she longs for her mother. She would like to be rocked in her mother's lap, with her head on her mother's shoulder and her knees drawn up. She remembers the short, plump, brown and grey haired mother in her best dress, to whom she waved goodbye on her wedding day.

The humiliations of Aggie's old age — her loss of bladder control, dignity and independence and her diminished power and pride — are from June's point of view the behaviour of a fat, greedy, old woman, who failed as a mother. June has looked after her mother dutifully, but Aggie sees this as a failure in her daughter. She would admire her if she said, "Go to hell. I want to be myself and be happy". Despite her sacrifice for Aggie, June knows her own daughter will not make the same sacrifice for her. Frances will point out what her grandmother taught her: that she is a separate individual, with her own life to live and she must get on with it.

June attempts to put her mother in a nursing home, against Aggie's wishes. Finally, sorting Aggie's things from the trunk in the attic, June recognises in her mother, not a mother, but a separate individual, a young girl with hopes, stitching with her own mother for her glory box. Through this act of detachment and separation, she realises her father was not the only disappointed one.

In summary, the journey toward mature mother-daughter relationships begins with emotional separation. It includes giving up the unrealistic, idealised image of mothers or daughters and acknowledging that mothers and daughters are not ideal. It requires the acceptance of each other — warts and all — rather than remaining locked into personal projections and expectations.

The Dying Mother

Mother-daughter relationships must survive many separations. The separation causing the greatest difficulty is often the final separation in death. For the daughter, the living mother may be an unrecognised emotional buffer- a security gate between herself and her own death. When the mother is dying, anxiety about the approaching loss of her mother and the daughter's heightened awareness of the inevitability of her own death can be compounded by feelings of guilt and anger about the imperfections of the relationship with her mother. This arouses ambivalence about whether she is doing enough and resentment about any unreasonable demands and expectations. The reversal of roles — becoming mother to the mother who may be seen as not having mothered her daughter enough — leads to tensions, wounds and wounding. For years to come, guilt about some of the things that were said or happened in the final years or days can linger and even destroy the daughter's feeling that she is a good person.

One novel which offers therapeutic suggestions for dealing with this kind of anguish and self-blame is Doris Lessing's, *The Diaries of Jane Somers*.[12] It appears to be a sequel to her Martha Quest novels and a way of working through a bad relationship with a mother after the mother's death. In this case, the unfinished business is completed through taking on the roles of both surrogate mother and daughter.

The novel addresses the ups and downs of learning to love an ageing and dying surrogate mother and the give and take, which is necessary in this complex and emotionally charged situation. It also underlines that mother-daughter relationships may develop without biological ties. It shows how childless women, spinster women, widow women, business women, women of all kinds, fill nurturing roles for each other — some successful and some unsuccessful.

Jane, or Janna Somers, is the successful and responsible editor of an upmarket women's magazine. She is impeccably dressed, attractive and efficient. Her flat is the essence of order and good taste. She has had a successful sexual relationship with her husband, although all other forms of communication between them were fairly superficial. He has recently died of cancer, during which process he protected her from the realities of his agony. She was a child wife.

Her role, as the selfish child in family relationships, is underlined for her when her sister asks that she take her share of responsibility for their mother, who now comes to live with Janna. Mrs Somers is an aged, heavy, respectable suburban matron, whose appearance embarasses her fashionable daughter. Not long after her arrival, Mrs Somers is diagnosed as terminally ill with cancer. Although the doctors had not been able to talk candidly to Janna about what was happening to her husband, they could talk openly to her mother about what was happening to her, because she could deal with it, with dignity and strength. For the first time, Janna wants to be like her mother. Now, wanting to do all the things daughters should, she cannot stand her mother's physical awfulness in her last stages of cancer — yellow, glistening skin, bones showing. She wants to kiss her mother and hold her in her arms at the end, when she is being brave:

> I couldn't touch her not really. Not with kindness. The smell ... and they say it isn't infectious, but what do they know? Not much. She used to look at me straight and open. And I could hardly make myself meet her eyes. It wasn't that her look asked for anything. But I was so ashamed of what I was feeling, in a panic for myself.[13]

When her mother is removed to hospital, Janna visits every day, hating every second, unable to think of what to say. She feels she has let both her husband and mother down and that that is the type of person she is.

After the death of her mother, she is attracted, while shopping, to the aged Mrs Maudie Fowler. Maudie with grime on her old neck and hands, has a sweet, sour, dusty smell, but once she had been as concerned for cleanliness as Janna. She is now one of the many sad, angry old ladies, who cling to their independence through the degrading incapacities and incontinence of their last years — old ladies, for whom the rare affections and treats of their childhood and their girlhood working years shine like rare jewels in a string of hard times. They have been mothers and surrogate mothers to many who have now forgotten them.

> Why aren't they in a home? Get them out of the way, out of sight, where young healthy people can't see them, can't have them on their minds.[14]

Because her mother has taught her she must keep promises, Janna goes back again and again to Mrs Fowler, to clean her house, prepare her food, show her her clothes. Maudie loves clothes. She was once a milliner's apprentice and enjoys admiring Janna's boots, and her crêpe de chine camisoles and walks around her laughing with pleasure at pretty things. In turn, she tells Janna fascinating stories of her sad childhood: of a philandering father, who cruelly neglected her mother; of her exploitation by the milliner and a married sister; of her own failed marriage and a loved child disappearing into a void, stolen from her by her neglectful husband.

Maud is an angry, difficult, old lady, so old that incontinence and failure to wash is habitual. She does not want to go into an old people's home. She is fiercely independent, ashamed of her incontinence, her ill-kept rooms, pleased when Janna is doing things for her. But her pride hurts. She expects a lot of Janna and is helpless and frantic because she does. Their relationship seethes with emotion, ambivalence and love.

Janna has become Maudie's surrogate daughter and does for Maudie what she would have liked to have done for her mother and could not. She washes Maudie, as she had not washed her mother, and finds the vitality beneath the skin and bones of the fierce, angry old lady who does not always say thank you, who is often stand-offish and who is so angry about her helplessness, that she can only acknowledge help grudgingly. Lessing's characterisations of Maudie and the old ladies in her neighbourhood offer marvellous and sympathetic insights into why these old ladies are angry and behave as they do.

Maudie too has cancer and must go to hospital, when care at home is no longer possible and the pain is unbearable. She is very angry at having to die because, she says, Janna's coming has made it the best time of her life. She is 92 and her life is in sharp contrast to that of her successful, surrogate daughter, Janna, but life is still precious. She struggles to survive, is put in an old people's home and cries when Janna visits her: "Lift me up. Lift me up". She begs to be taken home with Janna. It is painfully poignant, but Janna is sufficiently steadfast to know that it is unfair to herself to take on the exhausting full time task of looking after Maudie.

Janna is not with Maudie when she dies. The night nurse accidentally spilled her pain killing medicine. Did she die in pain? Lessing has a special skill in arousing the evocative, heart-rending images that remain with us after the death of someone who arouses guilt, love and anger.

While Janna is being surrogate daughter to Maudie, she is surrogate mother to her two nieces. One, Jane, takes her as a model and becomes successful in Janna's field of work. Janna provides a positive role, which Jane's mother could not. The second niece is a different matter. Her parents cannot face up to the fact that she is not a success. Not only is she not a success, she cannot take responsibility for her own survival; she lives off others like a parasite and in so doing is destructive toward herself and others. Janna's attempts to save this surrogate daughter do not work. In part, she must admit defeat but she can also end a relationship that is destructive.

These attempts at mothering and daughtering change Janna Somers' vision of herself and the world. She learns her own strength and how much she can give and take. In short, she has learnt who she is. She has worked through the guilt and disappointment of her relationship with her mother and has set herself free. At last, the inner space that is self is expansive enough to allow love and she falls in love for the first time. It does not have a happy ending, as the man is already contentedly married to a successful wife, but the loving and the experience is valued.

Positive Images of Separation

The most effective therapy is to know that a sense of separation can be achieved, alongside a warm and continuing relationship. The key is independence, in both mother and daughter. Indeed, in my research, it was notable how proud some daughters were of independent mothers. One daughter, Yvette, in her twenties, described a mother who was doing voluntary work overseas.

"It does a lot for my feeling of worth. Miriam's (a friend's) mother lies in bed all day demanding that she visit her constantly. She's a wreck worrying about it and now says she's just got to cut herself off from her mother. I love it when Mum's in town. We talk a lot. I like taking holidays with her too."

Another, Amanda, described her mother, in her eighties, with considerable pride.

"She's off on a holiday on the South Coast. She gets about a lot and looks very smart. It makes me feel good. I hope I'll be like that when I'm 82."

Both these daughters were as independent as the mothers they described.

"She's always told me I could do things. She's good for my self-esteem. Sometimes, when my friends have been difficult and prickly, I go through a down; then Mum turns up and I know that I'm worth a lot. Mind you it's not all apple pie. We have lots of arguments about attitudes to people and social issues, but the thing is that you feel that she digests what you are saying — maybe not today or tomorrow, but eventually. Of course, I recognise that it's a two-way process and I try to give her as much as she gives me."

The notable thing about Yvette and Amanda was that they did not use their mothers as sponges. They not only accepted them on their own terms, but theirs were reciprocal relationships of empathy and listening. They wanted to be and were close, because they were independent. As Joan had belatedly discovered in Margaret Attwood's novel, *Lady Oracle*, they knew that daughters, who blame their mothers, more often than not have themselves not let go. Independence and emotional separation are two-way processes.

Bella, aged 35, was a warm hearted mother of four and a popular schoolteacher. She said her own very unhappy childhood had taught her how important self-responsibility is.

"Daughters need to understand that once past 18, they are responsible for themselves. If they keep blaming their mothers, they will never be close. True closeness comes when you have learnt that you are a separate person."

It is refreshing when one comes across individuals who are largely unaffected by the negative images of mothers. It is even more therapeutic when one finds whole communities that have lived through generations of patriarchy and retained something of the valuing of mothers, typical of long past eras. An example comes from an interesting and important study conducted by Michael Young and Peter Willmott in the 1950s in Bethnal Green in the East End of London. The notable thing is that the mother-daughter relationship is good, because mutual respect allows both independence and closeness.

The Mothers and Daughters of Bethnal Green

The relationship between Bethnal Green mothers and daughters is in strong contrast to those of middle class daughters of the 1950s, who were struggling with their 'monster' mother images.[15] Bethnal Green mothers and daughters were close and supportive of each other. After marriage, many of these working class daughters lived in the same street or in the same neighbourhood, as their mothers. At least fifty percent of these daughters saw their mothers every day and most at least once per week. The mother-daughter relationship was highly significant to both mother and daughter.

Willmott and Young quote a typical example from the study — Mrs Cole has one child at school and two under five. She lives with her husband and three children in the same street as her mother and describes how much each day involves some interaction with her mother:

> After breakfast I bath the baby and sweep the kitchen, and wash up. Then I go up the road shopping with Mum, Greta (one of her married sisters who has a young child), and three children. After dinner I clean up and then round about 2 o'clock I go out for a walk if it's fine with Mum and Greta and the children. I come back about quarter to four to be in time for Janice when she gets back from school. She calls in at Mum's on her way home just to see if I'm there. This is an ordinary day. If anything goes wrong and I'm in trouble, I always go running round to Mum's.[16]

The daily lives of these women are not confined to the places where they sleep; they are spread over two or more households in which they regularly spend part of their time. They are extended families. The mother is the head and centre of the extended family and her home is its meeting place. Her daughters congregate at the mother's, visiting her more often than she visits any one of them. In addition to weekly meetings, which involve husbands and brothers as well, there are special family gatherings at the mother's house for birthdays and wedding anniversaries — Mum's own birthday being one of the occasions of the year. In one family, the daughter explained the significance of the event.

> "My Dad died when I was 14. Mum was a brick. Even if we never had shoes on our feet, we always had good grub. She always kept a good table. I'm going to get a special party together for next year when Mum is 80. Since we've had a family of our own, we realise how Mum's worked for us in the past."[17]

In Bethnal Green in the 1950s, Mum plays an important part in the life of her extended family. She is honoured and the warmth contained in the way "Mum" is said, conveys the respect in which she is held:

> "Since her status as 'Mum' is so high, it is derogatory to call her by any other name. Mrs Gould for one, thinks the use of any mere Christian name a disgusting example of the 'American' way of doing things."[18]

Most daughters take it for granted that Mum belongs on a pedestal. "I'm very devoted to Mum, of course, that's understood with mothers and daughters," says Mrs Warner and, like many others, leaves it at that, as a statement of the obvious, hardly worth making.[19] This is a far cry from the belief in the inevitability of hostility between mothers and daughters and the accompanying denigration of mothers.

The sentiment of affection for Mum in this East End sample is strong, partly because mothers, as well as acting as the organisers of social life, perform so many important services for their daughters. Helping at childbirth is one important service and the daughter draws on the knowledge of her mother, who has been through it all before. Her doubts, fears and hopes are discussed with the person who is the close companion of her daily life, and support is provided by relatives, not government services. Mum looks after her daughter's home during her daughter's confinement.

The 'expert' has not ousted Mum as he has in middle class circles. The daughter knows her mother has an advantage over the male expert, because she is a woman, and over the female expert, who may be unmarried and childless, in that she has been a mother herself. When the daughter gets contradictory advice from the welfare clinic and her mother, it is usually Mum to whom she listens. After the birth of the baby, Mum looks after him or her regularly, while the daughter shops. If a daughter and her husband want to go out for the evening, the children are taken to stay with the daughter's mother.

The relationship, between mother and daughter and her daughter's husband, is not entirely without conflict. The mother may uphold traditions with which the daughter and her husband may not agree, such as "churching" or going to church as soon as possible after the confinement to be "cleansed", for example. Even so, most daughters comply with their mothers' wishes and, even if they resent the interference, they accept them as a necessary presence in their lives.

In the grandparent hierarchy, it is the wife's mother who is paramount. On the whole, the Young and Willmott Bethnal Green study, found that the grandchildren saw more of the maternal grandmother than they did the paternal grandmother, although not to her exclusion.

In some kinship systems, alongside marriage, it is the relationship between fathers and sons that is important. In Bethnal Green, in the 1950s, the most significant relationship, alongside that of marriage, is between mother and daughter. The mother is not cut off from her daughter by marriage.

In school and in work, the daughter, as well as the son, withdrew from the mother's home. As long as she was working in a man's world, the daughter behaved in many ways like a man and, like her brother, clocked on at a factory and earnt her own money to spend as she chose. But when she marries, and even more importantly when she leaves work to have children, she returns to the woman's world and to her mother. Marriage divides the sexes into distinctive roles, and so strengthens the relationship between the daughter and her mother who has been through it all before. The old proverb applies:

My son's a son till he gets him a wife;
My daughter's a daughter all her life.

Overview

The ability to separate our inner selves from those of our mothers is the crucial factor in viable mother-daughter relationships. Separation has as many facets as there are developmental stages throughout childhood and adulthood. In the beginning, it involves a mother recognising that her newly-born daughter is an individual. It involves valuing her individuality, rather than surrendering to disappointment because she is not as expected or as wanted. The story of Aggie and June made this point and carried it further. It showed that defining mothers and daughters solely in terms of fixed roles and expectations results in stress and poor mother-daughter relationships. In adulthood, emotional separation — creating a separate identity each — is the key to good relationships. Often, daughters, who feel enraged and entrapped, have themselves not let go of their mothers.

There are many kinds of separation which mothers and daughters must negotiate.[20] The final separation in death may be the hardest, not only because of the finality of the loss, but because guilt about poor relationships has not been resolved. Working through unresolved guilt with surrogate mothers and daughters can be therapeutic. Illustrations were found in Janna Somers' relationships with Maudie Fowler and her niece, Jane.

There are other separations — imposed separations — perhaps the loss of a mother in childhood. In their novels, the Brontës have dealt with the effect of such a loss so evocatively — so much more vividly than psychology can — I have left this topic to a discussion of their lives in Book II.

This chapter concluded with some cheerful examples of positive mother-daughter relationships and how these had been achieved.

So far, we have explored many aspects of mother-daughter relationships, including self-esteem, just communities for mothers, the role of fathers, patriarchal stereotypes that put mothers and daughters asunder, unsatisfied needs for love in daughters, the crucial factor of emotional separation and other issues.

Throughout Book I, I have selected the most relevant parts of many theories to help in the interpretation of mother-daughter relationships and conflicts. Sometimes, there have been references to Freudian theory and psychoanalysis, with comments about their value or otherwise for mother-daughter relationships. These theories have had a pervasive influence on mother-daughter relationships and are much used by professionals. Some feminists have tried to reinterpret them. Others feel they offer a restrictive and erroneous view of mothers and daughters.

For the reader who hasn't the time to chase references but is interested in major trends in, and discussions of, these theories, I have selected a mixture of opinions by leading practitioners and feminists. These are outlined in the next chapter. It is not possible to look at the theories fully as feminist theories. Many books exist which review such matters. In the next chapter, I concentrate simply on those aspects of the theories, discussions and arguments that relate to mother-daughter relationships and the issues raised in this book.

❧

BIBLIOTHERAPY

Throughout this chapter, I've suggested some reading relevant to the issues it has raised: Margaret Attwood's *Lady Oracle*, Joan Barfoot's *Duet for Three* and Doris Lessing's *The Diaries of Jane Somers*. For the effect of separation through loss in childhood read any of Charlotte Brontë's novels and her Juvenilia and Virginia Woolf's *To the Lighthouse*, among others. These are discussed in Book II. For the difficulties of separating from a charismatic and publicly prominent mother, read Kim Chernin's, *In My Mother's House*. For the tragedy of a daughter who cannot separate from her mother, see Jean Bedford's *Love Child*

❧

CHAPTER 8

Freud and Feminists on Mothers and Daughters

Who Best Describes Your Case?

There are many self-respecting women who have established satisfactory relationships with their mothers, who say that psychoanalytic and feminist theories about mothers and daughters have no meaning for them. Said Rosslyn, a secretary in a large metropolitan hospital:

> "I know some psychoanalytic ideas, because I often type lectures and papers for the psychiatrists on the staff. When the book *My Mother My Self* by Nancy Friday, first came out, they and the family therapists were all reading it and said it was great. One of them lent me a copy and I recognised how much it had been influenced by psychoanalytic concepts. What the book had to say was nothing like my relationship with my mother. I felt Friday didn't like mothers and that she'd talked to a lot of therapists who didn't either. Nevertheless, I'm glad I read her book because I can see where these therapists are coming from and how careful anyone who goes to them for help needs to be."

Rosslyn's reactions are not unusual.

Trudi, a teacher, told how she was invited to a feminist meeting on motherhood.

> "I went along wanting some insight into how to avoid repeating, with my daughter, the stress that my mother and I went through. Unfortunately, it was all head talk — nothing they said was practical. I heard names like Irigaray and Kristeva, French and other feminist psychoanalytic writers. I was lent their books, but it was all semantics to me. These authors are talking to each other, like the women at the meeting. They are not trying to communicate with women like me; and what about black women, working class women, Aboriginal women and women who are not from white middle-class western culture? Where does all this wordiness help them when they want to work out how to get on with their mothers? So many feminist writers need to translate what they are saying into practicalities and throw their ideas open for discussion

among all kinds of women, not just themselves."

Trudi's attitude is also not unusual and it is for mothers and daughters like her that this chapter has been written.

Julia, a part-time solicitor with four daughters, also complained that many feminists, particularly professional and academic ones, are writing and talking for each other.

> "I'd like to know more about what they are trying to say, but I'm too busy to afford the luxury of spending days in libraries or going to meetings to talk endlessly about theory. They seem to have contempt for those of us who are at the coal face with our mothers and our daughters."

Julia and her friends urged me to set up some seminars where they could select and examine theoretical feminist and psychoanalytic material that made sense in relation to their own experiences. They were not specialists, but genuinely interested in what feminist and psychoanalytic theory might tell them about the hidden agendas in their relationships with their mothers. The participants monitored, not only their own attitudes but mine, at all the meetings.

> "We were so pleased when you stopped that argument about Melanie Klein[1] and Winnicott[2] and gave the protagonists a reading list of feminist discussions of these two. It was purely an argument for professionals and the rest of us were cut out."

or

> "We felt much better after you reminded that little clique in the front row that a great deal has been written on women and psychoanalysis and that the meeting wasn't about that, but what is in these theories for mothers and daughters."

There was a lot of laughter at these seminars and sometimes irritation and anger. What is written in this chapter is based on the preferences of the mothers and daughters as well as a few fathers, who attended. I've quoted critiques by well-known authors, but in all cases they've been chosen because they are similar to critiques produced by a general audience interested in practicalities. Some aspects of the feminist and psychoanalytic theories outlined here have already been mentioned in previous chapters, especially if they have practical applications. Here, to give more of the overall flavour, I introduce more detail than was previously possible.

Since his ideas are so crucial to many feminist and psychoanalytic theories about mothers and daughters, I begin with Sigmund Freud. I will try to summarise the few conjectures Freud made about mother-daughter relationships and the pertinent aspects of his theory of gender. As we have seen, gender is crucial to mother-daughter relationships.

Freud's View of Mothers and Daughters

Freud acknowledged that his theory of women, and his few conjectures about mothers and daughters, were based on how they responded to the coercions of patriarchy — an attitude that has been endorsed here. He addressed the bisexual disposition of human beings, which I discussed in Chapter 4. There, I explored how social coercions result in different outcomes for daughters and sons, in relation to their mothers. For Freud, the great puzzle was how that bisexuality became the socialised dichotomy, that is man and woman in the patriarchal family. From this promising beginning, Freud came to regard bisexuality in women as more problematic than for men. Because such generalisations on his part were based on his own interpretation of the experiences of the women who came to him for analysis, inevitably there are doubts about their validity.[3] The research evidence given in earlier chapters of this book suggests the reverse of Freud's views — in particular, it disagrees with Freud's view that the fluidity of women's sexuality has negative outcomes for mother-daughter relationships.

Freud's theory about mother-daughter relationships begins with the insatiability of a child's demand for love. Her, or his, inevitable frustration leads to violent feelings. The mother simply cannot give the baby enough and, according to Freud, this lays the foundation for many subsequent ambivalences and resentments. Although some evidence for this was presented in previous chapters of this book, the unequal responsibility of mothers in the caring role was taken into account. Freud did not always acknowledge such social factors and his literal and conjectural extensions of his observations are regarded as notorious male projections — for example, his claim that not only does a daughter blame her mother for the fact that she is a girl but also for her lack of a penis.[4] If the penis is intended merely as symbolic of the power men have, then the theory has some currency. But careful reading suggests that ultimately the intention is quite literal — girls, said Freud and his followers, suffer from penis envy.[5]

By the age of four, when a small girl discovers the anatomical differences between the sexes, she reacts to the absence of the penis by acquiring a castration complex. According to Freud, she imagines she has been mutilated and penis envy remains with her for the rest of her life. This arrogant phallocentricism is belied by the evidence. Women may envy men their power, but they do not envy them their penises. Far from it.[6]

At puberty, a daughter particularly blames her mother for the restrictions placed upon her sexual life. Again, Freud was not primarily concerned with the social and economic reasons for this. He was more concerned to show that later love patterns are built on the primary love relationship with the mother. The unsatisfied content of the love relationship of early years can be transferred to other love objects and particularly the husband, who replaces the mother in the daughter's affections. But there is insufficient exploration of the feminine perspective and the complex deprivations which mothers and daughters suffer in the patriarchal family. Nor are the positive aspects of the primary love relationship given sufficient attention. All these issues were addressed in earlier chapters of this book.[7]

Not only did Freud give little emphasis to the responsibility of the patriarchal family for children's ambivalent attitudes toward their mothers, he saw this ambivalence as more difficult for daughters than sons — an argument that has not found support in the research quoted in this book. Freud's reasoning will become apparent a little later, when the work of Jane Flax is discussed. He held that children try to master their ambivalent feelings in play and both boys and girls have a fear of being killed by the mother, which is transformed into an active death wish against her. Both also wish to give the mother a baby, or to have some hand in the birth of a new brother or sister. Freud's most famous description of this contention is the case of Little Hans.[8]

According to Freud, the five year old boy, in his anxiety about the power and anger of his father, gives up his sexual desire for his mother and identifies with the power and domination of his father. As a consequence, this strong identification with the father leads to the development of a strong superego, or moral conscience. Thus, the son resolves the oedipal conflict. The daughter, on the other hand, states Freud, does not have a strong figure with whom to identify, since she remains attached to her mother; hence her superego and moral conscience is weaker. The prejudices of this contention about the moral inferiority of women and their impact on mother-daughter relationships have already been examined in earlier chapters and will be addressed again later in the analysis of Carol Gilligan's work.[9]

Freud further exposes his Victorian proclivity for patriarchally biased interpretations when he goes on to say that the child-daughter envies her mother and tries to seduce her father[10] — an interpretation that should be noted for its projection of adult male ways of thinking onto the child. He goes on to say that the small daughter is frustrated that she cannot be like her father, but is compensated by the affection she inspires in him. She suppresses her incestuous wishes and this contributes to the development of her superego. Interpreting the affectionate ways in which young daughters approach their fathers, as having the same sexual objectives as adult coquetry, partly sanctions blaming children for child sexual abuse. It also sets up a stereotype of females competing for men and encourages mother-daughter conflict.

But more damaging interpretations follow. As a result of suppressing her oedipal desires for the father, says Freud, the daughter becomes passive. She salvages what is left of her sexual drive and devotes it to the passive aim of being loved. In order to be loved and in recognition of her "inferior" clitoris, a daughter compensates by offering her body as a sex object. She is prepared to accept the sexual desire of her partner for her body as a substitute for love.[11] Simone de Beauvoir who is discussed later in the chapter, argued that it is men who objectify women and their sexuality and that women's compliance is a result of coercion rather than initiation. Failing to recognise this, Freud claimed that a woman is both passive and vain.

The problem is that one cannot always ascertain whether Freud is talking about a fundamental disposition or an end product of social pressures. He does say that the outcome of the developmental processes he has described is a feminine personality which is suitable to the patriarchal society. Whatever his true understanding, many of his followers believed he was talking about a fundamental inferiority in the female. In this frame of mind, they accepted without question his contention that a daughter and her mother are both masochistic and passive and have a limited sense of justice. Masochism, or pleasure in pain, is an outcome of the turning of the wish for the satisfaction of the sexual and autonomous drives against the self. In the female, it is expressed in the wish to submit to copulation and child-birth and to get pleasure from pain. This, said Freud, is the feminine predicament.

As I have demonstrated here, this attitude that females are the weaker sex — physically, psychologically and mentally — has set mothers and daughters in contempt of each other. The attitude does not have to be accepted as fact and incorporated into a self-degraded view that keeps mothers and daughters at odds.

According to Freud, in the original resolution of the oedipal conflict, the boy made the break from the mother. The daughter's separation is delayed until adolescence and hence is of necessity quite radical and a source of much mother-daughter conflict. Some girls leave home but not their mothers. Freud wrote:

> When a mother hinders or arrests a daughter's sexual activity, she is fulfilling a normal function whose lines are laid down by events in childhood, which has powerful unconscious motives, and has received the sanction of society. It is the daughter's business to emancipate herself from this influence and to decide for herself on broad and rational grounds what her share of enjoyment or denial of sexual pleasure will be.[12]

There are several problems with this argument — the major one being the patriarchal fear of mother-daughter closeness. Secondly, if a woman decides she wants and assumes the same sexual freedom as men, she is likely to be seen as unworthy of her sex within patriarchal society. Thirdly, there are more positive ways of interpreting the mother's protective behaviour, as Flax indicates later in the chapter.

Nevertheless, Freud rightly stated that middle class families of his time, largely repressed any expression of sexuality in their daughters, in fear that they would not make good marriages. As a result, Freud believed many married women were able only to enjoy sex in adultery, when the condition of prohibition is re-established.[13] He spoke of the woman who was too "cowardly" or "moral" to console herself with another man, while remaining sexually unsatisfied with her husband. Such women, he believed, may find a substitute in neurosis, or in over-sexualising their relationship with their children. This cannot be tolerated because of the sexual taboo and so they establish the conditions for neurosis in their daughters. This, as Freud sees it, is the contradiction of the family under patriarchy.

Freud realised that his psychology of women was inadequate and admitted that his comments on infancy and the pre-oedipal period were fragmentary. He could not imagine what course psychological development would take outside the patriarchal family.[14] However, he did believe that such a family generated the conflict which lay at the heart of neurosis. He first suggested that this neurosis is a result of sexual seduction by a family member in childhood. Later, he decided that reports of seductions were fantasies, based on wish fulfilment[15] — a concept which was subsequently interpreted in such a way that sexual abuse, reported by children, was often denied. Until recently, generations of daughters have been left without human rights, by the very theories that were supposed to assist understanding of human behaviour.

Masochism in Women?

Let us now return to Freud's assumption that females are masochistic and take pleasure in pain — a damning view that turns women into willing victims and perpetuates mother-daughter disrespect. The assumption became even less valid when it was separated from its sociological basis. Followers of Freud tended to regard masochism as innate to the female sex and that view has influenced psychoanalysis for decades.

One of many feminist psychologists who has demolished this concept is Paula Caplan. In *The Myth of Women's Masochism*,[16] she asks why it is that women's behaviour is used as evidence of innate masochism, while men's similar behaviour is used as evidence that they are real men and good providers. For example, observe the sympathy for the businessman who drives himself to a heart attack to augment the more than sufficient income he already has. Compare him to the contemporary "superwoman", who may have three children and a full time job and is perpetually run off her feet. She is often denigrated as a masochist, when in fact she may relish living life to the full, enjoying both motherhood and employment.

The belief that women seek out pain and suffering — that they have an innate need for misery — derives from the old Christian adage that a woman's lot is to suffer. This adage survives and encourages women to see themselves derogatorily as victims. It is not a good model to hand on to one's daughter, especially when so called masochism in women most often has other explanations.

The theory of women's masochism is a no-win theory. If it is demonstrated that women do not consciously want to suffer, it is said the wish remains unconscious. If women do express righteous anger, it is said to be unfeminine. If women appropriately direct blame at the cause of their unhappiness, it is said to destroy close personal relationships — a guiding principle in women's lives. A misogynist society has created innumerable situations that make women unhappy and yet that same society uses the myth of women's masochism to blame the women themselves.

The myth that women like to suffer justifies pornographic descriptions of women in bondage (she enjoys it). It excuses wife battering (she brought it on herself). It sanctions Jewish mother jokes, teenage prostitution and, most appallingly, mental health workers' confident assumptions that their women patients are enjoying their suffering.[17]

In fact, the abused wife most often stays with her abusing husband, not because she enjoys pain and fear, but out of economic necessity, or terror that relatives, neighbours and the law will see her as having failed in her wifely and motherly duty. She may also have good reason to believe that, if she leaves, her husband will find and kill both her and her children.

More often than not, teenagers who work as prostitutes do so, not because they are masochistic, but for economic and other necessities. They work for the money and the power they have over clients. They like the admiration they sometimes receive for their bodies or sexual skills. Most significantly, they come from severely, emotionally deprived backgrounds and what they have now — however degrading — is better than anything they have known before.[18]

The myth of women's masochism is female psychology turned on its head to justify patriarchal injustice. Caplan points out that the behaviour in women that has been called masochistic is actually one of the following:

1. The ability to delay gratification, wait for rewards and pleasure, or attempt to earn happiness through effort;

2. The capacity to put other people's needs ahead of one's own;

3. The belief, based on past experience, that what one has is about all one can expect to get; or

4. The effort to avoid punishment, rejection and guilt.

In fact, concludes Caplan, the most extreme cases of masochism are men, plagued by guilt about sex and other matters. Our daughters need our explanations of these facts, so that they do not become prey to false labels and false blaming. Moreover, ridding ourselves of false and derogatory descriptions increases our self-esteem and improves the mother-daughter relationship.

Female masochism is only one among a number of conjectures about the moral inferiority of women found in Freudian and psychoanalytic theories.[19] That it is part of the propaganda directed at demoralising mother-daughter relationships becomes apparent in the lack of attention to scientific controls and to the uncontrolled intervening variables in many such psychoanalytic generalisations. These are commonly regarded as among its major flaws.[20] There is the added problem that psychoanalytic research is often based on individual examples rather than systematic research. Despite these shortcomings, it has a devoted following and is regarded by its critics as having the status of a religion rather than a science.

Nevertheless, before many of these issues were fully discussed, several feminists adopted Freud's theory. There are indeed useful insights to be found in his and other psychoanalytic theories and some have been used in this book, where there is research evidence for them.

Early Feminists and Freud

One early example of a feminist who explored the value of Freudian insights for women is Juliet Mitchell. In a sterling work entitled *Psychoanalysis and Feminism*,[21] she tried to define the affinity she thought women should find in the patriarchally oriented work of Sigmund Freud. She believed his theories attempted the beginning of an explanation of the "inferiorised" and "alternative" (second sex) psychology of women under patriarchy. Mitchell argued that his descendants and followers did not always understand that he was talking about mothers and daughters under patriarchy.[22] If this is so, argue his critics, then the confusion has been compounded by the fact that Freud himself often conveyed the impression that, what he was talking about, was in the nature of things and not subject to culture.

Indeed, Mitchell herself believed in the universality of the oedipus and associated castration complex in women (where is my penis? was it chopped off?). As we have seen this attitude is phallocentric and not based on how women view their sexual organs. She also believed that the cultural order had been invariably patriarchal. The evidence and arguments against this belief is found, not only in systematic research and modern feminist writings, but the writings of many neo-Freudians. Their arguments are discussed in Book II and are important in restructuring a social order which frees mothers and daughters of the patriarchal denigration that puts them asunder.

Later, in response to the misconceptions of theorists like Mitchell, Gerda Lerner,[23] whose work was introduced in the Preface, made some statements that many feminists found threatening. She argued that women have participated in the construction of their own subordination throughout history. They have participated in the androcentric or male-centred fallacy, because all too often they have lacked knowledge and experience outside the belief that the viewpoint of men embraces all human experience. In the past and to this day, many have so internalised patriarchal learning, that they have lost the ability to conceive of alternatives. Mothers and daughters need to examine where they have succumbed to this situation and lost the ability to measure each other in anything but patriarchal terms.

Lerner argues that not even the feminists can congratulate themselves that they are free of patriarchal bigotry. She admires and acknowledges the ground-breaking work of many modern feminists — some of whom are discussed in this chapter. However, she believes that their single-minded engagements in dialogues with patriarchal theorists mean they remain within the confines of patriarchal thinking. As long as they do this, sources of new insights are closed to them. She argues that feminists now need to step outside and beyond the patriarchal models they have borrowed from such as Freud, Marx, Engels, the Bible and other philosophies which have held sway from antiquity to the present.

Optimistically, she believes that historical development has now created the necessary conditions by which women can create their own philosophies, untainted by patriarchal bigotry. These can educate and bring about social organisations in which women are not the second sex. Once women have cast off the role of the second sex, they can look at their mothers and daughters with more clarity.

Are there any such feminist philosophies? Toward the end of this chapter, I discuss one by Carol Gilligan, who is leading the way to a genuine psychology of women. But first, I shall give an introduction to several who began the dialogues of which Lerner is speaking — dialogues in which women have tried to establish a rapprochement between feminism and the theories of Sigmund Freud. They were trying to go further than Mitchell and give a more female-centred approach. Here, the focus is on the outcome of their endeavours for mother-daughter relationships.

Rapprochement Between Freud and Feminism

Adrienne Rich's View of Mother-Daughter Relations

Adrienne Rich is one of several feminists who has used a Freudian or psychoanalytic framework to describe what she sees as the basis of mother-daughter conflict in contemporary society. Her work shows the value of an interdisciplinary approach. She follows in the footsteps of many members of the psychoanalytic school who look to history to illustrate the psychological arena.[24] Rich is particularly interested in prehistory, where she finds evidence that mother-daughter relationships were better than today because these societies were more women-centred.[25]

But women-centred societies were conquered by the early patriarchies, who set a pattern of investment in political and economic power to compensate for their inability to give birth. Their identity became synonymous with power over others, beginning with women and their children. As a result, women became colonised people and like all colonised people they came to be described as weak, incapable of self- government, ignorant, irrational and in need of firm control. Like all denigrated peoples, they sometimes turned on each other. Rich is not impressed with the characteristics that the men of power extol, such as "detachment", "objectivity", "sanity". She sees them as willfully ignorant of inner, psychic life. She believes that, under patriarchy, men become victims of "moral stupidity" and possessed of "inner chaos" and "emptiness".

Rich's philosophical feminism is derived from psychoanalytic research which has tried to assess socialising influences upon men and why they are so intent upon controlling and denigrating women and mother-daughter relationships. The psychoanalytic studies of male envy, by Karen Horney[26] and Bruno Bettelheim,[27] provided insights for her ultimate viewpoint. Along with Horney, Rich believes that under patriarchy, men have learnt to fear women and their power to create life and to see them as consumers of their sexual energies. Despite male dominance in every other sphere, a residual envy and resentment of women remains. This is denied by the psychological manoeuvre of devaluation. Patriarchy devalues femininity. It creates a dichotomy between feminine sexuality and motherhood. As a result, we have the sex symbol on the one hand and the mother on the other. Daughters find themselves in a dilemma: If I become/am a mother do I lose my sexual attractiveness?

Yet the mutual power to create life can provide a sense of continuity in mothers and daughters and a special bond between them. This is no doubt why it has always been prey to envy or attack of some kind. For example, Bruno Bettelheim has described male initiation rituals in which males try to imitate and magically share in the power of females to create life. The envious content of these ancient rituals can now be found in modern technology. Like many feminists, Rich argues that some of the highly dubious technology of obstetrics and the proliferation of hysterectomies, is a gradual attempt by a male dominated medical profession to extricate the process of birth from women and and call it its own.[28] One might add IVF programmes to this list.

The emphasis on sterilising women in the third world as a means of population control, rather than devoting more time to the study of new ways to produce and distribute food, also reflects a patriarchal need to control female reproductive power. Similarly, it is interesting that the emphasis on birth control in western society has, until recently, tended to concentrate on control of female reproduction, rather than male fertility.

Male fantasies about the power of women have found expression in tales, legends and art, since antiquity. Some of these are unpleasant, for example, woman as the vampire, controlling, castrating and guilt-provoking. Rich argues that these images contribute to an atmosphere of disrespect between mothers and daughters. Yet, women have tended to close their eyes to the patriarchal fear of female sexuality. They incorporate it into their concepts of themselves and avoid recognising its true nature. This is why women have accepted as just the patriarchal hatred of overt strength in women. They have allowed physical strength in women to be defined as a wish to castrate or control men. They have feared these tendencies in themselves. There is preference for dependent, malleable, gentle women. Mothers have handed on these proscriptions to their daughters and helped to perpetuate the powerlessness that puts mothers and daughters in contempt of each other.

Why is it that women have, for so long, overlooked men's secret dread of women? Women's obliviousness of this male dread, says Rich, is a manoeuvre to protect themselves from "anxiety and the impairment of self-respect". It is not successful. However much women try to render themselves pleasing and non-threatening, they still, to some extent, bear the imprint of the feared aspect of woman. As Rich interprets it: "Since politically and socially men do wield immense power over women, it is unnerving to realise that your mate or employer may also fear you".[29] And if a woman hopes to find not a master but a lover and an equal, how is she to meet this dread?

> If it brings to her intimations of a power inherent in her sex, that power is perceived as hostile, destructive, controlling, malign; and the very idea of power is poisoned for her. ... woman's primary experience of power till now has been triply negative; we have experienced men's power as oppression; we have experienced our own vitality and independence as somehow threatening to men, and, even when behaving with "feminine" passivity, we have been aware of masculine fantasies of our potential destructiveness.[30]

Rich recognises that daughters often feel angry and guilty about these contradictory expectations and that they direct their anger at their mothers because they share their predicament. Rich also observes that, as a result of their education, women deal with their anger by repressing it and then turning it against themselves. In particular, mothers take into themselves the cultural belief that all misfortunes in human psychological development stem from their inadequacies as mothers. At the same time, they act out their conflicts with their daughters, so these become the daughters' conflicts as well.

The inhuman expectations, involved in the concept of maternal responsibility and the subsequent guilt which is handed onto their daughters, is as central to Rich's theory as it has been to earlier chapters in this book. She describes the unbearable load of responsibility which becomes a woman's bondage and is often the cause of mother-daughter conflict. The research among mothers and daughters reported in this book provides testimony for her view.

The evidence in Chapter 6 gave support to another of Rich's tenets. A daughter's rejection of her mother may be an attempt to renounce the joint roles of the martyred mother, the super mum and the victim. Woman is not only the victim of exploitation and hostile projections as a mother. She is the victim in sadistic pornography and literary and television violence. She is the victim of patriarchy's violence, by rape on the streets and wife bashing in the home. Rich believes, and daughters have told us, that they are angry with their mothers for handing on this heritage.

The anger is compounded by a daughter's observation of the burdens her mother allows to be put on herself domestically and in the family. Her mother may bear the joint load of a job and most of the housework, without adequate help from a partner. She may be worn down by chronic worry over children and perhaps martyrdom to the demands of her male partner, which in some cases may be degrading.

The daughter's rage at her mother is likely to arise from the mother having relegated her to second class status, while looking to the son or the father for the fulfilment of her own thwarted needs. Rich writes:

> Many daughters live in rage at their mothers for having accepted, too readily and passively whatever comes. ... A mother's victimisation does not merely humiliate her, it mutilates the daughter who watches her for clues as to what it means to be a woman.[31]

Rich points to the fact that mothers, as victims, have carried their guilt and self-hatred over into their daughters' experience. Thus, in the past, not only the father, but the mother cast out the girl who was raped or bore a child out of wedlock. This self-hate among women who see themselves as victims and feel loathing for their mothers, who are also victims, is not unusual. Self-hate and loathing for others like them is generally found among people who are discriminated against, such as Jews, blacks and other minority ethnic groups.

Rich rejects these divisive ploys and argues that, because of their biologically alike bodies and biochemical affinities, there is the deepest mutuality between the mother and the female child.[32] Yet in patriarchal religion, art, literature and psychoanalytic theory, it is the mother and son who appear as the eternal, determinative dyad. This is not surprising, since throughout western history the patriarchs have controlled the selection of what shall be noticed, what shall be preserved or what shall be exhibited. They have tended to treat as significant only what men say and do.

Recent discoveries of exceedingly talented, but previously unknown, female writers and artists by feminist historians, offer support to these claims. Their research also indicates that female contributions to culture have been significant but disregarded as invalid, unreal, trivial or stupid. In this evaluative way, women's perceptions, experience and judgement have been excluded from the processes by which culture is created.[33]

In summary, Rich is saying that patriarchy has tried to ensure that all that mothers have to hand onto their daughters is a culture filtered through the perspective of men, which denies the experiences of their sex. She tries to counter this trend by offering evidence of ancient societies, where mothers and daughters had a central place and enormous pride in each other. This is a counter culture — a culture which provides mothers with a heritage to hand onto their daughters. In Book II, evidence of our heritage from antiquity to the present day is retrieved. The mother who introduces her daughter to the heritage of writings and portrayals, that are relevant to fighting for and establishing positive relationships, is laying the groundwork for a good relationship between herself and her daughter.

A Critique of Rich's Theory

Much of what Adrienne Rich has to say is highly pertinent to the experiences of the ordinary mothers and daughters, whom we have met in this book. Indeed, many of her valuable insights provided the framework for my initial research into mother-daughter relationships. Rich has obviously borrowed extensively from psychoanalysis and gained much from it.

Earlier in the chapter, I aired concern that feminists who limit themselves to the psychoanalytic model may unwittingly hand on patriarchal prescriptions about women which damage mother-daughter relationships. Are there any such problems in Rich's theory? Gerda Lerner's constructive criticism of Rich's approach suggests some answers to that question.

Lerner admires Rich's ground-breaking contribution to the psychology and history of women.[34] Nevertheless, she feels that there are some patriarchal assumptions — a major one being the emphasis on women as victims.

First, the "women as victims" theory is not helpful to the kind of consciousness-raising that improves mother-daughter relationships. It undermines women's feelings of power and their belief in their ability to change things. Secondly, it is an incorrect perception. While all women have been victimised in certain aspects of their lives, at certain times more than others, "women are structured into society in such a way, that they are both subjects and agents".[35] The complex pull of contradictory forces upon women makes them simultaneously marginal and central to historical events. "Trying to describe their condition by the use of a term which obscures this complexity is counter productive".[36]

Lerner aptly quotes from an unpublished paper by Michelle Rosaldo:

> By challenging the view that we are either victims of cruel social rule or the unconscious products of a natural world that (most unfortunately) demeans us, feminists have highlighted our need for theories that attend to the way that actors shape their worlds; to interactions in which significance is conferred, and to the cultural and symbolic forms in terms of which expectations are organised, desires articulated, prizes conferred, and outcomes given meaning.[37]

In other words, mothers and daughters can achieve the conditions that make for good mother-daughter relationships.

There is much of value in Rich's research, says Lerner, but it occasionally suffers from the deficiencies of some other feminist psychological theories which do not give sufficient attention to the social context. It generalises from middle class people in industrialised nations, to the universal. She also slots Rich into a long line of feminist maternalists, who reason that women have been outside political power in patriarchal societies, but have a special entitlement to equality.

The theory of the special entitlement of women as mothers has had many supporters and is an important one. A nineteenth century supporter was George Eliot who saw mothers as better equipped than men to improve society, because of the strength embodied in their maternal roles. It must be said that Rich would not settle for Eliot's idea that women should confine themselves to influencing men, rather than taking an equal role in the political sphere.

Others who believed in the uniqueness of the rights of women were the "New Women" — a political group that emerged at the turn of the twentieth century. They reasoned that they were entitled to equality, not only because they were citizens and thus enjoyed the same natural rights as men, but because they were spiritually and morally superior to men by reason of the special sensibilities of women.

The problem with the "entitlement" view is that it is justified by claiming an élitist sexist position. This, of course, is exactly what men have been doing since patriarchy began. An élitist position is difficult to justify on egalitarian grounds.

Nevertheless, it can be said that Rich has a point. The differences in the socialisation processes of the sexes give women better empathetic and other humanistic skills. This means they have the making of better agents for reform. Men have to learn to free themselves from traditional thinking and become comfortable with sharing power. There must be a just community for both men and women.

In summary, where Rich relies on a patriarchal psychoanalytical model, she sometimes gives a gloomy analysis of women's position and its consequent destructive effect on mother-daughter relationships. But it must also be said that she is one who has made a major contribution to consciousness-raising in women. She offered women a past — a history. She is saying that mothers and daughters can understand how they have become as they are. They can rebuild relationships, if they are aware of the pressures on them. They need to recover the symbols that testify to their strength and creativity.

Nancy Friday's My Mother My Self

Nancy Friday is another who used the psychoanalytic framework to analyse mother-daughter relationships. However, whereas Rich's approach is a scholarly one, Friday's is journalistic. She interviewed psychoanalysts and her data is based on these interviews and her own opinion and experience. In this way, she effectively highlights some of the delusions about mother-daughter relationships under patriarchy. For example:

> We are raised to believe that mother love is different from other kinds of love. It is not open to error, doubt or to the ambivalence of ordinary affections. This is an illusion.[38]

or

If the child is encouraged to enter into collusion with mother to pretend that the maternal instinct conquers all, both will be stuck ever after with the mechanisms of denial and defense which cut them off from the reality of their mutual feelings; gone is any hope of true relationship between them.[39]

or

How many of us who live away from home, periodically go back to mother, perhaps at Christmas or on a birthday hoping that this time 'Everything will be different'? Grown women ourselves, we are still looking for, still tied to the illusion of the all-loving good mother.[40]

Friday is interested in the ways in which women try to find the affection they believe they did not get from their mothers. These manoeuvres were discussed in the studies reported earlier in this book. In accord with these, she acknowledges the martyrdom of mothers and is concerned with their use of their daughters as narcissistic extensions of themselves.[41] She argues that the seeds for good mother-daughter relationships are sown when the mother is not "parasitic", but has a life of her own. If the mother indicates that she made the decisions and the choices about becoming a mother, pursuing a career, staying home, taking up yoga or embroidery or karate or whatever, then she validates herself as an independent person.[42]

However, Friday falls prey to many divisive negativisms about the mother-daughter experience, because she sees it largely from a patriarchal perspective. To quote Judith Arcana:

Friday's work, despite her occasional comments about how things are changing, reinforces only the resentment and anger many women feel for their mothers, and is heavily weighted with the words of gynaecologists and therapists.[43]

For example, she makes much of penis envy and of sexual rivalry for the father between mother and daughter. She assumes greater jealousy between girls than boys and posits the original relationship with the mother as the prototype of all other disturbed relationships, including those with husbands. Such concepts have not been validated in the general population and have been explored in earlier chapters in this book. They are age old patriarchal stereotypes which promote conflict between women, especially mothers and daughters. Friday blames mothers far too much and does not allow sufficiently for cases outside her experience in the southern states of America. Nor does she have much to say about daughters who successfully individuate from their mothers. To quote Arcana again:

...(she) seems to be describing a society in which everyone is middle class and heterosexual, and certainly going to get married. Her analysis evidences no political context; in her book it is as if our mothers, in their perversity, somehow decided to socialise us to our detriment. This kind of analysis is not what women need. What we want is a telling of truths about women.[44]

Friday's "blame my mother" kind of determinism is not constructive. Like many theories, it perpetuates the reactionary concept of supreme maternal responsibility. It absolves daughters from responsibility for their own development in adulthood. It implies that any growth, or solving of identity problems, must be in spite of the mother. It implies that we cannot change what we have become without rejecting our mothers.

This runs counter to the experiences of the many mothers and daughters whose cases have been reported in this book. They've confirmed that we can change what we are and that changing can improve our relationship with our mothers.[45] If we go on accepting theories that blame mothers, we will never become independent persons. *Lady Oracle* by Margaret Attwood illustrated this point well.[46] On the whole, mothers do their best within their limitations. Virginia Woolf is one of several examples given in Book II who was able to evocatively describe the importance of letting go of mother-blaming. When she ultimately came to terms with the value of letting go of blaming her mother, she was able to accept her as she was and actualise her own potential.

Women Who Analyse Freud's Assumptions About Mothers and Daughters

SIMONE de BEAUVOIR

Many feminists have written critical and thoughtful analyses of Freud's theory, which have implications for mother-daughter relationships. They underline the unfortunate and burdensome image which some aspects of his theory put upon mothers and daughters. For example, Simone de Beauvoir, the French philosopher, novelist and author of *The Second Sex*, took issue with Freud for the masculinity of his early model. She challenged his assumption that the boy is the norm and the girl a deviation from it. She pointed out that he'd not paid sufficient attention to historical and social factors when he made this generalisation.[47]

De Beauvoir argued that Freud presented women as receptacles for man's alienation. Under patriarchy, woman is "The Other", the object. Man is the subject. He does not engage in reciprocal relationships with females, but is the psychic oppressor. Men proclaim that love is women's supreme accomplishment, but do not want to accept it. Thus a woman's life is empty. Her best alternative is the pursuit of religion and the love of God, which are substitutes for the adoration of man. This substitution was typical of de Beauvoir's mother and many Christian women in the ninteenth and early twentieth centuries. As a result of observing the tragedy of it, de Beauvoir stressed that both men and women need to regard each other as equals. Only then will the self-respect that is the basis of good relationships be achieved. This extends to mother-daughter relationships.

The problems of ideal motherhood under patriarchy was underlined for de Beauvoir through her relationship with her own mother. Her mother was the model subservient wife and devoted mother. She was fervently pious. Like most females at the turn of the century, her entire education had convinced her that the greatest thing for a woman was to become the mother of a family. Her mother's fulfilment of this role required that Simone play the dutiful daughter, which Simone tells us in a novel of that name, she did until she was eight. As a result, she led a stiflingly respectable childhood.

But as she grew older, she resented the limited, impossibly ideal and unassailable model of motherhood which her mother provided. She became critical of the dependency model for daughters and the cultural indoctrination that women are inferior. To escape this, she determined not to have any children. She rejected all that her mother stood for, in a way that Freud would predict. Nevertheless, she was able to portray the relationship with her mother in its complexity from the feminine perspective which, she argued, Freud's theories did not because he was not a woman.

In order to develop a sense of independence and self-respect, she rejected the model that prevailed for her sex in France in the early decades of this century. She incorporated her father's declaration that she had a "man's brain". It gave her confidence to create her own independent philosophy. Like many others, she needed to identify with the "superiority" of men to give herself the self-assurance to achieve in a man's world.[48] Unfortunately, this identification puts the core of one's femininity at a lower level. This was an inescapable feature of Simone de Beauvoir's self-view — a feature that troubles many mother-daughter relationships.

Feminists who have found a model in de Beauvoir are disappointed to learn that she subordinated so much of herself to Jean Paul Sartre.[49] They are disconcerted by her ambivalence toward women and their bodies. We cannot blame de Beauvoir. We have seen in this book that these are the patriarchal coercions which many daughters cannot put aside. It explains much of de Beauvoir's early intolerance and conflict with her mother. The coercions of her time were even more insidious than they are now.

Simone de Beauvoir exhibits her belief in man's transcendence in other ways. She accepts the Freudian view that it is male psychology and biology that has provided the drive to build civilisation.[50] De Beauvoir also believed that women have no history, no past, no religion of their own, which is why they lack the concrete means of organising themselves in defense of their own interests. Another common patriarchal error is apparent in her conjectures about prehistory and her belief that hunting was, from the beginning of time, seen as a superior pursuit, carried out by men. In fact, research evidence is to the contrary.[51] The main food supply in early societies was provided by the gathering activities of women, who had relatively high status as a consequence.[52] It was precisely Simone de

Beauvoir's lack of knowledge of women's history and her reliance on the androcentric scholarship available to her at the time, that lead her to endorse erroneous patriarchal generalisations[53] — generalisations which are the basis of the propaganda that causes mothers and daughters to disrespect each other.

In a much later book, *A Very Easy Death*, de Beauvoir re-examined her mother. She was now able to see her as a person, not just a disappointing model of a long-suffering mother. In tune with feminism's more positive appraisal of mothers in later decades, she wrote:

> My mother was awkwardly laced into a spiritualistic ideology; but she had an animal passion for life which was the source of her courage.[54]

This reassessment is de Beauvoir's constructive contribution to mother-daughter relationships. We can both recognise the patriarchal limitations of some of her thinking and take pride in what she achieved as a daughter. By the last two decades of the twentieth century she was respected as a pioneer of modern feminism. The French vilified her when *The Second Sex* was first published. Thirty years later, her death was nationally mourned and her funeral was attended by intellectual and political leaders as well as huge numbers of ordinary men and women.

JANE FLAX

Throughout earlier chapters, mention was made of Jane Flax and her excellent work on the separation of mothers and daughters. Flax also takes issue with Freud on many points. She disagrees that the watchful guardianship of the mother over the daughter's sexual activity must be interpreted negatively. Freud saw it as generating hostile relationships between mothers and daughters.[55] Flax believes this early care can be reinterpreted positively. Mothers can be seen by daughters as the original love object and "guardian" of their sexual activity. Flax also asks why boys were not seen by Freud as developing a similar hostility toward their own sex, since fathers are so prohibitive about them loving their mothers.

Like many before her, Flax argues that Freud lacked sufficient clinical experience with children and that his belief in the daughter's discovery of her castration is tenuous. He does not explore the mother's role in depth. He makes naive male-centred statements to the effect that a mother's relationship with her son is more perfect than, and less prone to the ambivalences of, all other human relationships.[56] His account of civilisation concentrates on the human pathological outcomes of patriarchal domination of women. He doesn't explain why this domination takes place.

Moreover, says Flax, Freud assumed that aggression is innate to humans, rather than a problem with social roots. Like Hobbes, he excludes from centrality the traits which are culturally attributed to females. These include sociability, nurturance and concern for dependent and helpless persons, which are prime factors in infantile experience. The empathetic and sociable aspects of the period, in which women are powerful in their children's lives, are not given due emphasis in his theory. They are not given due emphasis in most patriarchal theories, thereby denying the value of the characteristics of women's relationships in general and mother-daughter relationships in particular.

Flax is not wholly critical of Freud's theory. She retains some of its tenets about mother-daughter relationships and amalgamates these with more recent theories in order to interpret the behaviour of her female patients. She accepts the psychoanalytic adage that girls will complete their infantile phases of development less successfully than boys. In Chapter 2 of this book, I put a counter argument. However, Flax sees the social complexity of her claims. She recognises that patriarchy has devalued the female sex. This devaluation inhibits the mother's full endorsement of her female infant and makes her less available to her emotionally than to her sons. Thus, because they've not had enough mothering, "women are therefore more likely to retain a wish to return to the infantile state".[57] This makes blows to her self-esteem harder to bear. While this may apply to many women, in this book I've given illustrations of women who create good self-esteem for themselves, sometimes in the face of terrible odds. They hand this onto their daughters and enjoy a close bond with them.

Certainly, there is ample evidence for Flax's claim that many daughters crave mothering throughout their lives. However, although she recognises the influences of patriarchy, the craving for mothering is sometimes framed by her in a way that the "deficiencies" of mothers can be construed as the crux of the problem. Unfortunately, this means we are back with the patriarchal syndrome, "blame mothers for everything". The poor emotional education of men and the undervaluing of relationship skills under patriarchy, are among many other considerations that must be taken into account. I documented evidence for this in earlier chapters and showed how mothers and daughters tackle the problem.

Flax explains that the relationship between mothers and daughters is troubled if the mother is ambivalent about giving up the symbiotic stage (absorbed closeness during infancy), or if she is "parasitic" (reliving her own infancy through the child). In these situations, the child will find it more difficult to take pleasure in her developing capacities. By two years, boys like to disengage themselves into the wider world but girls keep closer to mothers.[58]

Girls are not rewarded for autonomy and feel a need to stay fused with the mother, because early infantile experiences were inadequate. This need is compounded by the mother. Because of her own infancy, the mother does not wish her daughter to individuate. As an adult, the daughter repeats the process, by thwarting her daughter's move toward autonomy.

Here, in an otherwise valuable description of female development, we have some of the problems encountered in Rich's theory. There is a great deal of emphasis on the plight of females. In Chapter 2, I advanced an argument that there are positive outcomes to a daughter's close and consistent relationship with her mother. I explained how autonomy and closeness go together. It is necessary to step outside the tunnel vision of patriarchal thinking, in order to gain new and comprehensive insights into mother-daughter relationships.

In explaining the early mother-infant relationship, Flax also resorts to the Freudian concept of penis envy. Admittedly, she reinterprets it as a symbol of sexual access to the mother, who is the daughter's first love object. Thus, she says, the small daughter desires to have a baby with the mother, so that the original symbiotic unity, or sense of being one with the mother, can be maintained.

Flax claims support not only from Freud but from Margaret Mahler, who was interested in the psychological development which ensures that an infant grows out of the original symbiosis with the mother and becomes an individual. Mahler attributes behavioural differences between boys and girls, during their disengagements from their mothers, to the daughter's discovery that she lacks a penis. Although Flax stresses that it should be interpreted symbolically, she adds:

> Boys do not have to grapple fully with their fathers as rivals until later because at this point their magic organ seems unthreatened. Yet the mother, too, is now devalued — not only did she fail to give her daughter a penis; but she turned out to be 'just a girl' as well.[59]

The use of the penis, even as a symbol, is a patriarchally-oriented one, and the concept does not convey the way in which contemporary women see the hierarchy of power. To most it is involved with the lesser training of men in empathy and care of others and their greater training in achievement and competition. This is the symbolism that is meaningful to the experience of women. As Carol Gilligan points out, women's notions of power and justice are different, not inferior as patriarchy would have.[60] When mothers and daughters come to understand this, they learn to value their sex and each other.

While the insights of neo-Freudians such as Flax may be pertinent to disturbed mother-daughter relationships, they have been overextended by others as typical of mother-daughter relationships in general. This reinforces the view, discussed in previous chapters, that the mother-daughter relationship is inevitably pathological. Moreover, Freudian and neo-Freudian interpretations offer few realistic means of overcoming the dilemmas they pose.[61] In fact, most seem to exacerbate them, by implying that mothers need to be more perfect and daughters more autonomous.

This chapter began with the query as to whether the overuse of patriarchal models is hindering new insights into mother-daughter relationships. I wish to stress that many of Flax's insights are valuable. It is simply necessary to be aware of how they can be extended beyond patriarchal strait-jackets.

NANCY CHODOROW

Nancy Chodorow is a philosophical feminist who criticised Freud for his sexism and for overlooking cultural influences in his description of gender differences. Her work is largely filtered through a neo-psychoanalytic framework. She regards psychoanalysis as providing a helpful understanding of early development. Providing one regards this patriarchal aspect of Chodorow's discussions with care, for reasons already discussed, she has some helpful things to say about mother-daughter relationships.[62]

The most valued aspect of her feminist interpretation of psychoanalytic theory is that it offers some insights into the processes of development, whereby gender is created out of the fact that women mother children. My own description of this has already been put in Chapter 2. Along with Chodorow, I believe identity development in daughters is less conflicted and problematic than it is for sons. Daughters do not have to reject the female behaviours that were incorporated into their self-view in the early years when their mothers were the main care givers. Here we part company with Flax.

Chodorow's philosophy gives support to some of the other research findings presented in Chapter 2. From infancy, the relationship with the mother differs in systematic ways for girls and boys. Since mothers are opposite in sex from their sons, they do not identify with them as they do with their daughters. They relate to them as different from themselves. After a period of experiencing themselves as physically merged with their mothers, boys define themselves as quite different from them.

Girls and boys both learn to expect infinite love from their mothers, but they also observe her powerlessness. For boys, the escape from powerlessness is via identification with their fathers and learning to see themselves as other than their mothers. The way in which they reject their feminine aspects was described in Chapter 2. Boys turn away from emotional expression toward action in the world. They learn to define themselves as more separate and distinct, with a greater sense of ego boundaries and differentiation. Their identification with men is not so much through interaction, but on an impersonal basis, through observation of their roles. Thus, they grow up well-suited to the impersonal and changing role requirements of occupational work, but ill-suited to child care.

Girls identify with the mother who, because she mothers children, imparts experience as continuous with others. Thus a daughter's experience of self, contains more flexible or permeable ego boundaries. The basic feminine sense of self is connected to the world; the basic masculine self is separate.

Because they keep their close, primary relationship with their mothers, daughters are prepared for greater participation in the spheres of relationships, while sons prepare for the public arena. As a result, Chodorow believes women are more able to relate to and anticipate their babies' needs.

Chodorow argues that we must look to motherhood in patriarchal soci-ety and the structures and relationships it engenders, if we wish to alter the relationships between the sexes and end the subordination of women. The testimonies of mothers and daughters reported in this book confirm that argument.

Chodorow also warns against psychoanalytic interpretations, which take only the viewpoint of the child and leave the mother as an object, rather than a self. She emphasises the necessity of both mother and child developing separate identities. If this is achieved, then a daughter can recognise her similarity, commonality and continuity with her mother, because she has developed enough of an unproblematic sense of a separate self. True empathy is possible, when one is confident that one is a separate being. Throughout this book, through the use of research and case studies, I have illustrated the importance of a sense of personal autonomy. I have emphasised that this is not the same thing as abandoning closeness with the mother or breaking the mother-daughter bond.

In Chapters 2 and 3, I discussed another matter in which I find some agreement with Chodorow — children and adolescents may experience their mothers as both nurturing and denying. The outcome is ambivalence toward their mothers. Chodorow is particularly interested in what she describes as the infant's pre-oedipal experiences of being merged with the mother, who is seen as overwhelming and denying. Like Dorothy Dinnerstein,[63] she believes that the present tendency to see these processes as an entirely female problem is best tackled by male participation in, and equal sharing of, parenting. But as Janet Sayers aptly states:

> Chodorow's argument for shared child care is only compelling so
> long as one overlooks, as does the object relations version of psy-
> choanalysis on which it is based, the way that child care and family
> life generally are structured by external factors.[64]

There are substantial obstacles to shared parenting. It must make finan-cial sense for men to take time off to look after children. It also depends on whether a man is willing to share child care, as well as the domestic chores.

Paula Caplan is another who is cautious about accepting Chodorow as having all the answers to mother-daughter relationships. She believes her philosophy is contaminated by a patriarchal perspective because of its mother-blaming elements, especially in her descriptions of how mothers don't let go of their daughters.[65]

Gerda Lerner also believes we should be cautious about generalising from Chodorow's theory. Both Rich and Lerner speculate that the kind of personality formation which Chodorow describes did not occur in hunter-gatherer societies for example. Rather, because women's mother-ing and nurturing activities were associated with their self-sufficiency and competence in food-gathering and many varied life-essential skills, they must have been experienced, by men and women, as a source of strength and, probably, magical power.[66]

In these societies, women jealously guarded their knowledge of healing herbs. Their access to the secrets of healing, together with the mystery and awe which surrounded menstruation and birth, gave them an aura and sense of their participation in the mystic powers of the universe. In fact, women may have used menstruation as a symbolic weapon. In the light of this, while in "civilised" patriarchal societies it is girls who have the greater difficulty in ego formation, Lerner speculates that in primitive society the burden must have been on boys. On account of their fear and awe of the mother, they may have felt that their sex, and thus themselves, were inferior.[67]

In summary, Chodorow's philosophical theory supports many of the practical research outcomes and the ideas they generated, which I presented earlier in this book. The patriarchal aspects of her theory have been discussed constructively by Sayers, Rich, Lerner and Caplan.

Finally, I will look at a theory which is not influenced by any of the patriarchal assumptions of psychoanalysis. It belongs to Carol Gilligan. Gilligan's theory is a warning to mothers and daughters about the generalisations put forward by patriarchal psychiatry and psychology. We need to understand their assumptions and not be cowed by professionals who operate in their mould. She agrees with Lerner that women are now at a stage where they can see beyond the patriarchal framework and can construct a theory, which acknowledges that women are the other half of the human race. This is the basis for respectful mother-daughter relationships.

A Non Patriarchal Theory

CAROL GILLIGAN

Gilligan is taking a leading role in analysing the assumptions about women in psychology and psychiatry that undermine the relationship skills of women. She has looked critically and constructively at the work of patriarchally-oriented theorists such as Erikson, Piaget and Kohlberg — some of whose contributions I have already discussed in earlier chapters. She demonstrates that their theories of development are all plagued by the same problem, namely:

> ...the problem of women, whose sexuality remains more diffuse, whose perception of self is so much more tenaciously embedded in relationships with others and whose moral dilemmas hold them in a mode of judgement that is insistently contextual. The solution has been to consider women either as deviant or deficient in their development.[68]

Her concern is demonstrated in her analysis of the theory of Laurence Kohlberg, which is an extension of Freud's contention that in patriarchy, if not eternally, women are morally inferior to men. Kohlberg is viewed in psychological texts as an advance on Freud, because he paid more attention to the social context. This claim has distracted attention from the inadequacies in Kohlberg's methods. Kohlberg devised his theory about the moral immaturity of women, on the basis of an all male sample, and developed a six stage theory which was supposed to apply to both sexes. The ultimate sixth stage is a legalistic one, in which rights and non-interference predominate in judgements of justice. It is seen to be more typically attained by "mature" males. Women on the other hand, in this theory, tend to make "lower" third stage judgements which are concerned with relationships and pleasing others. Thus in Freud's footsteps, Kohlberg's criteria relegate women to a lesser sense of morality than men and, in doing so, judges them in male terms.

These outcomes have been possible, because the culture and knowledge created by men has been seen as a "universal" reality, independent of the knower. This assumption about knowledge permits the exclusion of the interpretations of women.[69]

Instead of dwelling upon where Kohlberg was wrong about women, or trying to salvage something of relevance from patriarchal psychoanalytic theory, Gilligan took a more constructive approach. She set about developing an independent theory of the morality of women. It is a positive theory that mothers can teach their daughters with dignity. First, she observed and listened to women. She found that when they were asked to construct their moral domain, a common thread was clear: the wish not to hurt others and the hope that in morality there lies a way of solving conflicts, without hurting anyone. The moral person is one who helps others. If possible, the moral person does this without sacrificing herself or himself.

Under patriarchy, we have two modes of judging in the moral domain. One is traditionally associated with masculinity and the public world of social power. The other belongs with femininity and the privacy of domestic exchange. Kohlberg formalised the prevailing patriarchal belief that masculine morality was superior. His theory of developmental inferiority in women, however, has more to do with the standard by which development has been measured, than with the equality of woman's thinking per se. Women's judgements are tied to feelings of empathy and compassion and are concerned more with the resolution of "real life". They are in contrast to the hypothetical legal dilemmas upon which Kohlberg's theory is based.

The conflict, between their own personal needs and accommodating to the rights and needs of others, constitutes the central moral problem for women. It is the conflict between compassion and autonomy, between virtue and power, which the feminine voice struggles to resolve in its effort to solve moral problems, in such a way, that no one is hurt. To inflict 'hurt' is considered selfish and immoral. It reflects unconcern, while the activity and expression of care is seen as the fulfilment of moral responsibility. Women's reiterative use of the language of selfishness and responsibility and the underlying moral orientation which their language reflects, sets them apart from the men whom Kohlberg studied. This difference is the critical reason for the hierarchy which Kohlberg produced, rather than the moral inferiority of women. The logic underlying an ethic of care is a psychological logic of relationships, which contrasts with the formal, legal logic of "fairness" and non-interference.

Whereas Kohlberg formulated his theory on legalistic power and property issues, Gilligan collected the data base for her theory by asking women about issues which are central to them in patriarchy. For example, she asked them about abortion, pregnancy and babies. She found that their moral judgements proceed from an initial "first stage" focus on themselves and their need to survive. This is followed by a transitional phase, in which this focus is criticised as selfish. The criticism signals a new understanding of the connection between self and others, which is given meaning by the concept of responsibility. The second stage is an elaboration of this concept of responsibility and its fusion with maternal morality, which seeks to ensure care for the dependent. At this point, the good is equated with caring for others. However, if others are legitimised as the only recipients of a woman's care, the exclusion of herself gives rise to problems in relationships. These create a disequilibrium that initiates the second transition.

In an effort to sort out the confusion between self-sacrifice and care of others, which is inherent in the conventions of feminine goodness, there is a reconsideration. This reconsideration leads to the third stage in women's moral development — a stage that focuses on the dynamics of relationships. It dissipates the tension between selfishness and responsibility, through a new understanding of the interconnection between other and self. Care becomes the self-chosen principle of any judgement. This is a psychological principle because it is concerned with relationships and responsibility. It is also a universal principle because of its condemnation of exploitation and 'hurt' in the wider world.

This ethic, which reflects a growing understanding of human relationships and an increasing differentiation of self and other, evolves around a central insight. Self and other are interdependent. The fact of interconnection informs the central recurring recognition that, just as the incidence of violence is, in the end, destructive of all, so the activity of care enhances both others and self. This moral imperative for women is in contrast to that for men, which conceives of obligations to others negatively, in terms of non-interference.[70]

Patriarchal morality, operating according to rules, separates the psychological and the legal and frequently does violence to the individual.[71] By constructing a feminist perspective, Gilligan is arguing that women must develop self-respect and know their own positive philosophy. I would add that by handing this feminine perspective onto their daughters, mothers are doing a great deal for mother-daughter relationships. The issue for women is to separate themselves as persons from the needs of others and to achieve and maintain personal autonomy and, at the same time, care about others. As long as care is seen as secondary to legality and non-interference, mothers and daughters will not value their talents for caring — nor will they value each other.

Overview

In this chapter, I have concentrated on theories which relate to some of the practical research findings reported earlier in the book. I have confined the discussion to aspects of these theories which concern mother-daughter relationships. Within these confines, I have selected insights which give positive understanding of mother-daughter relationships, together with those that critics consider do not offer constructive ideas about mending relationships. I have tried to explore the contention that, in the beginning, feminist dialogues with Freud gave much that was valuable. Now we are better equipped to recognise where they contain limitations. We need to construct research and generate substantiated theories which see mothers and daughters, not through the prism of patriarchy, but in their own light.

The next and final Chapter of Book I contains the full Bibliotherapy, which has been referred to throughout Book 1. It contains accounts of novels about relationships between mothers and daughters. More realistically than psychology can, these novels offer insights that may help us.

౪౩

READING

Reading of books by the theorists discussed in this chapter is recommended. It is important to discuss both their value and their patriarchal limitations and to apply this experience to all our reading. *The Standard Edition of the Complete Psychological Works of Sigmund Freud*, runs to so many volumes it is best to select from the index what interests you most. Other suggested reading is Paula Caplan, *The Myth of Women's Masochism*; Gerda Lerner, *The Creation of Patriarchy*; Adrienne Rich, *Of Woman Born*; Simone de Beauvoir, *The Second Sex* and *A Very Easy Death* ; Carol Gilligan, *In A Different Voice: Psychological Theory and Women's Development*. Papers by Jane Flax and Nancy Chodorow are listed in the Bibliography. If you want to keep up with feminist theory and the latest ideas about sexual differences in art, science, music and film, Oxford University Press publish a journal, *Women: A Cultural Review*. If you are interested in how men suffer under patriarchy, read *Beyond Patriarchy: Essays by Men on Pleasure, Power, and Change*, edited by Michael Kaufman.

౪౩

CHAPTER 9

Bibliotherapy For Mothers and Daughters

Novels and stories which candidly recount the lives of mothers and daughter often reflect our own lives. They become mirrors in which we can see ourselves, our joys, our sorrows, our actions and our mistakes. Such reflections sometimes help us to better understand ourselves and our relationships. Sometimes, observing the pain, the mistreatment, the pettinesses which others have suffered and overcome, sets off a stream of anger and will power that is cathartic. Observing that others have been as foolish, weak or self-indulgent as we have lightens our personal load of embarrassment. In these ways, novels and short stories, which genuinely portray the lives of mothers and daughters, can provide a bibliotherapy or a means for each of us to become our own therapist.

Contemporary women writers are endeavouring to rework, rethink, rediscover and establish a positive context for mother-daughter relationships. There is a growing literature which is reflecting and confirming mother-daughter experiences in a way that is relevant and cathartic. It is a validating literature which depicts a great range of genuine mother-daughter experience. Its images are ones in which mothers and daughters can find their own identity. Through these images they can know that their experiences of each other have been shared by other women.

At the same time, women can — and are — turning away from the patriarchally-oriented theories and biases in the counselling techniques of psychology and psychiatry. They are finding that the most vivid and therapeutic insights into life, as it is lived by mothers and daughters, come from their novels, their short stories and their poetry.

For this reason, in this final chapter of Book I, a collection of short stories, a play and five novels have been selected to highlight particular aspects of mother-daughter relationships. Each raises facets of mother-daughter relationships which have been explored earlier in this book. In précis, each tale is largely left to make its own point, so that mothers and daughters can find episodes relevant to their own situation, without the intervention of academic or psychological comment.

Short Stories as Therapy

Some of the stories I've chosen come from the collection, *Between Mothers and Daughters: Stories Across a Generation*, edited by Susan

Koppelman.[1] This collection exemplifies the openness with which women can and are exploring their relationships with their mothers. Until recently, stories about daughters who search for, and find, their identity in the world of women and the community to which their mothers belong, have been largely ignored in the public domain. This book makes such stories readily available, the first dating from 1848.

Here are testimonies of daughters' powerful love and respect for their mothers. They tell of their mother's oppression and confrontation with patriarchy, and of mothers with talent, repressed by fathers. There are stories of daughters who refuse to act out their mothers' submission and suffering, yet love and accept them. Mothers and daughters conspiring together, rather than in conflict, people this book.

We find mother-daughter stories where menarche is especially important, or where a mother is desperately trying to make her daughter understand what it means to be a woman in a man's world, sometimes with a cautionary tale of her own life. There are also ritual stories, which focus on life cycle events. The first phase of such stories is to remind the mother and daughter of some event in their collective past: "Hey remember the matching red blouses". These reminders resonate with the meaning of a shared history. The second stage is to assess their relationship, for example why something didn't work, and the third phase is a projection into the future together: "Next time we get together, the strawberries will be in season".

There are also stories of disgraceful and unconventional mothers, who violate narrow patriarchal rules for women — and their daughters' struggles to resolve their feelings about such mothers. These mothers may be depressives, alcoholics, slovenly, frazzled, impatient, or drug-addicted by medically prescribed medication. Some are mad or emotionally malfunctioning.

Several of these stories tell of daughters' resentment of their mothers' failure to fulfil conventional female roles, while disregarding their mothers' success as artists or professionals. Most end with a reconciliation between mother and daughter, if not in reality, then in the daughter's fantasy. The daughter may have learnt, sometimes with difficulty, that for her own psychological health and identity, she must accept her mother's separateness and her own guiltlessness in her mother's 'disgrace'.

Where the stories are written by artists who transcend their personal feelings and attitudes to their mothers, the fictional mothers are portrayed as vulnerable women, without power. In this vein, and of particular interest historically, is the story, *Recuerdo*, by Guadalupe Valdes. This story was written in 1963, when Valdes experienced disappointments as a young married mother, which she believed were her mother's fault:

> Until recently, it had not occurred to me that my mother has also been betrayed and trapped ... like so many women, she had also tried to follow the rules; to make sense of so many things that seemed unfair; and to hope that somehow, for her daughters, things would be different.[2]

Since she wrote the story, Valdes has recognised that her mother advised her as best she could: "Marry a man who doesn't drink". She also recognises that her mother had a lot to do with her ability to imagine herself as a writer: "I can remember bringing her the first poems I ever wrote. She found them brilliant, of course, and praised me warmly".

Tillie Olsen's story, written in 1956, is another of this genre. *I Stand Here Ironing* is a story of a mother who, wanting to do the best for her daughter, was often forced to do the worst. Economic exigencies had forced her to leave her daughter of eight months with a neighbour in their tenement. When she returned each day from work, her baby began to weep uncontrollably and could not be comforted. Later, there were her terrors about school bullies, her nightmares and then her thinness, which led her to be sent to a convalescent home. When her mother visited her on Sundays, there was the painful recognition that her daughter had taken on the ravaged appearance of all the other convalescent small girls.

This daughter was a child who had to be helper, mother, housekeeper and shopper for four younger siblings, running off each day to her huge school, where she was lost, suffering over her unpreparedness, stammering and unsure of her classes. She was a child seldom smiled upon, and with a gift for acting which could not be fostered due to lack of money. Her potential will not be able to bloom, but her mother wants her daughter to know that she is worth more than the dress she is ironing for her and that her ironing of it expresses her deep love and sadness for her daughter.

Mothers are largely silent, knowing their role is to give, to be criticised and to accept. There is an unspoken rule that daughters may hate mothers, but mothers cannot hate daughters or speak ill of them. *Every Day Use* by Alice Walker, breaks that tradition. It is about a black mother's critical feelings towards, and her ultimate rejection of, the values of an upwardly mobile daughter. Dee, the daughter, with the yuppie gold earrings hanging to her shoulders, believes she has found her identity by leaving home and developing an overbearing ego. She fails to recognise that her behaviour prohibits her from relating to the culture of her uneducated, big-boned mother, with rough, working man's hands.

Dee has become a typically smug member of the trendy suburbs, collecting memorabilia. She thinks her mother's churn will make a good centre piece for the alcove table and the quilts, pieced by her grandmother, will frame well and make excellent wall hangings. Dee believes that she values such things more than her mother and sister and that she understand oppression better than they do. She tells her sister, Maggie, who was to have the quilts for everyday use after her marriage, that she does not understand her heritage and that there is a new order for blacks and women alike, in which symbols of domestic servitude have no part.

Maggie, in reply, comments that she does not need the quilts to remember her grandmother and, since she taught her how to make them, she has her own resources to imbibe her traditions. Her mother's conclusion, that Dee's search for identity outside her female community is a farce and a failure, enables her to value her other daughter. She observes Maggie's search for identity in the women in her family. She realises Maggie is of her own ilk and bond and this boosts Maggie's self-esteem. Hitherto, she was regarded as the ugly duckling.

Ann Allen Shockley, in *A Birthday Remembered*,[3] testifies that mothering is something more than a biological accident. The spirit and activities of nurturance are gifts, not only of biological mothering across generations, but of teachers, stepmothers, mentors and friends. Biological mothering has certain external validations that other types of mothering do not, including those in lesbian relationships. Without external validations, such relationships may be forced into greater inter-dependency and greater awareness of persecution and bigotry. Trapped in socially devalued categories, they may exist in a constant state of insecurity.

The Quest for the Mother After Her Death

Many stories by contemporary women writers deal with the daughter's quest to rediscover the mother after her death — to know what it was like to be her. Most, who have experienced the death of a mother, know the almost immediately subsequent urge to seek her out in locations where time was spent with her when we were children. We may travel to the scenes of our mothers' childhood, retrace her footsteps on the road she took to school and find the house in which she lived. We look at her old photographs and talk to people who knew her in her youth. We recall things we did together and our actions toward her and perhaps for the first time wonder how she felt about those actions. In this way, we not only get to know more about our mothers, but more about ourselves — who we are — where we have come from.

In two short stories in *Something I've Been Meaning to Tell You*,[4] Alice Munro shares these evocative and pervading memories in her thumb nail sketches of a daughter's recollections of her dead mother. The daughter's fleeting reminiscences of her actions toward her mother prompt a re-examination of her mother and their relationship.

In the first story, *Ottowa Valley*, on the occasion of a funeral, mother and daughter return to the Valley where the mother grew up and where a former beau, now married, still lives. As they walk into the church on a sunny morning, the child-daughter notes that her mother is tastefully clothed in a flowered grey dress with matching hat and gloves. Looking back as an adult she writes:

> She must have planned and visualised it just as I now plan and visualise, sometimes, what I will wear to a party.[5]

Well-laid plans and effects are spoilt, when the elastic of the daughter's underpants breaks and the only pin available is that which holds up the shoulder strap of her mother's slip. She tries to encourage her daughter to go without panties, as no one will know. The daughter objects and is advised to sit in the car. As she reluctantly retreats, the mother calls her back and gives her the pin. As a result, with the former beau and his wife in view, her grey slip hangs down in a slovenly way when she leaves the church. The daughter, sure of her rights, did not say thank you. Now, after her mother's death she wants to understand her mother's feelings and hidden reactions in this situation.

The daughter is also ready to re-examine how her mother felt about herself as the spasms and tremors of Parkinson's disease overcame her when she was only in her early forties. She wonders if her mother was wounded by her childish indifference. She recollects that as a child she needed a promise, that she would not end up having to mother her, as her aunt had to with her mother's mother who died of cancer. Cruelly, she had pursued the topic of her mother's affliction, which her mother preferred to avoid. Her mother held out against her for the first time and she did not get her promise.

In the second story, *Winter Wind*, the daughter continues to re-examine her embarrassment on account of her mother's Parkinson's disease, and her feelings of shame because her mother was not like other mothers and needed her help to keep the house in order. Why was it that throughout childhood, she had argued with her mother whenever she could? She begins to realise that it had something to do with her bond with her mother. If there had been no bond, she would have preferred to retreat to the physical comfort and charm of her grandmother's house. Her grandmother had competed for her affection with domestic order, ironed sheets, eiderdowns and jasmine soap. Why did she prefer life at home with her mother? The daughter now realises that she found the fights, the confusion, the work, the opportunity to get lost in a library book, to drop a coat where she chose, to read with her feet in the oven and to argue, more attractive because there was room for everything. Through her recollections of her mother and her own actions toward her, she realises her mother gave her the freedom and opportunity to be an individual. It was not an ideal world, family or mother, but it made her as she is and the story is written with affection.

The need to try and rediscover her mother remains. She needs to illumine, to celebrate and rework the haunting memories of her. It will always be so.

Unfinished Business Between Mothers and Daughters

Quite different, are a daughter's guilty recollections of a dead mother from whom she cannot separate.

Such a situation is portrayed in the novel *Love Child*, by Jean Bedford. It also has two other themes central to mother-daughter relationships. One is the effect of a violent father. The other is the effect of family experiences which make it difficult for a daughter to accept her mother.

Grace, the mother, was a daughter who grew up in a slum tenement in London. As the eldest, there were seemingly endless new babies for her to look after and, although she did well at school and loved it, she had to leave to help support the family. When he was drunk, her father beat her mother and her sisters with his spare wooden arm. Grace would laugh later, telling her daughter and her friends about it, but it wasn't funny at the time, with the crockery smashing and the children silent, huddled, making themselves as small as possible behind the big armchair. "Slut!" he would shout at their mother and her daughter, Grace, and her sisters: "Slovenly whores, fit for the gutters!"

> They would eat, carefully, slowly, not looking at the clock. If he could only stay out until after the baby's feed, then everyone could be in bed pretending sleep when he came in. Not that this always worked. He had been known to rage through the children's room, flailing indiscriminately, with Grace trying to block the blows as she vaguely remembered her mother doing for her when she was smaller. She would not let herself think about what happened in the other small bedroom when she lay with the pillow pressed around her ears desperately not hearing the thuds, the muffled crashes, her mother's unwilling half-stifled cries. She had been used, all her life, to the fading and fresh bruises on her mother's thin body as she washed in her slip in the mornings.[6]

As the daughters grew older, their fear turned to contempt and they began to talk back, intervening for their mother. Puzzled at his loss of power, their father would complain to his cronies, "Pack of bitches. A man's home's not his own any more". There was laughter in the flat now, as the daughters tried out new hairdos and did things to their eyebrows with tweezers and black pencil. They took typing and shorthand classes and managed to send a younger sister to high school, all without their father's permission. Grace enjoyed her brief butterfly time before her marriage, which was not successful and perhaps a legacy of her violent father. Daughters, who have violent fathers, often have difficulties in relationships with men throughout their lives.

In blitz-torn London, she meets the solemn and serious Bill, a sensitive Australian sailor. They fall deeply in love and Grace leaves her husband to live with Bill, who, however, is often absent as a wartime sailor. She becomes ill and bears her illegitimate daughter prematurely. It is a time of great suffering, but the two marry and sail for Australia. Soon, the mismatch of the easy, kind, outgoing, pleasure-seeking Grace, with the legacy of the violent father, and the ascetic Bill, with his brooding disappointments, leads to open and bitter conflict. Grace's first husband and their sons remain a hidden part of her of which she never speaks.

As one who has experienced domestic violence as a child, Grace has no models or resources for a peaceful family life. Every night Anne, her daughter, lies in bed fearful, trying to block out her parents' fighting, trying to gain their attention so that she is the focus, rather than their bitter-ness for each other. Unlike her mother, Anne is not a survivor. Ultimately, her own vulnerability and lack of inner strength results in her mental con-fusion.

Anne says of her mother, Grace:

> When I was little, she was warm and held me often; later she became complaining, complicit and hesitant. Her favourite times were in her garden, the cat on a fence-post somewhere near. She wore rouge in pink round spots, she chain-smoked menthol cigarettes and swore. She laughed with her mouth wide open — sometimes you could see the dentures — but even in old age she was pretty.

> I loved her, my vulgar, laughing mother; I blamed her for every-thing. My memories of my father are soured by her muttering vindictive presence.[7]

Anne describes her embarrassment at her mother's flirtations, her care-lessness, her drinking. She was not as Anne thought a mother should be.

Anne leaves home, meets and marries the personable Steve and has a baby. Her father dies and her mother stays with them a while. Anne's irri-tation mounts at her untidiness, her paraphernalia and especially at how Grace and Steve play act with each other and enjoy it.

> I felt he diminished her, that she diminished herself with her elderly, rouged coquettishness. I still had an ideal of my mother perhaps, thought she should have grown old with some dignity, some serenity.[8]

But there are intermittent good times, when Grace is her expected mother again and helps with the fractious baby.

Anne not only has difficulty in accepting her mother's vulgarity, but in coming to terms with her ageing, for this will also be her own fate. After Grace has a stroke, Anne loathes bathing her withered body. She tries to avoid seeing the grizzled pubic hair, the wasted flesh, the skinny arms and legs and their hanging folds of unused skin. Why couldn't she say, "You are my mother, I love you. It is my privilege to look after you."? Why wouldn't Grace say, "I am old and lonely and frightened, you are all I have."?[9]

Grace is removed to hospital and, in order to be with her, Anne must leave her baby son and the husband of whom she is uncertain. Frantic with jealousy about Steve, she prepares to leave. The memory of her mother at that moment haunts her:

> When I said goodbye her terrible body convulsed under the blan-kets, her eyes widening into madness. It was too late then, I was going. But she knew me ... She knew I was leaving her alone to die.[10]

The tragedy in this relationship is that Anne fails to complete the unfinished business between her mother and herself before her mother's death. Her mother remains alive, somewhere inside her head and is not experienced as a separate person, even after death: "She has got into me and she can't escape". Ultimately, Anne tries to kill herself, to release her mother within her.

The tragedy is that emotional separation from a mother can be achieved by less self-destructive methods. This was the theme of Chapter 7. Ways of achieving emotional separation, even after a mother's death, were illustrated there in the discussion of Doris Lessing's novel, *The Diary of Jane Somers*.

Daughters of Charismatic and Publicly Prominent Mothers

In hindsight, it might be easy to suggest how Anne could have come to terms with her mother and her own identity. She needed to examine her unrealistic longing for the perfect mother and her false images of the malevolence of mothers. She needed to recognise that her mother was not a formidable person — she was just a working class mother with little power. But what happens if mothers are charismatic and powerful persons? How hard is it for their daughters to achieve a sense of self-esteem and identity in their own right?

Where the mothering role is compounded by an additional, publicly prominent one, the frequent expectation is that the relationship between mother and daughter is inevitably soured. It is therefore encouraging to read a novel, based on fact, that attests that this is not necessarily so.

The novel *In My Mother's House*, by Kim Chernin, is the story of the famous American communist leader, Rose Chernin, and her relationship with her daughter, Kim. Rose was a daughter who refused to be a victim like her mother. Kim was a daughter who engaged in the separation rituals with her mother, that are typical of most adolescents and young adults. Mother and daughter finally came to accept and understand the separate identities of each other. Kim's resolution of their relationship is in contrast to that of many offspring of the famous.

Rose Chernin was born in 1902 in a small village or shtetl[11] in Russia. Her mother is victimised by a brutal and abandoning husband, to whom she nevertheless feels bound and serves loyally whenever he demands it. In her early years, she has a courageous streak which Rose observes and emulates. At this time, she also has self-esteem, for she can read and write, which most other women of the shtetl cannot. Rose's self-esteem and confidence is also helped by a childhood that becomes increasingly happy after their father leaves them to make his life in America. Her mother and the children have the support of a delightful grandfather. The mother is loving and fun.

When their father calls them to the U.S.A in 1914, the mother becomes a complete victim, has no friends, does not understand the culture or the new ways of domestic life. She attempts suicide and is committed to a lunatic asylum by her husband, until Rose defies him and the authorities. Even so, she returns to her husband.

When Rose first stands up to her father and forbids him to strike their mother, she learns that no-one can break her. Rose does not have the making of a victim, nor is she overpoweringly guilt-ridden by the things that disturbed Anne, in *Love Child*. Although she knows her father will start beating her mother again, she makes a decision to become independent and make something of her potential and she leaves home. Her leadership qualities and concern for injustice gradually earn her the respect of trade unionists and she ultimately joins the communist party. From then on she is out fighting for justice for the poor, the unemployed and the immigrants.

It is worth noting that Rose has a supportive husband, who loves and admires her fiercely and is not threatened by her powerful personality. He also fosters a nurturing relationship with his daughter.

Rose survives gaol and the McCarthy witch hunts and grows in stature. She has charisma. Her indomitable spirit, her integrity, her joy in life and her positivism, means she is a woman of whom her daughter can be proud. The book burns with Kim's pride in her mother. Yet, with a mother belonging to a party that was spurned by mainstream society, she could have been a victim, embarrassed by her politics and ashamed of her. But, like her mother, Kim is not a potential victim and she thrives in the support, culture and way of life which communism provided for its members in the middle decades of this century.

At the same time, because she has her mother's spirit, Kim and her mother argue all their lives. Her adolescence was particularly stormy. This is not unnatural and Kim describes their arguing as the separation ritual. She rejects her mother's Marxism, and her admiration for the Soviet Union. She embraces religion and becomes a poet, instead of a political fighter. She instils in her own daughter, Larissa, values that are opposed to her mother's. Yet, when away from her mother, Kim misses her and finds herself feeling guilty if she behaves in a fashion which is contrary to her mother's values.

In her mother's old age, there is a reconciliation. Rose is willing to recognise that Kim's rejection of communism is not a rejection of her. Kim learns that beneath the charisma lay her mother's questioning that she may have harmed her children by her communist activities. Kim acknowledges that she would not have had her mother any other way.

Better known to us than Rose Chernin is Margaret Mead. How did she cope as a mother and as an internationally famous anthropologist? How did her daughter cope in the shadow of such a remarkable mother?

Margaret Mead:

Her Mother, Her Daughter and the Question of Self-Esteem

With the publication in 1928 of *Coming of Age in Samoa*, Margaret Mead, only in her twenties, was well on the road to fame. This was unusual for a woman of her time. Her autobiography[12] and the biographies by her daughter, Catherine Bateson,[13] and Jane Howard,[14] give the impression that Mead's mother and grandmother were seen by her as playing a significant role in these unusually early achievements and her later life and work. Because of this, she regarded motherhood and the relationship with a daughter highly and resented that the conflicting model should be presented as typical of American mothers and daughters.

There appears to have been a tradition of powerful women in her family. In *Blackberry Winter: My Earliest Years*, [15] Mead described her paternal grandmother as the most decisive influence in her life. She and Mead's mother combined domestic duties with intellectual and community pursuits and commanded widespread community respect. From Mead's and Bateson's account, it was because the grandmother and mother had such good esteem themselves that they were able to encourage it in their daughter. One of the principle arguments I have put forward in this book, is that mothers and daughters need self-esteem to build a good relationship. Mead had self-esteem and a positive relationship with her mother.

Mead describes how she knew she was a wanted child and was told continually by her mother and grandmother: "There's no one like Margaret". She described herself as "a child that both my parents wanted ... I was told from the time I was born that I was totally satisfactory. I had a chance to be what I wanted to be and I have always been able to be what I wanted to be".[16]

This endorsement of herself and her gender was reinforced as she observed her mother filling 13 notebooks with accounts of Margaret's deeds as a baby and a young child. Accordingly, Margaret grew up with two strong convictions: that being observed was wonderful and that observing others, far from being anything to feel guilty about, was more wonderful still.[17]

The women who were significant in her childhood were active in responding to external circumstances.[18] They were not simply reactive as were many of their contemporaries. They were not the homebound, long-suffering, self-effacing Edwardian mothers whom Simone de Beauvoir described as being typical of her mother.[19] Instead, in her mother and grandmother, Margaret Mead found models for an active, assertive approach to the world and adopted a similar behaviour. Mead believed that this healthy, self-actualisation was another factor in the good relationship between herself and her mother. She described how they were important in each other's lives. Communication was good and intimate and could survive and benefit from frank exchange and disagreement. They respected one another.

Mead's mother had four children, attained a doctorate, maintained an independent and active intellectual life and was involved continually in the rights of the disadvantaged — the poor, blacks and women. Without becoming a martyr, she was a loving parent, a continued and stabilising influence for her children, and provided her daughter, Margaret, with the best affordable education. She expected and did not resist independence in her daughter and this too, Margaret stressed, contributed to their good relationship throughout Margaret's adulthood, as in childhood. It is little wonder that Mead did not feel the need to reject her mother's life, as Simone de Beauvoir did. Instead, she modelled herself on her mother and her values and became an outstanding and strong woman in her own right.

Margaret Mead studied a wide range of cultures in the Pacific and did some valuable studies on childhood in New Guinea as well as Samoa. She observed the very considerable variation in gender rules and behaviour across societies. She helped present the evidence which began to change patriarchal views that innate characteristics predetermine specific sex roles. She exposed the inexorable cultural pressures that make men and women as they are. She wrote or co-authored 39 books and 1,397 other publications. She had 28 honorary degrees and 40 awards.[20] Hers was an esteemed life that did not succumb to patriarchy's prescriptions for women.

Born in 1901, at the height of Edwardian patriarchy, Margaret Mead, as a woman, relied on personal self-esteem and solidarity with other women to achieve her international reputation as an anthropologist. Her daughter, Catherine Bateson, and the journalist, Jane Howard, both give excellent insights into her situation. Howard, for example, documents the way in which her most famous field trip, which led to Coming of Age in Samoa, was seen in the second decade of this century. The field trip was planned in order to study women and children. As part of the discipline of anthropology which had concentrated largely on males, it was described as a study of "low things" by her male superiors.[21]

The same denigration of the female scholar was something she had to contend with in her later, much valued museum work at the American Museum of Natural History. It began with her boss, Dr Clark Wissler, describing museum work as fitted for women, "because it was like housekeeping".[22] She was not accorded appropriate status and position at Columbia University, where she lectured for many years.[23] Perhaps hardest of all was that she had to contend with intense hostility toward women, from her much loved third husband, Gregory Bateson. He is described by his daughter as having "darkly complicated feelings about women, starting from his own mother, whom he had heartily wanted to get away from".[24] To add to the ignominy, he and his group of colleagues developed the idea of the mother "as a double bind bitch". This theory was publicised during the 1950s and contributed to the open hostility toward mothers at the time. This patriarchal pre-occupation with mother-baiting was discussed in

Chapter 1 and illustrated through Doris Lessing's portrayal of Mrs Quest.

Mead is a good illustration of how women can maintain the kind of self-esteem that is the basis of positive mother-daughter relationships in a society which tries to destroy women's self-esteem. Throughout her professional life, she had to sustain her belief in the value of herself and her work and inure herself against the hostility she experienced from men within her own profession. Two of her most bitter critics were Edward Sapir and Derek Freeman, neither of whom is now remembered to the extent that Mead is. Freeman is remembered, if at all, largely for his attempt to discredit Mead after her death. Mead's daughter, Catherine Bateson, assesses his resentment as arising from having to work for 40 years in the shadow of a woman, especially as Mead became a more outstanding anthropologist than he did. Bateson found him to be "rigid, grim and competitive". Fortunately, there are men who are less paranoid about women and more concerned about scholarship. Professor Bradd Shoe of Emory University, in analysing Freeman's attack on Mead's work, which initially was given headlines in the world press, contended that, like most researchers, Margaret Mead was not completely wrong in Samoa. She was incomplete. He was not happy that Freeman had given the impression that anthropology was a "shooting gallery" instead of a subject for "scholarly discussion".[25]

Many of her colleagues have described Mead as having unquestionably pioneered in the ethnography of women and children, in the application of psychology to field work, in the study of national character and in the refinement of methods of observation. She made her own arcane discipline seem not only glamorous but useful.[26]

Mead's self-esteem and assurance made it possible for her to accept the diversity of cultures, individuals and the sexes. She argued with passion against moving from this concept to that of the superiority of one group over another.[27] Her grateful daughter, Catherine Bateson, describes how she learnt this lesson early. Margaret encouraged her to honour the diversity and rules of the various households belonging to relatives and Margaret's friends that formed, by her mother's design, part of her extended family.[28]

Mead, herself a product of an extended family, had admired big communal households, even before her first field trip to Samoa. The isolated nuclear family, she kept declaring all her life, was the worst possible place to bring up a child. Never would she have dreamed of bringing up her own child, especially an only child, without a great many people around.[29] Such a situation of course means that mothers do not have the undue burden of frustration and discipline described in earlier chapters. According to Mead and her daughter, their well chosen extended family arrangement contributed to their good relationship, as it had between Margaret and her mother.

Mead's life provided a model of the changing roles for mothers and daughters and women in general. Having outgrown her two first husbands, she cast her private troubles into ideas that later became acceptable.

She argued that, ever since women had begun to be educated, marriages have begun to be endangered by the possible development, or failure to develop, by both husbands and wives. The phrase "she outgrew him" would in time become as commonplace an explanation for why a marriage ended, as "he outgrew her".[30] She believed, and put into practice in her own life, that such separations should not be acrimonious. Rather, the positive aspects of the time together should be valued and her daughter was grateful for this attitude, when her father left Mead.

Understanding the difficult role of women and because of her good self-esteem, Margaret Mead urged and mothered many surrogate daughters into promising careers. One of her teaching assistants described how she said: "You've got to decide whether you want to be an anthropologist or not for the rest of your life. For several years you've spent entirely too much time becoming a woman and not enough becoming a person".[31]

Because of her esteem for her sex, she found classes of women more exhilarating to teach than classes of men. All told, she found women's thinking more congenial.[32] In this context, one can understand why one of her many protegees described how distressed she was when Margaret died of cancer in 1978 and had not lived to see her baby, because "by discovering me, Margaret had given birth to me as much as my own mother had". Many others likewise felt bereft of a surrogate mother and acknowledged the incredible structure of self-esteem and support she had given them. She had taught them to realise that they could stand on their own two feet.[33]

Her daughter describes with gratitude:

> "She brought me up in the fifties, before women had rediscovered the friendship and support they owe to each other, never, ever, to break a date with a woman in order to accept one with a man. At the same time, she also talked about the need for a woman to have real friendships with men, men who are not lovers, and the pleasure of friendship cultivated in the soil of passion".[34]

Bateson also writes:

> She believed that decent and caring human relationships are sustained by courtesy. Thus, in talking about sexuality and about the functions of the human body, she clearly wanted me to be both proper — respectful of external forms — free to play, pleased to be a woman and unconstrained by gender. Being female was fun. At the same time I was taught that there were no limits to what women of intelligence and determination could achieve.[35]

> There was no either-or involved, no acknowledgment that achievement as a woman would involve sacrifices or hard choices. 'You just have to learn not to care about the dust-mites under the beds', she said.[36]

Mead was both a product of, and a giver of, courageous mothering.

However, she did not fully escape the alienated character traits patriarchy can impose on women. She is described by Howard as needing to mother. Margaret herself recognised this and recalled how her adored paternal grandmother confided in her about her parents, in a way that confused her and made her sometimes feel that her parents were her children, as much as she was theirs. According to her first husband, throughout her life she was always looking for new mothers and she needed adulation. Yet total strangers thought of Mead as a mother and she did her best to oblige them, although she still needed mothering herself. She never stopped establishing new families and she had a way of making people feel connected to her and to one another.[37]

At least one of her friendships with a woman, the famed anthropologist, Ruth Benedict, had a sexual component. Benedict was her earliest and most lasting surrogate mother and one of her distinguished mentors. Like Virginia Woolf, Mead grew up at a time when deep involvements between women, sexual and otherwise, were nearly as common as obsessions about losing virginity.[38] Howard and Bateson both confirm that in Margaret, Benedict found the companionship, love and devoted affection denied by her aloof husband. According to one of Mead's close friends, Mead "fell in love with women's souls and men's bodies. She was spiritually homosexual, psychologically bisexual and physically heterosexual".[39]

Margaret Mead's surrogate mother-daughter relationship with Benedict was fluid in nature as are many such relationships. In some relationships, the roles are fixed, in others they alternate, depending upon the circumstances.[40] The fluidity of Margaret Mead's sexuality was not unusual and gives occasion to augment the description of self-concept development given in Chapter 2 and the description of sexuality in Chapter 4.

As far as mother-daughter relationships are concerned, the most notable aspect of Mead's life is her self-esteem and how she transmitted it to her daughter. Because of her self-esteem, she was able to survive the very distressing break-up with her beloved third husband and ensure that it did not damage her daughter's self-esteem.

Mothers Trapped by Social Convention and the Forgotten Influence of Fathers

I will now turn to a play and a novel which say something about the effects on the mother-daughter relationship of fathers who are absent or have absconded. Fathers have been accorded, and they themselves try to assume such a peripheral role in mother-daughter relationships, that one may well ask whether their departure matters? Certainly, their failure to nurture and encourage their daughters is not judged as harshly as the failures of mothers. Nevertheless, the research recounted in earlier chapters demonstrated that fathers are generally as crucial to a daughter's well-being and her relationships as mothers are.

Another important question is what happens to the mother-daughter relationship when both the mother and father are failing — the mother because she is totally warped by social convention and the father because he abandons all responsibility? This is a story told by many a daughter and is captured in one of Tennessee Williams' most memorable plays. It is also a play which depicts the "blame mother — forgive father" attitude.

Tennessee Williams, one of the twentieth century's most popular playwrights, is one of many who wrote about the lasting effects of the wounds and desolations created by mothers. In *The Glass Menagerie*, Williams uses the character of Amanda Wingfield to capture the feelings of guilt and hate that the failing mother can arouse. At the same time, he portrays the unbearably ambivalent situation in which some mothers found themselves in earlier decades — decades in which families and societies confined their daughters' possibilities to courtship and reproduction.

Amanda Wingfield is a deserted wife and the mother of Tom and Laura, whom she has raised on her own. A former southern belle, she has been warped by social conventions and her personality constrained by a man's world that expects her to be silly, snobbish and perpetually vivacious. She accepts the dependent lot of women in the male-dominated world of early twentieth century America and advises her daughter on the passivity and manipulation necessary for survival in such a world.

Williams recognises the courage that underlies Amanda's superficiality. She possesses valour and endurance, but her children's recognition of this creates a bond of guilt. Her love for her children is exasperating and suffocating, but she recognises that Tom will escape. It is her daughter, Laura, who has been most damaged by her mother's possessiveness, projections and expectations. When she has skipped secretarial college to spend her days in museum, park or zoo and is "found out", she pleads with her mother not to get "that martyred look. It makes me feel so guilty".

Laura is crippled. She is not perfect. Her mother, Amanda, refuses to notice or accept that Laura has any physical imperfection worth noting, or is any way disinclined to the standard behaviours of marriageable daughters. Her greatest disappointment is that Laura does not have as many gentleman callers as she wishes for her, nor does she receive proposals of marriage — things she wants to happen to her daughter in order to relive her own time of courtship. Because Amanda cannot come to terms with her daughter as she is, Laura is repeatedly thrust into situations where she fails her mother's expectations and retreats into her compensatory world of old phonographic records and the glass menagerie.

Amanda is obsessed with her past and her lost youth as a southern belle. It was her only time of importance. She dwells on these past memories, now illusions, and hopes they will come to fruition in her daughter. Nevertheless, she is in touch with reality. For her daughter, illusions have become reality and she is cripplingly neurotic. The fact that she has been allowed little autonomy and cannot become, or compensate for, the lost dreams of her mother, has played an important role in her situation. The tragedy is that the mother wants the best for her daughter, but can only conceive of that within the patriarchal strait-jacket.

However, Tennessee Williams' play falls short of full human experience because, despite its insights, it is a patriarchally-biased play. There is little hint of the effect on Laura as a small child of the father's departure. Is this another important reason why she lingers with the glass menagerie, a much loved toy of her childhood? The glass menagerie perhaps represents the softer emotions and the small and tender things that Laura needs. The play leaves her destroyed by her mother's projections. She must stay because she is a daughter. Tom, the son, is permitted to escape.

The novel, *Peeling*, by Grace Bartram deals with the effect on a mother-daughter relationship of a divorce initiated by the father. It also concerns the effect of the loss of a woman's identity as a mother.

Because they have been pressured to restrict personality development to the mothering role, many women may have spent their lives trying to prove they are good mothers. Some extend the role and mother men in general. Mothering men in patriarchal society may allow women to feel strong and wanted. They may need the neediness of others to be able to feel their own strength.[41] Deprived of this role after the divorce or death of a spouse, these women disintegrate as persons. This dependency on being needed can create special tensions between mothers and daughters and was discussed in Chapter 6.

The main character in *Peeling* is a mother, Ally, who is abandoned by her husband after 30 years of marriage. She cannot believe at first what has happened and goes through despair and disorientation. Her deeply conventional, sedate self is traumatised. She cannot and does not turn to her daughter, Jane. There is a huge gap of misunderstanding between them and the departure of Jane's father and Ally's inability to cope threatens to create an even wider gap between them. The father is so peripheral that he can have no positive influence on the situation.

Ally remembers that not even her daughter's birth was pleasurable. There was the ignominy of being shaved around the pubic region, having enemas administered without explanation, the pain, no one nearby who cared about her, and the impatience of the nursing staff. Her self-negating dependency on her father and then her husband, destroyed her ability to give love and support to her daughter.

In the course of getting to know herself, Ally finds that due to the anger of an emotionally distraught father, she has blamed herself for the drowning of her eight year old sister. This is a sad delusion which has had its effects on her daughter, Jane, who, as a child, could not help overhearing her mother's nightmares and the impatient reactions of her father.

Jane too has nightmares and is sent to a psychiatrist who rapes her. Her hysterical refusal to return to him is dismissed impatiently by her father. Her mother does not question her. Jane, angry at her violation, is not close enough to her mother to stumble into her arms and pour out the horror of the experience. She reflects sadly that perhaps, if she could have talked out much of the anger, she would not have been left years later with feelings of guilt. As it is, because she'd never spoken of it, she feels that she was in some way partly responsible for what had happened.

As a conformist mother, another problem for Ally is that she has lost her hopes for a married daughter. Many mothers and fathers are disconcerted about daughters who do not marry as they did. Ally is one of them. In her case, there is an additional issue. Jane has formed a lesbian relationship. Jane realises that her reticence in talking about her lesbian relationship is a stumbling block and she wistfully studies a photograph of a grey-haired mother marching in a gay rights demonstration in support of her daughter. By capturing such personal longings, this novel gives life to the issues concerning sexuality and the mother-daughter relationship that were explored in Chapter 4 of this book.

Eventually, Ally accepts her daughter's different way of loving. The change in herself is aided by the experience of helping in a women's refuge. Here, through communication with the care workers and the abused women, she finds an unexpected self. She confronts the fact that women cannot burden men with expectations of their happiness. She stops being scared of what people — including her daughter — are going to tell her about themselves. She stops feeling she must always be available, be needed, solve people's problems. She learns the impossibility of this in the context of the highly-charged demands of the women who come to the refuge. In fact, Ally, like many contemporary mothers, finds great pleasure in her new and independent life, once the anxieties of separating from a husband are worked through. The divorce becomes a catalyst for a new relationship with her daughter.

When her mother loses her apologetic incoherence and ceases to be the inconsequential, disappearing woman, Jane is proud. The path is still not smooth between them. But Ally knows she can initiate something better with her daughter and must not expect her to live by her rules.

Ally is a mother who learns in time not to crucify her daughter on her own martyrdom. Where martyrdom takes over, it can be destructive of mother-daughter relationships and this theme is explored by Marilyn French in her novel, *Her Mother's Daughter*. [42]

Martyred Mothers and Depressed Daughters

Almost every mother and daughter will find something that bears on their relationship in *Her Mother's Daughter*. It describes the effects on mother-daughter relationships of poverty, raging fathers, unwanted pregnancy and conflicts with adolescents. The central theme of the story is the imprisoning pattern of relationships repeated by four generations of mothers and their daughters. Each mother enmeshes her daughter in her own martyrdom, although each tries to help her escape. The second half of the book underlines repeatedly that outward appearances, good clothes, good food and material possessions can be a mask for the inherited suffering within many American families, and especially in their mothers and daughters.

The book is especially relevant to daughters of poor immigrants or holocaust survivors. The immigrant world it portrays and the emotions and conflicts, generated by the victimology of the holocaust survivors, has its support in psychological research. The guilt the children of such parents can suffer, and the tragedy of living with care-givers who believe their children can never understand their hardship and suffering, have been examined by among others, Barocas and Barocas,[43] Freyberg[44] and Heller.[45]

Freyberg observed that children of parents, who were holocaust survivors, had perceived their parents as having difficulties with close emotional attachments and suffering psychic numbness — a diminished capacity to feel, resulting in withdrawal, apathy, depression and despair. They tended to regard their children as possessions, meant to compensate them for what they had lost.

Holocaust offspring desperately needed the love and approval of their parents and especially of their mothers. There was intense concern for the mother's happiness and welfare and a deep sense of responsibility for her. At the same time, many harboured intense anger with their mothers for not meeting their needs for emotional relationships. The intensity of this need was extremely frightening to them and rigidly defended against.

Barocas and Barocas observed that children of concentration camp survivors may become transferential recipients of unconscious and unexpressed rage and death anxiety. The child is frequently forced to take on the burden of having to fulfil, not only her own developmental needs, but also her parents' unrealistic expectations that she must compensate for their sense of worthlessness.

Although she is not directly the daughter of a holocaust survivor, but a child of loss and unresolved mourning, Bella, the mother, in *Her Mother's Daughter* has all the symptoms of such an inheritance.

The story begins in the Bronx in the first decade of this century, with an immigrant Polish family and their four children. At first it focuses on Bella and her mother, Frances. Bella's father, Michael, is a tailor, charmingly egocentric to outsiders, but drunken and brutal at home. In 1913, when Bella is nine, he dies of uremic poisoning. He has deliberately not provided for his dutiful and submissive wife, in case she forms a liaison with another after his death. She is left in poverty. Welfare claims her children (the youngest is Euga, a girl of four), but allows her to keep Bella who is partially deaf. Bella, who is timid and does not understand her handicap, believes herself stupid and cannot understand why her mother chose to keep her.

Things are never explained to her. Herein lies the beginning of her self-rejection and longing for love, which remains with her all her life. It is compounded by the suffering of her mother, which she cannot appease, and a dreary and joyless childhood. This is not a book for blaming mothers, so one understands both the deep depression of Frances and the tragedy of Bella. Their relationship is stressed by poverty, unacknowledged reversal of child-parent roles and loss.

Frances works in a sweat shop ten hours a day for six days each week, for which she is paid $5.00. They must live in a back alley apartment. She is forever weary and lost in depression — frequently crying for her lost children — sometimes screaming. She is harsh to Bella and refuses to be comforted by her. So begin Bella's attempts to please and placate her mother and to ease her lot. The child cannot understand that there is no solution under patriarchy to the lot of martyred mothers such as Frances.

Bella tries to fill the dark void in her mother's existence, by taking on most of the home cleaning, shopping and cooking. There is little acknowledgement from her mother. She sleeps in the same bed, but her mother never caresses her or even says goodnight.

The orphanage cannot cater for four year olds and Euga is returned to Frances, who croons to her and hugs her as she never does Bella:

> Bella was silent, watching from her seat at the table, as Momma sat on the couch with the baby, rocking for a long time, kissing her forehead, holding her close. If she wondered if her mother would love her more if she'd gone to the orphanage, she did not let the question enter her mind. She just sat and watched.[46]

When the boys are able to go to work, the orphanage releases them and the economic situation improves for Frances. With all the children working, they are able to buy a house. Frances replaces the sweat shop for domestic service to her children, without complaint. It is said in the family that she eventually died of grief:

> Perhaps. For when had she a life of her own? Her children 'bettered' her by moving to the house on Manse Street, which was a nice enough house, but far from any neighbourhood where she might have heard Polish spoken, or made a friend. There was no old neighbourhood for her: they had moved too often, and she worked too hard to make enduring friendships. Her family, which had abandoned her when Michael died, was also dead or distant now. She devoted herself to her children as she had to him, became their slave, servant caretaker. She knew no other way of life.[47]

Long before her mother died and while she was still working in the sweat shop, Bella had joined her there. She'd had to leave school early, but she took night lessons in typing and shorthand. Eventually, she escaped the dreariness of the sweat shop to work in a more glamorous world — an interior decorator's shop. Later, she moved to an even better job on Wall Street and was studying to be an artist. Now, she could afford make-up, a fashionable haircut and an occasional meal in a restaurant. She felt that she was beginning to live her life at last and escape her mother's tragedy. But her fulfilment was brief. Despite her lack of enthusiasm for his embraces, her boyfriend, Ed, caused her to became pregnant.

Where was the justice? He wanted it, he urged it, he was hot with eagerness and she, lukewarm, had allowed it, merely allowed it, and she was the one to bear the shame and the punishment.[48]

Forced into marriage, she began to re-enact her mother's tragedy and her first daughter, Anastasia, was born of the unwanted pregnancy:

My mother cried. It must be my first memory. Alone in the dark narrow cold room, the two of us still bound together, she screamed and no one came and she cried. Once, the door opened and a sliver of light showed, but the nurse roughly asked why she was making so much noise, she wasn't ready yet. She kept screaming, the pain was so terrible. She wept, and from her pain, I emerged, I Anastasia, her punishment, the midge daughter.[49]

Thereafter, Anastasia feels that, midge-like, she developed inside her mother and devoured her, leaving behind only a chitinous shell.[50] While she could not understand why it was her fault that Jesus died or how he'd died for her, she had no trouble in understanding that her mother had died for her. So she and her sister, Joy, and their father laid their vitality at Bella's feet and tried to give her pleasure. This became increasingly difficult as she aged. There was a cold distance in her eye, and sometimes a sneer of contempt upon her lips: "Nothing, nothing you can do can console me for the loss of my life".[51]

As a child, Anastasia also tries to make up to her mother for her hard life, as Bella had done for her mother. She dreams of saving her from the past unhappinesses and of punishing the people who were mean to her, such as teachers impatient with her deafness, or Ed, who made her pregnant and yet had never ceased trying to make amends. Her mother's bad moods, her silences, her sinus headaches, the failed holidays, the looked-for hopes that always go awry, are incomprehensible to Anastasia, who forever blames herself as the cause. Sometimes, when there was nothing that would please her mother, Anastasia would accuse her of not loving her and Bella, lost in the suffering of her life, was incredulous at the injustice and cruelty of her daughter.

Anastasia reflects that emotional mothering is lost, where the physical struggle to survive is supreme and there is no energy for expressed love and acceptance. Even when times change and it is difficult but possible to make ends meet, the habit of investing all in the physical provision has become totally ingrained. There was no experience of anything else.

She knew above all the love her mother felt for her was there, in the dinner, in the food Mommy gave her, and somehow, although she loved food it was not enough.[52]

The tragedy of this situation is that, as a child, Bella had dreamed of how she would fill her daughter's life with the love and material benefits she had not had herself. In reality, she worked and scrimped and scraped to put both daughters through college, for Ed's wage was a meagre one. When Ed first vented his rage on the children, she'd stopped him, as her mother had never been able to stop her father. She was determined that her daughters would not become like her. Courageously, she had tried to invent a peaceful family life but she had no models, because the families she had known were all ripped apart by raging fathers and weeping mothers.

In her mature adulthood, Anastasia is able to recognise that her mother has no resources for mothering.

> She ... lived out her childhood in emptiness that was the eye of a violent storm, who was never held, never mothered, never once wrapped in warm strong arms so that she felt safe.[53]

But this understanding by Anastasia and her sister, Joy, is not enough and they continue to blame themselves for their mother's unhappiness: Joy says:

> "But she keeps asking me in her own silent way, to do something, to save her ... and I want to, I would if I could. But she's inconsolable. Oh, I love her. You know that. You love her too. We all do. Profoundly. She doesn't know what she does to us. She thinks she doesn't matter, she is sure she doesn't matter to us. And so she makes you feel it doesn't make any difference to her that you love her ... And it doesn't — her sorrow, her desolation are all that exist. ... She lies cold in the centre of my heart like a gravestone".[54]

Anastasia and Joy reflect that Bella is their favourite subject, the person who ripped them apart, the person who bonded them, the only thing in the world that told them they were sisters.

Anastasia's first steps toward living a life other than her mother's are not unusual. She denies being a woman and mixes primarily with boys. She does not finish college but acts out her mother's tragedy, becomes pregnant, is forced into marriage and her mother dismisses her. At the patriarchal style birth of her daughter, Arden, where she is allowed no sense of competence, Anastasia experiences the same joylessness that her mother had at her birth. She is locked into an arid marriage — an emotional and sexual desert. She has two dependent children, whom she cannot leave. Like her mother and her grandmother, she has no escape, due to financial dependency. Anastasia realises she has become like her mother.

But, as many daughters were beginning to do by the 1960s, she gradually makes a career of her own. When she becomes a successful photographer, her mother acknowledges her again. However, the career is hard-won and the novel takes us through many of the typical problems women face in the work-place — including being assessed for sexiness, rather than professional ability. She faces two divorces and above all children who make her feel guilty. There are the misunderstandings, the repetition of her own childhood, children who feel left out and who are not clear about their mother's motives. By adolescence, her children know how to rub the wound of their mother's guilt in salt. They misinterpret her pleasure in her job as a lack of love for them. They are never happy that she is happy in her work. She must secretly seek needed reinforcement from her mother who is as excited as she is at every achievement.

As part of her rebellion against Anastasia's believed inattention, her eldest daughter Arden marries, joins a commune and becomes the earth mother of three children. She believes she has chosen an alternative path to her mother, until she discovers she is repeating her grandmother's tragedy. She is weighed down by domestic drudgery and exploited by her man. She submits to his needs more than her own.

Anastasia is horrified to find that her daughters feel the same way about her moods, as she did about her mother's. She realises that, as a result of her hardships, she has become like her mother — inconsolable, unable to give up her clutched melancholia and her hopelessness.

> And I saw her inconsolability — mine, hers, her mother's before her — as the natural consequence of being alive for forty years as a woman.[55]

Eventually, Anastasia meets Clara, who encourages her to understand that she allows her children to demand too much. She is not responsible for every sorrow her mother has. It is presumed this habit gives her pleasure, or she would give it up. She also learns to value the attributes of women, their capacity for empathy, their capacity for the juice of life beyond 40. She resolves that women's work is important. In fact, the book has a great deal of domestic detail and the message is that the skills that go to feeding and clothing a family are as important and sometimes more important, than getting a car off the assembly line or any other skills respected by the male work-force.

Anastasia and her daughter discuss the past misunderstandings which are rooted in the problems of martyred mothers. They begin to learn to throw off self-sacrifice. Free of the imprisoning pattern of martyrdom, Anastasia is able to accept replacement mothering from other women and give it in return. She recognises that this is what women are good at.

An excellent example of replacement mothering and how invaluable it is in helping daughters survive oppression, can be found in the last novel to be discussed, *The Colour Purple* by Alice Walker.

Mothers and Daughters Surviving Multiple Oppression

Although *The Colour Purple* belongs to the genre that deals with the double oppression of mothers and daughters through colour and poverty, it highlights universal issues. Walker's characters are black mothers and daughters who survive not only racism, but commonly experienced obstacles and frustrations, including sexism, poverty and physical and mental abuse. These are exemplified in characters such as Sofia who describes her position thus:

> "All my life I had to fight. I had to fight my Daddy. I had to fight my brothers. I had to fight my cousins and my uncles. A girl child ain't safe in a family of men".

It is the story of two sisters who live in the American Deep South. The eldest, Celie, is raped continually by the man who is supposed to be her true father:

> "Then he push his thing inside my pussy. When that hurt I cry. He start to choke me, saying 'You better shut up and git used to it'".[56]

She is alienated from her mother by her step-father's sexual abuse of her and her mother's inability to recognise that her daughter is not willingly giving sexual services to her husband. After her mother's death, Celie tries to protect her younger sister, Nettie, from the abuse she has experienced. She becomes Nettie's surrogate mother.

Later, she learns that her true father is dead and the pseudo-father who has sexually abused her has disinherited her. She bears two children to this man, who takes them away from her at birth and leaves her to think they have been killed.

Tired of her, and seeing an advantage in it for himself, her 'father' gives Celie in marriage to the vain and bullying Albert. She is to look after him, his farm and his children. He too abuses her and she submits, but a spark of dignity remains in her bond with, and protection of, her sister. Nettie comes to live with them, but when Albert starts making sexual advances and attempts rape, she runs away with Celie's help. Celie's love for Nettie remains her source of survival, even though Albert ensures she never receives Nettie's letters.

The other source of strength is found in Shug Avery, a black singer, whom Albert loves. After the initial pain of rivalry, Shug Avery comes to act in the best tradition of surrogate mothers. Eventually, she leads Celie to a new independence and life of her own apart from Albert. Shug has fame and unlike Celie is assertive. Albert treats her royally, even humbly, and from her model Celie learns what women can be like.

This book is about the love and support of women, who hold the mirror one to the other, in order to show what each may be. The core of it is the strong support they provide for each other in developing self-esteem and a strong identity. It is one of the most endearing books about surrogate mothers and daughters.

Overview

This chapter has presented the outline of a number of short stories, novels and plays that deal with various aspects of mother-daughter relations. The tales have been told without comment so that readers can pin-point whatever is relevant for them. Some may want to go further and read in full the books that have particularly interested them.

All the stories recounted in this chapter relate to aspects of the psychology of the mother-daughter relationship that were discussed in previous chapters. In this chapter, fiction has replaced psychology and research and often describes fundamental feelings more vividly, because of the special talent the mothers and daughters who wrote the various pieces of fiction have for describing their own lives.

In this chapter we have met a suffocating mother who wanted her daughter to live out her own unfulfilled dreams, daughters coming to terms with disgraceful mothers and daughters facing the realisation that their mothers also had their own disappointments. It described the pain for mothers who did all they could, yet knew it was not enough. It dealt with daughters who find pride in the traditions of the women in their families.

The quest for a mother's past is a common experience, particularly after the death of a mother. Alice Munro's stories dealt with how the quest helped a daughter come to terms with a family and mother that were not ideal. Coming to terms involves recognising that our strengths spring from our non-ideal families and mothers.

Unfinished business between a mother and daughter led to mental confusion in the story of Grace and her daughter Anne. Grace was a kind, if vulgar mother. Anne dwelt on how her mother should be and therefore was unable to recognise that her mother could only be as she was. Anne was in a perpetual state of embarrassment about her mother's laughing, drinking, flirting, because her mother remained an extension of herself. Unable to find the resources to come to terms with her, she abandons her mother before her death. This is no solution, because her mother remains part of her. Eventually, guilt drives her to destructive self-punishment.

The next novel, two biographies and one autobiography asked whether identity formation and separation between mothers and daughters are very difficult if the mothers are overwhelming persons, by reason of their public images. Many daughters resent their mothers' public fame. Daughters of famous actresses have written at length about the inadequacies of their mothers. They may have needed to face up to the fact that their mothers were unpleasant people, in order to prevent resentment from consuming and wasting their lives. Or was it that they could not grow up and find the resources to create a separate identity from their mothers?

In the two stories here of charismatic mothers, the relationships are good. In the first, Rose Chernin learnt to be unlike her martyred mother. Her daughter, Kim, went through the usual adolescent and young adult separation rituals. Eventually, mother and daughter both came to acknowledge that each had a separate identity. This acknowledgement was the basis of their respect and love for each other.

Margaret Mead's story illustrated the importance of self-esteem for a good relationship between a famous mother and her daughter. Mead had to put up with a great deal of male chauvinism to become a functioning anthropologist. She formed a network of women and surrogate daughters who gave her more worthwhile support than her patriarchal colleagues. Her daughter was grateful for the model and values her mother provided about friendship between women, tolerance and respect for others and becoming a fulfilled person.

Grace Bartram's story offered something for daughters who are coping with a mother whose husband has left her and for mothers who are coping with an estranged relationship with a daughter. The resolution begins when the mother loses her apologetic incoherence and becomes her own person. These two factors do more for the mother-daughter relationship than anything else.

The novel by Marilyn French dealt with martyred mothers and their depressed daughters and how these stances can be handed on from generation to generation. It graphically illustrated how destructive these stances can be for mother-daughter relationships. Love by guilt is a prison.

The last novel looked at multiple oppression and how women can act as surrogate mothers to each other.

Novels like these can be used as a Bibliotherapy and encourage the realisation that we are not alone — that others have coped in this or that way. Self-realisation through Bibliotherapy is for those who want to take responsibility for change in themselves.

In the Conclusion that follows this chapter, the overall themes of Book I are summarised and given a final, unified direction.

ॐ

Conclusion to Book I

The Way Forward

Mending The Mother-Daughter Relationship

The path is not strewn with roses all the way. Like any other relationship, the mother-daughter relationship is very complex. It is not possible to give a one-directional answer to why a particular mother-daughter relationship is working or not working. Rather, mother-daughter relationships have to be approached on many fronts. Self-esteem, autonomy, gender, fathers, sexual attitudes, myths and stereotypes have been found to be particularly important. I have highlighted normal developmental upheavals and conflicts which may make a mother incorrectly feel that the relationship is failing when it is not. I have also discussed relationships that have become strained but are retrievable.

As this is a very common situation, in this conclusion to Book I, I shall review some of the ways in which mothers and daughters try to resolve their unhappiness with each other. Each resolution relates to a major theme of Book I. Here the main conclusions are summarised through some extended insights with the help of several mothers and daughters who are newcomers to my research and counselling programme. Their experiences demonstrate that, where some resolution is achieved, the first step is to acquire an awareness of the hidden and divisive cultural agendas that are influencing their particular mother-daughter relationship. Let us begin with Deidre who put her finger on a common, but often unrecognised agenda, that was disrupting her relationship with her mother — an agenda she and her mother had to rethink.

Changing:
Women are not the Second Sex

"I always thought my Dad was a great person. I was pretty antagonistic toward my mother. After I left home, I'd come back for occasional weekends and began to notice how Dad put Mum down — his generalisations about the neurotic, demanding nature of women. It suddenly hit me that this barrage was a major factor in my contempt for my mother. The problem was worsened by the fact that she always put him first and made us respect him. She made us be quiet when he wanted to sleep — but no one bothered when she needed to sleep during the day. If he was sick, she waited on him hand and foot and made us do the same. If she was sick, we'd rush her a bit of breakfast and that was it. She was expected to keep going.

I began to talk to her more and ask her more about herself, her hopes, her disappointments. It's taken a long time but I'm now beginning see that Mum has a lot of courage. She did her best out of the way she was brought up. She believed women must make themselves secondary to men. What has helped me get things into perspective is that she came into a little bit of money and became financially independent of Dad. She now stands up to him more. As he's retired and lost stature, she seems to have grown as a person. We are getting on much better. We've both had a talk to Dad and he's trying to stop his "put downs" of Mum and women."[1]

Mending this mother-daughter relationship started with building a respectful bond, which involved casting off the myth that devalues mothers and daughters — the superiority of men.[2] Mothers and daughters, who don't recognise the myth for what it is, find themselves subordinating their own needs to the male members of the household. They teach their daughters they are the second sex. They favour sons because they will become more powerful than daughters in the work-place. They are sad if their first born is not a son. They may compete for the attention of the father or sons.

The devaluing of femaleness leads to daughters' anger with their mothers for handing on their secondary status. If daughters can recognise what is making them angry and the trap which created their own and their mothers' secondary status, they have taken a huge step toward mending the relationship.

Giving Up the Ideal Mother Myth

The next step is to take another look at our mothers. At the end of Chapter 6 we met Michele Wandor and her humorous story "Meet My Mother"[3] which provides a good example. The daughter in this story had entombed her Jewish mother in stereotypes and could not talk to her. Her friend took a fresh look at this mother and found her more than willing to re-educate herself and escape the trap she was in. The tragi-comedy is that the daughter does not grow likewise and is left bemoaning the loss of a mother she loved to hate.

The problem for the daughter in Wandor's story is that she wants an "ideal" mother but her notion of "ideal" is ill-defined and contradictory. This is the core of her difficulty with her mother. It is not an unusual difficulty or at all surprising, since we are all indoctrinated by impossible definitions of the ideal mother. In short, such a mother is not humanly possible. She is a myth.

The pervasiveness of this myth was explored in Chapter 6, when daughters outlined what they expected of mothers, namely super mothering. They also told us that the ideal mother myth frightens them and that they are terrified they might fall short if, and when, they become mothers.

Because they've not had an opportunity to explore the inhumanity and ridiculousness of the myth, many daughters are angry because their mothers are not perfect. A daughter, whom I shall call Claudia, was no exception and told me of many incidents of which she was now ashamed. They were all trivial, as in the following example. She'd invited a friend, Ita, home to tea. Her mother had one of her close women friends there also and, as usual, they argued forcefully and amicably about current issues. The daughter was mortified. "You competed with one another and Ita noticed it", she accused her mother. Claudia wanted her mother to be the ideal, calm, unassertive mother. Her interaction with her mother was, as she put it, "teeming with stereotypes" which had to be surrendered before the relationship could improve. She is now working at accepting her mother as a fallible human being. She and her mother are finding the humour in their mutual fallibilities. Outings and visits together are now something to be looked forward to.

Said another daughter, Liliana:

> "I worked really hard at seeing my mother just as an ordinary fallible person. I now find I don't expect so much of her and we are getting on much better. Being angry with one's mother for not being some ludicrous supermum seems to be a difficult habit to get rid of."

Her mother, Ruth, said:

> "I know I haven't failed because Liliana is fatter than Twiggy and plans not to have any children. It's been hard to give up these myths about perfect daughters, but it has paid off. Liliana and I have some good close times and laughs together now."

Giving Up the Ideal Daughter Myth

The ideal daughter myth is as pernicious as the ideal mother myth. A mother is supposed to produce the ideal daughter. When the daughter isn't slim, beautiful, heterosexual, successful, well-dressed or agreeable, the mother may feel that she has failed.[4] In turn, daughters are distressed by their mothers' lack of endorsement and each becomes critical of the other.

Bianca described how she'd tried to be the ideal daughter all her life:

> "My mother and father used to have these awful rows and, after my father would storm out of the house, my mother would come and demand sympathy from me. I had to listen to all her troubles, help her with social events, fill in on all sorts of occasions and finally nurse her for four years before she died. I waited on her hand and foot. I never went out. I took a lot of abuse. Looking back on it, I'd have done better if I'd been like my brother and my sister who did what they could and no more. My sister used to say quite firmly, 'I

can't help you with that dinner party Mum, I've already got an engagement', or 'I've got to study' or 'I'm worn out', and Mum would accept it. The sad thing is that she liked them both better than me, probably because they didn't try to be perfect like I did."

Giving Up Negative Stereotypes

Daughters, along with their mothers, are undermined by many negative stereotypes. Often these stereotypes are attempts to diminish the caring skills of women. The belief that women's capacity for emotional response is neurotic is an example. Belief in this stereotype encourages mothers and daughters to fall into a self-fulfilling trap — the "we are crazy" trap — which is very destructive of respectful mother-daughter relationships. On the one hand, the stereotype becomes a false foundation for a daughter's contempt, not only of her mother, but of women in general and herself in particular. On the other hand, it makes mothers feel that their complaints are irrational.

Realistic examination of the situation of mothers is much more constructive than resorting to myths and stereotypes. Research shows women are coping with unjust and colossal burdens and frustrations and that their tears, complaints and depressions are not neurotic, but most often justified.

At the Australian Institute of Family Studies conference in November 1989, a number of research papers provided some of the relevant facts.[5] These papers revealed that even if the mother is working full-time, the expectation still exists that she should be "the always-there 'good' mother". Mothers are expected to "be there", fathers to "make time" to be with families.[6] While most agree with the theory that men should share equally in household tasks, in reality most fathers are as absent from home as were their forebears. Women are still performing the traditionally entrenched roles — preparing food, cleaning, doing the laundry, ironing, tidying, making beds and shopping. At the same time, they are also seen as primarily responsible for child care and the emotional well-being of their children.[7] The new, soft nurturant father is a myth. Fathers often express quite patriarchal attitudes about gender roles, parenting and their own masculinity.[8]

Quite apart from working outside the home and assuming the responsibility for most of the domestic work and child care, Caplan tells us that according to current estimates at least one third and probably closer to one half of mothers were victims of some kind of abuse.[9] In one third of families, fathers physically abuse mothers; in a larger number, they humiliate their wives.

Let us look at our mothers a little more closely and beyond their inability to match the perfect mother myths and stereotypes. Let us accept their fallibilities. Many of them are courageous and are survivors who have overcome substantial odds. These mothers often have an enormous capacity for emotion, for empathy and for forming relationships — the very that patriarchy sees as manifestations of the neurotic syndrome — the very attributes that daughters have absorbed by example from their mothers. Skills of caring and being a homemaker are underrated and invisible. At the end of the day, these skills don't always provide quantifiable and marketable outcomes — unlike producing cars on a production line or harvesting wheat. Work outside the home is more valued. Men's work has more status.

The trouble with patriarchal myths and stereotypes is that they are conflicting and "either" — "or". In fairy tales, mothers are either angels or witches. In psychological texts and in common parlance, mothering is supposed to be innate, yet the experts are supposed to know better. Mothers are accused of being too emotional, yet mothers must be caring.

Many daughters tell me that mutual discussions of myths and stereotypes and their contradictions has opened up their relationships with their mothers. A sense of humour helps. Said one daughter, "We actually got to the stage where Mum and I could laugh at how we acted out some of the stereotypes. Even Dad was ashamed of himself for using them to attack us and joined in the laughs too".

Looking at situations where mothers and daughters are not in conflict is also enormously helpful. Evidence of respectful mother-daughter relationships underline that the way things are is not fixed and inevitable, and has been provided here. For example, the mothers and daughters of Bethnal Green, who were described in Chapter 7, were mutually supportive. Similarly, Carroll Smith-Rosenberg's descriptions of mothers and daughters in the nineteenth century not only depicted closeness, but reminded us how much mother-daughter conflict is a product of economics.[10] Book II describes several societies and situations, unclouded by our current myths, where close mother-daughter relationships prevail.

Selecting a Therapist/Counsellor Carefully

Many mothers and daughters query the fact that they cannot get information about the myths that drive them asunder from the helping professions. They sometimes feel that the therapist is either not conscious of the myths or supports them. Even if they recognise them, their experience is that many therapists still operate within the framework of their traditional training. The drift of the therapy is that in order to be mentally healthy, they must accept their ambivalent attitudes to their mothers. Initially, this seems fine, until they find the direction means that they must recognise that their mothers are both "good" and "bad". The labels divert them from seeing their mothers as human beings who are fallible like anyone else. The therapy does not put the greedy expectation of the perfect mother in social context. It says nothing about patriarchal pressures for the impossibly ideal. Therefore, it cannot get away from the inference that mothers are partly bad — it cannot get away from mother-blaming.

For these reasons, many feel that therapy alienated them further from their mothers. These women are also often confused by what they see as the double bind of the conflicting messages they get from experts — namely, that 'good' mothering is essential to the mental health of their children and that mothers cause pathology in their offspring.

Experts, as we have seen from Chapters 1 and 8, face enormous difficulties. Child-rearing fashions change. Experts, especially one-theory experts,[11] disagree with other experts. Their knowledge may be based on untested theories that are divisive of mother-daughter relationships. Despite their disagreements, the experts usually have one thing in common — most are trying to make patriarchy work. In fact, as we saw in Chapter 1, they have a vested interest in keeping it going.

This is why traditional therapists so easily fall into mother-blaming. Many still genuinely believe that their hostile generalisations about mothers fit reality. Paula Caplan, in a review of articles in professional journals, found that mothers were blamed for 72 different problems ranging from bedwetting, schizophrenia, aggressive behaviour, learning problems to homicidal transsexualism.[12]

Cases in which a daughter's curable medical problem have been seen by the expert as due to the mother's pathology, are myriad.[13] In contrast are the large numbers of cases which have overlooked such matters as the paramount role of the father's depression in the emotional disturbances of his children — perhaps after World War II or the Vietnam War.[14] Its not unusual for his psychiatric disturbance to be added to the list of malfunctions said to be due to the mother.

Negative attitudes to mothers are influenced by theories which have a hard core of mother-blaming. Psychology and psychiatry are bedevilled by the jargon of mother-blaming. Mothers who stay with husbands who are, for example, violent alcoholics, are described as "co-dependent", "getting something out of the husband's problem", or indulging in the satisfaction of feeling "holier than thou". If these abused wives leave their husbands, they are often blamed for breaking up the family. Not infrequently, as a result of the mother-blaming ethos, a daughter of an alcoholic father will tell you that she blames her mother more and sees her as the cause of her father's alcoholism.

There has been a spate of feminist literature to combat mother-blaming, much of which I have discussed or listed in the Bibliography. Nevertheless, patriarchy is ever looking for the main chance — the opportunity to apply the myth that mothers are dangerous. For example, in the late 1980s it became the fashion for some experts to say that mothers are more likely to abuse their children. As Caplan points out, in general, these mothers spend more time with their children. Their husbands have left their families or are rarely home. So for each hour spent with the children, mothers actually abuse them far less than fathers do.[15] Moreover, the mothers' lack of support and poor self-esteem are not always addressed in the blaming process.

Caplan also sees a deterioration in the previously improved attitude to incest and a re-growth of mother-blaming in respect of it. Mothers are now said to coach children to give false claims of sexual abuse, because they are vicious, manipulative ex-wives taking revenge on their husbands. Caplan stresses that most reports of sexual abuse are true. She says scepticism about mothers prevents proper attention to abused children and illustrates her point in a story of a divorced mother's treatment. Her small daughter had said, "Daddy puts his thing in my pee-pee and it hurts a lot". Instead of thoroughly investigating the evidence, the sexual abuse team recommended that the mother take medication because they thought she might be a manic-depressive.[16]

Rejecting the Propaganda Against Closeness

The bias of some therapists and experts against mothers, even after several decades of modern feminism, was brought home to me in my work with parents and professionals as head of a Research and Community Liaison Unit within a University. Lecturers and volunteers came from every branch of the helping professions. Often mothers and daughters came together at seminars or worked together as volunteers. Invariably, there was a psychiatrist, a family therapist, a social worker, a psychologist, a teacher or an educationist, who queried the relationship. He or she would insist that mother and daughter were "too close". Usually, these experts knew absolutely nothing about the background of the particular mother and daughter, but were ready to judge that the close association was pathological.

Why is it that closeness with our mothers is attacked as unhealthy and pathological?[17] Closeness with a man is not seen in this way. There is little logic in this. Fear of closeness goes with fear of the mother-daughter alliance. Many a daughter is bullied by this fear. She is embarrassed to tell you that she rings her mother every day, enjoys visiting her or asks her advice on some issues. Yet in my experience, a daughter who has a genuinely close relationship with her mother is usually a secure and generous person. She is a person who is independent and knows her own mind and her mother is likewise. Both form good and stable relationships with a few well-selected friends and relatives.

Fortunately, there are mothers and daughters who are prepared to challenge the assumptions of the experts. For example, Eleni, who had sought help for post-rape trauma, talked about a session with a family therapist:

> "I asked her for evidence for her generalisations, that my relationship with my mother was my problem. I asked her on what her assumptions were based. I showed my anger at her prejudices that my close and friendly relationship with my mother meant I was overly dependent. I gave her some articles to read about prejudice against mothers among health professionals. She's becoming more tolerant. She said she'd not really stopped to think about the stereotypes her training had taught her to apply willy nilly."

This was a successful challenge because the therapist was open to rational change.

One, who didn't feel she had the background knowledge to challenge the experts, described her experience with a therapist:

> "I just had a gut feeling that it sounded like rubbish. He manoeuvred things so that I got angry with Mum, instead of the conditions under which Mum was raised. Mum is not marvellous; she's pretty old fashioned. I can see all that. But she did her best. Getting me angry with her doesn't get us anywhere. I could see my objections were threatening to the therapist and that he interpreted them as my being pathologically afraid of separating from my mother. I could have stayed with him and become neurotic, but I changed therapists. I'm now going to one who is very good. Perhaps we should have a directory of therapists in which they describe their position on a number of issues — just as Women's Electoral Lobby once issued a listing of politicians and their attitudes to women's issues."[18]

In order to quell the propaganda against mothers and their relationships with their daughters, we need to challenge the myths. We need to challenge the experts who support the myths. We can refuse to listen to anti-mother jokes and label them for what they are.

Giving Up Mother-Blaming

Mother-blaming is one among many forms of prejudice, but it's not included in psychological and sociological studies of prejudice in our universities. It is not socially acceptable to express prejudice against Aborigines or Jews, but prejudice against mothers is OK. Mother and mother-in-law jokes abound, but there are not many about fathers and fathers-in law. Insults, such as "son of a bitch", are commonplace. It is permissible to generalise about mothers as smothering and overprotective. It's regrettable to be a "Mummy's boy" but admirable to be a "Daddy's girl". Literature is overpopulated with Mrs Quests. The surfeit of this kind of propaganda gives us permission to blame our mothers and focus on where they failed and upset us.

Just as with any other form of prejudice, mother-blaming is meeting the needs of the prejudiced. Mothers have become the scapegoat for social and personal problems.[19] Mother-blaming perpetuates the unequal distribution of power between men and women. It keeps women feeling powerless and ashamed. It drains their energy, so they give up on justice for themselves. What is achieved by this divisiveness? It keeps mothers and daughters in conflict and it keeps them from understanding the part societal expectations play in that conflict.

Patriarchy isn't threatened by ignorant mothers and submissive daughters. Their ignorant and lowly position protects patriarchy from its fear of women's power — the power in their sexuality, their power to give birth, and the power mothers had over men when they were children. Many men are so fearful of women's power they must denigrate it to maintain their sense of manliness. Their fear of femininity in themselves has been turned into nightmares about engulfment — about being swallowed up by women's sexuality and mothering — about women's capacity for emotion and empathy.

Under patriarchy, men are afraid of being engulfed by love, as Simone de Beauvoir discussed so well in *The Second Sex.*[20] They do not realise how destructive this myth is of themselves and their relationships. One young man, who adored his new bride, described a sense of suffocation when he was ill and she nursed him. Even when he was well, he had to escape from her to the pub. He knew there was something wrong because his young wife was not dominating and controlling. He just couldn't stop himself from seeing her that way — like his mother. The myths, that wives are mothers and that mothers are engulfing, totally controlled his behaviour. They were destroying his marriage. We began some discussion of such myths — where and how he'd come across them in the past — and the insights he got from these discussions, about his fear of losing his manliness, put him on the path to self-understanding. He and his wife went on happily to have a family, a son and two daughters.

It is not only men who think they need mother-blaming to survive. Many a daughter has confessed to me that taking away her anger with her mother left her painfully facing up to her need to grow up. Mother-blaming had supplied the driving force of her whole existence. Many, many daughters describe how mother-blaming is all that they talk about with their women friends. They describe how it offers temporary relief from self-examination, but in the long run exacerbates their feelings of worthlessness.

Said one daughter, Marisa:

"Blaming is a cop out. It gets a relationship nowhere. I feel guilty for criticising my mother. I don't stop to get insight into why she irritates me so much. The myths allow me to use her as a whipping post."

This daughter went on to open up discussions with her mother. They set guidelines. Discussions were not to begin with blaming. Instead of "You make me feel ..." discussions began with "I feel ..." Marisa said it was quite a surprise. The many times she'd thought her mother had been uncaring or indifferent were times when her mother had been worried as to how to act in the best interests of her daughter. She said she could relate to the story of Kim Chernin and her mother given in Chapter 9.

Another daughter said,

"When I feel really angry with my mother, I try to see whether I am applying some stereotype — some myth. I find it really helpful to talk to my friends about this. We try to throw away the false labels. I've encouraged Mum to do the same with her friends. We are getting on much better. It's also helpful for each of us to know how much we are like everyone else."

One of many daughters who tried dealing with her problems by forming workshops in which adult daughters could share experiences, said, "You've got to set ground rules, otherwise the discussion degenerates into mother-blaming and every one tries to outdo everyone else".

For many a daughter, the worst outcome of a life of mother-blaming can follow the death of her mother. Often such a daughter expresses regret that she didn't make peace with her mother before she died. Mourning seems much harder. The unresolved ambivalences and problems become confused with the mourning process and can become destructive. In Chapter 7, we saw how Janna Somers tried to work through these feelings in relationships with surrogate mothers and daughters. Many women writers have found it therapeutic to write about their mothers after their death — Virginia Woolf being one of many women writers who tells us the value of this in Book II.

Not all of us can be brilliant authors, but many daughters find it beneficial to write to their mothers about the unfinished business between them.[21] For example, after having mourned unsuccessfully for her mother for over 20 years, Betsy told me:

> I write once a week and tell Mum where I think she was unreasonable and overlooked my feelings and needs. Before she died and we had that terrible row, she told me where I was short in respect of her needs, so I tell her where I think she was probably right or wrong. I tell her I regret we didn't air these things. I talk about our good times. I ask her questions and try and think up answers from her perspective and mine. It makes me feel less guilty.

Recognising That Our Worst May Be Our Best

Mothers are often in a double bind. While wanting to do the best for their daughters, they often do the worst. They know patriarchy has delegated them to produce the kind of daughter that guarantees the status quo — a mothering, nurturing, submissive daughter. Many mothers feel guilty and blame themselves if their daughters become the contrary — assertive, clever, perhaps swearing or arguing on equal terms with men. Did they do the right thing? Will their daughters drive potential husbands away and become lonely, even ostracised? Daughters don't always recognise that a mother's doubts and criticisms may come from patriarchal demands and are attempts to make life, as they see it, easier for their daughters.

Sometimes a mother finds pride in something that is traditionally advocated, but is not in the best interests of her daughter. For example, patriarchy has created the tenet that a daughter is her mothers' right arm. As a result, most daughters have to grow up more quickly than their brothers. This leaves daughters feeling insufficiently mothered. The double bind is that mothers who have been indoctrinated by the 'right arm tenet' are proud that their daughters are not as needy as their sons. But they have been prevented from recognising that the behaviour that gives them pride also signifies their daughters' deprivation.

Discussions of the origins of our neediness and ways of reworking it are important. A daughter, whom I shall call Caroline, told of her attempts to do this:

"I talked a lot with friends who had brothers and found their mothers behaved the same way. We asked why. We then realised the same thing had been done to our mothers and why we couldn't expect them to be revolutionaries. That moved us onto how to cope with the way we were running around looking for mothers. I realised I just had to stop looking for mothers in men and blaming Mum when it didn't happen. I'm working on mothering myself. When I pass an exam, I indulge myself. When I've worked hard, I do my favourite things or loaf in the sun. I praise myself for things well done. I'm going up so much in my estimation, that Mum's or anyone else's approval is becoming less important. It's good to have it for feedback, but if I don't get it, it's not the end of the world any more."

Should We Give Up On Some Mothers?

The single-minded pursuit of mothering from others is rarely fruitful in adulthood. It is particularly unfruitful if the target is unable to provide it. Sometimes, it is necessary to face up to the fact that a mother is an unpleasant person — mean, abusive, unresponsive, uncaring. The problem is that daughters of such mothers may feel guilty that they do not love their mothers or cannot grieve when they die. They often feel that they are bad. It is important to undo this inference. A daughter is not bad because her mother says so. Her mother may be a poor judge for many reasons. Nor are daughters deficient because they have poor mothers.

Sarah, whose mother was very selfish and rejecting, said:

"I used to feel that I was bad because my mother always told me I was — that I made her unhappy. I've thought about the awful childhood she had and can see that is why she's as she is — not because of me. It doesn't make me like her any better, but I stopped expecting her to be a perfect mother. I knew I could have no expectations of her — to long for them was self-destructive. I then started thinking about my good points — my talents. I concentrated on those. Actually, I realise that because of my unhappy experiences with her, I've got a lot of talents I wouldn't have otherwise. I'm pretty good at judging people's moods. I'm self-reliant. I'm a good listener . . ."

When they have stopped seeing their mothers as witches and simply as not very nice persons, many daughters find they lose the compulsion to get their mothers to change their attitudes toward them. They stop feeling guilty about not having the perfect mother and not being the perfect daughter. Some can then set limits on the relationship and on expectations. They can be firm and calm in their resolve to behave in certain ways with their mothers.

Said Terisita:

> "It helped me enormously to understand how my mother became such a cruel and abusive person. My Aunt Florent told me a lot about how she was sexually abused — what their father was like. Mum's a lost cause. Knowing doesn't make me want to see her more often, but at least I know I'm a good person. She was wrong about me. I don't need her approval anymore."

Humanising Our Mothers

Other burning issues for daughters are disgraceful or disabled mothers or mothers with idiosyncracies that embarrass. By way of illustration, I've already referred to Alice Munro's stories of a child whose mother had Parkinson's disease[22] and of a daughter whose mother, in her eyes, was gauche enough to sell encyclopaedias.[23] Jeanette Winterson told us about a militantly religious mother who had a horror of graven images and gave her a tortoise called "Psalms" in an effort to remind her to continually praise the Lord.[24] These imperfect mothers, say these daughters, made us as we are and we wouldn't have it any other way.

These writers are revisiting their mothers. They do this in many ways. They may write about their mothers' childhoods, because it helps them see their mothers not just as mothers, but as vulnerable human beings with funny quirks and perhaps courage. Incidents in their mother's childhood become a shared heritage. Attwood has done this in her short story, "Significant Moments in the Life of My Mother". Munro did it in "Princess Ida". Many daughters tell me that finding out about their mothers' childhood is a very effective way to humanise their mothers. Once mothers are humanised, daughters don't feel the same urge to turn their human faults into monstrosities.

Building Self-esteem

One of the major themes of Book I has been that self-esteem is a crucial factor in mother-daughter relationships. Assaults on women's self-esteem are found in negative myths about women, indoctrination about the superiority of men, and intolerance and prejudice toward mothers. But mothers and daughters do not have to accept this. Book II gives examples from antiquity to the present day of how they have mutually maintained self-esteem. For instance, at the height of Victorian patriarchy and its misogyny, women gave morale-boosting support to each other in the work-place and through mother-daughter relationships that were not nec-essarily based on biology.

The forgotten history of mothers and daughters is packed with similar examples, that have been overlooked in the writings of the medieval writer, Christine de Pizan, Jane Austen, Charlotte Brontë and many others. These women successfully faced and fought patriarchal prejudice for their own self-esteem and the esteem of other women. In this conclusion to Book I, three contemporary daughters, Sarah, Caroline and Terisita, have also described how they worked on their self-esteem. Like them, we can recognise our attributes and act upon them. We can find and build support networks to maintain self-esteem. We can expose and reject the myths that undermine our self-esteem. We can find pride in our mother-daughter heritage.

Courageous mothering and daughtering involves esteem building in ourselves and each other. The hardest thing for a daughter is a mother who criticises every move, as we saw in Chapter 6. The importance of building self-esteem in a child-daughter and how to do it was stressed in Chapter 2.

Daughters with poor self-esteem find themselves in double-bind situa-tions. They believe their mothers do not approve of them, yet desperately need approval from their mothers. They both blame their mothers and long for their mothers' approval. They are mortified when they don't get the desired praise. They long for closeness but experience their mothers as having the power to make them feel infantile and inadequate. They despair of pleasing, but feel they weren't mothered enough. They hate themselves for being so critical.

How can we deal with these ambivalent emotions? In practice, I find that daughters who deal with them successfully, have worked hard and long at acquiring good self-esteem. Good self-esteem is accompanied by a strong feeling that they are self-responsible persons. It goes with a sense of security about their judgements of themselves. They are no longer threat-ened by every criticism.

Lisa is one of many daughters who learnt to acknowledge that achiev-ing and maintaining good self-esteem depended on her taking responsibility for herself. After a long stretch of poor self-esteem that took the usual form of her depression, she said:

> You might wonder why I was doing so well for a whole year and then retreated back into depression. I suddenly realised in the weekend what I was doing. It's easier to have poor self-esteem. Everyone makes allowances for you. You don't have to try. You don't have to motivate yourself to realise all the potential you have. You can say, 'I could do it if I didn't have poor self-esteem'. Poor self-esteem is my cocoon. I didn't want to give it away for the effort and responsibility that good self-esteem involves.

Lisa is now working very hard at expressing her potential. Each new achievement builds her self-esteem and she makes sure she praises and rewards herself for it.

The Fear of Becoming Like Our Mothers

Because the female is seen as the second sex, because motherhood is under-valued, because they see their mothers' martyrdom, daughters fear becoming like their mothers. Daughters everywhere are working hard at getting rid of that fear, by showing the worth of their sex, rejecting the second sex stereotypes and understanding how these stereotypes damaged their mothers. One of many who has trodden this path successfully, is Chris. She described her now past fears of becoming like her mother and the measures she took to overcome these fears. They involved achieving a job she enjoys and a great deal of discussion with her mother and friends about patriarchal undervaluation of women:

> "Every step involved some set-backs. I think at first Mum was threatened by me when I was promoted at work. It made her feel a failure because she'd given up everything for us kids and Dad. I'd felt I had to be very careful about talking about my success. But we talked a lot about how society frustrates and puts women down and how things are changing. Then she wanted to hear about my work. She's now my greatest supporter. She's the one I can turn to for sympathy when the men at work make it tough for me."

Chris added that she could identify with the experience of Anastasia in relation to her mother, Bella, in Marilyn French's *Her Mother's Daughter*, discussed in Chapter 9.

Daughters who do not manage to communicate as Chris did, dread the recuring awareness that they sound, act, behave, react or look like their mothers. Kath says:

> "The feeling that something in you is like your mother is loathsome. It comes from identifying with the prejudices that women are second rate. Mum and I discussed where these prejudices in us came from and how destructive they are. We had to apply ourselves to enjoy being female. We started reading positive novels. We stopped reading about or watching movies about women as victims."

Embarrassment About Our Mothers

There is also the problem of feeling that everything our mothers or daughters do reflects on us. Alice Munro's story, "Princess Ida",[25] described an adolescent daughter's acute feeling that her mother's embarrassing sales' spiel about encyclopaedias reflected upon her. This is understandable in adolescence. Usually, by adulthood, a separate identity has been forged. If a sense of separate identity isn't achieved, the embarrassment continues.

One daughter, Liz, who had a very eccentric mother who was a well-known writer, described her embarrassment about her mother:

> "Mum would come to our school open days in old army gear. She seemed to delight in shocking the teachers and parents. Actually, looking back on it, I think they found her an enjoyable eccentric, because they liked to name drop that they knew her. At first, I dreaded open days. Then one day I decided she was doing all this potty behaviour for herself and I had no part in it. After that, I could joke about her to my friends, but I could do it with pride because she was a remarkable person."

This daughter was blessed with a great sense of humour which gave her the power to see her mother as other than an extension of herself. Some, like Kim Chernin, whom we met in Chapter 9, have to go through much longer and more divisive separation rituals to achieve the separation which enables them to accept their mothers as individuals in their own right.

At the end of these rituals, most daughters and mothers often express astonishment when they find each other's real motives for behaving as they do. An understanding of real motives is possible when each has humanised the other, given up interpretations based on myths and acquired the security of good self-esteem. Said Karen:

> It used to drive me mad when Mum wanted to do my shopping for me or help with the housework. It took me a long time and some careful listening to realise she wasn't trying to control me. She just felt she'd lost purpose without children at home and wanted to feel useful. After I realised what was really going on, I relaxed and found her help very useful.

During the processes of finding their individuality, some daughters are quite cruel to their mothers. They act against their involvement with them with violent rebelliousness. In later years, they speak sadly of a sense of alienation from their mothers and shame at their behaviour. Other daughters speak of the kind of alienation that makes them want to run away from their mothers because they cannot rescue them. Rose Chernin did her utmost to rescue her mother, but ultimately had to make a choice — her own survival. Such daughters tell me that insights into the social pressures on mothers and daughters, and understanding the psychology of the search for individuality, can put these problems into perspective. They benefit from airing their concerns with those who can recognise the often false sources of guilt.

Imperfect and Fallible Mothers Are Catalysts

The problem is that the patriarchal myth of the so-called "perfect" mother has created greedy and unrealistic expectations in daughters. It drives mothers to bow to their daughters' immature demands because they are inhibited by the myth that a "good" mother does not fight or argue with her daughter.

But by adolescence, the clash of opinion and perspective between mothers and daughters is an essential part of the maturing process. Dissonance between herself and her mother helps a daughter understand how she herself thinks and feels. It encourages her to define herself more clearly and cast off childhood. With "perfect" mothers, daughters would remain infantile. Their mothers would anticipate their every need, create their every comfort, and the daughter would never learn to take responsibility, cope with discomfort or negotiate the challenges of every-day living.

The developmental process of a daughter achieving independence can also be a time of growth in mothers. The challenges of a daughter can initiate the revision of old perspectives and the taking on of new roles. Mothers and daughters who express their difficulties with each other are working at renegotiating their relationships. Discussion of these issues began in Chapter 3 and continues throughout Book II.

Older Women Are Not Our Mothers

The excessive demands on women as mothers is often easier to observe in mothers other than our own. Good objective examples can often be found among older women, whom not only men but younger women expect to act as their mothers. Caplan reports a paper given by Rachel J. Siegel: "We are not your Mothers".[26] Siegel writes that people expect older women to be mothering, to understand and advise. They feel justified in getting angry if the expected nurturance and idealised behaviour is not forthcoming.

The case of Simone de Beauvoir is an excellent illustration. Television documentaries and biographies have recorded how many feminist saw Simone de Beauvoir as leading the way in a new deal for women.[27] In the process, they imagined her as an impossibly ideal and courageous mother figure. After her death and when it was discovered how fallible and human she was in her sometimes submissive relationship with Sartre, her criticism of other women and her personal living, the reaction was, "How could she?" "She's let us down".

The syndrome of idealising some women as mother figures contains conflicting and destructive elements. On the one hand, total nurturance is expected from the mother figure, on the other hand, mutual responsibility is ignored. Because the idealised replacement mother is expected to be infallible, there is no recognition that she too might need nurturance and support.

One colleague commented on a woman in her fifties who was head of a charity:

> "I was pleased when she told the staff and volunteers off for expecting her to be the ideal mother and described the bottomless pit her situation was. Everyone on the staff expected her to listen to their problems, but they never had time to listen to hers. They

expected her to fill in when they couldn't make it or forgot. They half did jobs and expected her to finish for them. They threw a fit if they were asked to take any responsibility. They wanted her to praise, praise, praise them — but never thought she might need a little self-esteem building too. If she didn't praise them, they were mortified. They thought they could speak insensitively to her but were as touchy as could be about their own feelings. Some of them threw tantrums like four year olds. They treated her like a super-mother. They expected and demanded too much. Now she's quit, they are sorry."

The same colleague pointed to the saying "Behind every good man there is a good woman" and said, "We need to act out a new saying, "Behind every good woman there are a myriad of good women".

Letting Fathers Off the Hook

Throughout history, the first of these sayings has allowed many an ambitious male egoist to exploit women as secretaries, supporters and drudges. Without these women, large numbers of causes and enterprises would never have left the ground. In the same way, we let father's off the hook in family interactions. Said one daughter, "I've got used to the fact that Dad sends me a birthday card about once every four years". The same daughter confessed she would be furious if her mother forgot her birthday. She was so grateful when her father did remember that she thought him more nurturant than her mother.

We also let fathers off the hook when considering personality formation in daughters. We often forget how important a role a father plays as a model for his daughters as well as his sons. For example, many daughters speak about their feelings of emotional emptiness. They blame their mothers, instead of looking to the model their fathers provided. In many cases, he was a person who suppressed his own emotionality in case he was accused of being effeminate. He portrayed emotionality as a devalued female characteristic.

Fathers spend less time with the family and are rarely involved in the daily grind of parenting.[28] This is why it is easier for children to idealise fathers. The effect of the disparity in child care responsibility on mother-daughter relationships has been discussed in Chapters 2, 5 and 6. Chapter 5 dealt with the profound effect fathers have on mother-daughter relationships. If daughters accept patriarchal prescriptions that fathers are superior and mothers inferior, they see themselves as inferior. This augers poorly for mother-daughter relationships.

Overview

In summary, mothers and daughters come to terms with their relationships through a great variety of individual solutions. However, there are basic consistencies that can be identified. Understanding the basic psychology of mother-daughter relationships gives an objective start. At the same time, some insight into the social and economic context in which psychological relationships take place, is necessary. For most of the women who took part in my research, this meant an awareness of the way in which patriarchy operates and the strains it puts on mother-daughter relationships. Resolving mother-daughter relationships for these women involved tearing the mask off the myths that mothers should be perfect, daughters should be perfect, mothers are to blame for everything, mothers are secondary, women are secondary, mothers are monsters, mothers are witches, mothers are engulfing, powerful, dangerous, mother-daughter closeness is unhealthy and so on.

Once this process of understanding was put in motion, mothers and daughters were equipped to identify their problems with each other more clearly. You will note that, in all the cases I've quoted, the next step was to give up mother-blaming and look at the human side of the mother, perhaps her childhood, her past. Many daughters then examined their own guilt and whether it was founded on reality or myth — whether the motives were as they thought. Most said that discussion with friends was enormously helpful. Above all, mothers and daughters found that building self-esteem was crucial. Without it, they could not give up criticism of each other and remained touchy about anything that was not fulsome praise.

Exploring the basic psychology of mother-daughter relationships has been the particular purpose of Book I. Its themes have been illustrated with cases taken from life, novels and short stories, some of which can be used as a Bibliotherapy. In Book II, I move onto a celebration of the mother-daughter relationship through a re-discovery and re-interpretation of the reading of our childhood and young adulthood. Many mothers and daughters claimed that developing a mutual sense of pride in their history enriched their relationship. It is to this end that Book II is dedicated.

ᘯ

BOOK II

Retrieving Our
Heritage

ॐ

Introduction

Literature and legend are excellent sources for in depth understanding of human relationships, including mother-daughter relationships. A good story can bring alive facets that may sound convoluted in the theories of psychologists, sociologists, anthropologists and psychiatrists, or in the recounts of clinicians. Unfortunately, so much was missed in the novels and legends we read at school, because these were interpreted from a patriarchal viewpoint.[1] Anything with as secondary a status as mothers and daughters have had under patriarchy was likely not to be paid much attention or, if it was, the insights were likely to have overlooked the feminine perspective.[2]

The following chapters overturn and attempt a re-examination of some of our school learning without the patriarchal myopism that makes mothers and daughters marginal.[3] The object is to contribute to the awareness and consciousness raising, which will enable men and women to see the equally central role of mothers and daughters in history and society. The concept of their marginality, as it presently stands, contributes to poor relations between mothers and daughters and conflict between men and women. People without the kind of good self-esteem that is derived from pride in their origins denigrate each other and accept secondary status, because it is all they have known.[4]

The marginality of mothers and daughters is incorporated, not only through the psychological processes by which they learn about their self-concepts and self-esteem, but by the literature they read about women. It is strongly reinforced by their lack of an acquired sense of history. While we learn a great deal about the exploits of fathers and sons in school, we are taught little about the role of mothers and daughters throughout history. Any literature by mothers and daughters, about themselves, is largely measured by a patriarchal yardstick or given a patriarchal emphasis. For example, Jane Austen's participation in the patriarchal denigration of sensibility is well taught, but her revolutionary portrayal of independent daughters is most often not. Charlotte Brontë is remembered for her literary talent, but not for the fact that she was an outstanding social historian. More often, she is seen as an 'odd ball' for her times, when in fact she was able to capture the every day experiences of mothers and daughters in the first half of the nineteenth century.

Many chapters in this book deal with the reaction of patriarchy to the friendships of some great women, which were often surrogate mother-daughter relationships. They include the nurture and protection of young female novices by the Abbesses of medieval convents and the creative support given by their close women friends to nineteenth and twentieth century authors, such as Colette and Virginia Woolf. Some of these friendships had a sexual component, others were loving without sexual content, and others were based on the pragmatics of similar interests and support in the work-place. Whatever their nature, it was when understanding, respect and support were generated in these friendships, that the mother-daughter relationship benefited. It was through their friendships with other women, that Colette and Woolf learnt to value their mothers. The following chapters address the imbalance of having heard so much about friendships between men or about strong men who provided opportunities for younger men, yet so little about great surrogate mothers or productive friendships between famous women.

In the first two chapters, we look to the myths of the Goddesses, which have intrigued men and inspired women. Is the idea of a Goddess rather than a God ludicrous? Many would say "No". The idea is used extensively in the consciousness raising literature for women. Moreover, in interviews with women in 1982, in a wide sample,[5] a large percentage recalled a fascination with Goddess legends during adolescence. It was conjectured that this was because, like fairy stories, they are among the few sources for observing strong female models during the crucial years of identity development. Also, some of the legends deal with aspects of male/female and sexual relationships, for example dominance and submission, which concern women. Many women recalled that they'd found these aspects of the Greek legends particularly disturbing during adolescence. The reasons for this may become apparent in Chapter 2.

Looking at the evidence surrounding Goddess legends leads to an examination of the contention that ancient matriarchies existed. If matriarchies did exist, were the relationships between mothers and daughters better because women had power and status? What are the facts? Gerda Lerner and other historians put the controversy in perspective in Chapter 3 — providing mothers and daughters with a more realistic awareness of the origins of their present condition, than do many patriarchal compensatory myths.

Some of course would argue that it matters not whether Goddess and women-centred societies ever existed. What matters is that for centuries man has had a fictional God to endow him with power and centrality. Why shouldn't women equally have fictional sources of inspiration?

History, by making male exploits central, has created the myth that women are marginal to the creation of history and civilisation, thereby profoundly affecting the psychology of women and men. According to Gerda Lerner, "It has given men a skewed and essentially erroneous view of their place in human society and in the universe".[6]

Gerda Lerner believes that, in appropriating the symbols of the communication system to create the centrality of men, the scholars and leaders of patriarchy have built a conceptual error of vast proportions into all their thought.[7] By taking the half for the whole, they have not only missed the essence of whatever they are describing, but have distorted it in such a fashion, that they cannot see it correctly.

The implication for mothers and daughters is that they most often see themselves in these false and partial metaphors and define themselves in relation to but half of reality, namely men. This inevitably leads to self-devaluation and conflict.

Lerner makes another important point:

> The androcentric fallacy, which is built into all the mental constructs of Western civilisation, cannot be rectified simply by· 'adding women'. What it demands for rectification is a radical restructuring of thought and analysis which once and for all accepts the fact that humanity consists in equal parts of men and women and that the experiences, thoughts, and insights of both sexes must be represented in every generalisation that is made about human beings.[8]

Women have largely lacked any knowledge of a history of female autonomy or alliance, or models of women who have lived without male protection, because patriarchal history obliterated or largely overlooked such information. This is why recovering this history is important to consciousness raising. It restores a sense of continuity to mothers and daughters and, in turn, the dignity of their relations with each other.

The marginality of women in the past was furthered in the denial of higher education for them, which limited their abstract skills for defining their own linguistic and ideological system. Ideas can only be generated when the oppressed have an alternative to the system of symbols and meanings belonging of those who dominate them.[9]

The few women who have been admitted to the centres of intellectual activity of their day have had first to learn to "think like a man", and usually so internalise that learning, that they lose the ability to conceive of alternatives. Fortunately, throughout history, there has been a tiny minority of privileged mothers and daughters, who have been able to free themselves of androcentric thought and give an alternative female perspective on art, philosophy and fiction — often at great cost. Mothers and daughters of this ilk, include Mary Wollstonecraft, Charlotte and Emily Brontë, Colette and Virginia Woolf, and their special insights are included here.

Some women have, in their time, been forced to live on the margins of society and their ideas considered so deviant and improper, that it was difficult for them to win influence and approval. Many were daughters with strong and supportive mothers, or at least with surrogate mothers, who had a profound influence on their lives. They all give us insight into what it was like for them to be a mother or a daughter.

Women's literary voices, marginalised and trivialised by the dominant patriarchal establishment, have also survived in the undercurrent of oral tradition- folksongs and tales of powerful witches and good fairies.[10] Women left records of the mother-daughter relationship in their embroidery, their diaries and their prayers. We can find mothers and daughters in the ancient myths and legends of Greece and Rome, in the records of early Christianity and in the romances of medieval times. We can see them in the plays of Shakespeare and in the letters they wrote to each other during the Renaissance and beyond. More realistically than psychology or psychiatry is able to describe them, we find mothers and daughters as Jane Austen, the Brontës or George Eliot depicted them in their novels. We can identify with Virginia Woolf's working through her relationship with her mother in her portrayal of Mrs Ramsay in *To The Lighthouse*. We can envy and aspire to Colette's acceptance and love for her fallible mother, when we read her many descriptions of her. These are the traditions of mothers and daughters, which are recorded in Book II.

By ignoring marginality and re-reading history and literature about mothers and daughters, with a strong, feminine orientation in mind, we can reconstruct our own symbols and consciousness. As mothers and daughters, we can see ourselves outside the patriarchal metaphors and self-fulfilling prophecies, which have put us in contempt of each other.

To sum up, this second book concerns a selection of readings that I have found mothers and daughters enjoy. They find them interesting and morale-boosting. Men have found them equally fascinating. The selection is deliberate — chosen entirely for the purpose of consciousness raising about mother-daughter traditions in literature and history. It is not comprehensive as that would run to several volumes. Nor is Book II a history in the usual sense of the word. Rather it focuses on neglected and little known issues which, when recalled, can help redress the imbalances of patriarchal records and put mothers and daughters back into history. It is largely a selection of events and writings that have been traditionally interpretated so that the mother-daughter alliance is obliterated. It shows how the mother-daughter tradition has survived in patriarchal literature and how it can be rediscovered.

Book II is intended for ordinary men and women, who might like to recover the misplaced pieces and participate in the consciousness raising necessary for rediscovering the mother-daughter alliance. It is about changing consciousness through re-reading novels and educational texts. It is about re-looking at famous literary figures and their lives and seeing them in a different framework from that imposed by school, university, work-place or society in general. By rethinking self, lifestyle, world view, historical view or personal view, we are taking political action. We must know that everyday relationships are political and a source for change.

The book begins by looking at societies where mothers and daughters are much more central than they are in our own. What are the outcomes for their relationships?

☙

CHAPTER 1

Societies in Which Mothers and Daughters Are Central

Matrilineal societies, where social identity, property and rights over land are transmitted through women, see male and female identities very differently from the way they are defined in post-industrial western society. Do these differences have any major effect on mother-daughter relationships? Among several historians and some feminists, who have researched into or theorised about ancient matrilineal societies, are those who say they do.[1] As matrilineal societies survive to this day, it is worthwhile looking at one existing example to see whether there are any factors within its organisation which throw some light on mother-daughter relationships. If there are, then the pursuit of the historical evidence and conjectures in later chapters becomes relevant to our present day situation. I therefore begin with an account of a contemporary matrilineal society — the Tubetube of Milne Bay Province in Papua New Guinea.[2]

Among the Tubetube, middle-aged women become leaders of their lineage groups by virtue of seniority and having the requisite personal qualities.[3] When a girl is born into the group, as a potential bearer of a future generation, her birth is celebrated. Women grow up knowing that they are essential members of their lineage and that they are the guardians of the land belonging to their group.

Tubetube fathers are indulgent and caring parents, who spend a lot of time with infants and are noticeably more engaged with them than most western fathers.

All the women of a single generation are mothers to each other's children. If a woman is ill or unable to attend to the needs of her biological children, the children live with another of their mothers. All adult women, regardless of their marital status, have children — not necessarily their biological children — of whom they take care. One of the observable results of this extension of child-parent relationships is an absence of disputes over the custody of children.

Physical and verbal violence are not condoned and adult offenders are required to pay compensation to anyone they hurt or insult. Both male and female children are inculcated with the same ideas of decorum and respect for others. There are few gender-specific behaviours. Women are economically independent. The brother-sister bond is central and each takes life-long responsibility for the other and their children. This contributes to the autonomy of Tubetube women. Sons and daughters perceive their interests as identical.

Thus here, in a matrilineal society, are caring fathers, multiple mothers, lack of violence and less oppression of the female sex. One can surmise that mother-daughter relationships are close and good, because of the equality of status and independence permitted females.[4]

Mother-Daughter Relationships in Pre-Patriarchal Societies

Although lineage and property rights are transmitted through women in matrilineal societies, this does not necessarily mean that women are the most dominant and powerful group.[5] Nevertheless, anthropologists and historians argue that ancient matrilineal societies, far from being savagely aggressive and cruel, were probably gentle, humourous and peaceable, like the Tubetube. They probably lived in small kin groups formed around a mother or mothers.[6]

Several anthropologists and historians who have taken an interest in ancient matrilineal societies, also suggest that it was through their experience of feeding and protection of the young, that women led the way to agriculture and house building. Through attempting to communicate with their infants and children, mothers developed language.[7] Mothers and daughters also figured prominently in all aspects of early civilisation. They can be found in a host of activities as merchants, ships' captains, farmers, chariot drivers, hunters and priestesses.[8]

In these early societies, because survival consisted largely of seeking protection from the elements and food gathering, it was easy to recognise that the most powerful act was the creation of another human being — the act of giving birth. The role of the male was not recognised until much later, as we shall see in Chapters 2 and 3. From awe at the act of giving birth, it is but a small step to a belief and a religion, that it was a woman who created the world and some of these creation myths are given in the next chapter.[9] In the early religions, the concept was of a Great Cosmic Mother, a grandiose version of a woman giving birth. As consciousness became more sophisticated, a Goddess was envisaged whose power was acknowledged by rites and sacrifices, inspired by the anxieties of her followers.[10]

Adrienne Rich has suggested that in many of these pre-patriarchal societies, mother-daughter relationships were dignified and their alliance strong, because these societies not only revered the work and contribution of women, but they shared certain kinds of woman-centred beliefs and woman-centred social organisations.[11] Women were venerated in several aspects — the primal one being maternal. The surviving mythology, sculpture, art and folk tales of these ancient eras attest to the presentation of women as beautifully strong — neither young nor old, and as self-possessed and calm. A woman was not portrayed as insipid, trivial, nor as a sex object, as is contemporarily the case.

Nor was she, like the female of the much later Christian period, depicted as absorbed in contemplation of the child at her breast. She is herself, even when nurturing her infant. She exists not to seduce or please man, but to assert herself. Rich conjectures that women of this period must have felt constantly validated by these images, which asserted that women are primary, awesome and central.[12]

Because of women's achievements and contributions and the high status of maternity in these pre-patriarchal societies, mother-daughter relationships and status were far more important than wife status. According to Rich, the foundation of all social bonds was seen as the one between mother and child and, from women's child-rearing functions, there flowed a natural division of labour. Above all, the mother-daughter relationship was regarded as most sacred; the rituals of art, creativity and birth were handed on from mother to daughter and there were temples, rites and Goddesses sacred to them.

Rich's belief in the more ascendant role of women in pre-patriarchal society was, in part, derived from the work of Erich Neumann.[13] He suggested that pottery making was invented by women and the art highly revered. Pottery made possible the long term storage of oils and grains and the cooking of a variety of foods, all of which had a civilising influence. Thus, the art of pottery came to be revered as a feminine force and transformation, and held to be as much a part of the creative activity of the time, as the making of a child. Examples of this are found in the ancient records from Neolithic Europe, where the pot was seen as having the body and the womb of the Great Mother. The clay, from which it was made, was believed to have a woman's soul and no man was allowed to see the female potter at work.[14]

Rich[15] and Neumann[16] see the invention of pottery as perhaps the most revolutionary creation throughout history. Women also decorated the pots and learnt, through experiment, how the colour changed with the firing process. Sjöö and Mor carry the argument further and state that there is evidence that women developed art and language out of the potter's craft.[17] This argument is based on the fact that the sacred pots were decorated with symbols and depictions of rituals, which were understood by the users and became standardised as a shorthand language over thousands of years.[18]

Certainly, recent discoveries of Neolithic/Chalcolithic scripts belie historians, who had long argued that the earliest example of written language was in later patriarchal societies. Sjöö and Mor, Shuttle and Redgrove and Miles also suggest that women, in women-centred societies, invented abstract notation, observational science and early mathematics, out of practical observations of the needs and rhythms of the human collective and their own bodies.[19] Their methods were distinct from later patriarchal mathematics and science, which is based on a desire to conquer nature. Several historians describe the Goddess-worshipping societies as embracing the time in which all the basic inventions essential to human culture were born. It is in these ancient cultures, that the earliest law, medicine, agriculture, metallurgy, wheeled vehicles, ceramics, textiles and written languages were developed.

On this basis, they argue that, if a society's state of advancement is measured in terms of equality between the sexes, artistic and creative output and material benefits of social use, then some of the most advanced societies were so-called pre-historical cultures. They included those of the Cretan, Etruscan, Dahomey and Ashanti peoples of West Africa and the Naya people of Kerala in South India and to some degree the Egyptian.[20] These feminist historians query the use of the term "pre-history" and see it as illogical and divisive, because it places a time when women and mothers and daughters were ascendant, at a lesser level.

These ancient Goddess-worshipping cultures were based on hunter-gatherer societies. There is evidence that the cultivation of grain and other foods and the associated agricultural labour was seen not only as a means of producing food, but as part of the basic unity of psychic, productive, sexual and cosmic power. Nature was valued as a common eco-life system. The exploitation of nature to increase consumption, production and profits, without taking the eco-life system into account and without conservation, as in industrial, patriarchal societies, would have probably been regarded as highly irrational by such cultures.[21]

It is largely held by the historians quoted here, and particularly those with a psychoanalytic orientation, that the ancient societies which supported Goddess religions, were not only matrilineal but matriarchal in organisation and structure. Matriarchal societies are usually defined as the reverse or mirror-image of patriarchal societies, with a woman as head of the family and held in the greatest awe. This implies that men were not the most powerful social group and that they participated in, and equally upheld, the worship of the Goddesses. Like matrilineal societies, matriarchies are described as peaceable.

Bachofen is one of many scholars who argues that a characteristic of matriarchal societies was a spirit of affirmation of life and a lack of destructiveness. In his history, matriarchal societies are described as relatively egalitarian, without hierarchy, unaggressive and based on kinship, not kingship. He believes that around 10,000 B.C., in the Near East, Neolithic culture, which followed the Palaeolithic or Old Stone Age of Western and Southern Europe, was matriarchal. Its women were responsible for, and revered for, the development of methods of agriculture and the maintenance of cultivation.[22]

There is much dispute as to whether the societies Bachofen described were truly matriarchal and the point is debated further in Chapter 3. Be they matriarchal or matrilineal, remnants of Goddess-worshipping cultures have been found throughout the Near East, Europe and Scandinavia. Recent excavations in the Orkney Islands of Scotland have revealed Neolithic villages of up to 60 houses, designed in the shape of the body of a Goddess. Goddess-cult shrines have been found from Crete to Ireland.

The Reverence for Women's Sexuality and Menstruation in Goddess-Worshipping Societies

Mother-daughter relationships are very much influenced by prevailing attitudes toward sexuality.[23] The revered view of sexuality in the ancient Goddess-worshipping cultures is seen as one of many conditions that enhanced mother-daughter relationships.[24]

In contrast, and well recognised, is the way in which sex has been debased and pornography has flourished in western patriarchal societies. The moment of life's origin, the fusing of male and female energies, is often seen as bestial or dirty and women's sex became impure and draining of male energy.[25]

The tragedy is that the negative sexual role of women in patriarchal society, with its ambivalent and hostile connotations, is one that mothers often hand on to their daughters, usually with much resentment on both sides. Several historians argue that this tension was not apparent in Goddess societies.[26] Images of sex in ancient tales and legends are quite different from present attitudes. Women were ascendant and held in awe for their creative birth giving powers. Female sexuality was seen as purifying and strengthening, as illustrated in the tale of Anahita, one of the most popular ruling divinities of the Persian Empire. She was the ruler of reproduction and said to purify the seed of males and the womb and milk of females.[27]

Similarly, there are the pre-Greek and Roman versions of the legends of the beautiful queen of the open sky and earth, who was the Goddess Diana. Diana was also the granter of conception. She was entirely a woman's Goddess and on her feast day, processions of women travelled to Africa to offer thanks for help in the past year and seek her continued support. Eventually, her worship moved to the Aventine Hill in Rome, where women flocked to invoke her protection. They also called on her support in childbirth.

Sex did not imply impurity or danger, but a powerful act leading to spiritual perfection. Festivals, which coincided with the times when special energy tides flowed strongly around the earth, were seen not only as providing a receptive time for humans to receive the Goddess spirit, but as times of healing and fertility. Ceremonial sex was practiced at these times and patriarchal historians, who have described these as fertility rites or orgies, miss the point entirely. Pious Romans were expected to make love freely at the festival of Anna. This has been mistakenly defined as promiscuity by some historians, because of their phallocentric view of history.[28]

Similarly, the notion of "sacred prostitution" is subjective, for it sees another age in terms of one's own. The fact, that women were free to take as many lovers as they chose in pre-patriarchal society and surrendered themselves to the Goddess by making love to strangers in her temple, has no relation to service to men. It was seen as a way for a woman to participate in the Being of the Goddess and to experience herself as at one with her at the moment of union. This was also the way that men could partake in the essence of the Goddess through the body of a women. Such participation, through ecstasy, can only be initiated by women who are equal and free partners.

The symbols of menstruation and the Moon Mother in Goddess-worshipping societies are also important. These relate to another difficulty between mothers and daughters, which appeared in advanced patriarchal societies, namely that mothers are often embarrassed to speak of menstruation to their daughters. It has unclean connotations and they lack pride in it. This is understandable, since Christianity and other patriarchal religions trace the evil of women to menstruation. This was the 'curse' God laid upon women for Eve's sin in Eden and as the 'curse' it is still described.

Pauline Wiedeger comments on how, in western society, at her first menstruation the daughter is made to feel that her body and its rhythms are a biological impediment and that a properly functioning body is male.[29] The daughter learns to distrust and be ashamed of her own body. The Jungian psychologist, Esther Harding,[30] sees such projections as creating an unnatural split in the human psyche, and relates them to the prime cause of the neurosis, illness and depression suffered by many modern women during menstruation.

In contrast, the ancient menstrual ceremonies allowed women to withdraw and revere their cyclic and primal selves. As Rich sees it, this is because, in pre-patriarchal societies, mothers and daughters had sufficient status to demand seclusiveness as a protection or respite.[31] Esther Harding suggests that a contemporary woman may still need to use her period as a time for withdrawal into privacy and self-reflection.

In Goddess-worshipping societies, women's monthly cycle had status and was observed to be of the same duration as the Moon's cycle and the Moon Mother was believed to bleed also. In most languages, there is a common root word for "Moon' or 'menstruation'. In English it is derived from 'menses', the Latin for month. Both relate to the word for 'moon' and 'measurement'.[32]

Researchers, such as Shuttle and Redgrove, go so far as to say that menstruation awakened in humankind the capacity to recognise abstracts, make connections and think symbolically. These were set in train when women first noted the relationship between the time of menstruation and the lunar cycle.[33]

The status accorded menstruation in ancient Goddess-worshipping societies is also described by Bruno Bettelheim in *Symbolic Wounds: Puberty Rites and the Envious Male.* [34] There he outlines the thesis that originally men's initiation rites were based on the desire to imitate women's menstruation and childbirth. Similarly, Australian male Aboriginals imitate female menstruation by cutting wounds in their penises and inserting stones to keep the wounds permanently open.

As patriarchal society developed, many of the ritual imitations of women's functions, and the original restrictions by women to protect their bodies and guarantee their sacred solitude during the moon functions, were turned into taboos of avoidance and hygiene.

Women began to be defined, during their menstrual periods and childbirth, as unclean and were banished to the menstrual hut as dangerous to man and his laws and gods. The more warlike and authoritarian a society, the stronger the need to overpower and devalue women and the stronger the menstrual taboo.

In summary, menstruation and female sexuality, which early Goddess-worshipping cultures saw as sacred and powerful for the generation of the whole group, became under patriarchal domination, filthy, dangerous and evil. Why? Bruno Bettelheim, Karen Horney and many others find the answer to that question in the evidence that men in patriarchal societies exhibit jealousy and fear of the sexual, mental and spiritual abilities of fully mature women. The menstrual taboo is one of the consequences of this fear, because women's menstrual sexuality is seen as castrating.

Women's Birth-Giving Powers Enhanced Mother-Daughter Relationships

Attitudes to birth and the birthing process also affect mother-daughter relationships.[35] Goddess-worshipping cultures and patriarchal monotheistic societies differ enormously in their attitudes to birth. In ancient times, the birth process was a female mystery, from which all males were excluded. The role of a daughter's mother in this process was central and the earliest, sacred precinct of the primordial age was probably that in which daughters, with the help of their mothers and other women, gave birth. It stands at the centre of all cults that are dedicated to the Great Mother as the Goddess of fertility.

By contrast in western contemporary society, gynaecology is male and technologically dominated. In Chapters 2 and 9 of Book I, the stories of Bella and Anastasia describe their loss of pride and sense of control in a technologically administered birthing situation, and how the consequent loss of self-esteem can affect relationships with a baby daughter. Nowadays, mothers have no formal role in the hospitalised birthing process and, in fact, many a daughter would confess to feelings of embarrassment even at the thought of the presence of her mother at the birth of her baby. Sadly, this embarrassment marks the lack of pride in shared experiences, to which many are reduced under patriarchy. There are of course exceptions and we saw a case of this in the mothers and daughters of Bethnal Green, in Book I, where mothers had not been ousted from their advisory and supportive roles.

Given the rosy picture some feminists and psychoanalytically-oriented historians give of ancient Goddess-worshipping or of "matriarchal" societies, the big question is why do they no longer exist? What happened to them?

ↄ৲

The Coming of the Patriarchal Hordes and the Twilight of the Goddesses.

Central to many psychoanalytic/feminist theories is the idea that matriarchies were defeated by patriarchal invaders.

Irrespective of whether these ancient societies were matriarchal or matrilineal in structure, there is evidence that the Goddess religions held sway across the ancient Near East and the continent of Africa. Avebury, in the Wiltshire Downs in the South of England, was the sacred centre of Neolithic civilisation in Britain, until the invasion of the patriarchal religions of Islam and Christianity. Because they were threatening to their economic and political position, the patriarchal Islamic and Christian invaders set about destroying the ancient religions of the Great Cosmic Mother. They stole the people's land and broke up the ancient maternal kinship groups.[36] They were also suspicious of close mother-daughter relationships, for these were the basis of kinship among women and threatening to patriarchal society.

The Christian Church waged a long fight before it conquered the common peoples' belief in the symbols of the Goddess — her sacred stones and rituals. Because the common people continued to respect the witches as the priestesses of the Goddess religions, the Church engaged in witch hunts well into the middle ages. During the many centuries it took for the Christian Church to destroy the relationship between the Goddess religions and the common people, it tortured and 'exorcised' thousands of witches and engaged in a vicious programme of propaganda against them. Its fear and hatred spilled over into a fear of women in general and millions of women were accused of being witches and burnt at the stake.

T. C. Lethbridge in *Witches*, puts forward the interesting thesis, that it was the development of metallurgy, originally by women, that brought the end to the Mother-Goddess cultures. The art was given to men by women in the division of labour, as women's development of agriculture made it less necessary for men to be away hunting for long periods of time. Larger and heavier metal weapons shifted warfare from a defensive skill to an aggressive one.[37]

Thus the Bronze Age brought the warrior tribes. Here begins the glorification of war in the epics and myths of the early patriarchies, as in Homer's *Iliad* and the epics of the Teutonic and Celtic peoples. Having gained economic supremacy, the patriarchal leaders needed to gain ideological supremacy over societies where men and women worshipped the Goddess. They were bent upon breaking up the Goddess worship of the conquered and establishing the Sky fathers, such as Zeus, who took over much of the ritual of the Great Mother. They developed myths of Gods, who raped and overcame Goddesses, symbolising the weakening of the Goddess and the devaluing of her function as a protecting powerful deity.[38] Robert Graves suggests that even the practice of homosexuality among the men of Classical Greece was an attempt to free themselves spiritually from the Goddess.[39]

The patriarchal tribes established themselves as the warrior élite, concerned mainly with military activities and administering conquered territories . Legends tell us of the Amazons, noted for their valour and beauty, who fought and lost to the patriarchy. There were men too who fought for the maintenance of the holistic practices of the Goddess societies. The threat of the psychic division within themselves, the split personality, the separation from nature that they feared, is depicted in many of the myths of early patriarchal societies. Examples are the myth of Adam and Eve, and the Hebrew myth describing how God the Father separated the originally bisexual twins.[40]

In establishing city states, the Greek and Roman civilisations began the process of separating man from Mother Nature. These, and subsequent patriarchies, set themselves up as the first factor among all living creatures and plants and no longer heeded the messages of nature, earth and the cosmos. Thus the city states, as patriarchies, were man's first attempt to become man made, born from himself rather than from Mother Nature. He no longer worked with the earth, he bought it. Moreover, the city states were organised around a professional, male priesthood and specialist workers, often living off artificially forced, agricultural supplies.[41] It was in the context of such economics and politics, that mother-daughter relationships began to change.

৩৩

Capitalism as an Explanation for the Defeat of the Female Sex

Frederich Engels offers a rather different interpretation of how women and mothers and daughters lost power. Of particular interest is his *Origin of The Family and Private Property and the State*, which describes "the world historic defeat of the female sex", as an event deriving from the development of private property.[42]

Engels based his generalisations on the work of nineteenth century ethnographers and theoreticians, such as Bachofen and Morgan, and postulated the existence of classless, communist societies, prior to the formation of private property. He believed the overthrow of private property would abolish the subjugation of women — a theory not supported by the research, which is discussed in Chapter 3.

Engels theorised that in tribal societies, the development of animal husbandry led to commerce and the ownership of herds by individual members of families. Surpluses from herding were appropriated as private property by men, who sought to secure it to themselves and their heirs by controlling women's sexuality. This heralded the demand for prenuptial chastity and monogamous marriage. Reflecting his Victorian sexist values, Engels reasoned that monogamous marriage was viewed by women as an improvement in their condition, since they acquired the right to give themselves to one man only.

Despite these biases, Engels made major contributions to our understanding of women's position in society and he certainly allowed them some history. In calling attention to the subjugation of one sex by the other and the consequent sexual conflict, which is built into the institution of marriage and private property, he was one of the first to recognise the relationship between socio-economic change and gender relations.

Gerda Lerner feels however that this, and the Marxist insistence that questions of sex relations must be subordinated to questions of class relations, is a dead end, in trying to explain why and how women have been marginalised. Nor should we simply offer the reverse and commit the error of regarding sexual relations as the only issue. Sayers, Evans and Redcliff are among the many feminists who support this view.[43]

They are also critical of Engels for limiting history to the public arena and confining women within the family, thereby displacing women from history. As they see it, Engels argued that it is only when they enter social production that women enter history. This is only possible with the advent of large-scale, capitalist development.

Engels also overlooked the existence of sexual divisions within capitalist production — even revolutionary organisations — which ensure that women perform particular categories of work, usually at the lower end of the occupational hierarchies, or in servicing the work of male leaders. It is such inequalities which lead the female sex to devalue itself in relation to men and gives substance to the general inferiorising, which divides women and particularly mothers and daughters.

Adrienne Rich is another feminist who disagrees with many of Engels' contentions in *The Origin of the Family*. She especially rejects that the "subjugation" of women in patriarchal society coincided with the beginning of private ownership. Rich argues that, although the theory has some currency, its stress on economic relations, to the exclusion of emotional and psychological factors, reflects a patriarchal point of view. As Rich sees it, from the beginning of the early patriarchies men invested in power to compensate for their inability to give birth. Under patriarchy, the identity of men became synonymous with power over others, beginning with women and their children.[44]

Engels was wrong when he said women enter history only when they enter the public domain of production. This thesis ignores the role of the family, domestic skills and care of others in the history and survival of the human race. He was, of course, not alone in his views. As we have seen, even feminists such as Simone de Beauvoir believed women were without a history.

In fact, mainstream history has defined the time in which women were creating civilisation as pre-history — a quite absurd concept. Later, history went further by concentrating on the exploits of men.

Whether women were dominant in so-called "pre-history" or not, mothers and daughters certainly existed and therefore have a history. Moreover, remnants of the Goddess-worshipping societies, where female figurines abound and far exceed those of men, suggest the powerful role mothers and daughters played in establishing culture and society.[45] These are sources for our sense of continuity and pride. If we choose, we can hand our realisations on to our daughters.

Another source of pride in the mother-daughter alliance can be found in ancient myths and legends. The later patriarchal societies acknowledge the mother-son relationship and the loss of the son has been a frequent tragic theme in literature. This literature has shown much less reverence for the mother-daughter relationship. History suggests that this was not always so. The Eleusinian mysteries of the Goddess-worshipping societies of 12,000 and 11,000 B.C., indicate that mothers and daughters not only had a special place as cultivators and creators of life and pottery and art, but a special bond between them, such that their separation, or loss, was seen to be a tragedy of epic proportion. This is illustrated in the tragedy of Persephone and similar legends, which are discussed in the next chapter.

❧

CHAPTER 2

The Mother-Daughter Alliance in Ancient Myths and Legends

Among the Australian, Aboriginal people, the earth's creators are the Djanggawul Sisters, Bildjiwuraroju and Miralaidji. These Goddesses were daughters of the sun and gave birth to all living creatures, plants, sacred articles and rituals. Their long vulvas broke off piece by piece, with each birth, producing the world's first sacred artifacts.[1] This reverend view of female genitals is in contrast to western, patriarchal cultures, whose negative perceptions are reflected in many derogatory terms.

Several religions of the Ancient East also held that the creation of the world was a female achievement.[2] Among the Hindu, it was the Goddess Devi who gave birth to all the forces inherent in physical phenomena and it is her energy that constructed form out of chaos. To these religions, cosmology was concerned with the transformation of energy into matter and into spiritual and psychic powers. The metamorphosis of motion into substance was symbolised by a spiral, continuously turning, thus bringing the universe into being and then to destruction. Often a dancer was the catalyst for the spiral, inhaling and exhaling the breath of the cosmos. In this fashion, the ancient Great Mother was described as coming into being and giving birth parthenogenically or without sexual union. She was the world's egg, containing the two halves of continuity and change, and occasioned the expansion and contraction of the universe. Under several generations of eastern philosophers, everything became classified under these two categories, including the sexes. Yin was female and Yang was male, constantly complementing each other to maintain cosmic harmony.

Such philosophies inculcated the belief and practice that all life was experienced as a spiritual wholeness with the Cosmic Mother. Through the dances and trances of the shamans and seers, one could communicate with the cosmic source. They translated the life sources and had healing powers.

One strikingly poetic version of a female as the world's creator is seen in the Pelasgian creation myth, in which Eurynome, the most ancient of Greek Goddesses, is described as rising naked from the primordial chaos. Her swirling dance separated light from dark and sea from sky and set in motion a wind from which she created a serpent Ophion, with whom she had intercourse. She then transformed herself into a dove and laid the universal egg, from which the earth and all upon it was hatched. Thereafter, she established herself high above the new earth on Mount Olympus and created the underworld to imprison Ophion, when he boasted that he had caused creation.

The Great Mother Goddess is not depicted as mating with a human, until well into late Neolithic times around 6,000 B.C.[3] So powerful were the beliefs behind the myths of a Great Mother as the sole creator of the world, that the idea that women were impregnated by the wind survived in common world-wide folklore, well beyond the matrilineal societies that inspired it.

The inclusion of the snake in the Pelasgian creation myth suggests that it comes from a transition period, when the Great Mother is no longer believed to give birth parthenogenically. Nevertheless, the concept of her powerful, all-embracing, creativity remains and the great snakes, which are common in the Neolithic Goddess temples, are seen as emanating from herself. Through the shedding of its skin and through its habitat, the snake symbolises rebirth and the abode of the dead, while its sinuous body symbolises the spiral of spontaneous life energy.

Most recorded pre-patriarchal cultures, except the Egyptian, saw the earth as a female divinity and patron of fertility.[4] Earliest religious images show pregnancy, birth and nurturing, as the worshipful state. Men imitated this experience by participating in the Goddess mysteries.

In this tradition, the Egyptians had a Water-jar Goddess called Nut, who was seen as nourishing the earth with her milky rain — symbolising the uterus that is broken at birth, pouring forth water like a well. Such imaginative and attractive concepts, derive from a society which sees body and mind as a subtle form of the cosmos, which transforms human bodily and mental systems with its energy, currents and structures. They contrast with the messy view of birth processes in societies where the power of the female body is not revered as it was by the ancients.

Other illustrations of how women were honored as creators of life-giving and life-sustaining forces are evidenced in myths and folklore which record that women first discovered how to produce fire. Again, so powerful is the concept, that even in patriarchal Rome the ritual survived and the maintenance of fire was entrusted to the Vestal Virgins. Fire was also seen as sacred to the Moon Mother. In this tradition, the nuns of Saint Brigid, who was formerly the Celtic Goddess Brigid, tended a perpetual fire at Kildare in Ireland. This practice lasted until the suppression of the monastries under Henry VIII.

More recent interpretations of the early creation and fertility myths hold that, in the beginning, pre-patriarchal societies saw the Great Mother as bisexual — hence the ability to impregnate herself.[5] If the theory is correct, then it is possible that there was an androgynous view of human behaviour in ancient societies. Rigid divisions of gender and heterosexuality, as we know them, may not have been the case. This androgynous view may well have survived beyond the early Goddess-worshipping societies and into the early patriarchal societies, where at first both Goddesses and Gods were still worshipped. For example, Gilgamesh was the hero of the patriarchal Sumerians and it was his task to overcome and slay the Mother. He is ambivalent in this task, loves another man and exhibits both male and female attributes in his behaviour. Similarly, the androgynous concept of human behaviour may well be exemplified in the Amazon myths.

Amazon Mothers and Daughters

The controversy as to whether the Amazons existed has not been resolved.[6] Plutarch assures us they invaded Athens. The ancient Greeks believed they existed in a country on the river Thermoda, on their borders. Generally, it is believed they dwelt in Asia Minor along the Black Sea from 1,000 to 600 B.C.

Whatever the facts of the matter, the mythology offers the Amazon as an example of the strong and assertive female. It is an image of feminine power which males in patriarchy largely fear, hence the ambivalent and derogatory jokes about any modern female who exhibits Amazon qualities. The Amazons deserve to be freed of negative stereotyping, for their legends are enthralling and an education that the present divisions of gender and relationships between the sexes is not the inevitable and the only way.

In the Amazon legends, daughters follow in their mothers' footsteps and are strong and powerful. One of the most vivid of these legends is the story of Aphrodite and Harmonia. However, one should be careful to distinguish the earlier pre-patriarchal version from that of the later Hellenic versions. In these, Aphrodite is rather insipid because she has been converted into the personification of the kind of physical beauty preferred by men, whose thinking had been shaped by patriarchal stereotypes. In short, she has been transformed, along with other women, into a sexual commodity — a development that is discussed in the next chapter.

In the Near Eastern version, Aphrodite's birth is an allegorical description of the sky impregnating the womb of the sea. As a result, the long haired Aphrodite rose from the waves riding on a mussell shell. Drops of sea water fell from her hair and turned into pearls, as she floated to the islands of Greece. There she was provided with a husband, Hephaestus, the crippled God of smithcraft. She had many divine and mortal lovers including Ares, the God of war.

Their daughter was Harmonia and from her the Amazons were said to be descended. At Harmonia's wedding, the Olympians bestowed magical gifts, including a necklace from Aphrodite, which gave irresistible sexuality to the wearer.

Harmonia is described as founding the dynasty of Thebes and as giving birth to the famous Dionysian women, Semele, Agave, Autonoe and Ino Semele, was worshipped in some legends as a Goddess of death and in others as the earth that devours life and, so fertilised, reproduces it.

The daughters, Agave and Autonoe, formed a new religion of the Bacchantes or Maenads, and followers were mothers and daughters who worshipped the Great Mother. Only women were allowed to participate in, or witness, the all night festivals and rites to the abundance of the earth, which were held in the privacy of forested mountains. During their rituals of dancing and drinking, they experienced themselves as part of the divinity of life.

Agave had a son, King Pentheus of Thebes, who unwisely spied upon the women's privacy. He was spotted and torn to shreds. The women bore his bloody remains back to Thebes and his mother carried his head aloft as a warning to intruders upon women's ceremonials.

The legends describe the Amazons as jointly ruled by two queens, one of whom attended to domestic matters and the other to defense. The military queen led a magnificent army of mounted warriors dressed in wild animal skins and equipped with double-bladed, battleaxes or brass bows and ivy shaped shields. They are said to have been the first to use horses in battle.

The Amazons were economically self-sufficient. They were noted for their artistic treasures which were part of the trade with neighbouring countries. Some legends hold that once or twice a year, they coupled with men from surrounding tribes, kept any daughters who were born and returned sons to their fathers' tribes.

In her Goddess directory, Patricia Monaghan[7] suggests that many interpretations of the Amazons represent ludicrous patriarchal anxieties and projections. For example, it was said that they were not women but beardless men or that they cut off the right breast, the better to draw the bow and throw the javelin. As is discussed later, patriarchal Greek society dealt with such anxieties about strong women by censoring the ancient Goddess legends. For example, a famous woman warrior, Hiera, general of the Mysians, fought in the Trojan war. She was edited from Homer's account because, says Philostratus, "This greatest and finest woman would have outshone his heroine Helen".[8]

Hyppolyte, 'The Stamping Mare', was one of the finest queens of the Amazons. She was beautiful and strong. She wore the golden belt which became the insignia of Amazon queens and was a gift from her father, Ares, the war God. The burly Hercules (named Heracles in later Greek legends) was assigned the seemingly impossible task of obtaining this fabulous belt, as punishment for his dastardly and murderous crimes, and led a large force of men to secure it.

Hyppolyte found Hercules attractive and, as was customary, wished to wrestle with him before she would make love to him. This was her usual way of testing the strength of her lovers, so ensuring she would not bear a weak child. Her loyal retainers thought the Greek strong man was attacking their queen and sprang to arms. Many warriors fell on both sides before the battle halted.

Such images are foreign to the contemporary mind. In the flesh, an Amazon would be sufficiently threatening to many contemporary men to render them impotent. Where potency is seen as power over women, impotence is a problem. The images of the past suggest that this was not always in the nature of things.

There is another version of the Hercules myth, which also runs counter to contemporary stereotypes. It concerns Omphale who ruled the southern empire of Libya. As an Amazon, she regarded men as inferior and not equal to a queen. Like other Amazon rulers, she enjoyed men as kings have enjoyed concubines and purchased many attractive slavemen, including the brawny Hercules, who had been put on sale for the murder of his wife and children. Omphale kept Hercules for three years, during which time his duties included weaving and spinning and wearing transparent purple dresses for Omphale's amusement. If he made mistakes she beat him. Eventually, she grew tired of him and sent him back to his homeland.

The story of the legendary Amazon queen, Thalestrus, also reverses contemporary stereotypes. As Monaghan points out, Thalestrus practised an early form of eugenics.[9] Instead of mating with anonymous males, as Amazons often did in the yearly fertility rituals, she looked at likely kings and princes to father her several children. For example, she recognised Alexander of Macedon as a superior specimen of manhood and invited him to fertilise her. He regarded this as a high compliment.

Most history books mention that Cyrus the Great died in a military campaign, but rarely that he was defeated and executed by the Amazon queen, Tomyris, ruler of the Massagetae of Scythia. When Cyrus, bent upon expansion, invaded Tomyris's country, she attempted to negotiate a truce. He refused and took her son prisoner. When her son subsequently committed suicide in shame, Tomyris forthwith destroyed Cyrus's entire army, captured him and beheaded him.[10]

Thus many ancient cultures myths and legends describe women, mothers and daughters quite differently from the way they are currently seen. There is no fixed nature in human relationships. It varies according to social scripts and expectations and can be changed, if one frees oneself from prevailing stereotypes and current social indoctrination. This understanding can contribute to the consciousness raising that enhances mother-daughter relationships.

Let us now look to the period of transition, when the belief in one Goddess, which gave women a special status, gave way to the belief in many, who shared power with the Gods. These polytheistic religions are well illustrated in the myths and legends of ancient Greece and Rome.

Mothers and Daughters in Polytheistic Cultures

During the early stages of the establishment of patriarchy and its mythology, the power of the concept of the "One Original Great Goddess" was weakened, by fragmentation of her image into her many aspects.[11] There emerged stereotyped partial Goddesses, such as Aphrodite, the Goddess of Love, Athena, the Goddess of Wisdom, Demeter the Mother and Persephone, the Daughter.[12] In these partial forms, the Goddesses were often set at war with each other. In pre-patriarchal societies this could not happen, because each different face of the Goddess was seen as part of the One Being.[13]

It took centuries to weaken and fragment the centrality and oneness of the Goddess in the minds and beliefs of the mass of the population and to establish the polytheistic cultures, where both Gods and Goddesses were worshipped. Even so, partial aspects of the Goddess retained strong imagery and following. For example, Greek legend retained that aspect of the great Goddess which represented family unity and particular kinship between mothers and daughters as founders of the family. In Greek legend, this aspect became Hestia, the Goddess of the hearth and the first born daughter of the Olympian Goddess. In patriarchal classical Greece, a new home was not considered established until a daughter brought fire from her mother's fire to light her own, thus symbolising the power of Hestia.

There also still survived, in the early polytheistic-worshipping patriarchies, enormous respect for the morality, intelligence and sense of justice in women, born of the days of the supreme religion of the Great Cosmic Mother. Thus, in contrast with recent and contemporary stereotypes that one cannot trust a woman, we find the ancient story of the Goddess Fides, who was one of the most ancient divinities of Rome. She was seen as the guardian of integrity and honesty between individuals and within groups. It was believed that without her there was no trust in the human community. On the first day of October each year, Rome's three major priests offered sacrifice at her sanctuary . The sacred ritual was carefully guarded from ill omen, for no other feasts were seen as more important than those which sanctified trust between people.

Not only do we find the former reverence for women partially retained in the legends of the ancient Near East, but also in ancient Scandinavia. Here for example, Freya was worshipped as the mistress of all the Gods, leader of the Valkyries and the ruler of death. She represented sexuality and was the one to whom love prayers were most effectively addressed. She was described as the most beautiful of all Goddesses and rode through the sky on a huge golden boar or in a chariot drawn by cats. It was said that she lived in a vast palace on Folkvangr, where she held the spirit hordes she claimed on the battlefields. She was the essence of the earth's fertility and it was believed that her absence from the earth, during autumn and winter, accounted for the fact that the leaves fall and the earth is mantled in snow. She was also the Goddess of magic.

The Freya legends have it that she took all the Gods as lovers, with none of the overtones of promiscuity by which such behaviour is judged now. Her favourite was her brother, Frey. She had a husband who was the father of her daughter, Hnossa, meaning jewel. Hnossa followed in her mother's footsteps and was the youthful Goddess of infatuation.

All Gods and Goddesses were sexually active, with many partners in and out of wedlock and within and outside the family. Most were not monogamous and notions of illegitimacy and incest were not of concern in ancient legends.[14] Divine maternity was not viewed as limiting the active powers and sexuality of the Goddesses. The divinities were seen as enjoying and enduring the vicissitudes of humans, in epic proportions. Goddesses and Gods loved and hated and were jealous and angry, just like humans.

Another legendary daughter of this era is Eos, the lovely, winged Greek Goddess of dawn, who was the daughter of the deities, Hyperion and Thea. She drove a chariot pulled by four magnificent horses across the sky, thus occasioning the light of day and the sunset. We are told that Eos had many lovers and often kidnapped handsome men to serve her. One mortal lover was Tithonis, of whom she was sufficiently fond to beg immortality for him, but she forgot to ask for his eternal youth. Tithonis wizened and Eos no longer found him attractive, but she took sufficient pity on him to turn him into a cricket. She installed him in a little cage and he was able to chirp goodbye to her, as she left on her light-giving journey each day.

Thus legends, which had typified the strength of mother-daughter relationships in pre-patriarchal society, remained in some version in the early polytheistic cultures. One of the best known is the myth of Persephone and her mother Demeter.

Demeter was the Goddess of agriculture, civilised arts and social order and was the sister of Zeus. With the consent of Zeus, Demeter's daughter, Persephone, was abducted and raped by their brother Hades and carried off by him to the underworld to become his queen. Her mother was inconsolable and in her grief she refused to do her work.

The earth became barren and humanity was threatened with starvation. The Olympian Gods demanded the return of Persephone on the condition that she had not eaten anything in the underworld. Hades, hearing of the heavenly verdict, pressed a single pomegranate seed into Persephone's mouth. As a result, she was condemned to spend one third of the year below ground. The rest of the time, she enjoyed the company of her mother on earth. When Persephone was with her, Demeter caused the earth to give forth an abundance of blossoms and fruits. While Persephone was absent and the earth Goddess mourned her annual separation from her daughter, the earth wilted and became barren.

Despite the survival of the theme of the mother-daughter bond, this version of the Persephone/Demeter myth exhibits the lessening of the power and unity of the Great Mother Goddess. Persephone's rape in the Greek myth can be seen as symbolising the power of men over women under patriarchy, and that the mother-daughter relationship is subject to the same power of men. In the original pre-patriarchal legend such was not the case. Moreover, in the original, the daughter, Persephone, and her mother, Demeter, are two aspects of the one Great Goddess.

Similarly, there are several versions of the story of Rhea and her daughter Hera. Whether or not Rhea Sylvia and Rhea, the mother of Hera, are one and the same person is not important here. What is important is how the patriarchal versions changed the images of women. The earliest version of a legendary female, known as Rhea — probably Rhea Sylvia — acknowledges her power by describing her as having intercourse with the war god Mars and as giving birth to Romulus and Remus.

Equally powerful is the Rhea, who was described as the mother of Zeus and other Olympian Gods and Goddesses, including Demeter. She coupled with Cronos and gave birth to a daughter, Hera. As Rhea's daughter, Hera was bequeathed special powers and became the Goddess of women and their sexuality and its changing nature throughout the timespan of their lives. For this reason, Hera was described as passing through three life stages. First, she was the virginal Hebe, symbol of the budding earth. In the second stage, she became the mature woman, Nympheuomene, the earth as summer, the mother in the prime of life. In the third stage, she grew into Theria, the woman beyond maternity, who again lives alone and to herself. Every one to four years, women came to a field near Hera's town of Argos and, with hair unbound, ran bare-breasted in the three age groups to honour the Goddess's three stages.

Subsequent forms of the Hera story demonstrate how ancient patriarchal society progressively destroyed the powerful and all protective image of the Goddesses of the societies they had conquered. In these, Hera is married to the unfaithful Zeus and is portrayed as unattractively jealous and vicious, as she hounds his consorts.[15]

The Hera/Zeus struggle typifies the theme of many patriarchal, polytheistic legends. It is seen as symbolising the political struggle for power between men and women in these times. As a result, divine mother-son relationships or husband-wife relationships are often portrayed as fraught with ambivalence, vengeance and sexual violence. In contrast, most mother-daughter relationships are described as supportive. This view of relationships is almost the reverse of the stereotypes in contemporary western culture and highlights the influence of social change on mother-daughter relationships.

The legends about mothers and daughters in Hellenic Greece are particularly good examples of an early, polytheistic, patriarchal society savagely bent upon supreme control of things feminine. The Greeks fought constantly to repress the awe for the Mother Goddess and their legends are records of some of the propaganda techniques used — 'legendary' rape being one.

Another technique was to remove all reference to the power of Goddesses. This is the fate of Hippodamia, who was originally a Goddess of pre-Hellenic Olympia and honoured in secret rites of women. In Greek legend, her importance related merely to the fact that she was the ancestral queen of King Atreus.

Yet another means of undermining the power of a Goddess was to portray her as dangerous or threatening. Robert Graves saw the Hydra myth as an example of the patriarchal attempt to exterminate the worship of pre-Hellenic Goddesses by these means. In Greek legend, Hydra was the many-headed daughter of the serpent Goddess, Echidne, and guarded the entrance to the underworld at Lerna. Her blood was depicted as so poisonous that to touch it was torture and it was believed that her blood killed Heracles. Heracles' wife, Deianeira, despaired of his countless affairs and wove a splendid garment for him. She soaked it in what a dying centaur, mortally wounded by Heracles, had told her was an infallible charm. The robe contained Hydra's blood and burned him to death.

Davidson and Broner[16] believe the story of Leda and her daughter, Clytemnestra, to be a good example of the use of 'legendary' rape to undermine the conquered populace's adherence to the Goddess religion. In Hellenic Greek literature, Leda is described as one of many Goddesses raped by Zeus's, which suggests she may have been a pre-Greek Goddess. In the shadowy stereotypes, into which the Greeks forced her, she is subject to the whims of the God Zeus and her mortal husband, Tyndareus. She produces four children, Castor and Pollux, Helen of Troy and Clytemnestra, who became more famous than she was.

The story of Leda and Clytemnestra also typifies the struggle of strong women to maintain the power that had been theirs in times when the Goddess was supreme. Like many others, Clytemnestra was conquered into the restricted wife-mother role. Her story also illustrates how the oral traditions about great mothers and daughters were picked up by Greek male poets.

As they described it, Clytemnestra was tricked by her husband, Agamemnon, into sacrificing her daughter, Iphigenia, to appease the Gods and arouse the winds, needed to sail his ships to Troy. The Greek myths portray a woman so full of desire to avenge her daughter's death, that she became unmotherly to her other children. Orestes, her baby son, had to be smuggled to another part of Greece to prevent Clytemnestra from killing him, in order to make sure there was no male heir to Agamemnon's throne. Her other daughter, Electra, is described as having a miserable life with her mother.

In her struggle to avenge her daughter, Clytemnestra attempted to gain power within the system, using the devious methods to which women must often resort for justice in patriarchal society. She took Aegisthus, her husband's worst enemy, as her lover and utilised him as her figurehead. She ruled the country in her husband's absence and enjoyed the power. She was unwilling to relinquish it and directed the plot whereby Agamemnon was murdered upon his return from Troy. Her son, Orestes, later slew Clytemnestra in revenge for his father's death. The legend tells us that the execution was directed by Apollo, which Washington and Tobal suggest, signifies a blow, by patriarchy, against independent women.[17] Although legend also tells us that Orestes was hounded for the crime of matricide, it is interesting that the Goddess, Athena, who cast the deciding vote in his favour at his trial, is described as motherless, having sprung fully armed from the head of her father, Zeus.

Clytemnestra had admired her mother and modelled herself upon her — a Goddess of the pre-patriarchy. She wished to be like her, not only in nurturing, but with the power to be a protector, guide and rewarder of her offspring and associates. Limited by the rules of patriarchy to her nurturing role and forbidden the influence of her other roles, she turned her back on her beneficent role and became an avenging fury. Davidson and Broner believe this kind of understanding must be applied to the violent women of Greek patriarchy.

A similar mother-daughter theme is found in the German folk epic, *Das Nibelunglied*, a legend about Kriemhild, her mother, Uta, and the loss of their power to the patriarchs. Although the later version does not emphasise it, in the earlier legend Uta was a strong mother, who, albeit indirectly, had the power to protect, guide and reward those around her and particularly her children. Kriemhild, her daughter, modelled herself on her mother's assertiveness and tried to become directly powerful in patriarchal society. She was not content with deriving power through her husband, Attila, the most powerful man in the world. Her attempts to achieve her ends involved revenge against the men, who deprived her of her wealth and power. This led to her ultimate defeat and her execution.

These are a few of the legends about heroic women who struggled to maintain a share in power and to uphold the mother-daughter alliance. They stand defiant on the brink of the subsequent dark age for mother-daughter relationships. They are part of the history of mothers and daughters.

Some questions remain. Were these women fighting for the rights their mothers and daughters had in egalitarian matrilineal societies or were they inspired by oral traditions about supreme maternal power in ancient matriarchies? Did matriarchies exist? Was there ever a time when society was the mirror image of patriarchy and mothers and daughters controlled politics and economics and dominated men and their sexuality? This last question is explored in the next chapter.

ɕɔ

CHAPTER 3

Matriarchies: Fact or Fiction?

We are so locked into to the androcentric explanatory system, that the alternate model that comes most readily to mind is usually that of the reverse — matriarchy. Many of the historians and feminists discussed in the last two chapters have been additionally reinforced by the psychoanalytic concerns with the power of the mother and therefore find it easy to conclude that there must have been matriarchies. Has there been any thorough research on this topic?

An impressive historical analysis, based on extensive scholarly research, is by Gerda Lerner in her book, *The Creation of Patriarchy*. [1] While not disputing ancient Goddess-worship and the totally different concepts of sex and birth in ancient societies, Gerda Lerner believes that looking for matriarchies and compensatory myths about a time when women ruled over men is ahistorical and unsatisfactory. She believes these manoeuvres will not emancipate women now or in the future.

She argues that there is no evidence for matriarchies — her definition of a true matriarchy being the mirror image of patriarchy, where women have power over men, where that power includes public and foreign relations and where women make decisions about the entire community and control the sexual behaviour of men. [2] Nevertheless, she offers ample evidence from ancient historical records of women having high status, of women holding power over an aspect of public life, and of them sharing power with men. She points to women's groups which had sufficient influence to check the power of men. [3]

Most of the evidence for female equality in the societies which are described in anthropological studies or in ancient history, derive from matrilocal societies which structure kinship in such a way that a man leaves his family of origin to reside with his wife or his wife's family. Evidence is also derived from matrilineal societies, where kinship is traced through the mother's family. In these cultures, the family group lived on land belonging collectively to the mother's kin group. A woman's husband, or husbands, lived with the woman or her kin group. Her children, regardless of the father's identity, remained with the mother and her family group.

Many sociologists and anthropologists conjecture that, in these ancient matrilineal cultures, fatherhood was a social role rather than a biological one. We've seen an example of this in the Tubetube — a contemporary matrilineal culture. [4] The mother may choose a social father from her many husbands or her brothers. Usually, the father is expected to win the children's affection and is not seen as having a right to it. It is argued that in such cultures where neither ownership nor hierarchy intruded, a closer bond developed between father and child than in patriarchal societies. This concept is somewhat suspect, since it extrapolates the pattern of the contemporary nuclear family to distant and foreign cultures.

Nevertheless, as the research of Lerner and others indicate, such societies confer certain rights and privileges on women, although it must be remembered, contrary to many psychoanalytic-feminist conjectures, that decision-making power within the kinship group rested with elder males.[5] Just as matrilineal descent does not indicate matriarchy, so patrilineal descent does not necessarily imply subjugation of women.

The Veneration of Women in Ancient Societies is not Synonymous with Matriarchy

There is however evidence to support the psychoanalytic-feminist contention that women caring for their helpless infants had the most incentive to develop food gathering and horticultural skills and that their role was crucial in advancing human development.[6] Women developed the weaving of bark and fibres and began the textile industries. They tanned skins into leather. Their knowledge of ecology, of plants, trees, roots and small animals and their properties as food or as dyes, hemp, yarns and clothing, made them man's equal, if not his superior.

There seems little to contradict the theory that women may have introduced the domestication of animals and stock breeding, or that they were the originators of cooking and built the first granaries and storehouses for provisions.[7] Both Lerner and Evelyn Reed[8] provide substantial evidence that, over thousands of years, women's knowledge of herbs and seed cultivation was developed into basic medical and agricultural science. Women's digging sticks were the first tools.

Remnants from the Neolithic period give ample indication of the veneration of women.[9] The veneration can be seen in surviving cave paintings and sculptures and these were, in all probability, a product of respect for women's agricultural knowledge and their capacity to procreate.[10] Correspondingly, the pervasiveness of the worship of the Mother Goddess in Neolithic and Chacolithic periods, is confirmed by the archaeological data.[11] There is a profusion of female figurines, all emphasising breasts, navels, vulvas, and usually in a squatting position, which was the position commonly adopted in childbirth. These are seen unequivocally as evidence of a widespread fertility cult. They correspond to later mythological and literary material celebrating the power of the Goddesses over fertility and fecundity. It is likely, says Lerner, that the female figurines indicate an even earlier period of Great Goddess worship, but this is not certain.

From the fourth millennium, the Goddess is shown amidst pillars or trees, accompanied by goats, snakes and birds. Eggs and symbols of vegetation are associated with her. These symbols indicate that she was still worshipped as a source of fertility for vegetation, animals and humans. She is represented by the Minoan snake Goddess, with her breasts exposed. She was venerated in Sumer as Ninhursag and Innana, in Babylon as Kubab and Ishtar, in Canaan as Anath and in Greece as Hekate-Artemis. Her frequent association with the moon, symbolised her mystical powers over nature and the seasons.

Such belief systems were monistic and animistic. They depicted unity between the earth and the stars, humans and nature, birth and death. Each and every aspect of that unity was embodied in the Great Goddess. Previous chapters have presented conjectures about the likely favourable effect of this supreme female role on mother-daughter relationships.

The belief in the supremacy of the Goddess has also been verified in the recovery of records of the earliest myths of origin. These celebrate the life-giving creativity of the female.[12] In these it is the Goddesses who alone give birth to the world, the Gods and humans. Later, the male God is decisively involved and the co-operation of the male is recognised, probably as a result of the educative effects of the domestication of animals and animal husbandry.

In these original, ancient societies, women may have favoured a sexual division of labour, whereby men did the big-game hunting and women the food gathering, since the latter could more easily be adapted to bearing and caring for infants.[13] However, the point is disputed, because it is a biological explanation which some find patriarchal in emphasis.[14] Whether right or wrong, the early accommodation to the capacity of women for reproduction is the only biological explanation Lerner accepts in accounting for the gender divisions of the sexes as we now know them. In the beginning, biology initiated a division of labour, but from then on sexual differences were created by culture and social structure and the consequent concepts of gender became confused with biology.

Under primitive conditions, the power of the mother over the infant and her ability to create life must have been seen as awesome. It is easy to conjecture that the ego formation of men must have taken place in a context of fear and awe of the female and led men to create their own social institutions to bolster their egos, strengthen their self-confidence and validate their sense of worth. There are however objections to this theory, since it suggests men acted in self-defence and thereby blames women for their subsequent subjugation by men.[15] It may be an androcentric interpretation. Moreover, one cannot necessarily transpose the modes of thinking within one social structure to an entirely different one.[16] It must also be emphasised that men willingly participated in Goddess-worship and fought hard to retain it. It remained embedded in the lives of many, particularly non-élite groups such as the peasantry, even until the middle ages.

While it qualifies them, the work of researchers such as Gerda Lerner and James Mellaart, substantiates many of the claims about Goddess-worshipping societies made by the feminists and historians who were discussed in previous chapters. Although they can find no evidence of matriarchies, their research offers hard evidence for the existence of alternate models to patriarchy — one being Catal Hüyük, a Neolithic settlement around 6,250-5,720 B.C.[17] In Catal Hüyük, authority appears to have been shared among the inhabitants and women appear to have created the religion and been the chief artists. They developed agriculture and controlled production. There is clear evidence of matrilocality and of Goddess-worship. Many similar societies where women were held in high esteem can be found in the Neolithic and the Bronze Ages.[18]

The Transition to Private Property — The Fertility of Mothers and Daughters Becomes a Commodity

In such cultures, the development of inter-tribal warfare during periods of scarcity, and the development of plough agriculture, fostered the rise to power of men in the tribe and also men of military achievement. These social processes altered the position of kin groups, women and their children and mothers and daughters.[19]

Military strongmen first became chieftains over villages and later established their dominance over previously communally held temple lands and herds, gradually pushing priests and priestesses into the background. Later, the strongest of these chieftains set themselves up as kings, further weakening the power of communal and kin-based structures.[20]

In seeking an explanation for these social and economic developments, Lerner resorts to some of the patriarchal concepts she admonishes others to free themselves from, when she uses the concept of bonding as a deductive argument. She speculates that men's bond to their children was not strong enough to ensure their submission for the sake of their children, but that it was through their bond to their children that women could be coerced.

However, the rest of her argument and evidence is convincing. Children, she argues, were an asset as potential labour in a tribal economy and women were captured and protected to bear them and bolster that economy. *Thus women's reproductive capacity was reified as an object and it was this that led to the concept of private ownership, not land, as Engels maintained*. It was also an agent in the transition from matrilineal to patrilineal societies.

In the Inca empire, for example, the conquerors extended their rule by forcing conquered villages to provide virgins for state service and as potential wives for Inca noblemen. This interference in the sexual and marriage patterns of the conquered, served a dual function. It undermined kinship structures and it singled out particular kin groups for alliances with the conquerors. At the same time, as in Mesopotamian societies, the institutionalisation of hierarchies within patriarchy created sharply defined boundaries between women of different classes — women of the élite were given power and privilege over the slave women.

The enslavement of women also laid the basis for the concept of a class hierarchy and the shift from kin-based to class-based societies. Societies developed in which both private property and the exchange of women, based on incest taboos and exogamy, were common.[21] We must not imagine this as a linear process which uniformly developed in different regions, but rather as a slow accretion of incremental changes, which occurred at different speeds in different regions and with varying outcomes.

Nevertheless, women were not yet completely stereotyped by gender. In the second and third millenniums, in documents from Lagash and Mari in Mesopotamia, there are records of ordinary women of the time, including slaves, who were employed diversely as spinners, wool workers, brewers, millers, singers and musicians. Elite women owned and managed property, could contract in their own names, could sue in court and serve as witnesses.

The fragments of evidence concerning Mesopotamian women in different cultures over a 400 year span provide ample evidence of societies in which the active participation of élite women in economic, religious and political life was taken for granted.[22] The documents from Mari, for example, also exhibit no distinction between male and female prophets, indicating the relatively equal status of élite women in Mari society. During the process of the establishment of written law codes, the state increased the property rights of upper-class women. However, this should not be taken to indicate thorough going equality — a mistake many historians make — because, at the same time, the sexual and reproductive capacities of mothers and daughters were increasingly commodified and sold in the interests of male family members.

Mothers and Daughters Become Deputies to Their Men

Women's dependence on and obligation to male kin, and/or husbands, was by now taken for granted. Male members of the ruling élite established power through patrimonial bureaucracy or by installing family members, including women, wives, concubines or daughters, in subordinate positions of power. There emerged the role of wife or daughter as deputy, as in the case of Queen Shibtu. As stand-in wife, during the absences of her husband, King Zimri-Lim, she served as her husband's deputy and achieved the highest power a woman could.[23]

The power of élite women derived entirely from the men on whom they depended. Nevertheless, their influence and actual role in shaping events was real, as was their power over men and women of lower rank, whom they owned or controlled. But in matters of sexuality, they were utterly subordinate to men. When wives or daughters could no longer provide adequate sexual services, as in the cases of Kirum or Kunshimatum, they were out of power at the whim of their lord.[24]

Kunshimatum was the secondary wife of King Yasmah-Addu of Mari and managed his palace. Yasmah-Addu was overthrown by Zimri-Lim and Kunshimatum became part of the victor's spoils. Like many genteel daughters of defeated kings, she became a domestic slave.

King Zimri-Lim arranged political marriages for his daughters and, when he married his daughter Kirum to Khaya-Sumu, the ruler of Ilansura, he also appointed her mayor of Khaya-Sumu's city. Kirum seems to have been quite a spirited daughter and exercised her authority as mayor. She also corresponded with her father concerning political matters and freely offered him advice. She eventually fell out of favour with her husband and, at her insistence, she returned to her father.[25]

King Sargon of Akkad also maintained power by astute patrimonial bureaucracy which included female kin. He was a Semitic ruler, who founded a dynasty which extended over sections of Sumur, Ahur (Assyria), Elam and the Euphrates Valley (ca. 2,371-2,361 B.C). He not only strengthened his rule by installing trusted persons as governors over the formerly independent city states, but made his daughter, Enkheduanna, high priestess of the Moon God Temple in the city of Ur. The Moon God temple was one of the temples of An who was the supreme God of Heaven. Since Enkheduanna was also the lifelong cultic devotee of the Sumnerian Goddess Innana,[26] her appointment symbolised the fusion of Inanna with the Akkadian Goddess, Ishtar. It appears that Enkheduanna was highly gifted and politically astute. She was a distinguished poet and her poetry and hymns to the Goddess Inanna survive her. After Sargon's death, the new ruler of Ur removed her from her position as high priestess.[27]

Thus, quite realistically, women came to perceive themselves as dependents of men and so began the female world of social contract. In exchange for protection, women, who were denied autonomy, bargained for the best possible deal for themselves and their children.

Women of all classes had traditionally been excluded from military power. By the turn of the first millennium B.C., they were excluded from institutionalised formal education. Even so, some powerful women lived on in cultic service, in religious representation, and in symbols. The effect of this on mothers and daughters is discussed later.

There was a considerable time lag between the subordination of women in patriarchal society and the declassing of the Goddess[28] and it is remarkable that the spiritual and metaphysical power of Goddesses remained active and strong. Mesopotamian men or women, in distress or sickness, humbled themselves before the Goddess, Ishtar, and other Goddesses like her, who had power in their own right. Men and women offering such prayers must have thought of women, just as they thought of men, as capable of metaphysical power and as potential mediators between the Gods and human beings.

This is a mental image, which is quite different from that of the Christians, who in later time would pray to the Virgin Mary to intercede with God on their behalf. The power of the Virgin lies in her ability to appeal to God's mercy; it derives from her motherhood and the miracle of her immaculate conception. She has no power for herself, and the very sources of her power separate her irrevocably from other women.[29]

In summary, the hard evidence of Lerner and others suggests that it was the development of plough agriculture, coinciding with increasing militarism, and the later rise of strong kingships in the archaic states, which brought major changes in kinship relations and the transition from matrilineal kinship and royal succession to patrilineal kinship and succession. This effected changes in religious beliefs and symbols.

The political aspects of this transition can be seen in Hittite society between 1,700-1,190 B.C. Early Hatti government was based on the system in which the right of succession lodged in the tawananna, the prince's sister. The Hatti royal household practised brother-sister marriage — similar to the kinship arrangement in royal families in Egypt. A male ruler married his sister who, as tawananna, was a priestess with considerable economic and political power, including the right to collect taxes from cities. Her male child inherited the right of succession, not because his father was king, but because the right of succession lodged in the tawananna. A succession of kings modified this traditional rule and quarrels were ultimately resolved by granting the king's son the right to succeed to the kingship. The king's daughter became the tawananna and exercised the office of priestess to the Sun Goddess. By this arrangement, the right of succession was subtly shifted to the king.[30]

Transference of the Act of Creation from Goddess to God, Symbolises the Reduction of Mother-Daughter Power

Accompanying these changes was the containing and reduction of the power of the Goddess. First the Mother Goddess was demoted; next came the ascendance and later dominance of her male consort/son, then his merging with a storm God into a creator God, who headed the pantheon of Gods and Goddesses. Finally, the power and creation of fertility was transferred from the Goddess to the God.[31] The concept of creation changed from being merely the acting out of the mystic force of female fertility. It became a conscious act of creation, involving first both sexes and later the male God. Creation was now symbolised in words. "And God said 'Let there be light', And there was light." (Gen. 1: 3). God's word, God's breath creates. The divine breath is life-giving. Naming gives meaning and order and this power is given by God to Adam. After the creation of Eve, Adam names her, as he names the animals. The naming is not only a symbolic act of creativity but it defines woman as created by man and part of him.[32]

Lerner argues that these changes appeared when writing was invented because it provided the abstract capacity to give names symbolic meaning. She sees written language as a great leap forward into abstract thinking. Again, there are other interpretations. For example, the work of Piaget demonstrated that symbolic thinking in young children and indeed throughout history is distinct from abstract thinking. It is restricted by egocentricity, animism and artificialism.[33] It seems more reasonable to suggest that it was this animistic type of symbolic thinking, which develops much earlier than abstract thought, that inspired the early androcentric assumptions and myths.

Whatever the reason, it is clear that the former Earth Goddesses began to appear as daughters and wives of vegetation Gods. As the kings took over the temples, the Mother Goddess not only lost her supremacy, but generally became domesticated and transformed into the supreme God's wife. Although the changing position of the Mother Goddess and her dethroning took place in many cultures at different times, the change was usually associated with the same historical process that has been described here.[34] Nevertheless, she remained firmly embedded in the culture in some form until the coming of Christianity.

Before this and up until the second millennium B.C., men and women stood in the same relation to the mysterious and awesome forces represented by the Gods and Goddesses. The kind of gender distinctions we find in the story of Adam and Eve were not yet used to explain the cause of evil and the problem of death. The cause of pain and suffering was the sinfulness of men and women and their neglect of their duty toward Gods and Goddesses. No matter how degraded and commodified the reproductive and sexual power of women was in real life, their essential equality could not be banished from thought and feeling as long as the Goddesses lived and were believed to rule human life. Women must have found their likeness in the Goddesses, as men found theirs in the Gods.

The reverence for the essential qualities of women, alongside the use of mothers and daughters politically by the rising patriarchy, was still evident in ancient Rome. There is hard evidence that by now mothers were participating actively in educating their daughters to serve patriarchy.

ক৩

Roman Mothers and Daughters

Unfortunately, the sources deal almost exclusively with Roman upper class society, not provincial life or the poor. The greatest interest is in political life, which is concerned with maintaining the power of a male élite. Thus, only the activities of a few powerful upper class women who impinged on political life are recorded. The writers are all men and their perceptions of mothers and daughters are coloured by their own attitudes and experiences. They depict strong women, whose strength has been channelled to the service of the patriarchy.

The Roman mother, for good or ill, was a powerful character, deeply involved in her daughter's life and exerting a controlling influence.[35] Most of this involvement had to do with the daughter's married life and this in connection with events that concerned politically-minded patriarchal writers. These included consequences of the political position of the daughters' husband or conflicts between mothers-in-law and daughters-in-law in political contexts. The daily and normal domestic life and human relational situations of mothers and daughters were not reported, presumably because they were seen as of less importance, or did not impinge on patriarchal politics.

Mothers were expected to and did take a strong role, if not the entire decision, in deciding whom their daughters would marry. Most of these arrangements were to further the husband's political ends. One of many examples is that of Octavia, last Roman wife of Mark Antony and sister to the emperor, Augustus. She not only brought up Antony's surviving children by Cleopatra with her own, but also, according to Plutarch, arranged the marriage of the girl, Cleopatra Selene, with the Numidian king, Juba.

There were mothers who decided when their daughters were to divorce and implemented the divorce to achieve their own ends. Here, the sources suggest that daughters generally participated willingly in these manoeuvres, as it was believed that the role of the daughter to her mother take precedence over the role of the wife to her husband.

An example appears in Plutarch's life of Pompey. Sulla was made dictator in 82 B.C. and on the advice of his third wife, Caecilia Metella, persuaded Pompey to divorce his current wife and marry Caecilia's daughter by an earlier marriage. The daughter was at the time married to someone else and pregnant. The object was to assure Sulla of Pompey's continued support. Plutarch and his source attribute the plan to the mother, who no doubt also had the role of ensuring her daughter's compliance. Another example is that of Sassia, who pressured one of her daughters into divorcing her husband, so that she could marry him herself.

The role of the Roman mother was to educate her daughter to the service of the patriarchy and the daughter's behaviour was seen as reflecting the training of her mother. The blame for a daughter who committed adultery or homicide was seen to rest with her mother and she was obliged to share in her failures. For example, it is said that Cornelia, the mother of the Gracchi, and her daughter, Sempronia, co-operated in the murder of Sempronia's husband, Scipio Aemilianus.

In 2 B.C., when Augustus sent his 37 year old daughter, Julia, to the island of Pandateria, her mother, Scribonia, voluntarily went into exile with her. Another woman of the imperial family, Messalina, the wife of the emperor Claudius, brought ruin on herself by her sexual adventuring and was helped to face the consequences by her mother, Domita Lepida. The crisis established a supportive relationship between the two, despite earlier difficulties.

Although they were often directed to the strengthening of male political power, there were expectations of strong ties between mothers and daughters in Roman society. Mothers were expected to be the allies and protectors of their daughters, to provide them with companionship, continued advice and training in married life, to attend them in childbirth and to come to their aid in time of need. Motherhood was a recognised social form, such that, even if the mother lived apart from her daughter due to divorce or remarriage, the mother's authority held good. Daughters were expected to be obedient to their mothers and defer to them. They were also expected to visit their mothers regularly after marriage.

Whereas there is much reported conflict between mothers and sons, there is little reported between natural mothers and daughters, although this may be an omission due to the lack of interest by male writers. Even so, the protective relation between mothers and daughters appears to have been much stronger than between mothers and sons. There are many instances of close lifelong relationships between mothers and daughters of sufficient interest to the male political writers of the time. The bond between Arria and Fannia is an example. Pliny admiringly reports how Fannia practised her mother's and her grandmother's principles and how she and her mother, Arria, stood shoulder to shoulder during the political vicissitudes of the family.

This chapter began by asking for hard evidence that matriarchies once existed. There is plenty of evidence of Goddess worshipping societies and reverence for women, mothers and daughters. But when matriarchy is defined as the mirror image of patriarchy, none can be found. Lerner's alternative thesis, about matrilineal and matrilocal societies and the later commodification of the reproductive power of mothers and daughters in order to establish and consolidate the political power of men in the early patriarchies, as exemplified in Mesopotamian and Roman times, is a powerful one. It explains the origin of private property and the marginalisation of mothers and daughters much more convincingly than many other theories.

I find Lerner's theory and research has meaning for mothers and daughters. They see it as making sense and giving insights into their present status. It certainly gives them a sense of their history and continuity. Not all will read *The Creation of Patriarchy* from cover to cover, but I find that many are interested in particular aspects of Lerner's interpretation of ancient history. For those who want to go further I have included many other sources and references in the footnotes.

We now move onto the final destruction of the Goddess religions under patriarchal Christianity and the loss of reverence for the mother-daughter relationship.

എ

CHAPTER 4

The Book of Genesis, Medieval Knights and Witches

Are Mothers And Daughters Vile?

Wommen are born to thraldom and penance,
And to been under mannes governance.
                    Chaucer, *The Man of Law's Tale*

The quotation from Chaucer encapsulates the attitude to women, after several centuries of Christianity. Christianity crushed polytheistic culture and religion with its remnants of reverence for the power of mothers and daughters. Wherever the monotheistic and patriarchal religion of Christianity came to power, the Gods and Goddesses of polytheistic cultures were regarded as heathenish and threatening. Mothers and daughters were no longer included alongside men in temple life as initiates, celebrants or priestesses. Instead, parts of the Bible represented men in a special and closer relation to God.[1]

The Book of Genesis

The book of Genesis gives insight into these early patriarchal, monotheistic religions. Here we see the development of strong leadership, under King David and Solomon, and the establishment of the corresponding symbols of gender.[2] How this came about is important for mothers and daughters to know, because it vividly demonstrates how much gender is a product of the accidents of history and the politics of power and economics. There is a history behind present gender relationships which marginalise women and put the mother-daughter relationship in a secondary and conflicting position.

The stories of the patriarchs in Genesis continue a transition we have already seen in Mesopotamia[3] — a transition from matrilocal to patrilocal and patrilineal family organisation. Examples are given in the marriages of Leah and Rachel. Jacob's seven years of service to Laban, for each of his daughters, would conform to the practice of matrilocal marriage. Similarly, the story of Jacob's courtship and his flight from Laban's house has been interpreted as implying the transition from matrilocality to patrilocality.[4]

In the earliest period, the patriarch or head of the family had undisputed authority over its members. The honour, even the lives of women, were at the disposal of the men of their families, who regarded women as interchangeable instruments to be used for their procreative services. For example, the story of the Benjamite war demonstrates how wars were ended and enemies pacified by matrimonial arrangements, which were entirely under the control of the men of the tribe. The men of Benjamin, whose wives and children had been killed by the Israelites, accepted new wives from among enslaved or captured women and thus formed new families. As for legal rights in respect of their persons or their bodies, there was no difference between free or slave women or virgins. The virgin daughters were as disposable as the concubines or the enslaved women who were captured in warfare.

In the Decalogue, the wife is listed among a man's possessions, along with his servants, his ox and his ass (Ex. 20:17). In this period, the father could also sell his daughter into slavery or prostitution. For example, Lot's right to dispose of his daughters, even so far as to offer them to be raped, is taken for granted. It does not need to be explained; hence we can assume it reflected an historical condition.[5] Such acts were later forbidden to fathers. Historical records show that as tribal leaders and feudal lords were united under monarchies and controlled by administrators of state, the father's power of life and death over his family members was no longer unlimited and unrestrained and there was an improvement in the position of daughters.

There is no question that the predominant family structure in the Biblical narrative is the patriarchal family. All Israelite women were expected to marry and they passed from the control of their fathers to the control of their husbands and fathers-in-law. Daughters were furnished with a dowry by their fathers and this took the place of their share of the inheritance. Thus, a daughter of a wealthy citizen had some measure of protection from abuse, since the return of her dowry in the case of a divorce might be of economic disadvantage to her husband's family.

In marriage, the wife was expected to produce male offspring. Women were valued for 'building up' their husband's houses by reproduction. Barrenness in a wife or the failure to bear sons was her greatest shame and a disgrace. It was a cause for divorce. For example, Sarah, Leah, and Rachel, in despair when they found themselves barren, offered their slave women to their husbands, in order that the slave women's children could be counted as their own.

In general, the married Jewish woman occupied an inferior position to that of her counterpart in Mesopotamian societies. However, Lerner also notes a strong upgrading in the role of women, as mothers, in the Old Testament. The fifth commandment enjoins children to honour father and mother equally and women are exalted as teachers of the young.

Nevertheless, Lerner can find no evidence to support the contention of some, such as Phyllis Trible, Phyllis Bird or John Otwell, that women were regarded as the equal of men and of high status.[6] She points out:

> Those who regard the Biblical narrative as showing advances for women point to the few heroic women mentioned in the narrative, speak of the role of the five female prophets mentioned in the text, stress the positive statements about women in the Proverbs and the erotic richness and praise of female sexuality in the Song of Songs. Unfortunately, the historical method does not support such a construction.[7]

In fact, the few women mentioned as having respected or heroic roles are quite overwhelmed by the many women described in servile, submissive or subordinated roles.[8]

In the early period of Hebrew history, women were recognised as prophetesses and there remained vestiges of the cultic leadership of a few great women. Deborah, Jael and Chuldah were described as strong individuals in their own right and as acting in close accord with God's purposes.[9] One of the oldest segments of the Old Testament, the Song of Deborah (Judges 4:5), tells us that Deborah was a prophetess and judge. She inspired Barak to rally the troops in resistance to the Canaanites and, in a passage quite exceptional in Biblical literature, her assumption of leadership over men was described.[10] Although we are told that the miracle of the defeat of the leader of the Canaanites, Sisera, was the Lord's, who enabled even a woman to kill a warrior, the passage is a remarkable celebration of physical and moral strength in a female.

In the later monarchy and thereafter, women cannot be found in such roles. As the Jewish tribes moved from confederacy to statehood, the Old Testament text shows a gradual restriction of a woman's public and economic role, a lessening of her public function and an ever increasing regulation of her sexuality.[11] Lerner believes that those feminists, who have tried to argue this meaning away, use linguistic arguments and optimism to describe something that does not exist.[12]

On the other hand, she argues that nothing points to the inevitability of an all male priesthood. It probably grew out of the prolonged ideological struggle of the Hebrew tribes against the worship of the Canaanite deities and the cult of the fertility Goddess, Asherah. This hardened the emphasis on male cultic leadership and the tendency toward misogyny. This may be why the Old Testament's male priesthood represented a radical break with millennia of tradition and with the practices of neighboring peoples. As Lerner concludes:

> The new order under the all-powerful God proclaimed to the Hebrews and to all those who took the Bible as their moral and religious guide, that women cannot speak to God.[13]

The Naming Process and the Theft of the Power of Mothers and Daughters

In line with this misogyny, the creation story in Genesis departs significantly from other creation stories in the region. In Genesis, naming is used to take life-giving away from women and the Goddess, in order to invest it in men and a God. God's word creates the world and he gives the power of naming to Adam, who names Eve and the animals. Naming in Genesis is not only a symbolic act of creativity, but defines woman as part of man's flesh, in an inversion of the relationship of mother to child. Naming is typical of early symbolic thinking. It is based on the belief that there is some special uniqueness and power in a name.[14]

Naming and renaming is a powerful activity and a symbol of sovereignty throughout the Bible. From this symbolic process of reasoning,[15] there grew the most powerful metaphors of gender. Woman was said to be created of Man's rib. Eve was named as the temptress who caused humankind to fall from grace. Lerner again:

> These have, for over two millennia, been cited as proof of divine sanction for the subordination of women, and have had a powerful impact on defining practices in regard to gender relations.[16]

The naming process was also used to convert the tracing of lineage and procreation into male spheres, in such a way that mothers were not involved. It inverted the symbolic belief that it was Ishtar, or other fertility Goddesses who opened the wombs of women, into the belief that it was God, who opened the wombs of Leah and Rachel. Man had become central in relation to God and in the procreative role. The major emphasis was on the implanting of the male seed in the womb and placing higher value on the issue of sons. For example, Sarah was described as the bearer of Abraham's seed. She and Abraham were blessed as progenitors of kings and a male community. Gone is the celebration of the birth of daughters and the powerful role of women in the creation and nurturing of life. Here is a major step toward marginalising mothers and daughters and women as a whole.[17]

Women's power and creativity were further diminished by numerous symbolic acts intended to establish the supremacy of men. Even the custom of circumcision may have originated in a symbolic rite making the penis central to procreation and fertility. By signifying their entry into patriarchal dominance in this way, young males may have been seen as following God's will and achieving his grace. To quote Lerner again:

> The image of the breasts of the fertility-goddesses nurturing the earth and the fields has been replaced by the image of the circumcised penis signifying the covenant contract between mortal men and God.[18]

To the same end, the symbols of the Goddess were taken over by patriarchal kings and rulers. Ears of corn, the bowl from which flows the water of life, the tree of life, the pomegranate, the date and the apple, began to decorate the insignia of male office and patriarchal temples.[19]

Biblical Stories Borrow Mother Goddess Stories and Reinterpret Them

Many Biblical stories were based on, or are reinterpretations of, Goddess stories. The Eve of Hebrew mythology bears a strong resemblance to the great birth and death Goddesses of the ancient Near East.[20] Ishtar, Kuli and Tlazolteotl symbolised that women, by bearing life, bring death as well. The difference in Judaeo Christian mythology is that Eve is secondary and guilty.[21] She is drawn from Adam's rib and becomes the cause of the loss of human innocence and immortality.

In earlier creation myths, Adam and Eve were described as being created simultaneously and Eve was Adam's instructor, rather than merely his helper. Like other powerful Mother Goddesses, Eve travelled beyond this world to win rebirth. As Adam lay near death, she travelled to Jehovah's throne to plead for his life, offering to take Adam's pain on herself and she won Jehovah's pity. Thus, the earlier version of the Eve story depicted her as saviour of mankind, winner of resurrection, mother of humanity and bearing responsibility for the downfall of her man.

Later, the story of Eve was converted into one that symbolised the destruction of the power of the fertility Goddess, through the role of the snake.[22] In the historical context of the times, the snake was associated with the fertility Goddess and symbolically represented her. This is why God put enmity between the snake and the woman, so severing female procreativity from female sexuality. Thus, by God's command, the free and open sexuality of the fertility Goddess was to be forbidden to woman and her sexuality was to find expression in motherhood.[23]

Fallen Eve was to take hope and courage from her redemptive role as a mother, but there were two conditions which defined and limited her choices, both of them imposed on her by God. She is to be severed from the snake, and she is to be ruled by her husband. If we understand the snake to be the symbol of the fertility Goddess, this condition is essential to the establishment of monotheism. As Lerner states:

> 'Here is the historic moment of the death of the Mother Goddess and her replacement by God the Father and the metaphorical Mother under patriarchy.'[24]

Henceforth, women's access to the purpose of God's will and to the unfolding of history is possible only through the mediation of men. Thus, according to the Bible, it is men who live and move in history.[25]

It is little wonder therefore that many biblical passages express profound ambivalence toward women. Women are often described, in comparison to men, as less capable of moral judgement. Female sexuality is conceived as endangering the pursuit of righteousness by men. The ambivalence toward women is carried over into patriarchal views of their importance as mothers.

Along with its secondary view of women, the Bible depicts the once sacred mother-daughter relationship as sometimes assuming aspects of abomination. For example, God says of Israel:

'Behold, everyone who uses proverbs will use this proverb about you: Like mother, like daughter. You are the daughter of your mother, who loathed her husband and her children...' (Ezekiel 16: 43-9).

In the midst of such ambivalence, *The Book of Ruth* is a charming oasis and a straightforward description of mother-daughter love. The action of the book was centred upon women and the narrators were women of the neighbourhood. It is the story of Ruth, who chose to leave her own people and country, because of her love for her surrogate mother, Naomi. The affection between the two outstripped their relationships with their husbands or sons.

Ruth worked to support Naomi in her middle and old age and when she presented Naomi with a grandson, the women of the village said to Naomi, "He shall be to you a restorer of life and a nourisher of your old age, for your daughter, who is more to you than seven sons, has borne him" (Ruth 4: 14-7). Naomi in turn provided a husband and status for Ruth.

Judith Ochshorn[26] believes that this moving story of Ruth and Naomi's love for each other originated in the era of close mother-daughter relationships apparent in the matrilinear societies of the ancient Near East. Ruth, the Moabite, came from a polytheistic society, where women might well have held higher status than they did in the later days of ancient Israel. Therefore, she may have shared in the autonomy, exhibited by other alien women such as the Queen of Sheba, Jezebel and Delilah. It must be noted however that, in the Bible, the outcome of the love and mutual support between mother and daughter was described as leading to the birth of the grandfather of David and the building of the patriarchal house of Israel. It was recounted in a way that gave it patriarchal value.

Throughout the subsequent centuries, Christianity became exclusively patriarchal, culminating in the authoritarianism of medieval societies.

ಬಿ

Mothers and Daughters in Medieval Society

Medieval Christian societies were rampantly patriarchal and exhibited all the tendencies that were discussed in Book I as making for uneasy relationships between mothers and daughters. They were largely hierarchical and conformist, hence femininity had low status and was seen as a deviance from the norm of masculinity. The powerful élite was authoritarian and concerned with maintaining patriarchal power and status. This meant they demanded unwavering loyalty to themselves and institutionalised rigid sets of rules about good manners, behaviour and appearance, in order to protect their exclusive right to rule. Inevitably, their attitudes were black and white and persons were judged according to appearances or whether their observable behaviours adhered to conformist expectations.[27] Patriarchal leaders in church and government were notoriously intolerant of beliefs other than those of their own group. They were obsessively concerned with following rules they believed to be inspired by God, but were more often a projection of their own arbitrariness.[28] Medieval knights, the standard bearers of Christianity, were tough and projected all the behaviours we now regard as 'macho'. Conquering heroes were glorified.

As is typical of patriarchal societies, medieval society was very confused about love and sex. Romantic love was regarded as purifying, but voluptuous sex was sinful. This is Troilus's dilemma in the story of Troilus and Criseyde.[29] The whole pattern of romantic or courtly love in medieval literature makes an interesting study of needs expressed in the fantasies of those who associate sex with sin, brutality, aggression and inexplicable breakthroughs in self-control.[30] Women's sexuality is somehow hideous and to be feared. These attitudes are a far cry from the celebration of sexuality in Goddess societies and their effect on the self-esteem of mothers and daughters is described later in this chapter in the story of Christine de Pizan.

Medieval romantic literature demanded that women be passive, subservient, sweet, kind, generous and pure. It asserted that women needed men to protect them. This view of women offered medieval man the opportunity to feel superior.[31] The man was likely to be described as master, while the woman highlighted his masculinity by being weak and dependent. The division of masculine and feminine characteristics was sharply made. Nevertheless, medieval and authoritarian males denigrated the very attributes they needed in women to make them feel masculine. They expressed their irritation at the dependency of women and described them as fickle, flighty and burdensome.

There was much of this kind of dichotomised thinking and contradiction in medieval attitudes to women. Medieval literature exhibited an ambivalent underlying disrespect for, and resentment against, women, often hidden behind excessive pseudo-admiration. On the one hand, its heroines are the essence of sweetness and purity as in the following description of Constance in The Man of Law's Tale by Chaucer.

> Peerles in beauty, yet untouched by pride,
> Young, but untainted by frivolity,
> In all her dealings goodness is her guide,
> And humbleness has vanquished tyranny.

> She is the mirror of all courtesy,
> Her heart the very chamber of holiness,
> Her hand the minister to all distress.

On the other hand and also from The Man of Law's tale:

> O satan, ever envious since the day,
> On which they chased you out of paradise,
> Our heritage! How soon you found the way
> Through Eve to woman! Our bondage is the price.
> And now this christian match by your advice
> Shall be undone. Of woman you have made
> The instrument by which we are betrayed!

Women were conceived as either marvellously good, or totally bad. This black and white thinking resulted in moral contradictions in belief and behaviour in many aspects of society.[32]

Christine de Pizan, a medieval woman, who is discussed later in this chapter, wrote that it was the kind of society in which mothers and daughters have little true status and learn to doubt themselves and their relationships. Her writings, as well as surviving medieval romances and records, indicate that women were primarily seen in relation to men for pleasure, good or evil. When they appeared in medieval courtly romances and stories of chivalry, the relation of a woman to the hero is much more important than that of a woman to her children. This is in part due to the fact that, in authoritarian medieval societies, motherhood had come to be viewed as being of service to patriarchal lineage and of no great value, beyond the nine months of bearing a child. Motherhood was no longer depicted as an occupation or a role, as it had been in earlier Roman society for instance.

The strength of the patriarchy was now such that husbands more or less owned their wives and children. A daughter's entire livelihood depended upon whether or not her father would provide a dowry, approve a husband or make arrangements with a nunnery. The father was of such socio-economic importance, that when parent-child relationships were depicted, they tended to be father-son or father-daughter relationships. Thus, the literature of the time portrays an emotional dependence on the father which, in this century, has been associated with mothers. This obscures records of mother-daughter relationships.[33]

An example of the emphasis put on the greater importance of the relationship of a woman to her husband, rather than to her children, is seen in the cruel story of Griselda, as told by the Clerk in Chaucer's Canterbury Tales. This story also reveals the lack of empathy for women, children and all who do not belong to the powerful and ruling patriarchal group.[34] As a test for her passivity, loyalty and utter compliance and obedience to him, as was expected of all good medieval wives, Walter, Griselda's husband, orders her to give up their small daughter, seemingly to be slain. The Clerk reports:

> Wel myghte a mooder than had cryd 'allas'!
> But natheless so sad stedefast was she
> That she endured al adversitee, ...

Later, when their son is born, Walter orders Griselda to give him up also. Finally, he instructs her to prepare for his marriage to another. Unbeknown to Griselda, the new bride is her own daughter, now grown into lovely girlhood. In her selflessness, which also suggests the fraternity and concern women had in those harsh times for potential daughters who were doomed to suffer as they had, Griselda says to her husband:

> O thyng biseke I yow, and warne also,
> That ye ne prikke with tormentynge
> This tendre mayden, as ye han doon moo; ...

Eventually, all is revealed and the story of Griselda's humility is seen as an allegory about the human soul. Nevertheless, the allegory portrays the relationship expected between the sexes.

An especial difficulty in finding mothers and daughters in medieval literature arises because most writers were men in a society which was sexually segregated. Medieval men would have had relatively little access to women in their own world. What the majority of women did was not recorded officially. Also, the available literature is that of an authoritarian, aristocratic culture, where contact between aristocratic mothers and high born children, of either sex, was limited.[35]

However, we do get glimpses of mothers concerned for their daughters. *The Wife of Bath's Tale* and *The Lives of Women Saints of Our Country of England*, for example, portray mothers eager to protect their daughters from the miseries of married life. In several legends, mothers and daughters enter a religious house together. It would seem that these mothers, in order to protect their daughters, encouraged them to be virginal and childless. The downside of this manoeuvre is that it invalidated the creative power of their sex, but these are the dilemmas of mothers and daughters in obsessive patriarchies. It is likely that along with mothers and daughters generally in such cultures, they lived in a state of siege, which in turn engendered a counter culture in which women and mothers and daughters took central roles. Phillip Verdier, as a result of his research, *Woman in the Marginalia of Gothic Manuscripts and Related Works*, believes there is considerable evidence that this was the case.

There certainly appears to have been a protective alliance among women in this period, which encouraged the development of surrogate mother-daughter type relationships between women with some power and those with less, or between older women and younger women. The weaker and the younger became a kind of daughter to the older and stronger and the two formed a supportive alliance against the oppression of patriarchy. Examples of such alliances may be seen in the roles and actions of some of the Abbesses of the period. Even though Abbesses were generally ultimately responsible to a male Bishop, there are many stories of them protecting surrogate daughters who entered their nunneries. For example, when Saint Ethelburge fled the house of her cruel father, she found a surrogate mother in Hildelitha and in turn became chosen mother and Abbess to many nuns.

Saint Elfede was another who found a surrogate mother in an Abbess, the Abbess Merwenne, who loved her as her own daughter. Even though these surrogate mothers also did the work of the patriarchy, since they taught their surrogate daughters humility,[36] there are many instances of their bravery in resisting male authority on behalf of such daughters. Even their teaching of humility can be interpreted as an attempt to help their daughters. It is one of the many survival techniques to which women resort in demanding patriarchal societies. It is one of the many manoeuvres that has both a positive and negative side for women.

As children, when we were told stories of medieval nunneries, knights and damsels in distress, witches and old hags, little or nothing was said about the most salient features of this literature — its fear of women and the mother-daughter relationship.[37] Without the help of developmentally appropriate comment, children who read these romances may incorporate their prejudices. These stories survive from a time when a sick fear of women permeated thought. They need frank scrutiny, for they are part of mother-daughter history .

In medieval society, the fear of women had a lot to do with a patriarchal and authoritarian Church, which held power by creating anxiety about sin and eternal damnation. Men were taught to be afraid of their own flesh, which the Church chastised as being full of bestial desires. Men, as the delegated guardians of patriarchy, were encouraged to project into women those propensities, which the Church taught them to hate in themselves. Anxiety, unbearable guilt and fear of their own impulses was relieved by this 'off-loading' or externalisation of their inner feelings.[38]

Sex had become the most disgusting of all impulses and therefore their sexuality was the most abominable aspect of women. The attitude divided men and women and turned Goddess-worship into the work of the Devil. Because of its connotations of the power and sexuality of women, Goddess-worship invited the threat of eternal damnation. If modern classifications of psychiatry were permitted, it might be possible to describe many medieval religious patriarchs as most dangerously deranged and insanely paranoid in their drive to exterminate any surviving relics of Goddess-worship and any vestiges of female power.

This state of mind engendered frequent images in medieval romantic and chivalrous literature of men in jeopardy for their status and their souls, due to the traps set by women and old hags. Old hags were widely believed to advise young women on how to set snares for men and this is probably the way men thought women counselled their daughters.[39] Medieval literature is fraught with the male fear of the bond between women and between mothers and daughters, as if an evil magical power lay in female generation.

In the medieval romances surrounding Sir Gawain and, in particular, the story of Sir Gawain and the Green Knight, the threatening nature of the Old Hag-Young Woman alliance is depicted:

> Most unlike to look on those ladies were,
> For if the one was winsome, then withered was the other.
> Hues rich and rubious were arrayed on the one,
> Rough wrinkles on the other rutted the cheeks.
> Kerchiefs with clear pearls clustering covered the one,
> Whose breast and bright throat all bare appeared,
> Shining like sheen of snow shed on the hills;
> The other was swathed with wimple wound to the throat
> And choking her swarthy chin in chalk-white veils.
> Trellised about with trefoils and tiny rings,
> Nothing was bare on that beldame but the black brows,
> The two eyes, protuding nose, and stark lips,
> And those were a sorry sight and exceedingly bleary.[40]

Medieval patriarchs believed that within every young woman lay the potential Hag and thus she would eventually become. Consequently, we soon discover that the beautiful young woman, who attempts to seduce Sir Gawain, is simply an aspect of the withered old crone. The two generations of women symbolise the threat of the mother-daughter alliance. They are depicted as especially dangerous to Gawain's manhood and his very life. The Old Hag represents the evil power and advice daughters were believed to get from their mothers.[41]

This sick fear of women, mothers and daughters, accounts for medieval constructs about witches and the medieval obsession with witch burning. Whatever one's political beliefs, the massacre of the witches has to be the most deranged aspect of medieval patriarchal culture.

ↄↄ

The Politics of Witchcraft and the Myth of Female Evil

George Bernard Shaw, feminist historians and many others have argued that the killing of the witches was a political act.[42] Its objective was the complete supremacy of the patriarchal religion. During medieval times, Christianity felt threatened because some of the practices of the ancient Goddesses still survived among the common people and the peasantry. Many of these practices related to illness, childbirth and birth control.

Knowledge of herbal contraceptives and abortives, as well as narcotics, that could ease childbirth had survived from a time when women had had control over their own fertility. Fertility control had been applied during harvest shortages and the sense of the practice was not lost to the peasantry over centuries. Legends were still circulated testifying that the arts of gynaecology, midwifery and healing were purely female domains, guarded by the witches who were priestesses of the Great Goddess.

One of these legends was about Diana-Artemis, who was the Goddess of the Witches and the Great Goddess of the Amazons. She was Queen of Heaven, the pure huntress of the Moon and protector of wild animals. Her followers were young women and no man could enter her temple. She, the virgin huntress untouched by men, was also the Goddess of childbirth, born of her mother without pain. She taught women the techniques of painless childbirth. She was a midwife. Once her cult had major centres around Marseilles, Syracuse and Ephesus. It is believed that her temple at Ephesus was built by Amazons ca. 900 B.C. The legend had been officially obliterated but it survived in the folklore of the peasantry. In every small village, the witch was the spiritual and political rival of the local priest, the Christian Church and the male-dominated medical profession.

The growing power of patriarchal Christianity had inevitably spawned a closed, male, medical profession to assist in the sexual oppression of women. The aim was to keep women ignorant of contraceptive methods and force them into compulsory and yearly child bearing. Being a woman became burdensome. The joy of birth and the pride in the mother-daughter alliance at birthing ceremonies gave way to anxiety.

Long after anaesthetics were medically available and as late as the nineteenth century, religious and medical authorities still opposed methods that might relieve women's suffering during childbirth. The traditional Christian belief was that women were meant to suffer for humanity's collective sin. Witches were accused, arrested and burned, for helping women in labour with their herbs and muscle-relaxing techniques.[43] Obliterated was the ancient closeness of mothers and daughters during the birth process. Instead, there began a tradition that it was a time of suffering, guilt and shame. Over the centuries, mothers and daughters learnt to be uncomfortable with each other about their ability to create life.

Whilst the medieval propaganda against witches could be compared with that against Jews by the Nazis, it was much more effective, because to this day, witches are generally depicted as dangerous and hideous. Justification for witch hunts was based on the pervasive, patriarchal myth of female evil.

Myths about the evil propensities of subjugated peoples are not unusual. They are projections of those who are anxious about losing power, and they are a means of justifying oppression. They are also effective propaganda, because they scare the populace into avoiding those who are labelled evil. It also undermines the self-confidence of those so labelled.[44]

An example of this propaganda is seen in *The Hammer of the Witches*, dated 1486, which was written by two Dominican monks and rationalised the patriarchal hatred and fear of women. It was used by the Inquisition to justify its mass persecution of women. It was used by priests, preachers and judges to sanction the arrest, torture and burning of millions of European women.[45]

Children of the condemned were forced to stand before the stake and watch their mothers burn. As they watched, they were whipped by the priests as punishment for being spawned of the Devil. These millions of children, orphaned and robbed of their homes and inheritances, were sent to wander as beggars or imprisoned in Christian orphanages.

The Christian witch burners were obsessed with sex and *The Hammer of the Witches* constantly equates the Devil with sexual activity. The sexual attractiveness of women to men was seen as a Devil-inspired power and as a threat to man's possession of his soul. According to Sjoo and Mor:

> Witches were accused of instigating extra-marital sex, of inhibiting potency, hindering conception, slaying infants in the womb — all threats to patrilineal property inheritance. Rape and sexual abuse of women by Inquisition torturers was blessed by priests as Devil exorcism.[46]

Christianity has an ugly record of religious intolerance and the centuries, over which the religion of the Goddesses and Witches was terrorised out of the people, are no exception. In the determination to remove the threat of the Goddess religions, books, libraries and entire cultures were destroyed. The records, monuments, knowledge and art of the Goddess societies were obliterated and the intellectual development of the human race was, in the eyes of feminist researchers, set back thousands of years.[47]

To sum up, the war against witchcraft was a war against the religion of the peasantry. It was a product of the authoritarian style thinking of the ruling élite. The ruling patriarchs were totally conformist, could not tolerate differences and lacked the ability to empathise with others. The killings of the witches was part of the grand design that led to the Christian Church's control of Europe. The religions of the Goddesses were wiped out. Women lost their sense of power and learnt to question and doubt the value of their feminity. Their doubt was handed on to their daughters.

In this context, the story of Joan of Arc has special meaning for mothers and daughters.

Joan of Arc

Joan of Arc is an interesting daughter of medieval times and the reasons for her ultimate persecution by the Church is still a source for debate, the most famous being George Bernard Shaw's St Joan. Several historians argue that, because the common people believed she represented the second coming of the ancient Goddess, she was a political threat.

Joan arrived on the scene when nations were not yet under the strong central control of the Church and one king. Instead, secular power was divided among many feudal lords, who, while often oppressive, allowed the peasantry a sense of security in their communal villages and the retention of their ancient customs.[48] It was under these conditions that the pagan religions survived and the priests of Christianity were instructed to accommodate these religions where they could not conquer. Thus both pagan and Christian deities are pictured in the reliefs and lintels of early Christian churches. The naked Goddess, with her legs spread wide to show the origins of life was depicted in many church lintels of the time. The tree and gift exchange of Christmas are pagan customs which survive to this day. Santa Claus originated in a Norse Goddess and Easter is a pagan festival of spring. Easter rabbits and eggs are fertility symbols of the Goddess.

During the middle ages, the Church became stronger by means of aligning with powerful kings who had conquered or persuaded the feudal lords to support central control. One means of securing such control was to establish a centralised city court system, but this necessitated eliminating the rival witchcraft systems, which held sway over the people of the countryside. Achieving control was made easier, because the Crusades had weakened many of the feudal lords, who fought and died in the Holy Land at the Church's instigation. At the same time, the Crusades posed a revolutionary threat to the Church and its push for centralised control because the poor joined in these Crusades. They often burnt the castles of the rich and the privileged. They believed in the coming of a female Messiah.

Into this situation stepped Joan of Arc. On the one hand, she helped the patriarchal Christian church in its drive for central control and led France against its secular enemies. On the other hand, she was a daughter of the peasantry and shared their beliefs and dreams. Her peasant backing generated paranoia in those anxious to see that the power of the authoritarian French Catholic Church was not challenged. It was feared she might go further and lead the people against the oppressive Church-State alliance. She might even become a secular and divine rival of the Church. To quell this fear, it was ensured that she became a scapegoat and was condemned by the Church to be burned at the stake as a witch.

One of the factors in Joan of Arc's condemnation was that she had dared to dress as a man and take on the role of a man. Such transvestism was especially threatening to the ruling patriarchy of the time. It was seen as a challenge to male supremacy. This reaction does not mean that Joan was a lesbian or accused of lesbianism. In fact, the patriarchs of the time did not conceive of, or see the possibility of, 'true sex' without a penis, such was the phallocentricism of a closed patriarchy.[49] Hence, the sexual aspects of women's friendships were not seen as a cause for anxiety. In fact, it was believed they were amusing and sexually stimulating for men. Moreover, they could be an apprenticeship or training for sex with a husband.

But should women dress and live as men, as many women did, to escape their female bondage, they were put to death. An instance is described in the early thirteenth century version of the French Romance, *Huon of*

Bordeaux. In this Romance, Ide, a woman in a man's dress, becomes a knight of the Holy Roman Emperor and, because of her achievements, is given the Emperor's daughter in marriage. After the marriage ceremony, she confesses and is condemned to be burnt to death. She is saved at the last minute by metamorphosis into the male sex.

In the midst of the rabid phallocentricism and misogyny of medieval patriarchal culture, the work of one woman, in particular, reinforces the earlier thesis that there was a strong underground of loyalty among women and especially mothers and daughters. The woman, who was both a mother and a daughter, was Christine de Pizan. Her achievements indicate that not all succumbed to the prevailing propaganda against feminine nature.

༄

Christine de Pizan

Christine de Pizan was born in 1364 in Venice. She was the daughter of a Bolognese physician and a Venetian noblewomen. Her parents moved to the court of Charles V of France, when Christine was four. Here she was able to obtain an unusually good education for a woman, in spite of her mother's concern that her morés would be ruined as a result.[50] Hers was the kind of protective and anxious concern that mothers have had over the centuries about the consequences for their daughters should they step outside patriarchal prescriptions for women. Christine disregarded her mother's concern because, as she saw it, only men who are foolish are displeased that women should know more than they.[51]

In her mid-teens, Christine married a court notary. Her husband encouraged Christine's studying and literary activity. He died in 1389 and Christine was widowed at the age of 25, with three small children to support and no inheritance.[52] Resourcefully, she set about obtaining economic security for herself and her children by her writing. By the early 1400s, Christine was known as a French woman of letters. The breadth of her scholarship was widely acknowledged.[53] She received numerous offers from princes to become attached to their courts, including an invitation from Henry IV of England.

Christine's work included poetry, treatises on the education of women and of her son, manuals on good government and on warfare. One of Christine's prime concerns was women and she argued that they should lead independent lives, irrespective of their relationships with men. She believed that history, as experienced by women, is very different from that recorded by men.

She debated vehemently against the portrayal of women in *Roman de la Rose*, the much acclaimed and quoted authority of the time, on chastity and avoidance of the sins of the flesh. While encouraging men to pursue religious ideals, its method was to present women as wicked and as defective versions of men, albeit in allegorical fashion.[54] Christine and other critics such as Jean Gerson, the Chancellor of the University of Paris, while recognising the device, argued that it was harmful to the status of women and that the *Roman de la Rose* contained much that vehemently degraded them.

The recounting of the debate on the *Roman de la Rose* by later authors throws some light on the treatment of female scholars by the patriarchal 'literati' over the centuries.[55] In 1969, John Fleming in his criticism of Christine's ideas wrote:

> Taken seriously, her arguments and her manner show the acumen (in the words of Jean de Montreuil) of the Greek whore who dared to write against Theophrastus.[56]

Christine's *The Book of the City of Ladies* (1405), is a spirited defence of women against such anti-feminism and uses allegory to discuss the history of women. It presents a psychological treatise on how women lose self-esteem if they succumb to the denigrating opinion of foolish men, and how they must trust their own experiences to know they are good and capable. She wrote of the process thus:

> I finally decided that God formed a vile creature when He made woman, and I wondered how such a worthy craftsman could have deigned to make such an abominable work which, from what they say, is the vessel as well as the refuge and abode of every evil and vice. As I was thinking this, a great unhappiness and sadness welled up in my heart, for I detested myself and my entire feminine sex, as though we were monstrosities in nature. And in my lament I spoke these words: "Oh God, how can this be? For unless I stray from my faith, I must never doubt that Your infinite wisdom and most perfect goodness ever created anything which was not good ... how could You go wrong in anything? Yet look at all these accusations which have been judged, decided, and concluded against women."[57]

While thinking these painful thoughts, she is visited by three women, the first of whom says:

> "... we have come to bring you out of ignorance which so blinds your own intellect that you shun what you know for a certainty and believe what you do not know or see or recognise except by virtue of many strange opinions ..."[58]

The woman asks Christine to note how philosophers contradict themselves and have never resolved truth or falsity, that poets deal in fiction, that words are not articles of faith and that no one has produced evidence of the evilness of women. She concludes:

> Come back to yourself, recover your senses, and do not trouble

yourself anymore over such absurdities. For you know that any evil spoken of women so generally hurts only those who say it, not women themselves.

Reassured in her beliefs, Christine insisted that given equal chances, women would do as well as men. It was the custom of not educating daughters that limited their knowledge:

...if it were customary to send daughters to school like sons, and if they were then taught the natural sciences, they would learn as thoroughly and understand the subtleties of all the arts and sciences as well as sons.[59]

The esteem in which she held the potential of women is seen in her *Ditie de Jehanne d'Arc* (1429) where she comments:

I have heard of Esther, Judith and Deborah, who were women of great worth, through whom God delivered his people from oppression, and I have heard of many other worthy women as well, champions every one, through them He performed many miracles, but He has accomplished more through this Maid ...

Oh! What honour for the female sex! It is perfectly obvious that God has special regard for it when all those wretched people who destroyed the whole Kingdom — now recovered and made safe by a woman, something that 5,000 men could not have done — and the traitors have been exterminated.[60]

Christine de Pizan did not see marriage as women's sole purpose in life, or as an excuse for not realising their potential. She saw marriage as a mutual relationship, rather than the subjugation of women to men. However, because she was a product of her times, she did not go further and analyse the bondage that marriage and child-rearing had created for the women of her era, where they often had unequal access to power and the means of earning a living. She accepted the medieval Christian view that later rewards flowed from present suffering. She was a medieval woman, concerned with the attainment of virtue, both individually and for the nation. Nevertheless, she stands at the threshold of the humanism of the Renaissance, which is discussed in the next chapter.

ℰℐ

CHAPTER 5

Mothers and Daughters in the Service of Patriarchy

Some Insights from Shakespeare

The humanists of the Renaissance could not accept that women were as base as medieval Christianity had held. While there was no change in the legal status of women and but rare possibility of their involvement in public life, humanistic scholars such as Sir Thomas More, Erasmus and the Puritan religious reformers, paid attention to the importance of women as mothers. Unlike their medieval forebears, these men believed women had potential for piety and learning. They argued that women should study, if not for their own sake, at least for their sons and daughters, that they may teach them.[1] Educated mothers gained some status as thinking and dignified human beings.

An examination of the writings of English Renaissance mothers finds them responding enthusiastically to the task of educating their daughters to give good service to patriarchy. They directed them to take active religious, social and familial roles, moderated by chastity, humility and temperance. These were the symbolic words which were used to control women's sexuality and power throughout subsequent centuries. None of these mothers showed dissatisfaction with the limits placed on their daughters' professional and public lives. Few even noted the distinction in the education of males and females.

The writings of these mothers are infused with the belief that women are capable of good sense and learning. They are concerned to provide their daughters with the knowledge that will make them good mothers. For example, Elizabeth Knevet Clinton, Countess of Lincoln (1574-1630?) wrote a treatise for her daughter which was a religious justification for breast feeding. Lady Grace (Sherrington) Mildmay (1552-1620) wrote a journal, in which she addressed her daughter, Mary, with her most intimate thoughts on the education of the young.[2]

Provided mothers and daughters abided by the patriarchal limitations on their sexual and gender roles, they were permitted a close and loving relationship. Many of the surviving upper class journals and diaries attest to a deep affection between many a mother and daughter.[3]

Did Shakespeare Renegotiate Misogynist Stereotypes?

Some of the most interesting insights into how an entrenched and authoritarian patriarchy, tempered by some post-Renaissance humanism, rated the role of mothers and daughters during the sixteenth and seventeenth centuries, come from the plays of Shakespeare. In particular, the dramatic devices he used suggest he was trying to say something about the stereotypes that were applied to the mothers and daughters of his time. Was he poking fun at these stereotypes? Was he going further and making a statement about the blurred distinction between male and female? Virginia Woolf thought so and described him as an androgynous author.[4] If he was, he was centuries ahead of most of his contemporaries, who on the whole, shared an entrenched belief in the opposition of, and division between, the sexes.[5]

It is of course difficult to be sure of Shakespeare's intentions, but there are some interesting questions. For example, why do Shakespeare's female characters pose and dress as males when their roles demand that they exhibit wisdom or initiate a romance with members of the opposite sex? Was Shakespeare trying to help the audience of his time renegotiate prevailing stereotypes about women? Is this why Portia, in *The Merchant of Venice*, dons the male apparel and robes of a counsellor at law, so that she might raise a point of logic and be accepted by the audience as wise enough to defend Antonio and save his life? Did the male attire encourage the Shakespearian audience to step outside the confines of their stereotyped expectations of female behaviour, so that they may admire the wonderful sagacity of the young counsellor?[6]

It is certainly remarkable that throughout the seventeenth, eighteenth and nineteenth centuries, when women were so often described as far less intelligent than men, that audiences were seduced by Shakespeare into accepting that Portia saved Antonio through her sagacity. She alone saw the flaw in the bond that Antonio had signed. Shylock could claim his pound of flesh, but there was nothing in the bond that permitted him to spill one drop of blood. It was this finding that saved Antonio and destroyed Shylock.

Shakespeare may have been trying to educate his audience — to get them to accept reality — that women are better and wiser than the then prevailing folklore would have. One can only speculate that through his dramatic devices he was consciously endeavouring to make it easier for his audience to accept an uncommon view. Perhaps it is significant that *The Merchant of Venice* is not the only one of his plays in which he had women disguise themselves as men before they assumed the characteristics of the "noble" sex.

Twelfth Night is another. In this case, the concerns are the conventions of courtship and it certainly seems that Shakespeare was poking fun at stereotypes when he wrote this play. The heroine, Viola, is twin sister to

Sebastian and the two look remarkably alike. They are separated in a shipwreck and Viola disguises herself as a male, calls herself Cesario, and becomes a page to Duke Orsino, whose land she reaches in a small boat. She falls in love with Orsino and in her disguise as a man is able to freely declare her love. Meanwhile, Olivia, the object of Orsino's bountiful love, falls in love with Cesario.

In an age when women were supposed to be reticent about such matters and men had to appear in control, freedom for Olivia to openly declare her love is dramatically possible, because the audience knows Cesario is really the gentlewoman, Viola. The conventions of gender eventually right themselves. Sebastian turns up and takes Viola's place in Olivia's affections and Orsino discovers Viola's true identity and loves her too.

This comedy of falling in love with the same sex is only amusing, if it is believed to be ridiculous, taboo or not possible.[7] The muddles and errors of the heroes and heroines are only comic if the audience believes that it is odd for a woman to initiate romance with, or propose marriage to, a man.

As You Like It is another story of a heroine, Rosalind who, once she adopts male clothing, acquires male rights. Disguised as Ganymede, she and her close and loving friend, Celia, escape from the court of Duke Frederick to Arden, where Rosalind's banished father lives. Here they purchase a shepherd's cottage. In disguise, Rosalind may assume the forward manner of a young male and this permits her to persuade Orlando, with whom she has fallen in love, to visit her and Celia. The story becomes comic because of its sexual convolutions. Rosalind, disguised as a male, can indulge in a seemingly mock courtship with Orlando. He thinks he is playing, while she knows she is in earnest. Eventually, Rosalind reveals her sex and returns to the conventions of her gender. This permits her to find her father and to marry happily.

Great literature such as Shakespeare's is commonly expected to give us insight into how real people lived, felt and thought. In his plays we can recognise the Elizabethan reverence for the so-called masculine virtues of courage and leadership. But Shakespeare had moved beyond the black and white characterisations of medieval knights. His heroes were not totally strong, wise and virtuous. Their tragedies arose out of their own vulnerabilities, their irrationalities or their rejection of the feminine principle — Othello being an example.

Despite this more mature view of men and women, some of Shakespeare's plays tell us that the definition of female still included the possibility of the witch, the hag, the monster.[8] His witches have little to distinguish them from the nastiness of medieval witches. He described women who influenced their men to do evil — Lady Macbeth being one.[9] She was a woman who deviated from the patriarchally prescribed female role and became a threat to men. She abandoned the womanly stereotypes of gentleness and motherliness and became a monster as a consequence. Her conniving and that of the witches, led to the destruction of Macbeth. Here we have the age-old theme of men's fear of the power of women to overcome their manliness. This is projected as the potential of women for cruelty, deception and destruction.[10] The hero, Macduff, is only able to save the day, because he is not susceptible to the spell of the witches and is undaunted by feminine power. Why? Because he was "not of woman born", but plucked forcibly from the womb.[11] Whether Shakespeare intended it or not, this is one of the most dramatic expressions of man's envy and fear of the generative power of women and his desire to be sole creator of his own life.[12]

Shakespeare's Missing Mothers

The evidence of a still prevailing ambivalence about women in Shakespeare's plays is accompanied by its correlate, an undervaluing of mothers. They are often missing from his plays. There are numerous daughters, such as Desdemona, Viola, Ophelia and Rosalind, whose relationships and connections with fathers are delineated, but rarely are their relationships with their mothers given much attention.[13] This suggests that Shakespeare's plays reflected a still popular view, that fathers were more important and endorses Myra Glazer Shotz's view, with which I agree, that the seventeenth century was a period not yet ready to accept the idea of the importance of mothers.[14]

An even better illustration of this point comes from *King Lear*, in which mothers are not only absent but loss of manliness occurs when paternal power is unwisely handed to female relatives — in this case, daughters. After Lear divides his kingdom among his daughters, Goneril and Regan, they show their true colours, become monsters of ingratitude and are wicked and cruel to their father, as a result of which he becomes mad.

Ostensibly, King Lear is a play about father-daughter relationships. Despite what was said earlier about Shakespeare's tendency to omit mothers, this play could be saying something about mother-daughter relationships and what happens when mothers are absent.[15] It might have been yet another attempt by Shakespeare to get his audience to renegotiate prevailing stereotypes. Is this play about an imbalance of paternal authority, untempered by the maternal? Does it imply that a little feminine intuition may have saved Lear from the tragedy of his own making?

Feminine perception may have checked his stupidity in not seeing through the exaggerated and phony protestations of Goneril and Regan, before he gave them his kingdom. Lacking feminine perception and advice, he couldn't recognise the sincerity of his truly loving daughter, Cordelia.

There is also the suspicion that Goneril and Regan are trapped, by Lear's perversities, into lust and violence. There is much to indicate that Lear is an utter misogynist. He dreads the female archetype and fears the female power to create life. He is obsessed by revulsion for female sexuality. He describes the monstrosities of his daughters in sexual terms:

> 'Down from the waist they are Centaurs,

Though women all above:
But to the girdle do the gods inherit,
Beneath is all the fiends.
There's hell, there's darkness, there is the sulphurous pit,
Burning, scalding, stench, consumption ...'[16]

Shakespeare may well have intended that Lear's misogyny be recognised as a major factor in his downfall in a time that was reluctant to acknowledge the value of women and mothers. His plays vacillate between this kind of acknowledgement of the female principle and a fear of women. It may reflect his own ambivalence or the shrewdness of a popular playwright who knows that progressive ideas need to be tempered with attitudes that do not disturb the status quo. Some of his plays very much reinforce the status quo. For example in *Pericles*, he dramatised the conflict between the mother-daughter bond and the need for fathers to control mothers and female sexuality. In fact, Myra Glazer Shotz could be right in diagnosing this play as a deliberate patriarchal re-working of the ancient story of the Mother Goddess, Demeter and her daughter, Persephone. In Shakespeare's version, mother and daughter are purged of their threatening feminine aspects and powers, such as rebirth, and it is the father, Pericles, and not the mother, who receives his daughter back from the brothel that symbolises Hades. [17]

The Mother-Daughter Bond in Two Shakespearian Plays

In contrast, in *The Winter's Tale*, Shakespeare offers a version of the ancient, Demeter-Persephone myth which is more faithful to the original theme of the strength of the mother-daughter bond. In this play, Leontes, the king of Sicily, becomes insanely jealous of his faithful and loving wife, Hermione. He is unduly anxious about his paternity. In Leontes' time, not even a king had sufficient power over a woman's body to be certain of his generative role in the lineage of offspring and Leontes is almost destroyed by his inability to cope with the limits of male power and creativity.[18] By comparison, his pregnant wife, Hermione, is omnific — a constant reminder of woman's power to create life.

In his obsession and doubt that he really is her biological father, Leontes cruelly abandons his baby daughter, Perdita. He imprisons his wife and it is reported that she dies of grief when Leontes will not accept the oracle's word that she is innocent of adultery.

Like Lear, Leontes then falls into madness. Is this because he has rejected Hermione, who symbolises the value of living in harmony with the feminine half of the family — the wife and the mother?[19] Is Shakespeare making a statement that without the feminine input into the family, men lose their good mental health? The rest of the story suggests there might be some truth in this interpretation.

Leontes' son and heir dies of grief because of his mother's shame and Leontes appears to have lost all possibility of retaining his kingdom and lineage. However, all is not as bad as it seems. Unbeknown to him, his daughter has been taken to Bohemia and reared by a good shepherd, and his wife has gone into seclusion with a close friend, Paulina. It is not until his daughter is found and restored to her mother and both rejoin the husband and father, some 16 years later, that Leontes returns to sanity. Albeit subsumed under its importance for the continuation of patriarchal lineage and mental health, *The Winter's Tale* is one of the few Shakespearian plays to acknowledge, or positively endorse, the mother-daughter bond.

Another is *All's Well That Ends Well*. Here, we are told of a surrogate mother, the Countess of Rousillon, who protects and advances the cause of her surrogate daughter, Helena, against her son, Bertram. Bertram is a foolish young aristocrat, who does not recognise the virtue and beauty of Helena, until he believes that he has lost her. The mother-daughter bond is also portrayed in the relationship between two secondary characters, Diana and her mother. This mother, a Florentine widow, advises her daughter against the enticement and promises of men.

The concern and advice both these mothers shower on their daughters is directed at protecting them from the callousness and deception of men toward young women. Their concern says something about how unjustly the social morés were stacked against female sexuality in the seventeenth century.[20] The loyalty of mothers and daughters is described as a source of strength in a male-dominated social order. Daughters are protected by the rational actions of their mothers, which include the measures taken to deceive Bertram. Shakespeare presents this deception as perfectly justified, given the foolish and unempathetic acts of Bertram toward women.

As in *The Winter's Tale*, the theme presents the final solution for the happiness of all as the perpetuation of patriarchal lineage. Nevertheless, the play also suggests that the importance of the mother-daughter bond was something Shakespeare's contemporaries were coming to terms with and that Shakespeare saw his plays as instigators of social change. Of course, Shakespeare's plays also underline how entrenched the reification of women's productive capacity had become.[21] We see it in his descriptions of daughters who are used by their fathers as assets to cement paternal power and augment estates through marriage. The tragic impact of these patriarchal arrangements on young lovers is depicted in *Romeo and Juliet*.

৽৩

Some Royal Mothers and Daughters

History certainly records the authenticity of this theme for royal daughters. Many of the powerful rulers of Shakespeare's era treated their daughters as political and economic commodities. Paradoxically, if daughters did gain power, they often participated in the same practices with their own daughters. This was possible because they had internalised the attitudes of patriarchy.

Catherine de Medici is a case in point. She was born in 1519, the daughter of Lorenzo de Medici and the French aristocrat, Madeleine de la Tour d'Auvergne. Her mother and father died within three weeks of her birth. She was brought up by aunts and later by nuns in a series of convents. Her uncle, Pope Leo X was said to be her protector. In fact, she was his pawn in the marriage market, utilised to increase his power. At 14, she was married to the Duke of Orleans, who later became King Henry II of France. Her eldest son, while he was Dauphin, married Mary Queen of Scots, who regarded her mother-in-law contemptuously as "the Florentine shopkeeper".[22]

However Catherine, because of her station, was ultimately able to wield power that other women of her time could not. When her husband and eldest son died within a year of each other and the new king was 10 years old, as Queen Mother she was able to take control. She is reported to have been an ambitious and shrewd ruler, who did everything she could to protect the interests of her children in the midst of the intrigues and battles for the French crown. Nevertheless, she had been educated to serve patriarchy and she used her daughters for political ends. One daughter was married to King Henry of Navarre, the protestant who became the first Bourbon King of France. Another was married to the King of Spain, the most Catholic country in Europe.

One queen, whose daughter was partly her undoing simply by the sin of being the wrong sex, is Anne Boleyn, the second of King Henry VIII's six wives. She married Henry in January 1553 and in September the hoped for heir was born. Henry was most disappointed because the new baby was a daughter. We are assured that Anne was intensely maternal,[23] but the daughter, Elizabeth, was removed from her at 3 months of age to Hatfield House in Hertfordshire, where she lived for the next 10 years. Anne had two more miscarriages and at the age of 28 was charged with treason and beheaded. Her daughter became Queen of England. She is said to have been greatly influenced by the fate of her mother and feared the power of men over women and hence resisted marriage.

Unfortunately, patriarchal historians have recorded few insights into the effects of these separations on mothers and daughters at an early age. They certainly give little account of what is contemporarily known as "later manifestations of separation anxiety". But in an age, when "bonding"[24] had not been reified to influence expectations, the effects may have been quite different.

By the eighteenth century, little had changed for royal mothers and daughters. For example, Maria Theresa bartered her daughter, Marie Antoinette, in a fashion established in the ancient, patriarchal kingdoms centuries before and continued ever since. Like Catherine de Medici, Maria Theresa became one of the most powerful women in Europe. She was a daughter of the Holy Roman Emperor, Charles VI, who was the last Hapsburg male heir. Before his death, he proclaimed that she should succeed him and this was accepted by the principal rulers of Europe. She became Empress and also Queen of Hungary and Bohemia and Archduchess of Austria. Frederick the Great of Prussia and others subsequently went back on their declared support for Maria Theresa, which led to the eight year war of the Austrian Succession. Throughout, Maria proved a skilful diplomat and stateswoman.

She married Francis, Duke of Lorraine, who became Emperor, but she kept control over most affairs of state and ruled for 40 years, in which time she was respected as wise, astute and innovative. She gave birth to 16 children. All her daughters were given the first name Maria. The tenth child was named Maria Antonia, which was later gallicized as Marie Antoinette. Despite the fact that Maria Theresa was in a powerful position as a woman to resist the practice of using daughters as sexual commodities, she did not. Instead, she used her unusually powerful position to negotiate Marie Antoinette's marriage to the King of France, in the most blatant traditions of patriarchal power-broking. Yet in no way did she prepare or educate Marie Antoinette for any of the skills necessary in state matters, although she'd had the match in mind for years.

In fact, she shared the prevailing patriarchal views on the poor intellectual capacities of daughters and left Marie Antoinette entirely to the indulgence of governesses and music and dancing teachers. Not until she sent her off, at the age of 15, in a cavalcade of over 50 carriages to join her husband in France, does she seem to have attempted to impart motherly wisdom. She began sending her daughter messages of advice. In a letter to the Austrian ambassador in Paris she wrote:

> 'I say outright that I do not want my daughter to have a marked influence upon affairs. I know only to well from personal experience what a weight it is to rule a huge kingdom. What is more I know my daughter's frivolousness and her aversion to concentrating — and she does not know a thing! All that makes me thoroughly afraid if she should try to govern a kingdom as ramshackle as France at the moment.'[25]

Maria Theresa died at the age of 63 in 1780. Her daughter's life ended at the guillotine during the French Revolution.

The cases of Maria Theresa and Catherine de Medici and their daughters, well illustrate Gerda Lerner's point that women are both objects and instruments of subordination and that the patriarchal system would not function without their co-operation.[26]

In this chapter, we have seen that by the sixteenth, seventeenth and eighteenth centuries, mothers were teaching their daughters how best to serve and survive patriarchy. The humanism of the Renaissance had tempered the medieval tendency to overlook mothers. Shakespeare's plays portray both the misogynist hangovers of medieval Christianity and a patriarchal recognition that there is something in femininity and the mother-daughter relationship that is important for the good mental health of men.

In school, had we explored the questions raised in this chapter about Shakespeare's negotiations of female stereotypes, we might have benefited from an early opportunity to poke fun at the tyranny and hierarchy of gender rules. With humour, we could have developed some resistance to their ridiculous impact on mother-daughter relationships. We could have derived more pride from the portrayal of Portia's wisdom. Unfortunately, questions about Shakespeare's dramatic disguises or the absence of mothers are rarely used to help make sense of the problems of the patriarchal view of women, the feminine principle and the importance of the mother-daughter relationship.[27]

If, during the seventeenth century, Shakespeare was trying to persuade his contemporaries to think more rationally about women, mothers and daughters, then his eighteenth century successor is the feminist, Mary Wollstonecraft, who is discussed in the next chapter. Mary's criticism of the destructive effect of patriarchy on mothers and daughters reminds us that feminism is not a modern phenomenon. She challenged many of the ideas of the major patriarchs of her day, including Jean Jacques Rousseau.

და

CHAPTER 6

Mary Wollstonecraft and a New Deal for Mothers and Daughters

Mary Wollstonecraft deserves a place in the history of mothers and daughters. She challenged the worst excesses of a society which saw women as morally, intellectually and physically weaker than men. She used her pen to good effect to attack the hidden agendas behind conventions that turned mothers into slaves and daughters into sexual commodities. She argued vehemently that mothers and daughters were deprived of education and employment in order to keep them subordinate and devised her own curriculum for daughters. One of her chief opponents was Jean Jacques Rousseau

Rousseau's Definition of Ideal Mothers and Exemplary Daughters

Rousseau has been given a place in history as an innovator in a number of areas, but most of all for advocating a new deal in children's education. In fact, in his work, we find daughters are given a raw deal. Their education was to be quite different from the education of sons — a point that even contemporary lecturers in education often by-pass.

Rousseau's theories of the mother-daughter relationship appeared in his novel *Emile* in 1762 and were serialised in *The English Ladies Magazine*, during 1780.[1] He wrote that daughters as future mothers should be trained to avoid willfulness, pride, energy and egoism. In no event should they be allowed to express anger or show the slightest impatience.

Rousseau pictured Sophie, Emile's wife, as the ideal mother. Sophie "rightly and nobly" taught her daughter the most fundamental tenet of all — that dependence is a natural state for women: "She will teach her to interrupt her games without complaint and change her plans to accommodate others". From this good habit, daughters will learn "the docility women need throughout their entire lives, since they never cease to be subject to men".[2]

His ideal daughter was homely, wearing the loose dress of Grecian women, rather than stays. She was to be reared in a rural environment, fed on cakes and cream, not meat,[3] and be entirely unable to run, for "women are not made to run".[4] A love of embroidery was natural to daughters and should be encouraged by their mothers.

Beneath his romanticism, Rousseau revealed the inevitable patriarchal ambivalence toward females.[5] On the one hand, he extolled shame and modesty in daughters. On the other, he wrote that skilful shrewdness, tending to duplicity, and love of embellishment and finery are inborn and instinctive to the female sex.[6] Since his concept of gender and how to maintain its inequality reinforced patriarchal prescriptions, it is little wonder that Rousseau became lastingly popular.

Rousseau and several English moralists set themselves up as experts on mothering. They chastised wealthy mothers who farmed their babies out to wet nurses. The very rich of Europe might abandon their children in this way for two to five years.[7] Many of these babies died. Equally, Rousseau admonished unwed mothers (mostly seen as immoral) and the poor who abandoned their newborns to doorsteps, institutions and gutters.[8] With little awareness of the pressures of convention and poverty, the fear of social ostracism and the inability to cope with another mouth to feed, Rousseau and his colleagues argued that all could be overcome, if mothers resumed nursing their children. Then morals would be reformed,

> natural feelings will revive in every heart, the state will be repopulated; this first step alone will re-unite everyone.

The pendulum had swung from the concept of the medieval mother, with little responsibility beyond reproduction, to the mother with the responsibility of nursing her children in order to save the world. Mothers and their families took on romantic overtones.

Affectionate family ties became increasingly important in the latter part of the eighteenth century and women's place was locked and enshrined therein. Art romanticised the blissful home and hearth, with the mother surrounded by her angelic brood.[9] Femininity was shifting from the emphasis on seduction, pregnancy, birth and producing a male heir, to a much larger role. Women were now expected, not only to bear children, but assume the responsibility for raising and mothering them.[10] A concept which had been introduced to the élite during the Renaissance, had become widely popular.

This phenomenon had much to do with the enclosure acts which were passed for the benefit of landed aristocracy and allowed them to deprive the peasantry, poor farmers and tenants, of their customary rights to common holdings. For example, during the first 33 years of the reign of George III (1760-1793), 1,355 such acts were passed and at least 3 million acres were transferred from poor farmers and tenants to influential well-to-do landlords. The displaced became the work-force of a burgeoning industrial society — an outcome of the preeminence Britain held in world trade.[11] Where men had to abandon cottage and rural-based occupations and absented themselves to factories and business, a division of labour was necessary.[12] Women became doubly important. They were charged with the responsibility of mothering and bearing and nurturing future workers for the new industries. This gave them considerably more status in the family than they'd had in medieval times, and women flocked to embrace the concept of motherhood. Motherhood became an overriding issue for radical and conservative writers and a philosophy emerged which placed mothers and daughters in a seemingly exalted position.[13]

Wollstonecraft Challenges Rousseau's Prescriptions for Mothers and Daughters

The following pages contain a selection of quotations from the work of Mary Wollstonecraft which suggests that the 'exalted' position of mothers and daughters was more fiction than reality. Wollstonecraft's comments give a fascinating insight into the actual position of mothers and daughters and the hypocrisy of the romanticism surrounding them. She exposed the crushing inequalities encouraged by Rousseau's ideas on the education of daughters. She believed that a mother who wished to give true dignity of character to her daughter must, "regardless of the sneers of ignorance", proceed on a plan diametrically opposed to that which Rousseau recommended.[14]

Daughters should be allowed more fresh air and not cramped by sedentary activity. They should be less encouraged by their mothers in embroidery, which keeps them "close and docile as men admire."

> The baneful consequences which flow from inattention to health during infancy and youth, extend further than is supposed — dependence of body naturally produces dependence of mind; and how can she be a good wife and mother, the greater part of whose time is to guard against or endure sickness.[15]

The politics of the counsel handed out by Rousseau and others like him did not escape Wollstonecraft. She saw that its intent was to ensure that women had no power, status or credibility. She recognised and hated all those practices which reduced mothers and daughters to objects of derision in order to enhance the masculinity and dominance of men.

She ridiculed the fashion that impelled eighteenth century mothers to teach their daughters "false descriptions of sensibility and artificial notions of delicacy" and to embrace poor health as beauty. Such women of fashion, she wrote, neglect their duties, yet self-complacently recline on couches, boasting of want of appetite as proof of delicacy.

Wollstonecraft condemned the exhortation that mothers encourage their daughters to pretend to be weak to arouse male desire, for such pretences occasion the disrespect and contempt of men. She asked whether women who have learnt notions of weakness and passive obedience have sufficient character to manage a family, or educate children, or make the best wives.

She particularly disliked the patriarchal fashion which encouraged mothers to commit their daughters to "coming out". She saw this fashion as nothing more than "putting a marriageable miss to market and on vulgar display".

Perhaps Wollstonecraft's most ardent criticism of the misguided influence of eighteenth century mothers on their daughters, was directed at the excessive attention paid to personal beauty, with the sole objective of marriage. While recognising the purpose of the preoccupation, since marriage offered women the best security they could expect at the time, she wrote that the one-sided attention to beauty made daughters ridiculous and useless, once their shortlived bloom of beauty was over. Then, lacking resources for self-fulfilment, they degraded themselves with affectation of weakness and infantile airs, in the hope of tyrannising men. Such cunning ploys "undermine self-esteem..." [16]

Emphasising the duplicity and the hypocrisy of women's status under eighteenth century patriarchy, Wollstonecraft went on to say that women should never be deceived into believing that they tyrannise over men in love affairs, as the word "mistress" suggests. Such deceptions are a stupid game, in which they hold a petty, limited and degraded position.

To Wollstonecraft, men had increased the inferiority of women, until they were almost sunk below the standard of rational creatures:

> Women are everywhere in this deplorable state; for in order to preserve their innocence, as ignorance is courteously termed, truth is hidden from them, and they are made to assume an artificial character before their faculties have acquired any strength.[17]

A man, she argued, cannot expect virtue from one he has ensured is a slave and ill-educated. Dependency breeds cunning and falsity. "Men are not aware of the misery they cause and the vicious weakness they cherish, by only inciting women to render themselves pleasing."[18]

Her argument was a radical one which was not widely valued by women for another century. To her credit, many of her views were derived from a realistic assessment of her own situation and insight into its meaning for women in general.

Wollstonecraft's Mother, Surrogate Mothers and Her Ideas About The Education of Daughters and Women's Rights

Mary Wollstonecraft was born in London in 1759, to Elizabeth and John Wollstonecraft. John had just inherited the means to become a gentleman farmer, but it was the time of the Enclosures and he lacked the skills to succeed as an independent farmer. As the family grew, his inheritance was rapidly depleted. He vented his fury and despair on his wife, and she in turn inflicted her misery on her daughter with impatient and excessive demands for obedience.[19]

Later, in *A Vindication of the Rights of Women*, Mary, speaking from bitter experience, exhorted parents not to expect blind obedience from their children. Parental affection, she wrote, is often an excuse to tyrannise.

Her early home life affected her deeply and she spent much of the rest of her life looking for substitute mothers among males and females alike. William Godwin, whom she married a year before she died, commented on her extreme love of domestic life, as if to compensate for her earlier deprivations. She was frequently depressed, a not uncommon outcome of such a childhood, and she speaks of her inability at times to control her emotions and of often weeping like a child.

However, it was perhaps her mother's demands and her own later determination that bred in her the need to achieve. Coping with the scenes which her father inflicted on the family, taught her to regard him with contempt and to be independent. This probably fortified her later ability to withstand her misogynist male critics.

One of her earliest loving relationships was with Fanny Blood, who was a mentor in her writing and her reading. Fanny and Mary, together with two of Mary's sisters, set up a school, during which time Mary wrote *Thoughts on the Education of Daughters*. In this, she expressed her opposition to the educational practices advocated by Rousseau. Contrary to his advice, she argued that girls should have plenty of time for fun, riotous holidays and self-expression, in like manner to boys.

Unconventionally for her time, she favoured co-education, because she believed it promoted better understanding between the sexes. She was very much against the then current fashion of entrusting the upbringing of children to hirelings. She believed children should not be confined to the company of adults, for in such circumstances children become dependent and do not learn to think for themselves. She favoured an educational situation where the child could return daily to the affection of the home, rather than remain in the tyranny and confinement of boarding schools.

Inspired by the storming of the Bastille in July 1789, she published a pamphlet attacking the well-known writer Edmund Burke for his willingness to support injustice. All the leading journals took note of her arguments and Wollstonecraft, her self-esteem boosted, wrote *A Vindication of The Rights of Women*, which established her place among the political writers of her time and as one of the courageous writers of feminist history.

In this treatise, she addressed herself to middle-class women, as she found aristocratic women in a state of "false refinement, immorality and vanity ... raised above common wants in a premature unnatural manner".

Wollstonecraft emphasised that the problem of the child-like quality of women's reasoning lay not in nature, but in their early education which was "disorderly", providing but a smattering of accomplishments, without understanding and without that degree of exactness in which men only were trained. Young daughters, she wrote, are obliged to sit for hours listening to the idle chatter of weak nurses or attending to their mother's toilet. They have only the vacuous behaviour of their mothers and aunts to emulate.

She described contemporary mothers as slaves "in every situation of prejudice", seldom exerting enlightened maternal affection, for they either neglect their children or spoil them by improper indulgence. She argued that unless the understanding, independence and character of women was enlarged by education, mothers would never have sufficient sense to manage their children properly. But Wollstonecraft did not fall into the chauvinistic trap of many women, by only blaming mothers for the parlous education of their daughters.

> ... alas! husbands as well as their helpmates, are often only overgrown children; nay thanks to early debauchery, scarcely men in their outward form — and if the blind lead the blind, one need not come from heaven to tell the consequences.[20]

Aware that the patriarchal theorists of her time argued that education would de-sex women, she responded:

> Would men but generously snap our chains, and be content with rational fellowship instead of slavish obedience, they would find us more observant daughters, more affectionate sisters, more faithful wives, more reasonable mothers — in a word better citizens.[21]

She also challenged the patriarchal restrictions on female occupations. Unfortunately, the few eighteenth century jobs open to women were menial and when...

> ...superior education enabled them to take charge of the education of children as governesses, they are not treated with the status and dignity accorded to the tutors of sons ...[22]

Wollstonecraft thought women well-suited to studying the art of healing and becoming physicians as well as nurses. Such studies would also permit them to understand their own anatomy and how to guard their health and that of their children and husbands.

> They might also study politics, and settle their benevolence on the broadest basis; for the reading of history will scarcely be more useful than the perusing of romances, if read as mere biography.[23]

Women, she argued, need to be encouraged to respect themselves and political and moral subjects should be open to them to "enhance their minds".

> Business of various kinds they might likewise pursue, if they were educated in a more orderly manner, which might save many from common and legal prostitution. Women would not then marry for a support ...[24]

Inevitably, she did not have an easy time among patriarchal critics and Horace Walpole, for one, described her as "that hyena in skirts". Even as late as 1947, she was said to be a psychiatric case, suffering penis envy.[25]

Wollstonecraft's Daughters and Husband

Wollstonecraft had two daughters of her own. While in France, writing a brief history of the French Revolution, she had a passionate affair with an American, Gilbert Imlay, and gave birth in Havre in 1794 to a daughter, whom she named after her friend Fanny. Imlay deserted her for another and, after months of protesting that she could not live without some "particular" affection, she attempted suicide by drowning. One can imagine the depressive effect this had on her baby daughter.

In William Godwin, the philosophical anarchist, she probably found the first true intellectual match of all her heterosexual relationships. The relationship lasted briefly, from 1796-1797, for she died 10 days after the birth of their daughter, Mary, later to achieve fame as Mary Shelley. Mary was persuaded by Percy Bysshe Shelley to elope with him when she was only 16 and, like her mother, suffered for living outside convention. When Shelley's wife drowned, they were married and, after his death, she devoted her life to making her son, herself and her family "respectable enough" for the title and the fortune he inherited.[26]

Wollstonecraft's eldest daughter, Fanny, was only three when her mother died. This separation, and her earlier experiences with her mother, suggest she became a depressive and, in her later teens, she committed suicide. She left a note: "Perhaps to hear of my death will give you pain, but you will soon have the blessing of forgetting that such a creature ever existed".[27]

Godwin published the story of Mary Wollstonecraft's life in *Memoirs*. The public, and even the feminists of the time, were shocked at her affairs outside marriage. This led to the neglect of her work until 1889, when Susan Anthony and Elizabeth Cady Stanton published the first three volumes of *The History of Woman's Suffrage* and included Wollstonecraft's name in their list of dedications.

∞

Romantic Friendships as a Means of Survival

In his story of her life, Godwin acknowledged and accepted Mary's love for Fanny Blood. Fashion in the seventeenth, eighteenth and nineteenth centuries encouraged women to fall passionately in love with each other. These women prized their friendships and the mutual support it provided. Lillian Faderman[28] suggests that for most there was little genital sexual content in these romantic friendships, especially as in the eighteenth century women's sexuality was denied. The 'ideal' woman was not sexual and suppression of sexuality was part of the training mothers were expected to transmit to their daughters.

However, lesbianism was now recognised as a possibility. But it could only be envisaged as a prototype of male sex. It was believed that the active partner stimulated the passive one with her larger than usual clitoris. Inevitably, lesbianism was dealt with pornographically in the male-oriented literature and in a manner to sexually excite men. Examples can be found in books such as *L'Éspion Anglois* (1777-78) by Francois Mairobert.

The active and dominant partner in a lesbian relationship was depicted as a corrupter of innocence. Usually, she was described as the older and was denigrated and hated as a threat, since she was deemed to be emulating male sexual roles and power. However, readers were assured that, at the first opportunity, a young woman, so corrupted, would run to the arms of a man.

On the whole, romantic friendships between young women were not regarded as lesbian in nature.[29] Lillian Faderman argues that this was because men of the eighteenth century were utterly phallocentric and strongly believed women lacked sexuality.[30] They regarded romantic liaisons between young women with patronising delight. They found the physical display of affection between women titillating and most believed it would not be enduring anyway. In Samuel Richardson's *Clarissa* (1748), the Colonel remarks, "Friendship, generally speaking ... is too fervent a flame for female minds to manage". The male-dominated fiction also suggests that men believed that women carried on these close friendships in order to be able to talk of their relationships with men.

None of these things were true. Friendships with each other, romantic or otherwise, were the mainstays of women, where divorce was extraordinarily difficult and marriages often a matter of alienation between the partners rather than companionship.[31]

Women of fashion pledged life-long devotion, openly embraced, walked hand in hand in public, addressed each other in frequent letters as "my heart" or "my queen" and wore portraits of the adored friend dangling from their wristbands. This was the age of sentimentality, when feeling, or sensibility, was valued for its own sake.

The eighteenth century abounded with romantic friendships between women, one of the most famous being that between Sarah Ponsonby and Eleanore Butler, two upper-class Irish women, who ran away together and lived in a cottage in Wales. They were intelligent and cultivated and befriended by the Duke of Wellington, Wordsworth, Southey, Josiah Wedgwood, Edmund Burke, Sir Walter Scott and Lady Caroline Lamb.

Romantic friendships were the way in which women coped with an age in which double standards for male and female sexuality exacerbated the tensions and alienation between the sexes. In contrast to the loving closeness between women, the patriarchal literature of the time often portrayed a potentially hostile situation between males and females. This can be seen in novels by popular authors such as Samuel Richardson. In *Pamela* or *Clarissa*, the seduction of a daughter is presented as amusing sport for men, especially as it meant the loss of her innocence, her most valued asset in patriarchy. The greater the agony of the woman, as a result of the male use of deceit to deflower her, the funnier.

Much of the literature exhibited complete lack of empathy for women. Eighteenth century novels and magazines abounded in the adventures of men who tricked daughters out of their virginity. Moreover, the brutality of men to women sexually had currency and accounted for the popularity of the Marquis de Sade.[32] Men and women were reinforced in an adversary situation and the daughter who valued herself learnt to distrust men.

What was sport for men was tragedy for daughters in an age when patriarchy emphasised that all depended on women retaining their virginity, as it was their only marketable commodity. It was pertinently described as their purse.[33] Fiction tells us that even loving parents of the period preferred their daughter's death to the loss of her virginity. Mothers warned their daughters of such a catastrophe.

The vulnerable position of middle and upper-class women was compounded in other ways. While in earlier centuries, women could find meaningful things to occupy their time, by the eighteenth century this was taboo.[34] For the glorification of their husbands' and fathers' social and economic status, eighteenth century women were supposed to be idle and unlearned and pure adornment.[35]

If they tried to air any cultivation of learning, they were denigrated as blue-stockings. Samuel Johnson, not untypically of the misogyny of the time, compared a woman preaching, to a dog standing on its hind legs. When intelligent women of note tried to form their own salons to discuss among themselves matters of learning, they were frequently ridiculed in satirical drama and poetry. For example, Molière in his plays, *Les Précieuse Ridicules*, *Les Femmes Savantes* and *The School for Wives Criticized*, mocked women who attempted to embrace learning.

Daughters could not even feel safe from patriarchal hostility, once they were married. Middle and upper-class marriages were commercial affairs, determined by the parents on the grounds of amassing fortunes or strengthening family power. The best a mother could do for her daughter was seek to arrange a 'good' marriage, which was measured in terms of the settlement. Daughters and sons were rarely consulted and there was little attention to personal compatibility or age differences. Richard Steele, editor of *The Spectator*, commented that parents were more often concerned with matching their estates, rather than their children.[36]

In her autobiography, Mrs Delaney,[37] a famous librettist, tells of having been married at 17 to a man of 60 whom she loathed and the sadness of leaving her home to be ruled by a tyrant, whom her training had taught she must and would obey. Her parents felt the match was a fine one, since the man was wealthier than they.

Eighteenth century novels, such as *Clarissa* and *Tom Jones*, [38] indicate that while daughters should not be forced into abhorred matches and that they may justifiably resist them, there was no justification for their marrying against their parents' will. Sadly, without any other possibility of economic independence, upper-class daughters often accepted their parents' choices, in the hope of escaping from parental tyranny through marriage. Daughters were advised by their mothers and fathers to close their eyes and ears if they found themselves married to someone of repulsive morals and tastes and put up with it. Most genteel daughters appear to have complied. Perhaps there was some solace, for husbands and wives who loathed each other were permitted to lead separate lives, attending only formal social occasions together.

However, once married, daughters were generally expected to be subservient to their husbands. At least an upper-class wife was better off than the wife of a peasant, who was often valued as less than his horse and subject to frequent beatings by her husband.

It is little wonder that in this hostile context, mothers and daughters turned to their own sex for some understanding and communication. Romantic friendships flourished in the eighteenth century, because of the segregation and alienation of the sexes, the lack of genuine and lasting affection between husbands and wives, and the belief that the very natures of men and women were opposite.[39] These factors also explain why women embraced the fashion of sensibility, which served to endorse the dual psychology of the time.

❧

A Literature of Their Own

Sensibility was derived from sentimentalism. Sentimentality was defined as a moral reflection and opinion about the rights and wrongs of human conduct, much influenced by emotion.[40] In the middle decades of the eighteenth century, novels, poetry, drama and essays were devoted to sentiment and pathos, which became the cult of sensibility. Large numbers of women contributed to this literature. Charlotte Lennox's *Euphema*[41] is one of innumerable examples. In this novel, the heroine looked forward not to a happy marriage, but to the sweetness of women's society.

Ultimately, the feminine influence on literature alarmed patriarchy, which denigrated sensibility as expressing the irrational benevolence of women and their tears, fainting fits and palpitations.

As Janet Todd points out:

'This fiction initially showed people how to behave, how to express themselves in friendship and how to respond decently to life's experiences. Later it prided itself more on making readers weep and teaching them when and how to weep. In addition it weep and teaching them when and how to weep. In addition it delivered the great archetypal victims: The chaste suffering woman, happily rewarded in marriage or elevated into redemptive death, and the sensitive, benevolent man whose feelings are too exquisite for the acquisitiveness, vulgarity and selfishness of his world."[42]

The concept of sensibility was about feeling — delicate emotional and physical susceptibility — and the ability to display compassion for suffering. Those who possessed it were said to have an innate sensitiveness, which gave rise to a variety of spontaneous activities, such as crying, swooning and kneeling.[43] The cult of sensibility valued the pure victim and had a poignant repertoire of nouns and adjectives: the heart is "kind", "honest", "tender" and "fond"; feeling is "melting", "swelling" or "overflowing" and sighs and tears are "pitying" and "sympathetic".

Initially, men were also influenced by sensibility and gave it expression in some of the famous sentimental novels of the period. Generally, in these novels, there was a plot of female friendship, which was deeply sentimental and full of emotional reunions and separations. For example, in Richardson's *Clarissa*, two persecuted and defenseless female friends clung together in a hostile world. Most of the authors of this kind of literature couldn't capture the genuine sentimental content of close friendships between women. They were a parody of the supportive friendships of real life, which Faderman describes in her research of the era.[44] Mary Wollstonecraft was one who was well aware of the falsity of these descriptions and she admonished mothers to have their daughters eschew sentimental novels.

Was Sentimental Fiction a Delusion for Mothers and Daughters?

Indeed, Mary Wollstonecraft began to express doubts about sensibility when she wrote *Mary:A Fiction*, which investigated her relationship with Fanny Blood. She found it did not match the sugary descriptions of female friendship in the sentimental literature of patriarchal authors such as Richardson. She also noted that the fashion for sensibility existed alongside social cruelty. She saw the pattern and effusions of sentimentality as no remedy for poverty and injustice.

In an excellent analysis, Janet Todd confirms Wollstonecraft's beliefs about the hypocrisy of much of the literature of sensibility. She wrote that there was "a stark opposition of fiction and reality: the sentimental elevation of the maiden or mother on the one hand and the possibly brutal reality of female economic and social impotence within marriage on the other".[45]

Mary Wollstonecraft also recognised the delusions surrounding the concept of romantic love between men and women — another favourite theme of sentimental fiction. Like many wishing to improve the condition of women in society, she recognised it as a fantasy — a wish-fulfilment of power — which obscured women's actual impotence and distracted them from acting for reform. In *The Wrongs of Woman*, written in 1798, she illustrated her point by portraying a heroine imprisoned in a madhouse by the husband she sentimentally chose. In *A Vindication of The Rights of Women*, she was concerned to attack the false sensibility adopted by mothers and daughters in the courtship game. She insisted that rationality, not false sentimentality, was the path to the reform of women's condition.

Sensibility also came to encompass the concept of free love. In a less patriarchal world, it could be advantageous to women.[46] In a strongly entrenched patriarchy, which largely limited women's means of support to marriage and which regarded virginity as an essential commodity in the marriage market, free love was only advantageous to men. For this reason it became fashionable, but Wollstonecraft recognised its hypocrisy for eighteenth century women and in doing so no doubt drew on her own unfortunate experience with Gilbert Imlay. Since chastity was required for women to flourish socially, she said, then sexual license became a trap for them. She described free love as a collusion by women in the libertine reveries of men.

How can we in the twentieth century judge Wollstonecraft's conclusions? They were right for her in the society and time in which she lived. As we have seen, she was well aware of how patriarchy brainwashes women. Her point about collusion anticipated Gerda Lerner's point that patriarchy can only function with the co-operation of women and supports Lerner's argument that women do this largely because they are denied a full understanding of their oppression.[47]

That the fiction of sensibility was full of enormous contradictions was aptly illustrated by Wollstonecraft's husband, Godwin, in his biography of her. Here he worked at severing sensibility from benevolence and humanitarianism, and associated his well-educated wife with sensibility and himself with rationality! This was the way in which the differences between the sexes were categorised over the next two centuries.

Because the philosophy of sensibility implied the natural superiority of women, since they were seen as the more emotional sex, as sensibility grew increasingly popular, it was attacked. It was also criticised because of its excesses and illogicalities. The attack upon sensibility came from diverse directions for different reasons and included misogynists, feminists and the moralists of the Christian Church. Fiction moved away from the eighteenth century sentimental novel and ideas of a special female sensitivity were questioned and denigrated.

Janet Todd rightly believes that the movement from sentiment was not wholly a gain, since it denied traditionally sentimental topics close investigation. Moreover, the association of sensibility with effeminacy, made the sentimental style possible only as a lapse from "masculine rigour and moral and social seriousness". Such an attitude, strongly entrenched in patriarchal circles ever since, limits the discussion of relationships, including mother-daughter relationships.

Fortunately, reality-based sentiment remained to good effect in several nineteenth and twentieth century novels. The novels of the Brontës are examples. Alice Walker's *The Color Purple* is another. Whenever and wherever the feminist movement has been strong, it has made it possible to expose the sentiment which is essential to good relationships.

This chapter has concentrated on the unfortunate outcomes of the limited education of daughters during the eighteenth century. Mary Wollstonecraft's criticisms give wonderful insights into the deliberate subordination of mothers and daughters. Even so, many mothers and daughters resourcefully nurtured themselves by forming romantic friendships with other mothers and daughters. They turned the cult of sensibility to their advantage, until it was parodied and jeered out of rational existence. The next chapter shows that, as always, mothers and daughters managed to secure something for themselves out of the economic and social changes of the late eighteenth and early nineteenth centuries. They also managed to establish a culture of their own, using the occupation of embroidery which Wollstonecraft saw as an unhealthy and imprisoning occupation for young daughters. In part it was, but mothers and daughters also used it to good effect to endorse their relationships.

෴

CHAPTER 7

Marriageable Daughters

Embroidery and The Novels of Jane Austen

Embroidery and the Mother-Daughter Relationship

In the eighteenth and nineteenth centuries, teaching a daughter to embroider became an accepted and traditionalised symbol of the unity of mothers and daughters and, as such, is recorded in the paintings and literature of the time.[1] For example, the well-known painting, "La Mère Laboreuse" by Jean Baptiste Chardin (1699-1799), depicts a mother and daughter embroidering together.

Patriarchy condoned the symbol. Mothers and daughters accepted it and subverted it into a counter-culture of their own. Embroidery by mothers and daughters, which can be found in museums, galleries and churches throughout England, Europe and America, tells us a great deal about mother-daughter relationships in the eighteenth and nineteenth centuries. Unlike its androgynous conception in the middle ages,[2] by the eighteenth century embroidery had become a feminine pursuit, indeed the hallmark of feminity. Application to embroidery signified the containment[3] and submission expected of women and their embroidered adornments became symbols of a leisured, aristocratic life-style. If a woman had time to embroider, it also meant she was not working and did not need to work. Thus, the feminine art of embroidery played a crucial role in indicating the class, position and economic circumstances of a man's household.[4]

As Roszika Parker indicates in her delightful history of women and embroidery, by the eighteenth century, embroidery and feminity were so fused that the connection was regarded as innate.[5] Being one of the few leisure pursuits permitted middle and upper-class mothers and daughters, they utilised it as a means of self-expression and a source of artistic pleasure. In their embroidery, women achieved praiseworthy levels of skill and reflected the womanly ideals which were demanded by patriarchy. Sometimes their embroidery subversively questioned their situation.

Parker also believes that the mutuality and the reciprocity of embroidery, as a joint leisure pursuit, summoned and sustained images of early childhood, where a primal and unproblematic unity between mother and daughter still existed. In the embroidered pictures and samplers of the eighteenth century, mothers are honoured and loved. The mother-daughter relationship is celebrated and idealised. Mothers and daughters are depicted in rustic settings, hands clasped, walking together. These outdoor settings appear to underline the naturalness and healthiness of the relationship. The daughter is a small replica of the mother, so illustrating the identification between the two and that the daughter is more of an extension of the mother than a son can ever be.

Just as in the literature of the time, it became fashionable for mothers to write instructive tracts or letters to their daughters with such titles as "An Unfortunate Mother's Advice to her Absent Daughter", so the samplers often followed suit and became a vehicle by which a mother imparted moral instruction to her daughter.[6] Sampler verses extolled a mother's love and moral duty and the daughter's absolute love and obedience, as in the following example:

> Behold the labour of my tender age
> And view this work which did my hours engage.
> With anxious care I did these colours place
> A smile to gain from my dear Parent's face
> Whose care of me I will ever regard,
> And pray that God will give a kind reward.[7]

A twentieth century observer may see guilt in these lines, but again we must take care in extrapolating the feelings of one age to another. The motivation expressed may have been more straightforward than the convolutions of many twentieth century mother-daughter relationships. Expectations and attitudes were not similar to those in the twentieth century. Attaining independence had different connotations.[8]

For example, Fanny Burney's diary, illustrates how at the age of 16 one may be both a good girl — as she clearly wanted to be — for one's mother, or stepmother in her case, and yet independently ration the time she was expected to spend on embroidery. This limitation of embroidery work by the stepdaughter, Fanny, was probably a symbolic act in her striving for autonomy as her adulthood approached. No doubt, for her part, the stepmother was trying to protect Fanny from becoming uncommonly bookish and 'unfeminine', by stipulating that she not devote all her time to reading. Fanny wrote:

> I make a kind of rule never to indulge myself in my two most favourite pursuits, reading and writing, in the morning -no, like a very good girl I give that up wholly to needlework, by which means reading and writing in the afternoon is a pleasure I cannot be blamed for by my mother, as it does not take up the time I ought to spend otherwise.[9]

Fanny's compliance with the current ideology of femininity and rebellion against it, using the medium of embroidery, sums up the dual role the art played in the lives of mothers and daughters for centuries. While conforming to the feminine ideal, mothers and daughters were able to use embroidery to make meanings of their own. Embroidery provided a source of pleasure and power for women, while being indissolubly linked to their powerlessness.[10]

The way in which embroidery came to signify femininity under patriarchy makes interesting history.[11] It demonstrates that the embroidery of mothers and daughters has little to do with their innate nature and everything to do with their place in society. Far from being a mark of femininity, in medieval times, embroidery was strongly associated with self-adornment as a mark of social power in men. Heraldry and other emblems of political allegiance and power made embroidery politically and artistically a leading art.[12] As far as women were concerned, there was a disjunction between their contribution to the art of embroidery and society in general and the Church's repudiation of women.[13]

In medieval times, crafts were open to women and the records indicate they were involved in a great variety of crafts such as shoemaking, ironmongery and candlemaking. They ran businesses and were members of guilds alongside their husbands and fathers.[14] As embroiderers, they played a significant role in creating and stitching some of the major tapestries of the time.[15]

By the time of the Renaissance, mothers and daughters were becoming increasingly detached from paid production[16] and their embroidery expressed their changed social position. Renaissance man, through the embroidery of his wife and daughters, was able to make a statement about his opulence and his power. The rich stitchery indicated both his nobility and the humility of his wife and daughters.[17] Below the level of the great landholders, the numbers belonging to the merchant class were increasing and their wealth growing. They emulated the nobility in their domestic embroidered furnishings and the embroidered clothes of their wives and daughters. In her time, Christine de Pizan had blamed these upwardly mobile men for encouraging vanity in women by using their richly embroidered garments as status symbols.[18]

The Renaissance also marked the beginning of the decline in the status embroidery once had. It extolled painting as evidence of the divinely inspired male individual and downgraded collective skills, including and especially embroidery because it was becoming a predominantly feminine pursuit.[19] Texts advocated needlework to promote the virtues of femininity — chastity, humility and obedience.[20] Embroidery became the expression of the ideology of sexual difference.

Although embroidery had come to indicate the subservient position of mothers and daughters, they managed to subvert it to exercise their wits and create private communication. A famous historical example can be found in Mary Queen of Scots' use of emblamatic embroidery. During her imprisonment, she used it to send secret messages or make obtuse comments on her situation. One of her embroideries shows a marmalade cat wearing a golden crown playing with a mouse and symbolised her relationship with Queen Elizabeth.[21]

By the seventeenth century, education for upper-class women was tolerated, but only when it was sufficiently differentiated from men's by the addition of music, dancing and embroidery. Embroidery permitted women to acquire a humanistic education without threatening the boundaries between masculinity and femininity.[22] This was the time of Cromwell and aggressive puritanism,[23] and puritan values had their impact on embroidery. A woman's skill with a needle increasingly came to imply chastity. Not that this was entirely new. Even Christine de Pizan, the medieval feminist, had seen embroidery as a means of avoiding the temptations that lay in idleness.[24]

The Puritans were concerned with discipline[25] and embroidery was utilised by them to inculcate obedience and patience in females. There was a new emphasis on more testing stitchery in embroidery.[26] As we have records of young daughters who protested, we can see that femininity, as defined through diligence to embroidery, did not come naturally to little girls.[27]

The church argued that embroidery was to prepare girls for housewifery. As ever, mothers and daughters expressed their resistance and resignation through the content of their embroidery. Famous and strong women of the Bible became popular. Embroiderers favoured stories about women who'd had power within marriage, such as Sarah and Esther. By the end of the seventeenth century, mothers and daughters had gained sufficient confidence to no longer need to invoke biblical heroines to make women recognisable as reasonable beings. Pamphlets appeared calling for the just liberty of the tender sex.[28]

By the eighteenth century, embroidery was coming in for some scornful attacks from women who wanted a better education for girls, Mary Wollstonecraft being one critic.[29] Regrettably, some found themselves in the same camp as men who belittled women's activities. On the whole, campaigners for women's education still took great care to include embroidery in their curriculum in order to make it acceptable to patriarchy.[30] With the spread of charity schools in the eighteenth century, even the education of working-class girls included the stitching of samplers.[31]

After the "Glorious" Revolution of 1689, which limited the power of the monarchy and established the oligarchy and the splendour and privilege of the aristocracy,[32] the industrious wife of the seventeenth century gave way to the aristocratic ideal of a leisurely feminine lifestyle. The helpless leisured lady made men feel masculine and powerful and embroidery became synonymous with female seductiveness. In *Pamela*, Richardson showed how the patriarchal view of femininity and embroidery was constructed and fused in men's minds.[33] With considerable ambivalence, he portrayed embroidery both as an instrument of seduction and a waste of time. The prevailing fear of, and contempt for, feminine endeavours and unity was well expressed by Addison who wrote mocking letters on the art of embroidery to *The Spectator* referring to its usefulness in distracting women from gossip and politics.[34] He ridiculed the embroiderers preoccupation with pastoral pictures and floral themes. By mid-century, these themes had given way to the happy peasant and the stitched shepherdess which reinforced the patriarchal ideology that femininity was natural and a cross-class characteristic. When the fashion of sensibility came along, the sampler verses testified to the crucial feminine quality of feeling.

Drawing also became a feminine occupation during the eighteenth century, but women were excluded from the best art academies and schools. They responded by developing creative alternatives. They worked with shells, feathers and paper collage. Mary Delaney[35] was one of many famous women in this period who was involved in shell work, feather work, paper collage and a diversity of creative arts.

While the eighteenth century believed that femininity was innate and that embroidery was a natural expression of it, it accepted embroidery as a creative pleasure. By the nineteenth century, the protestant ethic of the rising and powerful middle-classes had applied the concept of moral duty to embroidery. Unless performed in a spirit of selfless industry, it was seen to reflect aristocratic decadence and indolence.[36]

As long as it was intended for refurbishing the Church, embroidery in the drawing room was acceptable to Church elders because it combined domesticity and piety — highly acceptable traits in mothers and daughters. Women, who otherwise would not have been heard outside the home, found a public voice by embroidering church furnishings and writing books on the history and practice of the art of embroidery.[37] In these books, mothers and daughters asserted the value of the skill that signified their femininity, yet was devalued by their Victorian masters. They used their skill to redress their dissatisfaction with their position.

They gained vicarious pleasure from embroidering the exciting courtly romances of medieval times with their sexual overtones.[38] They believed medieval literature testified to a time when females had the status and freedom denied them by Victorian patriarchy.[39] They were misled, but their objectives have to be admired. In order to recapture a time when their ability to create life was honoured and when obstetrics was a female province, they incorporated fertility symbols and midwives in their tapestries.

Nineteenth century feminists became increasingly intolerant of embroidery, because it symbolised the oppression of women. Charlotte Brontë thought embroidery limited women's intellectual life.[40] In *Shirley*, she depicts 12 year old Rose Yorke protesting that embroidery is boring and trying to resist her mother's endeavours to get her to apply herself to it. The servant, Sarah, sympathises with one of the principal female characters, Carolines Helstone, for being "mewed up" with her embroidery.[41] Charlotte Brontë also described how the independent heroine, Shirley, uncharacteristically tried to use embroidery to conform to the ideology of femininity. By embroidering in the presence of her suitor, she hoped to make him feel masculine and prevent him from feeling threatened by her economic power. Charlotte Brontë takes pleasure in describing how the ploy failed.

Charlotte Brontë was not totally dismissive of the art of embroidery. Although critical of it, she relied on her reader's knowledge of it.[42] She also saw embroidery as an instrument of self-defence for the subjugated sex. With eyes downcast to their sewing, mothers and daughters could surreptitiously assess visitors and suitors.[43] They could use attention to the intricacies of embroidery to impose silence, even dominate. Mrs Gaskell was of the same opinion and demonstrated this point through the character of Mrs Gibson in *Wives and Daughters*.

Men both imposed embroidery as a definition of femininity and revealed their ambivalence toward women by lampooning it, mocking it and sneering at it from the seventeenth century onward. But embroidery is not only the history of the oppressive construction of femininity, it is also the history of the creative relationship of mothers and daughters to the art. Throughout the centuries they have subverted it to their own purposes. Even the suffragettes used it for making the slogans on their banners. Their handkerchiefs and their embroidered signatures expressed their solidarity.[44] By 1960 embroidery had become, not a selfless duty, but a manifestation of self. For example, the hippy use of embroidered jeans in the 1960s asserted individuality, creativity and non-conformity.[45]

But this anticipates a time of greater freedom for mothers and daughters. In the eighteenth century, the routines and art of embroidery gave mothers and daughters an opportunity to express themselves within the limits set for them by patriarchy. They made embroidery the symbol of their unity. It is hard to assess how much the patriarchal attacks upon embroidery were motivated by fear of that unity or genuine concern for the well-being of mothers and daughters. Embroidery certainly came under suspicion because of the growing patriarchal concern about motherhood.[46] William Buchan, in *Domestic Medicine, or a Treatise on the Prevention and Care of Diseases by Regimen and Simple Medicine*, 1769, argued that women, who have been accustomed to a sedentary life, generally run great hazard in childbirth.[47]

Social and economic changes were affecting the life-styles of mothers and daughter in other ways. The eighteenth century saw an increase in the middle-class population, due to the Enclosures, the invention of the steam engine and the new industries. Whereas during the seventeenth century arranged marriages were the norm, there was now a growing class of people who did not depend on large estates and for whom dowries and amalgamation of lineages were unimportant.[48] Without these constraints, their daughters were permitted greater freedom and the rituals of courtship began to change, such that daughters could briefly make decisions and choices.

The changes are reflected in the literary magazines for women. In 1744, *The Female Spectator* came out against arranged marriages and, by 1780, *The Ladies Magazine* was bravely asking why courtship should be confined to men and advancing the radical idea that ladies should be permitted to propose in leap years.[49]

As ever, these radical ideas were contained by patriarchal politics and economics. The long French wars, in which Britain was intermittently engaged from the early 1790s to 1815, promoted militarism and conservatism. These were alarmist times, full of suspicion of revolutionary ideas and giving rise to a cult of nationalism, with stress on restraint, self-control and stoical acceptance. These years coincided with the attack on sensibility, which was now felt to be demoralising, anti-Christian, childishly French and to have emasculated men.[50] Sensibility had been increasingly associated with women who, denied the classical education of the universities, had been reading and writing sentimental novels and poems in ever increasing numbers.

To many in Britain, the cult of sensibility seemed to have feminised the nation and given women undue prominence. Sheridan, Gibbon and Coleridge are among those well known for leading the conservative onslaught on sensibility. Jane Austen was another. Her criticism of sensibility was delivered through her portrayal of mothers and daughters in an upper middle-class world.

ॐ

Mothers and Daughters in the Novels of Jane Austen

In Austen's novels the clichés of sentimental fiction were overturned; living mothers were sometimes vulgar and limited; sentimental friends were a sham; there were no female victims and women engaged in rational discourse. She parodied and mocked the prose and posturing of sensibility. Instead of romantic fantasies, she presented real people as they were. The sentimental were the uneducated and ill-bred. For example, Lucy Steele in *Sense and Sensibility*, who displays sentimental attitudes, is one who speaks in vulgar jargon, comes from Plymouth,[51] where her uncle tutors boys for a living, and is described as in want of delicacy, rectitude and integrity of mind.

Austen was part of the eighteenth century development of the novel as a literary form, in which characters were portrayed in a three dimensional fashion and as a mixture of ordinary strengths and weaknesses, rather than in the two dimensional dichotomy of either lily-white or totally evil proportions, which typified much of the previous patriarchal literature. Her novels also demonstrated that special ability some women writers have for portraying the daily joys, cares, feelings and hopes of family life.

Using this talent, she was able to capture the greater freedom permitted middle and upper middle-class daughters in a conservative world. She depicted daughters who believed they were able to steer a self-directed course, within the rules of the courtship game, and win the men they wanted and loved. Her daughters displayed a new independence and an acquisition of good sense.

One way in which Austen allowed the daughters in her novels greater freedom was through the use of a literary convention, which portrayed mothers as absent or inadequate. Ideally in the eighteenth century, one of the most important tasks of a mother was to assist her daughter's social contacts, maintain her daughter's propriety and ward off her undesirable suitors. The mother's absence or inadequacy in these tasks and the daughter's successful maturing processes in subsequent trials are the stuff of Austen's novels.

When mothers are dead or absent and unable to shield their daughters from the trials of attaining adulthood, then their daughters are obliged to develop some self-assertion and independence.[52] Emma, Jane Fairfax and Harriet Smith are daughters without mothers in the novel, *Emma*. Some of the men in this novel are also without mothers, including Knightley and Frank Churchill. Darcy, the Bingleys and Wickham, in *Pride and Prejudice*, the Tilneys in *Northanger Abbey* and the Elliots and Captain Wentworth in *Persuasion* are similarly situated.

That Austen used this device intentionally is suggested in *Northanger Abbey*, where she remarks of Catherine Morland:

> Her mother was a woman of useful plain sense, with a good constitution. She had three sons before Catherine was born; and instead of dying in bringing the latter into the world, *as anybody might expect*, she still lived on — lived to have six children more — to see them growing up around her, and to enjoy excellent health herself.[53]

However the device was not entirely artificial. The death rate in childbirth was high and death was a much more common occurrence in families than it is today. Many daughters were indeed without mothers. In such cases, daughters were brought up by stepmothers or aunts and chaperoned in their journeys from home by older married or respected women who were family acquaintances or friends.

In Austen's novels, such surrogate mothers are often inadequate, indeed they sometimes expose their charges to dangers. In *Persuasion*, Lady Russell is the surrogate mother who tries to replace Anne Elliot's dead mother as an adviser during her courtship. At first she persuades Anne to give up Captain Wentworth and encourages her to accept the proposal of her cousin, which would enable her to preside where her mother had. "The idea of becoming what her mother had been ... was a charm she could not immediately resist". Her cousin is her inferior and wisely Anne rejects the potentially disastrous advice of her surrogate mother and marries Captain Wentworth and is happy. Susan Peck Macdonald[54] believes that here we see a representation of the seduction of becoming like the mother, who belongs to the fashion of an earlier era. Anne is of the new breed of daughters and acts according to her own inclination which is to be independent of her mother's past and lot.

However, even biological mothers were inevitably flawed and pale in comparison to the conception of ideal motherhood put forward by Rousseau and the romantics. As Wollstonecraft underlined, female education was often inadequate to the task of motherhood.[55] Thus reality provided another convention, the flawed mother, which permitted Austen to safely describe a daughter's increasing independence, without flouting patriarchal insistence that "good" mothers supervise their daughters in every respect.

In *Pride and Prejudice*, Mrs Bennett is an example of a flawed mother whose actions precipitate many of the trials suffered by her daughters. Mrs Bennett's improprieties hinder good social contacts and negatively affect suitors for Elizabeth and Jane. It is not until she goes to Pemberley, away from her mother, that better understanding develops between Elizabeth and Darcy and he proposes marriage.

These independent daughters, Elizabeth and Jane, win the love of rich and eligible husbands, which is of course all that Mrs Bennett could have hoped for. Lydia, the daughter with whom she is closest and who remains dependent on her, is as silly as her mother — a recreation and an extension of her — a mirror image of the dependent daughters of previous eras. Because she is her mother's daughter, she marries poorly. Susan Peck Macdonald believes that the moral is that independence in daughters is the healthiest way for them to behave. It was also, in Austen's creations, most likely to achieve the best marriages.

These devices, the absent mother and the flawed mother, leave patriarchy intact. Daughters obtain their independence through an omission or deficiency in their mothers. There is another particular advantage in the absent mother tradition. Motherhood can be idealised through the dead mother and any shortcomings can be separated and projected onto the living scapegoats. Only thus is the patriarchal ideal of the mother a possibility. Any questioning of the patriarchal system and its ambivalent expectations and impossible ideals is safely contained. The result is a good, undisturbing novel of the heroine's tribulations and her arrival at independent maturity.

This comment is not intended to support the patriarchal stereotypes about Austen, which define her work as restricted in its range and complacent in its celebration of the status quo.[56] On the surface of it, she seemed not to pay attention to the great historical events of her time — the French Revolution, the turmoil surrounding the emergence of the English working class, the controversial arguments found in the writings of contemporaries such as Edmund Burke and Thomas Paine.[57] But she was more aware of these things than the conventional view of her allows.[58] It is true she held many Tory sympathies and she upheld patriarchy in many ways, but she was also highly critical of her society and used her heroines to express her values about the important role women could play in it.

Her devotion to "marriageableness"[59] is often held against her, but in Austen's world marriage was the means by which mothers and daughters survived economically. Austen saw it as imperative that daughters struggled for the right kind of marriage — a marriage that allowed them not only economic security but the possibility of rewarding lives as women. She also saw the "good" marriage as indispensable for the renewal of society.[60] Her novels depict many ill-suited couples in marriages which are imprisoning, boring and miserable and have terrible effects on their households, estates and morals. Her female characters who choose unwisely, as did Fanny Price's mother, end up in coarse and degrading circumstances.

The community Jane Austen was writing about was based on landed interests and the sacredness of property. Austen was no doubt impressed by the arguments of respected philosophers and authors, such as John Locke and Dr Johnson who held that the rights of property were linked with the general order and stability of society.[61] The landed class could exact the bonds of obedience that held society together, only if they were just, merciful, generous and paternalistic. Austen recognised and accepted that this exchange involved collusion, mystification and selectively distorting and censoring many aspects of society.[62] This is no doubt why the poor and the potentially violent are contained and silenced in her novels. Current national and European upheavals were not allowed to intrude adversely on the ideology she was advocating. This is not to say she was unaware of them. She dealt with them by talking about ways of containing them as I will discuss later.

The concern with just and gracious paternalism and the way her characters uphold it is crucial in the ideology of Austen's novels. In the early part of the eighteenth century, the ruling class had often been associated with every degree of moral laxity and boorishness. This is why Jane Austen placed such emphasis on necessary and proper conduct in all areas of social behaviour. Bad manners in the landed gentry were symptoms of a sickness of their class, manifested in neglect of their responsibilities which could end in the same fate as the French aristocracy — on the guillotine.

Jane Austen's heroines needed propertied men, but they also needed men with good manners and morals. The ideology of property in the eighteenth century came to be indissolubly linked with propriety. Property was a necessary but not sufficient basis for a stable and ordered society.[63] Jane Austen used this concept to emphasise the importance of women and the new breed of sensible daughters. Women had no property but they had propriety. Property without propriety ended in disorder and degeneration. The ideal happy marriage united property and propriety and regenerated society. The fascination of many of her novels revolves around daughters who in the beginning lack propriety and the trials and tribulations their own fallibilities land them in. Emma, in the novel of the same name, is a good example. Emma's lack of propriety makes her most endearing and how she matures and incorporates propriety without becoming a bore is what the novel is about.

By internalising the proprieties of a well-ordered society, Austen's marriageable daughters contribute to its preservation. The locations into which they are born, or in which they live, are not always ideal but her heroines struggle to redeem their circumstances and make an authentic place for themselves in their community. They achieve this through marriages of propriety — their best possibility of security under eighteenth century patriarchy.

Inevitably, Austen's heroines have difficulties in distinguishing truly good manners in the men who court them. Often they are profoundly deceived by the people in their immediate circle and their attempts to sleuth the facts read like a good detective novel. Learning to perceive genuineness is one of the many tests which tutor and mature her heroines. In this process, Austen's mothers and daughters, suitors and relatives, help each other to recognise proper conduct and truly good manners. But sometimes they hinder each other and this adds to the intrigues of the plot. Anne Elliot is one heroine who has to educate herself to recognise genuine manners after being miseducated by Lady Russell.

Austen uses conversation and the strategic use of silence to mark those who are well educated in good manners and those who are not. Vulgarities of speech tell us much about the misplaced ambition of the character. The deployment of abstract concepts may indicate a facade of rationality and morality.[64] The conversation of the Crawfords in *Mansfield Park* is deceptively attractive. In such cases, Austen turns the patriarchal expectation of feminine silence to the advantage of her sex and describes it as an effective and proper way of dealing with shams. And this is exactly how Fanny Price rejects the Crawfords. Her silences are indications of her virtue, honesty and propriety.

The patriarchal ideology of femininity is used to advantage in other ways by Austen. Her language is controlled and rarely goes in for vigorous active verbs or violent nouns and adjectives.[65] Movement is largely confined to mind and heart. She crafted a style of writing which Virginia Woolf saw as well-suited to describing the lives of women. She believed Austen had laughed at the male sentence and devised "a perfectly natural, shapely sentence proper to her own use and never departed from it". She adds:

> There is no reason to think that the form of the epic or of the poetic play suits a woman any more than the sentence suits her. But all the

old forms of literature were hardened and set by the time she became a writer. The novel alone was young enough to be soft in her hands.[66]

The Enigma of Fanny Price

The patriarchal ideology of femininity tried to force mothers and daughters into submission and an unnatural feebleness.[67] Austen's spirited daughters are usually its antithesis. But one of Austen's characters, Fanny Price, is not. Fanny epitomises the passivity and helplessness that patriarchs admire because it makes them feel masculine. Her helplessness excites her suitors in a way that Mary Wollstonecraft would have described as contemptuous. Fanny seems to triumph because she does absolutely nothing. She is one of the few Austen heroines who is never wrong. She is a prig and a rather unpopular heroine.

What were Austen's intentions in creating the heroine of *Mansfield Park*? The novel was written between 1811-1813 and this timing may give us some explanation. England was on the verge of violent social change. Economic speculation was creating a climate which favoured acquisition of wealth and irreverence for the old proprieties that Austen valued so much.

In the beginning of the novel, Fanny Price emerges from the disorder and impropriety of her family in Portsmouth, a town which often represented coarseness and instability in Austen's novels — a portent of the state into which the whole of England may fall. At Mansfield Park, Fanny is badly treated and has to contend with landed gentry who have forgotten the obligations of their rank. To add to her problems, the Crawfords try to take her in with their insincerity, boredom and disregard for the moral imperatives of rural life. The Crawfords come from London, which in Austen's novels has links with selfish pleasure and the degeneracy of aristocracy.

These contrasting ways of life teach Fanny Price to value all that Mansfield Park should stand for. Moreover, the reader is left with the impression that her character enshrines the domestic and feminine codes of the traditional ideals of the inherited estate, and through her the old values of the landed gentry can be be redeemed and keep England a green and pleasant land. Fanny becomes the mistress of Mansfield Park by acting out every facet of the ideology of eighteenth century femininity. She is helpless. She is still. She blushes and cries and suffers poor health. She becomes the "angel in the house", marries and purifies Edmund and saves Mansfield Park.[68] Are we to take it that Fanny represented the kind of femininity that Austen thought was needed to save England? Is Fanny the embodiment of the political ideals Austen wanted to express in this novel?

Many find Fanny Price quite nauseating. Those who are left with this feeling often ask whether Austen was being ironic about the patriarchal ideology of femininity, when she created this particular character.[69]

Fortunately, most of Austen's daughter-heroines can be adored by the reader for their fallibility, independence, energy, rationality and willingness to learn. Emma and Elizabeth Bennett are two of Austen's most ebullient and enthusiastic characters. These spirited girls negotiate the constraints of eighteenth century patriarchy to achieve the best possible deal for themselves.

Jane Austen's Relationship With Her Mother

One guesses that Austen's novels partly reflect the relationship with her own mother. Her mother, Cassandra Leigh, was born on September 26th, 1739. She was the daughter of an eminent English family, which had included a Mayor of London in the days of Queen Elizabeth I. At 25, she married the handsome Reverend George Austen, Rector of Steventon — a small, charming village in wooded Hampshire. Austen was a classical scholar and his social standing was slightly lower than his wife's.[70]

Cassandra bore nine children, oversaw domestic matters and looked after the pupils of her husband's school. She loved the Hampshire countryside and was an excellent horsewoman. From all accounts, it was an affectionate good-tempered family with talented parents whom their children appreciated. There was also a convivial extended family and an active social life among good neighbours. It is unlikely in these circumstances that mother and daughter were subject to the psychological intensity of contemporary nuclear or single parent families. Mothers in the middle and upper classes probably had as little to do with their children as contemporary fathers, and the mother-daughter relationship was less fractious as a result.[71] Indeed, some distancing was evident from the moment of birth.

As was common at the time among those who could afford it, the Austens' babies were put out to be nursed in the first one or two years and the parents visited constantly. These situations cannot be assessed in terms of modern theories of maternal deprivation. Mrs Austen's letters give pictures of happy children of whom she was proud. When her eldest daughter, Cassandra, came back from her nurse, she reported that she talked all day long and was a very entertaining companion.

Mrs Austen kept up a warm correspondence with Mrs Walter, the wife of George Austen's half-brother, and many of her letters were about her children and are the source of much of the following information.[72]

She is described as a strong-minded woman, who embarrassed her daughters by mending in the front parlour for visitors to see. She had no use for ostentation and her tastes, like her husband's, were simple. Probably, like Mrs Morland of *Northanger Abbey*, she gave her small daughters their first education. She was apparently affectionate, but never close to Jane. Nevertheless, her practical good sense and the warm family life and schooling, which she provided, shine through in the optimism and security of Jane's novels.

At seven, Jane went with her sister to a boarding school in Oxford. Her mother regarded her as rather young to go away to school and had intended to send only the elder sister, Cassandra, but her common sense and tolerance were allowed to prevail and she wrote, "If Cassandra were going to have her head cut off, Jane would insist on sharing her fate". The school was moved to Southampton, from whence they were hastily retrieved by their parents, when "putrid fever" broke out. They were then sent to the Abbey School at Reading, which seems to have been a kindly and casual place.

In 1786 or 1787, they returned home to the advantages of a father who was a classical scholar and who had an excellent library to which his daughters had free access. This was the enlightened Georgian Age and Jane was brought up in its frank atmosphere. Jane read avidly; classical authors as well as Fielding, Richardson, Goldsmith, Smollett and Sterne. She had all the usual accomplishments of an eighteenth century daughter. She read French and Italian, could play the piano, sing and dance and was excellent at embroidery.

She had good intimate friends among her large extended family and was very close to her sister Cassandra, with whom she corresponded regularly in gossipy, sometimes maliciously intimate letters, when they lived apart. She formed supportive friendships with members of her own sex. She had an especial woman friend, Mrs Lefroy of Ashe, who died as the result of an accident in 1804. Another friend, Martha Lloyd, came to live with Jane and Cassandra and their mother, after the death of her own mother. Apparently, this enabled Mrs Austen's daughters to visit others freely, without fear of leaving their mother alone. Jane had several romances with men and exhibited some of the independence of her heroines in these. In 1801 she and a young clergymen fell in love. The romance ended tragically in his death.

The family held private theatricals in their barn. Many family members were fond of writing, including Mrs Austen, who wrote passable doggerel verse. When Jane wrote her novels, she read them to her family with much enjoyment on all sides. Indeed, by the age of 12, Jane was writing profusely and throughout her teens wrote jokingly of deformity, injury, death, drunkenness, childbearing and illegitimacy, about which Georgians were considerably less pious than the Victorians. Jane Austen died on the threshold of the Victorian era, just as the Georgian Age was making way for the self-righteousness of nineteenth century patriarchy. After her death, one of her favourite nieces wrote advising her daughter to avoid the coarseness of her aunt. Thus social change left Jane Austen with a reputation that belied her concern with propriety.

In 1801, when Jane's father was 69 and in poor health, the family retired to Bath, which was to figure in Jane's novels, although she found it rather boring after the warm social networks of Hampshire. Their father died four years later, leaving his family ill-provided for. Mrs Austen and her daughters returned to their beloved Hampshire to a cottage at Chawton, near the town of Elton. Mrs Austen became a keen gardener and a hypochondriac, a not uncommon fashion among mothers and daughters of the time. In 1798 Jane wrote to her sister Cassandra:

> My mother continues hearty, her appetite and nights are very good, but her Bowels are still not entirely settled, and she sometimes complains of an Asthma, a Dropsy, Water in her Chest and a Liver Disorder.[73]

Jane took over the domestic chores and between times wrote her novels. Observers report a hospitable, convivial atmosphere in the cottage. Jane made a fond and much loved aunt, indeed a surrogate mother, to her many nieces and nephews. She took aunting seriously, listening and caring and overseeing attempts at authorship. She died, aged 42, presumably of Addison's disease.[74] Her mother lived on at Chawton for 10 more years until she died, aged 88, in 1827.

Jane Austen's novels and eighteenth century embroidery have a great deal in common. Most obvious is the way in which each gives value to the self-expression of the mothers and daughters of their time. Embroiderers were concerned with skill and how to stay within the ideology of femininity, yet subvert it to their own needs. Austen gave women and particularly marriageable daughters, a central role in restoring and maintaining a stable and benevolent patriarchy. Mothers may seem unnecessary in Austen's kind of society, but that she made much of their absences and flaws is a right and proper comment on the unrealism of the angelic mothers invented by Rousseau.

At this distance, many of Austen's concerns may seem to do little more than endorse the patriarchal status quo, but this is because so often the patriarchally minded have selectively concentrated on what pleases them in Jane Austen. In particular, they have praised her attack on sensibility. Some lauded it as an attack on the "silliness" of her own sex. Perceptive mothers and daughters have seen it rather differently. To them Austen was saying that if they learn to be genuine, they are capable of rational discourse and the kind of propriety that maintains a good and just community. But not all agree. At least one of her near contemporaries saw Austen's attack on sensibility as the least admirable of her achievements. This was Charlotte Brontë.

ༀ

CHAPTER 8

The Brontë Daughters

The Loss of a Mother and Sexual Passion

The painful and fascinating story of five little girls, deprived of their mother before the oldest was seven, and how the tragedy and the mourning and the need to compensate for their loss inspired two of the daughters to write some of English literature's most evocative novels, has become the Brontë legend. Within the space of a few years, after the death of the last three daughters at a youthful age, the legend assumed the characteristics of a cult. Its accoutrements can be seen in pilgrimages to their home village, Haworth, and in Brontë replicas and relics made for tourists. Harrods sells "Brontë" cakes and liqueurs.[1] A kind of spiritual identification with the heroines, who recorded the tragedies of their lives in *Wuthering Heights* and *Jane Eyre*, overtakes men and women alike.

What is the reason for this extraordinary fascination? It is worth analysing because it made vividly public, facets of the nature of mothers and daughters and their relationship, which were not acknowledged at the time and still stir something at a deep level of consciousness.

Daughters Struggling with the Sin of Their Sexual Passion

Historically, part of the fascination lay in the ability of Charlotte and Emily Brontë to change the female literary tradition. They exposed mothers and daughters to some fundamental aspects of their identities that had been repressed and denied by patriarchy. First, their heroines are passionately sexual beings. Secondly, they made it clear that female sexuality is shaped and distorted by social forces. An example of this distortion is found in pornography which demeans the female sex and colours the public attitude to women.[2] Victorian pornography was preoccupied with the titillating idea of female masochism and salacious stories of the flagellation of young girls.[3] It was coupled with a moral edict about the necessity to chastise female flesh, because of its dark underside.

When we recognise that while trying to honour her own sexuality,[4] Charlotte had to battle the taboos of a phallocentric society that used morality to justify pornography, then her descriptions of social attitudes and institutions acquire meaning for mothers and daughters.[5] In *Jane Eyre*, Lowood school is not just an awful school, it tells us a great deal about the patriarchal ideology behind the education of daughters.[6] Lowood school, where Jane Eyre is sent by Mrs Reed, used deprivation of all sensory gratification in order to mortify, in its female pupils, the lusts of the flesh and what the Victorians saw as the animal-like qualities of female sexuality. Food is scarce, hair is cropped and clothes are harsh and drab. Charlotte's description of such discipline is juxtaposed with disturbing images of the mad cat, the witch, the vampire and the animalism of female sexuality. There are evocative descriptions of Bertha Mason in her foul den. She represents female passion as a potentially dangerous force that must be constrained. Her attacks come when the moon is blood red, reminding us of the powerful patriarchal myth of the dangers of the peak of the female menstrual cycle.[7]

These images are powerful enough to evoke inexplicable emotions of anger, resentment or self-revulsion in women — emotions whose sources are not always recognised. They are sensuous perceptions which illuminate the conflicting reflections of themselves that mothers and daughters experience under patriarchy. They also tell us a great deal about Charlotte and Emily, as daughters in early Victorian England.

Charlotte's letters, her juvenilia[8] and the vivid imagery of her novels give both personal and social insight into how the Victorians made their daughters fear their own sexuality. In her juvenilia, Charlotte expressed anxiety about the sensual dreams she began to experience in adolescence. Sensual dreams are not unusual in normal people. But Charlotte believed they were sinful, especially as hers were so vivid that they caused her to pant and their interruption made her physically sick. Because the patriarchal taboos about sexuality in females had such punishing moral overtones, Charlotte had to struggle with her sense of sin in order to write as vividly as she did later about heterosexual love. Christine Alexander, in an interesting analysis of the juvenilia of Charlotte Brontë, emphasises that the process of writing about sexual love was never easy for Charlotte.[9]

In an outstanding biography of Charlotte Brontë, Winifred Gérin concludes that Charlotte's struggle with her own awakening sexuality reached the proportions of religious melancholia in adolescence. She sees this as due to the moral ascendancy over her of her devoutly religious friend, Ellen Nussey. In her own unhappiness in her family, like many daughters of the period, Ellen preached the acceptance of the will of a fiercely puritanical God and made it her task to see that Charlotte wrestled with her passionate feelings. As a result, Charlotte underwent moral anguish about her delight in stories of love and sexual passion.[10]

She found little support anywhere. One publisher reprimanded her that, in writing, she neglected duties proper to a woman for a frivolous occupation.[11] Another, Hartley Coleridge, to whom she sent her first novel, censored her for her proliferation of fanciful and unconventional characters. Some of the fascination of her novels, especially Jane Eyre, lies in Charlotte's extraordinary ability to express in words the emotions she had undergone in a life-long struggle between wanting to be seen as an honourable and talented person and the prevailing social attitudes which tried to rob her of that right. For Victorian mothers and daughters, her writing offered the quintessential expression of a dilemma which a patriarchal society had tragically created for them.[12] The theme still strikes a chord in the late twentieth century.

Seeking Compensation for The Loss of a Mother's Love In Heterosexual Love

The desperate and unsatisfied longing for love in her childhood became fused with sexual longings as Charlotte became an adolescent. In her young adulthood, it was very much heightened by her unrequited love for her French professor, Constantin Heger, with whom she studied in Brussells. Adrienne Rich has written an informative, psychoanalytic discourse on the tragedy of daughters who look for mothers in their lovers and husbands.[13] Charlotte exposes the pain of it with literary genius.

Charlotte's search for love became even more painful in its sexual phase, because it had become ambivalent.[14] As Gérin sees it, on the one hand, Charlotte tragically came up against the rigidity of Victorian moralism through Ellen Nussey. On the other hand, she was a child at the height of the Romantic period and was allowed by her father to read all the great writers of that movement. She and her sisters were especially influenced by the romances of Scott and Byron. In particular, Byron's ill-fated lovers, with their contempt for convention and their bold unsociability find prototypes in the Brontë novels. Heathcliff, in *Wuthering Heights*, is clearly modelled in this style. His love and passion for Cathy Earnshaw is mixed with sadistic torture.

Charlotte's early adolescent writings exhibit how much she had constructed an imaginary world of amoral, unscrupulous Byronic heroes. Mr Rochester, with his French mistress and illegitimate daughter and his attempts to seduce the virtuous Jane Eyre belongs to this genre. That Jane was able to love him, in spite of his "immorality", shocked the moralists of the day.[15] But Charlotte was a realist, writing about accepting and loving men who are fallible, not just as a Calvinistic virtue, but as an act of heterosexual love.

By the time she was a mature writer, Charlotte had discarded the literary tradition of unrealistic, noble heroes. She replaced them with non-idealised male characters who were a complex mixture of worthiness and unworthiness. In short, she portrayed men realistically and as most of the mothers and daughters she knew saw them. Robert Moore, the leading male character in *Shirley* and Crimsworth in *The Professor* are in this mould. They arouse the conflicts and pain that real men occasion in daughters and mothers. Since she was so talented at capturing the social behaviours of her time, it would have been extraordinary if Charlotte had portrayed men any other way. Along with her sisters, she had first hand evidence of the human imperfections of men in the male members of her own family, including her brother Branwell, the flawed hero, who failed all expectations and became a drug and alcohol addict.

The Brontë Daughters Under Attack

Jane Eyre was first published under the male pseudonym, Currer Bell, and readers recognised the author's rare capacity for moving and emotional prose. However, the acclaim was reversed when it was discovered that it had been written by a parson's daughter, or simply a daughter for that matter, since it exhibited with such intensity and feeling an understanding of so much that was proscribed the female mind. Daughters were expected to be sexless and passive.[16] Charlotte was said to have forfeited the society of her sex. Her godmother considered *Jane Eyre* a bold, wicked, irreligious, unwomanly book and desired to see her no more.[17]

A similar fate met *Shirley*, written much later. This novel looked honestly at the status of mothers and daughters in Victorian England. The heroine, Shirley, is a motherless daughter, who steps outside the Victorian stereotypes of femininity, often usurps the masculine role, aligns herself with feeling and disregards current concern with status and convention. The process is possible, because she has "guineas of her own", as Virginia Woolf put it so aptly three quarters of a century later.[18] These themes utterly flouted patriarchal convention and *Shirley* was described as disgusting and vulgar by reviewers. Gérin records Charlotte's sense of isolation in the face of these attacks on her veracity and taste, when in fact she saw herself, justifiably, as portraying life as it was.

Wuthering Heights, which was published after *Jane Eyre*, was regarded as even more unpleasant. Passion, cruelty, blasphemy and a near sexual attack on the dead were seen as utterly alien to the female mind. In fact, what Emily portrayed in *Wuthering Heights* must have had much affinity with the explosive emotions of the men in her own family and indeed the men in many Victorian families.[19] But it was the double standards about sexuality that most occasioned the rejection of these two novels.[20]

Anne, the youngest of the Brontë sisters, was able to capture this double standard in *The Tenant of Wildfell Hall*, but without the hypnotic sexual undercurrent apparent in her older sisters' writing. It is an unconventional novel for its time, about a daughter, an orphan, who marries a profligate and drunkard, as Anne's brother, Branwell, was. The scenes of drinking husbands, behaving uncouthly to their wives, abandoning them for the pleasures of London and encouraging their tiny sons to be masculine, by being insolent to their mothers, indicate vividly the lot of many daughters.

In Anne's novel, the daughter reveals an initiative and independence not encouraged in Victorian England, by leaving her disastrous marriage to support herself and her son by her painting. Convention is observed when she obediently returns to her husband as he lies on his death bed. She is ultimately rewarded by a happy marriage. Despite its unconventional aspects, the ending was infinitely more satisfying to the Victorians and when the book was published, in June 1848, it was an instant best seller. Subsequently, it sank into oblivion, until a recent revival by a feminist publisher.

The Realistic Portrayal of the Lives of Mothers and Daughters

What is the source of this ability to portray a reality which punishing convention usually inhibits? Despite their isolation in a little village on the edge of the Yorkshire moors, the Brontë daughters were extremely well-read. They had access to their father's broad library. Their frequent use of the library in the nearby town of Keighley, their subscriptions to a wide range of serious periodicals, and the books posted to them by London friends, kept them in touch with fashion, politics and prevailing attitudes. Charlotte is described as paying exceptional attention to every aspect of the portraits and engravings in the literature she read. This accounts for much of the realistic detail of clothes, paintings and furnishings in her novels — details of which she would not always have had first hand experience.

But a great deal of the realism of the Brontës was derived from immediate experience, not only in their family, but in the social suffering that surrounded them. The Brontës lived in a period which was profoundly affected by the Napoleonic wars and the Industrial Revolution. The consequent social dislocations were not only visible but, from an uncommonly early age, Mr Brontë engaged his children in constant discussion and reading about these events. Thus, the Brontë sisters were very much daughters of their times.

Charlotte, in particular, became an outstanding social historian — an aspect of Charlotte, which Andrew and Judith Hook, in their excellent introduction to *Shirley*, see as underrated and neglected. Charlotte brings together the world of romantic feeling and love and the real world of social suffering and social responsibility and she hoped her novel would bring about change. She explores how the feelings and responses of individuals are moulded by social attitudes and realities over which they have no control. She analyses a society which ignores the world of feeling and the feminine principle. She was not impressed by Jane Austen's attack on sensibility.

Like her father, she was a Tory and accepted a middle-class paternalistic view of much of the grinding poverty caused by the Napoleonic wars. But she was never a prisoner of her own view. This accounts for her feminism. She had the intellectual flexibility and insight to be able to interpret the reality of her observations and her experiences. Perhaps the models provided by her mother and her aunt, both of whom were unusually well read and intelligent women, played an important part in her approach to the world. Indeed, her mother, Maria Branwell, composed a religious tract, "The Advantages of Poverty in Religious Concerns", which was published some 100 years after she wrote it.

That Charlotte was able to objectively analyse the dislocation created by Victorian patriarchal attitudes is remarkable, when all the evidence indicates that the Brontë daughters acquiesced in a household in which the feminine principle was very much accorded a secondary status. Perhaps the attitude was less so before the death of their mother. But after it, masculine virtues and masculinity were upheld as supreme. Even writing was very much a male domain and the Brontë daughters seem to have accepted this as in the nature of things. It was Branwell, the son, who was cherished and valued most and taught the classics and who was to have a career as a professional writer and artist. When his sisters had their work published, they hid the fact from him, in case it wounded him and underlined his own failure, especially as his failure was seen as contributing to his self-destructive drinking and opium addiction.[21]

It is well known that in childhood and adolescence, the Brontës indulged in a rich, imaginative world of their own.[22] What is not so well known is that, at first, Branwell's masculine status enabled him to direct his sisters' early games toward war and colonisation. He dominated their juvenile writings and, at his dictation, the Brontë daughters impersonated men. Female characters were absent.[23] This appears to have had such an effect on Charlotte, that she did not dispense with the male narrator until she wrote *Jane Eyre*. Throughout childhood and adolescence, with but occasional rebelliousness, she submitted to Branwell's macho themes of cruelty and horror. When away at school, she was disturbed and anxious lest he destroy the characters she had introduced into their collaborative writings.

Their juvenilia indicated that, whenever the girls were free of Branwell's influence, their tales and games had a different flavour. This can be seen in the *Islanders' Play*, in which female characters (princesses and fairy godmothers) have a part. Emily and Anne were less dominated by Branwell and their girlish contributions to the *Chronicles of Gondala* portrayed heroines to whom male characters were secondary.

Christine Alexander in her study of the early writings of Charlotte Brontë, emphasises how much Branwell contributed to Charlotte's development as an author.[24] But we must ask how much his domination delayed the development of her genius in portraying female and male characters outside the stereotypes of the time.

Once free of Branwell's influence on her writing, Charlotte had to contend with the phallocentric insults of some male literary critics. As we have seen, when *Jane Eyre* was first published under the male pseudonym of Currer Bell, it was heralded as a masterpiece and a monument to masculine perspicacity. In the light of the discovery of its female authorship, it was subsequently criticised as showing the weaknesses of the female mind. In her biography of Charlotte, Mrs Gaskell described how Charlotte suffered the condescension of male authors, such as Thackeray and G.H. Lewis. Charlotte herself wrote of their unjust sexism in judging her writing by standards deemed becoming to her sex.

It is little wonder that some characters in Charlotte's novels, and in particular *Shirley*, give critical insight into the arrogance of the conventional male of the period and his belief in his utter superiority over women in general and his daughters in particular. An example is the curate, Mr Helstone, who at heart could not abide sense in women. He liked to see them as silly, light hearted, vain — as open to ridicule as possible — because they were then in reality what he wanted them to be, namely inferior and toys to play with, to amuse a vacant hour and to be thrown away.

Shirley is predominantly about the predicament of women in their relationships with men and under male dominance. It is about daughters looking for love, daughters suffering from unrequited love and women who will never be loved or respected in a patriarchal society. Charlotte looks beneath the cruel stereotypes. She finds the starved longing for appreciation by spinster women, who lose themselves in good works to compensate for the derogatory labels put upon them because of their lack of husbands and children. She feared the same state in herself. She was as vehement as Mary Wollstonecraft in her belief that patriarchy should permit females to step outside the limits of their restricted education and limited opportunities in the work-force.

At least, in the example of their mother and in the free access to their father's library, Charlotte and her sisters were able to break out of some of the confines of the standard Victorian education for daughters, but not so in their choice of profession. Governessing and teaching were about all that were open to educated women. The low status of governesses meant that they could, and often did, suffer the arrogance of their charges and were expected to spend long hours on demeaning tasks, such as mending and sewing, as well as teaching. Charlotte hated her time as a governess and hoped, by portraying its mortifications and exploitation in her novels, to change conditions and attitudes.

She also suffered because of another patriarchal stereotype, the demand for beauty in women. Charlotte's lack of beauty was one of her greatest sorrows. Like her mother she was plain. This plainness became the inspiration for her novels.

Mrs Gaskell was one of the first to recognise that Charlotte's mother, her appearance and the circumstances of her death, had enormous impact in shaping her novels and their heroines. She describes Charlotte's mother as very small, not pretty, but very elegant, and always dressed with a quiet simplicity of taste, which accorded well with her general character. Most of Charlotte's heroines are presented in such a manner and dress.

In particular, *Jane Eyre* clearly has parallels in the intensely personal experience of Charlotte herself and her unhappiness about her lack of beauty.[25] Jane, like Charlotte, was poor, undersized and plain, the antithesis of the nineteenth century heroine. Like Jane, she suffered in a charity school and became a private governess — earning her living by work she hated and experiencing all the miseries of dependence on strangers.

A New Breed of Daughters

These heroines are daughters with whom we can identify. The heroine of the fashionable writing of previous eras,[26] who was beautiful, aristocratic and saintly, midst the seductions of lush boudoirs and estates, may provide flights of fancy and light relief, but never arouses our deepest feelings. Even when she lost her aristocracy and became the sweet and submissive heroine favoured by Thackeray and Dickens, she is so pathetic that it is hard to identify with her.

The fact that the influence of *Jane Eyre* on Victorian heroines was revolutionary and alarmed patriarchal critics, suggests that at last daughters were stepping out of novels as real people. The post-*Jane Eyre* heroine, according to the periodicals, was plain, rebellious, passionate, without status and likely to be a governess. One male critic, reported in literary studies of the Waverley novels, complained "the purchaser of a novel is a victim on finding that he has only to peruse a narrative of the conduct and sentiments of an ugly lady".[27]

The heroines of the Brontë novels also fly in the face of the dependent heroines so much favoured by the Victorians — incomplete without their mandatory heroes who save their honour. Instead, Charlotte's heroines not only survive prejudices and social obstacles, they overcome frailty and exhibit strength and independence, which prevents their loss of honour and self-respect. They are neither victims nor masochists at the mercy of male sexual power. That scenario is discarded for a more optimistic view of female character, without glossing over a deeply personal insight into the need to be loved and the many guises the desperate search for motherly love can take, as one grows and finds friends, peers, lovers and husbands. Charlotte's heroines undergo painful battles with rejection, loneliness and indifference, yet in a way that is seen as contributing to personal maturing.

The inner life processes, during the search for a secure and supporting love, are portrayed with genius, through evocative symbolic devices, such as dreams, visions, mythological illusions, furnishings, colour, weather and landscape.[28] These symbols arouse deep-rooted archetypes or universally shared emotions and unconscious wishes and yearnings that are common to us all. This power of expression not only contributed to the Brontë legend, it offered conclusive evidence that daughters are capable of a touch of genius in literary creation. That genius had much to do with their utilisation of the emotions and feelings generated by the loss of their mother and mother surrogates.[29]

Had they been restricted by a conventional mother, such as Mrs Yorke in *Shirley*, the result may have been quite different. In Mrs Yorke and her relationship with her two daughters, Rose and Jessy, Charlotte depicts the limited model that most mothers provided for their daughters in Victorian England. Rose is an original child who longs to travel and to lead a life rich in experience. She rebels against the barren future of duty and domesticity recommended by her mother. She will not bury her talents in the dust of household drawers, imprison them in the linen press or hide them in a tureen of cold potatoes. To Rose and Jessy, their mother represents what they dread becoming and they turn away from her. The Brontës' mother did not project such an unwanted image. Her education and their longing for her, after her early death, made her appear quite different.

Discarding Traditional Emphases

Studies tend to dwell upon the Brontë daughters' relationship with their father and their brother, a not unusual tendency in patriarchal analysis. Certainly, Charlotte's relationship with her father is of consequence in her novels. It is commonly accepted, for example, that the tenderness of Jane Eyre toward the blinded Rochester has its counterpart in Charlotte's care of her father, during his partial blindness after a cataract operation. Harold McCurdy, in an old but fascinating analysis of the Brontë sisters, demonstrates that the male characters, in many of Charlotte's and Emily's novels, are similar to their profligate brother Branwell, whom they believed to be a self-destructive genius.[30] Such studies are frequent and it is not my aim to repeat them here.

Instead, by freeing ourselves of traditional lines of thinking or primarily patriarchal modes of approach, we can find relationships that are important to mothers and daughters. We can begin to appreciate that the relationship with their mother or mother substitutes, the mother's death, memories of her, fantasies about her, her passionate relationship with their father, her appearance and behaviour, her conceived role toward them, even in death, had an all pervading impact on the Brontë daughters.[31] Their attempts to compensate for the early loss of their mother and work through unfinished mourning is the source of much of their creativity and genius as writers.

The Brontës' Mother and Her Daughters' Attempts to Compensate for Her Death

The tragedy of the Brontës' mother, Maria Branwell, is well known.[32] She was born in 1783, the third daughter of a Penzance merchant who was a staunch Wesleyan. In 1812, after her parents' death, Maria stayed with her uncle, the Reverend John Fennell, in the West Riding of Yorkshire. There at 29 she married Patrick Brontë, a handsome, vain and loquacious Irishman — a Cambridge graduate, who became an Anglican minister.

As newlyweds they set up house in Hartshead, Yorkshire, where Maria gave birth to her first daughter, named after her, in 1813, and a second, Elizabeth, in 1815. They moved to Thornton, another parish near Bradford, where Charlotte was born in 1816, Branwell in 1817, Emily in 1818 and Anne in 1820. In 1820, they moved to Haworth, ten miles west of Bradford, to a grey stone parsonage of doubtful sanitation on the edge of the moors. The house and situation were bleak and damp and the mother, Maria, became seriously ill with cancer. Over the last eight months of her life, she tried to come to terms with the abandonment of her precious children which her death would occasion, and finally she questioned her faith.[33]

For a number of months before her death, Mrs Brontë was confined to her bedroom upstairs, suffering greatly, rarely, if ever, seen by her children and perhaps mentally deranged by excruciating pain. Some of the images portrayed in the Brontës' novels find similarity in folklore about mad women and Victorian psychiatry, which gave coin to the concept of moral madness in women. But how much was contributed to these images by the dreadful and agonising process of their mother's death? How did it appear to her young daughters? Did it contribute, for example, to the disturbing description of the ghost of Cathy, trying to enter the house where she had lived, in *Wuthering Heights*. The enormity of the Brontë children's loss was compounded by their father's suffering and grief following the death of his wife.

After their mother's death, the children were sent to the semi-charitable "Clergy Daughters' School" at Cowan Bridge, which later became involved in scandals concerning harshness and neglect. The school's situation was unhealthy, the girls were ill-fed and exposed to frequent outbreaks of typhoid and there was no adequate medical attention. The gifted Elizabeth was, according to Charlotte, badly treated and she and Maria became consumptive. They were removed from the school by their father, only to die, as was the fate of several other daughters in the school.[34]

The tragedy had lasting effects on Charlotte, and the school to which Jane Eyre was banished was identified in Mrs Gaskell's life of Charlotte Brontë as the prototype of the one to which the Brontë daughters were sent.

The children sought compensation for mothering care and nurture in an imaginative life among themselves. Since a kitchen servant, Tabitha Aykroyd, was their only regular adult company and supervisor, they were free to roam the moors, which opened to the rear of their home. They learnt the landscape, the vegetation and the wind directions. The hidden glens and the hollow rocks were turned into a fantasy world and an imaginary land. Here, or at home by the fire on long winter evenings, or in their tiny children's study, they acted out a secret play life of imaginary companions, fugitives and romantic sagas, which they recorded in a precocious literature, entitled in their juvenilia with such names as: *Tales of the Islanders*, *The Young Man's Play*, *The Glass Town Saga*, *The Angrian Legend* and *The Gondal Chronicles*. Their fantasies became their refuge, compensation and escape from their motherless and sometimes affectionless childhood.[35]

Christine Alexander and Mrs Gaskell tell how the little Brontës huddled together for emotional security, of their reading and whispering in the children's study, and of their painful shyness on village social occasions. They had no idea of the games that ordinary children play. Although

Alexander assures us that their father believed in a liberal education, fostered their natural inclinations, set an example of a love of literature, and was a source for their extraordinary imagination, the fare he gave them was not typically that of childhood.[36] He conversed with them as one would with adults, about military, literary and political events and figures of the day, such as Wellington, Peel, George IV, or the Luddite riots. Incongruously, these often became central to their childish fantasies.

The significant factor is not that they were extraordinarily imaginative, but that their imaginary world frequently took over in a fashion that was clearly compensatory. For example, at the Roe Head boarding school, with its kindly headmistress, where Charlotte and her sisters were later sent and Charlotte became a teacher, we find Charlotte's juvenilia record instances when she became so severely depressed and homesick, that the imaginary figures of the legends she and Branwell had created at Haworth became real. The imaginary world became an obsession. She began to live in two conflicting worlds, so that the intrusion of the one on the other had the force of physical pain. She became frightened of her morbidly vivid realisations. She had visions of the people and places she had helped to create in the Angrian legends. She lived in dread that Branwell would kill or destroy her favourite characters in her absence.[37]

When she became a teacher and then a governess, loathing both occupations, her depression became chronic and her imaginings a habitual way of dealing with loss. This is not unusual, when grief is unresolved in childhood. Her writing is trance-like and she told one publisher that she only had to close her eyes to see her characters, with a life beyond their creator, and she described her writing as an escape from a desolate and depressing world.

Christine Alexander, in her thorough examination of Charlotte's juvenilia, confirms that her imaginative world became an important sense of security and gave her a sense of "belonging". While observing that it took on proportions which blurred the distinction between fantasy and reality, she questions whether it is not strange that the imaginative world of childhood continued to preoccupy her until she was 23. She suggests that the hypnotic attraction of the legends that she and Branwell created, stunted her development as a writer of realistic fiction. "It was only grudgingly, over a period of years, that childhood gave way to the balanced perception of reality that marks her mature work."[38] Yet, it is well-documented that the slow surrender of childhood and compensatory fantasies are not unusual where there is a lack of sufficient mothering in childhood. I believe the emotions that created the Brontës' compensatory fantasies and their ability to express them are the roots of the Brontë genius.

Themes of abandoned children, children deprived of parental love, children who have foster parents, disowned children, are an obsession in Charlotte's juvenilia. Loving mothers die young, surviving mothers are shallow and devious, scorned by their more intelligent daughters. The motherless heroines of Charlotte's later writings all have their precursors in her juvenilia.[39] The change, as she grew older, from the typical legends of abandoned children to a more realistic theme of estrangement, indicates how much the theme has autobiographical significance.

Charlotte's early loss of motherly love established a lifelong and unbearably painful fear of losing any loved one and a conviction that she would ultimately lose him or her. When she fell in love with her French professor, Constantin Heger, in Brussels, and he ultimately refused even her friendship, she asked what she could do with her life without love.[40] Reflecting her own experiences, her novels became detailed and painfully realistic descriptions of the way motherless young women, or insufficiently mothered young women, uncertain of love, suffer and behave.

A single theme runs through all four of Charlotte's novels, *The Professor*, *Jane Eyre*, *Shirley* and *Villette*. It is the struggle of an orphaned daughter to achieve a close mother love-type relationship in a difficult world. To her new friend at school Jane Eyre says:

> "I know I should think well of myself; but that is not enough: If others don't love me I'd rather die than live — I cannot bear to be solitary and hated, Helen. Look here; to gain some real affection from you, or Miss Temple, or any other person whom I truly love, I would willingly submit to have the bone of my arm broken, or to let a bull toss me, or stand behind a kicking horse, and let it dash its hoof at my chest."[41]

This passage typifies the situation at the beginning of most of the Brontë novels where, because of the early death of their mothers and the consequent loss of their protection and their teachings of self-worth, depression is common to their heroines, as it was to Charlotte, Anne and Emily throughout their short lives. There is poor self-esteem and a sense of inferiority and hostility, occasioned by depriving others. Mrs Reed, Jane Eyre's unloving surrogate mother, and Mr Brocklehurst, her cruel headmaster, induce all these qualities in Jane. With courage she overcomes the hurdles they create to her forming good relationships at school, and is able to find loving friends in Helen Burns and her teacher Miss Temple. Later, she secures the good opinion and affection of the housekeeper, Mrs Fairfax, in the house where she gains a position as a governess. Finally, against all odds, through her love for Rochester, the master of the house, her brave and principled character is fulfilled. Her progress is testimony that a daughter's personality can be strengthened by overcoming the scars left by losing a mother.

Significantly, there is also the frequent theme that the loss of love makes the heroine ill and depressed and its certainty restores her. Caroline Helstone, in *Shirley*, longs in her childhood for the mother she has lost and, in adulthood, she becomes gravely ill when she believes that she has lost the love of Robert Moore. It is the return of her long lost mother that restores her to her former bloom and health.

In emphasising the restorative nature of motherly love or its later sexual manifestation, heterosexual love, Charlotte was expressing her feelings about her own lack of mothering. She believed the lack had left her vulnerable. Throughout her life, Charlotte suffered poor health and accompanying depression, often exacerbated by the unexpected departures of close and loved friends. Her friend, Mary Taylor, recalled that not to be loved was Charlotte's ultimate dread since childhood.[42] The nightmare of her schooldays was the vision of her beloved dead sisters returned, but changed toward her and unloving and censorious. Summing up Lucy Snowe's anguish in *Villette*, Charlotte said that it was contained in the insufferable thought of not being loved any more.

The strength of Charlotte's belief in the omnipotent role of mothers as healers, helpers and protectors, is reflected in her portrayal of the power of Jane Eyre's mother, even after death. It also reflects the then socially sanctioned view, that mothers were responsible for their daughters' morality and virginity. When Jane is begged by Rochester to become his mistress, the ghost of her dead mother warns her to flee temptation and leave Rochester and Thornfield. Jane does and ultimately this advice, combined with her own independence, means Rochester becomes her lawful husband. In this episode, it can be seen that the positive power of the mother has another and condemning aspect, which often presents itself to Charlotte's young heroines on the verge of sexual love. Depressive attacks and hallucinatory images, such as Jane Eyre experienced, are common after a declaration of love from a man or a proposal of marriage, reflecting the strong patriarchal taboos about sex and women in nineteenth century England.[43]

It would appear that in the Brontës' case, the patriarchal dichotomy of the protective and the threatening mother was actualised.[44] Miss Branwell, the severe aunt who came to look after the Brontë children when their mother died, was indeed seen as the reproving mother and the dead Mrs Brontë became a symbol of the idealised, protective, educative mother. The high mortality of mothers probably made this a not uncommon experience of nineteenth century daughters and contributed to the marked dichotomies in the descriptions of Victorian mothers.[45] These descriptions are unlike the portrayals of mid-twentieth century mothers, when both the protective and reproving stereotypes became fused in the one mother, with the condemning aspects uppermost. A good example is Martha Quest's mother in the novel of the same name by Doris Lessing which was discussed in Book I.[46] Indeed, by the 1950s, the mother's condemning and prototype behaviour, as in the case of Mrs Quest, are portrayed as major problems.[47] Drastic separation from her mother is presented as the best solution for her daughter, Martha, in her search for independence.[48] Such a course was not encouraged in the first half of the nineteenth century.

The Particular Effect of Maternal Deprivation on Emily Brontë

Unfortunately, only Charlotte's letters remain and hence much more is known about her than her sisters. In view of the attacks upon the Brontë daughters' morality, due to the realism of their novels, it was feared their letters might create further scandals and Emily's and Anne's letters were destroyed by Charlotte and their friends after their deaths. The little information there is about them comes from outside observers.[49]

One of these was Mrs Gaskell, who described the differences in Charlotte's and Emily's personalities as due to Charlotte's advantage in remembering their mother.[50] Emily Brontë was two years younger than Charlotte and only three when her mother died. This was followed by the almost immediate departure of servants who had cared for her, and the advent of an aunt who had little control over her. Emily was said to have been the prettiest of the girls and, as the youngest attender, the pet nursling at school, but she pined for the moors of home whenever away from them, so the school nurturing was short lived.

In fact, it appears that Emily's need for love became invested in life on the moor. Mrs Gaskell tells us that only when she was unrestrained on the moors did Emily appear to become alive, even gay, and her fundamental kindness show itself. Generally, researchers claim that she became a mystic, who had exceptional spiritual experiences and devoted herself to a sense of the supreme importance of the natural universal soul.[51]

But Katherine Frank, in her biography, *Emily Brontë: A Chainless Soul*, argues that Emily's trance-like states were not due to mysticism but were symptoms of self-starvation or anorexia nervosa. Some evidence for Emily's familiarity with the condition of the anorectic can be found in the powerful imagery about hunger and food which pervades her writing. *Wuthering Heights* is a book concerned with food, hunger and starvation and is largely set in kitchens.[52] The heroine, Catherine, starves herself and refuses food when not allowed to have her way. Her refusal to eat is portrayed as an act of rebellion and despair.

There is also much evidence that in real life, by refusing to eat, Emily was able to control not only herself, but others and that this reached such proportions it was clearly a device for warding off anxiety about unmanageable and terrifying confusion. As several psychiatrists and feminists, such as Hilde Bruch, Susie Orbach, Kim Chernin and Joan Jacobs Brumberg point out, anorexia nervosa is not merely an eating disorder but a psychological disturbance centred on a fear of chaos and an obsession with order and control. The big question, in Emily's case, is how much her self-enforced physical hunger related to her emotional need for secure motherly love. How much did attempts at self-control by starvation ward off an overwhelming anxiety that disintegration and disorder might follow the loss of love or any major change or separation? Young children feel profoundly insecure when they lose a mother. If the mourning and panic is not worked through, anxiety attacks about impending chaos recur throughout life.

In Emily's case, the childish sense of powerlessness, exacerbated by the loss of her mother, was compounded as she grew older, by her situation as a woman in Victorian patriarchal society. In Victorian England, women were largely powerless and the first chapter of Book I described how they fought back through illness. Anorexia nervosa was one of many social maladies which gave Victorian women an illusion of power and through it they turned their feelings of helplessness, frustration and rage against themselves. The Brontë daughters were no exception. As we have seen, they were raised in a very patriarchal family where Branwell's career, fulfilment and value were put ahead of his sisters'.[53] They were all more talented than he, yet felt obliged to hide their talent and to work as governesses to help pay for his education. Refusal to eat and consequent poor health was often their only way of coping with situations they found intolerable. They used it more than once as a means of escape from positions as governesses which they loathed.[54]

Emily is known for other feats of physical control. For example, villagers and servants reported how on one occasion when she terminated a village dog fight by dousing the dogs with pepper, she was bitten by a rabid dog. She cauterized the open wound with a red hot iron from the kitchen fire.[55]

Emily's need for control took hold of every aspect of her life. Several have described her tyranny over Charlotte.[56] Constantin Heger, the professor at the school which she and Charlotte attended in Brussels, and English friends, the Wheelwrights, described how Emily prevented Charlotte from making friends at the school and resented any intrusion on their twoness. By creating an exceptionally narrow existence for herself at the school, Emily maintained a fragile illusion of control.[57] Only at home in Haworth, when household and family events remained constant, did she feel secure. Observers describe her as eating heartily when she succeeded her aunt as head of the kitchen and Charlotte came to defer to her in household arrangements.[58]

Obviously, the pursuit of order and control, through self-starvation and resistance to changes in her environment, may well be due to many complex factors. How much is due to the arrival of Aunt Branwell, who at the behest of Patrick Brontë ran a spartan house with authoritarian punctuality? The villagers said you could set your clock by the routines of the parsonage.[59] A childhood subject to over-regulation may well have played a role in Emily's insecurity about change and fear of interaction with unfamiliar others. It is reported that from an early age, she refused social activities. Instead, she retreated into a fantasy world, in which she had power over events and people. Her childhood fantasy world of Gondal continued as a means of retreat as an adult. She poured her wishes and dreams into a stream of poetry and prose writings and unlike Charlotte, she suffered no guilt about her imagination as a means to peace and fulfilment.

Ellen Nussey, Charlotte's close friend, was one of several who came to know Emily in adolescence and adulthood and commented that she always found her uncommunicative, as though afraid of revealing herself. She was shy and withdrawn. Her smile was apparently rare and often the only acknowledgement of thanks for a present. Mrs Gaskell confirms Ellen Nussey's observations. By adolescence, Emily was markedly defensive of her inner life and increasingly uncommunicative. She shunned social contact and averted her gaze when a stranger spoke to her.

It is well-documented that consistent early attachments are needed for the development of a secure and confident sense of self and an accompanying ability to act reciprocally with others — an ability which Ellen Nussey's and Mrs Gaskell's accounts suggest Emily lacked. How much did the longing for consistent love in childhood and the lack of a fully nurtured sense of self, account for the way in which Emily treated the passionate, sexual relationship between Cathy and Heathcliff in *Wuthering Heights*?[60] It is portrayed as being needed to achieve a realisation of self and Cathy says of Heathcliff, "Nelly, I am Heathcliff".[61]

When their brother Branwell became profligate and fell from grace, Emily warmed to him and succoured him. In Branwell's behaviour, Emily witnessed the lasting effect of their mother's death and the death of their sister Maria, who had become his mother substitute. In his young adulthood, he claimed to have had a most unhappy affair with a married woman[62] and the consequent discovery and enforced separation — a repetition of the previous separations by death — rightly or wrongly, was seen as precipitating his self-destructive drinking. Within a month of her brother's death, Emily refused to eat and would not answer when spoken to, and died not long after of a most rapid consumption, almost as though she'd willed it. Perhaps she lost hope at this final of many partings.

Winifred Gérin in her biography of Emily Brontë, believes Emily had suffered on account of Branwell's suffering and saw, in his death, the destructive power of the loss of love. Given her early childhood experiences and her observations of her brother, there is little wonder that *Wuthering Heights* so powerfully captured the effects of the loss of love. Death is seen as a liberation of the imprisoned spirit and a longing for reunion.

Charlotte was two years older than Emily and five when her mother died. During the rest of her life, she was able to form a fond relationship with her difficult father and female and male friends alike. In school, she formed a close and lasting attachment with Ellen Nussey, whose battlemented house became the model for Thornfield Hall in *Jane Eyre*. She was fond of her publishers, one of whom she came close to marrying, as she did Ellen Nussey's brother. She rejected them as husbands, even though or because she valued their friendship. She was also befriended by Harriet Martineau and Mrs Gaskell. Anne seems to have been similarly equipped for relationships. It is said she had more surrogate mothering than the others when she was little, because she was the one of whom her aunt was most fond. Although the aunt's love took the form of subjecting Anne to her oppressive religious outlook, she nevertheless became a kind, if somewhat overcontrolling, Calvinistic, surrogate mother to her.[63]

Mother Substitutes

In the behaviour of the Brontë daughters, there is ample illustration of the fact that children who lose, or lack, mothers and do not have adequate, loving, mother-substitutes, often spend the rest of their lives turning any likely association into a mother-child one. It may be that friends, neighbours, colleagues, even brief acquaintances, are expected to fill the role of the loving mother or the reproving mother. From Charlotte's letters, it can be seen that the friends of whom she was fond were quite often seen as loving surrogate mothers. Her letters to them are full of yearning for some succour. Ellen Nussey, who, in Gérin's view, contributed to Charlotte's tragedy by trying to save her soul, was certainly seen by Charlotte as a source of support throughout her life. Whether this was a lesbian or a romantic friendship,[64] whether it suffered under the then current fashion against sentiment, whether it was destructive or nurturing or both, is open to debate, but Charlotte's letters leave no doubt that she wanted a nurturing love from Ellen Nussey.

Another shorter friendship, from which Charlotte would have liked some mothering affection and endorsement, was with Harriet Martineau. This was why Harriet's disapproval of Charlotte's obsession with love was hurtful to her. Mrs Gaskell was very much valued as a good and supportive friend and indeed, after Charlotte's death, wrote a biography with the aim of protecting Charlotte's name from the accusations of unfeminine behaviour.

It is not surprising therefore that, reflecting their own situation, the Brontë novels are peopled with surrogate mothers in many guises. Some are supportive of the heroine or partially help her in particular situations, but many are inadequate or bad surrogate mothers. They may hinder, even create substantial obstacles for the heroine to overcome. This of course contributes to the theme that through adversity, motherless daughters become stronger persons. This appears to have been how the Brontë children saw their situation with their aunt, Elizabeth Branwell, who very much regretted having to leave her previous life in Penzance in order to look after her nephew and nieces. It was the advent of this authoritarian aunt which united the children in self-defence. Her arrival encouraged them to be mutually supportive, acting as mother surrogates to each other.[65] Her sternness reinforced their need to escape into their fantasy worlds of Gondol, Angria or Glass Town.

The only tribute the girls were able to pay Miss Branwell, in later life, was that she inculcated in them a sense of duty, order and punctuality. In tune with a typical mother's education of her daughters at the time, she made the girls practise the sewing of samplers for long hours as a form of self-discipline. She discouraged any other creativity.[66]

Later Charlotte told Mrs Gaskell that the unsympathetic character Mrs Reed, the substitute mother who took charge of the orphan, Jane Eyre, was modelled on her aunt.[67] Mrs Reed is unremittingly mean to Jane Eyre. She persuades people to dislike Jane, and ruins, in advance, her relationships with others by misrepresenting her character. She describes Jane as having a deceitful disposition, to Mr Brocklehurst the headmaster of Lowood school, where she is to be sent. Jane says:

> "Well might I dread, well might I dislike Mrs Reed; for it was her nature to wound me cruelly: never was I happy in her presence: however carefully I obeyed, however strenuously I strove to please her, my efforts were still repulsed and repaid by such sentences as the above. Now uttered before a stranger, the accusation cut me to the heart: I dimly perceived she was already obliterating hope from the new phase of existence which she destined me to enter; I felt, though I could not have expressed the feeling, that she was sewing aversion and unkindness along my future path; I saw myself transformed under Mr Brocklehurst's eye into an artful, noxious child, and what could I do to remedy the injury."[68]

Charlotte regarded the surrogate mothering by her elder siblings more positively. During Mrs Brontë's illness, Maria and Elizabeth, then seven and six, mothered the youngest siblings, teaching them to read and singing them to sleep at night. Charlotte and Branwell worshipped them and were totally convinced of their cleverness and goodness. Maria's and Elizabeth's death, as a result of the harsh conditions at school, accounts for Charlotte's bitterness in portraying a similar school in *Jane Eyre*.[69]

Later, Charlotte became the mothering sister to the youngest and, as the living eldest, was conscientious in her duties. In later life this was fraught with much ambivalence, for she disapproved of Branwell, while Emily defended him. At times, she was overly concerned for the independent Emily. She was often critical of both her sisters, thought *Wuthering Heights* verged on the immoral and believed Anne's novel not worth a great deal. Winifred Gérin believes Charlotte was wrong in assessing Anne's mental state by her frail physical condition. Not until after her death, when her posthumous papers fell into her hands, did Charlotte discover Anne's strengths and the depth of her emotions. She was surprised to learn that, as close as their physical existence had been in their home at Haworth, she had been unaware that Anne had silently suffered over unreciprocated love for a young curate, who died suddenly. Emily does not seem to have taken on a motherly role with Anne, but was more disposed to treating her as an equal.

Despite there being much the sisters did not share with each other, they were in many ways very close and discussed and shared their writing. With Branwell's death, Charlotte became convinced that her sisters were beings from whom she could derive life and purpose. Their death, within a few months of each other, wrought a deep depression, saved only by the expression of her literary talent. It took her, she said, out of a dark and desolate reality. *Shirley* was written as a tribute to Emily after her death.[70]

Female servants are also often portrayed as partial mother surrogates in the Brontë novels, as they were in their lives and that of many daughters of the time. For example, after the arrival of their aunt, two servants who had been close to Anne and Emily, were replaced by a 56 year old widow, Tabitha Ackroyd, a Methodist. She was a sharp-tongued disciplinarian who nevertheless had a warm and generous nature and took all the children to her heart, especially Emily. We find her immortalised in *Wuthering Heights* as Nelly Dean. Tabitha had memories stretching back to the 1780s, when villagers believed in fairies, when stone farms dotted the hills, and when conditions were hard and primitive. She told vivid tales of those times and Emily was so influenced by them, that she set *Wuthering Heights* in this period, and many of the settings and characters are similar to those described by Tabitha. This is also the time of the childhood of the Brontë's mother, Maria.[71]

Some surrogate mothering was found among teachers and this was Charlotte's positive experience at the "Clergy Daughters' School". She recounted it in Maria Temple's caring for Jane Eyre. Other substitutes were found among relations reflected, for example, in Anne Brontë's *The Tenant of Wildfell Hall* where the heroine, Helen, is motherless, with a good but not very effective mother surrogate in her aunt.

Thus, the Brontë daughters found some mothering among teachers, servants, sisters and friends. That these did not satiate is clear from their novels. Charlotte, the most prolific writer, in all her novels conspicuously expresses a longing for complete fulfilment of the motherly love she lost. This does not mean that she did not see how the potentially constructive love of mothers for their daughters is perverted to the cause of patriarchy. Charlotte portrays it with its sad confusions. Discipline is administered to her female heroines (daughters), by women (mothers), who are agents of men. Thus, it is the beloved Bessie who locks Jane up and the kindly Miss Temple who starves the girls at Lowood school.[72] It is Grace Poole who is Bertha Mason's gaoler, all of which signifies the painful realisation that, under patriarchy, daughters grow up in a world without female solidarity, not even from their mothers. While this was more so in Victorian England, it cannot be said that the theme has lost its appeal in the late twentieth century.

◈

CHAPTER 9

The Hand That Rocks the Cradle Rules the World!

George Eliot, Female Influence and the New Woman

The saying that the hand that rocks the cradle rules the world is part of our folklore. It began to appear widely in patriarchal literature in the Victorian age and many women fell for the idea that as females they had enormous influence. The concept was of course a distractor, a false image, which belied the experience of mothers and daughters, yet beguiled them into the compensatory fantasy that they shared in power.

Female influence, as it was sold to nineteenth century mothers and daughters, is probably best typified in the life and times of the nineteenth century novelist, George Eliot. First, in her family, social and intellectual life, Eliot had to contend with the expectations and taboos of Victorian patriarchy which ensured that women were powerless.[1] Secondly, despite Eliot's personal belief in female influence, nothing shows up the hypocrisy of the concept more than her novels.

Yet, how often was this aspect of Eliot's work discussed, when her novels were introduced as part of our secondary school reading? Many women have told me that they remembered Eliot with distaste and that her heroines depressed them, until they were encouraged to understand their significance for themselves as women living under patriarchy. She became less dull, once they came to appreciate that she was describing life as it was for the ordinary women of her time and that her novels are part of the politics and history of mothers and daughters.

George Eliot's Political Statements About Mothers and Daughters

The Mill on the Floss is probably the best known of Eliot's novels and a good introduction to the situation of ordinary nineteenth century mothers and daughters. In this novel, Eliot captured the feeling of intellectual and general inferiority that was imparted to daughters in the Victorian era. We are caught up in this feeling early in the novel, when the leading character, Maggie Tulliver is told by her beloved brother Tom:

> "I don't want your money, you silly thing. I've got a great deal more money than you, because I'm a boy. I always have half sovereigns and sovereigns for my Christmas boxes, because I shall be a man, and you only have five shilling pieces, because you're only a girl."[2]

Even when Maggie proves faster than Tom at learning, those who represent patriarchy will not accept it. Tom says to his male teacher, "Girls can't do Euclid can they, sir?" "They can pick up a little of everything, I dare say," said Mr Stelling. "They've a great deal of superficial cleverness, but they couldn't go far into everything. They're quick and shallow".[3]

If Maggie is a political statement about keeping women powerless under patriarchy, then Mrs Tulliver, Maggie's mother, is a political statement about how limiting the role of motherhood was for many Victorian women. She can interact with others only by caring for their digestion, food intake and their laundry. When her son Tom is to go away to school, she is obsessed with worry that he will not get an egg for breakfast, or that she will not be able to care for his shirts.

Of her, Mr Tulliver says, in stereotypically Victorian patriarchal fashion:

> "... I picked the mother because she wasn't o'er cute -bein' a good looking woman too an' come of a rare family for managing; but I picked her from her sisters o' purpose, 'cause she was a bit weak, like; for I wasn't a-goin' to be told the rights o things by my own fireside."[4]

The tragedy for Mr Tulliver is that his daughter inherits his brains, while his son is none too bright, like his mother.

Eliot's books abound in such women, who are political statements about the dehumanising effects of the treatment and position of mothers and daughters in nineteenth century England. Some of the most disturbing illustrations are found in women such as Maggie's Aunt Moss, "pulled down by children and toil".[5] These women, many of the poorer classes, were forever cleaning, cooking and bearing children. Mothers and daughters were enmeshed in an oppressive stereotype of asexual innocence, which barred them from any knowledge of contraception.

On the one hand, Eliot makes it apparent that the submissive and tearful mothers of the Victorian era, who are not allowed an identity beyond their maternity, were very restrictive models for daughters. On the other, she seems to be saying that becoming the ideal mother, whose self is entirely expressed and lived through others, is the best possibility for women. Her novels are full of anger and resentment toward women who will not endorse or act out this role.

In an interesting analysis of her ideology, Bonnie Zimmerman[6] argues that Eliot used the ability or unwillingness to bear children, as a political and moral principle by which she rewarded or criticised her heroines. An example, says Zimmerman, is the egotistical Rosamond, in Eliot's novel, *Middlemarch*, who miscarries when she goes riding in defiance of her husband's advice. Another is Gwendolen Harleth, in *Daniel Deronda*, who is consumed by anxiety lest she become a mother because she has self-indulgently married a man, who has a common law wife and children. Women who rebel or step beyond the social and biological limitations set for Victorian femininity and women who defy its sexual standards, rather than submit, are punished by sterility.

Eliot's heroines and their fate seem somewhat of a contradiction in view of her own life. She confined her heroines within strictures from which she herself escaped. She violated Victorian respectability.[7] She did not become a biological mother. She made a lot of money and was adulated by the famous and the gifted. She was described by many as quite the reverse of the submissiveness expected of women of the time. Indeed, some found her overbearing and superior in manner. They were angered by her disinterest in close friendships with other women and felt rejected and despised by her.[8]

The seeming contradictions between Eliot's heroines and her own life have inevitably aroused controversy — even anger. Her passive, renouncing, martyred mothers and daughters have been described as oppressive and poor models for women. But we cannot judge Eliot from the perspective of our own time, with its greater freedom, tolerance and less stringent standards. In historical context, she has meaning for mothers and daughters and she gives a great deal of insight into how mothers and daughters tried to cope in Victorian England. The use of drugs is a case in point.

In Eliot's time, drug addiction was predominantly a problem for married women and her references to opium have special significance. Women resorted to headache remedies, medicines and sleeping draughts which contained a high percentage of alcohol and opium,[9] in order to escape from the hopeless monotonies and restrictions of their lives and to ease their disappointments, mental inaction and seclusion. A contemporary, Florence Nightingale, diagnosed the narcissism, depression and addictiveness of Victorian women as suppressed anger. Eliot's novels seethe with that anger and frustration.

It is there in her exploration of the passionate experience of remorse and the polarisation of maleness and femaleness. It drives her attempts to negotiate a social order that left no room for intelligent and passionate daughters like Maggie Tulliver. Maggie longs for knowledge, sexual love and freedom but Victorian stereotypes prevent her from achieving them. The possibilities accorded males are denied her, but she cannot bond with other women. They are not clever. They gossip.

When mothers and daughters must depend on men for their livelihood, experience and very identity, they become like Maggie Tulliver. Maggie is pitifully dependent on the love of her brother, Tom. She turns her anger against herself and becomes neurotic and self-destructive.

In portraying daughters like Maggie, Eliot was concerned with the question of whether the only form of heroism open to women was martyrdom.[10] She exposed the double bind in which the mothers and daughters of her time found themselves and Maggie epitomises it when she questions the story of the old woman who is thrown into the water. If she swims she is a witch. If she drowns, she is innocent. But what good would that do her? This is Maggie's question and her own dilemma. If she doesn't drown she will be judged guilty. If she drowns, then she is innocent. In the end, she quite literally drowns in the torrent of the flooded river, held in a passionate, even incestuous embrace by her brother, Tom, whom she loved more than any other man.[11] The symbolism of the event lies in the fact that death is a region beyond blame. Are there any other such regions?

Eliot's contemporaries saw her preoccupation with love as an overwhelming enthralling force in both men and women, as inconsistent with feminine delicacy.[12] She was also criticised for the "ordinariness" of her characters, their lowly and insignificant status, but Eliot was concerned with the importance of the disregarded. Her heroines stood in for many and as such their anger and their powerlessness have meaning even today.

But the question remains, why did Eliot direct so much anger against women who did not take on the role of the ideal mother? She certainly never idealised women. Unlike Charlotte Brontë's heroines who fulfil themselves, Eliot's are self-destructive and their anger, aggression and frustration are menacing. Was she frustrated and angry about her own lack of mothering?[13] Was she projecting anger against herself and her own violations of Victorian standards? Each of these factors was no doubt important, but more important was her belief that motherhood gave women power.[14] She argued that by accepting responsibility for her children's upbringing, the middle-class woman improved her personal status. Eliot saw motherhood as a political weapon and became enamoured of the myth that the hand that rocks the cradle rules the world.

This secondary power, known as "female influence", was something that patriarchy tried to sell to women. That patriarchy also joked about it is a measure of its insincerity and anxiety about the concept. However, women accepted it as the truth. They could, it was argued, influence their men, rather than usurp them in places of management. In fact, this rationalisation meant that patriarchal authority was maintained in the 'real world'. But this reality was not immediately apparent and women clutched at "female influence", as a way to reconcile power and powerlessness.

In adopting this position, along with many of her generation, Eliot had been influenced by Louis Aimé Martin's *The Education of Mothers: or the Civilisation of Mankind by Women*, in which he claimed that the future destiny of the human race depended on maternal love. He also argued that, instead of disturbing the status quo by demanding legal reforms and equal right to the vote and employment, women should concentrate on influencing their husbands and educating their children to just and humane behaviour. He favoured education for women to equip them for this important responsibility and Eliot supported his arguments with enthusiasm. Thus, women, such as Dorothea in *Middlemarch*, by accepting their limited domestic role, hold the nation together.[15]

Through many such characters, Eliot expounded the ideology of motherhood in the hope that it would satisfy women's longings and leave undisturbed the family basis of society. While this attitude reflected the prevailing political view, it also probably derived much from her own unsatisfied longings in relationship to her mother. Her family life was not all it might have been and, in many of her novels, she created her own wish fulfilments.

Eliot's Relationship with her Mother and her Surrogate Mothers

She was born Mary Ann Evans (later known as Marian) in 1819 to Christina and Robert Evans, a well-to-do estate agent. According to Kenyon's *Consuming Flame*, which is an attempt to glean the story of Eliot's life from the very few surviving records, the Evans family lived at Griff House, a large red brick house on the road between Nuneaton and Coventry. Christina was Robert's second wife, and Mary Ann was her third child. Two years after Mary Ann's birth, she bore short-lived twins and, as a result, became an invalid.

Robert was in awe of his wife and very fond of his daughter, Mary Ann, but Christina's favourite was her son. She tended to reject Mary Ann and was hard and censorious toward her. If we are to accept Kenyon's story, she frequently commented on Mary Ann's lack of conventional prettiness and her plainness and preferred her older daughter, who appears to have been a model girl. In support of Kenyon, Redinger,[16] who has done some psychological sleuthing about Eliot, suggests that her mother was probably like Mrs Poyser in *Adam Bede*, who dominates by verbal criticism. Mrs Tulliver is perhaps another who reflects Mary Ann's mother, in that she is disapproving of her daughter's lack of typically feminine ways and not encouraging of her intelligence.

The sense of deprivation of affectionate attachments, which is present in Eliot's novels, may also have its origins in the fact that, at five, Mary Ann was sent to boarding school. Here, away from her beloved brother and father, there began a lifetime of night terrors. Typically, critics have dwelt on the influence of the male members of her family, the brother and father, yet her novels suggest that the search for a loving mother and her anger with mothers, who are unloving, had the greater effect on their conception. Her life was marked by a seeking of substitutes who could give motherly love and attention. This may have been why she was not able to make friends among the other girls at her schools, although she did well academically.

One of her earliest influential surrogate mothers was probably Miss Maria Lewis, the headmistress of her second boarding school, Wallington Academy at Nuneaton. She encouraged her avid reading, "improved" her Midlands accent and influenced her to become a devout Evangelist, to the horror of her brother, a High Church Anglican. Later, Mary Ann found mother substitutes in her very close friends, Clara Bray and Sarah Hennell.

After her mother's death in 1836, Mary Ann's formal education ceased and she became housekeeper to her father and brother. When her brother married, she and her father, now retired, moved to a small house in Coventry and she cared for him until his death. In Coventry, she was able to make a wider circle of friends, which included friendships with Charles Bray and his wife, who were local, progressive intellectuals and who influenced her to discard her evangelicalism and its puritanical fanaticism. She became a free thinker and, after much conflict, she attended Church, only to please her father. Through the Brays, she met John Chapman, the publisher, who made her his managing editor when he purchased the *Westminster Review* in 1851. As a reviewer and critic, she was witty and radical. There was little reference to motherhood, as such, in this early work.

She moved to London and became part of its radical intelligentsia. In London, she met active feminists, such as Bessie Raynor Parkes, Clementia Taylor, Jane Elizabeth Senior and Barbara Bodichon, who became her friends.[17] Nevertheless, unlike many women of her era who formed romantic friendships with members of her own sex, Eliot later complained that she had never been truly at ease in her earlier friendships with women and always found those with men more comfortable. After she entered into a de facto relationship with George Henry Lewes, she formed no reciprocal friendships with women. In this, Eliot anticipated a trend that influenced married women over the next 100 years. As I will explain later in this chapter, romantic friendships between women came to be regarded as a threat to men, and women were persuaded to regard their female friendships as trivial and even as dangerous.

The Influence of the Father-Daughter Alliance and Eliot's Relationship with her de facto Husband

Eliot's preference for opposite sex friendships perhaps repeats the early pattern of her childhood, since she was never comfortable with her mother, who disapproved of her. In contrast, her father doted on her. The preference is also typical of a phallocentric patriarchy, wherein friendships between women were described as less rewarding for them than their friendships with their husbands. It was said that women's friendships were not as stable, profound and deep as those between husband and wife or man and man.[18] George Eliot was not immune to this propaganda.

Her attitude may have had a lot to do with George Lewes' influence upon her. He was one of the writers, whose criticisms of her work and character, Charlotte Brontë resented because of their sexism.[19] We also know that George Eliot suffered her share of sexism. For example, in her early years in London literary circles, she met Herbert Spencer, whom she nearly married, but he found her "morbidly intellectual" and therefore unlikely to meet his very traditional expectations of a wife . These and other experiences of sexual discrimination could well have induced Eliot to develop her ideology of compromise, which Charlotte Brontë was not so prepared to do.

There may be another key to Eliot's preferences. Riegel[20] and Welter,[21] in studies of nineteenth century feminists, found many of them had fathers who had moulded their education, while their mothers were impassive and uninvolved. These daughters developed close ties with their fathers and attempted to take on board patriarchal interests and attributes because they provided a power not otherwise accessible to females.

Inevitably, their mothers became models which these daughters wanted to reject. Unfortunately, while their masculine-style education meant they became more independent than most daughters, society still treated them as inferior. Consequently, they became angry with patriarchy, rejected marriage and strove for a career. Although this behaviour pattern, as described by Riegel and Welter, is typical of many of the outstanding women of the nineteenth century, it is not completely typical of Eliot. She made many concessions to patriarchy, including an insistence that her relationship with Lewes was a conventional marriage.[22]

In 1856, she and George Henry Lewes, the versatile man of letters, decided to live together. As a result, she was ostracised by family, some friends and Victorian social attitudes because Lewes was separated from his wife, with no possibility of divorce. Eliot and Lewes lived together until his death in 1878. Lewes encouraged her to move from philosophy to fiction and during their years together, under the pseudonym, George Eliot, she wrote *Scenes of Clerical Life*, *Adam Bede*, *The Mill On The Floss*, *Silas Marner*, *Romola*, *Felix Holt*, *The Radical*, *Middlemarch* and *Daniel Deronda*. Jane Lilienfield questions, whether the story of George Lewes urging Eliot to authorship is not a red herring and a rationalisation to obviate the fact that Eliot, in the Victorian era, could not admit to her own aggressive motivation for fame and success as a writer.[23]

That Eliot felt she had to deny her female talent by writing under a male pseudonym, in order to be accepted as a writer in nineteenth century patriarchy, is another indication of how shallow the concept of female influence was.[24] Due to the attitudes of the time and her own, she was obliged to give up her 'respectability' and her family. She felt that, in her position, she must forgo the possibility of becoming a biological mother. Instead, her books became the children of her union with Lewes and he created a cult that bestowed upon her a holy maternal aura.[25] She began to sanctify family ties, became guardedly conservative and after 1856, references to mothers abound in her novels. Her idealisation of motherhood and the domestic model intensified during the 1860s and during the final decade of her life.

Eliot's Surrogate Daughters

Eliot believed she had an unused stock of motherly tenderness and became the all- nurturing, "Mother Goddess" to scores of young women. This gives some hint of how much her rejecting mother influenced her behaviour. It is not uncommon for rejected daughters to assume a mothering role to others. It's a way of compensating for and denying that there is insufficient motherly love in one's life. It protects from one's vulnerability.[26] According to Zimmerman,[27] whose insights into Eliot contribute to the ideas here, she was known as "little mamma" at school, suggesting that the compensatory behaviour was an early characteristic.

While she could not befriend women as equal partners, she could be a mother figure and provide them with the attention she had lacked as a daughter. At any party, George Eliot was surrounded by an adoring crowd of women, all waiting their turn to say a word. Much of the admiration from these 'spiritual' daughters was influenced by notions of romantic friendship, but it was also inspired by the model which Eliot provided. She had freed herself of many of the restrictions imposed on nineteenth century women. She was intelligent and intellectual and she was outstanding in her career, all of which were attributes regarded as open only to men. She provided her surrogate daughters with an achieving, unstereotyped identity and demonstrated that women could be strong within the patriarchal system. According to her model, they could at the same time maintain their femininity and their domestic life, and need not become revolutionaries. In George Eliot, they believed they had found the ideal nurturing and affectionate mother, together with the longed-for courageous mother.

One of her passionately worshipful surrogate daughters was Edith Simcox, whose fascinating autobiography tells much of George Eliot and how Eliot's admiration and praise of her intellect directed her to a constructive life. Indeed, a good part of Simcox's social work, her zeal on behalf of the oppressed, her writing, her books, her causes such as co-operatives, education, trade unions, women's suffrage or conditions in China, were stimulated by a desire to please George Eliot. She took her as her muse and her model. She wished to be worthy of her love.

In the nineteenth century, such loving and inspiring relationships between women were perhaps among their few motivational sources for generating any desire or strength to achieve in a male-dominated world. There are records of many such relationships.

෴

Surrogate Mother-Daughter Relationships in Women's Friendships

Lillian Faderman's *Surpassing The Love Of Men*, gives an excellent and feminine insight into these relationships and why they continued to thrive under nineteenth century patriarchy, despite the attack on sensibility. As far as mothers and daughters are concerned, a climate which encourages friendships between women is obviously better for their relationships.[28] Unfortunately, in the nineteenth century, the toleration of women's friendships had much to do with continued and arrogant phallocentricism.

Throughout the Victorian age, sex continued to be regarded as an activity in which virtuous women were not interested and did not engage, unless to gratify their husbands or to procreate. A sexual act between women was still believed to be impossible, as patriarchy held unequivocally that it required a male initiator and a penis. Moreover, good and normal women were seen as having no sex drive, therefore there could be no sexual relationships between them.

Because there was seemingly no possibility that women would want to make love together, they continued to be permitted a latitude of demonstrative affection which, in the twentieth century, would be labelled lesbianism. They slept together at school and as friends. They had an obligation to the deepest intimacy and the demonstration of the tenderest of feelings toward their friends, sisters and mothers.

Many of the scenes in nineteenth century novels depicting women's friendships are of this closely loving, asexual nature. For example, Christina Rossetti, in the 1860's, describes the two heroines in *Goblin Market* thus:

> Golden head by golden head,
> Like two pigeons in one nest,
> Folded in each other's wings,
> They lay down in their curtained bed:
> Like two blossoms on one stem,
> Like two flakes of new fall'n snow ...
> Cheek to cheek and breast to breast
> Locked together in one nest.[29]

Not only were such friendships seen as entirely asexual, they were experienced by women as exalting. For example, in the German novel by Elisabeth Dauthendey, *Of the New Woman and Her Love: A Book for Mature Minds*,[30] the central character, Lenore, refuses to form a relationship with a man, because men have not yet evolved as highly as women. She falls in love with Yvette, a 'normal, healthy' woman and distinguishes her love for her from the impure (sexual) advances of the sapphists (lesbians).

Margaret Fuller, an early feminist who admitted to loving another woman passionately, also saw her love as "purely intellectual and spiritual, unprofaned by any mixture of lower instincts".[31] The same theme is found in Louisa May Alcott's stories which were sanctioned by mothers and fathers as good moral stories for their daughters. In *An Old Fashioned Girl*, Alcott presents the loving friendship between Rebecca, a sculptor, and Lizzie, an artist, as promoting their mutual well-being.

Another example is seen in Henry James' novel, *The Bostonians*. Twentieth century critics misread James and see his depiction of romantic friendships between women as a study in abnormality. In fact, he was describing a typical nineteenth century relationship between independent middle-class women. Such friendships abounded in the New England with which he was familiar.

The Bostonians depicts a wealthy young feminist, Olive Chancellor, who forms a passionate love for Verena Tarrant and tutors her in the Woman's Cause. Verena blooms in Olive's company, but she only half returns the attachment and eventually Olive's self-satisfied cousin, Basil Ransom, inveigles her into an unpromising marriage. The selfish and manipulative Basil, then proceeds to undermine her former values. He wants to transform her into a submissive "stay-at-home" wife.

James would have been puzzled by those who see Olive as a lesbian, suffering perverse sexuality, and Basil as her saviour from a terrible fate. His complex drama has no winners or losers, no heroes or heroines, and he pokes as much fun at Basil as he does at Olive. James believed, as did others of his time, that a romantic relationship between women was not sick, but had the constructive potential for the self-actualisation of the women involved.

In fact, he had such a relationship to observe first hand in his own family. The one positive relationship in his sister Alice's life was with Katharine Loring. With a formidable father and two famous brothers, Alice became a recluse and a hypochondriac, until Katharine loved her and involved her in her Boston charities and betterment programmes. James regarded Katharine's love for his sister as noble and generous and as having the most positive effect on her.

These friendships, which were often surrogate mother-daughter relationships, flourished throughout the nineteenth century, because middle-class men and women occupied separate spheres and regarded themselves as different species. One of many who portrays the situation is the French writer, Theophile Gautier. In *Mademoiselle de Maupin*,[32] he observed that men and women were entire strangers to each other, as if they were inhabitants of different planets, with not the slightest intellectual or physical link existing between the two sexes. Men not only believed that good women were asexual but, as Tennyson put it, "Nature made them blinder motions bounded in a shallower brain: woman is the lesser man".[33]

Nineteenth century patriarchy, bent upon building an industrial society and amassing material goods, urged men to deny the female in themselves, to suppress emotion and heart, and to be resolute in their capacity to be rational, active and achieve. They should not fall prey to female seductiveness and softness. The lure of the image of fathers and sons, in unity, establishing the material prosperity of the nation, was considerable. Fathers advised their sons to test the virtue of the women they wished to marry by making sexual advances to them. If they did not react with due abhorrence, they would not make good wives.

Mothers were obliged to teach their daughters the dangers of seduction, to deny their heterosexual urge and not to show feelings, even to the men they loved. They learnt that they must not be open with men. They were taught that only with women could they be trusting and unrestrained in their affections. Carroll Smith-Rosenberg's research demonstrates that women survived by seeing themselves as kindred spirits, who inhabited a world of interests and sensibilities alien to men.[34] This meant mothers and daughters were expected to, and did, form close bonds based on feelings, sensibility and mutual love. Matters of heart and feeling were seen as the entire and only sphere of women.

Women turned to each other for support, because of the almost siege-like condition in which they lived under nineteenth century patriarchy. They were stereotyped as possessing minds which were alien to the best practices of men. Because they were often regarded with the hostility and suspicion shown toward subjugated peoples, they were sometimes endowed with magical and evil properties. For example, in the folklore of the time it was held that if a syphilitic man raped a virgin, he would be cured. Even in the 'learned' debates in 'scientific' and medical journals, anxiety about female powers was evident. Such issues as whether ham would be spoiled if cured by a menstruating woman, were argued with amazing credulity.[35]

If mothers and fathers handed these sick images of femininity onto daughters, imagine the disgust that could be incorporated into their daughters' view of themselves and the ambivalence generated by the accompanying and reverse messages, that they were also asexual and pure. It is little wonder that many fell into madness or found their wedding nights such a shock, they developed a traumatic aversion to heterosexuality.

Marriage was sold to mothers and daughters as the only way to fulfil themselves, yet the high male mortality, during the American Civil war and England's wars in Europe and the numbers of men emigrating, meant that millions of women would not find husbands. By 1851, there were two and three quarter million unmarried women in England.[36] This was another reason for the tolerance of intimate female friendships under nineteenth century patriarchy, which regarded unmarried women as objects for pity. Therefore, if single women could find partial compensation in the affection of other women, it was acceptable, but it was held that any such arrangement could not match the expectations they might have had in marriage. In view of the conditions of married women which Eliot portrayed in her novels, this attitude is a good example of myopic patriarchal arrogance.

The 'redundant' or 'superfluous' women, as unmarried women were called in the nineteenth century, were seen as a vast social problem. Among many novels which described their situation was the German novel by Gabriele Reuter, *Aus Güter Familie* (From A Good Family). It depicted the tragedy of an unassuming daughter, whose whole education had been directed towards becoming a perfect wife, a nurturer and a good housekeeper. She failed to 'catch' a suitable husband and became a pitiable spinster, dependent upon the generosity of her brother.

Whereas in medieval times, women had participated in family businesses and trades, social change and the advent of industrialisation had separated work-place and home. This meant that middle-class women were barred from working at men's work.[37] Since the surplus of women meant that large numbers would not marry, women were forced to agitate for jobs and education to support themselves. Teaching was the one profession that had been open to women until around 1870, when they were given some political rights in England. These enabled them to fill a few public positions such as churchwarden, medical officer in a work house, membership of a parish council, or clerk in the Post Office. The invention of the typewriter in 1873 opened up further employment opportunities.

Many of these significant changes were initiated by women themselves. The belief that women were a different species, their exclusion from public events and male haunts, parties and sports, and the segregation of the sexes even at the few heterosexual social gatherings there were, meant women of the middle-class had the leisure, the motivation and the opportunity to meet and compare grievances and act for reform and equal rights.

Despite the stigma patriarchy put upon spinsters, there had been some advantageous changes in their position. Middle-class women were not obliged to marry to merge large estates, as their aristocratic sisters were. Nor did they always need to marry to survive as was often the lot of lower-class women. They were inspired by the French Revolution and had the time and support to initiate and participate in humanitarian and betterment movements. Among their many achievements was gaining access to higher education — for example, Queen's College London in 1848, the University of Zurich in 1867, and the College de Sevigne in the 1880s.[38]

In the later decades of the nineteenth century, as women joined men in the work-place and engaged in public and organised reform among the poor and the oppressed, their support for each other became more and more important. They capitalised upon, and took seriously, the patriarchal tongue in cheek saying that they were spiritually and morally superior to men. They argued that the state of patriarchal, industrial, Victorian England, and the outcomes of wars between men, demonstrated the deficiencies of the 'powerful' male sex.

As a patriarchal expediency, women had been taught that love between women was spiritually uplifting. They now used it as a form of sustenance and impetus to achieve in a male-dominated work-force. In the offices, the schools, the universities, the publishing houses, the hospitals, or wherever they were able to take up positions, women looked to other women for the support they needed to maintain their self-esteem. Even though they were themselves confident of their intellectual capacities, they knew men would not take their abilities seriously. They craved respect and found it in other women. Anna Mary Wells, who wrote of a romantic friendship between two academic women, Mary Wolley and Jeannette Marks, observed that in women's colleges, twosomes were an established fact. Women, who lived by their brains and their skills, found in other women the profound supportive friendships which were essential to their pioneering role.[39]

The Irish writer, Edith Somerville, had such a friend in Violet Martin. The two women collaborated on numerous books and Edith insisted that they continued to collaborate, if in name only, even after Violet's death in 1915. Both had mothers who were suffragettes, not frail impassive women. Edith was encouraged in 'masculine' activities and was brought up with a fine sense of herself and her capabilities, both intellectual and physical. Unlike most women of her time, she was given a higher education. To Edith and Violet, the spiritual and supportive aspects of their relationship were vital to their survival. They saw it as a perfect marriage, but carnality had no place in it.

In these relationships, there was often equality, but also one of the pair sometimes became helpmate to the more accomplished one. During the last four decades of the nineteenth century, one such example is found in Bertha Vyer, daughter of a French countess, who gave up her talent as a painter to sustain Marie Corelli, then fiction's queen of the best sellers. Bertha created Marie Corelli, just as Alice B. Toklas can be said to have created Gertrude Stein.[40] Both were mothers and loving friends to their chosen daughters and, like proper Victorian mothers, had little conscious resentment of their generally secondary position in the mothering role.

Eventually, nineteenth century patriarchy was also prepared to recognise that women's friendships might help in bad marriages, especially as divorce was difficult. Thus, we find George Meredith, in *Diana of the Crossways* (1885), depicting a love between Antonia and Lady Dunstane, that helps them through the dismal failure of male-female relationships. However, the recognition is qualified, because his heroines must also attach themselves to a man, since they are seen as incapable of coping in the world otherwise. Longfellow's *Kavanagh* (1849) and Oliver Wendell Holmes' *A Mortal Antipathy*, follow suit. The women in these books may love one another as an expediency but their attachments to males are portrayed as more serious.

To women, romantic friendships were much more. For example, in the letters of Geraldine Jewsbury to Jane Carlyle, the wife of Thomas Carlyle, we read how she helped Jane in the face of Carlyle's overbearing personality and his disparagement and neglect of her. Geraldine believed she was the luckier because she was single. Similarly, Florence Converse in her novel *Diana Victrix* (1897), shows women sustaining each other as a husband generally could not and would not. She extols the 'New Woman', a popular image for the newly emerging independent women of the time.

Romantic Friendships Misinterpreted and Attacked.

By the end of the century, lesbianism had been identified, but as a 'medical problem', and was believed to occur only in abnormal women who were masculine or hysterical. In 1928, a very unphysical novel about lesbian relationships, *The Well of Loneliness* by Radclyffe Hall, had been censored with public approval. This occurred, despite the fact that Radclyffe Hall's novel subscribed to the current patriarchal view that a lesbian was a male trapped in a female body and a congenital abnormality. She argued that, if God had created her a freak, then she had a purpose in his scheme of things. Homosexuals, she argued, could lead constructive lives, needed merciful toleration and society should not try to convert them. For this reason, the book was considered a justification of perversion and condemned. Nevertheless, because of its accord with patriarchal views and because it aroused suspicion about female friendships, the book had a damaging effect. Mothers gave copies of it to their daughters to warn them against the sinfulness of sexual perversion and to demonstrate its lonely outcomes. Women began to be embarrassed about their friendships with other women.

Another even more significant influence on attitudes to mothering-type friendships and mother-daughter relationships at this time was the work of Sigmund Freud. Freud raised the ogre of lesbianism and described it as arrested development. It was an outcome, he believed, of daughters not resolving the oedipal complex the second time around in puberty. Instead of allowing the love for the mother to expand into heterosexual attractions, lesbians were said to remain fixated on their mothers. Freud reinforced the patriarchal notion of "butches" and "femmes", since he knew no other model of sexual love than that of heterosexual marriage.

He wrote a famous paper, 'The Psychogenesis of a Case of Homosexuality in a Woman'[41] about a young woman who, in adolescence, according to him, had a secret dream that her father should give her a baby. When instead, he gave one to her mother, her consequent subconscious guilt and anger caused her to turn her sexual feelings away from men. She feared becoming her mother's rival and became 'unnaturally' solicitous of her and fell in love with a woman very much like her. We are told there had been a history of attachments to older women, including a teacher. She was also said to suffer penis envy, which is Freud's reinterpretation of her anger at women's secondary status and her envy of the freedom permitted her brother because he was a male.

In her female friendships, the young woman said she had never gone beyond kisses and embraces and spoke often of the purity of her love. The problem was that Freud appeared to be unfamiliar with the romantic friendships of women or did not understand their political and social context. Had his 'patient' lived a decade or two earlier, in all probability she would have been regarded as perfectly normal and her friendship interpreted otherwise. Had she lived today, an interpretation might be that she was at an age when her drive for autonomy was central, but it was frustrated by her difficulties with a puritanical and tyrannical father. As a result, she became concerned about the secondary and exploited status of women.

Indeed, these factors may have accounted for the young woman's greater understanding of her mother at this stage. Certainly, her mother was more supportive of her romantic friendships, which the father found most threatening. Today, with hindsight, she seems a perfectly normal girl, not altogether impressed by Freud's interpretation of her condition, a fact which he found disconcerting enough to give it a neurotic interpretation.

According to Faderman,[42] like other patriarchal sexologists of his time, Freud made the mistake of not recognising that, even in lesbian relationships, sex is rarely the primary interest. The focus is the mutuality and closeness in which men are not especially trained. Men, who are obsessed with sex, are convinced that lesbians are not only obsessed with sex, but that any friendship between women must have sexual intercourse as its prime motive.

The theories of Freud and his followers helped to rationalise the increasing anxiety about the growing freedom of women and their solidarity, by interpreting loving friendships between them as sex-laden perversions and cases of arrested development. By the end of the first quarter of the twentieth century, romantic friendships between women had lost their 'innocence' and women were rewriting their history. For example, when they were being prepared for publication in the twentieth century, Martha Dickinson Bianchi edited out large sections of her aunt Emily Dickinson's nineteenth century love letters to her sister-in-law, Sue Gilbert, lest she be accused of being a lesbian.[43]

These anxieties about, and denigration of, friendships between women, spilled over into mother-daughter relationships. They were increasingly regarded with hostility and suspicion and ultimately, by mid-century, mothers and daughters were persuaded that they could only be in conflict. These were some of the sad consequences of the early stages of greater freedom for women in the twentieth century.

Not all women were prepared to submit to these attitudes, but their rebellion put them in an alienated and conflicting situation. The belief that women occupied a spiritually and morally superior world of sensibility, apart from the world of men, had contributed to same sex love becoming highly fashionable among the "new" women of the literary and bohemian circles of the early twentieth century. By the 1920s and 1930s, it was seen as typifying cosmopolitan chic, with connotations of excitement and sin.

Women were anxious to experience it and talk about it and some found themselves in a painfully ambivalent situation over it.

They had to contend with popular authors who endorsed patriarchal attitudes such as Marcel Proust, who wrote of the bitter ecstacy, shocking desires and decadence of sexual love between women. Yet most of these women were concerned with bonds that went deeper than fleeting sexual passions.[44] Their attitude was typified in the words of Colette, who spent 6 years in a lesbian relationship, in an attempt to recover from an unhappy marriage and overcome an overwhelming urge to return to her mother:

> "What woman would not blush to seek out her amie only for sensual pleasure? In no way is it passion that fosters the devotion of two women, but rather a feeling of kinship."[45]

The most famous of these relationships was that of Vita Sackville-West and Violet Trefusis, described with sensitivity and empathy, by Vita's son, Nigel Nicolson, in his book *Portrait of a Marriage*. This was first published in 1973, 11 years after his mother's death and in it Nicolson depicts the relationship between Vita and Violet as a tempestuous one, charged with guilt and joy. Vita was also the sometime lover of Virginia Woolf and the subject of her novel *Orlando*. While these women obtained inspiration and support from each other, they were sufficiently influenced by convention to suffer self-loathing. They were disturbed by the moral images, increasingly created by patriarchy, which depicted lesbians as violent, sick and disreputable.

Thus Vita saw herself as a Jekyll and Hyde personality, with her love for her husband (and it was a happy marriage) as the good side of herself, and her love for women as a product of her androgynous heredity and as evil. On the one hand, she described her marriage to Harold Nicolson as a rescue from everything that was vicious and violent and, on the other, had fun in dramatising the roles in which she found herself in her loving friendships with other women. Sometimes, she acted the part of a gypsy man to his heroine and sometimes she wore a bandage round her head in the pose of a boy wounded in battle and returning to his mistress.

In recent decades, many women writers have tried to put the point of view of women in such relationships. Adrienne Rich[46] is one who endorses Faderman's view that these sexual relationships between women were neither perverse nor cases of arrested development, but served to inspire a realisation of the possibility of spiritual and physical intimacy between women and mothers and daughters. She believed they enabled them to become more aware of their sensuality, more accepting of their bodies and their female physical selfhood, and more appreciative of the bodies that bore them. All too often, each of these factors is a source of ambivalence for women and between mothers and daughters.[47] Jane Lilienfield[48] likewise believes that in their loving relationships with other women, daughters found understanding of the physical and nurturing characteristics of their mothers and she provides evidence for her belief in the novels and lives of Willa Cather,[49] Colette and Virginia Woolf.

Certainly, in their writings, each of these women offered refreshing insights through the portrayal of their relationships with their own mothers. Had it not been for the heady women's movements of the late nineteenth and early twentieth centuries, what they had to say about mothers and daughters might never have been written or published. It is no coincidence that their acclaim came after women had agitated for and achieved the right of women to enter the work-force and higher educational institutions, and for legal changes to implement equal rights. In 1882 in England, *The Married Woman's Property Act* enabled women to inherit, bequeath and own property. There was great optimism and enthusiasm among women that such measures would ensure the advance of equality.

In this climate, middle-class mothers were casting off images of the ineffectual, absent or worn out with child-bearing mothers of the eighteenth and early nineteenth centuries. Women writers began portraying a new breed of mothers, mothers who did not provide models which restricted their daughters to the biological and mental inferiority of previous eras. In the following chapters, I shall comment on three daughters who wrote of such mothers: Henry Handel Richardson,[50] Sidonie-Gabrielle Colette and Virginia Woolf. These writers came from different backgrounds, cultures and countries, but shared a common wish to celebrate the strong mothers who allowed them to develop beyond the confines of the daughters of past centuries.

ல

CHAPTER 10

Henry Handel Richardson

Daughters with Strong Mothers

Fiction has left us with many an account of strong and courageous mothers. They seem to have flourished most in the literature of the last decades of the nineteenth century and the early decades of this century. We would know little of the courage, adaptability and heroism of this generation of mothers, if some of their daughters — daughters like Henry Handel Richardson, Sidonie Gabrielle Colette and Virginia Woolf — had not become outstanding novelists and left records of them.

Women were still less valued than men, still denied equal access to education and power and continued to be denigrated because of this, but the heady women's movements of the late nineteenth and early twentieth centuries created an atmosphere which made it possible for the mothers of Richardson, Colette and Woolf to openly express their indomitable spirits. It is true their sphere of influence was confined to their domestic and family lives, but here they were magnificent organisers of complex and demanding households. They are portrayed as strong characters who reigned like queens in their families. Even coping with the demands of extremely difficult husbands did not diminish their spirits. Their daughters had models of active, managing and independent mothers — mothers with vision. While there were times of anger and rebellion, they were all thankful and admiring of their mothers, because they inspired them to be independent persons.

Henry Handel Richardson, known as Ettie as a child, probably had the most difficult and rebellious relationship with her mother, Mary. While Richardson did not get on particularly well with her mother, she was a scrupulously honest and fair writer. Against a background of the emergence of a liberal democracy in Australia and the sophistication and culture of Europe, her novels tell us of her mother's courage, as well as her short-comings, and her complex relationship with her. The flow of her narrative is among the finest in English fiction and her psychological understanding and her capacity for creating characters and their emotions place her among the great European novelists of her time.[1] Her novels, the letters between her parents and the accounts of observers and biographers, tell of a conflicting mother-daughter relationship better than psychological texts can.

Richardson's Father and his Influence on her Relationship with her Mother

As in most mother-daughter relationships, her father, Walter Richardson, had a profound effect on Ettie and her relationship with her mother, Mary. It is therefore important to pay equal attention to him in this story. Walter was a medical practitioner and came of a line of landed Irish Protestant gentry, clergy and military officers and saw himself as embodying the values and position of an eighteenth century gentleman. Maybe he was attracted to Australia because, as a young colony, it protected many eighteenth century conventions, including a determination to keep power from the masses.[2] Walter was an egoist, concerned with class, pride and status. Throughout his life, he wrote articles on medical subjects in which he shows the vanity of a man who likes to be always right.[3]

His background and an intelligent mother, inclined him to an interest in the most fashionable subjects of his time: namely, science, truth and improving the lot of mankind. As a medical student at Edinburgh University, he was much influenced by the Professor of Midwifery, James Young Simpson, who introduced the use of anaesthesia by inhalation as a means of dulling the pains of childbirth and fought against those who thought it was good for women to endure the pains of labour without relief.[4] There is strong evidence that Walter contracted syphilis while he was a student and thought himself cured by the then conventional mercury lotions and medicines. The fact that he was not cured and inevitably died of the consequences — general paralysis of the insane — when he was 53, obviously placed immense strain on Ettie and her mother and their relationship with one another.

In 1852, Walter sailed for Melbourne and headed for Ballarat, the largest goldfield in Australia. He was not admitted as a general practitioner in Victoria until 1856. The character and behaviour of Richard Mahony, in Richardson's trilogy, *The Fortunes of Richard Mahony*, describe much of his life and how he experienced Australia. Richardson later said there were so many books about people who had emigrated successfully to Australia, she wanted to tell of the misfits who were mentally and physically incapable of adapting themselves, as was her father, a fastidious, highly strung, self-absorbed man. Actually, Richard Mahony is not a very likeable or admirable person, but such is Richardson's unsparing honesty and gift for examining the manifestations of his character, that he grows to almost heroic proportions.[5] He fails in adjustment not only to the new colony, but to life itself. One of the few positive things about him is his love for his wife, Mary, who was modelled on Ettie's mother.

Richardson admitted there was something of herself in the portrayal of the father she hardly knew in *The Fortunes of Richard Mahony*. She said she was haunted more and more by what he had gone through and came to identify herself with him fully. She also adopted his mixed attitudes of love, respect and condescension to her mother, Mary.

Richardson's Mother: The Unromantic Survivor

In contrast to Richard, the Mary of the novel and of real life, adapted to the new land and her personality became buoyant, spacious, frank and free. She had an affirmative view of life and, in the end, her character and actions say something about the vitality of women. She is also described as standing up to members of the opposite sex in the way English women never did.[6] Mary came from an old Leicester family and she had emigrated to Victoria with her eldest sister, Sarah, and her brother William in 1853 to join two other brothers. She married Walter in 1855, when she was 20 and he was 30.

Walter was attracted to Mary because of her timidity and because she was very competent domestically, with a talent for making a room comfortable and attractive with few resources.[7] Her letters, during their courtship, express an unassuming and deferential attitude to Walter, whom she at first saw as wise and fatherly. Later, she learnt that she was expected to mother him. In the trilogy, Richardson presents the fictional Mary as slowly coming to recognise her husband's egoism. To Richard, it is his pride that matters, not hers. He cannot give her anything positive. From seeing him as a superior being, she moves to accepting that he is a gifted wayward person, whose happiness depended on her. In real life, Walter's letters to Mary, when they are apart, show an hypochondriacal and insecure man, who needed plenty of attention and reassurance from his wife.[8]

Like the fictional Mary, the real life Mary was not a romantic and had no great interest in artistic pursuits. This enabled Walter to take a tolerant but superior attitude to her — an attitude that influenced Ettie's attitude to her mother and later created tension between Walter and Mary and Mary and Ettie.[9]

Ettie described her mother as having no intellectual interests, but questions whether circumstances prevented her from realising her talents. As a child, she watched her mother whitewash walls, repair upholstery and dig trenches to irrigate the garden. Mary loved pottering over broken sewing machines or stopped clocks and enjoyed getting them to work. It was Mary's good and practical sense that ultimately became the strength of the marriage and ensured not only the survival of herself and her daughters, but an exceptionally good education for the girls, after Walter's descent into insanity and death.

Mary and Walter were very much in love. They mutually admired and appreciated one another and the expressed affection was evident until Walter's irrationality made living with him very difficult.[10] In The Fortunes of Richard Mahony, Richardson describes how, as Richard declined mentally, his picture of Mary as the comforter whose love had the touch of the divine and as a person who was utterly selfless, patient and infinitely forbearing, gave way to suspicion, distrust and hate. This is no doubt as it was in real life and like the fictional Mary, the real life Mary never doubted that her husband was a good man. She had more faith in Walter than he had in himself and she "showed a young Victorian wife's devotion to her older and better educated husband".[11]

Mary seems to have had many miscarriages and Ettie was not born until 15 years after the marriage, in 1870. Ettie assures us she was passionately welcomed. Mary adored children.[12] A little more than a year later, Mary had another daughter, Lillian who came to be known as Lily or Lil. Throughout childhood, the sisters were forced into close companionship because, for reasons of class, their parents did not allow them to play with most other children or go to State schools. Mary insisted that they had a daily governess and a nurse, as befitted their rank, even when money became short. The sisters were both intelligent and eventually became gifted musicians. They remained very close throughout their lives.

Two Entirely Different Daughters

In 1874, the family went on a Grand Tour of Europe, during which time Walter's financial troubles began.[13] Mary kept a diary of their voyage home and this provides the earliest details of the personalities of her daughters and her attitude to them. Ettie was then five and described as clever, independent and troublesome. Ettie seems to have inherited her father's extreme sensitivity. She was encouraged to think of herself as special. Increasingly, Ettie is described in open conflict with her mother over starchy clothes that chafed her skin and hair painfully twisted into curls. In old age, Richardson presented these as conflicts between a robust mother with no intellectual interests and a child who was abnormally sensitive.[14] Ettie was not the daughter Mary had dreamed of and in many ways they were temperamentally different, although in some ways uncomfortably similar. They both had violent tempers.

Lil who was three and a half during the voyage, was described as shy, compliant and chubby, with golden curls. She was eminently cuddly. Ettie was not and did not want to be. She was described by observers as over-confident, showy and forward and her appearance as unprepossessing — long nose, dark straight hair and a port-wine birth mark which ran from shoulder to hand on her right arm. Her parents were very upset by the birth mark. Walter tried unsuccessfully to obliterate it by cutting. He compounded the child's embarrassment by photographing it. Ettie felt there was something shameful in her appearance. She felt inferior and jealous of her younger sister and coped by dominating her and making her act as her flunky.[15] Her poor self-esteem made it hard for her to cope with her mother's discipline, however mild.

An Insecure Childhood

Walter was never satisfied in whatever situation he found himself, as a consequence of which the family was always moving. This insecurity and her father's restlessness and deterioration turned Ettie's childhood into a nightmare. By 1876, Walter was showing marked signs of mental instability and probably recognised that he was in the early stages of general paralysis of the insane. In his youth, he had been reckoned the most distinguished-looking man in any room. Now he was a pathetic, decrepit figure, old before his time.[16] His nerves were frayed and he suffered bouts of depression. He struggled with his condition and tried to establish practice after practice in Melbourne and the country, but they all quickly failed and Mary was left to organise yet another move, preserve the family honour and look after its practical interests, while Walter sought fresh horizons.

During this time there was little money to live on. Mary is described as coping with this crisis with the same courage, dignity and practical sense she had demonstrated in all other adversities.[17] She secured a position as postmistress in Koroit, a small country town in Western Victoria. The position of postmistress was one of the few occupations then open to women and Ettie moved for the eighth time in her eight years of existence. Their mother's unusual absence in training and later at work, added to the insecurities of the little girls. Lil lived in constant dread that her mother would not return. In his biography of Henry Handel Richardson, Axel Clark describes Ettie at eight, as a badly disturbed, morally confused and socially alienated child.[18]

Ettie knew her father was ill and that something had gone deeply wrong in her life.[19] She heard her parents' quarrels and began to walk in her sleep. By day she occupied herself by obsessively bouncing her ball on the verandah of the house and creating fictions to escape from a life that was intolerable. There are no records of what the girls suffered at this time, except the accounts in *The Fortunes of Richard Mahony*. Like Cuffy Mahony, whom Richardson described as her alter ego, the girls were probably humiliated by the public spectacle of their father's madness, his lunatic delusions and his weeping like a frightened child.

Cuffy Mahony is a memorable child and the only character with whom Richardson clearly identifies. Through him, she succeeds in giving us a child's thoughts, consistently and dramatically, without sentiment. Since she understood how children think and was able to convey this better than any psychological text, Cuffy's childish literalness contributes to the pain of many of the scenes of her father's deterioration. Richardson's insight reminds us that under stress, even the most loving parents ignore children's feelings and that their injunctions can cause pain and confusion. She understands the guilt children feel when their parents quarrel. Cuffy also feels guilty about his sister's death and his father's madness. Richardson makes us privy to the child's developing sense of self, through Cuffy's determination and will to survive in a family that puts children at risk. One observer believed Ettie came to hate her father and angrily rebelled against her situation, while Lil submitted and became socially crippled by her timidity.[20]

Before they went to Koroit, their father was admitted to a government asylum at Yarra Bend. Mary brought Walter from Yarra Bend to Koroit to die. Medical records show his speech had become incoherent and that he was liable to fall when walking. Perhaps Ettie and Lil had to take the shameful, stumbling wreck that was their father out on walks as Cuffy and Luce had to in *The Fortunes of Richard Mahony*. Walter died on August 1st, 1879, aged 53. Ettie was relieved.

Ettie's formative years were harrowing, spent in insecurity, embarrassment and terror. This environment contributed to basic features of her personality — persistent fearfulness and dissatisfaction — which did not make her relationship with her mother an easy one. After her father's death, Ettie was left with a severe nervous tic and her ugly and uncontrollable facial twitches were greeted with mirth and ridicule.

After Walter's death, Mary was promoted to the position of postmistress at the larger and more pleasant town of Maldon. Some indication of the courage Mary needed to hold this position in a male-dominated society, is given in the annoyance expressed in a letter published in the *Argus* about her appointment and "placing ladies in charge of grown men".[21] The model of a mother who worked and patriarchal attitudes toward her, must have left a lasting impression on Ettie. It no doubt influenced her tendency to portray courageous women characters and her later strong friendships with women.

In Maldon, the cramped quarters they'd lived in at Koroit, were replaced by a well-built brick villa of six rooms and there was a large garden. Richardson remembers the house and the prosperous town of Maldon as something of a paradise.[22] The girls were given more freedom than they'd ever had before; they were now allowed to play with other children and as their lives became more pleasant, they became more confident and sociable. Mary no longer felt she had to keep up appearances as the wife of a medical practitioner who believed in his own superiority. She made many friends in Maldon and the children moved beyond the confines of their immediate family as never before. Ettie became interested in the odd characters that legends are usually built around in country towns such as Maldon and this probably nourished her imagination and her later talent for describing the personalities of a wide range of people.

Despite the lesser tensions of her home life, Ettie still retained the need to dominate, feel superior and show contempt, traits she'd acquired from her father and which compensated for her own insecurity. She came into conflict with her mother's strong will and practical good sense — the very traits that had held the family together. Ettie was not the ideal daughter and her negativeness had much to do with her own inner turmoil.

Because of her unmanageability, her mother sent her to Melbourne to become a boarder at the Presbyterian Ladies College in 1883. Despite their conflicts, Mary was immensely proud of her clever daughter. The school was an excellent choice. Founded in 1875, it had from the outset been the leading Australian institution in the movement for higher education for women and put into practice the belief that, given the proper education, girls were as intellectually capable as boys. The school achieved excellent results and provided a large proportion of the women studying at the University of Melbourne after their admission in 1881.

At school, Ettie, always on the watch for slights, suffered badly from snobbery, social isolation and her own outstanding intelligence, about which she could be arrogant. Her family was considered unacceptable and her clothes and manners wrong, much of which she portrayed in *The Getting of Wisdom*. In this novel, through the character of Laura, she describes the awakening of girlhood, the problems of adolescence and the vicissitudes of young adulthood, with devastating truth and gaiety.[23] Laura seeks the wisdom needed to cope with a number of questions. Can a growing girl ever understand and co-operate with what her mother expects from her? How can one be a lady without being a snob? Are women's brains unreliable and inexact and how could a girl be a woman and also clever? How to conform? Is it possible to accommodate the wish for personal success with humility? How to succeed for the sake of one's mother?

As is sometimes the case with insecure children, Ettie told artful tales to ingratiate herself with the other girls and gained a reputation as a liar. Lying is something that confuses children greatly and not until they are about nine do they really understand what a lie is.[24] The problem is parents and teachers rarely understand this. Distinguishing between fact and fantasy is not an issue for very young children and Ettie's fanciful tales from an early age were misunderstood, leading her to believe there was something morally wrong with her. She defended her sensitivity with a growing cynicism which unnerved most of her fellow students, but at least two of her school friends recognised that she was an intelligent, but not very happy child.[25]

She did well academically and musically and was attracted to the idea of being a musician — an attitude endorsed by her mother, who began planning to help her study in one of the great musical centres of the world. Later Richardson was to complain that her mother had thwarted her desires to be a writer, but it certainly seems that at 16, it was she who wanted to be the musical genius. The attitude that she should go out in the world to support herself, reflected a common attitude of the College staff and pupils in response to the feminist ideals popular at this time.[26] This, and the example of her mother, encouraged Ettie to believe in the right and capacity of women to independence and intellectual equality.

At school, she developed an infatuation for an exceptionally beautiful girl, two and a half years older than herself, who became "Evelyn" in *The Getting of Wisdom*. The two kept in touch until the death of "Evelyn" and according to Nettie Palmer, Richardson confessed later that the attraction she felt for this girl was so strong, few others surpassed it.[27] During her life she developed strong attachments to a number of women and became involved in several women's issues, such as the suffragette movement. At one stage, she set about introducing German women writers to the English speaking public.[28] She was always interested in the vitality of women and the actions of her female characters are rather different from the Madame Bovarys and Anna Kareninas of her time, even though their dilemmas are similar and she was a great admirer of their authors. In her novel, *Maurice Guest*, Louise, unlike Madame Bovary, is not shamed into taking her own life, despite her many affairs. And although George Eliot — another well-known writer of the time — wrote about egotistical women, Louise's boredom and egoism are on a grander scale than shown by any of Eliot's women characters.

The character of Louise was based on the famous actress Eleanore Duse. After seeing her on stage in London in 1894, Ettie developed an enduring passion for her. Ettie longed to be loved utterly and the objects of her passion were recreated in her private imagination — in reality, they knew little or nothing of how she felt.[29]

Ettie and her Mother in Europe

By 1880, Mary's financial affairs had improved. She gave up postmistressing and took her musically talented daughters to Leipzig to study music. En route, they stayed with relatives in England, which Ettie disliked because of the stuffiness of its people, the dismal slums, the weather and the dirt. Having completed a liberal education in a country which was in the vanguard of progress towards liberal democracy, she was repelled by her relatives' snobbery and narrow-mindedness. The curriculum of her Australian school had been broad and included classical and scientific studies as well as a good grounding in the classics of English literature. This and her talent for languages, meant she escaped the parochialism, prejudices, unquestioned beliefs and narrowness of much of the English education of the time. She found the then popular novelists such as Thomas Hardy alien and George Eliot "intolerably prosy and long winded".[30] European literature was more congenial to the broad horizons of her birthplace and the psychological experiences of her childhood.

By her own account, Ettie's years in Leipzig were the happiest she had yet known. She made friends, went to every available concert, played tennis, danced and hugely enjoyed being a student in a cosmopolitan European city.[31] She was fascinated by the notion of becoming a great musician. Her mother devoted all to helping Ettie realise her dream and although Ettie remained dependent on her mother, she enjoyed a new sense of her independence and importance. In Leipzig, they set up house with Martha (Mat) Main, Ettie's closest friend. Mat observed how pleased Mary was to run the household and described her as a splendid manager.[32] Mary never complained about the loud dissonant sounds from surrounding apartments where musical students practised day and night. She organised parties and dances. Mat recalled that she loved taking charge and providing the refreshments.

Ettie had her male admirers, but after a childhood and adolescence of believing she was ugly in physique, morals and social skills, she found it difficult to reciprocate the tender feelings of men and not all recognised that she was afraid of them. They teased her unmercifully in order to overcome their awe of her.[33]

She transferred her need to dominate and be at centre stage from Lil to Mat and used Mat in the same way as she had Lil — as a flunkey. Mat observed that she was a ruthless competitor on the tennis court and in relationships with those close to her. She preferred competing with men rather than women, whom she terrorised. But she also put herself to the test and was unsparing in her self-assessment, which indicates how much her behaviour sprang from her own insecurity. Although happy in Leipzig, she continued to find it hard to return her mother's affection, no matter how much they needed each other. She remained a difficult, demanding person and quarrelled frequently with her mother. The issues were her mother's expectations of the ideal daughter and Ettie's tendency to discount everything her mother did for her. For example, Mat described how Ettie's mother made all her clothes, but Ettie was unco-operative about fittings and Mary was left to struggle along as best she could.[34]

By 1890, to Mat's pain, Ettie found a close companion in a bespectacled, reticent and intellectual young Scotsman called George Robertson. He was an exceptionally gifted scholar of European literature and Ettie found his companionship stimulating and congenial. Their attachment was probably intellectual rather than romantic.[35] He suggested Ettie read an abundance of Russian, French, Danish and Norwegian books in German translations, German being a language in which she was fluent. She was already familiar with Stendahl, Flaubert, Tolstoy, Bjornson, Ibsen and Dostoevsky, whom she greatly admired. She'd also read Zola, Goethe and Nietzsche. By now she knew she was never going to be a musical genius and announced she was going to give up her musical studies and marry George. Mary gave her a supper to celebrate her engagement, but it was followed by a stormy scene in which she vented her anger and frustration on Ettie. Once more Mary resigned herself to making the best of things.

Ettie felt she had let her mother down and became depressed. The quarrels between them became chronic. Ettie expressed contempt for her mother, believing her to be insensitive, without imagination and completely deficient intellectually and artistically. Mother became the enemy.[36] Mary continued to be generous and sympathetic toward Ettie and it was she who made it possible for her to marry George with a wedding present of £300. On the first evening of her honeymoon, Ettie wrote a brief, grateful letter to her mother.[37]

Very soon George was offered a post at Strassburg University. Later, after the publication of his history of German literature in 1902, he was invited to become the first professor of German at London University. Although she regretted having to live in England, henceforth Richardson had the financial security and psychological encouragement and support to write her novels. She found the intellectual mothering she craved in her husband. She decided not to have children, seeing herself as ill-equipped to be a mother after her own harrowing childhood. She poured all her creativity into her novels.

In the early period of her marriage, Ettie wrote to her mother for advice on housekeeping and Mary responded with hints on how to manage servants, keep the flat warm, economise and an avalanche of recipes. Mary had set up house in Munich to further Lil's musical studies, and had become ill with an undiagnosed disorder, later thought to be bowel cancer. Ettie described how she never thought that the mother she had always been able to rely upon without thinking, could die. She was about to lose a parent she'd always been inclined to discount. Mary was only 57 when she died and was buried in Munich. Her death left Ettie shattered and angry and for the rest of her life she wrestled with her feelings of affection, dependency, resentment and rejection toward her mother.[38]

Richardson's Tribute to her Mother

In the short story, Mary Christina, Richardson wrote about the details of her mother's bitter death with great honesty, but for all that, it is not a particularly remarkable short story.[39] The trilogy, The Fortunes of Richard Mahony, was her greatest tribute to her mother. In the first part, Australia Felix, we see Mary grow from an innocent child-wife into an independent, assertive person. We become as interested in her as we are in Richard. At first, her negative censoring attitude to Richard makes the reader unsympathetic toward her, but by the second part of the trilogy, The Way Home, it is clear that Mary has resources that can save Richard from his inner self-destructiveness. In the third part, Ultima Thule, Mary's will and sense of responsibility have shaped her into a woman of initiative and courage.

She rises to her full height after Richard's breakdown. In the early part of their marriage, she had invested all her ambitions in him, but when he gives up medicine, she finds her own resources, casts convention aside and ignores his status as head of the household. However, it is not until Richard's admission to the asylum, that Mary feels totally free to make her own decisions and begins to demonstrate her true strength. Before that, her abilities had to be controlled lest they threaten her husband's authority. Richardson is not interested in sexual stereotypes. The threat lies in Richard's view of himself, rather than patriarchal imperatives. Mary negotiates the threat with sense, but once it has gone, she is magnificent.

In the last part of Ultima Thule, Mary is portrayed as stepping beyond the limiting dimensions of her domestic sphere. The scene in which she battles for Richard to be returned to her care before he dies, shows her at her fighting best.[40] In her mothering of Richard and her children, undaunted by many catastrophes, she embodies the regenerative forces of women. This is a very positive view.

But Richardson was too much of a realist to turn the Mary of her fiction and the real life Mary into a super Mum. Her mother is not spared and we are forced to recognise her limitations. Richardson knows how we feel about our mothers and describes how she stole from the room in shame and pain whenever her mother tried to sing in public. She was almost tone deaf. We are not spared her bad taste, her occasional lack of sensitivity to her children and her thick skin. The good woman is a very difficult character to present in fiction, but Richardson's honesty and insight into the manifestations of her mother's personality, quicken our sympathy for the fictional Mary and help us to recognise that there is something noble, not just in mothers like Mary, but in humanity in general.

The model her real mother provided gave Richardson a vision beyond the downtrodden Victorian mothers, whom George Eliot portrayed. That vision, her childhood experiences, her education, her interest in the European tradition and her reading of philosophers such as Nietzsche, trained her to keep an open mind about the moral values and psychological imperatives of her characters.[41] Whereas George Eliot's women feel morally trapped, Richardson's characters create their own moral worlds. Whether male or female, all her characters, through their choices and their interpretations of those choices, are the arbiters of their own destinies.[42] They speak for themselves in their own language. They are free. There is no pact with the reader as to with whom sympathies should most lie.[43] Instead, Richardson prefers to present multiple points of view and multiple truths and had a remarkable ability to do so. For example, in the story "The Professor's Experiment", we begin with a jaundiced view of the Professor's sister, the prim old maid, Annemarie, but by the end of the story and the death of the Professor's wife, we see how much Annemarie has been deprived by her selfless devotion to her brother, the egoist.

We see Laura in *The Getting of Wisdom* as vulnerable to the rejections and criticisms of her schoolmates, but also as arrogant about her abilities, heartless with her mother and heartbreakingly lonely and craving for love. The novel moves from one set of observations to others, at different angles. Whereas Charlotte Brontë passionately identifies with Jane Eyre, Richardson's Laura is tempered by the multiple perspectives of Laura's actions.[44] The book is also about Laura's own kind of triumph, although she is not the perfect daughter. She is not crushed by her setbacks. Her education of herself has been subversive, but she is still herself.

In *The Fortunes of Richard Mahony*, Richard, like Walter, has to adjust to his wife's lack of intellectual and artistic interests. But we also see that Mary has to make larger and much more sustained adjustments. We cannot stay with the question, "Is Mary the right wife for Richard?". There is the other question, "Is Richard the right husband for Mary?"[45] Richardson's great talent is that we understand both the experience of being Richard and of being Mary.[46]

Whereas Eliot saw submission to the demands of others as the highest good, Richardson's characters are egotistical, driven by their own needs and desires. Richard is ruthless to Mary because he pits his welfare against hers. Usually, egoists are monsters in English fiction, but in Richardson's work they become heroic as they face their shortcomings, live intensely and make an effort to live by their own moral imperatives. The results are not the important issue. Ostensibly, Richard Mahony, the embodiment of Ettie's father, is a failure. As Richardson sees it, he created his own tragedy, because he tried to live by the outmoded standards of an eighteenth century gentleman and because of his pride, his fastidiousness and his inner compulsions. Richard believed in his status as a gentleman in a society where the concept was irrelevant. He was a man divided against himself — a man who would never be satisfied anywhere. But he constantly probed himself and fought to understand himself and to keep his sanity. When he failed to commit suicide, he chose to endure the last stages of his illness. The impact of this decision on himself, his wife and their children is described in its complexity, without according blame.

Richardson's characters are driven by their own will and standards rather than by a sense of duty to others. They embrace suffering and celebrate intense feeling, because this is life. They struggle to understand life and themselves and see themselves as responsible, even when they must grapple with arbitrary circumstances. To give up the struggle, to try to understand, as Agnes Ocock does in The Fortunes of Richard Mahony, is contemptible. In real life, Mary did not give up. In her mother, Richardson had a model of a female who was a survivor.

The Fortunes of Richard Mahony has been rated among the world's great novels.[47] It explores a marriage and its impact on the children of that marriage, with a depth and subtlety that has been likened to the perceptions of Tolstoy's epics. In previous Victorian fiction, there had always been someone to blame if a marriage went wrong. Richardson examined the relationship by understanding both her characters on their own terms. Richard and Mary walk into marriage full of partial truths about each other and perceptions determined by their own expectations. We see Richard Mahony as he sees himself and as he sees his struggles to retain his standards. We also see him as his family and acquaintances see him. To his wife and friends, his actions are a series of crazy rejections of what is good for him. On the one hand, Mary seems heartless about Mahony's breakdown; on the other we see how much she cannot give up her belief in him and therefore cannot accept his insanity. She has been immensely ambitious for him, but he is a failure. She co-operates with his emotional needs; he rarely does with hers. The marriage began with the patriarchal convention of Mahony protecting Mary. It gives way to the much more powerful one of Mary protecting Mahony. She becomes the mother figure, he the child.[48] Although Richardson probably didn't consciously intend it that way, the outcome is a reversal of the myths of patriarchal society and portrays the reality for a great many mothers and daughters.

After her marriage and settling in England, Richardson was described as immensely shy, fierce, avoiding all but intimate friends and putting all of her energy into her writing. She was scarcely known to the English literary world. Europe was her intellectual and moral centre.[49] *Maurice Guest* set in Germany, was published in 1908, *The Getting of Wisdom*, set in Australia, in 1910. Over the next 20 years she wrote her trilogy *The Fortunes of Richard Mahony*, the last of which, *Ultima Thule* was published in 1930. It was an immense success in America and Australia, running into many editions and was translated into several European languages. Her last novel about Cosima Wagner was a failure, presumably because the facts were known and she could not give her characters their usual freedom.[50] Her short stories — of which she wrote a number throughout her life — also generally exhibit less talent than her early novels. Finally, in the summer of 1939 she began writing her memoirs — an autobiographical fragment which ends with her marriage. It was published under the title, *Myself When Young*, and provides much of the information for the account of her early life given here.

Richardson is well known in Australia, but although she spent most of her life in England, it was not until 1985 that the first British study of her work appeared. It is by Karen McLeod, who considers why Richardson has been so neglected in Britain since the initial resounding success of her first novels.[51] She concludes it has to do with Richardson's reclusive life, the fact that she was not pre-occupied by class differences which particularly interested her English contemporaries, that her style and direction is not English but European and because she didn't choose to join or concern herself with the ethos of the English literary upper middle-class, as did Virginia Woolf and all the great English writers of her period. Richard, Mary and Cuffy are quite original characters and outside a specific, recognisable group preferred by the influential critics and writers belonging to this particular ethos. McLeod thinks that, as a novelist, Richardson is greater than any of them and deserves to be read more than she is. She certainly needs to be read by anyone interested in a realistic portrayal of the complexity of mother-daughter relationships.

☙

CHAPTER 11

Colette

Daughters with Strong Mothers

Sidonie-Gabrielle Colette and Henry Handel Richardson share many similarities in their experiences of the mother-daughter relationship. Both found models of strong women in their mothers. Yet there are also many differences. Colette, who was born just three years after Richardson, on the other side of the world in the Burgundian village of Saint-Sauveur-en-Puisaye in 1873, openly and fully admired and adored her mother. It was an unreserved love — the kind that Richardson could never give her mother. This difference in emotional feeling had a lot to do with differences in Richardson's and Colette's childhood experiences. Colette wrote repeatedly that her childhood was a period of deep happiness.

Colette's Admiration for Her Independent and Fallible Mother

Her mother, Sido, was mistress of her house, a garden burgeoning with flowers, and an adoring and adored second husband. She handed on her love of animals, plants and close observation of all things to her daughter and provided the model for the love between them. This is expressed in many passages in her letters to Colette, such as the following, where she describes Colette, as a child, in her garden:

> "I can still see your graceful little form wandering about in it while you dreamed of a thousand and one things...How far away that is! Yes, you were my golden sun. I used to tell you too that when you came into a room where I was you brought more light in to it."[1]

In return, Sido is Colette's most adorable and most lasting character. Perhaps one of the most telling passages about her, from *My Mother's House*, describes her mother lost in observing the beauty of a thieving blackbird, until reminded by Colette of the stolen cherries:

> "Into those eyes there flickered a sort of wild gaiety, a contempt for the whole world, a light hearted disdain which cheerfully spurned me along with everything else. It was only momentary, and it was not the first time I had seen it. Now that I know her better I can interpret those sudden gleams in her face. They were, I feel, kindled by an urge to escape from everyone and everything, to soar to some high place where only her writ ran. If I am mistaken, leave me to my delusion."[2]

Such expressions of security in exchanged love, are frequent themes in Colette's writing and are generally accompanied by the necessary recognition of the autonomy of both mother and daughter. For example, in another famous passage Colette demonstrates both her confidence in her mother's love for her and her acceptance of her need for independence. She admiringly describes an occasion when Sido decided against visiting her daughter in order to await the rare blooming of her pink cactus. In the same vein, Colette remembers how, in earlier childhood years, her mother called for her, her sister and her brother, "'Where, oh where are the children?" ... tormented by her inability to watch over them enough.'" They found no need to reply from their hiding places, escaping her, not responding, but taking her calling as an indication of her secure love for them.

Like Mary Richardson, Sido was not a forerunner of the late twentieth century super-mum, chivied into an impossible perfectionism by two centuries of pseudo-Rousseaus and neo-Freudians. Nor was she the mother victim, impossible to identify with, who arouses anger, resentment and anxiety because of her submissiveness. Sido enjoyed her children, was fallible, faulty, did not always understand and sometimes allowed her jealousies to take hold.

Occasionally, in her own anxiety and love, she was also unwittingly selfish and did not perceive the perspective of her daughter — a matter which Colette could later accept in the give and take of their relationship. For example, in *My Mother's House*, Colette describes her joy after her elder sister's marriage, because she inherited her room, wallpapered in cornflowers on a pearl-grey background, and her bed, curtained in white lace and lined with blue. Her happiness was threatened because her mother was anxious, since the young Colette's new room was several rooms and a staircase removed from her own. She says to Colette, "Last night I dreamed again that you were being kidnapped". Colette does not reply for she knows no cure for her mother's anxiety. "And is that all you care about it you little monstress?". "Well hang it all, mother! What do you want me to say? You look as though you blamed me for its being only a dream."[3]

Not long after this conversation, Colette's fears, that she might have to return to her old room to allay her mother's uneasiness, are realised. One night, in the midst of a storm, Sido anxiously moves her sleeping daughter back into her old garrett-bedroom next to her own. Thus, Colette tells us, she was abducted out of childhood into ungrateful adolescence.

Sido expressed her mind, but she knew how to temper it with love and impart worth and self-esteem to her daughter; again in *My Mother's House*, Colette describes this characteristic:

I would tremble and blush under her barbed praise, her piercing look, and her voice with its rising final inflexions, so surely pitched. She never called me 'daughter' except to underline a criticism or a reproof. But both voice and look were swift to change:

O my Jewel-of-pure-gold, it isn't true, you're neither stupid nor pretty, you're just my peerless little girl. Where are you going?

Absolution lent me wings, as it does to all mercurial creatures, and having been duly kissed I was already light- heartedly preparing for flight.[4]

Colette also admired her mother's spunk and integrity and, as an example, reports that Sido was once asked to comment about the forced marriage of a young woman, three months pregnant, to her seducer. Her answer is not submissive to patriarchal moralisms:

What would I do? I should say to my daughter: 'Carry your burden, my child, not far from me, but far from that man, and never see him again! ... a man who was capable of taking you in the dark, under the windows of your sleeping parents. To sin and scourge oneself, to sin and then drive forth the unworthy one, is not irreparable shame. Your ruin begins from the moment you consent to become the wife of a knave; your fault lies in hoping that the man who has stolen you away from your own hearth has a hearth of his own to offer you'.[5]

A Daughter's Physical Love for Her Mother and the Influence of Her Father

There are several other factors in Colette's relationship with her mother which provided the basis for their later devotion to each other. For one, she acquired the capacity to admire her mother's physical being, beautifully expressed in the following passage:

A swift hand stopped mine. Why did no one ever model or paint or carve that hand of Sido's, tanned and wrinkled early by household tasks, gardening, cold water, and the sun, with its long, finely-tapering fingers and its beautiful, convex, oval nails?[6]

The physical love and admiration accorded by her daughter, had much to do with Sido's own pride in her femininity, helped by her husband's admiration and love for her. Colette tells us that, while adoring of her husband, Sido was not as demonstrative as he and she found pride in observing that her mother was obliged to shyly submit to his frequent public kisses on his demand of "Pay up, or I won't let you pass!".

Only once, on a summer day, when my mother was removing the coffee tray from the table, did I see my father, instead of exacting the familiar toll, bend his greying beard and bearded lips over my mother's hand with a devotion so ardent and ageless that Sido, speechless and as crimson with confusion as I, turned away without a word. I was still a child and none too pure minded, being exercised as one is at thirteen by all those matters concerning which ignorance is a burden and discovery humiliating. It did me good to behold, and every now and then to remember afresh, that perfect picture of love: the head of a man already old, bent in a kiss of complete surrender on a graceful, wrinkled little hand, worn with work.[7]

While the admiration and respect of her father for her mother was important in the good relationship between this mother and daughter, Colette reports that she knew her father very little. "My attention, my fervent admiration, were all for Sido and only fitfully strayed from her."[8] Outwardly, Captain Colette took little interest in his children and his daughter recognised "The curious shyness of fathers, in their relationships with their children"[9] and, in *My Mother's House*, portrayed him with the same humanity and complexity as she did her mother. We learn he had a bad temper, was hopeless with money and lost Sido's fortune. He was kind, but resented the children for disturbing the longed for tête-a-tête with his wife.

Not until after his death did he assume his true shape in Colette's thoughts and she guessed that he, a passionate man, a poet with a love for literature and science, a townsman, a former military hero with one leg, had missed his former active life and found the country a cultural desert. Even his attempts at local politics and education were endearing failures. All that sustained him was his love for Sido.

Coping with Marriage and Separation from Sido

When Colette fell in love with Willy Henri Gauthier-Villars and married him, she described the event as losing a mother, rather than gaining a husband.[10] The outcome is well known. Willy, a plagiarist, exploited Colette's literary talents, and locked her for hours in a dark room to miserably write the Claudine novels under his name.[11] The novels contained first hand accounts of an adolescent girl's experiences, not easily accessible to males, and Willy sensed their best seller possibilities. They made Willy famous and rich.

Jane Lilienfield asks whether blaming her husband was Colette's way of hiding her own aggressive drive for fame and success as a writer, in an age when women didn't admit to such tendencies.[12] Obviously, Colette was not wholly a victim. She had talent and this was the beginning of an esteemed career. Willy taught her the discipline of writing, perfectionism in her craft and how to utilise the commercial market. She called the six Claudine novels, their six daughters.

Willy also taught her how to be her own best saleswoman and because she always needed money to support herself, she never forgot her training.

Unlike Henry Handel Richardson, she became a well-known popular author. But she was never greatly respected as a substantial writer and intellectuals avoided her, until the feminist movement began underlining the originality of her talent.[13]

By the end of the first year of her marriage, Colette was desperately unhappy, but she did not want to worry her mother, whose husband and other daughter had recently died. She fell into a fever and it was Sido who came and nursed her back to health. Colette left Willy and fought her unutterable yearning to go back to her mother, for she wished to develop the autonomy that Sido had planted in her. She coped more successfully than Juliette, her half sister from Sido's first marriage. Juliette, a withdrawn girl, married disastrously against her mother's wishes and yet it was Sido who sold her beloved house and garden to provide her with a dowry. Juliette's husband and his family encouraged her to break completely with her mother and the campaign involved the traditional malevolence about mothers and mothers-in-law. There followed law suits between Sido and her son-in-law's family[14] and there was litigation to keep her at a distance from Juliette. Autonomy is of course not won by law suits, but comes from within oneself.[15]

Despite her falling out with her mother, Juliette lived next door. When she was giving birth, her cries reached Sido and Colette observed her mother going through the motions of birth in an anguished attempt to assist her ungrateful daughter survive her ordeal.[16] Finally, in her state of conflict and unhappiness, Juliette resorted to suicide.

In contrast, Colette learnt how to cope with separation and independence through the love of another woman, the famous Missy (the Marquise of Morny). In the worst moments of her adult life, Colette was able to recollect the bliss, strength and protectiveness of her mother's body, which is why she sought comfort in Missy. To many theorists this kind of replacement is not abnormal because they believe that all women are initially homosexual, since their first love object is also female.[17] Certainly, it benefited Colette and she describes how Missy brought back her deepest feelings for her mother and her determination to be like her. She tells us that through this supportive relationship, she increased her awareness of her own selfhood. It was Missy who gave her a house in Brittany by the sea, where she recreated Sido's hospitable and cheerful home.

Colette's open relationship with Missy was not unusual. Paris had become the mecca of lesbianism in the late nineteenth century — a trend that was not discouraged because it was fashionable among men to see lesbianism as titillating.[18] When she married Willy, Colette knew nothing of the lesbian world of Paris. It was Willy who had encouraged Colette to include some adolescent lesbianism in the Claudine novels, knowing there was a ready voyeuristic audience. Willy tolerated, even encouraged, her lesbian affairs. But as she outgrew the Claudine novels, Colette presented lesbianism, not as seeking the kind of sexual gratification that titillated men like Willy, but as a sisterly refuge under patriarchy.[19]

From Colette's portrayal of her, Missy becomes a moving study of why so many of the unmothered try to mother others.[20] Missy was a neglected, vulnerable child of an aristocratic family, abandoned to abusing servants.[21] In Colette, she found someone to mother and in Sido she found a needed mother figure. Sido accepted Missy as the kind companion of her daughter and her affection for her grew as she saw how protective and generous she was to Colette. She sent her gifts of fresh country eggs and water chestnuts. Sido cared about Colette's happiness and was appalled when Colette forsook her stable relationship with Missy and married the penniless Henry Jouvenel, a baron and the editor of Le Matin. Missy lost Sido too when she lost Colette, and she died derelict and alone.

Colette's feeling of freedom to change husbands, when they did not suit her, might have found some sanction in the fact that Sido had had two husbands but, unlike Sido, she was not lucky the second time. Jouvenel left Colette for a wife with a fortune and because Colette was having an affair with the adolescent son of his first marriage. The son, Bertrand, was willingly seduced by Colette, who initiated him sexually and also mothered him.

Colette continued to deal therapeutically with her uncompleted separation from her mother in her writing. She pursued her relationship with her in Break of Day, where she examined Sido's example, wisdom and bequests to her. Each section of the book begins with a letter from Sido and describes how Colette enriched her own life with her mother's selfhood. Unfortunately, by the mid twentieth-century, this example of a daughter achieving autonomy by consciously modelling herself on her mother became an uncomfortable one — a situation that was discussed in Book 1 and illustrated in Doris Lessing's novel, Martha Quest. [22]

Colette Becomes a Mother

Colette had a daughter, Bel Gazou, by her second husband. Some understanding of Colette the mother comes when she refers to teaching her little daughter embroidery, which she did under pressure from friends, lest she fail as a mother. While friends applauded the nine year old Bel Gazou's application to feminine skills, Colette had her doubts. Her daughter's stillness, while embroidering, suggested repression and subjugation and her silence, separateness from her mother. She also describes the inadequacy all mothers feel in answering Bel Gazou's questions on the rightness of relationships between men and women: "I let it drop. I feel inadequate, self-conscious, displeased with myself. I should have answered differently and I could not think what to say".[23]

Bel Gazou was sent to boarding school, perhaps because her mother wanted her to have more space than she had had, but she became a silent withdrawn child. Nicole Ward Jouve suggests that Colette was more motherly to Bertrand.[24] But we need to know more about Jouvenel and his relationship with his daughter and her mother, before we follow the age old pattern of focusing blame on the mother. Jouve also believes Colette was in some ways ruthless and 'mothered' her writing rather than her daughter. Of course, had Colette been Bel Gazou's father, rather than her mother, the attitude would be less harsh. Fathers are allowed to forgo their parenting responsibility in the interests of their work.[25] One cannot help wondering if perhaps Eliot and Richardson were wise when they decided not to have children, because they saw how much their novels became their 'children' and the consumers of all their creativity.

Traditional Prejudice versus Colette's Positive View of Her Mother

We frequently see the same tendency to mother blaming in the literature about Sido. Some critics present her as destructive because she was too motherly and point to Juliette's suicide and the character of her two sons. One never got over his mother's death. The other never lost his longing for his childhood. These were the offspring of Sido's union with her first husband, a violent man known as 'le Sauvage'. After the death of 'le Sauvage', Sido's second husband, Captain Colette, could not provide a strong nurturing substitute father figure. Perhaps, without Sido, the children may have been utterly destroyed. We hear that she stood up to the violent behaviour of 'le Sauvage' and once threw a burning lamp at him.

It is pretty clear that Colette sought both father and mother substitutes in her husbands.[26] She appears not to have been able to make a satisfactory choice of a male partner until she started living with Maurice Goudeket in 1925. She married him in 1935 and lived with him in Paris until her death in 1954. Like Captain Colette, Goudeket's business ventures floundered. During the Nazi occupation, he was arrested because he was a Jew and put in a camp in Compiègne.[27] Colette remembered that her mother had protected her children from the Prussians and managed to get him out, but he spent the rest of the occupation in fear and hiding. This is said to have contributed to Colette's slow paralysis with arthritis. Pain meant her writing took deep concentration, but like her mother she had plenty of courage and did not give up.

Unlike Richardson, who complained that her mother did not encourage her writing, Colette was aware that her mother believed she had talent for writing and wanted to foster it. She tells us how Sido introduced her children to plants, animals, flowers, woods and birds and taught them their names. From an early age, she saw Sido scribbling in odd corners and Sido's letters to Colette indicate her talent and love for words and images. Colette was greatly influenced by her mother's love of words and it shows in her writing. She developed a special capacity to make words interact and give enticing images of everyday life. It is little wonder that, with gratitude, Colette dedicated her writing to Sido.

With the power of her words, Colette overturned domestic experience and is able to engage us in admiration for the mother on whom she modelled herself. Colette's greatest pride is in her mother's defiance of traditional behaviours which she saw as meaningless, stupid or unkind. She presents her mother's common sense as subversive, because it challenges the entrenched prejudices of the existing social order. Colette tells us how Sido took the dog to Church, kept open house for pregnant servants and stray animals, resisted dogma and was annoyed by the catechism her children were taught. Readers of Colette's stories of her mother are encouraged to admire Sido's original religious and moral convictions and her utter confidence in them.

Colette was never interested in theory. Her talk was never bookish and we are told that even when Sartre and Simone de Beauvoir later came to admire her, she talked to them about fertilisers, baking bread, plants and animals, as her mother would have.[28] As a result, Nicole Ward Jouve describes Colette as the twentieth century recipe against the kind of neurosis, Freud, her contemporary, was describing in women.[29] Colette was totally uninterested in Freud.

The Mothers of Colette and Richardson: A Comparison

Mary Richardson was a courageous mother. She stepped outside the submissive and martyred role that mothers of her time were expected to adopt. She fought for her husband, she fought for her daughters and she fought for her own survival. She was not crushed by the egotism and failures of her husband. She had the courage to flout convention and usurp the dominant position of men if it achieved the best for her daughters and herself. She took setbacks in her stride, including her failed ambitions for her husband and her eldest daughter.

Sido Colette was an original — a kind of omnipotent Mother-Goddess. Whereas neither mother put marriage before their daughter's potential, Sido seemed to be challenging the absurdity of patriarchy. She found it ridiculous that daughters leave their mothers to marry men they hardly know.[30] She didn't mind her children having affairs, but she disapproved of them getting married.[31]

Mary Richardson was more concerned at the loss of potential talent in a world where married women devoted all to their husbands. Her daughter achieved the best of both worlds. She wrote and had a husband who not only provided her with economic security to write, but actively encouraged it.

When Mary Richardson began earning "guineas of her own", she grew in stature.[32] In Colette's family, Sido had guineas of her own from the start. She brought a fortune from her first marriage to her second and Captain Colette squandered it, but it gave Sido a power and status which most mothers did not have. Neither Mary nor Sido did the patriarchal thing and worshipped money for its own sake and neither did their daughters. None of Colette's women characters, who make money by their looks, charm and street wisdom, is affected by their seeming monetary bondage. They never allow their situation to reduce them to commodities or victims.

Probably because of the stature and power their mothers had, both Richardson and Colette suggested new relations between men and women — an equality. We have seen how both Colette's and Richardson's fathers were failures in terms of many of the patriarchal expectations of men. Their fathers were not more powerful or more dominant than their mothers and as a result their daughters had room in which to become independent as females.[33] Walter Richardson's lack of power was contributed to by his insanity, Captain's Colette's by having one leg, which forced him into a sedentary life. Like Walter, he lacked the capacity to realise his ambitions and was a failure to the end. After his death, his family discovered that the bound volumes on his bookshelves contained blank pages. They represented what he wanted to write but never did. Colette wrote her books on those blank pages and recognised her father's bequest to her.

Walter Richardson and Captain Colette both loved their daughters' mothers obviously and openly. Both mothers were endorsed by the patriarchal representatives in their families and, as well, were loving and powerful enough in their own right to give their daughters the confidence to do what they wanted. Captain Colette respected Sido more than Walter did Mary and this may be significant in Colette's open and easy love for her mother. She had her early conflicts with her, but was able to work through these in her writing about her mother and ultimately achieve a lasting respect for her, alongside an acceptance of her fallibility.[34] Richardson's respect for her mother was tinged with resentment for her fallibilities to the end.

One of many marked differences in the childhood development of Richardson and Colette is that Colette's mother told her she was beautiful and this was reinforced constantly in words, actions and affection. Colette was able to take enormous pleasure in her physical self and the feminine body of her mother. In contrast, Richardson, de Beauvoir and Eliot are among many women writers, discussed here, who did not like their own bodies, and this may be crucial to their more difficult relationships with their mothers. If a woman rejects her female body, it is very difficult to respect her mother, who is also female.[35] Whereas de Beauvoir tried to cope with what she felt to be the secondary status of women by escaping into the world of her father and of Jean Paul Sartre and participated in male pursuits,[36] Colette did not find it necessary to abandon her mothers' interests, values and morals, because her female self-esteem was not undermined by example or teaching.

Despite their dissimilarities, there was something about the mothers and childhoods of Richardson and Colette that made them both respect women and have many lasting friendships with women throughout their lives. In *My Apprenticeships*, Colette describes how, not long after her marriage to Willy, she felt jealous when she found him with another young woman who raised a pair of scissors against her. Colette decided not to regard her as the enemy and stretched out her hand. They later became friends.

One could go on to explore many other similarities and differences in the relationship Richardson and Colette had with their mothers, but the significant factors accounting for these will be apparent to the reader in the light of the discussion in Book 1. Suffice it to conclude here that Mary and Sido were two strong and assertive mothers who were in refreshing contrast to the weeping, victimised mothers of previous decades. Their daughters benefited enormously as a result.

Meanwhile, in England, another famous daughter, nine years younger than Colette, had also been exploring her relationship with her mother through fiction. This was Virginia Woolf and the final discussion here of the impact of strong mothers on their daughters, prior to the double bind image of the mid-twentieth century, concerns Virginia and her mother, Julia.

℘

CHAPTER 12

Virginia Woolf

Daughters with Strong Mothers

Virginia Woolf's mother, Julia Stephens, had intelligence and talent. Like most women of her time she was limited to the domestic sphere, but there she had enormous power. She brilliantly managed a complex household of eight children (including one retarded daughter from her second husband's first marriage) and seven servants. She supervised the children, helped in the education of her daughters, controlled the finances and entertained leading writers and intellectuals of the time.

Virginia's Perception of Her Mother

According to Virginia Woolf, her portrayal of Mrs Ramsay, in her novel *To the Lighthouse*, tells us how she and her sister Vanessa perceived their mother. Observation of Mrs Ramsay suggests that Julia enjoyed managing the lives of others and generally had her own way, believing it to be for everyone's good. She gave shape and order to the chaos of family life.[1] She was the pivot, the presence, around which they all revolved, as in Virginia's evocation of her:

> Mrs Ramsay sitting under the rock, with a pad on her knee, writing letters. ... That woman sitting there, writing under the rock resolved everything into simplicity; made these angers, irritations fall off like old rags; she brought together this and that and then this, and so made out of that miserable silliness and spite ... something — this scene on the beach for example, this moment of friendship and liking — which survived.[2]

Julia wished her daughters to have a more systematic and adequate education than she had received. She and her husband agreed that daughters should be as well educated as sons, have independent interests and pursue a profession. Unfortunately, the agreement was more theoretical than practical. While Virginia's brother, Thoby, went to Cambridge as a matter of course, as was typical in middle-class families in Edwardian England, Virginia, the daughter, studied at home. Women of her time were expected to be available at all times for the social demands of their men. Her father was no exception, expecting his daughters to preside at the teas and dinners for his numerous literary visitors. Nevertheless, Julia took her daughters' education in hand and they were given every encouragement to read widely and, in such a literary household, had advantages many other daughters did not.

That the model of Julia, as a woman, invoked admiration in her daughters is clear. Virginia, for one, reflected — perhaps strove after — her mother's accomplishments. Julia had a passion for literature, she wrote stories for her children and published one book with a tone similar to that of Virginia Woolf's essays.[3]

The outstanding memories that both Vanessa and Virginia retained of their mother were of her beauty both in appearance and character and her remarkable insight and intuition. These images are often evoked in *To The Lighthouse* and the following passage suggests how remotely beautiful Virginia found her mother and how she admired her and longed for her attention. It is given expression through the effect Mrs Ramsay has on the tedious Mr Tansley:

> …she was the most beautiful person he had ever seen. With stars in her eyes and veils in her hair, with cyclamen and wild violets — what nonsense was he thinking. She was fifty at least; she had eight children. Stepping through fields of flowers and taking to her breast buds that had broken and lambs that had fallen; with the stars in her eyes and the wind in her hair — He took her bag.[4]

The reverence their mother's beauty and empathy aroused and her confidence in her role was recaptured in another passage about Mrs Ramsay:

> And like some queen who, finding her people gathered in the hall, looks down upon them, and descends among them, and acknowledges their tributes silently, and accepts their devotion and their prostration before her ... she went down, and crossed the hall and bowed her head very slightly, as if she accepted what they would not say: their tribute to her beauty.[5]

According to all accounts, Julia was tall, unfashionable in dress and as beautiful as Virginia believed her to be. In 1867, at 21, she fell in love with and married a handsome and courteous lawyer, Herbert Duckworth. Swiftly she bore two children, George and Stella, and was pregnant with a third, Gerald, when Herbert died suddenly in 1870. The continued longing in secret moments for this early life, with its less complex and more straightforward love than she experienced in her second marriage, is fleetingly evoked by Virginia in her portrait of Mrs Ramsay.

Widowed at age 24, Julia was prevented by the newborn child and well-meaning friends from giving full expression to her grief.[6] She became morbid and longed for death. In 1878, she married a neighbour, the intellectual man of letters, Leslie Stephens, son of a puritanically astringent couple and descendant of a long line of intellectual, legal and literary men. His scientific humanism, love of literature and agnosticism, attracted Julia, for they confirmed her own ideas.

Her Father Influenced Virginia's View of Her Mother and Herself

Like Mr Ramsay in *To The Lighthouse*, Leslie was an exceedingly difficult and demanding man, utterly dependent upon women for all his needs. On the one hand, he was affectionate with his children, setting them examples in regularity and dedication and, on the other, melancholic, self-pitying, self-absorbed and full of unsatiated ambition. He was touchy, irritable and suffered poor health. He made rapacious emotional demands on those close to him, particularly Julia, from whom he hated to be parted. He worshipped Julia. Like Mrs Ramsay she, in turn, "looked after his every need, soothing away his irritations and warming his intelligence with her sensibility".[7]

Through the character of Mrs Ramsay, Virginia pondered what this cost her mother:

> Nothing would make Mr Ramsay move on. There he stood demanding sympathy.
>
> Mrs Ramsay, who had been sitting loosely, folding her son in her arm, braced herself, and, half turning, seemed to raise herself with an effort, and at once to pour erect into the air a rain of energy, a column of spray, looking at the same time animated and alive as if all her energy were being fused into force, burning and illuminating (quietly though she sat, taking up her stocking again) and into this delicious fecundity, this fountain and spray of life, the fatal sterility of the male plunged itself, like a beak of brass, barren and bare. He wanted sympathy.[8]

Leslie projected a public image of calm and reasonableness, but in private expected subordination from his daughters and self-indulgently threw tyrannous tantrums which he clearly and immaturely wanted his wife to moderate and contain.[9] *To The Lighthouse* gives insights into Virginia's resulting ambivalent attitude toward him. Through Cam (with whom she identifies her childish self) she contemplates her father:

> For no one attracted her more; his hands were beautiful to her and his feet, and his voice, and his words, and his haste, and his temper, and his oddity and his passion... But what remained intolerable she thought ... was that crass blindness and tyranny of his which had poisoned her childhood and raised bitter storms, so that even now she woke in the night trembling with rage and remembered some command of his; some insolence:'Do this', 'Do that', his dominance: his 'Submit to me'.[10]

Virginia loved her father intensely and found it difficult to resist him, all of which is worked through in her description in *To The Lighthouse* of Mr Ramsay and his relationship with James and Lily Briscoe.

Alma Halbert Bond, in a psychobiography of Virginia Woolf, makes some interesting points about Virginia's relationship with her father.[11] She believes that Virginia's recognition that those close to her father had to shut their eyes to his shortcomings and had to flatter and admire him, while ignoring his self-deceptions, was a contributing factor to her personality disorders. For psychological survival, children of such parents have to distort reality, in order to maintain the idealised image required by the parent.[12] As Virginia described it, Leslie's demanding, mercilessly dominating and emotionally, dishonest attitudes left her little room to exist — to be an individual separate from him.

Virginia's way of coping with her ambivalent attitude to her father was to identify with him. She turned her rage toward him against herself, in order to keep her love for him (and her mother) intact. The pity of it is that she made a self-destructive choice to solve her conflicts. By taking him as her model, she learnt that cruelty and self-indulgence, at the expense of others, is personally and socially acceptable. She adopted his fluctuating moods and is described by her nephew, Quentin Bell, as a difficult person, who gave people clashing and confusing messages. Identifying with her father did not solve her problems and years later she still carried her inner rage against him. After his death she wrote in her diary: " Father's birthday ... His life would have entirely ended mine. ... No writing, no books ...".[13]

Jane Lilienfield is another critic who looks at the influence of Virginia's father. She points out that, after his death, Virginia's position as a writer was as powerful and prestigious as her father's had been and she questions whether this achievement did not make her feel that she was at last equal as his adversary, as she had never been during his life.[14] She argues that this realisation added to Virginia's confidence.

Phyllis Rose also feels that we must pay attention to the role Virginia's father played in her behaviour and personality. She agrees with the point I am making that Virginia's father was typically patriarchal in his view of women: he combined a theoretical veneration of women with actual condescension and harassment, demanding their total dedication to his needs.[15] In this context, picture a young daughter observing a father, who requires his wife to give up her own needs in order to meet his self-centred claims.[16] In the normal flow of events, a little girl chooses to identify with her mother but, to Virginia, her mother appeared to have surrendered her selfhood and her identity to her husband. This was a nightmare for Virginia, who already feared that her will and identity might be obliterated by her father. In To The Lighthouse, she endeavoured to work through these disturbing confusions and found that she could love her mother without modelling herself on her emotionally. She also began to understand that, despite the restrictions and injustices of her life, her mother had managed to construct a belief system that gained her some selfhood — albeit a belief system that Virginia could not accept for herself.

Virginia's Craving for Maternal Attention

Alongside her fear of engulfment by her father and her dread of becoming the martyred female, Virginia was also obsessed with securing her mother's love. The year after her second marriage, Julia bore Vanessa, the next year Julian Thoby, in 1882, Virginia and in 1883, Adrian. If we are to accept Bond's psychoanalytic interpretation, which acknowledges that jealousy is an emotion that appears in infancy, then Virginia must have seen the newborn Adrian as a rival. When she felt that she had been replaced by her new brother, in order to continue receiving expressions of love from her mother, Virginia gradually learnt to control her anger with her. As she grew older, she pushed the true reason for her anger from consciousness and turned her anger against herself. This left her vulnerable to depression and psychological collapse.[17] It inhibited the learning of good self-esteem and autonomy and the healthy control of emotions and impulses. As a result, the childish rage occasioned by her father's demands and her repression of her anger with her mother lay smouldering within, until it finally burst forth to power her manic attacks.[18]

The frequent open commitment of her mother to others in her large step-family caused Virginia a great deal of pain. In her autobiographical notes, she captures the childish longing this situation aroused by writing that she felt as though her mother "shone out of reach" when she craved for her attention. "Can I remember ever being alone with her for more than a few minutes? Someone was always interrupting".[19] The hypothesis about insufficient attention from her mother, whether founded in fact or not, certainly influenced how she saw herself and her behaviour. In some ways, she adopted the characteristics of a rejected child; for example, tantrums were frequent and there was excessive seeking of the attention of her surrogate mother-come-sister, Vanessa, throughout her life.[20]

Bond is certain that, although Julia Stephens had to ration her attention to her children by the time they were older, she ensured that she was a super-mother to them when they were babies and provided them with a luxurious, sensual atmosphere. Virginia later claimed that her memories of her babyhood were idyllic and "the base upon which life stands". She described one of her first memories as a state of intoxication with her mother: "My mother would come out on her balcony in a white dressing gown. There were passion flowers growing on the wall; they were great starry blossoms, with purple streaks and large green buds".[21] From this intoxication, the uniqueness of Virginia Woolf emerged.

Her feelings and longings continued beyond childhood and in *To The Lighthouse* were given expression through the character of Lily Briscoe, with whom Virginia identified her adult self. She describes Lily, returning to the Ramsays' holiday house several years after Mrs Ramsay's death, hoping to find some intimation of her presence in the old rooms and in the garden — something to hold onto and give her comfort. Because she cannot find what she needs, the old memories of Mrs Ramsay's overcommitment to others overwhelm her. "Mrs Ramsay! Mrs Ramsay! she cried feeling the old horror come back — to want and not to have. Could she inflict that still?"[22]

Virginia's yearning for her mother's attention was aggravated by the patriarchal preference for sons -a situation into which women had been inducted, often betraying their daughters in the process. Just as Mrs Ramsay prefers her youngest son, James, to her daughter, Cam, so Virginia's mother was seen to love her youngest son, Adrian, best.[23] Again, if we take Mrs Ramsay as the replica, then Virginia's mother felt that sons and husbands — men in general — needed to be protected, while women and their daughters could take care of themselves.[24] This was a source of Virginia's resentment against her mother, and its complexity was therapeutically explored in her novels about mothers and families.

Virginia also describes how difficult she found it to separate from her mother and how she used her writing to achieve it. She described her mother as "The Angel in the House" — intensely sympathetic, utterly unselfish, sacrificing herself daily and excelling in all the difficult arts of family life. As Virginia wrote of Mrs Ramsay, so great was her mother's capacity...

> ...to surround and protect, there was scarcely a shell of herself left for her to know herself by; all was so lavished and spent; and James, as he stood stiff between her knees felt her rise in a rosy-flowered fruit tree laid with leaves and dancing boughs into which the beak of brass, the arid scimitar of his father, the egotistical man, plunged and smote, demanding sympathy.[25]

As with most mothers at the turn of the nineteenth and the beginning of the twentieth centuries, Julia's sacrifice of her life to others had been ingrained in her from her childhood and her charity and goodness to her neighbours, her lessers and her extended family, knew no bounds.[26] Similarly, Mrs Ramsay attends to the poor and needy in her life, and writing about her helped Virginia to put these attributes in perspective so that she could reject them for herself without rejecting her mother. The process of learning to see herself as other than her mother — to separate from her — was one of the keys to Virginia's early talent as a book reviewer and later as a writer.

Virginia's Writing About the Loss of Her Mother Was Therapeutic

In 1895, when Virginia was 13, her mother died of rheumatic fever. Virginia, a vulnerable, sensitive child, experienced a severe breakdown not long after. The loss of her mother was compounded by other factors. At 13, daughters are on the verge of forming their adult identities. As *The Diary of Anne Frank* records so well, at this stage they are frequently critical of their mothers, because they are seeking to define their own values and hopes as emerging, independent persons.[27] To lose a parent at this critical stage can arouse guilt about remembered criticisms or a mistaken belief that insufficient love may have caused the death. These are common immediate reactions after loss, even in the strongest of children and adults. Loss through death can also arouse anger stemming from a feeling — albeit unfounded — that the parent has abandoned them.[28] A combination of these reactions may mean that a vulnerable child becomes overwhelmed with an unmanageable guilt.

At first, Virginia could not fathom the anger she felt at her mother's death and sought meaning through her exploration of several of the characters, whom she created in her novels. An example is Delia in *The Years*, who denies her feelings and represses her anger at her mother's death.[29] Another is Lily Briscoe who openly expresses her vehement feelings toward Mrs Ramsay: "Giving, giving, giving, she had died — and had left all this. Really she was angry with Mrs Ramsay".[30]

Much of Virginia's writing explores the emptiness her mother's death left for her. Again it is captured through the character of Lily Briscoe and her reactions upon returning to the Ramsay's empty holiday house, years after Mrs Ramsay's death:

Suddenly, the empty drawing-room steps, the frill of the chair inside, the puppy tumbling on the terrace, the whole wave and whisper of the garden became like curves and arabesques flourishing round a centre of complete emptiness. 'What does it mean? How do you explain it all?'[31]

In the process of coming to terms with the loss of her mother, Virginia exquisitely evokes the presence, the lingering meaning, the wistfulness of a lost dream, the questioning of what her mother's true self was, through the character of Mrs Ramsay, as in the following two passages:

But what have I done with my life?', thought Mrs Ramsay, taking her place at the head of the table, and looking at all the plates making white circles on it.[32]

One wanted most some secret sense, fine as air, with which to steal through the keyhole and discover as she sat silent, knitting talking, her thoughts, her imagination, her desires. What did the hedge mean to her, what did the garden mean to her, what did it mean to her when a wave broke? ... And then what stirred and trembled in her mind when the children cried, 'How's that. How's that?' cricketing? She would stop knitting for a second. She would look intent...[33]

Virginia also examined her negative feelings about her parents. She said she found it a disturbing process until she came to understand that she did not have to retain an idealised image of them in order to be a good person.

She claimed that by turning the light onto Mr and Mrs Ramsay she did for herself what psychoanalysts do for their patients[34] — in other words she became her own therapist For example, she was able to use Lily Briscoe's criticism of Mrs Ramsay to explore her resentment of her mother. Through her, she found it easier to accept her own belief that her mother was not perfect and to recognise the hypocrisy, the unattainability and the ambivalence of the patriarchal image of the perfect mother which sets mothers and daughters in conflict.[35] This acceptance and recognition allowed a much less demanding view of her mother and herself.

Through Lily, she could also come to terms with the fact that there were probably people who disliked her mother very much or found her beauty too much of a good thing or criticised her for her weakness with her husband and for being too earnest, remote and grave. Then there was her mother's conventional attitude to marriage. Clearly, Virginia had mixed attitudes to marriage and resented her mother's belief that marriage is a superior condition. Through Lily Briscoe, Virginia is able to gloat that the marriage Mrs Ramsay encouraged between Minta and Paul failed as a model of fidelity in the Ramsays' sense, yet was a friendship between a man and a woman in a way that Mrs Ramsay could not comprehend.[36]

Re-inventing her family in *To The Lighthouse*, enabled Virginia to expose the patriarchal traditions of marriage and the male-female relationships of her time, which she found suffocating — even destructive. This was therapeutic because she could also recognise their complexity. She acknowledges the love of sacrifice that lit up many women's faces, including Mrs Ramsay's, when their emotions were drained and they had to cope with the mundaness of family life or attempt to stem the tempest created by raging husbands and banging doors and flying plates. She observed their plaintiveness, weariness and an inability to overcome the violent and stormy behaviour of their menfolk. But she also observed that all this was combined with such love between her mother and father, that it took precedence over the children. Her portrayal of the profound jealousy that this occasioned in Mrs Ramsay's small son is another complexity and an insightful look into the mind of a child. It perhaps symbolises how all the Ramsay or Stephens children felt. For Virginia, writing about James' jealousy, was no doubt therapeutic.

Mrs Ramsay's daughters dreamed of a place, a life, a freedom, that was different from their mother's, yet they were proud of her and could admiringly observe: "That's my mother". With this ability to acknowledge and accept her mother in her own context, Virginia's criticism of her mother, through Lily Briscoe, helped her go beyond her limiting example to her own identity. It inspired her later novels, in which she continued to portray the complexity of family life, and came to realise that her family and her mother were not unique, but an expression of the limitations of patriarchal relationships. Her father's and Mr Tansley's male chauvinistic attitudes to women, their belief in their sensibility, not their intelligence, are exposed for questioning. The patriarchal dichotomisation of the potential of men for intelligence and women for intuition is recognised as limiting both sexes.[37]

As Virginia saw it, there is the inner barrenness of the male, who pursues truth and does not consider feeling, particularly apparent in both Mr Tansley's and Mr Ramsay's insensitivity to little James's hope to visit the lighthouse. The female may embrace feeling but there is the restriction of intellectual subordination. The therapy for Virginia in writing *To The Lighthouse* was that she allowed Lily Briscoe to rebel and advance beyond the model provided by the Mrs Ramsay she loved.

That Virginia constructively worked through her relationship with her mother in her writing is not always recognised. Patriarchal critics find it hard to give up mother-blaming. Julia is blamed for Virginia's mental illness. It is said she was too remote and had too many children to give each one proper attention. Even her time-consuming kindnesses to others is described as a deficiency — all of which demonstrates that mothers cannot win under any circumstances under patriarchy and how nebulous and rapacious its standards of motherly perfection are. Julia Stephens, like Mrs Ramsay, brilliantly protected and cared for her husband and his household, bore seven children and carried out charitable works, in the best traditions of her time.

Julia has also been condemned for sometimes leaving her children in the care of no less than seven servants and a husband, while she attended her ailing mother. But all the facts need to be considered. Julia's father had been a leading physician in Calcutta. Julia's mother, Maria Prattle, had to cope with a man who was completely dedicated to others, which meant that when his wife, due to ill health, had to return to England with their children, he did not rejoin her until his retirement, seven years later. The mother appears to have displaced her need for some return of affection onto her daughters and turned to them for sympathy. For this, she is seen in the 'mother is all' tradition as totally damaging, while the father's absence is little emphasised.

Her illnesses, during which Julia cared for her, also need to be set in the context of the times. Edwardian patriarchy saw women as neither strong nor stable creatures and ill health was something it trained husbands to accept in their wives, rather than face up to their need for love. This provided the script for Julia's relationship with her mother, which centred around ill health, either her mother's or someone else's. If this was the convention for expressing or achieving concern, to which women were relegated, why see it as abnormal?

The relationship between Julia and her mother has also been condemned as 'too close'. What does 'too close' mean and for whom? Was it too close for Julia, or was it too close for her husband, who was left to stand on his own two feet, without his nurturing wife, from time to time? Why must a daughter's closeness with her mother be necessarily regarded as unhealthy by patriarchy?[38] Julia cared for her mother. She also enjoyed nursing for the power and sense of achievement it gave her[39] and perhaps it was a recuperative 'time out', which provided strength to survive with her husband.

More recently Virginia's relationship with her mother is being freed of these patriarchal myopisms, omissions and biases and seen in its greater complexity. Moreover, Virginia's admiration for her mother is now recognised, as is her acknowledgement of the forces of patriarchy which limited her. She explored these, built upon them and moved beyond them. To dwell on patriarchal myopisms about Julia's mothering is to ignore Virginia Woolf's considerable contribution as an independent woman.

As with most patriarchal analyses, the role of the father in his child's development is often ignored. We frequently hear how fond Virginia's father was of his children, but the general recognition of his emotionally draining egocentricity is rarely considered in relation to his daughter's developing selfhood. Only a few researchers question whether his demanding behaviour may have instilled in Virginia overwhelming doubts about herself, which contributed to her schizophrenia and her punishing voices. Neither, until recently, was there much questioning of why a father, who worked at home, could not have been adequate to his children, when his wife was absent.

The Victorian Patriarchal Family was a Dangerous Place

Another factor that needs some attention is that Virginia lived in a family which was a second marriage for both her mother and father, each of whom had lost their first spouse through death. For children, step-families involve changed hierarchies, jealousies, rivalries and hard to manage conflicts.[40] In fact, there were vast differences in the personalities and values of Virginia's half siblings from her mother's first marriage and those of her second, to which Virginia belonged. In particular, Virginia and her sister, Vanessa, had to contend with an overbearing half brother and his indecent sexual explorations[41] and perhaps, after the death of their mother, protracted incest. Children do not always report sexual abuse, even in the best of families, and it can have lasting effects of identity confusion and self-loathing. These things could have played a role in the punishing voices which Virginia experienced in her periods of mental anguish and indeed she hinted at it.[42]

Louise DeSalvo, who has written a fascinating insight into Virginia's childhood and adolescence, believes that most patriarchal biographers have not read the facts clearly portrayed in Virginia Woolf's juvenile writings. She argues that Virginia had to deal with trauma and threat and her responses were a way of coping and should not be seen as mad.[43] Even if one looks at Virginia's most famous juvenile contribution,"The Experience of Pater-familias" in 1892 in the family journal, "Hyde Park News", it shows that very early in life, she understood the violence that patriarchy does to children. DeSalvo believes and provides evidence that Virginia was reared in a household where sexual abuse, sexual violence and abusive behaviour were the pattern, as they were in many Victorian households. This is no doubt why every child in Virginia Woolf's novels is either betrayed or ignored or at risk or abused. Virginia wrote about what it was like to be a child in a Victorian patriarchal family, long before child abuse was legitimised as a cause for concern. We have seen how patriarchy denied child abuse in order to hide its inherent violence, so there is little wonder that patriarchal writers have wanted to overlook this aspect of Virginia's life.

Surrogate Mothers

On the positive side, Virginia Woolf's life demonstrates the important role that surrogate mothers can play, albeit often unacknowledged. Virginia had several surrogate mothers who figured strongly in her life. One of the first was her half sister, Stella.

During Julia's frequent absences, due to her mother's illnesses, Stella, the elder daughter of the first marriage, took charge and mothered the children of the second marriage. It was not an easy task for one so young. For example, Virginia had a volatile nature, was somewhat fractious and possessed a vivid imagination. Even at five years, she entertained her siblings with elaborate tales. One gets the impression of intense childish emotions, needing an understanding adult to establish right and order. The father who worked at home, while not unfond of his children, favoured reclusion and attended to his major work, *The History of English Thought in the Eighteenth Century.*

Stella was a daughter in her mother's image, utterly dependent on her and emulating her selfless concern for others. There is some evidence that Julia saw her as an extension of herself and was unduly harsh to her as a result, which added to Stella's suffering passive affection for her. Julia was as demanding of Stella as her own mother had been of her. But, if she was like Mrs Ramsay, we also know that she was not unaware of her own inadequacies and the pathos of her daughter's devotion.

> But she let them take their time to choose: she let Rose particularly, take up this and that, and hold her jewels against the black dress, for this little ceremony of choosing jewels, which was gone through every night, was what Rose liked best, she knew. She had some hidden reason of her own for attaching great importance to this choosing what her mother was to wear. What was the reason Mrs Ramsay wondered, standing still to let her clasp the necklace she had chosen, divining through her own past, some deep, some buried, some quite speechless feeling that one had for one's mother at Rose's age. Like all feelings felt for oneself, Mrs Ramsay thought, it made one sad. It was so inadequate, what one could give

in return, and what Rose felt was quite out of proportion to anything she actually was.[44]

Because she was the eldest and so much like her, Stella was immediately cast in her mother's role, after her death. As surrogate mother, she faced the same demands as her mother had, which left the children still in second place to their father. In a similar fashion to Mr Ramsay, after the death of his wife, Leslie was inconsolable and self-pitying and the house at Hyde Park Gate was plunged into a nightmarish gloom. Virginia described their lives as increasingly restricted by her father's demands and said they were forever battling against his interference in their affairs.

He was as rapacious of Stella as he had been of Julia, and was reluctant about her marriage to Jack Hills, a young solicitor. After her honeymoon, Stella became critically ill and Virginia, at 15, faced with this second loss of a mother figure, was distraught. Inevitably, she had an ambivalent attitude to her saintly, mothering, older half sister and, once she believed Stella would recover fully, her diary indicates she was not always willing to help in her convalescence.[45] Quentin Bell believes that Stella's ill health and Virginia's mental health were linked in this period, and that one special aspect of Virginia's anxiety and feeling of guilt toward her surrogate mother-sister was a fear of going out in the streets of London.[46]

Stella recovered, became pregnant and died suddenly later in the same year. Vanessa believed her death had much to do with her inability to live without her mother.[47] Few critics have explored the possibility that it had something to do with guilt, arising from the emotional rapaciousness of her step-father, who'd made her feel that she was selfishly abandoning him in wishing to marry. DeSalvo also reminds us that there is evidence that the half brothers sexually abused Stella as much as they did Virginia and Vanessa and believes that her feelings of shame accounted for her withdrawn behaviour and illness.

After her death, the legend of Stella's saintliness and that of her mother Julia was a constant and gloomy theme in the family and must have exacerbated guilty feelings about past unkindnesses in an adolescent as vulnerable as Virginia was. Moreover, the house at Hyde Park Gate was inundated with Virginia's extended family — a family replete with the usual quota of saintly mothers in the Victorian mould. Exhausted and washed out, they carried the weight of their families with courage and punished them with their sacrifice by manipulating guilt — their only weapon in their oppression.

Vanessa then filled Stella's place as surrogate mother of the household. Vanessa was in many ways also like her mother and Virginia's relationship with her, over the years, varied from good close periods to more difficult ones. It seems that Virginia demanded of her the time she'd not had with her mother and was frequently intrusive. She was often jealous of others for whom Vanessa cared.[48]

Bond's psychobiographical research suggests that Vanessa and Virginia had a sadomasochistic relationship, which began in early childhood, when Virginia found that her mother was unavailable and turned to her siblings, particularly Vanessa. The more Vanessa and Thoby teased her, the more desperate Virginia became in her attempts to make her sister love her. As they grew older, for all the reasons outlined here, neither Vanessa nor Virginia were able to develop a secure sense of their own selfhood. As Bond points out, "Individuals unsure of their identity are afraid to love a fully available person, because of their fear of losing what fragile sense of self remains. A sadomasochistic relationship is a halfway measure that puts distance between two individuals who are involved with each other".[49] That this was understood by Virginia is exemplified by Jenny in *The Waves*, who says, "Our hatred is almost indistinguishable from our love".

Nevertheless, Vanessa served as enough of a mother substitute and the relationship partially satisfied both, without threatening the fragile autonomy of either. Virginia would demand some demonstration of love and affection and would nag, until Vanessa reluctantly gave in to her pleas. But the insatiability of Virginia's neediness for love could not be endured indefinitely. To quote Bond, "There frequently comes an instance when the underdog wakens to reality and belatedly seeks to rescue his or her selfhood."[50] Thus at times Vanessa rejected Virginia.

Vanessa had so many demands on her, it was difficult to be herself. For example, like women of her class, she was expected to be at home at four in the afternoon everyday to serve tea to her father's guests, even though she had a hard-won place as an art student in the Painting School of the Royal Academy.

According to Virginia, her father had learnt from his mother, that he could expect care and commiseration from women, and pity had figured in her mother's decision to marry him. Like a spoilt child, he expected others to restrain his rampant egotism and rages.[51] Julia, Stella and Vanessa resorted to small deceptions to rid him of irrational anxieties, just as Mrs Ramsay did with her husband in *To The Lighthouse*. Little wonder his daughters, Vanessa and Virginia, were described as shy, aloof and silent.[52]

Leslie Stephens was given a knighthood for his contributions to literature and died of abdominal cancer two years later. Vanessa was relieved by her father's death and flung herself into her painting and other interests with new vigour. Virginia, now 22, who had formed a special relationship with him in his last years, felt guilty that she had not given him the affection he demanded and was distressed by Vanessa's indifference. During her next bout of mental instability, this developed into hatred and distrust of her. This may have been a projection of her own guilt because there is evidence of Virginia's immense relief at her father's death, "For so long as he lived, he left her no room to exist".[53]

No doubt Virginia resisted her father's demand for sympathy, as Lily Briscoe did Mr Ramsay's, and felt determined, confused and inadequate as a result. Guilt, as discussed earlier, is not uncommon after the death of a parent or spouse. It can result in serious breakdown, when guilt has become so much part of one's personality that one cannot control it. Thus, in this next breakdown, we may see the likely impact of Leslie's rages and demands on Virginia. Even Vanessa dreamed that she had murdered him.

To escape the gloom that had become habitual in their father's house, Vanessa moved the family to Gordon Square, Bloomsbury, soon after he died. The new house, its decor and furniture, represented freedom and a less cluttered and restricted life. When she was well enough, Virginia came there with great pleasure, but was a ceaseless source of anxiety to her sister. However, it is worth pointing out that the psychoanalytic interpretations of Virginia's behaviour, given in this chapter by such as Alma Bond, were not yet in vogue and her doctor believed her nervous condition resulted from a physical disorder and recommended good food and rest.

In Bloomsbury, the atmosphere changed from the male-dominated atmosphere of their father's household to a socially and intellectually free atmosphere. Thoby brought his intellectual friends from Cambridge and there began the famous "Thursday Evenings", which sowed the seeds for the Bloomsbury set. Here Virginia and Vanessa met the men they later married: Leonard Woolf and Clive Bell.

Leonard's and Virginia's marriage was punctuated by Virginia's periods of mental instability, in which she became lost in a world of mind-tormenting demons. Amidst these, there were stretches of creative inspiration, in which Leonard Woolf felt she "left the ground" to give forth a "lyrical description of an event, place, or person".[54] It seems that Virginia and Leonard were a successful couple, each compensating for the shortcomings of the other.[55] In the Woolf household, Virginia played the dominating, self-centred role of her father and Leonard the sympathetic, supportive role of Julia, Leslie's long-suffering wife. In the case of the Stephens, the pecking order was based on gender. In the marriage of Virginia and Leonard, it was based on religious background, for he was Jewish. According to Phyllis Rose, "She managed to turn the tables of Victorian patriarchy, but did so by substituting one form of bigotry by another".[56] Ultimately, Virginia became disillusioned with Leonard, lost his support and was unable to function. His departure set off the rage she had suppressed against her father all her life and was a contributing factor in her suicide.[57] Suicide may also have been a means of avoiding identification with her ageing father: "I cannot bear to become the wretch my father became when he reached my stage of life".[58]

It was during her creative periods, after her marriage in 1912, and with the nurturance given by her husband and a number of women friends, that Virginia completed her first novel, *The Voyage Out* (1915).

Virginia and Vita

One of Virginia's most famous surrogate mothers was the friend of her early twenties, Violet Dickinson, who gave her the job of reviewing for *The Times*, which provided her with some initial confidence. Violet encouraged Virginia's talent for writing and nursed her when she was ill. Later Virginia became passionately involved with Vita Sackville-West, who was in many ways like her sister, Vanessa and her mother. Vita was a mother, an artist, socially prominent, restless and magnetic. By now, Virginia was an acknowledged, experimental writer and could present herself as witty and successful to Vita, so the attachment had its triumphant aspects. It may also have given opportunity to challenge and overcome the aloofness and distance of both her mother and Vanessa and thereby enhanced her growing self-confidence. Lilienfield asks whether a sexual relationship with a woman similar to her sister, Vanessa, and her mother, Julia, acted out a buried fantasy of physical closeness with the mother beyond her reach.[59]

Whatever its basis, the relationship with Vita has occasioned much salacious probing by patriarchal writers and the inevitable casting of a close relationship between women in the heterosexual model. It certainly involved sensual attraction and, according to Nicolson, Vita's son, perhaps two or three passionate beddings, which need understanding in the context of the independent romantic bohemianism of the women's movements of the early twentieth century.[60] He is certain that the physical element of their friendship was tentative and not very successful, lasting only a few months. A letter written by Vita to her husband Harold suggests that sexuality was not its prime purpose:

> I love Virginia — as who wouldn't? But really, my sweet one, one's love for Virginia is a very different thing; a mental thing, a spiritual thing, if you like.[61]

Nicolson portrays the value of the relationship, when he describes how Harold, Vita's husband, was as grateful to Virginia for enriching Vita as Vita was herself. As for Virginia, she wrote that Vita, "lavishes on me the maternal protection which, for some reason is what I have always most wished for from everyone."[62]

Bond doesn't agree with Nicolson's description of Vita's and Virginia's sexual relationship. After examination of Virginia's diaries and letters within a psychoanalytic framework, Bond believes it was a sexually passionate one and continued for many years. Whatever the truth of it, she agrees to the value of the relationship and goes further to describe Vita as the love of Virginia's life. She describes the two women as programmed to each other by similar sadomasochistic experiences in childhood. Vita, who was unable to remain faithful to anyone, duplicated Virginia's relationship with Vanessa, in the sense that Virginia was always the one who pleaded for love, while both Vita and Vanessa resisted her demands. Virginia expressed a conscious pleasure in the small abuses Vita caused her to suffer.[63]

However, there were therapeutic aspects to Virginia's relationship with Vita. Vita admired her literary genius and this enabled Virginia to win her back in a way she could not win back her mother after her death. Through Vita's departures and returns, she mastered the loss of her mother and sisters again and again. She learnt to cope with jealousy more effectively through anger, rather than depression. She unearthed her original anger and its source and through her love for Vita was able to integrate a mother figure into a loving relationship and put her conflict with her mother at rest. She discovered her love for her mother was the bedrock of her creativity. Love was also the basis on which her life stood and the loss of Vita's love, with her final departure, perhaps ended her life.[64]

Vita sparked a most creative period in Virginia's life and inspired the writing of some of her greatest works: *Mrs Dalloway*, 1925; *To The Lighthouse*, 1927; *A Room of One's Own*, 1929 and *The Waves*, 1931. As long as Virginia was in love, her creativity flourished. Without it, she felt she lost the art of writing. She was also driven by her father's perfectionism and her standards were so high, that she rarely regarded her work as satisfactory. Her suicide headed off the supreme disaster — that the quality of her work would deteriorate further.[65]

Vita herself had a conflicting relationship with her mother and their true selves were hidden behind the masks of motherhood and daughterhood.[66] Her mother, Lady Sackville, had contended with her husband's chronic infidelities and his sullenness by forming her own liaisons with prominent and wealthy men. Thus, Vita had two parental models of infidelity, which she acted out in her behaviour with Virginia. Like Virginia, she was engaged in a never-ending search for unconditional love. In her case, this was partly because she'd believed her mother couldn't love her because she was an ugly, sloppy child and in order to get some semblance of love, Vita constructed a false self. She acted the part of the ideal daughter and began the never-ending search for unconditional love for her true self. Virginia Woolf came closest to meeting this need, but Vita was not able to accept what she had to offer, because she'd neither resolved her relationship with her mother, nor learnt to fully accept herself. Instead, she used Virginia to stand in for her mother and sought revenge by abandoning her.

Virginia Woolf's story is both a celebration of mothers and a cautionary tale of the tragedy of the failure to establish an independent selfhood. It includes fathers and siblings and surrogate mothers, jealousy, hate and love. It engenders discussion and illustration of almost every aspect of the mother-daughter relationship which has been explored in this book.

☙

Conclusion

Casting Off the Strait-Jackets

The life stories and writings of Richardson, Colette and Virginia Woolf give us an insightful summary of some of the major facets of the real life psychology of mothers and daughters, which have been addressed in Book I. We see the influence of the patterns set in childhood in which fathers play such an important role. We are reminded of our own longings and confusions in adolescence and recall our early struggles for autonomy which had more to do with ourselves than anyone else. As adults, we see the value of working through mother-blaming and the futility of trying to be the perfect daughter.

The importance of self-esteem for good mother-daughter relationships is vividly underlined in the accounts of the lives of Colette, Richardson and Woolf. Colette had most opportunities to develop good self-esteem in her childhood. She was not simply an empty vessel into which self-esteem was poured by her mother. She worked on it herself. She struggled to develop her autonomy. As she became more confident and sure of herself, she could honour her mother for what she was. She accepted her mother's fallibilities and saw the humour of them. She took pride in their battles.

Each of these writers, and Colette most of all, makes it clear that within the patriarchal family structure, mothers are the catalysts for their daughters' growing autonomy and independence. Patriarchal writers describe the conflicts which this generates, negatively. Some describe them as destructive. In fact, conflicts between mothers and daughters are mostly constructive. Without them a daughter would remain an infant. A blind adoring relationship would leave us little girls for the rest of our lives. Mothers are usually secretive about their conflicts with their daughters and react by feeling guilty that they have failed. Perhaps they should boast about them for what they are — a robust impetus to autonomy and individuality. Colette took pride in the conflicts between herself and her mother. She saw them as constructive, as human and as humorous. Contemporary women writers such as Attwood, Winterson and Wandor are doing likewise.

Resolving the unfinished business of childhood is part of the essence of adult growth. It makes us independent and autonomous persons. With perfect mothers, no unfinished business and no need to work through relationships, we'd all be stuck in infantilism. Colette would say, "Thank God for my imperfect mother".

Patriarchal psychology has taught us that the best thing to do is to break free of our mothers. Not true, says Colette. Her mother told her repeatedly that she was her creation and Colette heard the pride in her mother's voice and felt she was special. She expanded her selfhood with a sense of continuity in learning from her mother's skills and values. She made it clear that working through her relationships with her mother was an essential voyage of self-discovery and self-development. To her it was as much a part of becoming a person as learning to read or speak was.

Colette's and Virginia Woolf's descriptions of their lives remind us of what was so apparent in the studies of the adolescent daughters described in Chapters 3 and 4 of Book I. Most daughters longed to be close to their mothers, but were confused by an awareness that it was not officially sanctioned. They felt that mother-daughter closeness was not healthy and that conflict and storm and stress was the cultural prescription. Preoccupied by finding out who they are, adolescents are vulnerable to the powerful images of patriarchy and torn between them and their own urges. Families which legitimise the mother-daughter relationship and put storm and stress in perspective are rare in our culture.

Colette also recognised something Richardson never quite resolved. Mothers and daughters get on better when they respect the separateness of each other and this involves accepting responsibility for one's identity. It is easier to blame a poor childhood or an inadequate mother for our present unhappiness, than to work at developing our own self-esteem. We are not puppets or putty — we can change ourselves. How many achieve this was discussed throughout Book I, in practical rather than theoretical terms.

Virginia Woolf didn't hide behind theory. She had to come to terms with the realisation that there is no perfect mother. There is no perfect daughter. Over-expectations and demands for perfect love and support are destructive of relationships. She learnt that she must step outside the strait-jackets of patriarchal prescriptions and theories and that pursuing an impossible ideal did herself and her mother injustice. Like Colette, she learnt to live with her mother as a fallible person, who helped her in some respects and could not in others. Virginia fought hard to take responsibility for herself and accept herself as she was. What probably prevented her from making as good an end as Colette was the sexual abuse of her childhood and its legacy — a tormented view of herself — an outcome of a patriarchal society which protected sexual abuse by refusing to recognise it and thus denied the reality of her experience.

Consciousness Raising

The independent attitudes of Colette and her mother reminds us how much we need some consciousness raising in order to become independent of patriarchal obfuscations and strait-jackets. This is one of the purposes of Book II. It has tried to renegotiate a few of the omissions in our early learning. It has highlighted that throughout the centuries there are writers who have been saying important things about mother-daughter relationships, but patriarchal education chose to ignore them.

Henry Handel Richardson's Irish forbears saw no need to record mothers and daughters in their family tree, unless they brought property to the patriarchal family.[1] This has been the problem with our history on a global scale. As a result, even Simone de Beauvoir was deluded into thinking mothers and daughters had no history, because it wasn't recorded in the way that the history of fathers and sons is.[2]

We have a right to protest against this discrimination. In school, our daughters and sons need to hear more about cultures other than patriarchal ones, in order to induce some reflection and a realisation that present attitudes to mothers and daughters are not the only, or necessarily the right and proper ones.

The notion of pre-history needs to be exposed for its suppression of the contributions of mothers and daughters to civilisation. Stories of Gods and Goddesses need to be put in the context of the war against Goddess religions and the ancient reverence for mothers and daughters. We were told the story of Demeter and Persephone but not the context of its ancient significance for mothers and daughters. Can't we celebrate the beauty and strength of the mothers and daughters in the early creation myths and legends as well as admiring the sons of Sparta and the warring Greek patriarchs? We hear about gladiators but not the powerful relationships between mothers and daughters in ancient Rome.

A little awareness of the ancients awe for the creativity of the birth-giving power of mothers and daughters may encourage more sexual responsibility and offer a positive alternative to the destructive attitudes in societies, such as our own, which objectify and commodify sex. It may arouse discussion and humour about contemporary oddities — the preponderance of male obstetricians for example.

The politics of early patriarchal Christianity need de-mystifying. The patriarchal propaganda in the story of Eve can be discussed without killing Christianity — its acknowledgement might make for more respectful equality between the sexes. More frequent celebrations of Ruth and Deborah, and others like them, would make mothers and daughters prouder Christians.

Yes, we can enjoy the stories of medieval courtship, while understanding their inherent pseudo-admiration of women and all it implies for mother daughter-relationships. One can appreciate the fantasy. Accompanied by the reality, it might have taught us earlier about stereotyping and prejudice between the sexes in a lighthearted way. By the time we can cope with statistics and heavy sociological interpretations, sexism is ingrained.

The origins and role of the witches need telling, so that mothers and daughters cease to carry the myths of their evil propensities. Popular medieval tales are full of images of woman, the sperm drainer, the temptress, but there's not much about the goodness and skills of medieval mothers and daughters. There were many remarkable medieval mothers like Christine de Pizan. Boys can take pride in the stories of King Arthur and numerous brave bands of knights and kings and their oaths of loyalty. The bravery of the surrogate mothers in the nunneries would temper the exclusively male saga of adventures. Women mothered other women, protected young women from harm, but were of little interest to the male historians who had access to the means for ensuring that records survive.

The Renaissance looms large in our history books. We admire male painters and inventors. But what did the Renaissance do for mothers and daughters?

Then there is Shakespeare. Who'd have thought he had so much to say about mothers and daughters and the prejudices against them. Who recognised that he was arguing that the wisdom and creativity of mothers and daughters had been underestimated and was crucial to the proper functioning of the family? Most of us felt a little pride for our sex when Portia showed her sagacity, but neither teachers at school nor lecturers at university said a word about feminine pride. Did we ever recognise how much the great Mother-Queens of history were pawns in the patriarchal game and that they subverted their daughters — their Marie Antoinettes — likewise?

Promoting Counter Arguments

We struggled through the list of male achievers we were asked to admire in history books. A little colour might have been added had we been allowed to see what male chauvinists some of them were — Rousseau for example. Why did he think daughters should eat only cream and cakes?

Surely, we should have heard the counter argument before we were induced into giving Rousseau an unchallenged place in history. Mary Wollstonecraft, who was a daughter and a mother, challenged Rousseau for his sexist views on the education of daughters. She called attention to hidden agendas. Women were allowed only a little education in case they gave up their slavish obedience to men. She tried to point out the obvious — mothers needed some education in order to raise children. She mocked the phallocentricism of the seventeenth and eighteenth centuries, which tried to dictate that mothers and daughters be idle, unlearned and little more than adornment for their menfolk.

This was a time when the favourite 'gentlemanly' sport was tricking daughters out of their virginity. Mothers and daughters fought back with liaisons of solidarity — romantic friendships. These were often a surrogate mother-daughter relationship — the most famous being the runaways, Sarah Ponsonby and Eleanore Butler, the Ladies of Llangollen.

Mothers and daughters also used embroidery to create a world apart from patriarchy — even used it as a weapon against it. It became subversive. It was highly significant in the history of mothers and daughters, but did any of us ever recognise its message of creativity and the unity of mothers and daughters? More often we accepted the patriarchal denigration of it.

Jane Austen, ever a realist, killed the myth of the ideal mother, from the moment she put pen to paper. Instead, she said a great deal about how flawed mothers are and how important their fallibilities are to a daughter's independence. She showed how the mothers and daughters of her time and class were able to subvert patriarchal institutions such as marriage, by directing their energies to ensuring that property did not become the controlling issue in human relationships. In her novels, mothers and daughters represented the kind of morality and manners that made marriages decent and bearable and Austen used her heroines to popularise fundamental feminist values about the important role women could play in making society more humane. Patriarchal literary theory and analyses led us to believe she supported the status quo. This is not true.

Austen also developed a style of writing that captures the feminine perspective. The tradition of stepping outside the formalities and restrictions of the patriarchal sentence and patriarchal clichés was continued in the writings of the Brontës, Richardson, Colette and Woolf.[3] As a result, all these women pictured the complexity and reality of mother-daughter relationships in a way that most patriarchal writers cannot.

The Brontë sisters have never been neglected. Their following has reached cult proportions, but many do no understand why. It has much to do with their ability to capture images, feelings and emotions that tell us about mothers and daughters under patriarchy. Their books outshine any psychological text in their understanding of what it is to lose a mother in childhood. They encouraged mothers and daughters to recognise themselves as sexual beings.

That the Brontës dared to write about the realities of the nature and the lives of mothers and daughters aroused the patriarchs to frenzied denigrations. More acceptable to them were the fantasies of George Eliot, that the hand that rocks the cradle rules the world. There is no better illustration of a fantasy that is used to compensate and subdue women by making them feel that they are a threat to power. George Eliot tried to get Victorian women, pulled down by child bearing and toil, to believe that the fantasy was a reality. Her books seethe with anger about the position of mothers and daughters.

In the works of Eliot, we see mothers and daughters in a Victorian abyss of submission and oppression. They seem to have become hostages to the patriarchal heads of their households. They have no right to education or to work in the male work-place. They cannot own property or vote. They have no access to contraception. Hostages contemporarily tell us how they felt when their captors had all the power and held them prisoner.[4] They fought against losing the sense that they were individuals and tried to demonstrate to their captors and themselves that they were still human beings. They became grateful as well as ingratiating to their captors for small mercies. They remind us of what is known as the Stockholm syndrome, as demonstrated in the example of a woman, held hostage for several days, who married her captor, a bank robber.

Fighting Back

George Eliot's anger and Virginia Woolf's insight tells us that mothers and daughters — hostages or not — fought back. They used guilt as a weapon, until the patriarchal experts of the early decades of the twentieth century undermined it. Guilt is threatening to patriarchy. Therefore, it drives guilt underground, abuses it and hems it in by excluding the essential evidence. Mothers and daughters are bringing their guilt out in the open, using it constructively to mend relationships and change the circumstances that cause it. Colette and many contemporary women writers are able to admire the way their mothers used guilt. They also see the humour of it and turn it into family folklore.

In summary, Book II has been an extension of the Bibliotherapy with which Book I concluded. It stretches back much further in time, indicating how important mother-daughter relationships have always been. It has also tried to provide a perspective beyond our present condition. It began with some challenging ideas about a time when the mother-daughter relationship was revered. It described the ascent of patriarchy, the commodification of the sexuality of mothers and daughters and the attempts to make them the vessel and reflection of men. As always, mothers and daughters found techniques for survival and one of them was meekness. They turned meekness into a genuine Christian virtue and a strength — a sign that they were morally and spiritually superior in a way that men, encumbered by their masculinity, could never be.

Book II has shown how mothers and daughters not only coped but fought back in many such ways in ancient societies, in medieval times, during the Renaissance and with the help of Shakespeare, Jane Austen and the Brontës in the seventeenth, eighteenth and nineteenth centuries. Subsequently, the mothers of Richardson and Colette became antidotes to the weeping mothers of the Victorian age described by Eliot. Spurred on by the heady women's movements of the late nineteenth and early twentieth centuries, they reminded us how strong and creative mothers and daughters can be.

Unfortunately, the era of the honoured strong mothers, exemplified in the lives of Colette, Richardson and Virginia Woolf, gave way to the mid-twentieth century which was perhaps the most rapacious of recent eras in its expectations of mothers. We are still struggling with its images, which put excessive strain on mother-daughter relationships. But the history of mother-daughter relationships tells us that whenever the women's movement has become strong, then so has the mother-daughter relationship. We are in the midst of such a revival now.

An Improving Climate

Nowadays, it is easier to find other women who are eager to share mutual interests than it was mid-century. The 1960s and 1970s witnessed a resurgence of feminist movements which exposed patriarchal arrogance and prejudice to scrutiny. One outcome is that currently women's friendships are more readily acknowledged as relationships of substance than they used to be. More books are published on topics that concern women than ever before. Friendships and books provide information and support. We have seen how important the support of other women was to Richardson, Colette and Woolf, in achieving autonomy and finding the space to honour their mothers.

My objective has been to try to explore some of the facets of history, literature and psychology, which have smothered us in the kinds of delusions and misconceptions that have contributed to poor mother-daughter relationships. Book I looked at mother-daughter relationships from birth, through adolescence, young adulthood to old age and death. It examined the complexity and hidden agendas in issues such as separation and autonomy. It looked at well-known theories and common practices and asked whether they served the mother-daughter relationship. It talked in practicalities and provided a Bibliotherapy.

Hopefully, there are sources and ideas here to help readers work through their mother-daughter relationships. As I've tried to show throughout these two books, there are no clear answers, easy solutions or magic wands. Expecting magic solutions is generally a sign that a person has difficulty with self-responsibility. It may even mean a desire to always overlook, defend against understanding or fail to capitalise on suggestions for improving the mother-daughter relationship. The objective of this manoeuvre is clear — a determination not to change, because without conflict with their mothers or daughters such persons cease to have motivation or purpose in their lives. Mother-blaming is the basis upon which their personalities rest.

Each one of us needs to question our own situation and try to understand it on many fronts. We need to work on our own self-esteem and autonomy, because patriarchy will not do it for us. Acquiring a sense of our history and our importance in the writings of some of literature's most famous women authors, is one of many ways of contributing to a new consciousness about the nature of women and the relationship between mothers and daughters.

For those who may be fathers and husbands, mothers and daughters, there are many more facets to explore and many more ways to contribute to the new consciousness. The journey has just begun.

～

Footnotes

Book I

PREFACE

1. For a fuller discussion of this point see writings by Carol Gilligan, 1979 and 1982, which are listed in the Bibliography. Also see publications by S. Phillips, 1980 and 1983, which overview some of the relevant research.

2. *Don't Blame Mothers* by Paula Caplan, 1989 is an example of a book that tries to be constructive.

3. Research by Paula Caplan, 1989 and Lucy Fischer, 1987 is among the little systematic research there is. By systematic, I mean research that pays attention to scientific principles and tries to achieve some objectivity by taking measures to ensure validity and reliability, for example by rechecks of interviews etc..

4. Stanley and Wise, 1985, who are committed feminists, discuss this point much more fully than I can here.

5. An example, among many, is Barbara Thiering who presented a critique of Christianity's myth making on Australian ABC television during April 1990.

6. This is important and for male insight into it read the 1987 publication by M. Kaufman.

7. This view is common to many researchers — Clare Burton, 1985, is an example.

8. Gerda Lerner, 1986 p.217. For more detail of Lerner's impressive research see Chapter 3 in Book II.

9. Note that Lerner is adding weight to the earlier point, which is covered by footnote 4.

10. See S. Phillips, 1983 and 1986, for other references containing discussion of this process. Chapter 8A by S Phillips in Bain, 1983, discusses this more fully and refers to supporting research.

11. Gerda Lerner, 1986 p.224.

12. This aspect of patriarchy was defined earlier in the Preface. It's illustrated in many parts of the book and particularly in Book 11.

13. Dale Spender, 1990 — see Bibliography.

14. Clive James, *May Week Was in June*, Jonathan Cape, 1990 is also one who makes this point and discussed it on ABC Radio National, First Edition, 31st May, 1990. Edward de Bono, 1990, is another who tries to step outside patriarchal thinking.

CHAPTER 1

1. The series is composed of five novels: *Martha Quest, A Proper Marriage, A Ripple from the Storm, Landlocked* and *The Four Gated City.*

2. I'm referring to patriarchy which was briefly defined in the Preface and is discussed in Chapter 3 in Book II.

3. Katherine Fishburn, 1980, offers an excellent analysis of the mother-daughter theme in Lessing's novels, some of which is referred to here. For details see

Bibliography.

4. Lessing was influenced by psychoanalysis and its view of mothers and daughters. This is discussed in Chapter 8 of Book 1. Fishburn is very aware of the psychoanalytic interpretation and gives more detail than I need to here.

5. This is discussed by Adrienne Rich, 1977.

6. The insight can also be found in Fishburn, 1980.

7. "Biology is destiny" is discussed in several chapters in Book 1. See the discussion of Erikson's theory in Chapter 3. See also Chapter 8.

8. Patriarchy has a long history of being opposed to this. Why and how is described in Book II.

9. See Karen Elias-Button, 1980.

10. Ibid. Carroll Smith-Rosenberg, 1985, also makes this point. See Bibliography.

11. The behaviour of hostages was discussed by Paul McGeogh in 'Innocents in the Front Line' in Section 3, Spectrum, *The Sydney Morning Herald*, 25-8-1990, p.65.

12. Patriarchal societies have always tried to justify their power structure by myths of female inferiority. Their beginnings are discussed in Book II.

13. Ehrenreich & English, *For Her Own Good: 150 Years of the Experts Advice to Women.* pp98-9

14. This is the time of the slave trade and such cruel rationalisations about Negroes eased the Christian conscience.

15. A male gynaecologist described women in childbirth in these terms on a recent Australian ABC national radio programme about children, entitled "Offspring".

16. Ehrenreich & English, pp125-6

17. The story of Eve's betrayal and why women 'should' suffer in child-birth is discussed in Book II.

18. Some evidence for this is given in Chapter 6.

19. For more details of these developments see Book II.

20. This is not necessarily the case. Chapter 7 of Book I tells of the mothers of Bethnal Green whose daughters preferred to consult them rather than the experts.

21. For an overview of this movement and the chief contributors to it, see S. Phillips, 1976.

22. Ibid.

23. Ibid. The "means of production" concept is borrowed from Engels, 1971, Marx, 1974. See Bibliography.

24. For an introduction to Watson's work, see S. Phillips, 1976 and the many references given there.

25. Ibid. Also see Ehrenreich and English, 1979.

26. For a very brief outline of these theories and relevant references see Phillips, 1976. For those wanting to pursue Freud's theories further, the best source is obviously *The Standard Edition of The Complete Psychological Works of Sigmund Freud.*

27. A commonly used psychological text book which discussed this situation in this period was Conger, 1977. That research has been duplicated many times and is found in reality based contemporary psychological texts — ie those that include fathers in their analyses. A source for the contemporary situation in Australia is research done by the Australian Institute of Family Studies, Melbourne.

28. One of the first texts to collate research on this subject was by Helen Bee in 1978. It is a much respected text and still holds good today. Much of the research has been duplicated since then.

29. Ibid.

30. Chapter 8 explores and compares psychoanalytic and feminist views of the mother-daughter relationship.

31. See E.M. Broner's *A Weave of Women*, 1978, which was written while this attitude prevailed. For a more recent discussion see Susan Weidman Schneider, *Jewish and Female*, 1985.

32. See Chapters 3 and 6 for further exploration of this tendency.

33. Lawyers were particularly inclined to justify this situation by quoting John Bowlby. Bowlby's views on the important role of mothers can be found in his books, *Attachment, Separation and Loss* and *The Making and Breaking of Affectional Bonds*, listed in the Bibliography.

34. For an overview of the research and references on the problems of children involved in divorce, see S. Phillips, 1986. It includes references to research on Australian children from The Institute of Family Studies in Melbourne.

35. Ibid.

36. S. Phillips, 1979 and 1986.

37. S. Phillips, 1986.

38. There were plays and novels by feminists that reinforced this trend. While it does not denigrate mothering, *Gaining Ground* by Joan Barfoot, 1985, is an example of a novel that demotes mothering. The mother in this book sees herself as important only in her children's very early years. After that, she believes they can fend for themselves. She leaves her children to live in the wild without the trappings that control housewives and mothers — mirrors, clocks and the emotional coercions of "ought" or guilt. She forsakes all responsibility except to herself. She expects her daughter to do likewise.

39. For further discussion of this theme see the paper on Toddlers by S. Phillips, 1988.

40. For a discussion of the effect of language on girls and some of the significant research in the area in this period see the chapters by S. Phillips in Bain, *The Sociogenesis of Language and Human Conduct*, 1983. Many other chapters in the book are worth reading.

CHAPTER 2

1. For a more detailed discussion of self-esteem, see S. Phillips, 1986. Note that self-esteem should not be equated with arrogance and aggression. People who have a confrontationist style are usually on the defensive. They fear that others are as aggressive as they are. Arrogance is a manoeuvre to intimidate others before they attack them. Their self-esteem is poor.

It must also be said that in some other cultures, even subcultures within our own, where multiple mothers or extended families are the norm, the concept of self and mother-daughter relationships can develop diffferently from the way that is described here. What is said here is associated with the pressures of western society and a society in which the care of an infant is largely the responsibility of one mother.

2. A most famous case is that of Sybil in the book of the same name by F.R. Schreiber, Middlesex, Penguin, 1979.

3. Chapters 4, 5, and 6 in Book I examine self-esteem, in relation to adolescent girls and their mothers, and Chapter 7 in relation to adult daughters and their mothers. Chapters 10-12 in Book II, which discuss Henry Handel Richardson, Colette and Virginia Woolf and their mothers, highlight how differences in the degree of self-esteem affect the mother- daughter relationship.

4. All the case studies described in this Chapter come from a research project which I began in 1982. Permission to quote has been given in each case. All names are fictitious.

5. Methods for doing this are given throughout the book. The Conclusion to Book I gives a summary of the some of the measures mothers and daughters claim to be most effective. In Book II, the measures taken by Richardson, Colette and Woolf are of especial interest.

6. See Chapter 6 for evidence from contemporary women.

7. Some of these feelings arise out of ugly patriarchal teachings about the animal and sinful nature of women and their sexuality and similar conflicting feelings about being female.

8. Marilyn French, *Her Mother's Daughters*, p.181.

9. Judith Traill reported this study at the Tavistock Clinic in London in 1983. As late as 1990, concern about unnecessary technological intervention during the birth of a baby was expressed by a number of early childhood nurses and midwives who were interviewed on national radio Australia in an Offspring programme on 8th May of that year. They felt strongly that male dominance in obstetrics has resulted in the devaluing of the role and power of women giving birth — issues that are discussed in historical perspective in the early chapters of Book II. Fetal monitoring which results in unnecessary caesarian births, for which Australia has notoriously high figures, still goes on. Hospital births continue to be dominated by a male perspective, yet there is evidence that there is a lower incidence of interventions and post natal depression when a midwife, rather than an obstetrician, is helping at the delivery. Other important issues are that midwives are trained for normal births, while obstetricians are trained for the abnormal; that women need more information and need to be protected by a birthing contract which assures them against the kinds of indignities and unnecessary interventions described here.

10. Another hazard for the self-esteem of mothers can be breast feeding — how successful one is at it. Moreover, social attitudes put women in a conflicting position. Under patriarchy the breast is primarily seen as erotic to men. Topless bars are fun places. On the other hand, breast feeding in public is given an obscene connotation. Women have to negotiate these absurd ambivalences.

11. The concept of bonding has been subject to much questioning. See Deidre

James, 'Bonding: Mothering Magic or Pseudo Science. A Critical Review of Some of The Research in The Area', Selected Paper No 40, F.C.Y.S. 1985, published by Hampden Press.

12. Erik Erikson is the most famous exponent of the trust theory. See Bibliography.

13. Paulson, Stone and Posto, 1978, are among the first modern advocates of this attitude.

14. See accounts of the Tubetube in Chapter 1, Book II.

15. These findings come from a study of adult attitudes to children. See S. Phillips, 1982, (a) & (b) and 1986.

16. Lorraine Riach from the Melbourne Teachers College has done research in this area. She reported it at the 2nd International Child Development Conference in Melbourne in 1982. See also S. Phillips, 1982 and 1986.

17. Child development books written by women such as Greta Fein and Helen Bee are good sources for descriptions of infant development. Even their books of the late 1970s are much ahead of some of the more patriarchally-oriented texts of today. The emphasis here on the differentiation process is from my own research, 1986.

18. For further references and a review of the research in this area, see S. Phillips, 1986.

19. Ibid.

20. Ibid.

21. Ibid.

22. The reasons for this are explored more extensively in Chapters 4 & 6 of Book I.

23. See Chapter 6 for illustrations of this.

24. See Bibliography, Jane Flax, 1978, p.174.

25. See Levine, 1983.

26. For more details see S. Phillips, 1982 and 1988.

27. The development of gender is explored further in Chapter 4. Also see Peterson, 1984.

28. For more details see S. Phillips, 1986 and 1988.

29. Ibid.

30. For a discussion of the hostile approach see de Mause's *History of Childhood*, 1971. For more recent data see S. Phillips, 1986.

31. For more references and details of the research, see S. Phillips, 1986.

32. See Fabian and Loh, 1980.

33. The way in which children construct their self-view has been explored extensively by sociologists and psychologists. See Fein, 1978, Hamachek, 1978, Peterson, 1984.

34. Stead, 1984, p.410.

35. For more details of research findings see S. Phillips, 1986.

36. Helen Bee was one of the first who collected together research in this field. Her book, 1978, is still in advance of more recent publications.

37. See S. Phillips, 1979 and 1986 for details of the research.

38. After I had completed and written about my research on this topic, I came across the philosophical feminism of Nancy Chodorow, who has made similar observations. Her work is briefly referred to here.

39. This is based on the findings of my own research, 1979, revised, 1986 — again, supporting evidence from others is quoted in the 1979 and 1986 publications.

40. Ibid.

41. Ibid.

42. Susi is a fictitious character. Her story is one told by scores of little girls in their early primary school years and an even greater numbers of adult women. In only one case was there a solution as given in this story.

43. This situation has much improved in the last couple of decades, due in part to the re-appearance of feminism and the recognition of the strength of women's friendships with other women — an observation previously belittled by patriarchs. However, my colleagues and I are often surprised at the numbers of women who don't honour women but support old patriarchal attitudes. For example, recently a woman, who was head of an accountancy firm, told me she didn't respect women's abilities, so she didn't employ them. In another case, some male academics refused to lunch with some social workers on the grounds that their conversation " would probably be the usual women's junk about their operations". A female colleague agreed with them. In fact, the social workers were well known and interesting researchers and academics.

44. For a discussion of this point, see Bate, 1975.

45. See Lakoff, 1973.

46. See S. Phillips, 1983 for further references and research about and discussion of this point.

47. For a summary of research see S. Phillips, 1979 and 1983.

48. See S. Phillips, 1983, for further references and research about and discussion of this point.

49. See Bettelheim, 1976.

50. See Phillips, 1983, for a list of references and a summary of the research in this area.

51. Here I'm referring to the work of Carol Gilligan, 1977 — another pioneer whose books over the past 15 years have more to offer women than the latest glossy child development texts.

52. There are many psychiatric texts that refer to this situation. This is taken from Dacey's summary of the research in 1979.

CHAPTER 3

1. Patriarchal anxiety about the mother-daughter alliance and the reasons for it are discussed in more detail in subsequent chapters. Some of its propaganda has been discussed in the Preface and Chapter 1. Throughout the Book, I give case studies and explore its effects on mothers and daughters. The conclusion that daughters want to be close with their mothers comes from my research about mothers and daughters. (The research began in 1982 and is ongoing. Details of its approach are given in later chapters.) My findings are reinforced by the work of Dalsimer, 1986 and Apter, 1990. During 1931-33, Freud admitted to under estimating the importance and duration of a daughter's

bond with her mother. But he continued to write that ultimately the relationship with the father took the place of the mother and the attachment to the mother terminated or ended in hate. Helen Deutsch, 1944, was among the first to insist that he'd made a mistake. She recognised the importance of the mother-daughter bond. She saw the task of adolescence as giving adult forms to the old, much deeper and more primitive ties with the mother.

2. D. W. Winnicott has written of the mirror role of mothers, 1971.

3. Jane Austen, *Persuasion*, 1978, p.73.

4. Contemporary evidence for this point is given in Chapter 6.

5. Frank, 1953 — see Bibliography.

6. Some ways to ease the ambivalence were also discussed in Chapter 2.

7. S. Phillips, 1986, explains this characteristic further and gives other references.

8. Terri Apter, 1990, also comes to this conclusion.

9. Ibid.

10. Ibid.

11. See books by John Janeway Conger and Anne C. Peterson, 1984, Kathleen Stasse Berger, 1983, Candida Peterson, 1984, John W. Santrock, 1984, L.J. Stone and J. Church, 1983.

12. Marilyn French, *Her Mother's Daughter*, 1987, p.642.

13. Rosenberg, 1979 — see Bibliography.

14. See S. Phillips, 1986, for a discussion of cognitive development in adolescents and relevant research.

15. Helm Stierlen, 1973. For a further discussion of the games families play and other matters which relate to adolescents separating from their parents, see Rickarby, 1984.

16. Rickarby, 1984 — see Bibliography.

17. The youth cult became marked by the 1970s and discussions of it are found in the psychological texts of the time. See Sebald, 1977. Since then there has been widespread discussion of the phenomenon. An even more savage indictment of it is found in Postman, 1985, where he states that television is destroying the traditional demarcation between childhood and adulthood. As he sees it, everyone tries to look as though they are somewhere between 20 and 30, until senility sets in.

18. Sebald was one who began discussing this phenomenon in 1977. David Bennett's book on teenagers, 1987, gives a more light-hearted approach to this and other aspects of adolescent development.

19. See Sebald and more recent adolescent development books by Conger, Kagan or Peterson etc. There are many others which discuss this point.

20. Baumrind has worked with the Family Research Institute, attached to the University of California, Berkeley. Her publications are continually being updated and can be obtained from her at the Institute.

21. One of the earliest books which was brave enough to talk about this described teenage behaviour as tyrannous. See Grace and Fred Heckinger, *Teenage Tyranny*, quoted in Sebald.

22. See footnote 11 for helpful references.

23. Erik Erikson, 1968 and 1974, discussed adolescent identity-seeking characteristics during the youth movements of the 1960s and 1970s. With modifications his theory is still applicable.

24. See S. Phillips, 1986 for a discussion of punks and a list of references on the topic.

25. Permission from this father to quote his case was requested and given, as with all other case studies throughout the book. After coming to understand more about adolescent development and that their case was not unique, this father and mother stopped feeling rejected by their adolescent.

26. The Australian Institute of Family Studies also has research evidence about parental concern over downward mobility of their offspring.

27. Since 1982, I have been conducting research on mother-daughter relationships and this was one of many similar case studies that were given to me by participants. More details of the research and how it was conducted is given in later chapters.

28. See footnotes 5, 8, 11 and 14 for useful references.

29. The discussion of therapy in the next section is explored further in Chapter 8.

30. See Erikson, 1963 and 1975 — the latter contains Erikson's views on women's liberation and revises his earlier theory of the female inner space.

31. Lerner & Spanier, 1980 — see Bibliography.

32. Ibid. p.379.

33. Adrienne Rich, 1977. Evidence for this is discussed in later chapters.

34. In *Between Mothers & Daughters. Stories Across A Generation*, edited by Susan Koppelman.

35. Ibid. pp.146-147.

36. Ibid. p.150.

37. Paula Caplan, 1989.

38. This topic has been discussed extensively in feminist books about women and therapy — one of the earliest and most famous being Phyllis Chesler's, *Women and Madness*.

39. Buczik, 1981 — see Bibliography.

40. Ibid., and Armitage, Schneiderman and Bass, 1979.

41. Ibid.

42. Ambromowitz, Ambromowitz and Weitz, 1976.

43. The same unawareness is apparent in the "therapeutic" works of several feminist writers, such as Nancy Friday. These are discussed in Chapter 8.

CHAPTER 4

1. For a fuller account than is appropriate here, see Katherine Dalsimer's charming account of this book, 1986.

2. Previous chapters have already drawn attention to some of the negative patriarchal folklore about women's sexuality. Also see Chapters 6 and 8.

3. Katherine Dalsimer, 1986. Also see Chapter 8 of Book I.

4. See Chapter 6 for further discussion. For the origin of some of these problems, see Book II.

5. All quotes in this chapter come with permission from mothers and daughters who have taken part in my research studies. This research was begun in 1982, while I was a senior academic at the University of New South Wales. In the first study more than 300 mothers and daughters, largely from middle to lower class backgrounds, were interviewed. The women were aged 18 to 70 years and educationally were a representative group. In roughly equal numbers, they included those who left school at 15 years or younger, those who had completed secondary school, those who had additional training or had completed an apprenticeship and those who had completed a university degree. The expected controls of variables and statistical analysis were carried out by my research assistants to whom I'm indebted. The first reports of this study appeared in the *Sydney Morning Herald* in 1982, and the Selected Papers of the Unit for Child Studies at the University of New South Wales. Since 1982 the research has been repeated in many settings and confirmed by overseas studies, for example see Fischer, 1987 and Bassoff, 1988.

6. Merlin Stone, 1984 — see Bibliography.

7. Anne Frank, 1953. pp.116-117. That stories of Goddesses can be used as morale-boosting folklore is considered in Book II.

8. Ibid., p.117.

9. For further explanation of this psychoanalytic view, see Chapter 8. Also see Dalsimer, 1986 and H. Deutsch, 1944.

10. Anne Frank, 1953, p.117.

11. For examples of pride in menstruation and female sexuality, see Margaret Mead and Tess Slesinger, whose work is discussed later in this chapter and in Chapter 9.

12. This has been discussed in previous chapters and the Introduction. It is discussed further in Chapters 6 and 8 and Book II.

13. This quote came from a participant in my ongoing research

14. Ibid.

15. This child-rearing practice in relation to female infants is an outcome of earlier patriarchal preferences for non-sexual women, discussed in subsequent chapters and Book II.

16. This knowledge has been around but underground for generations. Discussion of it began appearing in standard psychological texts in the 1970s — for example Furstenberg, 1976. Since then there have been innumerable conferences and books on the topic. Little headway has been made for reasons given in this chapter.

17. Ibid.

18. Again the issue has been discussed for some time. One could find excellent discussions of the topic a decade or so ago — for example, see Stassenberger, 1980. Yet lectures and books for adolescents still do not always indicate an understanding of how adolescents think. Most parents still have problems.

19. For a discussion of the distinction between authoritarian and authoritative, see S. Phillips, 1986.

20. Rich, 1977, p.248-249.

21. Ibid p.249.

22. From a participant in my research study.

23. Colette and her relationship with her mother is discussed in Book II.

24. In Koppelman, *Between Mothers and Daughters: Stories Across A Generation*, 1985.

25. Dinnerstein, 1976 — see Bibliography.

26. Chodorow, 1978 — see Bibliography.

27. These issues are discussed further in Chapter 6 and Book II.

28. For instances of how psychology and psychiatry have given a neurotic interpretation to the psychology of women, read Carol Gilligan, 1982, who is discussed later in this book. Also read Chapter 8 on psychoanalysis.

29. See Paula Caplan, 1989, who describes how women are told they are dependent and immature if they remain close to their mothers. I've given an example of a theory used to drive a wedge between mothers and daughters in Chapter 3. The issue is discussed further in Chapter 6.

30. H. Deutsch, 1944, gives some clinical descriptions of these friendships.

31. See Chapters 6 and 8 for further discussion of this point.

32. See Freud 1961 and Jung, 1982.

33. For further discussion of this point, see Fairchild and Hayward, 1979, p.88.

34. Golden, Éspin and Shuster, all 1987, explore this issue.

35. Stanley and Wise, 1983, give more attention to the evidence than I am able to here.

36. This was discussed in Chapter 2.

37. Shuster, 1987, discusses this point.

38. Fairchild and Hayward, 1979.

39. Shuster, 1987, is one of many sources of evidence for this point.

40. Golden, Éspin & Shuster, all 1987.

41. See Book II for discussion of the lives of Colette and Virginia Woolf.

42. Golden, 1987, pp.30-32.

43. Fairchild and Hayward, 1979.

44. Ibid.

45. Éspin, 1987, provides evidence for this.

46. Shuster, 1987 — see Bibliography.

47. Boston Lesbian Psychologies Collective, 1987.

48. Dunker, 1987, discusses this point. It is certainly most evident in my research.

49. Éspin, 1987.

50. Shuster, 1987, discusses this point.

51. Fairchild and Hayward, 1979, provide evidence for this.

52. Jeffreys, 1989.

53. Bettelheim, 1976 — see Bibliography.

54. Ibid., p.202.

55. For the origins of the belief that menstruation is a curse in patriarchal society see Chapter 1, Book II.

56. Bettelheim, 1970, p.204.

57. The effect of the prescriptive use of "he" on the self-concept of females was discussed in Chapter 2. Reputable international humanistic journals reject the use of 'he' to cover both sexes.

58. Bettelheim, 1970, p.207.

59. Ibid. p.p. 206-207. Freud described the narcissism of women under patriarchy. This is discussed in Chapter 8.

60. The next chapter in this book looks at what mothers and daughters say about the realities of supposed sexual competition between mothers and daughters.

61. Bettelheim, 1970, p.206.

62. Ibid. p.207.

63. Ibid. p.208

64. Ibid. p.209.

65. Psychoanalytic theory uses the term "latency" and, as indicated, sees it as a period, during primary school, when children inhibit their sexuality and boys and girls avoid one another. Research suggests that the avoidance has more to do with boys' anxiety about their own femininity. This was discussed in Chapter 2. Also see S. Phillips, 1979, pp.91-96.

66. Bettelheim, 1970, p.211.

67. Ibid. p.213.

68. Ibid. p.214.

69. This is discussed in the Chapters, 5 -6 and Chapter 1, Book II.

CHAPTER 5

1. Appleton, 1982, explores father-daughter relationships and these behaviours. Fischer, 1986 also reports on fathers who behave as "sexual guardians".

2. These reports and cases come from my research. They cover innumerable examples.

3. Permission was given to quote this and all other statements in this chapter.

4. This daughter revealed an exceptionally good understanding of her father's behaviour and how it was affecting her. Not all adolescent girls can see the situation so clearly.

5. The attitudes in the community reinforce and contribute to this deprivation. These issues were discussed in Chapter 1.

6. Herman and Hirschman's book, *Father Daughter Incest* is one of many sources for more information. See Bibliography.

7. See Chapter 2, this book for a full discussion of how the behaviours of significant others affects a child's self-concept.

8. Adrienne Rich, 1977, explores this reaction in her book, *Of Woman Born* — see Bibliography.

9. Throughout that year the press contained many reports of this case. Some articles still refer to it as a benchmark.

10. See Herman and Hirschman, 1981. Also see Alice Walker's, *The Color Purple*.

11. See DeSalvo, 1989, for a discussion of Virginia Woolf's childhood -also Chapter 12, Book II.

12. These and the following findings are taken from my research on mother-daughter relationships. The research used interviews and questionaires — there were also rechecks and observations to control validity and reliability.

13. See Chapter 2 in Book I for the emergence of this trend in boys and why it is so. Adrienne Rich, Karen Horney, Bruno Bettelheim, Nancy Chodorow and others also talk about how males fear feminity in themselves. Their discussions are included in Chapter 8.

14. Flax, 1978, p.179.

15. Rich, 1977.

16. These reports are taken from my own mother-daughter research.

17. Outside influences can undermine good attitudes within families, unless patriarchal propaganda against mothers and daughters is exposed and discussed.

18. The beginnings of this projection were discussed in Chapter 2.

19. Petra is a pseudonym for one of the volunteers in my research. She stands in for many such women.

20. Colette is discussed in Book II, Chapter 11.

21. See Howard's, *Margaret Mead. A Life*. 1985, p.34.

22. These women are not unlike Doris Lessing's Martha Quest, who was discussed in Chapter 1.

23. Howard, 1985, p.374

24. Barbara, as with all others quoted here, gave me permission to include her comments.

25. See Bassoff, 1988, for supporting evidence of this and other points made here.

26. These reports came from my extensive research studies on mothers and daughters. See footnote 12.

27. The social forces that influence the production of these attitudes under patriarchy have already been discussed.

28. Virginia Woolf, 'A Room of One's Own', In Rossi, 1974, p 633.

29. Coopersmith, 1967 was one of the first and most famous researchers to establish this fact. Since then the research on self-esteem has burgeoned and almost any reliable text on the subject will confirm the point. Lowenthal, Thurnher and Chirabago, 1975, pay attention to lowered self-esteem in mothers.

30. Lucy Fischer, 1987, also reports on a research study in America with similar findings to my own.

31. Ibid.

32. Ibid.

33. Ibid.

34. Ibid.

CHAPTER 6

1. This refers to the study begun in 1982. See footnote 12, Chapter 5.

2. This is a daughter who took part in my research and gave permission to be quoted. Her name and all others are fictitious.

3. Arcana, 1984. See Bibliography.

4. When these results were first reported in a leading article in the *Sydney Morning Herald* in 1982, the news was syndicated round the western world — in particular in the U.S.A. and Germany. The reaction and reports indicated that the idea that some mothers did not enjoy being mothers was one of astonishment — even shock. Since 1982 attitudes are a little more informed, but there remain the doubts about women who don't want to be mothers, as I have discussed.

5. Lessing's novel was discussed in the introduction to Chapter 1 of this book.

6. This point is discussed further in the next chapter.

7. Refer to Rich, 1977, for further discussion of this point.

8. Flax, 1978.

9. Ibid., p.179.

10. Ibid., p.175.

11. Arcana, 1984.

12. See footnote 12, Chapter 5.

13. This was discussed in Chapter 2.

14. This quote comes from a daughter in my research study. The name is fictitious.

15. This was discussed in Chapter 2 and Chapter 5.

16. Again, as in the rest of the chapter, the name is fictitious and permission was given to use the quote.

17. The story can be found in *Close Company*, edited by Park and Heaton, 1987.

18. Winterson, 1990.

19. Rich, 1977.

20. After the birth of three daughters of her own, this daughter has developed a close relationship with her mother and is constructively critical of her earlier attitudes.

21. For more details of the research see Footnote 12, Chapter 5.

22. Arcana, 1984.

23. A case of this is given in George Eliot, whose life is discussed in Book II.

24. This story is in *Close Company*, edited by Park and Heaton, 1987.

25. Ibid., p.31.

26. Ibid., p.36.

CHAPTER 7

1. Lorna Irvine, 1980 — see Bibliography.

2. Ibid., p.243.

3. Details of this research have been explained in Footnote 5, Chapter 4 and in other footnotes throughout the book.

4. Colette is discussed in Book II, Chapter 11.

5. As indicated throughout, all names are fictitious and permission to quote has been granted.

6. For a discussion of this point, see Chapter 2 this book.

7. Attwood, 1976 — see Bibliography.

8. Barfoot, 1985 and 1986 — see Bibliography.
9. Barfoot, 1985, p.174.
10. Barfoot, 1986, p.179.
11. Ibid., p.53.
12. Lessing, 1984.
13. Ibid., p.13.
14. Ibid., p.33.
15. This was discussed in Chapter 1, this book.
16. Young and Willmott, 1962, p.47.
17. Ibid., p.49.
18. Ibid., p.49.
19. Ibid., p.50.
20. See Chapters 2 — 4 for discussion of these.

CHAPTER 8

1. M. Klein, 1932, J. E. Sayers, 1988.
2. D.W. Winnicott, 1957 and 1971.
3. Critical commentaries and summaries of Freud's thinking abound. Among these, one which reproduces and sharply criticises several "classic" experiments purporting to demonstrate the validity of Freud's hypotheses is by Hans Eysenck and Glen Wilson, *Experimental Study of Freudian Theory*, New York: Harper & Row, 1973. Richard Wolheim has edited a collection of philosophical essays and methodological criticisms of Freudian ideas, *Freud. A Collection of Critical Essays*, New York: Doubleday, 1974. Also see Jeffrey Monosaieff Masson, 1984, listed in the Bibliography. There are many feminist criticisms relevant to mother-daughter relationships in particular e.g Badinter, 1981 and Ehrenreich and English, 1979.
4. See Freud's *Complete Psychological Works*, listed in the Bibliography.
5. Ibid.
6. See Caplan, 1989, p.102: "Many feel what I call penis pity. Some people of both sexes think that penises are funny, strange-looking, wobbly, out of control, and vulnerable to harm ... Little girls at this age (2-4 years) may regard themselves as lucky: they needn't try to control something that dangles and swings willy nilly, nor protect something that is externally exposed, sensitive and easily hurt, nor struggle to maintain privacy and avoid embarrassment about visible, easily observable genitalia."
7. See Chapter 2 in particular.
8. Freud's *Complete Psychological Works*.
9. Gilligan is discussed in the last section of this Chapter.
10. Freud's *Complete Psychological Works*.
11. Ibid. While the Freudian explanation in this instance illustrates the kind of assertions to which Simone de Beauvoir is objecting, note that in this case it is the child who is said to objectify herself. This is another example of the reversal and projection of the adult male's style of thinking onto the child. For a discussion of the tendency of adults to fail to understand how children think,

read Phillips, 1986.

12. Freud's *Complete Psychological Works* — quoted from 1915 writings.

13. Ibid., quoted from 1912 writings.

14. Ibid., 1961 edition.

15. Ibid., 1896 writings.

16. Caplan, 1985.

17. Ibid. Caplan provides evidence for this observation.

18. Ibid.

19. Statements about the moral inferiority of women abound in Freud's *Complete Psychological Works*.

20. See footnote 2 and references to Eysenck, Wilson and Wolheim. We have already seen that the generalisations of Freud's follower, Erikson, about destiny and biology have been researched in contemporary samples of women and found inapplicable. See Lerner and Spanier, 1980 and Gilligan, 1977 and 1979.

21. Mitchell, 1974.

22. Ibid.

23. Gerda Lerner, 1986 — see Bibliography.

24. The combination of these two themes, the psychoanalytic and women's history , are the basis of Rich's book, *Of Woman Born*, which has had considerable impact.

25. This aspect of Rich's theory is explored further in Book II.

26. Horney, 1967.

27. Bettelheim, 1968.

28. Rich, 1977.

29. Ibid., p.56.

30. Ibid., p.56.

31. Ibid., pp.246-7.

32. Ibid., 1977. Margaret Mead also made this point, 1975.

33. For further discussion of this point see Phillips, 1983.

34. Lerner, 1986.

35. Ibid., p.234.

36. Ibid., p.234.

37. Ibid., p.250.

38. Friday, 1981, p.21.

39. Ibid., p.27.

40. Ibid., p.26.

41. Ibid.

42. This point was made strongly in Chapter 7 of this book.

43. Arcana, 1984, p.3.

44. Ibid., p.4.

45. See Chapters 2, 6 and 7.

46. See Chapter 7.

47. de Beauvoir, 1957.

48. de Beauvoir does not make this point in this way. I have construed it from her account of her life, 1984.

49. See Deidre Bair's biography of de Beauvoir, 1990, for further details.

50. See Lerner, 1986, for discussion of this point.

51. Ibid.

52. Ibid., p.17.

53. Ibid., p.281.

54. de Beauvoir, 1969.

55. Freud, 1972.

56. Freud, 1964.

57. Flax, 1978, p.175

58. Ibid., p.177.

59. Ibid., p.178.

60. Gilligan is discussed later in the chapter. The mothers and daughters in my study showed no wish for the "magic" organ. They preferred their own sexual organs and were quite emphatic about this
   — see footnote 5.

61 Caplan, 1989, also makes this point. Motherhood as pathology was discussed in Chapter 1 of this book.

62. Chodorow, 1978 and 1982.

63. Dinnerstein, 1978.

64. Sayers, 1987, p.68.

65. Caplan, 1989.

66. Lerner, 1986, p.64.

67. Ibid., p.45.

68. Gilligan, 1977, p.274.

69. See Hextall, 1976, for discussion of this point.

70. Gilligan, 1982.

71. An example of this is seen in the way children are subsumed under adult motives and ways of thinking by lawyers and the legal process — also in the way that the legal process cannot cope with many children's issues.

CHAPTER 9

1. Koppelman, (ed.), 1985 — see Bibliography.

2. Ibid., p.188.

3. Ibid., p.285. This was written in 1980.

4. Munro, 1985. See Bibliography. Also see a more recent collection of Munro's short stories, 1990, *Friend of My Youth*, particularly, the first story which has the same title as the book.

5. Ibid., p.230.

6. Bedford, 1986, p.4.

7. Ibid., p.108.
8. Ibid., p.81.
9. Ibid., p.92.
10. Ibid., p.98.
11. "Shtetl" — a German/Yiddish word for a small village in the country.
12. Mead, 1972 — see Bibliography.
13. Bateson, 1984.
14. Howard, 1985.
15. Mead, 1972.
16. Howard, 1985, p.399.
17. Ibid., p.5.
18. Lynn Bloom, 1980, in an interesting study of mothers and daughters in autobiographies, explores these points.
19. Simone de Beauvoir, 1984.
20. Howard, 1985, p.441.
21. Ibid., p.65.
22. Ibid., p.87.
23. Bateson, 1984.
24. Ibid., p.62.
25. Howard, 1985, p.436.
26. Ibid., p.440.
27. Bateson, 1984, p.169.
28. Ibid., p.81.
29. Howard, 1985, p.236.
30. Ibid., p.287.
31. Ibid., p.333.
32. Ibid., p.365.
33. Ibid., p.428.
34. Bateson, 1984, p.144.
35. Ibid., p.102.
36. Ibid., p.103.
37. Howard, 1985. p.5.
38. These involvements are discussed in Book II.
39. Howard, 1985, p.367.
40. Shuster, 1987.
41. Rich, 1977. This issue was discussed in Chapter 6 of this book.
42. French, 1987.
43. Barocas and Barocas, 1973.
44. Freyberg, 1980.
45. Heller, 1982.
46. French, 1987, p.99.

47. Ibid., p.324.
48. Ibid., p.160.
49. Ibid., p.151.
50. Ibid., p.6.
51. Ibid., pp.6-7.
52. Ibid., p.257.
53. Ibid., p.258-9.
54. Ibid., p.718.
55. Ibid., p.681.
56. Walker, 1983.

CONCLUSION to Book I

1. The names given in the Conclusion, as elsewhere in Book I, are fictitious. Events recounted in each case study are slightly altered to preserve anonymity. Often the cases are composites, as so many individuals tend to recount similar problems, attitudes and solutions.

2. The origins of this myth are discussed in Book II.

3. This story was outlined in the Overview to Chapter 6. See Wandor, M. in the Bibliography.

4. Paula Caplan, *Don't Blame Mother*, 1989, offers a good discussion of the expectations of the ideal daughter in the U.S.A. The expectations are similar in many ways to those I outline here.

5. I've mentioned the Australian Institute of Family Studies before as a good source for research on families. This particular conference was the Institute's Third Australian Family Research Conference.

6. This paper was by Lyn Richards from La Trobe University's Sociology Department and is reported on p.43 of *Family Matters*, April 1990, No 26.

7. From research by Frances Baum, Richard Cooke, Kaye Crowe and Michael Traynor, reported in *Family Matters*, April, 1990, p.43.

8. Papers on Fathers by Naomi White and John Wilson reported in *Family Matters*, April 1990, p.43.

9. Paula Caplan, 1989, p.155.

10. Carroll Smith-Rosenberg, 1985. This was first mentioned in the introduction to Chapter 1, Book I.

11. The problem of the single theory expert, who is authoritarian about the theory on which his or her practice or teaching is based, was discussed in the Preface. Eclectic practitioners are generally more flexible and may use several theories according to the needs of the situation and keep their eyes open for the fallacies in the theories they use.

12. Paula Caplan, 1989, p.47.

13. Paula Caplan, 1989.

14. Ibid.

15. Caplan, 1989, p.49.

16. Caplan, 1989, p.60.

17. Caplan, 1989, also reports this situation in the U.S.A. As she rightly points out,

therapists are not always accountable for the tragedies they create. An outstanding example of this in Australia was given in media reports of the enquiry into the events at Chelmsford Hospital. A psychaitrist who experimented with deep sleep therapy was accused of causing the deaths of a large number of his patients.

18. The Women's Electoral Lobby is a women's organisation that did much to publicise the poor representation of women politically in Australia in the 1970s.

19. Mother-blaming has been described in feminist literature, some of which has been quoted in this book. Mother-blaming shifts responsibility from social organisations to mothers. If mothers couldn't be blamed, we'd have to face up to a total rethink of responsibilities in families. Bureaucrats would have to re-organise social services. The professions would need to overhaul the training of social workers, psychologists and psychiatrists. See books by Jan Harper and Betsy Wearing, 1984.

20. de Beauvoir, 1957.

21. Some find it beneficial while the mother is still living.

22. Alice Munro, 'Ottawa Valley' in *Something I've Been Meaning to Tell You*, 1985.

23. Alice Munro, 'Princess Ida' in *Close Company*, edited by C. Park and C. Heaton,, 1987.

24. Winterson, 'Psalms' in *Close Company*, edited by C. Park and C. Heaton, 1987.

25. In Park & Heaton, (eds.), 1987.

26. Caplan, 1989, p.193.

27. See biographies of de Beauvoir. Here the one by Deidre Bair is listed in the Bibliography.

28. Australian studies by Graeme Russell, at Macquarie University, provide data on this. Caplan, 1989, reports the same situation in the U.S.A.

Book II

INTRODUCTION

1. An example is given in Chapter 4. Since men fear some aspects of women, they may not find medieval legends about witches and hags incongruent. Women absorb them as acceptable. Thus children are given recounts of medieval stories of witches, hags, and damsels in distress without discussion of the fear of women underlying them. Early discussions of these topics would help girls and boys alike. When they first hear these stories many children ask pertinent questions about them.

2. Examples are given throughout — one of the most outstanding being the general disregard of all that Charlotte Brontë had to say about mothers and daughters under patriarchy. The relationship of the Brontë sisters to their brother and father is given prime attention.

3. This is not to say that men do not suffer under patriarchy. Michael Kaufman, 1987, has passionately explored how much men need to contribute to the

struggle against patriarchy, for their own benefit.

4. These issues were discussed in Chapter 2 of Book I.

5. The details of this study were given throughout Book I.

6. Gerda Lerner, 1986, p.222.

7. Gerda Lerner, 1986.

8. Ibid., p.220.

9. Ibid., p.222.

10. Lerner, 1986, discusses some of these oral traditions.

CHAPTER 1

1. The footnotes to this chapter and Chapter 3 give many of the references to this work. See Gerda Lerner, 1986, pp.29-31, M. Kay Martin and Barbara Voorhies, *Female of the Species*, New York: Columbia University Press, 1975 and Michelle Rosaldo, Michelle and Louise Lamphere, *Women, Culture & Society*, Stanford: Stanford University Press, 1974.

2. My source is Martha Macintyre's interesting account, 1986.

3. Ibid. This is not unusual. See Rosalind Miles, 1988, p.34 and Marilyn French, 1988, pp.35-6.

4. This is not spelt out in Macintyre's account.

5. Refer to Lerner, Kay and Voorhies, Rosaldo and Lamphere as in footnote 1 for the evidence. The point and evidence for it is discussed further in Chapter 3.

6. See Marilyn French, 1988, for a discussion of the suggestion.

7. Ibid., p.16. See also Alexander Marshak, 'Some Implications of the Paleolithic Symbolic Evidence for the Origin of Language' in *Origins and Evolution of Language and Speech*, ed. S.R. Harnard, H. D. Steklis and J. Lancaster, New York: Academy of Sciences Conference Proceedings, Vol. 280, Sept. 22-25, 1975.

8. See M. French, 1988, p.26. Mirija Gimbutas, *The Gods and Goddesses of Old Europe*, Berkeley: Univ. California Press, 1974 p.55. John Chadwick, *The Mycenean World*, New York: Cambridge Univ. Press, 1976, pp.61, 93, 94.

9. The following have examined the time when the supreme deity was female: Merlin Stone, *The Paradise Papers: The Suppression of Women's Rites*, 1976. Elizabeth Gould Davis, *The First Sex*, New York: Putman, 1971. Elizabeth Fisher, *Woman's Creation: Sexual Evolution and the Shaping of Society*, New York: Anchor Press/Doubleday, 1979. Many of these more contemporary writers draw on the earlier work of the following: Erich Neumann, *The Great Mother: An Analysis of the Archetype*, London: 1955. E. O. James, *The Cult of the Mother Goddess: An Archaeological and Documentary Study*, 1959. Robert Graves, *The White Goddess: A Historical Grammar of Poetic Myth*, 1948. C. Kerenyi, *Eleusis: Archetypal Image of Mother and Daughter*, London: 1967. There are many others.

10. Wilber, 1983, discusses the evolution of thought in relation to the Goddess.

11. Rich, 1977. Miles, 1988, p.35 argues strongly in support of this conjecture.

12. French, 1988, Lerner, 1986 and others support this view. Among Aborigines in Australia, there are myths that in the time of creation women owned or controlled many of the most sacred songs, rites, myths and objects, but men

took control of them through trickery, theft and persuasion. See Catherine H. Berndt, 'Interpretation and Fact in Aboriginal Australia', in Frances Dahlberg, (ed). *Woman the Gatherer*, New Haven, Conn: Yale Univ. Press, 1981.

13. Neumann, 1972. Evidence is also found in James, 1959, Elizabeth Gould Davis, 1971, Stone, 1976 as in footnote 9 and Josef Wolf and Zdenek Burian, *The Dawn of Man*, London: 1978. R. Miles, 1990 and M. French, 1988 are among many other feminists who support Rich's view.

14. Neumann, 1972, Rich, 1977.

15. Rich, 1977.

16. Neumann, 1972.

17. I have already given the argument that language was developed out of a mother's attempt to communicate with her infants. See footnote 7. R. Miles, 1988, thinks women's recognition of the link between the lunar cycle and menstruation played an important part in the use of words and relational thinking. Penelope Shuttle and Peter Redgrove, *The Wise Wound: Menstruation and Everywoman*, London: 1978, support this view.

18. This situation along with the factors indicated in footnote 17 are probably a few among many influences that played a part in the development of language.

19. Sjöö and Mor, 1981 and Shuttle and Redgrove, 1978.

20. Sjöö and Mor, 1981.

21. Ibid.

22. Johann Bachofen, 1967. Robert Briffault, *The Mother*, 1927, is another who argued the case for matriarchies. He also observed matrilocal and matrilineal societies and found plenty of evidence for female-centred practices. Some of his ancient sources are no longer considered valid, but there is still enough to suggest that women were central in many ways.

23. This was discussed in Book I, Chapters 4 and 5.

24. Sjöö and Mor, 1981, Rich, 1977, French, 1988, Miles, 1990 are among the many who argue this point.

25. The most intense of these attitudes is seen in medieval times and is discussed in Chapter 4. Remnants of authoritarian patriarchal thinking about sex still have influence.

26. Monaghan, 1981 is one of many.

27. Ibid.

28. Miles, 1990, p.54. M. Stone, 1976, pp.168-78.

29. Weideger, 1975.

30. Harding, 1955.

31. Rich, 1977. Miles, 1988.

32. Sjöö and Mor, 1981.

33. Shuttle and Redgrove, 1978.

34. Bettelheim, New York: Collier, 1968.

35. This was discussed in Chapter 2, Book I.

36. Sjöö and Mor, 1981.

37. T. C. Lethbridge, 1962. Also see Miles, 1988, p.64 and Nigel Calder, *Timescale*,

London: 1984, p.160.

38. See Chapter 2 for a discussion of this process.

39. Graves, 1955.

40. Sjoo and Mor, 1981

41. Ibid.

42. Engels, 1971

43. Sayers, Evans and Redcliffe, 1987.

44. Rich, 1977. R. Miles, 1988 goes further in this claim, pp.56-58.

45. Gerda Lerner, 1986.

CHAPTER 2.

1. I'm indebted to Adrienne Rich, Patricia Monaghan, Sjöö and Mor and many others for the legends recounted in this chapter.

2. These accounts are documented in Sir James Frazer, *The Golden Bough*, 1922. Margaret Mead, *Male and Female. A Study of the Sexes in a Changing World*, 1949. Jacquetta Hawks, *Dawn of the Gods*, 1958, *Prehistory*, 1965 and *The First Great Civilisation*, 1975. S.G. F. Brandon, *Creation Legends of the Ancient Near East*, 1963.

3. Ibid. Also see Sir Arthur Evans, *The Palace of Minos at Knossos*, 4 Volumes, London: 1921-35.

4. See Marilyn French, *Beyond Power. On Women, Men and Morals*, 1988, p.33. Elizabeth Fisher, *Woman's Creation*, 1979. Also Sanday, Peggy Reeves, *Female Power and Male Dominance*, New York: Cambridge Univ. Press, 1981 for discussions of the many cultures that have a female divinity and female creation myths.

5. Sjöö and Mor, 1981.

6. Abby Kleinbaum, *The War Against the Amazons*, New York: McGraw Hill, 1983 surveys most of the literature on the Amazons and concludes that they never existed and that the myth of their existence served to reinforce patriarchal mythology.

7. Monaghan, 1981.

8. Monaghan, 1981, p.138.

9. Monaghan, 1981.

10. Ibid.

11. Robert Briffault, 1969 is one of many who argues that Greece had a matricentric past. The theory of the fragmentation of the original great Goddess is found in Joseph Campbell, *The Masks of God. Occidental Mythology*, New York: 1970 and Lerner, 1986.

12. Joseph Campbell, 1970, Davidson and Broner, 1980, Lerner, 1986.

13. Ibid.

14. Ochshorn in Davidson and Broner, 1980, is among many who make this point.

15. Gilbert Murray, *Five Stages of Greek Religion*, Garden City, New York: 1955, Monaghan, 1981.

16. Davidson and Broner, 1980.

17. Washington and Tobal in Davidson and Broner, 1980.

CHAPTER 3.

1. Gerda Lerner, 1986. The following are among those who have argued that matriarchies existed: Johann Bachofen, *Myth, Religion and The Mother-Right*, Princeton: 1967. Friedrich Engels, *The Origin of The Family*, 1884. Robert Briffault, *The Mothers*, 1927. Evelyn Reed, *Woman's Evolution*, New York: 1975. Elizabeth Fisher, *Women's Creation*, 1979. Elizabeth Gould Davis, *The First Sex*, 1971 and Rayna Reiter, *Towards An Anthropology of Women*, London: 1978.

2. Gerda Lerner, 1986. A number of feminists support this view. Miles, 1988, pp.45 — 6. Recent arguments are that matriarchy was something conjured up by men to justify domination of women under patriarchy.

3. Miles, 1988, pp.47 -8 is among those who provide evidence to support this view.

4. Chapter 1, Book II.

5. Some feminists would not support this contention, but I find Lerner's sources more satisfactory. Marilyn French, 1988, pp.37-39 and her evidence supports Lerner's evidence as does that of M. Kay Martin and Barbara Voorhies, *Female of the Species*, New York: Columbia Univ. Press, 1975.

6. Elaine Morgan, *Descent of Woman*, 1972, Elsie Boulding, *The Underside of History*, Colorado: Westview Press, 1976, Rayna Reiter, (ed). *Toward an Anthropology of Women*, New York: Monthly Review Press, 1978, Gerda Lerner, 1986, Rosalind Miles, 1988. Also see Chapter 1 for evidence from other sources.

7. Lerner, 1986.

8. Evelyn Reed, 1975.

9. E. O James, 1960, M. Gimbutas, 1982, G. Lerner, 1986.

10. Lerner, 1986.

11. Female figurines are in the overwhelming majority from the Upper Neolithic, through the Neolithic, Bronze and Classical periods to the threshold of the Christian era. See M. Gimbutas, 1982, J. Ochshorn, 1981, G. Lerner, 1986, M. French, 1988, pp.22-28.

12. Lerner, 1986.

13. See references in footnote 6. Read R. Miles, 1988 for an argument against this contention, p.21.

14. Ibid.

15. G. Lerner, 1986, p.45. Lois Paul in Rosaldo and Lamphere, 1974, pp.297-99, describes a twentieth century Guatemalan Indian village in which women use menstruation as a symbolic weapon.

16. S. Phillips, 1972 and 1974 discusses this point in relation to judging medieval attitudes by twentieth century ways of thinking.

17. J. Mellaart, 1967, G. Lerner, 1986, M. French, 1988, Chapter 1.

18. Lerner, 1986. Also see Chapter 1 for other sources.

19. Ibid. Chapter 3. Lerner derives much of her information from the following: G. Child, 1936, C. Redman, 1978, J. Hawkes and L Woolley, 1963.

20. Ibid.

21. Lerner, 1986, p.53.

22. G. Lerner, 1986, B. Batto, 1974, R. Briffault, 1969, W. Hallo, 1968.

23. Ibid.

24. Lerner, 1986.

25. Ibid.

26. G. Lerner, 1986. For a discussion of Inanna and Enkheduanna see Paul Friedrich, 1978.

27. Ibid.

28. G. Lerner, 1986, p.141.

29. Ibid., p.143.

30. Ibid., p.156.

31. Ibid., p.145.

32. Ibid.

33. J. Piaget, 1950. At this early stage in the development of thinking, naming and words are seen as having special power. For example, the word cat is not just a word, it embodies everything to do with cats and they could be called by no other name. Piaget has written about the evolution and development of human thinking throughout history. Also see Wilber, 1983.

34. G. Lerner, 1986, p.154.

35. I'm indebted to the research of J. E. Phillips, 1978, for many of the details of the activities of Roman mothers and daughters, upon which I have based my interpretations.

CHAPTER 4.

1. Judith Ochshorn in Davidson and Broner, 1980, discusses this point.

2. Gerda Lerner, 1986.

3. See Chapter 3, Book II.

4. G. Lerner, 1986.

5. G. Lerner, 1986, p.173.

6. Trible, 1973, Bird, 1974, Otwell, 1977.

7. G. Lerner, 1986, p.176.

8. Ibid.

9. J. Ochshorn in Davidson and Broner, 1980.

10. G. Lerner, 1986, p.   165.

11. G. Lerner, 1986, p.177.

12. G. Lerner, 1986.

13. G. Lerner, 1986, p.179

14. This point was discussed in Chapter 3. See footnote 33.

15. I have explained in Chapter 3 that I cannot agree with Lerner's definition of abstract in this context. Symbolic thinking is qualitatively different from abstract or logical processes of thought which use deduction and induction.

16. G. Lerner, 1986, p.182.

17. G. Lerner, 1986, p.100.

18. Ibid., pp.192-3.

19. R. Miles, 1988, describes this hijacking process in a number of religions, pp.86-7.

20. P. Monaghan, 1981.

21. Ibid.

22. G. Lerner, 1986.

23. R. Miles, 1988 pp.85-87 argues that although early Christianity has been presented as a plot against women, since it put them in a subordinate position to men, it also had strong appeal to women. In a reward and punishment system, the more women submitted and suffered the greater the final pay off. In early Christianity, women found not merely a role, but an instrument of resistance to male domination in choosing to be a bride of Christ. Women helped build the church not only in good works but with their lives and blood.

24. G. Lerner, 1986, p.198.

25. Ibid., p.201.

26. J. Ochshorn, 1980.

27. The following information about medieval society comes from my own research, 1972, 1973, 1974, 1979.

28. Although one needs to be careful about extrapolating contemporary styles of thinking to past societies, there do seem to be parallels between some aspects of medieval thinking and what has been described as the authoritarian personality, see Phillips, 1979 (b).

29. Geoffrey Chaucer, c. 1340 -1400.

30. See footnotes, 27 and 28. These attitudes are often obfuscated by all manner of conventions. There are obviously many illustrations in contemporary attitudes also.

31. The attitude survives. See Virginia Woolf's pertinent description of this situation in Chapter 5, Book I or in 'A Room of One's Own', in Rossi, 1974, p.633.

32. Refer to footnotes 27 and 28.

33. Nikki Stiller, in Davidson and Broner, 1980.

34. Refer to footnotes 27 and 28.

35. N. Stiller in Davidson and Broner, 1980.

36. Ibid. Refer to Book I for discussion of contemporary mothers who try to hand on survival techniques to their daughters.

37. Children are sometimes puzzled, even upset, by these portrayals and ask questions which, if answered appropriately can provide a good foundation for later understanding of negative descriptions of women. These stories, unless discussed can have a negative effect on self-esteem in girls and encourage macho attitudes in boys. See Chapter 1, Book I. They need not be censored or removed from children but rather used as a way to recognise prejudice.

38. The situation finds parallels in the scapegoating of Jews in Nazi Germany.

39. Refer to footnote 27 and Stiller in Davidson and Broner, 1980.

40. *Sir Gawain and The Green Knight*. Trans. p.Stone, Penguin Classics, 1959, p.947.

41. Refer footnotes 27 and 28.

42. Bernard Shaw, *St Joan*, Kors and Peters, 1972, French 1988, Chapter 3.

43. K. Thomas, 1971, E. Boulding, 1976, M. French, 1988, p.164.

44. See the discussion on self-esteem in Chapter 1 of Book I.

45. Sjöö and Mor, 1981, give this figure but the exact number is disputed. See M. French, 1988, p.164, Bridenthal and Koonz, 1977, Ehrenreich and English, 1979.

46. Sjöö and Mor, 1981, p.67.

47. Sjöö and Mor, 1981.

48. Ibid.

49. See Lillian Faderman, 1981. Faderman has researched women's friendships since the middle ages and set them in the context of this kind of phallocentricism.

50. Christine de Pizan, *The Book of the City of Ladies*, 11.36. 1405, published Pan, 1983.

51. Ibid.

52. Earl Richards in the Introduction to Christine de Pizan, *The Book of The City of Ladies* and Enid McLeod, 1976.

53. Rebecca Bishop, 1985.

54. Ibid.

55. R. Bishop, 1985, also makes this point.

56. J. Fleming, 1969, p.47.

57. Christine de Pizan, 1405, Pan, 1983, 11.2.

58. Ibid., 12.2.

59. Quoted in Bishop, 1985.

60. Ibid.

CHAPTER 5

1. For an excellent discussion of Renaissance mothers see Betty

S. Travitsky, 'The New Mother of the English Renaissance: Her Writings on Motherhood', in Davidson and Broner, 1980.

2. Clinton, Elizabeth, Countess of Lincoln, 1622 and Lady Mildmay, in Rachel Wiegall, 1911 — see Bibliography.

3. Supporting evidence comes from S. Travitsky, 1980.

4. Virginia Woolf in 'A Room of One's Own' in Rossi 1974, first published in 1929. Also see Carolyn Heilbrun, *Toward a Recognition of Androgyny*, 1973 and Juliet Dusinberg, *Shakespeare and the Nature of Women*, 1975.

5. For a detailed discussion of the attitude to women in the sixteenth and seventeenth centuries see Faderman, 1981.

6. Myra Glazer Shotz, 1980, 'The Great Unwritten Story: Mothers and Daughters in Shakespeare', in Davidson and Broner, 1980, believes the answer is yes. Her research and sources contribute to and support several of the ideas presented here.

7. Ibid.

8. This concept of women in medieval times was discussed in Chapter 4. It is also

discussed in Book I as still being applicable.

9. Unlike medieval writings about "evil" women, Shakespeare's characterisation of Lady Macbeth is more complex. He shows the tragic effect of her ambition on herself.

10. Using women projectively was legitimised by patriarchal religion. See Chapter 4, Book II and the Preface and Chapter 1 of Book I.

11. Presumably he was born by caesarian section.

12. This point was discussed in Chapter 3 of this Book. The psychology of it was discussed in Book I.

13. Shotz, 1980, also makes this point.

14. Ibid.

15. Shotz, 1980 and Joyce Carol Oates, 1974, argue that it is.

16. W. Shakespeare, ed. W. J. Craig, 1955, pp.934-5.

17. Shotz, 1980.

18. The devices used by patriarchy to try to cope with the limits on male creativity were discussed in Chapter 3, Book II. See also Book I and the theories of Bruno Bettelheim, 1968, Karen Horney, 1967 and Adrienne Rich, 1977.

19. The Renaissance and Elizabethan periods placed great emphasis on the family and it seems likely that Shakespeare was making a statement about a feminine lack within it rather than simply men without women. Shotz, 1980, believes he was saying that female mysteries are essential to male well-being.

20. There are of course many hangovers to the present day.

21. This issue was discussed in Chapter 3, Book II.

22. See Ehrlich, 1976, for more detail.

23. Ibid.

24. Bonding was discussed in Chapter 1, Book I.

25. Quoted in Ehrlich, 1976.

26. This point was discussed in the Preface to Book I and in Chapter 3, Book II.

27. I remember one fellow student asking if Ophelia would have gone mad if she'd had a mother to support her? The question was dismissed as irrelevant. I was therefore delighted to see that Myra Glazer Shotz gave the same question a place in print on p.53 of Davidson and Broner, 1980.

CHAPTER 6

1. The quotations in this and the next four paragraphs come from Rousseau's *Emile*. Supporting evidence for my comments come from R. Parker, 1984, reprinted, 1989 and from Will and Ariel Durant, *The Story of Civilisation*. Volume 10, *Rousseau and Revolution*, 1967.

2. Rousseau, *Emile*, 1762.

3. Meat was seen as nurturing masculinity.

4. Rousseau, *Emile*, 1762.

5. Rousseau's writings indicate that he feared dominating, immodest women and argued that they were taking over and making men effeminate. Durant, 1967, offers evidence in agreement.

6. R. Parker, 1984, also discusses this point, p.123.

7. de Mause, 1974.

8. Rousseau, 1762.

9. Roszika Parker, 1984, gives examples of this in art and embroidery.

10. William Buchanan, *Domestic Medicine, or a Treatise on the Prevention and Care of Diseases by Regimen and Simple Medicines*, 1769, quoted in R. Parker, 1984, p.129.

11. Carlton J.H Hayes, *A Political & Cultural History of Modern Europe*, pp.462-69, 716-717.

12. The sources for the historical background are numerous. Two which provide basic material are K. O'Morgan, 1988 and H. J Habakkuk and M. Poston, 1965.

13. R. Parker, 1984, p.128, provides supporting data.

14. M. Wollstonecraft, *Thoughts on the Education of Daughters*, 1786.

15. Wollstonecraft, *Vindication of the Rights of Women*, p.57, Rossi Edition, 1974.

16. Ibid., p.43.

17. Ibid., p.57.

18. Ibid., p.65.

19. The details of Wollstonecraft's life can be found in Alice S. Rossi, *The Feminist Papers*, 1974.

20. Wollstonecraft, *Vindication of the Rights of Women*, p.46, Rossi Edition, 1974.

21. Ibid., p.71.

22. Ibid., p.69. Charlotte Brontë, who is discussed in Chapter 8, Book II, indicated that governesses were still treated very badly in the early nineteenth century and that there had been a tradition of parents allowing their children to behave disrespectfully toward their governesses. Governesses were often expected to do menial tasks such as mending and were dealt with like servants.

23. Wollstonecraft, *Vindication of the Rights of Women*, p.69, Rossi Edition, 1974.

24. Ibid.

25. Lundberg and Farnham, 1947:149, 150, 159, quoted in Rossi, 1974, p.37. Rossi criticises these authors for using a narrow psychoanalytic bias in their interpretation of Wollstonecraft's life that was more fancied than factual. She points out that these kinds of attacks and ridicule are often directed at pioneers who move outside the thought and action approved by their society.

26. Rossi, 1974.

27. Quoted in Rossi, 1974.

28. Lillian Faderman, 1981.

29. Ibid. It depends on how lesbianism is defined. See Lesbian History Group, 1989.

30. Lillian Faderman, 1981, is one of many who support this conclusion.

31. Ibid.

32. The Marquis de Sade took the brutality that existed between the sexes to its gruesome extreme. It was thrilling to torture women. Faderman, 1981, pp.95-96 discusses the hideousness of some of the "sadism" toward women in this period.

33. Faderman, 1981.
34. R. Parker, 1984, reprinted 1989, gives supporting evidence for this.
35. Ibid.
36. Quoted in L. Faderman, 1981, p.98.
37. Mary Granville Delaney.
38. *Clarissa* by Samuel Richardson was published in 1748. *Tom Jones* by Henry Fielding was published in 1749.
39. Support for this conclusion comes from many sources. One of the best is Lillian Faderman, 1981. See also *Ladies of Llangllen*, by Elizabeth Mavor, 1974.
40. Janet Todd, 1986, provides some excellent research material about the fashion of sensibility for those wanting to pursue the matter further than can be done here.
41. First published in 1790. Quoted in Todd, 1986, p.117.
42. Janet Todd, 1986, p.4.
43. Todd, 1986.
44. Lillian Faderman, 1981, provides some fascinating evidence about women's friendships from the Renaissance to the present.
45. Janet Todd, 1986, p.135.
46. This was discussed in Chapter 1, Book II, in relation to matrilineal societies.
47. Lerner's point was discussed in the Preface to Book I and in Chapter 3, Book II.

CHAPTER 7

1. Roszika Parker, 1984 — 1989 is an excellent source for the history of embroidery.
2. At this time both men and women were embroiderers. See discussion later in the chapter.
3. Roszika Parker discusses how the silence of the embroiderer suggested self-containment which became implicated in a stereotype of femininity and was represented as seductiveness. A picture by Marcus Stone, 1888, *In Love*, in the Castle Museum in Nottingham captures the stereotype beautifully. It is reproduced in Parker, 1989.
4. Source for evidence is R. Parker, 1989.
5. Ibid.
6. Ibid.
7. Ibid., p.131.
8. This point was discussed in the Introduction to Chapter 1, Book I. Because daughters had few options, they accepted their mothers' way of life. They served an apprenticeship with them and this became a supportive alliance. See Carol Smith-Rosenberg, 1985.
9. Quoted in R. Parker, 1989.
10. Ibid.
11. See R. Parker, 1989 for more details than I can give here.
12. Museum collections of medieval embroidery attest to this. Also see Parker, 1989, pp.42-3.

13. This point was discussed in Chapter 4, Book II.

14. Eileen Power, in M. M. Postan, (ed.), *Medieval Women*, Cambridge: Cambridge Univ. Press, 1975.

15. Twentieth century historians have largely accepted the Victorian assumption that professional embroiderers were mostly men. See Chapter 3 of Parker, 1989 for evidence to the contrary.

16. R. Parker, 1989, Chapter 4. Ruth Kelso, *Doctrine for The Lady of The Renaissance*, Urbana: University of Illinois Press, 1956. Ian Maclean, *The Renaissance View of Women*, Cambridge: Cambridge Univ. Press, 1980.

17. Ibid.

18. Christine de Pizan cited in R. Parker, 1989, p.68.

19. R. Parker, 1989, Chapter 4.

20. Ibid.

21. Margaret Swain, *The Needlework of Mary Queen of Scots*, New York: Van Nostran Reinhold, 1973.

22. Parker, 1989.

23. One of many sources for the attitudes of Cromwell and the Puritans is C. J. H. Hayes, *A Political and Cultural History of Modern Europe*, New York: Macmillan, 1935. Also see O'Morgan, 1988.

24. Christine de Pizan, *Le Livre des Trois Vertus*, 1497.

25. See footnote 23.

26. R. Parker, 1989, pp.84-5.

27. Ibid, p.88.

28. The sources for information in this and the previous paragraph come from pamphlets and poems of seventeenth century women, for example, Bathsua Makin, *An Essay to Revive the Ancient Education of Gentlewomen*, London: 1693. Many are cited in Cora Kaplan, *Salt and Bitter and Good*, London: Paddington Press, 1975, Roberta Hamilton, *The Liberation of Women*, 1978 and R. Parker, 1989.

29. Wollstonecraft was discussed in the previous chapter.

30. R. Parker, 1989, p.105.

31. Ibid., p.107.

32. After the unpopular three year reign of the Catholic, James II, who believed in the divine right of kings, Parliament re-asserted itself. In 1689 William of Orange and his wife, Mary, were invited to the English throne and helped establish its protestant nature. Sources for more detail are Hayes, 1935, Cristopher Hill, *Reformation to Industrial Revolution*, London: Penguin, 1975, O'Morgan, 1988.

33. S. Richardson, *Pamela*, 1740.

34. Cited in Parker, 1989.

35. Ruth Hayden, *Mrs Delaney: Her Life and Her Flowers*, London: Colonnade, 1980.

36. R. Parker, 1989

37. Ibid.

38. Alice Chandler, *A Dream of Order: The Medieval Ideal in Nineteenth Century Literature*, London: Routledge & Kegan Paul, 1970. Martha Vicinus, (ed.) *Suffer and Be Still: Women in the Victorian Age*, Indiana Univ. Press, 1972.

39. The underlying attitude to women in medieval times was discussed in Chapter 4, Book II.

40. Charlotte Brontë, *Shirley*, first published 1849.

41. Ibid.

42. Ibid.

43. Ibid., Chapter 9.

44. Examples of an embroidered suffragette banner and handkerchief can be seen in the Museum of London and in R. Parker, 1989.

45. Christine Risley, *Creative Embroidery*, London: Studio Vista, 1967.

46. See the discussion of Rousseau's influence in the previous chapter.

47. Cited in R. Parker, 1989, Chapter, 6.

48. Hayes, 1935, Faderman, 1981.

49. Irene Danciger, *A World of Women: An Illustrated History of Women's Magazines*, London: Gill and Macmillan, 1978. R. Parker, 1989.

50. Janet Todd, 1986.

51. Jane Austen uses Plymouth as a symbol for the disorder and coarseness into which England could fall.

52. Susan Peck MacDonald, 1980, also develops this interpretation.

53. The tradition can be seen in novels such as *Evelina*, 1778, by Fanny Burney. In this genre the heroine is plunged into trials due to the lack of a living mother's support and protection. Austen's comments about this tradition are obviously ironic, although she herself borrowed it to good effect.

54. In Davidson and Broner, 1980.

55. Wollstonecraft was discussed in Chapter 6.

56. Tony Tanner, 1987, gives a full discussion of this point of view.

57. Edmund Burke, *Reflections on the French Revolution*, 1790 and Thomas Paine, Rights of Man, 1791.

58. Tony Tanner, 1987, also develops this argument much more fully than I can here.

59. The American writer, Ralph Emerson, who thought Austen vulgar and sterile, said Austen had but one problem in mind — "marriageableness" — a term I have borrowed. His view depended on a patriarchal perspective and entirely missed the point of Austen's feminine ideology.

60. This point is also made in Tony Tanner, 1987. He gives more of the background than I can here.

61. John Locke, 1690, *The Second Treatise of Government*. Tanner, 1987, p.19, summarises the main points in Dr Johnson's theory.

62. For a more extensive discussion of the complexities of the social contracts of the eighteenth century, see the Introduction to Tanner, 1987.

63. Ibid.

64. Ibid.

65. Ibid.

66. Virginia Woolf, *A Room of One's Own*, 1970.

67. The point was also illustrated in the previous chapter.

68. Elaine Showalter, 1982, p.14, sums up "The Angel in the House" as part of the patriarchal ideology of the proper sphere and behaviour of a woman — to be a perfect lady, contentedly submissive to men, strong in her inner purity and religiosity and Queen in her realm, the Home.

69. Some who find Fanny Price distasteful include C. S. Lewis, D. W. Harding and Lionel Trilling in *Jane Austen. A Collection of Critical Essays*, ed. Ian Watt, Englewood Cliffs: Prentice Hall, 1963.

70. Laski, 1977, is one of many sources for biographical information about Jane Austen.

71. This issue was discussed in Chapter 2, Book II and subsequent chapters.

72. Cited in Laski, 1977.

73. Ibid.

74. Ibid.

CHAPTER 8

1. I'm indebted to Showalter, 1982, for this piece of information.

2. The way in which patriarchy teaches mothers and daughters to disrespect their sexuality was discussed in Book I.

3. The patriarchal myth of female masochism was discussed in Chapter 8, Book I.

4. This is discussed later in the chapter.

5. The important influence social attitudes have on female sexuality and how these affect mother-daughter relationships was discussed in Book I, especially Chapters 4 and 5.

6. The objectives of Lowood School are made clear in the writings of its prime mover and overseer, the Reverend William Carus Wilson. See *Letters: The Brontës: Their Lives, Friendship and Correspondence*, ed. T.J. Wise and J.A. Symington, 4 Vols, Oxford: Shakespeare Head Press, 1932, 1, pp.70-72. These letters are the source of much of the information in this chapter. .

7. Showalter, 1982, also stresses the power and meaning of this imagery.

8. Childhood writings include: 'Tales of the Islanders', 'The Green Dwarf'. 'A Tale of the Perfect Tense', 'Something About Arthur', 'The Foundling', 'Lily Hart', 'The Politics of Verdopolis' and many others. See Penguin collection.

9. Christine Alexander, 1983.

10. *Letters*, ed. Wise and Symington, give insight into Charlotte's anguish, for example Vol. 1, pp.147-8.

11. Ibid., p.155.

12. This issue is discussed in Chapter 4, 6 and 7 Book II and in Chapter 4, Book I.

13. Rich, 1977. Also see Chapters 6 and 8, Book I.

14. This still applies to adolescent girls and women today — the confusion, between valuing sexuality and the taboos that create the attitude that good girls don't, is discussed in various contexts in Book I, for example Chapters 3, 4 and 5.

15. Lane, 1966, discusses this fact.
16. The history of this prescription was discussed in Chapters 6 and 7 Book II.
17. These episodes are reported in Gérin, 1979.
18. Woolf, 1970.
19. Many accounts of life in Victorian times refer to raging husbands, for example Marilyn French, 1987, (Chapter, 9, Book I) and Charles Dickens.
20. In Victorian England men could have their mistresses but women had to be chaste and monogamous. To this day the double standard remains in some form. See Chapters 4 and 5, Book I for a discussion of attitudes to the double standard during adolescence.
21. Gérin, 1967.
22. Apart from the evidence of their juvenilia, Mrs Gaskell, 1971, and Christine Alexander, 1983, describe the Brontë children's imaginative pursuits.
23. Alexander, 1983, discusses the evidence for this.
24. Ibid.
25. Margaret Lane, 1966, also considers this of importance.
26. I exclude Jane Austen from this tradition.
27. 'The Waverley Novels', *Literary Studies*, 11, London, 1879, p.167.
28. Showalter, 1982, also draws attention to the Brontës' symbolism.
29. In this context, by mother-surrogates, I mean Elizabeth and Maria, the two little mothering sisters who died of consumption.
30. Sources for this information include Charlotte's letters and Gérin, 1967.
31. *Letters: The Brontës: Their Lives, Friendship and Correspondence*, ed. T.J. Wise and J.A. Symington, 4 Vols, Oxford: Shakespeare Head Press, 1932. Vol. 1 pp 9-18 indicate that Maria was passionately in love with Patrick and that she harboured misgivings that her love exceeded human bounds. This example of passionate love could well have provided a model for the love between Jane Eyre and Rochester, through childhood memories and Charlotte's reading of her mothers' letters after her death.
32. Gérin, 1967, is one of many sources.
33. Gérin, 1979. Also see Patrick's accounts of his wife's death in *Letters*, ed. Wise and Symington, Vol. 1, pp 58-9.
34. Lane, 1966.
35. Lane, 1966, Gérin, 1979.
36. Alexander, 1983.
37. Alexander brings these episodes together in her research into Charlotte's juvenilia, 1983.
38. Ibid., p.246.
39. See the Penguin collection of Charlotte's juvenilia and Alexander, 1983.
40. Gérin, 1967.
41. Charlotte Brontë, *Jane Eyre*, 1966, p.64.
42. Reported in Gérin, 1967.
43. McCurdy, 1947, who wrote some of the earliest psychoanalytic appraisals of

the Brontës, makes this point.

44. The dichotomised presentation of mothers has been discussed in many parts of Book I, for example Chapters 1, 3, 5, and 6.

45. The major contribution to the splitting of mothers into good and bad aspects comes from patriarchal attitudes and these were discussed in Book I.

46. Doris Lessing, *Martha Quest*, 1952.

47. By prototype behaviour, I mean that mothers are supposed to provide the models which daughters adopt.

48. Book I discusses the over-emphasis under patriarchy of the need for separation between mothers and daughters and the anxieties that generate this over-emphasis. It also indicates that physical separation is not the solution to mother-daughter conflict.

49. Gérin, 1967.

50. Mrs Gaskell, 1971.

51. Mrs Gaskell and Gérin support this view.

52. Frank, 1990, p.220 comments on this fact.

53. See *Letters*, 11, ed. Wise and Symington, p.261, for Charlotte's acceptance of this situation.

54. *Letters*, ed. Wise and Symington, 1932, Gérin, 1967 and Frank 1990 all describe periods of deep unhappiness where poor appetite and ill health permitted escape back to Haworth; for example Charlotte as a teacher at Roe Head and governess at the Sidgwicks' or Emily as a teacher at the Law Hill School.

55. Frank, 1990, p.136.

56. Sources are Mrs Gaskell, and Gérin, 1967, p.207.

57. Frank, 1990, p.171, discusses this further.

58. *Letters*, ed Wise and Symington, Vol 11, p.78. See also Frank, 1990, pp.181-220.

59. Frank, 1990, p.42.

60. The development of the self-concept and how we become separate identities is discussed in Book I, Chapter 2.

61. Daiches, 1985, also thinks this fusion of self with Heathcliff has something to do with Emily's limited awareness of self and others.

62. Frank, 1990, suggests that Branwell may in fact have been sacked for instigating a homosexual affair with his pupil and employer's son and spread the rumour about a liaison with the boy's mother to protect and arouse sympathy for himself.

63. Gérin, 1967.

64. Miller, 1989, argues that it was a lesbian relationship. It all depends how lesbianism is defined.

65. Gérin, 1967 and 1979.

66. Gérin, 1967.

67. Gérin, 1979.

68. Charlotte Brontë, *Jane Eyre*, pp.27-28.

69. Gérin, 1967.

70. Gérin, 1979.

71. Ibid.

72. Showalter, 1982, makes this point.

CHAPTER 9

1. Some of Eliot's experiences are given later in the chapter.

2. George Eliot, *The Mill on the Floss,* p.32.

3. Ibid., p.151.

4. Ibid., p.16.

5. Ibid., p.285.

6. Zimmerman, 1980.

7. A little of Eliot's life is given later in the chapter.

8. For more detail see Gillian Beer's account of Eliot's life and work, 1986.

9. Showalter, 1982, pp.129-130.

10. This is an issue to which Eliot constantly returned. Beer, 1986, discusses it at greater length than is possible here.

11. Beer, 1986, Chapter 4, refers to the incestuous implications of the drowning of Maggie and Tom.

12. Beer, 1986, quotes some of the criticisms of Eliot, pp.105- 106.

13. This has strong currency. Eliot's relationship with her mother is discussed later in the chapter.

14. Zimmerman, 1980, offers an excellent insight into Eliot's beliefs about the power of mothers.

15. Ibid.

16. Redinger, 1975.

17. Zimmerman, 1980.

18. Faderman, 1981, discusses these attitudes in full.

19. See Chapter 8, Book II.

20. Riegel, 1963.

21. Welter, 1974.

22. Haight, 1986.

23. Lilienfield, 1980.

24. Beer, 1986, disagrees with this suggestion. She argues that Eliot chose a male pseudonym simply to give her characters more objectivity.

25. Zimmerman, 1980.

26. This issue was discussed in Chapter 6, Book I. It is also discussed by Adriennne Rich, 1977.

27. Zimmerman, 1980.

28. This issue was discussed in Book I.

29. Quoted in Faderman, 1981, pp.171-172.

30. Published in 1900.

31. Quoted in Faderman, 1981, p.160.

32. Published in 1835.

33. Locksley Hall, 1842, quoted in Faderman, 1981.

34. Smith-Rosenberg, 1985.

35. Quoted in Faderman, 1981.

36. Ibid.

37. The history of the division of labour between men and women was discussed in Chapter 7, Book II.

38. Faderman, 1981.

39. Ibid.

40. Ibid.

41. Freud, *Complete Psychological Works*.

42. Faderman, 1981.

43. Ibid.

44. Ibid.

45. Colette, 1967. pp111

46. Rich, 1977.

47. These factors were discussed in Chapters 4 and 5, Book 1I.

48. Lilienfield, 1980.

49. Willa Cather 1873 — 1947 was a major American writer whose novels and short stories captured America's pioneering past. She was concerned about the loss of the kind of community-oriented security and human values which this period represented and the emergence of materialism and impoverishment. Her style is remarkable for its clarity and deceptive simplicity. She had a special skill for evoking feeling.

50. Richardson was born in Australia, but lived most of her adult life in England and Europe. Australia was the inspiration and setting for her writing.

CHAPTER 10

1. Nettie Palmer, 1950, and Karen McLeod, 1985, are two of several critics who make and provide evidence for these descriptions.

2. Palmer, 1950, who knew Richardson, makes this point. See p.72. The officials of the new colony preserved the conventions of the eighteenth century, after these had been replaced in Europe by industrial ethics. They were formal, stiff in spirit and unwilling to adapt themselves to the strange conditions of a new country. On the positive side, the eighteenth century had its virtues from which the new country benefited greatly, including the interest in science and discovery.

3. Axel Clark, 1990, p.35.

4. Ibid., pp.6-7.

5. Palmer, 1950, p.87, discusses the point further.

6. Richardson, 1982, *The Way Home*, Part 1, Chapter 8, p.414.

7. Clark, 1990, p.20.

8. Ibid., p.31.

9. The attitude of fathers to mothers in families and their powerful influence on the mother-daughter relationship was discussed in Chapter 5, Book II.

10. The evidence is provided in their letters to each other. See Clark, 1990, p.30.

11. Ibid.

12. Richardson, *Myself When Young*, Heinemann, London, 1948.

13. The issue is not as straightforward as I have represented it here. See Clark, 1990, p.65.

14. Richardson, *Myself When Young*.

15. Clark, 1990, p.71.

16. Richardson, *Myself When Young*.

17. Clark, 1990, p.74.

18. Ibid., p.108.

19. Richardson, *Myself When Young*.

20. Clark, 1990.

21. Ibid., p.118.

22. Richardson, *Myself When Young*.

23. Palmer's assessment, 1950.

24. For a discussion of the research, see Phillips, 1986.

25. Clark, 1990, p.153.

26. See the previous chapter for a description of this movement.

27. Palmer, 1950, p.22.

28. Palmer, 1950, p.27.

29. Clark, 1990, p.222.

30. Richardson, *Myself When Young*.

31. Ibid.

32. Clark, 1990, p.180.

33. Ibid., p.183.

34. Ibid., p.184.

35. Ibid., p.191.

36. Richardson, *Myself When Young*.

37. Clark, 1990, p.230.

38. This is apparent in her account of her life, her stories and her novels. Clark, 1990, who has researched all the letters, notes and accounts, relating to Richardson and written an excellent account of his findings, confirms the point.

39. Karen McLeod, 1985, who has written an excellent literary analysis of Richardson's work, discusses this point in more detail than is possible here.

40. Nettie Palmer, 1950, provides a good discussion of the growth of Mary, in Chapter VI of her study of the works of Richardson.

41. Karen McLeod, 1985, provides an excellent discussion of this aspect of Richardson's talent as a novelist.

42. See footnote 40.

43. For example, in Jane Austen's novels, we know at whom we should laugh or of whom we should approve. George Eliot makes it evident where anger

should lie. There is more freedom in Virginia Woolf, but there is a pact about the irrational mind. See Karen McLeod, 1985, Chapter 11, for a discussion of this difference between Richardson and other writers.

44. See Karen McLeod, 1985, for further exploration of the multiple perspectives of Laura.

45. See Chapter 6, 'Husband and Wife' in McLeod, 1985.

46. Ibid.

47. See Palmer, 1950, McLeod, 1985, for some of the assessments of Richardson's work by famous authors of her day and their own views. Some indication of the reception is that the last part of the trilogy, *Ultima Thule* was taken up by the Book of the Month Club in America, just after its publication.

48. See Chapter 6, 'Husband and Wife', Karen McLeod, 1985, for further exploration of this point.

49. The point is an obvious one to anyone who reads Richardson. Karen McLeod, 1985, discusses it in Chapter 2, 'The Education of an Expatriate'.

50. See Chapter 10, Karen McLeod, for a discussion of why this novel is not in the same league as Richardson's other novels.

51. McLeod, 1985.

CHAPTER 11

1. Quoted in Senhouse's Introduction to *My Mother's House*, 1968, p.12.

2. *My Mother's House* p.156.

3. Ibid., pp.40-41.

4. Ibid., p.160.

5. Ibid., p.117.

6. Ibid., p.153.

7. Ibid., p.177.

8. Ibid., p.164.

9. Ibid.

10. For a good discussion of this point, see Jane Lilienfield, 1980.

11. Willy employed an army of hack writers to write articles and books for him. From his point of view, Colette was part of the team.

12. Lilienfield, 1980.

13. If the reader is not familiar with the work of Colette and how much it creates the feminine perspective in words and imagery, I suggest they read Nicole Ward Jouve, 1987, Chapter 10.

14. Sources for this are many. See *My Mother's House*, Letters from Sido to Colette and Jouve, 1987.

15. The issue of autonomy is not expanded here because it was discussed in Book I, Chapters 2, 3, 6, and 7 and the reader is expected to make his or her own extrapolations.

16. *My Mother's House*, p.85.

17. This issue was discussed in Book 1, Chapters 2 and 8.

18. See Chapters 8 and 9 Book II and Jouve, 1987, p.86, for a discussion of this point.

19. Faderman, 1981, makes this point about lesbianism strongly and I have referred to her research in Chapters 8 and 9, Book II.

20. This psychological defense was discussed in Book I, Chapter 6.

21. Colette, *The Pure and The Impure*, Secker & Warburg, 1968.

22. See Chapter 1, Book I for more information on this situation.

23. *My Mother's House*, p.133.

24. Jouve, 1987, p.114.

25. This issue was discussed in Chapters 2 and 5, Book I.

26. The reasons for, and the problems of women who look for mothers in their husbands were discussed in Chapter 6, Book I.

27. Jouve, 1987, p.201.

28. Jouve, 1987, p.176.

29. Ibid., pp.74-75.

30. Colette, *Break of Day*.

31. Ibid.

32. I'm referring here to Virginia Woolf's famous declaration that women need economic independence to gain confidence and autonomy. See *A Room of One's Own*, 1974.

33. See Chapter 5, Book I for a full discussion of this point.

34. The need to accept our mothers as human and fallible rather than chase the super-mum myth, is crucial to good mother-daughter relationships and was discussed in Book I.

35. See Book I and particularly Chapter 4 for a discussion of this fact..

36. This aspect of de Beauvoir was discussed in Chapter 8, Book I.

CHAPTER 12

1. Apart from my conclusions drawn from Virginia's writings, Spalding, 1983, provides supporting evidence from letters, comments by family members and observations of friends and acquaintances of the Stephens' family.

2. *To The Lighthouse*, first published by Hogarth in 1927. Here the edition by Grafton is the source, 1985, p.150.

3. Spalding, 1983.

4. *To The Lighthouse*, p.18.

5. Ibid., p.78.

6. Spalding, 1983.

7. Spalding, 1983 provides additional evidence, based on observations of the Stephens' household. See footnote 1.

8. *To The Lighthouse*, p.38.

9. Apart from my own conclusions from Virginia's writings, see Bell, 1982, p.63.

10. *To The Lighthouse*, p.158.

11. Bond, *Who Killed Virginia Woolf?*, 1989.

12. Laing, *Sanity, Madness and The Family*, 1964, explores this issue more fully than I can here.

13. For further discussion of the impact of Leslie on Virginia see Leaska, 1983 and

the discussion, pp.461-462.

14. Lilienfield, 1980.

15. Rose, 1978.

16. Bond, 1989, describes Leslie's demands as narcissistic.

17. Rather than express anger against her mother, Virginia chose to regard herself as unworthy — the problem. Depression is often an outcome of poor self-esteem. It is closely associated with poor self-esteem, if not identical. See Phillips, 1986 for an overview of the relevant research.

18. Bond, 1989, p.45.

19. Virginia Woolf, 1976.

20. Quentin Bell, Vanessa's son, describes how his aunt's, ie Virginia's intrusiveness made life very difficult for his mother. Much of the work he draws on is unpublished and his book is a mine of information about Virginia and Vanessa, 1982.

21. Virginia Woolf, 1967, p.66.

22. *To The Lighthouse*, p.186.

23. Virginia Woolf, 1976.

24. Lilienfield, 1980, also discusses this issue. See Chapter 6, Book 1, for more insight into why women need to mother men.

25. *To The Lighthouse*, p.39.

26. Bell, 1982. See footnote 20.

27. This was discussed in Chapter 3, Book I.

28. See Phillips, 1986, for an overview of the research on this topic.

29. Lilienfield, 1980, also makes this point.

30. *To The Lighthouse*, p.140.

31. Ibid., p.166.

32. Ibid., p.78.

33. Ibid., p.182.

34. Virginia Woolf, 1976.

35. This issue has been discussed at length in Book I, and particularly in Chapter 6.

36. Lilienfield, 1980, also comments on this outcome.

37. This issue was discussed in Chapter 2, Book 1.

38. This is another issue that has been explored throughout Book 1.

39. Spalding, 1983, provides evidence for this.

40. For more details of the research into blended families, see Phillips, 1986.

41. Apart from Virginia herself, Spalding, 1983 is one of many sources for this.

42. Bell, 1982.

43. DeSalvo, 1989, *Virginia Woolf: The Impact of Childhood Sexual Abuse on Her Life and Work.*

44. *To The Lighthouse*, p.77.

45. Virginia's unresolved ambivalence toward her mother, at this stage, meant she transferred the same ambivalence to mother substitutes.

46. Bell, 1982.
47. Spalding, 1983, p.23.
48. Bell, 1982.
49. Bond, 1989, p.114.
50. Ibid., p.160.
51. Spalding, 1983, p.25.
52. According to DeSalvo, their father's aggression was compounded by their brothers' sexual abuse and incest. The withdrawn behaviour of Vanessa and Virginia is not an untypical way of coping with such physical and psychological violations.
53. Apart from Virginia's own testimony, which I quote in this chapter, Bond, 1989, brings this evidence together, p.51.
54. Leonard Woolf, *Beginning Again*, London: Harcourt Brace, 1963, pp.30-31.
55. This is the judgement of Bond, 1989.
56. Rose, 1978, p.88 and Bond, 1989, p.80.
57. Bond's analysis, 1989.
58. Virginia Woolf, 1975, p.125.
59. Lilienfield, 1980.
60. See Chapter 9, Book II for a description of these.
61. Nicolson, 1978, p.212.
62. Quentin Bell, *Virginia Woolf*, Vol. 11, pp.117-118.
63. Bond, 1989, pp.118-136.
64. Ibid., p.144.
65. Virginia Woolf, 1980, pp.485-6, Rose, 1978, p.161 and Bond, 1989, pp.62-3.
66. Vita Sackville-West, *Behind The Mask*, 1910, unpublished work, quoted in Bond, 1989, pp.130 -132. Also see Glendinning, *Vita: The Life of Vita Sackville-West*, 1983.

CONCLUSION

1. Axel Clark, 1990.
2. Simone de Beauvoir was discussed in Chapter8, Book 1.
3. It was Virginia Woolf who said Jane Austen took the patriarchal sentence and laughed at it and constructed a style that better suited her subject matter. See Chapter 7, Book II. Virginia Woolf, of course, constructed a special style of expression which captured the emotions and feelings of women. Colette's and Richardson's styles were discussed in Chapter 10, Book II.
4. Paul McGeogh, *Sydney Morning Herald*, 25-8-90, Section 3, 'Innocents in the Frontline', p.65, describes and quotes from the experience of hostages.

છ

Bibliography

Alcott, Louisa May. *Little Women*. New York: Grossett & Dunlap, 1947.

Alexander, Christine. *The Early Writings of Charlotte Brontë*. Oxford: Basil Blackwell, 1983.

Ambromowitz, C.V., Ambromowitz, S.L. & Weitz, L.J. 'Are men therapists soft on empathy? Two studies in feminine understanding'. *Journal of Clinical Psychology*. 1976, 32, 434-437.

Appleton, W.S. *Father's and Daughters: A Fathers Powerful Influence on a Woman's Life*. London: Macmillan, 1982.

Apter, Terri. *Altered Loves: Mothers and Daughters During Adolescence*. London/New York: Harvester Wheatsheaf/St Martin's Press, 1990.

Arcana, J. *Our Mothers' Daughters*. London: The Women's Press, 1984.

Armitage, K.J., Schneiderman, L.J. & Bass, M.A. 'Responses of physicians to medical complaints in men and women'. *Journal of the American Medical Association*. 1979, 241, 2186-2187.

Attwood, M. 'Significant Moments in the Life of My Mother' in *Close Company: Stories of Mothers & Daughters*. (eds.) C. Park & C. Heaton, London: Virago, 1987, pp. 5-20.

Attwood, Margaret. *Lady Oracle*. New York: Avon, 1976.

Austen, Jane. *Emma*. 1816, Middlesex: Penguin, 1966.

Austen, Jane. *Mansfield Park*. 1814, Middlesex: Penguin, 1985.

Austen, Jane. *Northanger Abbey*. 1818, Middlesex: Penguin, 1985.

Austen, Jane. *Persuasion*. 1818, Penguin, 1978.

Austen, Jane. *Pride and Prejudice*. 1813, Middlesex: Penguin, 1985.

Austen, Jane. *Sense and Sensibility*. 1811, Middlesex: Penguin, 1985.

Bachofen, J.J. *Myth, Religion and Mother Right*. 1870. *Selected Writings of J.J. Bachofen*. Trans. Ralph Manheim, Introduction by Joseph Campbell, Princeton: Univ. Press, 1967.

Badinter, Elisabeth. *The Myth of Motherhood*. Trans. R. De Garis, London: Souvenir Press, 1981.

Bain, Bruce. (ed.) *The Sociogenesis of Language and Human Conduct*. New York: Plenum, 1983.

Bair, Deidre. *Simone de Beauvoir: A Biography*. London: Jonathan Cape, 1990.

Barfoot, Joan. *Duet for Three*. London: Women's Press, 1986.

Barfoot, Joan. *Gaining Ground*. London: Women's Press, 1985.

Barker, P. *Basic Child Psychiatry*. 2nd ed. London: Crosby Lockwood Staples, 1976.

Barocas, H.A. & Barocas, C.B. 'Manifestations of Concentration Camp Effects on the Second Generation'. *Am.J.Psychiatry*. 1973, 130, 7, 820-821.

Bart, P. 'The Reproduction of Mothering' in *Mothering: Essays in Feminist Theory*. (ed.) J. Tebilcot, Totowa, N.J.: Rowman & Allenheld, 1983, 147-152.

Bartram, Grace. *Peeling*. London: Women's Press, 1986.

Bassoff, Evelyn. *Mothers & Daughters: Loving and Letting Go*. New York: NAL/Penguin, 1988.

Bate, B.A. 'Generic man, invisible woman: Language, thought and social change' in *Michigan Papers in Women's Studies*. 1975, 2, 1-13.

Bateson, M.C. *With A Daughter's Eye*. New York: Washington Square Press, 1984.

Batto, B. F. *Studies on Women at Mari*. Baltimore: John Hopkins Univ. Press, 1974.

Baumrind, D. 'Parental disciplinary patterns and social competence in children'. *Youth & Society*. 9, 3, March, 1978.

Baumrind, D. 'Reciprocal rights and responsibility in parent/child relations'. *Journal of Social Issues*. 1978, 34, 7.

Bedford, Jean. *Love Child*. Ringwood, Vic.: Penguin, 1986.

Bee, Helen. *Social Issues in Developmental Psychology*. 2nd ed. New York: Harper & Row, 1978.

Beer, Francis. (ed.) *The Juvenilia of Jane Austen and Charlotte Brontë*. Middlesex: Penguin, 1986.

Beer, Gillian. *George Eliot*. Brighton: Harvester, 1986.

Bell, Anne Olivea, (ed.) A Moment's Liberty. The shorter diary of Virginia Woolf, London: Hogarth, 1990.

Bell, Diane. *Generations: Grandmothers, Mothers and Daughters*. Fitzroy Vic.: McPhee/Gribble, 1988.

Bell, Quentin. *Virginia Woolf*. Suffolk: Triad/Granada, 1982.

Bennett, D. *Growing Pains: What to do when your children turn into teenagers*. Sydney: Doubleday5, 1987.

Berger, Kathleen Stassen. *The Developing Person Through The Life Span*. New York: Worth, 1983.

Berndt, Catherine, 'Interpretation and "Fact" in Aboriginal Australia', in Frances Dahlberg. (ed). *Woman the Gatherer*. New Haven, Conn.: Yale Univ. Press, 1981.

Bernstein, R.M. 'The development of the self-system during adolescence'. *Journal Genetic Psychology*. 1980, 136, 231-245.

Bettelheim, B. *Symbolic Wounds: Puberty Rites and the Envious Male*. New York: Collier, 1968.

Bettelheim, B. *The Uses of Enchantment: The Meaning and Importance of Fairy Tales* London: Thames & Hudson, 1976.

Bird, Phyllis. 'Images of Women in the Old Testament' in Rosemary Ruether. (ed.) *Religion & Sexism: Images of Women in the Jewish and Christian Traditions*. New York: Simon & Schuster, 1974.

Bishop, R. 'Christine de Pisan — A Medieval Feminist'. Paper presented to the *Women's Studies Conference*. University of Sydney, 20-22 September, 1985.

Bloom, L.Z. 'Heritages: Dimensions of Mother-Daughter Relationships in

Women's Biographies' in *The Lost Tradition: Mothers and Daughters in Literature*. (eds.) C Davidson, & E Broner, New York: Frederick Ungar, 1980, pp 291-303.

Bogan, Louise. *The Blue Estuaries: Poems 1923-1968*. New York: Eco Press, 1968.

Bond, Alma Halbert. *Who Killed Virginia Woolf? A Psychobiography*. New York: Insight Books, Plenum, 1989.

Boston Lesbian Psychologies Collective. (eds.) *Lesbian Psychologies: Explorations and Challenges*. Chicago: Univ. of Illinois Press, 1987.

Boulding, Elise. *The Underside of History*. Boulder, Colorado: Westview Press, 1976.

Bowlby, J. *The Making and Breaking of Affectional Bonds*. London: Tavistock, 1979.

Brandon, S.G.F. *Creation Legends of the Ancient Near East*. 1963.

Bridenthal, Renate & Koonz, Claudia. (eds.) *Becoming Visible: Women in European History*. Boston: Houghton Mifflin, 1977.

Briffault, R. *The Mothers*. New York: Johnson Reprint, 1969

Broe, M.L. 'A Subtle Psychic Bond: The Mother Figure in Sylvia Plath's Poetry' in *The Lost Tradition: Mothers and Daughters in Literature*. (eds.) C. Davidson & E Broner, New York: Frederick Ungar, 1980, pp. 217-230.

Broner, E.M. *A Weave of Women*. New York: Holt, Rinehart & Winston, 1978.

Bronfenbrenner, U. 'Nobody home: The erosion of the American family'. *Psychology Today*. 1977, 10, 12, 40.

Brontë, Anne. *The Tenant of Wildfell Hall*. 1848, Middlesex: Penguin, 1979.

Brontë, Charlotte. *Jane Eyre*. 1847, Introduction by Margaret Lane, New York: Dutton, 1966.

Brontë, Charlotte. *Shirley*. 1849, edited by Andrew and Judith Hook, Middlesex: Penguin, 1974.

Brontë, Charlotte. *The Professor*. 1857, *Tales From Angria, Emma A Fragment*. 1860, London: Collins, 1984.

Brontë, Charlotte. *Villette*. 1853, London: Hightext, 1983.

Brontë, Emily. *Wuthering Heights*. 1847, Middlesex: Penguin, 1985.

Bruch, Hilde. *Eating Disorders: Obesity, Anorexia Nervosa & The Person Within*. London: Routledge & Kegan Paul, 1974.

Bruch, Hilde. *The Golden Cage: The Enigma of Anorexia Nervosa*. London: Open Books, 1978.

Brumberg, Joan Jacobs. *Fasting Girls: The Emergence of Anorexia Nervosa as a Modern Disease*. Harvard: Harvard Uni Press, 1988.

Bucik, Francis Wells. *Mothers Talk: Sharing the Secret*. New York: St Martin's Press, 1986.

Buczik, T.A. 'Sex biases in counselling: counsellor retention of the concerns of a female and male clients'. *Journal of Counselling Psychology*. 1981, 28, 1, 13-21.

Burton, Clare. *Subordination: Feminism and social theory*. Sydney: Allen & Unwin, 1985.

Bushell, Alma. (ed.) *Yesterdays Daughters: Stories of our past by women over 70*.

Melbourne: Nelson, 1986.

Calder, Nigel. *Timescale*. London: 1984.

Campbell, Joseph. *The Masks of God: Occidental Mythology*. New York: Viking Press, 1970.

Caplan, Paula. *Dont Blame Mothers: Mending The Mother-Daughter Relationship*. New York: Harper & Row, 1989.

Caplan, Paula. *The Myth of Women's Masochism*. London: Methuen, 1986.

Cather, Willa. *A Lost Lady*. London: Virago, 1980.

Cather, Willa. *Sapphira and The Slave Girl*. London: Virago, 1986.

Chadwick, John. *The Mycenean World*. New York: Cambridge Univ. Press, 1976.

Chandler, Alice. *A Dream of Order: The Medieval Ideal in Nineteeth Century Literature*. London: Routledge Kegan Paul, 1970.

Chapian, Marie. *Mothers & Daughters*. Minneapolis: Bethamy House, 1988.

Chernin, Kim. *In My Mother's House: A Daughter's Story*. London: Virago, 1985.

Chernin, Kim. *Reinventing Eve: Modern Woman In Search of Herself*. New York: Harper & Row, 1988.

Chernin, Kim. *The Hungry Self: Women, Eating & Identity*. London: Virago, 1985.

Chernin, Kim. *Womansize: Reflections on the Tyranny of Slenderness*. London: Women's Press, 1983.

Chesler, Phyllis. *Mothers on Trial: The Battle for Children and Custody*. New York: McGraw Hill, 1986.

Chesler, Phyllis. *Sacred Bond: The Legacy of Baby M*. New York: Times Books, 1988.

Chesler, Phyllis. *Women and Madness* New York: Avon Books, 1973.

Chess S. & Whitbread, J. *Daughters: From Infancy to Independence*. New York: Doubleday, 1978.

Chess, Stella. 'The Blame the Mother Ideology'. *International Journal of Mental Health*. 1982, 11, 95-107.

Child, Gordon. *Man Makes Himself*. London: Watts, 1936.

Chodorow, N. & Contratto, Susan. 'The Fantasy of the Perfect Mother' in *Rethinking the Family: Some Feminist Questions*. (ed.) B. Thorne & M. Yalom. New York: Longman, 1982, 54-75.

Chodorow, N. *The Reproduction of Mothering: Psychoanalysis and the Sociology of Gender*. Berkeley: Univ. of California Press, 1978.

Clark, Axel. *Henry Handel Richardson: Fiction in the Making*. Brookvale, Australia: Simon & Schuster, 1990.

Clinton, Elizabeth, Countess of Lincoln. *The Countess of Lincolnes Nurserie*. Oxford: John Lichfield and James Short, 1622.

Colette. *Break Of Day*. London: Women's Press, 1979.

Colette. *My Mother's House* and *Sido*. Middlesex: Penguin, 1968.

Colette. *The Claudine Novels*. Middlesex: Penguin, 1979.

Colette. *The Pure and the Impure*. New York: Farrar,Straus & Giroux, 1967

Conger, J.J. *Adolescence and Youth: Psychological Development in a Changing World*. 2nd ed. New York: Harper & Row, 1977.

Conger, John Janeway & Petersen, Anne C. *Adolescence and Youth*. New York: Harper & Row, 1984.

Connell, W.F., Stroobant, R.E., Sinclair, K.E. Connell, R.W. & Rogers, K.W. *12 to 20. Studies of City Youth*. Sydney: Hicks Smith, 1975.

Coopersmith, S. *The Antecedents of Self Esteem*. San Francisco: Freeman, 1967.

Cross, J.W. *George Eliot's Life as Related to Her Letters & Journals*. arranged & edited by her husband, 3 Vols. London: Blackwood, 1895.

Dacey, J.S. *Adolescents Today*. California: Goodyear, 1979.

Daiches, D. 'Introduction' in Brontë, Emily. *Wuthering Heights*. Middlesex: Penguin, 1985.

Dally, Ann. *Inventing Motherhood: The Consequences of an Ideal*. New York: Schocken Books, 1982.

Dalsimer, Katherine. *Female Adolescence. Psychoanalytic Reflections on Literature*. New Haven: Yale Univ. Press, 1986.

Danciger, Irene. *A World of Women: An Illustrated History of Women's Magazines*. London: Gill & Macmillan, 1978.

Davidson, C.N. & Broner, E.M. (eds.) *The Lost Tradition: Mothers and Daughters in Literature*. New York: Frederick Ungar, 1980.

Davis, Elizabeth Gould. *The First Sex*. New York: Putnam/Penguin, 1971.

de Beauvoir, Simone. *A Very Easy Death*. Middlesex: Penguin, 1969.

de Beauvoir, Simone. *Memoirs of a Dutiful Daughter*. Middlesex: Penguin, 1984.

de Beauvoir, Simone. *The Second Sex*. New York: Alfred A Knopf, 1957.

de Bono, E. *I Am Right. You Are Wrong*. London: Viking, 1990.

de Mause, L. (ed.) *The History of Childhood*. New York: Harper & Row, 1974.

de Pizan, Christine. *Ditie de Jehanne d'Arc*. 1429, republished in a version edited by Angus J. Kenneth Varty, Oxford: Society for the Study of Medieval Languages and Literature, 1977.

de Pizan, Christine. *The Book of the City of Ladies*. 1405, translated & introduced by Earl Jeffery Richards. Foreword by Marian Warner, London: Pan Books, 1983.

de Pizan, Christine. *The Treasure of the City of Ladies or the Book of the Three Virtues*. Harmondsworth: Penguin, 1985

DeSalvo, L. & Mitchell, Leaska. *The Letters of Vita Sackville-West to Virginia Woolf*. New York: William Morrow, 1985.

DeSalvo, Louise. *Virginia Woolf. The Impact of Childhood Sexual Abuse on her Life and Work*. London: Women's Press, 1989.

Deutsch, H. *The Psychology of Women*. 2 Vols. New York: Grune & Stratton, 1944.

Dinnerstein, Dorothy. *The Mermaid and the Minotaur: Sexual Arrangements and Human Malaise*. New York: Harper & Row, 1976.

Dodd, Celia. *Conversations With Mothers & Daughters*. London: Macdonald Optima, 1990.

Duncan, Erika. 'The Hungry Jewish Mother' in *The Lost Tradition: Mothers and Daughters in Literature*. (eds.) C. N. Davidson & C. M. Broner, New York: Frederick Ungar, 1980.

Dunker, B. 'Aging Lesbians: Observations and Speculations' in *Lesbian Psychologies*. (eds.) the Boston Lesbian Psychologies Collective, Chicago: Univ. of Illinois Press, 1987, 72-78.

Durant, Will & Ariel. *The Story of Civilisation*. Vol 10, *Rousseau and Revolution*. New York: Simon & Schuster, 1967.

Dusinberg, Juliet. *Shakespeare and the Nature of Women*. London: Macmillan, 1975.

Ehrenreich, B. & English, D. *For Her Own Good. 150 Years of the Experts Advice to Women*. London: Pluto Press, 1979.

Ehrlich, R. (ed.) *Mothers. 100 mothers of the famous and the infamous*. London: Paddington Press, 1976.

Eichenbaum, Luise & Orbach, Susie. *Between Women*. New York: Viking Press, 1988.

Elias-Button, K. 'The Muse as Medusa' in *The Lost Tradition: Mothers and Daughters in Literature*. (eds.) C. Davidson, & E.M. Broner, New York: Frederick Ungar, 1980, pp. 193-206.

Eliot, George. *Middlemarch*. Middlesex: Penguin, 1965.

Eliot, George. *Scenes from Clerical Life*. Middlesex: Penguin, 1973.

Eliot, George. *The Mill On The Floss*. Middlesex; Penguin, 1979.

Ellis, A. & Greiger, R. *Rational Emotive Therapy: Handbook of Theory and Practice*. New York: Springer, 1977.

Ellis, Albert & Dryden, Windy. (eds.) *The Practice of Rational-Emotive Therapy*. New York: Springer, 1987.

Engels, F. *The Origin of the Family, Private Property and the State*. New York: International Publishers, 1971.

Erikson, E. *Childhood and Society*. New York: Norton, 1950.

Erikson, E. *Dimensions of a New Identity*. New York: Norton, 1974.

Erikson, E. *Identity, Youth & Crisis*. New York;, Norton, 1968.

Erikson, E. *Life, History and The Historical Moment*. New York: Norton, 1975.

Éspin, O.M. 'Issues of Identity in the Psychology of Latina Lesbians' in *Lesbian Psychologies*. (eds). the Boston Lesbian Psychologies Collective, Chicago: Univ. of Illinois Press, 1987, 35-55.

Evans, Sir Arthur. *The Palace of Minos at Knossos*. 4 Vols., London: 1921-35.

Fabian, S. & Loh, M. *Children in Australia. An Outline History*. Melbourne: Hyland House, 1980.

Faderman, Lillian. *Surpassing The Love of Men. Romantic Friendship and Love between Women from the Renaissance to the Present*. New York: William Morrow & Co, 1981.

Fahey, M. 'Your Child's Self Esteem and Self Esteem a Family Affair', *Selected Papers. Foundation for Child and Youth Studies*. No 7, 1980. Sydney, Hampden Press.

Fairchild, B. & Hayward, N. *Now That You Know. What Every Parent Should*

Know About Homosexuality. New York: Harcourt Brace Jovanovich, 1979.

Fein, G. *Child Development.* Englewood Cliffs, New Jersey: Prentice Hall, 1978.

Fielding, H. *Tom Jones.* Middlesex: Penguin, 1969.

Firman, Julie & Firman, Dorothy. *Mothers and Daughters: Healing the Relationship.* New York: Crossroad, 1989.

Fischer, Lucy R. *Linked Lives: Adult Daughters and Their Mothers.* New York: Harper & Row, 1987.

Fishburn, K. 'The Nightmare Repetition: The Mother-Daughter Conflict in Doris Lessing's Children of Violence' in *The Lost Tradition: Mothers and Daughters in Literature.* (eds.) C.Davidson & E.M. Broner, New York: Frederick Ungar, 1980, pp. 207-216.

Fisher, Elizabeth. *Women's Creation: Sexual Evolution and the Shaping of Society.* Garden City, New York: Anchor Press/Doubleday, 1979.

Flax, Jane. 'Mother-Daughter Relationships: Psychodynamics, Politics, and Philosophy' in *The Future of Difference.* (eds.) Eisenstein & Jardine, Boston: G.K. Hall, 1980.

Flax, Jane. 'The Conflict Between Nurturance and Autonomy in Mother-Daughter Relationships and Within Feminism'. *Feminist Studies.* 1978, 4:2, 171-189.

Fleming, John V. *The Roman de la Rose: a study in allegory and iconography.* Princeton: Princeton Univ. Press, 1969.

Frank, A. *The Diary of a Young Girl.* New York: Pocket Books, 1953.

Frank, Katherine. *Emily Brontë. A Chainless Soul.* London: Hamish Hamilton, 1990.

Frazer, Sir James. *The Golden Bough.* London: Macmillan,1980

French, Marilyn. *Beyond Power. On Women Men & Morals.* London: Abacus/Sphere Books, 1988.

French, Marilyn. *Her Mother's Daughter. A Novel.* London: Heinemann, 1987.

Freud, S. 'Femininity' in 'New Introductory Lectures in Psychoanalysis' (1932). *The Standard Edition of The Complete Psychological Works of Sigmund Freud.* Vol. 22, trans. James Strachey, London: Hogarth & Inst of Psychoanalysis, 1964.

Freud, S. 'On the universal tendency to debasement in the sphere of love' (1912) in *The Penguin Freud Library.* Harmondsworth: Penguin, 1972.

Freud, S. 'Some psychical consequences of the anatomical distinction between the sexes' (1925) in J. Strachey. (ed.) *The Standard Edition of the Complete Psychological Works of Sigmund Freud.* Vol 9, London: Hogarth Press, 1961.

Freud, S. 'The aetiology of hysteria' (1896) in *The Standard Edition of the Complete Psychological Works of Sigmund Freud.* Vol 3, London: Hogarth, 1961.

Freud, S. 'The Psychogenesis of A Case of Homosexuality in a Woman' (1920) in *The Standard Edition of The Complete Psychological Works of Sigmund Freud.* Vol 18, (ed.) J. Strachey, London: Hogarth Press, 1973.

Freyberg, J.T. 'Difficulties in Separation-Individuation as Experienced by Offspring of Nazi Holocaust Survivors'. *Amer. J. Orthopsychiat.* Jan. 1980, 50 (1) 87-95.

Friday, Nancy. *My Mother My Self.* Glasgow: William Collins, 1981.

Friedan, Betty. *The Feminine Mystique.* New York: Norton, 1963

Friedrich, Paul. *The Meaning of Aphrodite.* Chicago & London: University of Chicago Press, 1979.

Furstenberg, F.R. *Unplanned Parenthood: The Social Consequences of Teenage Child Bearing.* New York: Free Press, 1976.

Gaskell, Elizabeth. *The Life of Charlotte Brontë.* London: Everyman, 1971.

Gee, E. M. & Kimball, M.M. *Women and Ageing.* Toronto: Butterworths, 1987.

Gérin, W. *Charlotte Brontë.* Oxford: Oxford Univ. Press, 1967.

Gérin, W. *Emily Brontë A Biography.* Oxford: Oxford Univ. Press, 1979.

Gesell, A. *The First Five Years of Life.* London: Methuen, 1954.

Gilligan, Carol. 'In A Different Voice: Women's Conception of Self and Morality'. *Harvard Educational Review.* 1977, 47, 481-517.

Gilligan, Carol. 'Woman's Place in Man's Life Cycle'. *Harvard Educational Review.* 49, 4, November, 1979.

Gilligan, Carol. *In A Different Voice: Psychological Theory and Women's Development.* Cambridge Massachusetts: Harvard Univ. Press, 1982.

Gimbutas, Marija. *Goddesses & Gods of Old Europe.* Berkeley: University of California Press, 1982.

Glendinning, Victoria. *Vita: The Life of Vita Sackville-West.* New York: Knopf, 1983.

Godwin, W. *Memoirs of Mary Wollstonecraft.* New York: Richard Smith, 1930.

Golden, C. 'Diversity and Variability in Women's Sexual Identities' in *Lesbian Psychologies.* (eds.) the Boston Lesbian Psychologies Collective, Chicago: Univ. of Illinois Press, 1987, 18-34.

Gordon, Taula. *Feminist Mothers.* London: Macmillan, 1990.

Graves, R. *Greek Myths.* Vols. 1 & 2, Middlesex: Penguin, 1955.

Graves, Robert. *The White Goddess: A Historical Grammar of Poetic Myth.* Faber, 1952.

Grieve, N. & Burns, A. (eds.) *Australian Women. New Feminist Perspectives.* Melbourne: Oxford Univ. Press, 1986.

Griffin, Vicky. *Like Mother, Like Daughter.* Sydney: Angus & Robertson, 1990.

Habakkuk, H. J. & Poston, M. *The Cambridge Economic History of Europe.* Vol. V1, Part 1. *The Industrial Revolution and After.* Cambridge: Cambridge Univ. Press, 1965.

Haight, G. S. *Selections from George Eliot's Letters.* Newhaven & London: Yale Univ. Press, 1985.

Haight, Gordon. *George Eliot. A Biography.* Middlesex: Penguin, 1986.

Hall, J.A. & Halberstadt, A.G. 'Masculinity and femininity in children: development of the children's personal attributes questionnaire'. *Developmental Psychology.* 1980, 16, 4, 270-280.

Hallo, William W. & van Dijik, J.J. *The Exaltation of Innana.* New Haven: Yale Univ. Press, 1968.

Hamachek, D.E. *Encounters with the Self.* New York: Holt Rinehart & Winston, 1978.

Hamilton, Roberta *The Liberation of Women.* London: Allen & Unwin, 1978.

Hanscombe, Gillian & Forster, Jackie. *Rocking the Cradle: Lesbian Mothers. A Challenge in Family Living*. Boston: Alyson, 1982.

Harding, Esther. *Women's Mysteries: Ancient and Modern. A Psychological Interpretation of the Feminist Principle as Portrayed in Myth, Story and Dreams*. New York: 1955.

Harper, Jan & Richards, Lynn. *Mothers and Working Mothers*. revised ed., Melbourne: Penguin, 1986

Hawkes, Jacquetta & Sir Leonard Woolley. *History of Mankind. Vol 1: Prehistory and the Beginnings of Civilisation*. New York: Harper & Row, 1963.

Hawkes, Jacquetta. *Dawn of The Gods*. London: 1958.

Hayden, Ruth. *Mrs Delaney: Her Life and Her Flowers*. London: Colonnade, 1980.

Hayes, Carlton J. H. *A Political and Cultural History of Modern Europe*. New York: Macmillan, 1935.

Heckinger, G.F. & Heckinger, F. *Teenage Tyranny*. New York: William Morrow, 1963.

Heilbrun, Carolyn. *Toward a Recognition of Androgyny*. New York: Knopf, 1973.

Heller, D. 'Themes of Culture & Ancestry Among Children of Concentration Camp Survivors'. *Psychiatry*. 1982, August, 3, 45, 247-261.

Herman, Judith & Hirschman, Lewis. *Father-Daughter Incest*. Cambridge: Harvard Univ. Press, 1981.

Hextall, I. 'Marking Work' in G. Whitty & M. Young (eds.) *Exploration in the Politics of School Knowledge*. Driffield: Nafferton Books, 1976.

Hiatt, L. R. 'Ownership and Use of Land Among Australian Aborigines' in Lee & Devore. *Hunter*.

Hill, Christopher. *Reformation to Industrial Revolution*. London: Penguin, 1975.

Horney, Karen. *Feminine Psychology*. New York: Norton, 1967.

Howard, J. *Margaret Mead. A Life*. New York: Ballantine, 1985.

Irvine, L. 'A Psychological Journey: Mothers and Daughters in English Canadian Fiction' in, *The Lost Traditon: Mothers and Daughters in Literature*. (eds.) C. Davidson & E. Broner, New York: Frederick Ungar, 1980, pp. 242-252.

James, Clive. *May Week Was In June*. London: Jonathan Cape, 1990.

James, E. O. *The Ancient Gods.: The History and Diffusion of Religion in the Ancient Near East and the Eastern Mediterrenean*. London: Weidenfeld & Nicolson, 1960

James, Edwin, O. *The Cult of the Mother-Goddess: An Archeological and Documentary Study*. London: Thames & Hudson, 1959.

Jeffreys, Sheila. 'Butch and Femme Now and Then' in *Not a Passing Phase. Reclaiming Lesbians in History*. 1840-1985. (eds.) Lesbian History Group, London: Women's Press, 1989.

Jouve, Nicole Ward. *Colette*. Brighton: Harvester, 1987.

Jung, C.J. *Aspects of The Feminine*. Princeton: University Press, 1982.

Kaplan, Cora. *Salt and Bitter and Good*. London: Paddington Press, 1975.

Kaufman, M. *Beyond Patriarchy: Essays by Men on Pleasure, Power and Change*.

Melbourne: Oxford Univ. Press, 1987.

Keesing, Nancy. *Dear Mum. Australian Mothers then and now*. Sydney: Angus & Robertson, 1977.

Kelso, Ruth. *Doctrine for The Lady of The Renaissance*. Urbana: Univ. of Illinois Press, 1956.

Kenyon, F.W. *The Consuming Flame. The Story of George Eliot*. London: Hutchison, 1970.

Kerenyi, C. *Eleusis: Archetypal Image of Mothers and Daughters*. London: 1967.

Klein, M. *The Psychoanalysis of Children*. (1932) New York: Seymour Lawrence/Delacorte, 1975.

Kleinbaum, Abby. *The War Against the Amazons*. New York: McGraw Hill, 1983.

Kohlberg, L. 'From is to Ought. How to Commit the Naturalistic Fallacy and Get Away with It in the Study of Moral Development' in T. Mischel, (ed.) *Cognitive Development and Epistomology*. New York: Academic Press, 1971.

Koppelman, Susan. (ed.) *Between Mothers & Daughters: Stories Across A Generation*. New York: Feminist Press, 1985.

Kors, Alan, C. & Peters, Edward. *Witchcraft in Europe:1100-1700. A Documentary History*. Philadelphia: Univ. Pennsylvania Press, 1972.

Laidlaw, Toni Ann, Malmo, Cheryl and Associates. *Healing Voices. Feminist Approaches to Therapy with Women*. San Francisco: Jossey Bass, 1990.

Laing, R.D. & Esterson, A. *Sanity, Madness, And The Family*. London: Tavistock Publication, 1964.

Lakoff, R. T. 'Language and Women's Place'. *Language and Society*. 1973, 2, 45, 45-80.

Lakoff, R. T. *Language and women's place*. New York: Harper Colophon Books, 1975.

Lakoff, R.T. 'Women's Language' in D. Burtuff & E. L. Epstein (eds.) *Women's Language and Style*. Akron, Ohio: Univ. of Akron, 1979.

Lamb, M. E. *The Father's Role: Applied Perspectives*. New York: Wiley, 1986.

Lane, M. 'Introduction' in Charlotte Brontë. *Jane Eyre*. Middlesex: Penguin, 1966.

Laski, Margharita. *Jane Austen and her World*. London: Thames & Hudson, 1977.

Le Francois, G.R. *Adolescents*. Belmont, California: Wadsworth, 1976.

Leacock, E. 'The Changing Family and Levy Strauss or Whatever Happened to Fathers'. *Social Research*. Summer, 1977.

Lerner, Gerda. *The Creation of Patriarchy*. Oxford: Oxford University Press, 1986.

Lerner, Harriet Goldhor. *The Dance of Anger*. New York: Harper & Row, 1985.

Lerner, Harriet Goldhor. *The Dance of Intimacy*. New York: Harper & Row, 1989.

Lerner, R.M. & Spanier, G.B. *Adolescent Development: A Life Span Perspective*. New York: McGraw-Hill, 1980.

Lesbian History Group. *Not a Passing Phase. Reclaiming Lesbians in History.1840-1985*. London: Women's Press, 1989.

Lessing, Doris. *A Proper Marriage*. London: Panther, 1964.

Lessing, Doris. *Landlocked*. Plume Books, 1958.

Lessing, Doris. *Martha Quest*. Plume Books, 1952.

Lessing, Doris. *The Diaries of Jane Somers*. Middlesex: Penguin, 1984.

Lessing, Doris. *The Four Gated City*. Bantam, 1969.

Lethbridge, T.C. *Witches*. 1962.

Levine, L.E. 'Self definition in two year old boys'. *Developmental Psychology*. 1983, 19, 4, 544-49.

Lilienfield, Jane. 'Reentering Paradise: Cather, Colette, Woolf', in *The Lost Tradition: Mothers and Daughters in Literature*. (eds.) C.N. Davidson, & E.M. Broner, New York: Frederick Ungar, 1980, pp. 160-175.

Livesley, W.S. & Bromley, D.B. *Person Perception in Childhood and Adolescence*. New York: Wiley, 1973.

Llanover, L. (ed.) *The Autobiography and Correspondence of Mrs Delaney*. revised edition, Boston: Roberts Brothers, 1882.

Loewenstein, S. 'An Overview of the Concept of Narcissism'. *Social Casework*. 1977, 58, 136-142.

Lowenthal M. Thurnher, M. & Chirabago, D. *Four Stages of Life*. San Francisco: Jossey Bass, 1975.

Macdonald, S.P. 'Jane Austen and The Tradition of the Absent Mother' in *The Lost Tradition: Mothers and Daughters in Literature*. (eds.) C.N. Davidson, & E.M. Broner. New York: Frederick Ungar, 1980, pp. 58-69.

Macintyre, M. 'Female Autonomy in a Matrilineal Society' in N. Grieve & A. Burns (eds.) *Australian Women. New Feminist Perspectives*. Melbourne: Oxford Univ. Press, 1986.

Maclean, Ian. *The Renaissance View of Women*. Cambridge: Cambridge Univ. Press, 1980.

Mahler, M. S. *On Human Symbiosis and Individuation*. New York: International Universities Press, 1968.

Mairobert, M.F. *L'Espion Anglois*. 1777-1778, reprinted London: John Adamson, 1851.

Maron, C. 'Children's Feelings About Themselves'.*Selected Papers. Foundation for Child and Youth Studies*. No 1, 1979. Sydney, Hampden Press.

Marshak, Alexander, 'Some Implications of the Paleolithic Symbolic Evidence for the Origin of Language' in *Origins and Evolution of Language and Speech*, (eds.) S. R. Harnand, H. D. Stecklis & J. Lancaster. New York: Academy of Sciences Conference Proceedings, Vol 280, Sept. 22-25, 1975.

Marshak, Alexander. *The Roots of Civilisation*. New York: McGraw Hill, 1972.

Martin, M. Kay & Voorhies, Barbara. *Female of the Species*. New York: Columbia Univ. Press, 1975.

Marx-Engels-Lenin. *On Women And The Family*. Dublin: Repsol, 1983.

Masson, Jeffrey M. *Against Therapy*. London: Fontana/ Collins, 1990.

Masson, Jeffrey M. *The Assault on Truth*. New York: Farrar, Straus & Giroux, 1984.

Mavor, Elizabeth.*The Ladies of Llangollen*. Harmondsworth: Penguin, 1974

McCarthy, M. *The Group*. New York: Harcourt, Brace & World, 1954.

McCrindle, Jean & Rowbotham, Sheila.*Dutiful Daughters*. Middlesex: Pelican, 1983

McCurdy, H.G. 'A Study Of The Novels Of Charlotte & Emily Brontë As An Expression Of Their Personalities'. *Journal of Personality*. Vol. 16, 1947-48, pp. 109-152.

McFarland, Dorothy Tuck. *Willa Cather*. New York: Frederick Ungar, 1972.

McLeod, Enid. *The Order of the Rose: The Life and Ideas of Christine de Pisan*. London: 1976.

McLeod, Karen. *Henry Handel Richardson. A critical study*. Cambridge: Cambridge Univ. Press, 1985.

Mead, M. *Blackberry Winter: My Earlier Years*. New York: Simon & Schuster, 1972.

Mead, M. *Male and Female. A Study of the Sexes in a Changing World*. New York: Morrow, 1975.

Mellaart, James. *Catal Hüyük*. London: McGraw Hill, 1967.

Miles, Rosalind. *The Women's History of the World*. Glasgow: Collins, 1988.

Miller, Elaine. 'Through All Changes and Through All Chances: The relationship of Ellen Nussey and Charlette Brontë' in Lesbian History Group (eds.) *Not A Passing Phase. Reclaiming Lesbians in History 1840-1985*. London: The Women's Press, 1989.

Mitchell, Juliet. *Psychoanalysis and Feminism*. Middlesex: Penguin, 1974.

Mitchell, Leaska. *Pointz Hall*. New York: University Publications, 1983.

Modjeska, Drusilla. *Poppy*. Ringwood, Vic.: McPhee Gribble/Penguin, 1990.

Monaghan, P. *Women in Myth & Legend*. London: Junction Books, 1981

Montemayer, M. & Eisen, M. 'The development of self-conceptions from childhood to adolescence'. *Developmental Psychology*. 1977, 13, 4, 314-319.

Morgan, Elaine. *Descent of Woman*. New York: Stein & Day, 1972.

Munro, Alice. *Friend of My Youth*. London: Chatto & Windus, 1990.

Munro, Alice. *Something I've Been Meaning To Tell You*. Ontario: Penguin, 1985.

Murray, Gilbert. *Five Stages of Greek Religion*. Garden City, New York: Columbia Univ. Press, 1925.

Neumann, Erich. *The Great Mother*. Princeton, N.J: Princeton Univ. Press, 1972.

Nicholson, Joyce. *The Heartache of Motherhood*. Middlesex: Penguin, 1983.

Nicolson, Nigel. *Portrait of A Marriage*. London: Futura, 1978.

O'Morgan, Kenneth. *The Oxford History of Britain*. Oxford Univ. Press, 1988.

Oates, Joyce Carol. 'Is This the Promised End? The Tragedy of King Lear'. *Journal of Aesthetics and Art Criticism*. 75, 1974.

Ochshorn, Judith, 'Mothers and Daughters in Ancient Near Eastern Literature' in C. N. Davidson & E, M. Broner (eds.) *The Lost Tradition: Mothers and Daughters in Literature*. New York: Frederick Ungar, 1980.

Ochshorn, Judith. *The Female Experience and the Nature of the Divine*. Bloomington, Ind.: Indiana Univ. Press, 1981.

Olsen, Tillie. 'I Stand Here Ironing' in *Between Mothers and Daughters*. (ed.)

Susan Koppelman. New York: Feminist Press, 1985, pp. 177-187.

Olsen, Tillie. *Mother to Daughter, Daughter to Mother: A Daybook and Reader.* New York: Feminist Press, 1984.

Olsen, Tillie. *Tell Me a Riddle.* New York: Dell, 1986.

Orbach, Susie. *Hunger Strike. The Anorectic's Struggle as a Metaphor of Our Age.* London: Faber, 1986.

Osborn, Judith, 'Mothers & Daughters in Ancient Near East Literature' in *The Lost Tradition: Mothers and Daughters in Literature.* (eds.) C. Davidson & E. Broner. New York: Frederick Ungar, 1980.

Otwell, John. *And Sarah Laughed. The Status of Women in The Old Testament.* Philadelphia: Westminster Press, 1977.

Palmer, Nettie. *Henry Handel Richardson. A study.* Sydney: Angus & Robertson, 1950.

Park, C. & Heaton, C. (eds.) *Close Company. Stories of Mothers and Daughters.* London: Virago, 1987.

Parker, Rozsika. *The Subversive Stitch. Embroidery and the making of the feminine.* London: Women's Press, 1984. Reprinted, 1989.

Paul, Lois, 'The Mastery of Work and the Mystery of Sex in a Guatemalan Village' in M.Z. Rosaldo & L. Lamphere. *Woman, Culture & Society.* Stanford: Stanford Univ. Press, 1974, pp. 297-99.

Paulson, M. Stone, D & Sposto, R. 'Suicide potential and behaviour in children ages 4 to 12'. *Suicide & Life Threatening Behaviour.* 1978, 8, 225-242.

Payne, Karen. *Between Ourselves. Letters Between Mothers and Daughters.* London: Pan, 1984Peterson, Candida C. *Looking Forward Through The Life Span: Developmental Psychology.* Sydney: Prentice Hall, 1984.

Phillips, J.E. 'Roman Mothers and The Lives of Their Adult Daughters'. *Helios.* 1978, 6, 1, 69-80.

Phillips, S. 'Adult Attitudes to Children and Child Rearing Practices in Sydney: the Implications for Social Influences on Child Development' in T. Cross & L. Riach [eds] *Issues and Research in Child Development.* Melbourne Institute of Early Childhood Development and Melbourne College of Advanced Education, 1982, 254-267, (b).

Phillips, S. 'Attitudes to Children and Child Rearing Practices in Sydney: Social and Educational Implications'. *ANZAAS Proceedings.* Section 22, May 1982, 1-26, (a)

Phillips, S. 'Authoritarianism: Factor Structure of A Middle-Childhood Scale'. *Child Study Journal.* 1979, 9, 1, 21-35. (a)

Phillips, S. 'Current Issues in Maternal and Paternal Deprivation'. *Selected Papers, Unit for Child Studies.* Univ. New South Wales, No 6, 1980.

Phillips, S. 'Facets of the Externalisation of the Concept of Self in Literature 1350-1400'. *Literatur.* 1974, 42, 4, 35-44. (a)

Phillips, S. 'Identifying Social Concepts in Medieval Literature'. *English Studies.* 22,1, 1972. (b)

Phillips, S. 'Notes on the Salient Features of the Authoritarian Personality and Parallels in English Literature 1350-1400'. *Gemini.* 1972, 1, 6, 2-11. (a)

Phillips, S. 'Self Concept and Sexism in Language' in *The Sociogenesis of Language and Human Conduct*. (ed.) B.Bain. New York: Plenum, 1983, Ch. 8A, 131-140. (a)

Phillips, S. 'Self Concept and Sexism in the Language of Children: A Middle Childhood Survey' in *The Sociogenesis Of Language and Human Conduct*. (ed.) B. Bain, New York: Plenum, 1983, Ch 8B, 141-151. (b)

Phillips, S. 'The Concept of Motivation in Medieval Romances'. *English Studies*. 26, 3, 1974. (b)

Phillips, S. 'The Contributions of Psychology to Education'. *Oxford Review of Education*. Vol. 2, No 2, 1976, 179-196.

Phillips, S. 'Toddlers'. *Selected Papers: Foundation for Child and Youth Studies*. No 58, 1988. Hampden Press.

Phillips, S. *Relations With Children. The Psychology of Human Development in A Changing World*. Sydney: Kangaroo Press, 1986.

Phillips, S. *Young Australians. The Attitudes of Our Children*. Sydney: Harper & Row, 1979. (b)

Phillips,S. 'Conventionalism and Pseudo Admiration of Women in English Literature 1350-1400'. *Literatur*. 1973, 41, 4, 26-34.

Piaget, Jean. *The Psychology of Intelligence*. London: Routledge Kegan Paul, 1950.

Postan, M. M. *Medieval Women*. Cambridge: Cambridge Univ. Press, 1975.

Postman, N. 'The Disappearance of Childhood'. *Childhood Education*. March/April, 1985, 286-293.

Rabuzzi, Kathryn Allen. *Motherself: A Myth Analysis of Motherhood*. Bloomington In.: Indiana Univ. Press, 1988.

Redinger, Ruby. *George Eliot. The Emergent Self*. New York: Alfred Knopf, 1975.

Redman, Charles. *The Rise of Civilisation: From Early Farmers to Urban Society in the Ancient Near East*. San Francisco: Freeman, 1978.

Reed, E. *Woman's Evolution: From Matriarchal Clan to Patriarchal Family*. New York: Pathfinder, 1975.

Reisman, D. *The Lonely Crowd*. New Haven: Yale University Press, 1961, first published 1950.

Reiter, Rayna. (ed.) *Toward an Anthropology of Woman*. New York: Monthly Review Press, 1978.

Rich, Adrienne. *Of Woman Born*. New York: Bantam, 1977.

Richardson, Henry Handel. *Myself When Young*. London: Heinemann, 1948.

Richardson, Henry Handel. *The End of A Childhood and Other Stories*. London: Heinemann, 1934.

Richardson, Henry Handel. *The Fortunes of Richard Mahoney*. Penguin, 1982

Richardson, Henry Handel. *The Getting of Wisdom*. London: Heinemann, 1960.

Richardson, S. *Clarissa*. (1748), Middlesex: Penguin 1985

Rickarby, G. 'Adolescents Separation From Their Families'. *Selected Papers: Unit for Child Studies*. Univ. New South Wales, 1984.

Riegel, R. *American Feminists*. Middlesex: Penguin, 1963.

Risley, Christine. *Creative Embroidery*. London: Studio Vista, 1967.

Robbins, Joan H. & Siegel, Rachel J. *Women Changing Therapy: New Assessments,*

Values & Strategies in Feminist Therapy. N.Y.: Harrington Park, 1985

Robinson, F.N. (ed.) *The Complete Works of Geoffrey Chaucer.* 2nd ed. Oxford: Oxford Univ. Press, 1957.

Rosaldo, Michelle & Lamphere, Louise. *Women, Culture & Society.* Stanford: Stanford Univ. Press, 1974.

Rose, Phyllis. *Woman of Letters: A Life of Virginia Woolf.* London: Oxford Univ. Press, 1978.

Rosenberg, M. *Conceiving the Self.* New York: Basic Books, 1979.

Rossi, A.S. *The Feminist Papers. From Adams to de Beauvoir.* New York: Bantam Books, 1974.

Roth, Phillip. *Portnoy's Complaint.* New York: Random House, 1969.

Rousseau, J.J. *Emile.* 1762, trans. Barbara Foxley, London: Dent, 1911.

Rowe, Penelope. *Tiger Country.* Sydney: Allen & Unwin, 1990.

Russ, Joanna. 'Autobiography of My Mother' in *Between Mothers & Daughters,* (ed.) Susan Koppelman. New York: Feminist Press, 1985, pp. 265-277.

Sackville-West, Vita. *Behind the Mask.* 1910, unpublished work.

Sackville-West, Vita. *Passage to Teheran.* London: Hogarth Press, 1926.

Sanday, Peggy Reeves. *Female Power and Male Dominance.* New York: Cambridge Univ. Press, 1981.

Sanford, Linda Tschirhart & Donovan, Mary Ellen. *Women and Self Esteem: Understanding and Improving the Way We Think and Feel about Ourselves.* Middlesex: Penguin, 1984.

Santrock, John W. *Adolescence. An Introduction.* Dubuque, Iowa: Wm. C. Brown, 1984.

Sarton, May. 'The Muse as Medusa', *Collected Poems.* Guilford, Ct: Norton, 1984.

Sarton, May. *Collected Poems.* New York: Norton, 1974.

Sayer, Mandy. *Mood Indigo.* Sydney: Allen & Unwin, 1990

Sayers, J. Evans, M. & Redclift, N. (eds.) *Engels Revisited. New Feminist Essays.* London: Tavistock, 1987.

Sayers, Janet, 'Feminism and Mothering: A Kleinian Perspective' *Women's Studies Int. Forum.* 1984. Vol.7, No.4. pp.237-241.

Schneider, Susan Weidman. *Jewish and Female.* New York: Simon & Schuster, 1985.

Sebald, H. *Adolescence. A Social Psychological Analysis.* 2nd ed. Englewood Cliffs, N.J: Prentice Hall, 1977.

Sexton, Anne. *Live or Die.* Boston: Houghton Mifflin, 1966.

Shakespeare, William. *Complete Works* (ed.) W.J. Craig, London: Oxford Univ. Press, 1955.

Shepherd, Trish. *Motherhood.* Sydney: Angus & Robertson, 1989.

Sherfey, M.J. *The Nature and Evolution of Female Sexuality.* New York: Random House, 1972.

Shockley, Ann Allen. 'A Birthday Remembered' in *Between Mothers and Daughters,* ed Susan Koppelman. New York: Feminist Press, 1985, pp. 285-293.

Shotz, M.G. 'The Great Unwritten Story: Mothers and Daughters in Shakespeare' in Davidson, C. N. & Broner, E.M. (eds.) *Mothers and Daughters: The Lost Tradition.* New York: Frederick Ungar, 1980, pp. 44-54.

Showalter, Elaine. *A Literature of Their Own. British Women Novelists from Brontë to Lessing.* London: Virago, 1982.

Shuster, R. 'Sexuality as a Continuum: The Bisexual Identity' in *Lesbian Psychologies.* (eds.) the Boston Lesbian Psychologies Collective. Chicago: Univ. of Illinois Press, 1987.

Shuttle, Penelope & Redgrove, Peter. *The Wise Wound: Menstruation and Everywoman.* London: Grafton Books, 1978.

Sjöö, M & Mor, B. *The Ancient Religion of The Great Cosmic Mother of All.* Trondheim, Norway: Rainbow Press, 1981.

Smith-Rosenberg, Carroll, 'The Female World of Love and Ritual: Relations Between Women in Nineteenth Century America'. *Signs: Journal of Women in Culture and Society* 1, Autumn, 1985, 1-29.

Spalding, Frances. *Vanessa Bell.* London: Papermac, 1983.

Spender, Dale. *The Writing Or The Sex.* London: Pergamon, 1990.

Sperling, Leone. *Mothers Day.* Glebe, N.S.W.: Wild & Woolley, 1984.

Spock, B. *Baby and Child Care.* New York: Cardinal/Pocket Books, 1957.

Spock, Benjamin. *Problems of Parents.* Greenwich, Connecticut: Crest/Fawcett Publications, 1955.

Stanley, L. & Wise, S. *Breaking Out: Feminist consciousness and feminist research.* London: Routledge & Kegan Paul, 1983.

Statham, June. *Daughters and Sons. Experiences of Non-Sexist Childraising.* Oxford: Blackwell, 1986.

Stead, Christina. *The Man Who Loved Children.* Middlesex: Penguin, 1984.

Stephen, Leslie. *The Mausoleum Book.* Oxford: Clarendon Press, 1977.

Stierlen, Helm, 'Adolescent as delegate of his parents'. *A&NZ Journal of Psychiatry.* 1973, 3a, 349-355.

Stiller, Nikki, 'Eve's Orphans: Mothers and Daughters in Medieval English Literature' in C.N. Davidson & E. M. Broner (eds.), *The Lost Tradition. Mothers and Daughters in Literature.* New York: Frederick Ungar, 1980.

Stone, L. J. & Church, J. *Childhood & Adolescence. A Psychology of the Growing Person.* New York: Random House, 1984.

Stone, Merlin. *Ancient Mirrors of Womanhood. A Treasury of Goddess and Heroine Lore from Around the World.* Boston: Beacon Press, 1984.

Stone, Merlin. *The Paradise Papers: The Suppression of Women's Rites.* 1976.

Stone, P. (trans.) *Sir Gawain and The Green Knight.* Middlesex: Penguin, 1959.

Straayer, Arny Christine, 'High Heels' in *Between Mothers and Daughters,* (ed.) Susan Koppelman. New York: Feminist Press, 1985, pp. 279-284.

Strom, Kay & Strom, Lisa. *Mothers and Daughters Together.* Grand Rapids, Mi.: Baker Book House, 1988.

Swain, Margaret. *The Needlework of Mary Queen of Scots.* New York: Van Nostran Reinhold, 1973.

Tan, Amy. *The Joy Luck Club.* London: Minerva, 1990.

Tanner, Tony. *Jane Austen*. London: Macmillan, 1987.

Taylor, Ina. *George Eliot. Woman of Contradictions*. London: Weidenfield & Nicolson, 1989.

Thomas, Keith. *Religion and the Decline of Magic*. New York: Scribner, 1971.

Todd, Janet. *Sensibility. An Introduction*. London: Methuen, 1986.

Todd, Janet. *Women's Friendships in Literature*. New York: Columbia Univ. Press, 1980.

Trautmann-Banks, Joanne & Nigel Nicolson, (eds.) *Complete Letters of Virginia Woolf*. (6 Vols.), London: Hogarth, 1975-80.

Trautmann-Banks, Joanne, (ed.) *Congenial Spirits. The Letters of Virginia Woolf*. London: Hogarth, 1990.

Travitsky, B. S, 'The New Mother of the English Renaissance' in *The Lost Tradition. Mothers and Daughters in Literature*, (eds.) C. Davidson & E. M. Broner. New York: Frederick Ungar, 198O, pp. 33-43.

Trebilcot, Joyce, Ed. *Mothering: Essays in Feminist Theory*. Totowa, N.Y: Rowman & Allenheld, 1983.

Trible, Phyllis, 'Depatriarchalizing In Biblical Interpretation'. *Journal of the American Academy of Religion*. Vol 41, No 1, March 1973, 30-48.

Trible, Phyllis, 'The Creation of a Feminist Theology'. *New York Times Book Review*. Vol. 88, May 1 1983, 28-29.

Valdes Guadalupe. 'Recuerdo' in *Between Mothers and Daughters*, (ed.) Susan, Koppelman. New York: Feminist Press, 1985, pp. 189-196.

Vicinus, Martha, (ed.) *Suffer and Be Still: Women in the Victorian Age*. Indiana: Indiana Univ. Press, 1972.

Walker, Alice. 'Everyday Use' in *Between Mothers and Daughters*, (ed.) Susan Koppelman. New York: Feminist Press, 1985, pp. 229-239.

Walker, Alice. *In Search of Our Mothers' Gardens: Womanist Prose*. San Diego, Ca.: Harcourt Brace, Jovanovich, 1983. (b)

Walker, Alice. *The Color Purple*. London: Women's Press, 1983. (a)

Walters, M. Carter, B. Papp, P., & Silverstein, O. *The Invisible Webb: Gender Patterns In Family Relationships*. New York: Guilford, 1988.

Wandor, Michele. 'Meet My Mother', in *Close Company*, (eds.) C. Park & C. Heaton. London: Virago, 1987.

Watt, Ian. (ed.) *Jane Austen. A Collection of Critical Essays*. Englewood Cliffs: Prentice Hall, 1963.

Wearing, Betsy. *The Ideology of Motherhood*. Sydney: Allen & Unwin, 1984.

Weideger, P. *Female Cycles*. London: Women's Press, 1975.

Weideger, P. *History's Mistress*. Middlesex: Penguin, 1985.

Welter, B. *Dimity Convictions*, 1974.

Wiegall, Rachel, 'An Elizabethan Gentlewoman'. *QR*. 215, 1911, pp. 119 -135.

Wilber, K. *Up From Eden: A Transpersonal View of Human Evolution*. London: Routledge & Kegan Paul, 1983.

Williams, Sherley Ann. 'The Lawd Don't Like Ugly' in *Between Mothers & Daughters*, (ed.) Susan Koppelman. New York: Feminist Press, 1985, pp. 241-264.

Williams, Tennessee. *The Glass Menagerie*. Middlesex: Penguin Plays, 1959.

Winnicott, D. W. 'The mirror role of mother and family in child development' in *Playing and Reality*. London: Tavistock Publications, 1971, pp. 111-118.

Winnicott, D.W. *Mother and Child: A Primer of First Relationships*. New York: Basic Books, 1957.

Winterson, Jeannette. 'Psalms' in *Close Company*, (eds.) C. Park & C. Heaton. London: Virago, 1988.

Winterson, Jeannette. *Oranges are not the only fruit*. London: Pandora, 1990.

Wise, T.J. & Symington, J.A. (eds.) *Letters: The Brontës: Their Lives, Friendships & Correspondence*. Oxford: Shakespeare Head Press, 1932.

Witting, Amy. *I for Isobel*. Melbourne: Penguin, 1989.

Wolf, Josef & Burian, Zdenek. *The Dawn of Man*. London: 1978.

Wollstonecraft, Mary, 'A Vindication of the Rights of Women' in *The Feminist Papers. From Adams to de Beauvoir*, (ed.) A.S. Rossi. New York: Bantam Books, 1974.

Woolf, V. *The Diary of Virginia Woolf*. 5 Vols. 1915-1941, (ed.) Anne Olivea Bell. London: Hogarth 1977-1984.

Woolf, V. *The Letters of Virginia Woolf*. 6 Vols. 1888-1944, (eds.) Joanne Trautmann Banks & Nigel Nicolson. London: Hogarth, 1975-80.

Woolf, Virginia, 'A Room Of One's Own' in *The Feminist Papers:From Adams to de Beauvoir*, (ed.) S. Rossi. New York: Bantam Books, 1974.

Woolf, Virginia. 'A Sketch of the Past' in *Moments of Being: Unpublished Autobiographical Writings*, (ed.) Jeanne Schulkind. Sussex: Univ. of Sussex Press, 1976.

Woolf, Virginia. *Between The Acts*. London: Harcourt Brace, 1941.

Woolf, Virginia. *Collected Essays*. Vol 2, London: Harcourt Brace, 1967.

Woolf, Virginia. *Jacob's Room*. Middlesex: Penguin, 1971.

Woolf, Virginia. *Moments of Being*. New York: Harcourt Brace Jovanovich, 1976

Woolf, Virginia. *Mrs Dalloway*. London: Hogarth Press, 1968.

Woolf, Virginia. *Orlando*. London: Harcourt Brace, 1928.

Woolf, Virginia. *The Voyage Out*. London: Granada, 1982.

Woolf, Virginia. *The Waves*. London: Harcourt Brace, 1931.

Woolf, Virginia. *The Years*. Middlesex: Penguin, 1971.

Woolf, Virginia. *To The Lighthouse*. London: Grafton, 1985.

Young, M. & Willmott, P. *Family and Kinship in East London*. Middlesex: Penguin, 1957, revised edition, 1962.

Zimmerman, B. 'The Mother's History in George Eliot' in *The Lost Tradition: Mothers and Daughters in Literature*, (eds.) C.N. Davidson & E.M. Broner. New York:Frederick Ungar, 1980, pp. 81-94.

℘

Index